STUDIES IN THE
HISTORY OF
ITALIAN MUSIC
AND
MUSIC THEORY

STUDIES IN THE
HISTORY OF
ITALIAN MUSIC
AND
MUSIC THEORY

Claude V. Palisca

CLARENDON PRESS · OXFORD

1994

Oxford University Press, Walton Street, Oxford OX2 6DP

Oxford New York Toronto
Delhi Bombay Calcutta Madras Karachi
Kuala Lumpur Singapore Hong Kong Tokyo
Nairobi Dar es Salaam Cape Town
Melbourne Auckland Madrid
and associated companies in
Berlin Ibadan

Oxford is a trade mark of Oxford University Press

Published in the United States
by Oxford University Press Inc., New York

British Library Cataloguing in Publication Data
Data available

Library of Congress Cataloging in Publication Data
Data available
ISBN 0 19 816167-0

1 3 5 7 9 10 8 6 4 2

Typeset by Best-Set Ltd., Hong Kong
Printed in Great Britain
on acid-free paper by
Biddles Ltd.
Guildford & King's Lynn

To Carl and Madeline

PREFACE

UNLIKE some retrospective collections of essays, this is not intended to be a panorama of a life's work. Rather, it unites widely dispersed strands that beg to be drawn together into a coherent web. The studies are focused on several of my central and abiding interests: the transition from strict counterpoint in the mid-sixteenth century to the experimentation with new, freer, idioms at the beginning of the seventeenth; the search for verifiable scientific truth as a basis for music theory; the ascendancy of the power of the verbal text in musical settings; and the recovery and imitation of the musical culture of antiquity. It is no accident that they all concern Italian music and thought, because this was the principal terrain of musical innovation in this period.

Of the nineteen essays, originally published between 1956 and 1986 (apart from one still unpublished paper), eleven first appeared in Festschriften, conference reports, and multi-authored books, one only in German translation, and almost all are out of print. The studies were selected because of their relevance to current research in Italian music and music theory, as evidenced by their continued citation in publications, papers read at meetings, and dissertations. I have not included studies that were absorbed or reworked in my previous books. For example, my very first scholarly piece, 'Mei: Mentor to the Florentine Camerata' (*Musical Quarterly*, 40 (1954), 1–20), was expanded and corrected in my book on Mei's letters to Galilei and Bardi. Similarly, much of 'The *Camerata fiorentina*: A Reappraisal', *Studi musicali*, 3 (1974), 313–46, was largely repeated in the introduction to Bardi's discourse addressed to Caccini in *The Florentine Camerata: Documentary Studies and Translations* (New Haven, Conn.: Yale University Press, 1989).

The previously published essays are reprinted without revision, except that they were edited to conform to Oxford University Press standards, and a few errors of fact, bibliographical reference, and of translation were corrected. In addition, some footnotes were enriched with current literature, the recent dates betraying these accretions. Where extensive quotations from relatively inaccessible sources were originally represented only in English translation, the original text is now given in footnotes or parallel columns, and, in the case of Essay 4, 'Marco Scacchi's Defence of Modern Music (1649)', on facing pages.

Preface

Each essay is preceded by a prefatory note, sometimes extensive, more often brief. A few of these notes may be read more profitably after the essay, since my purpose was to recall the context of my research and to review responses to it and recent developments in the field.

I acknowledge with appreciation the kindness of the copyright owners for consenting to republication: of Essays 1 and 17, the Staatliches Institut für Musikforschung Preußischer Kulturbesitz, Berlin; 2, the American Musicological Society; 3, Faber and Faber Limited; 4, the Department of Music of Harvard University; 5, W. W. Norton; 6, the University of Notre Dame Press; 8, the Princeton University Press; 9, the International Musicological Society; 10, the University Press of New England; 12 and 14, Oxford University Press for the *Musical Quarterly*; 13, the University of Pittsburgh Press; 15, The Cornell University Press; 16, Albert Mell for Queens College of the City University of New York; and 18, Oriel Press Limited.

This project was born in conversations with Bruce Phillips, Music Books Editor of Oxford University Press, and I thank him warmly for his encouragement. I had the exceptional good fortune of having the manuscript edited by Bonnie J. Blackburn, whose sharp eye, fine sense of style, linguistic virtuosity, and broad learning contributed much to the accuracy and consistency of the whole book. Leofranc Holford-Strevens helped resolve at last some lingering and troubling problems of translation from the Latin, particularly in Essays 9, 10, and 17, for which I am deeply grateful. I thank Kendall L. Crilly of the Yale Music Library for obligingly procuring microfilms and otherwise lending expert assistance. To my wife, Elizabeth A. Keitel, I owe thanks for just being there and looking over my shoulder, always an energizing, loving, and soothing presence.

C.V.P.

Hamden, Connecticut

CONTENTS

Contents

LIST OF ILLUSTRATIONS

PART I

Studies in the
History of Italian Music Theory

1

The Revision of Counterpoint and the Embellished Style

This essay was first published in a German translation as 'Die Neuordnung des Kontrapunkts und der verzierte Stil' in *Italienische Musiktheorie im 16. und 17. Jahrhundert: Antikenrezeption und Satzlehre*, volume 7 of Geschichte der Musiktheorie, edited by Frieder Zaminer (Darmstadt: Wissenschaftliche Buchgesellschaft, 1989), 265–92. This is one of four chapters in a section entitled 'Die Jahrzehnte um 1600 in Italien' (221–306) that I was commissioned to write by the Staatliches Institut für Musikforschung, Preußischer Kulturbesitz, Berlin. I submitted the English version of the essay published here in July 1980.

Although there is some overlap with Essays 2, 3, and 4, the redundant material is here placed in a larger context, and it seemed worthwhile to preserve the English version in this way. Of my other chapters in the German compilation, the first two, 'Der Zusammenbruch der universalen Harmonie. Das Problem der Stimmung', and 'Die humanistische Wiederbelebung der antiken Tonsysteme. Die Auflösung der Kirchentonarten', are covered in English more expansively in my *Humanism in Italian Renaissance Musical Thought* and are therefore not included in the present volume. The fourth chapter, 'Peri und die Theorie des Rezitativs', is represented in Essay 17.

Liberalization of the Counterpoint Rules

IF the theory of counterpoint in the mid-sixteenth century was dominated by Willaert's pupils, Zarlino and Vicentino, that of the last quarter of the century was dominated by Zarlino's disciples, Artusi and Galilei. To these names should be added that of Tigrini, who, although never a pupil of Zarlino, derived most of his teachings from him.

Artusi

Artusi's first treatise, *L'arte del contraponto ridotta in tavole* (1586), is a compendium of aspects of both speculative and practical music theory that Artusi considered essential to the composer. It includes some of the material from parts i, ii, and iv of Zarlino's *Le istitutioni harmoniche*, but the primary emphasis is on the rules of counterpoint of part iii. These are given in tabular outlines that constitute not only a simplification but also a clarification of Zarlino's often prolix prose.

With the *Seconda parte dell'arte del contraponto* (1589) Artusi set out in an independent direction, modernizing the rules, particularly in so far as dissonances were concerned. Whereas Zarlino maintained that dissonances were incidental to counterpoint, Artusi contends that earlier theorists unduly downgraded them, for actually there are more dissonances than consonances in counterpoint and they are very useful to a composer to express words of grief, sorrow, tears, and pain.

Artusi's most original contribution in this book is the clarification of the separate roles of the two voices in a suspension. He calls the two voices that meet in the dissonant interval of the suspension the 'agent' (*agente*) and 'patient' (*patiente*). The patient is the part that holds a note from the previous consonance and suffers (*patisce*) the agent to form a dissonant interval against it. Artusi states the general rule that the patient must descend a step—a tone or semitone—to a perfect or imperfect consonance, or, occasionally, to another dissonant interval. The agent is free to move to this interval by step or leap. This is a freer treatment than allowed by Zarlino, who obliged the voice that Artusi calls the agent to remain stationary while the syncopated voice, Artusi's patient, descends to the nearest consonance. Artusi insists that any rules stricter than his own are 'sophistries'. However, he does not agree with those who would free the patient to proceed by leap, as in Ex. 1.1.[1]

EX. 1.1

One of Artusi's models remains Adrian Willaert, but he more often cites works of Cipriano de Rore, Clemens non Papa, Costanzo Porta, Claudio Merulo, and Andrea Gabrieli. It is evident throughout this book that Artusi was bringing the theory of dissonance practice into line with recent usage. He particularly sought to liberalize the employment of the diminished fifth and augmented fourth, which he found to be the source of many beautiful effects, applicable 'with much elegance' both on the down-

---

[1] Giovanni Maria Artusi, *Seconda parte dell'arte del contraponto* (Venice: Giacomo Vincenti, 1589), bk. ii, ch. 1, pp. 27–8.

Ex. 1.2

Ex. 1.3

Ex. 1.4   Ex. 1.5 (*a*)   (*b*)   Ex. 1.6

beat and up-beat. Zarlino had already noted that the diminished fifth could resolve the suspended fourth, as in Artusi's example (Ex. 1.2).[2]

The diminished fifth itself may also be the dissonant interval of a suspension, when it is resolved by the major third (Ex. 1.3),[3] and the augmented fourth may similarly be resolved by the minor sixth (Ex. 1.4).[4] A diminished fifth may thus appear on a down-beat (*posata*) as well as on an up-beat (*levata*) (see Ex. 1.3). For its occurrence on the up-beat, Artusi gives several interesting examples, noting that the interval may be 'natural', that is, caused by notes within the mode (Ex. 1.5), or 'artificial', caused by accidental notes (Ex. 1.6; see also Exx. 1.3–4).[5]

Artusi also shows that a dissonant interval need not always be followed by a consonant one: two, three, or more dissonances may occur in succession. (Exx. 1.7*a*, *b*; the last of these shows six dissonances in succession).[6]

Although two dissonances of the same size may not be used in succes-

---

[2] Zarlino, *Le istitutioni harmoniche* (Venice, 1558), pt. iii, ch. 42. Artusi, *Seconda parte*, bk. ii, ch. 7, p. 34.

[3] Ibid.

[4] Ibid., ch. 11, p. 40.

[5] Ibid., ch. 7, p. 34.

[6] Ibid., bk. i, ch. 13, pp. 41–2. The 1589 edn. has a C-clef on the second line, making the first note in the superius F. It has been corrected to a G-clef.

Ex. 1.7 (a)   (b)

Ex. 1.8 (a)   (b)

Ex. 1.9 (a)   (b)   (c)   (d)

(e)

sion, this progression is permissible if it occurs through diminution. Artusi gives both the diminished version (Ex. 1.8*a*) and the simple one (8*b*) of such a case.[7]

Another way in which diminution compounds the incidence of dissonance occurs in the ornamented resolution of a suspension (Exx. 1.9*b*, *c*, *d*, *e* are all embellishments of 9*a*; 9*c* is from Rore's madrigal *Un'altra volta la Germania stride*).[8]

For stepwise notes of 'local motion' (*moto locale*) Artusi modifies the rule that consonance and dissonance should alternate on down- and up-beats; the third or both the second and third of four notes may be dissonant, as in Ex. 1.10.[9]

[7] Ibid., ch. 14, p. 43.
[8] Ibid., ch. 15, 44.
[9] Ibid., ch. 15, pp. 44–5.

Ex. I.10 (*a*)   (*b*)   (*c*)

In 1598 Artusi issued a second edition of the two parts of his counterpoint treatise of 1586–9 in a single volume.[10] In this edition he appears anxious to dissociate himself from the theories and the music of the previous generation. He urges composers to avoid unvocal lines with angular leaps and various *ostinationi*, such as forcing lines into fugues and other subtleties, while missing opportunities for agreeable *passaggi*, which bring much grace to a work. He praises Andrea Gabrieli, Palestrina, and Clemens non Papa, 'who, having eschewed such *ostinatione*, have given pleasure to everyone'.[11] The usefulness of counterpoint is now measured by the delight it can provide the listener, not by the combinatorial and fugal complexities it permits.

In view of Artusi's interest in modern dissonance practice shown in his second book of counterpoint of 1589 and his espousal of recent trends in the edition of 1598, the negative reaction of the interlocutor Vario in the dialogue, *L'Artusi, overo delle imperfettioni della moderna musica* (1603) to Monteverdi's licences is surprising. But if Vario voices Artusi's viewpoint, as appears likely, since of the two interlocutors he is the professional musician, Artusi chastises Monteverdi for crossing the fine line between tolerable and abusive licence. Artusi's own position, however, is not all that clear, because the dialogue form was often used to air issues to which there was no decisive resolution, where there was more than one valid point of view, and where the author preferred not to commit himself in print. Artusi allows the amateur, Luca, to justify Monteverdi's licences, and this with sound reasons—sounder, indeed, than those advanced by Monteverdi's brother some years later.

Each of the examples cited by Artusi in score violates one or more rules

[10] Artusi, *L'arte del contraponto, novamente ristampata, et di molte nuove aggiunte, dall'auttore arrichita* (Venice: Giacomo Vincenti, 1598).

[11] Ibid. 38: 'che per hauer fugita quella ostinatione, hanno dato tanto piacere a tutti'. That composition was now seen as a much more demanding art than simply writing good counterpoint is exhibited in the seven criteria enumerated by Zacconi for judging polyphonic music (*musica armoniale*): (1) artfulness (*arte*), (2) good part-writing (*modulatione*), (3) delight given to the listener, (4) texture (*tessitura*), (5) counterpoint, (6) invention, and (7) good arrangement (*buona dispositione*). See James Haar, 'A Sixteenth-Century Attempt at Music Criticism', *Journal of the American Musicological Society*, 36 (1983), 191–209.

Ex. 1.11. Monteverdi, *Cruda Amarilli*, bars 12–14

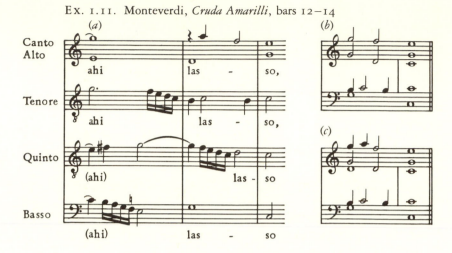

Ex. 1.12. Monteverdi, *Cruda Amarilli*, bars 41–2

of the strict style as taught by Zarlino and liberalized and augmented by Artusi himself. Ex. 1.11*a* is faulty because the upper parts do not accord with the bass. (Artusi prints only the second and third bars.) Since the dissonances made by the runs in the Tenor, Quinto, and Bass are essentially like those of Ex. 1.10*c*, these must not have offended Artusi. Rather it is the A of the Soprano, entering after a rest, which fails to accord with the Bass, G. Luca explains that this is 'accented singing'. Indeed, the offending A may be said to arise from what Zacconi calls an 'accento' (Ex. 1.11*c*, Soprano) applied to what is otherwise a normal progression of voices (Ex. 1.11*b*).[12]

A more dubious rationalization is that by which Luca excuses the sixth of

[12] Artusi, *L'Artusi overo delle imperfettioni della moderna musica* (Venice: Giacomo Vincenti, 1600; facs. edn., Bologna: Forni, 1968), Ragionamento 2, fo. 41ʳ.

Artusi's quotations from Monteverdi's *Cruda Amarilli* (Ex. 1.12, Artusi's no. 9):[13]

Osservano questi Musici, che	These musicians observe the
quella parte, che fa la	rule that the part which makes a
dissonanza con la più grave,	dissonance with the lowest part
habbi corrispondenza Harmonica	be in harmonic correspondence
col Tenore; di maniera	with the Tenor in such a way
che accorda lei,	that the [first] part accords
con tutte l'altre parti;	with all the other parts, and
e 'l più grave accorda lui ancora	the lowest part also accords
con tutte l'altre; & cosi	with all the others. Thus they
fanno una mistura a lor	make a melange in their own
modo.	fashion.

Artusi here refers to the rule for singing *contrapunto a mente*. The older method, described by Tinctoris, required that each part observe the laws of consonance with the tenor part alone.[14] Banchieri shows that the modern method was to observe consonance with the bass rather than the tenor.[15] Zacconi likewise emphasizes that when counterpoint is made in churches against a cantus firmus, this is in the bass, because it is the part that is never diminished.[16] If Monteverdi followed the rule of improvised counterpoint in this example, he did so with respect to the tenor, for all the voices behave properly with respect to it but not to the bass.

In appealing to improvised diminution, embellishment, and *contrapunto a mente* as justifications for some of Monteverdi's licences, Artusi astutely identified contrapuntal practices that were accepted in written composition only after listeners became habituated to them through hearing them improvised.

For some of the dissonant effects introduced by Monteverdi in his madrigals even Luca, however, cannot find anything positive to say. The three excerpts in Ex. 1.13 (Artusi's *caselle* 2, 3, and 9) are rejected outright. Luca declares that the semidiapente that enters after a rest in Ex. 1.13*b*, 'used and taken absolutely' in this way, 'cannot have a good effect'. The sevenths in Exx. 1.13*b* and 13*c*, 'used absolutely and openly', are condemned by Vario as against the teaching of the ancient masters, and Luca admits this is a new paradox.[17]

---

[13] Ibid., fo. 43ʳ.

[14] Johannes Tinctoris, *Liber de arte contrapuncti*, ed. Albert Seay (American Institute of Musicology, 1975), bk. ii, ch. 20, p. 107.

[15] Adriano Banchieri, *Cartella musicale nel canto figurato, fermo & contrapunto* (Venice: Giacomo Vincenti, 1614; facs. edn., Bologna: Forni, 1968), 230.

[16] Zacconi, *Prattica di musica, seconda parte* (Venice: Alessandro Vincenti, 1600), bk. ii, ch. 1, p. 59.

[17] Artusi, *L'Artusi*, Rag. 2, fos. 43ᵛ–44ʳ: 'quelli intervalli . . . usati & posti assolutamente, discostandosi da quel modo da loro insegnato, non possono fare buono effetto'.

Ex. 1.13 (*a*)   (*b*)   (*c*)

The only constructive word said in the controversy about these open and absolute diminished fifths and sevenths is by L'Ottuso Accademico, the otherwise unidentified author of a letter quoted by Artusi in the *Seconda parte dell'Artusi* (1603). L'Ottuso insists that to express new passions and sentiments the composer must devise new harmonies or *concenti*. A seventh is such a new sonority. In reply to Artusi's claims that such a dissonance cannot be a *concento,* which must be a product of rational intervals, L'Ottuso declares:[18]

... non essendovi alcuna dissonanza per se, che per accidente non possi farsi buona rispetto alli accompagnamenti, coi quali sarà fraposto quello interuallo dissono ... ma per il contrario come accento, et come inganno, overo come dissonanza sì, ma radolcita dallo accompagnamento delle altre parti; senza dubbio non solo farà buono effetto, ma come cosa nova sarà di maggior diletto all'udito, che non sarebbe stata l'ottava suposta; & perchè ella ne desidera la demostratione; da ottimo Poeta accordi la metafora al proposito, & così invece di settima vi ponghi l'ottava ...

... there is no interval that is in itself dissonant that through circumstances cannot be made good with respect to the accompaniments among which it is placed ... As an accent, as a deception, or, indeed, as a dissonance, though sweetened by the accompaniment of the other parts, it [a seventh] will undoubtedly not only have a good effect, but, being something new, will give greater delight to the ear than would the supposed octave. And since you desire proof, you will draw it very easily from this: you allow an excellent poet the metaphor purposefully used; similarly, the seventh is taken in place of the octave.

[18] Artusi, *Seconda parte dell'Artusi overo delle imperfettioni della moderna musica* (Venice: Giacomo Vincenti, 1603), 16.

The octave is 'supposed', but the seventh is actually written, as in a metaphor the normal word is suppressed and one with stronger associations is substituted. The idea of 'supposition' was later taken up by French theorists as an explanation for non-harmonic tones.[19]

Tigrini

By contrast with Artusi, Orazio Tigrini (*c.*1535–91) had almost nothing original to say in his *Il compendio della musica* (1588).[20] This treatise, dedicated to Zarlino, is in large part a summary and simplification of part iii of *Le istitutioni harmoniche*, with some material drawn from part iv and the other two parts, though many of the musical examples are new. Tigrini is more eclectic than Artusi, however, and derived some of his theories from Boethius, Gaffurio, Burzio, Vicentino, Aron, and Dentice, among others. Tigrini's is an extremely useful compilation that circulated widely in both its first and subsequent editions (1602 and 1638). Among the helpful features are examples of cadences in various modes in three, four, five, and six voices, instructions for written composition on plainchants,[21] and for improvising *contrapunto alla mente* on plainchants.[22]

Cerreto

Scipione Cerreto (*c.*1551–*c.*1633), in his *Della prattica musica vocale, et strumentale* (1601),[23] returns to the tradition of Gaffurio's eight rules, not ignoring Zarlino altogether, but building on other foundations. He was influenced particularly by two authors associated with Naples, Luigi Dentice and Rocco Rodio.[24] Cerreto's treatise is a comprehensive one, dwelling on a mixture of speculative and practical matters, including long sections on plainchant, psalm tones, and modes, and on musicians and musical life in Naples. The section on counterpoint[25] is insufficient for instructing a beginner but contains some novel observations. He classifies counterpoint into three *maniere*: (i) free (*sciolto*); (ii) bound (*ligato*), that is

---

[19] See Albert Cohen, '*La Supposition* and the Changing Concept of Dissonance in Baroque Theory', *Journal of the American Musicological Society*, 24 (1971), 63–84; and Palisca, 'The Artusi–Monteverdi Controversy', below, Essay 3.

[20] Orazio Tigrini, *Il compendio della musica nel quale brevemente si tratta dell'arte del contrapunto* (Venice: Ricciardo Amadino, 1588).

[21] Ibid., bk. iv, ch. 10.

[22] Ibid., bk. iv, ch. 11.

[23] Scipione Cerreto, *Della prattica musica vocale, et strumentale* (Naples: Giovanni Iacomo Carlino, 1601).

[24] Rocco Rodio's *Regole di musica* is extant only in an edition of 1609 (Naples: Gio. Giacomo Carlino e Costantino Vitale, 1609), but Cerreto (244) cites from an earlier edition, as 'just published (nouamente stampato)', therefore probably of 1600.

[25] Cerreto, *Della prattica*, bk. iv, chs. 1–7, pp. 241–312.

with suspensions; and (iii) syncopated (*sincopato*), consisting entirely of consonant suspensions.[26] The free *maniera* he divides in turn into two species, of mixed consonances and dissonances, and of all consonances. Cerreto's categories apply equally to written and improvised counterpoint. An interesting rule, which he credits to Rodio (while criticizing his language), is that when making a counterpoint above a tenor cantus firmus, the counterpoint should ascend after major consonances and descend after minor. In counterpoint below a tenor cantus firmus, one should descend after major consonances and ascend from minor ones.[27] These strictures are subject to exceptions, as when the counterpoint is obliged to conform to canon, *perfidia* (an ostinato), or repetition, or in order to remain within a mode.

Diruta

Neither Artusi nor Tigrini arrived at any general rules for the movement of consonances, retaining in their books the bewildering complexity of the instructions left by Zarlino.[28] Cerreto's general rule applies only to thirds and sixths. A more synthetic approach was attempted by Girolamo Diruta in the *Seconda parte del Transilvano Dialogo* (1622).[29] Intended as a guide to instrumental counterpoint within a treatise on organ-playing, his four principal rules of consonant progression or *movimenti* was adopted by almost every counterpoint theorist after him. The four movements are: (i) in going from a perfect consonance to another, contrary motion is required; (ii) the movement is free from an imperfect consonance to another; (iii) it is also free from a perfect consonance to an imperfect; (iv) contrary motion is obligatory in proceeding from an imperfect consonance to a perfect one, when one voice must move by semitone.

Diruta's conditions represent a stiffening of the rules. Whereas Zarlino allowed certain parallel movements towards perfect consonances, Diruta forbids them all. The reason given for requiring contrary motion in both the first and fourth movements is that otherwise hidden fifths or octaves will occur (Ex. 1.14).[30]

In addition to laying down the four movements, Diruta cautions the contrapuntist to alternate major and minor thirds and sixths so as to avoid cross-relations, and, when writing a third after a sixth or vice versa, to

---

[26] Ibid., bk. iv, ch. 3, p. 265.
[27] Ibid., ch. 1, p. 243.
[28] Zarlino, *Le istitutioni*, pt. iii, chs. 29–38.
[29] Girolamo Diruta, *Seconda parte del Transilvano dialogo* (Venice: Alessandro Vincenti, 1622), bk. ii, pp. 1 ff.
[30] Ibid. 3.

Ex. 1.14

make one major and the other minor, unless one of the parts remains
stationary.

Diruta continued the tendency already evident in Cerreto of providing
exercises or examples in various species or modes of counterpoint.[31] His
examples illustrate the following types: (i) note against note (*contrapunto di
nota contra nota*); (ii) minims against semibreves in the subject (*contrapunto
di minime osservato*); (iii) consonant suspensions (*contrapunto di note legate di
consonanze*); (iv) dissonant suspensions (*contrapunto ligato con le dissonanze*); (v)
counterpoint of black notes—that is, mixed quarter- and eighth-notes
(*contrapunto di note negre*); (vi) free counterpoint (*contrapunto di fantasia*). All
these categories belong to the *contrapunto osservato* or strict counterpoint.
Diruta also demonstrated a laxer standard that he called *contrapunto commune*, in which the only firm rule was that two perfect consonances of the
same species in succession were prohibited.[32] This common counterpoint
was that practised when improvising at the organ or in writing such pieces
as toccatas.

Galilei

The authors on counterpoint considered up to now were conservative,
determined to maintain the status quo of *contrapunto osservato*. On the other
hand, Vincenzo Galilei, although a consummate contrapuntist, saw no
reason to revere the ancient rules when they were daily violated in practice.
Modelling his precepts on the practices of the generation led by Cipriano de
Rore, he sought not simply to control dissonance and to mitigate its
crudeness but to exploit both consonance and dissonance to serve the
expression of the affections of a text. The text for him was the soul of
music, the notes the body; the soul must animate the body.[33]

He recognized no firm boundary between consonance and dissonance,

---

[31] Ibid. 9–14.
[32] Ibid. 14–15.
[33] Vincenzo Galilei, *Discorso intorno all'uso delle dissonanze*, Florence, Biblioteca Nazionale Centrale,
MSS Galileiani 1, ed. Frieder Rempp, in *Die Kontrapunkttraktate Vincenzo Galileis* (Cologne: Arno Volk,
1980), 77–161.

certainly no numerical sanctuary of consonance such as Zarlino's *senario* and the *numeri armonici*. 'It is as natural to delight in the concording of the octave as it is natural to be displeased by the discording of the seventh, the first conforming, the second not, with our sense [of hearing].'[34]

Galilei was on the whole satisfied with the rules governing the use of consonances in note-against-note counterpoint. But as normally understood and stated by Zarlino, they were more suited to instrumental music and through it for the delight of the ear and for pure recreation. For nobler ends, such as those sought by the ancients—to move souls of listeners to different passions and attitudes—these rules were sometimes superfluous, at other times insufficient. For example, two parallel major thirds or two parallel minor sixths were prohibited by Zarlino, because false relations occurred between the parts. Yet these very progressions may express what a text requires:[35]

Et perche due Seste minori usate nella mostrata maniera, hanno del mesto, et dell'allegro due maggior' Terze; non so per qual cagione il Tritono et la Semidiapente concorrendo alla qualità di questi effetti, mi habbino a ritenere che io non l'usi per espressione di quei concetti che con tali intervalli hanno conformità, et che con il mezzo di essi prendono forza et vigore, et questo sia detto per l'uso di tutti gl'altri Intervalli, et della natura loro.	Because two minor sixths used in the way shown [Ex. 1.15] have a sad feeling and two such major thirds a happy one, and since the tritone and semidiapente concur in the uniformity of these effects, I do not know under what heading I should be restrained from using them for the expression of those thoughts that conform with these intervals and that by means of them acquire form and vigour. And this goes for the use of all the other intervals and for their natures.

EX. 1.15

Galilei's counterpoint treatise is in two parts or discourses, *Il primo libro della prattica del contrapunto intorno all'uso delle consonanze*, and *Discorso intorno all'uso delle dissonanze*. Three drafts of each treatise are preserved in the Biblioteca Nazionale Centrale in Florence. External evidence shows that Galilei was completing a draft of the first book in 1588; he was still

[34] Galilei, *Il primo libro della prattica del contrapunto intorno all'uso delle consonanze*, MSS Galileiani 1, fo. 61ʳ: 'tanto è adunque naturale il dilettarci l'Ottava con il consonare; quanto è naturale il dispiacerci della settima con il dissonare: quella come conforme, et come disforme questa con il nostro senso' (ed. Rempp, 15).

[35] Ibid., Gal. 1, fo. 74ʳ (ed. Rempp, 33).

revising the two books in 1591, the year he died.[36] Some of the ideas in
the two discourses may have been communicated to a small circle of
Florentine musicians, but there is no evidence that it was ever copied and
circulated. Its importance cannot therefore be measured by its impact on
theory or practice; rather it is important as a document of the reflections of
a sensitive, highly cultivated musician who had taken the trouble to score
and intabulate, according to his own confession, 14,000 works by a large
number of composers.[37]

The book on consonances has many original ideas and corrects or refutes
Zarlino's rules. It admits welcome fresh air into a closed system. In it the
teaching of counterpoint falls into step with what was currently practised.
For example, the orientation of parts around a tenor was no longer a
realistic view of composition. 'It should be understood that the lowest part,
and not the tenor, as Zarlino would have it,[38] is that which reigns and
governs and gives air to a composition, and, whenever it does not move,
the composition will not be varied or only slightly so.'[39] It is in this book
on consonances that Galilei makes an important distinction between two
manners of treating dissonances:[40]

Nella Cantilena si usano le dissonanze in due maniere; una delle quali è parte principalissima del contrapunto; et per ch'ella è atta a mostrare la suffizienza del contrapuntista, è da lui grandemente considerata. L'altra è poco reputata da esso, come quella che è poco attenente a dimostrare il suo sapere, et aggiugnere la bellezza alla Cantilena di lui. La considerata et apprezzata dal contrapuntista, è quella nella	Dissonances are used in a vocal composition in two manners. One of these is the most essential part of counterpoint, both because it is capable of demonstrating the sufficiency of the contrapuntist's technique and because it is carefully considered by him. To the other he attaches little importance, as it is of little purpose for demonstrating his erudition or for adding beauty to his work. The manner considered and appreciated by the contrapuntist

---

[36] For an index to the Vincenzo Galilei manuscripts see 'Galilei' in *MGG* iv (1955), 1267. For a detailed study of the treatises concerning counterpoint see Palisca, 'Vincenzo Galilei's Counterpoint Treatise: A Code for the *Seconda Pratica*', below, Essay 2, and Rempp, *Die Kontrapunkttraktate*, 185–312.

[37] Gal. 1, fo. 101ᵛ (ed. Rempp, 73).

[38] Zarlino, *Le istitutioni*, pt. iii, ch. 58.

[39] Galilei, *Discorso . . . delle dissonanze*, MS Gal. 1, fo. 76ᵛ: 'è da sapere, che la parte grave, et non il Tenore come piace al Zarlino, è quella che reggi et governa, et quella che dà l'aria alla Cantilena, e' tutta uolta ch'ella non varia corde, la Cantilena non è varia o poco' (ed. Rempp, 38).

[40] Ibid., fo. 78ʳ (ed. Rempp, 40).

quale mi sono affaticato in dimostrare perfettamente il suo uso. L'altra poco da lui considerata è quella che consiste particolarmente nel modulare che si fa con le Note di non molta valuta, come sono le minime et le semiminime che per movimento congiunto per molti gradi procedano, ascendendo, o discendendo; delle quali (et questo ci servirà per Regola) per l'ordinario se ne costuma porre nel contrapunto una consonante, et dissonante l'altra; resolute per lo più, da consonanze fuore del commun'uso di quelle dell'altra più importante maniera: il qual modo di procedere più negli strumenti conviene, che tra le voci et massimamente nell'esprimere dell'Oratione.	is the one whose use I have been striving to demonstrate perfectly. The other, little considered by him, consists specifically in moving with notes of smaller value, like minims and semiminims proceeding by conjunct movement ascending and descending through many steps, of which (and this will serve as a rule) it is ordinarily customary to make one consonant and the other dissonant. These dissonances are resolved, for the most part, by consonances outside the common usage of that other more important manner [the regular resolutions]. This way of proceeding is more appropriate for instruments than for voices, especially when the latter are expressing a text.

The non-essential dissonances variously described by him as *cattive*, *dissonanze sciolte*, or *note di moto locale* are discussed and demonstrated in the first book. As a general principle, any dissonances that occurred among parts moving quickly and gracefully against each other were tolerated. When four semiminims occur, besides the alternation approved by Zarlino—Consonance–Dissonance–Consonance–Dissonance (CDCD)— Galilei admitted DCCD, CDDC, DCDC, and occasionally three dissonances in a row.

The essential dissonances are those to which Galilei dedicated his second book. After announcing a series of sweeping claims, such as 'that dissonances may be resolved no less by skipwise movement of one of the parts than by conjunct movement',[41] Galilei proceeds to show how each dissonant interval may be resolved by other than the traditional 'nearest' interval and how any consonance may be succeeded by any dissonance.

The suspended second, for example, may be resolved not only by the fourth and unison, but by the fifth, with the syncopated voice leaping down a fourth (Ex. 1.16). It is not the leap that makes this resolution

---

[41] Galilei, *Delle consonanze*, MS Gal. 1, fos. 105ᵛ–106ʳ: 'ch'elle [le dissonanze] possano risolvere non meno col movimento separato di una di ambedue le parti; non altramente che col congiunto' (ed. Rempp, from later draft, fos. 148ᵛ–149ʳ, p. 78).

Ex. 1.16   Ex. 1.17

Ex. 1.18   Ex. 1.19

harsher, Galilei contends, but the character of the resolving interval, for the same leap resolving into a different interval is more satisfying (Ex. 1.17).[42]

Still another example shows a resolution by a leap of a fifth (Ex. 1.18). Other instances illustrated involve a leap by the non-syncopated voice (Artusi's agent), among which one of the most extraordinary is Ex. 1.19.[43]

These examples, Galilei declares, illustrate the principle that 'the quality and nature of the consonance that succeeds the dissonance has the power to make the dissonance more or less pleasing to the hearing rather than the quality and nature of conjunct or disjunct motion'.[44]

Having shown that the second may proceed to any consonance, Galilei reverses the process and shows how from the unison one may reach any dissonant interval (Ex. 1.20).[45] Although some of these progressions would not have been disputed by earlier theorists, others boldly flout the current rules. Galilei's purpose in the exhaustive repertory of examples is to enlarge the expressive vocabulary.

Galilei demonstrates movements to and from the other dissonances in a similar fashion, taking up the fourth, tritone, and semidiapente (diminished fifth). Some of the more striking usages proposed are in Ex. 1.21.[46]

Further, Galilei demonstrates that several dissonant intervals, whether of the same or different size, may occur simultaneously, each properly

---

[42] Ibid., fo. 110^v.

[43] Ibid., fos. 119^v, 113^r.

[44] Ibid., fos. 110^v–111^r (ed. Rempp, 88, from third draft, fo. 156^r): 'più la qualità et natura della Consonanza che alla Dissonanza succede, ha forza di farla più, et meno grata all'udito; che non ha la qualità et natura del congiunto, o del separato movimento . . .'.

[45] Ibid., fo. 114^v.

[46] Ibid., fos. 117^v, 119^v, 119^v.

Ex. 1.20 (*a*)   (*b*)   (*c*)   (*d*)

(*e*)

Ex. 1.21 (*a*)   (*b*)   (*c*)

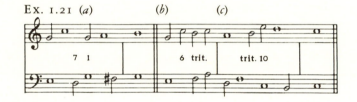

Ex. 1.22

(*a*)   (*b*)   (*c*)

resolved, and, besides, a chain of such dissonances may occur (Ex. 1.22).[47]

Dissonances resulting from suspensions may resolve ascending as well as descending (Ex. 1.23).[48] Dissonances may be used on the up-beat in the same way they are used on the down-beat, that is essentially rather than ornamentally (Ex. 1.24).[49]

[47] Ibid., fos. 127ʳ, 132ᵛ, 126ʳ.
[48] Ibid., fo. 136ʳ.
[49] Ibid., fo. 137ᵛ.

Ex. 1.23 (*a*)   (*b*)

Ex. 1.24 (*a*)   (*b*)

Galilei's treatise is filled with these quite extraordinary, yet plausible, examples. He admitted that he did not dare use some of them himself in published music before setting them out systematically in his book, which he never lived to see come to light. It is a pity, because his book would have been one of the landmarks in the history of theory, in the company of Zarlino and Rameau.

The Plurality of Contrapuntal Standards: The *Prima* and *Seconda Pratica*

In the years around 1600 it became evident that more than one standard of good counterpoint needed to be recognized. Pietro Pontio taught that what was proper to one genre of composition might not be to another. Galilei maintained that the rules for strict imitative counterpoint were adequate when writing for an ensemble of instruments, but they had to be relaxed for the vocal expression of the meaning and feeling of a text. Claudio Monteverdi proclaimed that besides the practice of composition taught by Zarlino there was a second practice so far as the use of consonances and dissonances was concerned. The novelty of this second practice was clarified by his brother Giulio Cesare, who explained that in it the harmony or part-writing was subordinated to the demands of the text. Finally, those who later adopted the *prima—seconda pratica* division emphasized that they were both viable alternatives for a modern composer, and that as coexistent styles they demonstrated the richness of resources then available.

The trend towards a plurality of standards for contrapuntal writing is already clear in the 'Ragionamento quarto' of Pietro Pontio's *Ragionamento di musica* (1588).[50] In this dialogue Don Paolo instructs Don Hettore that it is necessary to know what manner (*modo*) or style (*stile*) to choose for a given composition, depending on whether it is a motet, mass, psalm, madrigal, or some other genre. The style of a motet or mass should be severe and calm (*graue & quieto*).[51] The bass part, particularly, should move slowly and the subjects (*invenzioni*) should be severe. Assuming alla breve measure, a syncopated minim and rests of a semiminim or less should be avoided, and passages in chromas (eighth-notes), semichromas (sixteenth-notes), and continuous semiminims are inappropriate. Although in the same basic style, a mass differs from a motet in that the Kyrie, Gloria, Credo, Sanctus, and Agnus should all begin alike and also have parallel final endings, whereas in a motet the *secunda pars* calls for an invention different from that of the *prima pars*. In writing psalms the parts should mostly proceed together, with the words pronounced almost simultaneously, but in the Magnificat, Benedictus, and Nunc dimittis a more learned style is required in which all the parts imitate the plainsong or other subject. Both in the regular psalms and the Magnificat the median cadence and the mode are carefully observed.

In composing a madrigal the invented subjects should be short in comparison to those of a mass or motet, not longer than two or three semibreves, and the semiminim and minim may be used in syncopation, that is to say, in suspension. The parts may proceed together with minims and semiminims, and fast and slow movement may be contrasted to illustrate the text. A ricercare differs from all these in that it demands lengthy subjects and imitative entrances distant from one another. The same subject may be used again and again and even throughout a piece.

Diruta made a more general distinction—between *contrapunto osservato*, the normal counterpoint written for voices that strictly follows the rules, and *contrapunto commune*, practised when improvising at the organ or writing toccatas and such pieces, in which the only firm rule was that two perfect

---

[50] Pietro Pontio, *Ragionamento di musica* (Parma: Erasmo Viotto; facs., ed. Suzanne Clercx, Kassel: Bärenreiter, n.d.), 153–61.

[51] Ibid. 154. Pontio defines the severe style as follows: 'Severity and the severe style are observed in this way: when two voices sing and one of the parts has a breve, the other will move by minims or semiminims or with a value of a semibreve on the up-beat of the measure, and not by *crome* or *semicrome* or continually by semiminims, for then the composition would not have in itself any severity at all because of the fast, indeed, exceedingly fast movement. (Si serva la gravità, e' lo stile grave in questo modo, che quando due parti cantano, & ch'in una di esse parti si trova una figura di Breve, l'altra si moverà poi con figure di Minime, over di Semiminime, over con una figura di Semibreve, posta in elevazione della misura; & non per chrome, o Semichrome, over continuatamente di Semiminime; perchè non havrebbe la cantilena gravità alcuna in sè, per esser il moto veloce, anzi velocissimo . . .)' (154).

consonances of the same species in succession were prohibited.[52] Adriano Banchieri took up this division of counterpoint in his *Conclusioni nel suono dell'organo*. In the category of *contrapunto misto* or *commune* he included not only instrumental music but any music that must depart from the normal to imitate the affections. No rules can be devised for this kind of composition, which has no other principles than that the sense of hearing be pleased and that the listener be moved. The composer should imitate the perfect orator, of whom Cicero said: 'Optimus orator est vir canorus, qui in dicendo animas audientium delectat, & permovet.'[53]

To this end the composer may depart from the mode, change key (*muta chiavi*), and otherwise violate the usual precepts:[54]

. . . in somma la Musica deve osservarsi con gli buoni precetti, senza parole come sono toccate, recercari, & quando le parole nelle composizioni non ricerchino inosservanza, la quale inosservanza devesi usare per imitare la parola, essendo quella (come già s'è detto) la quale esprime gl'affetti di perfettissimo Oratore.	. . . in short, the good precepts should be observed in music without words, such as toccate, recercari, and when the words of the composition do not require inobservance, but this inobservance must be used to imitate the text, since this (as has already been stated) is what expresses the affections of the most perfect orator.

It is evident that Banchieri perceived the dichotomy differently from Diruta, for Banchieri goes on in this passage to defend as a model 'inosservatore' Monteverdi, whose 'artful expressions are truly worthy of complete commendation, for in them are discovered every affective trait of the perfect oration, industriously explicated and imitated with harmony equal to them'.[55]

Banchieri had obviously read Monteverdi's short defence of his own madrigals in *Il quinto libro de madrigali* (1605) and Giulio Cesare's explication of this statement in the *Scherzi musicali* (1607).[56] Claudio Monteverdi,

---

[52] Diruta, *Seconda parte del Transilvano*, 14.

[53] Adriano Banchieri, *Conclusioni nel suono dell'organo* (Bologna: Heredi di Giovanni Rossi, 1609), 57–8. A somewhat revised discussion of this distinction is in the essay 'Moderna pratica musicale', dated 1613 and included in his *Cartella musicale* (1614), 161 ff.

[54] Banchieri, *Conclusioni*, 60.

[55] Ibid.: 'poi che gli suoi artefiziosi sentimenti in vero sono degni d'intera commendazione, scoprendosi in essi ogni affettuosa parte di perfetta orazione, industriamente spiegati, & imitati d'armonia equivalente . . .'.

[56] Monteverdi's letter and his brother's 'dichiarazione' are printed in G. Francesco Malipiero, *Claudio Monteverdi* (Milan: Fratelli Treves, 1929), 71–85, and Domenico de' Paoli, *Monteverdi, Lettere, dediche, e prefazioni* (Roma: De Santis, 1973), 391–407, and in translation in Oliver Strunk, *Source Readings in Music History* (New York: Norton, 1950), 405–12.

though he promised a theoretical statement, made none; Giulio Cesare did make a number of theoretical statements, but it is not clear to what extent they represented Claudio's point of view or how much, if at all, Claudio participated in the drafting of the explication.

Giulio Cesare bases his main argument on Plato's dictum: 'Melodiam ex tribus constare, oratione, harmonia, Rithmo . . . quin etiam consonum ipsum et dissonum eodem modo, quandoquidem Rithmus et Harmonia orationem sequuntur non ipsa oratio Rithmum et Harmoniam sequitur.'[57] Giulio Cesare employs the Italian term *melodia* to render the Latin *melodia*, which had been *melos* in Greek. The Italian *melodia* was not then much used in technical discussions; what modern Italians mean by *melodia* was indicated by the term *aria*. *Melodia* signified the entire composition or song, which is a composite of the various elements of music. Zarlino used the term in this way when he stated 'Song (*Melodia*) is composed . . . of text (*Oratione*), rhythm (*Rhythmo*), and harmony (*Harmonia*), of which, since the text (*Oratione*) is the principal part, the other two are as if her servants'.[58] The first modern commentator to point out the significance of Plato's definition was probably Bishop Jacopo Sadoleto:[59]

. . . cum constet chorus ex tribus, sententia, rhythmo (hic enim numerus nobis est) & uoce, primum quidem omnium & potissimum sententiam esse, utpote quae si sedes & fundamentum reliquorum, & per se ipsa ualeat non minimum ad suadendum animo uel dissuadendum: numeris autem modisque contorta penetret multo acrius: si uero etiam cantu & uoce fuerit modulata, iam omnis intus sensus & hominem totum possideat.	A chorus consists of three elements, the sense of the words, the rhythm (which we call number), and tone. The words are the first and most important of the three as being the very basis and foundation of the others. By themselves the words have no mean influence on the mind, whether to persuade or restrain. Accommodated to rhythm (*numerus*) and metre (*modus*), they penetrate much more deeply. If in addition they are given a melodic setting, they take possession of all the inner feelings and of the whole man.

[57] Plato, *Republic* 398C–D.

[58] Zarlino, *Sopplimenti musicali* (Venice: Francesco de' Franceschi, Sanese, 1588; facs. edn., Ridgewood, NJ: Gregg Press, 1966), bk. viii, ch. 1, p. 277. Zarlino used the term also in *Le istitutioni*, pt. ii, ch. 12, p. 80.

[59] Jacopo Sadoleto, *De liberis recte instituendis* (Venice: Io. Antonium et Fratres de Sabio, 1533), fo. 42ᵛ.

Whereas Zarlino and, before him, Sadoleto understood Plato's term, *harmonia*, correctly as successive high and low pitches combined through consonant and dissonant intervals in a proportionate or harmonious whole,[60] Giulio Cesare incorrectly assumed that *harmonia* referred to part-writing or counterpoint, like Zarlino's *harmonia propria*.[61] For Giulio Cesare, then, *melodia* (melos or song) consisted of the text, harmony (in the modern sense), and rhythm (including tempo, metre, and rhythm), of which the text should be the prime component. The second practice differed from the first in that the text reigned over the other elements, whereas in the first it was the harmony that was sovereign. The second practice is based on a different usage of consonances and dissonances from that practised by Adrian Willaert and taught by Zarlino; the practice of Monteverdi was that begun by Cipriano de Rore and continued by Marenzio, Wert, Luzzaschi, Peri, and Caccini. Monteverdi aimed to write a book, *Seconda pratica o vero perfetioni della moderna musica*, which would constitute a second *practica* but not a new *theorica*, for he would leave speculative theory to those more erudite, such as Ercole Bottrigari. Whereas Zarlino's rules led to the perfection of *harmonia*, Monteverdi's would tend towards the perfection of *melodia*, that is the composite work that comprises *harmonia* and *rhythmus* and is dominated by the text.

Monteverdi never wrote that treatise on *musica practica*, but the idea that there were two different norms inspired others to consider the implications of such a broadened view of musical resources. Banchieri, as we saw, was one. Marco Scacchi was another. Unlike Giulio Cesare, who thought of the second practice as replacing the first, they perceived them as alternative options. Scacchi pushed this idea to its ultimate conclusion, in that he divided modern music into two practices and three styles.[62] The three styles are likewise indebted to Monteverdi, who, in his letter to the readers of the *Madrigali guerrieri, et amorosi, libro ottavo* (1638),[63] divided the manners of performance into three: oratorical, harmonic, and rhythmic, and the genres of court music also were threefold: theatre, chamber, and *da ballo*. These three genres of music, he noted, were marked in his collection by the qualifications 'guerriera, amorosa, and rappresentativa'. Monteverdi's

---

[60] Zarlino, *Sopplimenti*, bk. viii, ch. 1, p. 277.

[61] Zarlino, *Le istitutioni*, pt. ii, ch. 12, p. 80.

[62] The two main sources for Scacchi's view of styles are: *Breve discorso sopra la musica moderna* (Warsaw: Pietro Elert, 1649), trans. in Palisca, 'Marco Scacchi's Defence of Modern Music (1649)', below, Essay 4; and Scacchi's letter to Christoph Werner of around 1648, published in Erich Katz, *Die musikalischen Stilbegriffe des 17. Jahrhunderts* (Inaug. diss., University of Freiburg im Breisgau, 1926), 83–9.

[63] Malipiero, *Monteverdi*, 89–91; De'Paoli, *Monteverdi, Lettere*, 416–18.

manners of performance, genre of composition, and category of madrigal appear to form a scheme of coordinates:

manners of performance:	oratorical	harmonic	rhythmic
genre of composition:	theatre	chamber	*da ballo*
category of madrigal:	*guerriero*	*amoroso*	*rappresentativo*

The madrigals of Book VIII do not fall so conveniently into these categories, however. For the *Combattimento di Tancredi e Clorinda*, listed among the *canti guerrieri*, is also labelled 'rappresentativo', while the Ballo, *Movete al mio bel suon*, is a *canto guerriero*, and the *Ballo dell'Ingrate*, a *canto amoroso*, is in *genere rappresentativo*.

Scacchi's scheme utilizing these notions is more rational.[64] His system of stylistic options was adopted by his pupil Angelo Berardi (*Ragionamenti musicali*, 1681),[65] and it was further developed by Christoph Bernhard (*c.*1660)[66] and Johann Mattheson (*Der vollkommene Capellmeister*, 1739).[67]

Scacchi's analysis of stylistic categories came out of his endeavour to defend modern styles, particularly in church music, against the attacks by conservative composers and teachers, both in Rome and Danzig. 'I do not see the necessity', he responded to them, 'of reducing music to a single style of Palestrina . . . For the art of music could be rich with so many varieties of different styles composed almost throughout the world that it would be a marvel.'[68] Scacchi insisted that the modern style was altogether appropriate for the church, even though it was first used in the theatre. Two kinds of recitative style should be distinguished, the *semplice rappresentativo* and the *recitativo imbastardito* or mixed style, 'which will go on for a while representing the text in the recitative style and then, all of a sudden, will be varied with *passaggi* and other melodic effects'.[69] Only the latter is appropriate in church. To those opponents of the modern styles who charged that *ariette*, *barzelette*, and *serenate* were being sung in church he retorted that 'just as the church employs prose and verse, so the judicious composer uses airs for the verse and the severe style for the prose'.[70]

---

[64] See below, Essay 4, 91.

[65] Angelo Berardi, *Ragionamenti musicali* (Bologna: Giacomo Monti, 1681), 134.

[66] Christoph Bernhard, *Tractatus compositionis augmentatus*, printed in Joseph Müller-Blattau, *Die Kompositionslehre Heinrich Schützens in der Fassung seines Schulers Christoph Bernhard* (2nd edn., Kassel: Bärenreiter, 1963), 40–131, chs. 3 and 35.

[67] Johann Mattheson, *Der vollkommene Capellmeister* (Hamburg: Christian Herold, 1739; facs. ed. Margarete Reimann, Documenta musicologica, Kassel: Bärenreiter, 1954), Erster Theil, Hauptstück 10, pp. 68–93. Mattheson knew the manuscript letter to Christoph Werner, which he saw in the public reading-room of the St. Johannis monastery in Hamburg. The letter was later classified as MS ND. VI, 5573 in the Hamburg Staatsbibliothek.

[68] Scacchi, *Breve discorso,* sig. C1ʳ; Italian text below, Essay 4.

[69] Ibid., sig. C1ʳ⁻ᵛ; Italian text in Essay 4.

[70] Ibid., sig. C2ᵛ; Italian text in Essay 4.

In his letter to the composer Christoph Werner (*c.*1619–50) Scacchi detailed concisely some rules for composing in each style. Some of those for the older styles obviously derive from Pontio, probably through Cerone.[71] Particularly notable are his instructions for the polychoral and concerted styles. Works for several choirs, such as motets for four to six voices, whether with tutti and soli, are considered to follow the precepts of the first practice, though some licences are allowed, but motets and sacred concerti in modern style should follow the principle that the text is the mistress of the harmony, yet be distinguishable from the scenic and chamber styles.

The Figurative and Embellished Style

The *seconda pratica* was one path to the new styles of music that conquered Europe in the seventeenth century. Another path was the art of embellishment and the cultivation of the sensuous surface, as opposed to the expressive essence—the beautiful line, the florid, fluent, bel canto. The authors of the treatises on embellishment from Ganassi to Caccini aimed their writings at performers rather than composers. Their tracts belong, therefore, to the theory of performance rather than of counterpoint. However, the instructions they gave operated within a contrapuntal framework and assumed as readers performers who were conversant with the rules of counterpoint. Thus the instructions on diminution expanded contrapuntal practice along lines that composers would soon follow. Such a progression from improvised embellishment to composed counterpoint was hastened by the circumstance that many of the forward-looking composers and theorists were themselves singers—Caccini, Peri, d'India—or instrumental performers—Diruta, Frescobaldi, Marini, Banchieri, Viadana, and Agazzari.

The books on embellishment or diminution (as it was also called), of which Giovanni Battista Bovicelli's *Regole, passaggi di musica*[72] may be taken as an example, present several types of melodic progressions that are to be ornamented. The simplest is a single interval, consisting of the passage from one whole note to another by step or leap. The diminution normally begins on the first note, occupying the time of this note, and proceeds to the second note of the interval or to its octave. Sometimes the first note is approached through an ornament, or the embellishment may borrow from

[71] Pedro Cerone, *El Melopeo y maestro. Tractado de musica theorica y pratica* (Naples: Juan Bautista Gargano y Lucrecio Nucci, 1613). Scacchi depends upon Cerone for much of the historical information in his *Breve discorso*. He does not mention Pontio.

[72] Giovanni Battista Bovicelli, *Regole, passaggi di musica* (Venice: Giacomo Vincenti, 1594; facs., ed. Nanie Bridgman, Kassel: Bärenreiter, 1957).

Ex. 1.25. Bovicelli, *Regole*, 25

Ex. 1.26. Bovicelli, *Regole*, 32–3

the second note's duration (Ex. 1.25). Another technique is to ornament a voice, particularly the top voice, of a cadence (Ex. 1.26). A common type of demonstration that shows the application of these diminutions is the ornamentation of a complete voice part in a madrigal or motet, usually the top voice. A favourite model for this purpose was Rore's *Anchor che col partire*. Ex. 1.27 shows diminutions of the same passage of the soprano part by Girolamo dalla Casa (1584), R. Rogniono (1592)—both vocal and instrumental—Bovicelli (1594), and Spadi.[73]

That the art of diminution affected the theory and practice of composition is evident from some of the writings considered earlier in this chapter. In Artusi's dialogue of 1600, Luca defends some of Monteverdi's usages as diminutions, and in his book on counterpoint Artusi notes that at times parallel seconds, for example, may seem to result (as in Ex. 1.8*a* above) but that this is merely a diminution of a consonant progression (Ex. 1.8*b*), or a seventh may seem to be attacked by leap, as in Ex. 1.9*c*, an embellishment of a simple suspension (Ex. 1.9*a*).

Both Zacconi and Diruta incorporated diminution into their treatment of counterpoint. Diruta expects that in *osservato* counterpoint smaller notes, whether semiminims, *crome* (eighths), or *semicrome* (sixteenths), will follow the rule that those on the beat are consonant except for the combination minim–semiminim–semiminim (or proportionate faster notes), when the first of the short notes may be dissonant. All notes involved in a leap and boundary notes of a run (*li fondi & le cime*) should be consonant.[74] Zacconi makes explicit reference to the practice of embellishment when he admits *crome* and *semicrome* into the vocabulary of counterpoint.[75]

---

[73] See Imogene Horsley, 'The Diminutions in Composition and Theory of Composition', *Acta musicologica*, 35 (1963), 124–53, from which Ex. 1.27 is taken (150–1).

[74] Diruta, *Seconda parte*, bk. ii, ch. 11.

[75] Zacconi, *Prattica, seconda parte*, bk. ii, ch. 45, p. 93.

Ex. 1.27. Diminutions on the soprano of Rore's *Anchor che col partire*

L'ultime figure di diminuzione	The smallest durations in
(come sono le Crome e Semicrome),	diminution, such as *crome* and
se bene sono figure che più	*semicrome*, although more useful
serbano a' Cantori per fiorire &	to singers for adorning and to
a' Sonatori per abellir le Musiche	players for embellishing music
e l'armonie, non però sono	and counterpoints, nevertheless
talmente bandite da i Contrapunti,	should not be entirely banned
che solamente in caso	from counterpoint so that they
de communi, o composte accadenze	are used only in the case of
se ne possino seruire, che anco	common [i.e. somewhat
in altre occorenze le possano	embellished] or compound
adoprare come in obligation di	[florid] cadences, but they may
fughe o d'altro, e anco con	be employed as well in other
semplici occasioni di	situations and in obligations of
Contrapunti ordinari.	fugues and in simple cases of
	ordinary counterpoint.

Diruta and Zacconi appear to be overly cautious when judged against the evidence of the embellishment manuals. The virtuoso singers are quite unconcerned about keeping to such limitations as theirs. Although they make no explicit statements on the question, their examples show that a diminution usually begins on a long written note, which is always consonant, and ends on the next written note, which is also consonant. What happens between these consonant notes is free of restraints. Galilei was probably closer to the mark when he said that in rapid runs and figures played by instruments almost any combination of consonances and dissonances is accepted by the ear and that therefore this liberty should be extended to written 'notes of local motion'.[76]

A subject that the embellishment manuals do not address is the relationship of diminutions and *passaggi* to the sense of the text. Bovicelli is careful to point out that the length of syllables should be taken into account in making divisions, but he does not reach beyond the sound of the words to their meaning and feeling.[77] Giovanni Bardi, on the other hand, in the essay he addressed to Caccini (*c.*1578), concentrates upon the communicative aspect of the art of singing. As Sadoleto and Zarlino before him and Galilei and G. C. Monteverdi after him, Bardi recalled Plato's definition of *melos*. More correctly than his predecessors, Bardi interprets it as a definition not of melody or polyphony but simply of music: 'la musica essere un componimento di fauellare, d'armonia, e di ritmo'—music is a composition of speech, harmony, and rhythm.[78] He restores to the word

---

[76] Galilei, MS Gal. 1, fo. 143r.

[77] Bovicelli, *Regole*, 7.

[78] Giovanni Bardi, 'Discorso mandato a Caccini sopra la musica antica e 'l cantar bene', ed. C. V.

'harmony' its Greek meaning of proportion between low, high, and median pitch in voices and instruments, among long and short syllables and faster and slower motion, and of the harmony of all these elements in combination. After a long disquisition on the harmonic aspect of music, he returns to Plato's definition to emphasize that harmony and rhythm, according to him, must follow speech. He then reminds Caccini that Aristotle pointed out that in rhythms are images of fortitude and other moral qualities, and for this reason the longs and shorts of poetry must never be distorted in singing. If Caccini wishes to make some *passaggio*, he should do so on the sixth or tenth syllable of the endecasyllabic line and do it with moderation. 'Nor should it seem to you too little if from one stanza of eight lines you draw sixteen charming, varied, delightful florid passages, keeping the verse free and beautiful, without doing it any violence.'[79]

Caccini took this lesson to heart, and in his preface to the readers of *Le nuove musiche*, he notes that he has avoided making *passaggi* on short syllables, indulging at the most in a bit of decoration.[80] He attacks those who use long *passaggi* indiscriminately, for nothing is more inimical to affective expression. He used them in his songs, he says, with restraint, always on long syllables, mostly at final cadences, and mainly in the less affective pieces. He has also subordinated to the expression of the affections both contrapuntal art and the application of various graces, tremolos, trills, *esclamazioni*, crescendos, and decrescendos. Thus the art of singing gracefully of the sixteenth-century embellishment manuals becomes in the seventeenth century the art of composing expressively for the voice.

Counterpoint theory during the years covered by this essay, approximately 1580 to 1630, was in a state of flux. It had not yet hardened into a scholastic method that would be passed almost unchanged from generation to generation. It was adjusting during these years to the changing practices of the most advanced composers with respect to the treatment of dissonance, to the norms and licences customary in certain conventional genres, and to the admission of smaller note-values and embellishment figures. With the exception of recitative, which at first was outside contrapuntal theory, composition was still largely under the control of precepts that could be and were taught and expressed in counterpoint manuals.

Palisca, in *The Florentine Camerata: Documentary Studies and Translations* (New Haven, Conn.: Yale University Press, 1989), 92–3.

[79] Ibid. 120–1.

[80] Giulio Caccini detto Romano, *Le nuove musiche* (Florence: I Marescotti, 1601/2), ed. H. Wiley Hitchcock (Madison, Wis.: A-R Editions, 1970), 46–7.

2

Vincenzo Galilei's Counterpoint Treatise:
A Code for the Seconda pratica

This essay first appeared in 1956 in the *Journal of the American Musicological Society*, 9 (1956), 81–96. A shorter version was read on 28 December 1955 at the annual meeting of the Society in Princeton, New Jersey. This was not a time when much attention was paid to the work of theorists of the distant past, whether published or not. Scholars went to them mostly to solve problems of transcribing and editing early music and to seek answers to questions on how to perform it. Thus treatises of Johannes de Garlandia, Franco of Cologne, or Tinctoris (on proportions) were probed for the keys to transcribing medieval and early Renaissance notation. Other treatises were scanned for hints about *musica ficta*, because transcribers recognized that the written notation, once it could be accurately interpreted, had to be supplemented by an editor's judgements about the resolution of conflicts between smooth part-movement and harmonic correspondence between parts. This led to a certain interest, too, in the rules of counterpoint that might be applicable. But unless theorists could provide some answers to the practical problems of transcription, editing, and performance, there was little interest in them. *Urtext* and 'authenticity' were the buzz-words.

For analysts and interpreters to take a period-oriented point of view in confronting the music was an aspect of authenticity only seldom recognized. Although Knud Jeppesen, in *The Style of Palestrina and the Dissonance* (1946),[1] took note of some comments by Zarlino, Vicentino, and Cerone, he set out to reconstruct Palestrina's counterpoint methods not by relying on their formulations but through objective and statistical analysis. The outcome of his study agreed on most points with the teaching of these authors, but Jeppesen did not feel compelled to depend on this agreement for support. At the other end of the spectrum, some analysts completely ignored the older theoretical traditions. Felix Salzer, in his *Structural Hearing* (1952),[2] applied the methods of Heinrich Schenker (1868–1935) equally to the analysis of medieval and Renaissance music as to that of later centuries, and a periodical dedicated to this method, *The Music Forum*, founded by him and William Mitchell in 1967, offered detailed analyses of sixteenth- and seventeenth-century music by scholars of similar persuasion. That many details of these analyses were quite out of line with the way composers thought and worked, as evidenced

---

[1] Knud Jeppesen, *The Style of Palestrina and the Dissonance*, with an introduction by Edward J. Dent (2nd edn.; Copenhagen: Munksgaard, 1946; London: Oxford University Press, 1946).
[2] Felix Saltzer, *Structural Hearing* (New York: Charles Boni, 1952).

by what the verbally articulate among them said, did not much bother this school of interpreters.

On the other hand, music historians in the 1950s, in their commentary on the music of the Renaissance, dwelt to a large extent on the use of borrowed material—whether plainchant, tenors, or entire polyphonic compositions—and rarely came to terms with the method of composition. A publisher dedicated to issuing critical texts of music and writings about music, approached in the 1950s with a proposal to publish Galilei's counterpoint treatises, responded that it was too esoteric a subject.

The prospect that theorists and critics might lead us better to understand and appreciate the creative work of their contemporaries was nevertheless beginning to stimulate translations and editions of early writings. With great foresight Oliver Strunk began in the 1940s to compile an anthology of literary documents in the history of music, which was published in 1950.[3] The International Musicological Society sponsored a series of facsimile editions through Bärenreiter-Verlag under the title 'Documenta musicologica' of major theoretical works by authors such as Salinas, Vicentino, Coclico, Praetorius, and Mattheson. Soon other publishers initiated similar series: the Gregg Press of Ridgewood, New Jersey, Arnaldo Forni of Bologna, Minkoff of Geneva, Da Capo Press, and Broude Brothers of New York. Yale University's Music Theory Translation Series was inaugurated in 1965 with Francesco Gasparini's *The Practical Harmonist at the Harpsichord*. By the 1980s being well read and grounded in the theoretical documents was considered essential, and university courses in the history of theory had become common. The edition of Galilei's counterpoint treatises became the project of a doctoral dissertation by Frieder Rempp presented in 1975 at the Eberhard-Karls-Universität in Tübingen, and this led to his published edition of the treatises in 1980.[4]

The subtitle of my article, 'A Code for the *Seconda pratica*', which was intended to suggest that Monteverdi's *seconda pratica* had already been codified by Galilei, also marks my article as mid-twentieth-century musicology. Unless one could relate a minor luminary like Galilei to one of the major stars in the musical firmament, there was little chance that his historical significance would be appreciated. There was still a tendency to think of the course of music history as determined by the composers whose music survived the test of time and taste of our time. No responsible scholar today would entitle a book *Monteverdi: Creator of Modern Music*, as one did in 1950,[5] because, even if we could define what 'modern music' is, we would be reluctant to assign responsibility for it to one or even a group of composers. Were I writing the article on Galilei's counterpoint treatises today, I would concentrate more on his methodology, his rationalizations, and deal with the licences he proposed in the context of the practice of his contemporaries. But, with the texts of his treatises now all in print,[6] this is something anyone with a reading knowledge of Italian can do.

[3] Oliver Strunk, *Source Readings in Music History* (New York: Norton, 1950).

[4] Frieder Rempp, *Die Kontrapunkttraktate Vincenzo Galileis* (Cologne: Arno Volk, 1980).

[5] Leo Schrade, *Monteverdi: Creator of Modern Music* (New York: Norton, 1950; London: Victor Gollancz, 1951).

[6] The manuscript treatises not included in Rempp's edition are edited, with English translations, in my book, *The Florentine Camerata: Documentary Studies and Translations* (New Haven, Conn.: Yale University Press, 1989).

IN 1605 Monteverdi promised in his preface to the *Fifth Book of Madrigals*[7] to undertake the defence of the new school of composers of which he was the protagonist. Artusi had accused Monteverdi and some of his contemporaries of sinning against the precepts of good composition by indulging in certain licences in the treatment of dissonances.[8] That the manner of using dissonances was the crucial issue of the day, Monteverdi readily acknowledged. The established considerations for their use as taught by Zarlino, he declared, were now superseded by a second scheme of considerations, and this constituted a *seconda pratica*. He planned to show in a subsequent treatise that the new approach to composition was not unbridled anarchy but a deliberated method, a new practice, different from the earlier *prima pratica*. In 1633 Monteverdi confessed that he had still not written the treatise but was driving himself back to this task and would call the work *Melodia, ovvero seconda pratica musicale*.[9] It probably never reached beyond the planning stage.

That we now lack the treatise, whether for Monteverdi's failure to write it or its failure to survive, has been much lamented and is indeed regrettable. But if destiny has robbed us of Monteverdi's promised theoretical testament, it is only neglect that has deprived us up to now of an authoritative exposition of the new practice by one of his older contemporaries. Sixteen years before Monteverdi wrote his famous letter to the 'studious readers' of his madrigals, the task he set for himself there as spokesman for the new practice had been largely discharged by Vincenzo Galilei. In a little-known treatise now in the Biblioteca Nazionale in Florence,[10] Galilei had already set down and defended the principles of the *seconda pratica* in 1588. He had spent the last years of his life expounding the new doctrine and had finished revising his treatise for publication shortly before he died in 1591. In many respects the counterpoint treatise is Galilei's most significant achievement. For prophetic vision, originality, and integrity, it has few equals in the history of music theory.

What the principles of the new harmony were, who practised it, and who were its founders—these are questions to which Galilei and Monteverdi gave consentaneous answers. Giulio Cesare Monteverdi's 'Explication of the

---

[7] Prefatory letter, 'Studiosi Lettori', in *Il quinto libro de madrigali a 5* (Venice: R. Amadino, 1605), repr. in G. Francesco Malipiero, *Claudio Monteverdi* (Milan: Fratelli Treves, 1929), 71–2.

[8] Giovanni Maria Artusi, *L'Artusi, ouero delle imperfettioni della moderna musica* (Venice: Giacomo Vincenti, 1600), Rag. 2, fos. 39 ff.

[9] Letter, Venice, 22 Oct. 1633, to an unidentified correspondent, but evidently Giovanni Battista Doni, printed in Malipiero, *Monteverdi*, 293. For a translation, see Denis Stevens, *The Letters of Claudio Monteverdi* (London: Faber and Faber, 1980), 410.

[10] Florence, Biblioteca Nazionale Centrale, MSS Galilei (hereafter Gal.), vols. 1–2. The treatise is edited in Rempp, *Kontrapunkttraktate Vincenzo Galileis*.

Letter Printed in the Fifth Book of his Madrigals',[11] which can be accepted as an authoritative statement of his brother Claudio's beliefs, lucidly sets forth the guiding principles of the new school. According to this declaration, the modern composer did not consider it necessary to follow obsequiously the rules of counterpoint laid down for the first, the sixteenth-century practice. If the new counterpoint was not 'observant', it was because above the rules reigned a more essential consideration: the expression of the text. Perfection of 'melody' (that is, song) was placed above perfection of 'harmony', (that is, counterpoint), which was relegated to the position of servant to the text. The new practice of harmony differed from the old chiefly in the manner of employing dissonances. Although Galilei never used the term *seconda pratica*, the foregoing, it will be seen, were also his guiding principles. He began his treatise with a commentary on the rules regarding the use of consonances. He then outlined a new practice of dissonance, keyed to the expression of a text and emancipated from the artificial restrictions of the *contrapunto osservato*. Finally, he showed how the principles of melody already expounded in his *Dialogo della musica antica, et della moderna*[12] were to be applied within the new practice.[13]

Neither Monteverdi nor Galilei claimed responsibility for the foundation of a new school. Giulio Cesare Monteverdi named Cipriano de Rore as the father of the second practice. After him, Giulio Cesare said, it was being carried on by Marco Ingegneri, Luca Marenzio, Giaches de Wert, Luzzasco Luzzaschi, Jacopo Peri, Giulio Caccini, and the 'Heroic School' of gentlemen-composers, among whom he named the Prince of Venosa, Emilio de' Cavalieri, Count Alfonso Fontanella, the Count of the Camerata (Giovanni Bardi?), Cavaliere Turchi, and Tommaso Pecci.

Galilei, too, honoured Rore as the founder of the new music. Among composers whose works he had examined to establish the new principles he named 'Josquino, Gian Moutone, Gomberto, Morales, Adriano [Willaert], Cipriano [de Rore], Giannetto [Palestrina], Strigio, Orlando [di Lasso], Giaches Wert, Giaches Bus, Annibale [Padovano], Claudi [Merulo], and Giuseppe Guami'.[14] Galilei's leadership in the group that included Jacopo Peri, Giulio Caccini, and Giovanni Bardi is already well known. The

---

[11] 'Dichiaritione della lettera stampata nel quinto libro de suoi madrigali', in *Scherzi musicali* (Venice: R. Amadino, 1607); repr. in Malipiero, *Monteverdi*, 72–85; trans. in Strunk, *Source Readings*, 405–12.

[12] V. Galilei, *Dialogo della musica antica, et della moderna* (Florence: G. Marescotti, 1581).

[13] Galilei's contributions in these manuscripts to the theory of melodic composition and its relation to harmony are considered in Essay 12, 'Vincenzo Galilei and some Links between "Pseudo-Monody" and Monody'.

[14] Gal. 1, fo. 138ᵛ. In Gal. 1, starting from fo. 94 (incorrectly numbered 93 in the manuscript), the numbers given here exceed by one those pencilled in the manuscript and given in Rempp's edn.

omission of their names from his list is understandable, since in 1588 their musical reputations were still in the making.

One of the reasons for the long neglect that Galilei's treatise has suffered, apart from the fact that the manuscripts are no models of good penmanship, is that many scholars have refused to believe that Galilei, the arch-enemy of counterpoint, could have contributed anything of value to its theory. In effect, however, Galilei not only never abandoned the practice and teaching of counterpoint; he saw no opposition between counterpoint as he understood it and the ideal of expressive monody. Pietro Bardi, in his letter to Doni, recalled how Galilei, encouraged by Giovanni Bardi and his comrades, whom he used to entertain as a lute-player, took up the study of theory and history and became a 'good teacher of the theory of every kind of music'.[15] Galilei's reputation as a teacher evidently travelled widely, for Artusi, in his diatribe *Trattato apologetico* (1589), conferred on him the titles: 'Signor Dottore Vincenzo Galilei nobile Fiorentino Mathematico, Musico Teorico, Pratico: Sonatore di Leuto et Mastro da Scola'.[16] Galilei must have still been teaching counterpoint in 1584 when his 20-year-old son, Michelangelo, published the *Contrappunti a due voci*.[17] These duets, intended primarily as exercises for playing and singing, undoubtedly served also as models of two-part counterpoint. It should not have surprised his contemporaries, therefore, that in 1587 Galilei published a second book of madrigals[18] and that in 1588[19] he announced the imminent publication of a discourse on the use of dissonances in counterpoint.

Galilei's treatise on counterpoint originally comprised two parts, *Il primo libro della prattica del contrapunto intorno all'uso delle consonanze* (The First Book of the Practice of Counterpoint concerning the Use of Consonances) and *Discorso intorno all'uso delle dissonanze* (Essay concerning the Use of Dissonances). Later he decided to add an essay called *Discorso intorno all'uso dell'enharmonio, et di chi fusse autore del cromatico* (Essay concerning the Use of the Enharmonic and concerning the Author of the Chromatic). To this last

---

[15] Printed in Angelo Solerti, *Le origini del melodramma* (Turin: Fratelli Bocca, 1903), 144.

[16] [G. M. Artusi], *Trattato apologetico in difesa dell'opere del R. Zarlino de Chioggia giuditio musicale del S. Cabaleo Nobile di Pocceia, Academico Infarinato intorno alle differenze note frà il dottissimo Zarlino, et il S. Dottore Vincenzo Galilej nobile Fiorentino . . .* The letter of dedication is addressed to Galilei and dated 8 Apr. 1590. This work is not extant, but the above title and subtitle, the incipits of the letter of dedication and of the treatise, and the last words of the treatise are given by Bottrigari in his *Aletelogia*, Bologna, Civico Museo Bibliografico Musicale, MS B-43, 111.

[17] V. Galilei, *Contrappunti a due voci* (Florence: G. Marescotti, 1584); transcription by Louise Rood (Northampton, Mass., 1945). See Alfred Einstein, 'Galilei and the Instructive Duo', *Music and Letters*, 18 (1937), 360–8; 'Vincenzo Galilei e il duetto didattico', *Rassegna musicale*, 11 (1938), 108–16.

[18] *Il secondo libro de madrigali a quattro, et a cinque voci* (Venice: Angelo Gardano, 1587).

[19] In *Discorso intorno all'opere di Messer Gioseffo Zarlino da Chioggia, et altri importanti particolari attenenti alla musica* (Florence: G. Marescotti, 1589; letter of dedication dated Aug. 1588), 37.

essay he eventually wrote a short supplement, entitled *Dubbi intorno a quanto io ho detto dell'uso dell'enharmonio con la solutione di essi* (Doubts concerning what I have said about the Use of the Enharmonic, with their Resolution). No general title exists for the whole work, but the first book begins with the words, 'L'arte et la pratica del moderno contrapunto', which Galilei proposed there as his main subject.[20] Three versions of each of the two main parts of the treatise have reached us in the author's own hand. All three are in a collection of manuscripts at the Biblioteca Nazionale Centrale in Florence called 'Manoscritti anteriori a Galileo', which forms part of a larger collection of manuscripts pertaining to and by Galileo Galilei.[21]

The treatise can be dated without difficulty. The years 1589–91 assigned to it by Fabio Fano[22] are approximately correct. The date 1588, rather than 1589, for the completion of the earliest version of book ii is established by references to the treatise in Galilei's *Discorso intorno all'opere di messer G. Zarlino*. There Galilei mentioned an essay 'made already some months ago concerning the use of dissonances, which should be published soon'.[23] The *Discorso* was published in 1589, but the letter of dedication bears the date August 1588. Therefore the first draft of book ii must have been finished no later than 1588. In a correction, inserted and then crossed out, in the second draft of book ii of the counterpoint treatise, there is evidence that Galilei was revising the manuscript in 1590: to a list of composers whose music he said he had scored Galilei added the phrase, 'and subsequently others later than these and those who flourished in the same times as the above up to the year 1590'. In a still later third draft of this passage Galilei deleted the list of composers and made the passage read simply: 'compositions from Josquin to the present, and we are now in the year 1591'.[24]

Anticipating the controversy his treatise would invite, Galilei dedicated a long introduction in the first book to a review of his principles and a

---

[20] Gal. 1, fo. 55ʳ.

[21] Earliest draft: bk. i, Gal. 2, fos. 3ʳ–54ᵛ; bk. ii, Gal. 2, fos. 55ʳ–136ʳ. Second draft: bk. i, Gal. 1, fos. 6ʳ–51ᵛ; bk. ii, Gal. 1, fos. 104ʳ–147ᵛ. Third draft: bk. i, Gal. 1, fos. 55ʳ–103ᵛ; bk. ii, Gal. 1, fos. 148ʳ–196ᵛ; *Discorso intorno all'uso dell'enharmonio*: Gal. 3, fos. 3ʳ–34ᵛ; *Dubbi*: Gal. 3, fos. 62ʳ–68ʳ.

For an index to the Vincenzo Galilei manuscripts, see 'Galilei', in *Die Musik in Geschichte und Gegenwart* (hereafter *MGG*), iv (Kassel and Basle: Bärenreiter, 1955), 1267. Two more general catalogues also cover this collection: Bianca Becherini, *Catalogo dei manoscritti musicali della Biblioteca Nazionale di Firenze* (Kassel: Bärenreiter, 1959) and Angelo Procissi, *La collezione Galileiana della Biblioteca Nazionale di Firenze* (Rome: Istituto Poligrafico dello Stato, 1959), vol. i.

[22] Introduction to facs. edn. of the *Dialogo della musica antica, et della moderna* (Rome: Reale Accademia d'Italia, 1934).

[23] Galilei, *Discorso intorno all'opere di Zarlino*, 37.

[24] Gal. 1, fo. 186ᵛ, ed. Rempp, 143.

renewed critique of vocal polyphony as currently practised. He made it plain that his philosophy had not changed since the *Dialogo*. But he spoke out now with less invidiousness and greater assurance, for, though the opposition of the musical schoolmasters had not subsided, the tide of Aristotelian aesthetics and scientific empiricism that had first swept him along was now overflowing into a new era of enlightenment, and the victory of his cause seemed inevitable.

Galilei saw a desperate need for a return to the standards Aristotle had set for a music worthy of free men. The Greeks, according to Aristotle, had a music for free citizens, which moved the soul to various passions, and another for plebeians, which was worthless beyond the simple amusement and contentment it provided the sense of hearing. The latter Galilei likened to the artful sensuous instrumental music of his day. This he did not wish to banish, as Plato would have done. Nevertheless he saw no necessity for considering it in his treatise, because it had already reached a state of supreme excellence. But the vocal music, which among the ancients possessed such remarkable emotional powers, he wished to see rise again to its former glory.

Galilei was drawn to Aristotle, the naturalist, by the same affinity that compelled him to follow the Stagirite's aesthetic premises. Rather than accept the dogmas about numbers propagated by the Platonists and Pythagoreans, Galilei experimented with strings of various material, pipes, and other sounding bodies, to ascertain how universal the sacred numbers were. As his son, Galileo, was to do later, Vincenzo questioned the validity of equating certain ratios with particular consonances. While the lengths of the monochord could be depended upon to demonstrate the traditional ratios for the consonances, when other sounding bodies, such as discs, solid objects, and bells, were used to produce these consonances, the ratios of volumes or areas did not match the accepted proportions.[25] What disturbed Galilei even more than this was that the contemporary musical number science, so consistent within itself, failed to correspond to the acoustical realities of musical practice. Galilei was sceptical of a process of thought that began with nature as the occasion for some idea but left it to elaborate theories never further subjected to verification by controlled observation of nature.

The laws of composition set down by Zarlino constituted such a theory,

---

[25] *Discorso particolare intorno alla diversità delle forme del diapason di V. G.*, Gal. 3, fos. 44^r–54^v, ed. and trans. in Palisca, *The Florentine Camerata*, 180–97. Galileo Galilei came to a similar conclusion in *Discorsi e dimostrazioni matematiche intorno a due nuoue scienze*, 1st edn. (Leiden: Elsevirius, 1638), in *Opere* (Florence: G. Barbèra), viii (1898), 141 ff. The fact that the lengths on the monochord gave certain ratios 'did not seem to me sufficiently conclusive to justify assigning the duple and 3 : 2 ratios to the octave and fifth as their natural forms' (144).

evolved from an ideal view of nature, leaving the immediate facts in the distance. Zarlino had classified intervals as consonant and dissonant according to their numerical ratios. The consonances could be expressed in numbers from 1 to 6, the numbers of the *senario*.[26] The rules for handling these consonances and for subordinating the dissonances to them were determined by their relative positions in the hierarchy of ratios. Thus, for Zarlino, the proprieties of counterpoint had the authority of natural law. Galilei, on the other hand, considered numerical ratios irrelevant to the artist, and the rules of counterpoint a product of the demands of taste, experience, and aesthetic purpose. A musician should no more confuse physical facts with sensations than a scientist would take external appearances of objects for their true intrinsic properties. Such properties of moving bodies as numerical ratios were the concern of the physicist. The musician dealt with superficial qualities of sounds, such as could not be measured except by the listening ear. The only interval with a determinate ratio was the octave; the others were subject to endless variety. Galilei says:

Of the musical intervals . . . those outside the parts of the *senario* are as natural as those contained in it. The ditone in the 81 : 64 ratio is as natural as that in the 5 : 4 proportion. For the seventh to be dissonant in the 9 : 5 ratio is as natural as for the octave to be consonant in the 2 : 1 ratio.[27]

Separating thus the provinces of science and art, Galilei cleared the air, still laden with Pythagorean mysticism, for an empirical theory of harmony.[28] Galilei's musical spectrum, like Giordano Bruno's universe of

---

[26] In later writings, Zarlino extended the range to the *ottonario*, which had the virtue of being the first cubic number and contained the numbers from 1 to 8. This admitted the minor sixth. See Zarlino, *Dimostrationi harmoniche* (Venice: Francesco dei Franceschi Senese, 1571), Rag. 2, Definitioni 1 and 2. Zarlino distinguished here between *consonanza propriamente detta* (consonance properly speaking), and *consonanza comunemente detta* (consonance commonly speaking). Consonances of the first kind were limited to the *senario*.

[27] *Discorso intorno all'opere di Zarlino*, 92–3: 'poi tanto sono naturali (com'io ho detto) quelli contenuti tra le parti del Senario, quanto gl'altri che son fuore di esse parti. E tanto è naturale il Ditono contenuto dalla sesquiquarta quanto, quello che è contenuto dalla super 17 partiente 64. Si come ancora tanto è naturale l'accordare dell'ottaua drento la dupla, quanto è naturale il dissonare della settima drento la super 4. partiente quinta . . .'.

[28] Girolamo Mei deserves some credit for Galilei's empirical orientation. In a letter to Galilei of 17 Jan. 1578, Mei suggested an experiment with variously tuned strings to determine the ratios used in singing: Rome, Biblioteca Apostolica Vaticana, MS Regina lat. 2021, fo. 48ᵛ, in Girolamo Mei, *Letters on Ancient and Modern Music*, ed. Palisca (2nd edn.; Neuhausen-Stuttgart: Hänssler, 1977), 140. Mei also pointed out to Galilei the essential cleavage between the paths of science and art. 'The true end of the sciences is altogether different from that of the arts . . . The science of music diligently investigates and considers all the qualities and properties of the constitutions, systems, and orders of musical pitches, whether these are simple qualities or comparative, like the consonances, and this is for no other reason than to know the truth itself, the perfect goal of all speculation, and as a by-product the false. It then lets art exploit as it sees fit for its own ends, without any limitation, those same pitches about which science has learned the truth' (letter of 8 May 1572, ibid., fos. 19ᵛ–20ʳ, *Letters*, 103, trans. in Palisca, *The Florentine Camerata*, 65).

infinite numbers of solar systems, admitted an infinite number of intervals, though, he said, the number of dissonances 'was a greater infinity than that of the consonances'.[29] Of these, the musician used only a small number—those best known to the sense of hearing, which was the sole judge of their acceptability.

As observation and experiment were the paths to a true knowledge of the natural world, musical experience was the source of the precepts of composition. For Galilei this was a collective experience, and he enumerated the composers whose works he had diligently examined to learn what should and should not be done.[30] Cumulatively, the scores and tablatures he had personally made of all kinds of contrapuntal music totalled 14,000. He urged readers of his text to follow his example and spare themselves no labour copying out and scoring all the works they could, especially those of Cipriano de Rore. 'No other means is more efficacious than the compositions of Cipriano de Rore, for without further labour, the contrapuntist will acquire from their diligent examination all that he can possibly wish.'[31]

The acceptance of a new empirical classification of musical intervals, Galilei recognized, could, as a wedge, widen the harmonic resources of his time. He proposed such a new classification at the outset of his treatise.[32] The consonances were: the octave, thirds, fifth, and sixths, including the much maligned minor sixth; the dissonances were the seconds and sevenths. The fourth, augmented fourth, and diminished fifth he placed in an intermediate category, because they sounded less harsh to the ear and were subject to fewer restrictions than the other dissonant intervals.

Galilei then proceeded to a discussion of the rules of counterpoint that pertained to the use of consonances. He was on the whole satisfied with the conventional rules for the progression of consonances note against note in two parts. These could still serve for the composition of simple duets without words. But if a duet had to be composed to a text, the rules needed to be relaxed to give breadth for the expression of the affections. Moreover, if any effect at all were to be operated on the hearer through consonances exclusively, no piece should be composed for more than two voices, 'because many parts sung together always destroy one another's nature and effect'.[33] One of the rules that should not be taken literally, he

---

[29] Gal. 1, fo. 60ʳ, ed. Rempp, 14.
[30] Gal. 1, fo. 138ᵛ, ed. Rempp, 143.
[31] Gal. 1, fo. 101ᵛ, ed. Rempp, 72.
[32] Gal. 1, fos. 60ʳ ff., ed. Rempp, 14 ff.
[33] Gal. 1, fo. 66ᵛ, ed. Rempp, 22.

Ex. 2.1

said, was the prohibition of certain movements that produced false relations, such as two parallel major thirds or minor sixths, as in Ex. 2.1.[34]

Galilei defended the composer's right to use these progressions, 'because two minor sixths used in the way illustrated have a mournful feeling, and the two major thirds a cheerful feeling . . . I do not know under what heading I should be restrained from using them for the expression of those ideas that are in accordance with these intervals and that through these intervals acquire form and vigour.'[35]

If, on the subject of consonances, Galilei had few quarrels with the conventional rules, on the treatment of dissonance he stands out as an innovator, the codifier and prophet of the *seconda pratica*. Galilei's was a new positive view of the function of dissonance, opposed to the typical sixteenth-century outlook reflected in this definition of Zarlino:

The dissonance is an interval between low and high sounds that cannot mix or unite with one another because of their contrary natures. It strikes the ear harshly and without any pleasure and is born of numerical proportions different in denomination from those found in the *senario* or *ottonario*.[36]

Dissonances were tolerated, in Zarlino's view, because the contrast they permitted with the consonances made these seem more beautiful and sweet. When used properly, say the authors of the Zarlinian school, the dissonances lose their sting and blend smoothly with the consonances.

Far from wishing to efface the harsh quality of the dissonances, Galilei meant to exploit it, as he says:

In the use of these [dissonances] I have not sought that which Zarlino (*Istit*. 2. 12) says practical musicians desire, namely that the dissonances blend in harmony with wonderful effects; but rather that the sense become satisfied with them, not because they harmonize, as I said, but because of the gentle mixture of the sweet

---

[34] Gal. 1, fo. 74ʳ (R 33). (R 33 stands for Rempp edn., 33, and similarly for subsequent examples.) Rempp's edition was based on the third draft of the two treatises, whereas my examples were drawn from the third draft of the treatise on consonance but the second draft of the treatise on dissonance, which appears to be more complete, since it contains marginal postils missing in the third draft.

[35] Gal. 1, fo. 74ʳ, ed. Rempp, 33.

[36] Zarlino, *Dimostrationi harmoniche*, Rag. 2, Def. 3, p. 85: 'La Dissonanza è distanza di suono graue & di acuto: che insieme per loro natura l'uno con l'altro mescolare, ouero unire non si possono: & percuote l'udito aspramente: & senza alcun piacere: & nasce da proportioni differenti di denominatione da quelle, che, si trouano in atto tra le parti del Senario, & l'Ottonario numero, collocare.'

and strong, which . . . affect our ears not unlike the way in which taste receives satisfaction from both sugar and vinegar.[37]

Galilei objected, further, to the idea that dissonances should be used in vocal music only 'per accidente', as Zarlino put it, or incidentally.[38] Rather, he regarded them as the most important part of counterpoint. Galilei could not have better epitomized, than by this bold acceptance of the dissonance for itself, the restoration through the Baroque of the ugly and asymmetrical as positive aesthetic values.

Galilei's method in the second book of the treatise is to take up the three principal dissonances—the seconds, fourths, and sevenths—in numerical order. Then the tritone and diminished fifth are considered. The principles of the new counterpoint are elaborated by example rather than by precept. The examples are written in two, three, four, and five parts. The traditional rules, alongside the contemporary practices, are discussed in relation to the preparation and resolution of each dissonant interval.

Galilei himself gave the best summary of his *Discourse concerning the Use of Dissonances* in the sixteen points that he outlined at the beginning of the second book:[39]

I shall demonstrate first: (1) . . . what dissonance is; (2) in what manner it is generated; (3) the reasons for its being what it is; (4) how many kinds of it are found; (5) and which is more dissonant and which less.

(6) I shall next show in what and how many manners dissonance can be used in two and more voices so that the hearing is pleased; (7) that a consonance need not necessarily follow immediately after it; (8) how many dissonances may be used one after another without the intervention of any consonance; (9) how many dissonances of the same species may be used at the same time with four and more parts; (10) and how many of diverse species can be used with the same number of parts.

(11) It will be made known, further, that the suspension [*sincopa*] of one of the parts is not necessary for the use of dissonance; (12) nor that the consonance that succeeds the dissonance need be the nearest; (13) what is the particular interval that is most proper for the resolution of each dissonance; (14) and that dissonances may be resolved no less by skipwise movement of one of the parts than by conjunct movement.

(15) It will be made known, finally, that dissonances can be resolved ascending as well as descending; (16) and that they can be used equally well on the first and second beats of the measure without being deprived of their rightful justification or offending the sense any more than by other manners of treatment.

Galilei distinguished between two manners of treating dissonances. They are approximately analogous to the two categories that Knud Jeppesen has

---

[37] Gal. 1, fo. 77ᵛ, ed. Rempp, 39.
[38] Zarlino, *Le istitutioni harmoniche* (Venice, 1558), pt. iii, chs. 2, 27.
[39] Gal. 1, fos. 105ᵛ–106ʳ, ed. Rempp, 78.

called respectively primary and secondary dissonance.[40] Galilei explained these two manners in book i as follows:

Dissonances are used in a vocal piece in two manners. One of these is the most essential part of counterpoint, both because it is capable of demonstrating the sufficiency of the contrapuntist's technique and because it is carefully considered by him. To the other he attaches little importance as it is of little purpose for demonstrating his erudition or for adding beauty to his piece. The manner considered and appreciated by the contrapuntist is the one whose use I have been striving to demonstrate perfectly. The other, little considered by him, consists specifically in moving with notes of smaller value, like minims and semiminims, proceeding by conjunct movement, ascending and descending through many steps, of which (and this will serve as a rule) it is ordinarily customary to make one consonant and the other dissonant. These dissonances are resolved, for the most part, by consonances outside the common usage of that other more important manner [the regular resolutions]. This way of proceeding is more appropriate for instruments than for voices, especially when the latter are expressing a text.[41]

This passage is illustrated in Ex. 2.2.[42]

Ex. 2.2

Illustrated here are secondary dissonances—*dissonanze sciolte*, loose or untied dissonances, which include *cattive*, that is, passing notes, and *note*

[40] Jeppesen, *The Style of Palestrina and the Dissonance*, 94–5.
[41] Gal. 1, fo. 78ʳ, ed. Rempp, 40.
[42] Gal. 1, fo. 78ʳ (R 40).

Ex. 2.3 (*a*)   (*b*)

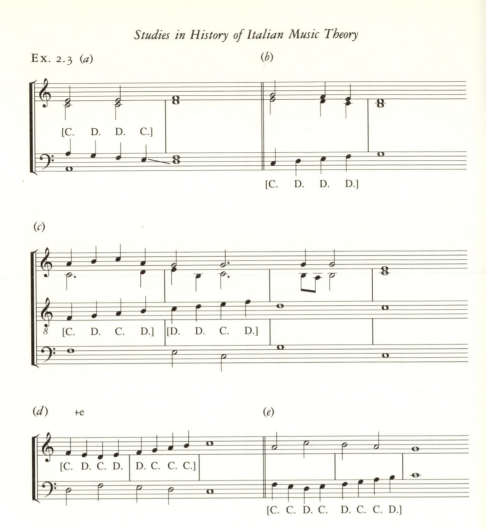

di moto locale, that is, auxiliary notes. Occasionally, he added, skips of a third might be used instead of conjunct movement, as in Ex. 2.3*c* (last dissonance).

The general rule accepted by musicians, Galilei said, was that when the value of the dissonant note was equal to one beat (a minim), secondary dissonances should occur on the up-beat (*alzare*) of the measure but never on the down-beat (*bassare*). With notes of smaller value, he said, they allowed consonant and dissonant notes to alternate without respect to beat.

Although the manner of treating secondary dissonances just described is freer than that taught by Zarlino or practised by Palestrina, Galilei wished to remove the few restrictions that remained. He declined to make a fast rule for the passing or ornamental dissonance. His general principle was, in his own words:

> Whenever two or more parts move over one another gracefully according to the decorum of the art of counterpoint, whatever dissonance occurs among them not only will be tolerated by the sense, but it will take delight in it. All extremes, however, should be avoided with mature judgement as vicious.[43]

One rule Galilei did specifically reject. He recalled that it was usually learned by heart that of four semiminims the second and fourth might be dissonant but the others had to be consonant. He advised memorizing instead that the two extreme notes, the two central notes, or the second and fourth, or any others, in fact, might be dissonant. In other words, Galilei approved not only the pattern Zarlino considered acceptable (where C stands for Consonance, and D for Dissonance), C D C D, but allowed also D C C D, D C D C, and occasionally others. As many as three *cattive* may occur in succession (Ex. 2.3*b*).[44]

The primary dissonance in counterpoint remained for Galilei, as for his predecessors, the *sincopa* or suspension. Galilei's contribution in this sphere was the relaxation of the rules for the resolution of the suspended dissonance. In the traditional resolution the tied dissonant note moved down conjunctly to the nearest consonance while the voice against which the dissonance occurred remained stationary. Artusi, in his second book on counterpoint of 1589, had permitted some licences; for example, voices other than the suspended one might move while the tied note resolved to a consonance other than the expected one, and a tritone or diminished fifth might take the place of a consonance in the resolution.[45] Galilei now permitted several more variations from the norm: the tied dissonant note might resolve by skip into a consonance; the note of resolution might be preceded by an ornamental figure or by another consonant note; the suspension might resolve ascending as well as descending; two voices might be suspended over the same note; and two or more suspensions might occur simultaneously in music of many parts. Several of these irregular resolutions occur frequently in the music of the fifteenth and early sixteenth centuries. Sixteenth-century rule-givers frowned upon them, however, and composers tended to avoid them. Galilei thus restored the limited variety of treatment enjoyed before sixteenth-century practice became standardized and added,

---

[43] Gal. 1, fo. 143ʳ, ed. Rempp, 152.

[44] Gal. 1, fos. 144ʳ (R 153), 126ʳ (R 113), 143ᵛ (R 153), 144ʳ (R 154), 144ʳ (R 154).

[45] Giovanni Maria Artusi, *Seconda parte dell'arte del contraponto nella quale si tratta dell'utile & uso delle dissonanze* (Venice: G. Vincenti 1589), bk. ii, ch. 3, p. 29.

Ex. 2.4

for the first time in theoretical literature at least, several irregular resolutions that have since become inseparably bound up with the suspension technique.

1. Skipwise resolutions (Ex. 2.4).[46]

In exonerating the traditionally prohibited skipwise resolution, Galilei stated:

The quality and nature of the consonance that succeeds the dissonance has more power to render it more or less satisfying to the ear than the quality and nature of the conjunct or separate movement, and, while the first is more satisfying, the latter is not to be disdained.[47]

2. Simultaneous motion towards resolution (Ex. 2.5).[48]

Ex. 2.5 (*a*)   (*b*)

3. Ornamental resolution (Ex. 2.6).[49]

Ex. 2.6

---

[46] Gal. 1, fo. 118ʳ (R 99).
[47] Gal. 1, fos. 110ᵛ–111ʳ, ed. Rempp, 88.
[48] Gal. 1, fo. 110ᵛ (R 88); 118ᵛ (original barlines and tie) (R 100).
[49] Gal. 1, fo. 111ʳ (R 88).

4. Resolution into another dissonance (Ex. 2.7).[50]

Ex. 2.7

5. Ascending resolution (Ex. 2.8).[51]

(*a*) Tied note is properly resolved in another voice (Ex. 2.8*a*).

(*b*) Note of resolution does not appear in another voice (Ex. 2.8*b*).

Ex. 2.8 (*a*)   (*b*)

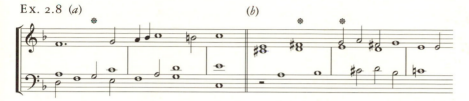

Among the examples Galilei used to illustrate how several dissonances might occur simultaneously are a number of double and triple suspensions.

6. Double suspensions (Ex. 2.9).[52]

Ex. 2.9 (*a*)

(*b*)

[50] Gal. 1, fo. 130ʳ (R 120).
[51] Gal. 1, fos. 124ᵛ (R 110), 136ᵛ (R 139).
[52] Gal. 1, fo. 133ᵛ (not in R); 131ᵛ (R 123).

7. Triple suspensions (Ex. 2.10).[53]

Ex. 2.10

The dissonant intervals varied in the freedom with which they might be introduced outside the suspension. Those deserving the greatest freedom of treatment, according to Galilei, were the augmented fourth, diminished fifth, and fourth. The preferential treatment accorded the first two, Galilei felt, was justified by an inherent characteristic 'of moving in their parts not only by contrary motion, but by a semitone, in which resolution one discerns a certain something that is beautiful in the order and qualities of musical intervals'.[54] The conservative manner of treating the diminished fifth is seen in the example from Zarlino (Ex. 2.11*a*).[55] According to Galilei, the augmented fourth and diminished fifth might be treated, like any other prepared dissonances, as passing notes or regularly and irregularly resolved suspensions. When treated this way they might be succeeded by any consonant intervals (Ex. 2.11*b–d*).[56] But, when resolved by their

Ex. 2.11 (*a*)   (*b*)

(*c*)

(*d*)

---

53 Gal. 1, fo. 134ʳ (R 132).
54 Gal. 1, fo. 122ᵛ, ed. Rempp, 107.
55 Zarlino, *Istitutioni*, bk. iii, ch. 30.
56 Gal. 1, fos. 119ᵛ (R 102), 119ᵛ (R 102), 122ʳ (R 106).

proper consonances, that is, the minor sixth for the augmented fourth, and the major third for the diminished fifth, these two intervals might be introduced as freely as consonances (Ex. 2.12).[57]

EX. 2.12

Besides the regular resolution, Galilei permitted a chromatic resolution for each of these intervals (Ex. 2.13).[58]

EX. 2.13 (a)   (b)

Always keeping in mind that dissonances were vehicles for expression, Galilei showed how these two intervals might be placed to sound more or less harsh. 'When the dissonance is caused by the lower voice [Ex. 2.14b]', Galilei observed, 'it will be less hard than when it is caused by the upper voice [Ex. 2.14a], and it will be hardest whenever it is caused by the concurrent movement of both voices [Ex. 2.14c].'[59]

Galilei accorded to the fourth the same freedom that he claimed for the diminished fifth and augmented fourth. His general rule was:

The fourth, as an interval that is not absolutely dissonant, is properly used, irrespective of syncopation, down-beat, or up-beat, any time that it is succeeded by

EX. 2.14   (a)   (b)

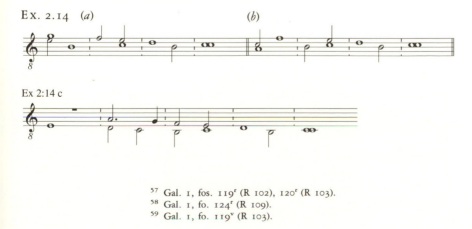

Ex 2:14 c

[57] Gal. 1, fos. 119ʳ (R 102), 120ʳ (R 103).
[58] Gal. 1, fo. 124ʳ (R 109).
[59] Gal. 1, fo. 119ᵛ (R 103).

Ex. 2.15 (a)   (b)

Ex. 2.16

Ex. 2.17

Ex. 2.18

the sixth, whether major [Ex. 2.15*b*] or minor [Ex. 2.15*a*], provided the parts proceed by contrary motion as shown.[60]

The licences permitted in introducing the fourth and diminished fifth might on occasion be allowed for the second and seventh. Free introduction of dissonances came under the last of Galilei's sixteen points: 'that they can be used equally well on the first and second beats of the measure'.

That the fourth, augmented fourth, and diminished fifth may be used on this . . . [weak beat] of the measure has already been shown and of these two the following example [Ex. 2.16] will refresh the memory. From the succeeding example [Ex.

[60] Gal. 1, fo. 115ᵛ, ed. Rempp, 95.

Ex. 2.19 (a)　　　　　　　　(b)　　　　　　　　(c)

2.17] it is evident that the second and seventh are not wanting this just licence, without obligations of ties or anything else.[61]

Regarding another example in which a free seventh is introduced (Ex. 2.18), Galilei warned, 'nor should those who are little expert believe that it is used in the next to the last beat as a passing dissonance *(cattiva)*'.[62] This seventh, he wished to emphasize, is an integral part of that chord.

A number of examples (see Ex. 2.19)[63] exhibit seconds and sevenths introduced by skip on a relatively accented beat (though still Galilei's *alzare*), that is, what we would call appoggiature. Galilei acknowledged that 'some delicate ears' might deny him this usage in two-part writing 'because of the extraordinary offence that might be felt when dissonances are used by skip between only two parts'.[64] Nevertheless, he employed them quite freely in his examples (Ex. 2.19b, c).

Galilei was nowhere more emphatic than in upsetting the rule that only two voices may form a dissonance in a four- or five-voice texture at a given time.[65] The ninth and tenth headings of Galilei's plan for the second book were: how many dissonances of the same species can sound simultaneously in four or more parts; and how many dissonances of different species, with the same number of parts? Under the first heading, he demonstrated with examples how two seconds, two fourths, and two sevenths could be built one on top of another. He cautioned, however, that this could not be done with two augmented fourths or two diminished fifths, at least not in the tuning commonly sung. For an augmented fourth above F–B, for example, is B–E♯, and this E♯ does not make a perfect octave with the lower F unless played on an instrument tuned in equal temperament. A similar difficulty arose in trying to build a chord on diminished fifths. Two augmented fourths or two diminished fifths could be heard at the same time, however, if they were not conjunct, and he gave examples of how this

---

[61] Gal. 1, fos. 137ᵛ–138ʳ, ed. Rempp, 141. The *tactus* here is evidently the semibreve, since Galilei considered the third minim as the 'alzare della battuta'.

[62] Gal. 1, fo. 137ᵛ, ed. Rempp, 141.

[63] Gal. 1, fos. 116ᵛ (R 98), 119ᵛ (R 101), 109ʳ (R 85).

[64] Gal. 1, fo. 109ᵛ, ed. Rempp, 86.

[65] Zarlino, *Istitutioni*, pt. iii, ch. 46.

could be done. Not only two but even three seconds, fourths, or sevenths could be built one on the other and used in harmonic progressions.[66]

Galilei attacked the second question—how many dissonances of different species could sound together—statistically. There were fifteen ways of pairing the six principal dissonances, that is, the second, fourth, augmented fourth, diminished fifth, seventh, and ninth. There were twenty ways of combining these six so that three different dissonances sounded together. These are, in fact, the total number of permutations, if these intervals are arranged indiscriminately. That all the possibilities were musically practicable, he demonstrated by providing a musical example for each one.[67]

In the manner of the *ars combinatoria* that became popular in seventeenth-century theory books, Galilei presented two tables showing the possible combinations using two and three dissonances at a time.[68] Like the *loci* and *tropi*, which the rhetoricians gave pupils to aid them in elaborating their orations, here was a guide for the invention of *concenti* to fit almost any expressive purpose.

Galilei was far more progressive in his views on vertical tonal combinations than in his limited appreciation of the necessities of horizontal chordal progression. Sixteenth-century theorists characteristically faced the problem of chord progression as if they wore blinders that prevented them from seeing more than two chords at a time. The extent of their scope was the passage of one consonance to the next, the suspension and 'saving' of dissonances, and cadence patterns made up usually of two intervals or chords. Galilei did not broaden appreciably this circumscribed vision.

His treatment of resolutions and cadence patterns nevertheless constitutes a substantial advance over the theories of most of his predecessors. He distinguished between progressions most suitable for final cadences and those best suited for internal cadences. The cadence in which a suspended fourth sounded against the bass and in which the bass moved, after the resolution, down a fifth or up a fourth was best for final endings (Ex. 2.20*a*). Cadences with the suspended seventh above the bass and with bass movement by a tone or semitone were best for internal endings (Ex. 2.20*b*). One of his examples shows a final cadence in which the seventh is entered freely (Ex. 2.20*c*).[69]

---

[66] Gal. 1, fos. 126ʳ ff. ed. Rempp, 114 ff.

[67] Gal. 1, fos. 128ᵛ ff. ed. Rempp, 118 ff.

[68] Gal. 1, fo. 129ʳ, ed. Rempp, 118; and 132ᵛ, ed. Rempp, 127. These tables were undoubtedly meant to parallel those given by Zarlino in *Istitutioni*, pt. iii, ch. 58, which show the combinations of consonances possible in three and four parts.

[69] Gal. 1, fos. 139ʳ (R 144), 144ᵛ (R 155), 139ʳ (R 144), 145ʳ (R 156).

Ex. 2.20 (a)   (b)

(c)

(d)   (e)

The choice of cadences was governed also by the affections of the text. A 'completely happy, peaceful, and cheerful' affection, Galilei observed, is conveyed by the archaic final cadence of Ex. 2.20*a*. A progression he characterized as 'disdainful' is shown in Ex. 2.20*b*, while one that he called 'effeminate and lascivious' because of the 'many softenings and the quantity of semitones in the outer voices' appears in Ex. 2.20*d*. For a doleful effect Galilei suggested following the example set by Rore in the final cadence of the first part of *Mia benigna fortuna*, which closes with a minor instead of a major triad (Ex. 2.20*e*).[70]

Galilei's concern with vertical sonorities in a book on counterpoint leads us to question whether 'counterpoint' meant to him in 1588 what it means to us. In the *Dialogo* modern counterpoint had been associated with the practice of singing several different 'airs' at the same time. Thus understood, counterpoint was to be condemned as a hindrance to musical expres-

[70] Gal. 1, fo. 145ʳ, ed. Rempp, 156. Rore, *Il secondo libro de madrigali a 4 voci* (Venice: Antonio Gardano, 1557); *Opera omnia*, ed. Bernhard Meier, iv. 79.

sion. Less than ten years later, Galilei had reached a compromise. He had extracted from polyphony what furthered his ends: the plurality of voices necessary for a variety of consonant and dissonant chords. He had discarded what hindered his purpose: the rhythmic and melodic independence of voices that had been considered an essential ingredient of good counterpoint until then. From the compromise there emerged a new structural frame for composition—chordal harmony dominated by a single melody or bass. Galilei never tired of repeating that in music of several parts it was either the bass or soprano that 'gave the air', as he expressed it, or movement to the piece and determined its key or mode. His treatise, then, is in reality a treatise on harmony, perhaps, indeed, the first treatise on harmony in the usual modern sense.

Galilei did not believe that the art of combining melodies should be neglected altogether. It had its place in the training of musicians and was necessary for writing elegant and easily sung lines when composing for many voices. But he did not intend to deal with this art himself. He hoped that perhaps Alessandro Striggio, who was such a master of it, would some day write a treatise on this aspect of composition.

It would be a mistake to attribute the bold experiments in harmony that we find in this treatise entirely to Galilei's invention. His intention was to report the 'modern practice of counterpoint' common to a group of avant-garde expressionistic composers. As a teacher and theorist Galilei prided himself on being up to date, and rightfully so, for almost every other theorist of the sixteenth century was a generation behind his own time. Coclico, Glareanus, Zarlino, and Artusi were compilers of rules and guardians of traditions. They passed on the wisdom of their revered masters—Josquin and Willaert—rather than their own experience as working composers and musicians. Galilei, on the other hand, was summing up the experience of his own contemporaries.

Yet he claimed some credit for the originality of his examples. Early in book ii he declared:

After these conceits of mine, the greater part of which I repute to be most new and useful, have been seen and understood, I know the majority will say of my examples that they knew them already many many years before they had seen them written in my present discourse, because for those versed in this faculty they are easy to learn from my clear examples. Nevertheless those who take the trouble to examine the works of these men will find that they put them to use only after learning them here. Not even I have been willing to put these examples into practice in my compositions published up to now, so that they might first appear all together, set forth in an orderly manner.[71]

[71] Gal. 1, fo. 114^{r-v}, ed. Rempp, 93–4.

The closing words of the second book of the treatise are those of a man confident of having found the path to the music of the future:

Now, if someone reading this discourse of mine fears to drown traversing with his feeble wings this river, suddenly become so wide and rapid, he should follow the example of the great Philoxenus and turn back to traverse it where it takes its origin, until I myself or others draw the arches over these fundamentals I have cast, stretching across its banks a bridge spacious and capable of taking everyone.[72]

[72] Gal. 1, fo. 148ᵛ, ed. Rempp, 161.

3

The Artusi–Monteverdi Controversy

Giovanni Maria Artusi, like Eduard Hanslick, made the mistake of tangling with a great composer. Thereby he earned the fate of the Beckmessers of this world, to be branded a hopeless reactionary and a philistine unable to appreciate true genius. Music historians have had few kind words for Artusi. He has even been charged—unjustly—with composing a polemic pamphlet against his teacher Zarlino,[1] when, actually, the pamphlet was a eulogy, and it was as Zarlino's defender that he entered the debates on the rules of counterpoint.

There is no denying that Artusi was a contentious critic, but he was neither reactionary nor lacking in understanding of modern music. Indeed, no commentator of the period revealed greater insight into Monteverdi's compositional methods. By choosing the dialogue form, Artusi was able to present both a critique and a defence of Monteverdi through the sparring of the open-minded Luca, who is fascinated by the innovations of the avant-garde composers, and the conservative Vario. Although Artusi does not reveal his own opinion, it may be assumed that it is closer to Vario's than Luca's, since Luca is usually forced to yield to Vario's superior authority. But it is not a dialogue between teacher and disciple in which the teacher is always right. Artusi evidently wanted to air both sides and to do so without offending Monteverdi, whose name the interlocutors never mention. Even in 1603, when Artusi answers the letters of the Ottuso Accademico, a defender of Monteverdi who apparently is not a fictional chararacter, he conceals the composer's identity in the tag 'Sign. Etc.'. Artusi was eager to keep the discussion on a non-personal, intellectual plane.

The Artusi–Monteverdi exchange needs to be put into the larger context of the quarrels in Bologna in the decades around 1600. It is well to remember also that music-theoretical quarrels were endemic to that city. In the 1480s Ramos de Pareja in Bologna debated with John Hothby in Lucca. The debate continued in the next generation, as Giovanni Spataro of Bologna defended his teacher Ramos against Franchino Gaffurio of Lodi. Later, in the seventeenth century, Giulio Cesare Arresti and Maurizio Cazzati crossed musical swords.

---

[1] Hans F. Redlich in the article 'Artusi' in *MGG* i (1949–51), 747–9 makes this accusation: 'Vicenzo Galileis theoretische Dispute mit Zarlino und mit Artusi selbst kulminierten schließlich nach des ersteren Tode in Artusis Angriffen auf den einstigen Lehrer, zusammengefaßt in der Streitschrift *Impresa del molto rev. Gioseffo Zarlino da Chioggia . . . dichiarata.*' This pamphlet, issued by Artusi in Bologna in 1604, is a eulogy of Zarlino by way of an explication of his device, or emblem.

Artusi's opponents were several: Ercole Bottrigari, against whom Artusi presumed to take the side of the late Annibale Melone; Vincenzo Galilei, against whom he defended Zarlino; L'Ottuso, who defended Monteverdi; and eventually Monteverdi himself, whom Artusi apparently now confronted directly, but under the pseudonym Antonio Braccino da Todi. The multilateral exchange may be outlined as follows.

1589. Artusi, in his *Seconda parte dell'arte del contraponto*, enumerated some of the imperfections to which *concerti* or ensemble performances were susceptible. These were principally: (i) instruments and voices were not situated properly in relation to each other, or their numbers were in the wrong proportions, (ii) compositions were poorly constructed, and (iii) the disparate bass parts of different choirs did not provide a sufficient foundation for the total texture.[2]

1593. Ercole Bottrigari took up the invitation by Francesco Patrizi in his *Della poetica, la deca istoriale* (1586)[3] to all friends of the truth to correct any errors in his book. In *Il Patricio*[4] Bottrigari offered friendly corrections to Patrizi's book vii, where tunings of the Greeks were discussed. Artusi later rose to Patrizi's defence.

1594. Ercole Bottrigari, without acknowledging that Artusi had first proposed the problem of the imperfections of modern ensembles, dedicated to it an entire book, *Il Desiderio overo de' concerti di varii strumenti musicali, dialogo di Alemanno Benelli*,[5] in the form of a dialogue between Gratioso Desiderio and Alemanno Benelli, who was named on the title-page as the author. But the name was an anagram for Annibale Melone, a leading musician of the town, who, Bottrigari later explained, used to spend three hours daily at Bottrigari's house discussing music theory, both ancient—in which Bottrigari was particularly erudite—and modern. In the dialogue Bottrigari put forward the view that the principal weakness of ensemble music arose from the different systems of tuning used by different instruments, which he divided into those with fixed or stable tuning, those that were stable but alterable, and those that were altogether alterable in intonation.

1599. When Bottrigari heard that people were attributing the authorship of *Il Desiderio* to Melone, he published it under his own name, with a preface explaining his action.[6]

1600. Artusi, *L'Artusi, overo delle imperfettioni della moderna musica*.[7] In the first *ragionamento* or discussion Artusi returns to the question of what is required in a good *concerto* or ensemble performance. He proposes eight criteria, the last of which is that all the instruments should be tuned to the same temperament by a single ear, as happens with the ensemble of the convent of San Vito in Ferrara. In the

---

[2] Giovanni Maria Artusi, *Seconda parte dell'arte del contraponto, nella quale si tratta dell'utile et uso delle dissonanze* (Venice: Giacomo Vincenti, 1589), ch. 16, 'Opinione intorno alli conserti musicali', 47.

[3] Ed. in Patrizi, *Della poetica*, by Daniello Aguzzi Barbagli (Florence: Istituto nazionale di studi sul Rinascimento, 1969–71).

[4] Bottrigari, *Il Patricio, overo de' tetracordi armonici di Aristosseno* (Bologna: Vittorio Benacci, 1593; facs. edn., Bolgna: Forni, 1969).

[5] Venice: Ricciardo Amadino, 1594. Desiderio was also the name of one of the interlocutors of Gioseffo Zarlino's *Dimostrationi harmoniche* (Venice: Francesco dei Franceschi Senese, 1571).

[6] *Il Desiderio, overo de' concerti di varii strumenti musicali, dialogo del M. Ill. Sig. Cavaliere Hercole Bottrigaro* (Bologna: Gioambattista Bellagamba, 1599; facs. edn. with extended introduction by Kathi Meyer, Berlin: Martin Breslauer, 1924).

[7] Venice: Giacomo Vincenti, 1600; facs. edn., Bologna: Forni, 1968.

course of the discussion of tuning (p. 8), the interlocutor Luca mentions that 'someone' has made a classification of instruments into fully stable, fully alterable, and stable alterable. Vario accepts the first two classes but rejects the third. He then revives the classification that Zarlino had made: (i) instruments tuned with equal whole tones and unequal semitones, such as organs and harpsichords; (ii) those that bend to any tuning, such as voices, trombones, and rebecs; and (iii) those that are tuned with the whole tone divided into two equal semitones, such as lutes and viols. Artusi ends the discussion with a defence of Aristoxenus, then a brave stand in support of an anti-Pythagorean author. The second *ragionamento*, discussed in the essay below, was dedicated to a critique of Monteverdi's madrigals.

1601. Artusi claims to have discovered a copy of the *Desiderio* in Melone's hand among the papers he got from his widow—Melone, who was accustomed to copy out all Bottrigari's writings, died in April 1598—and accuses Bottrigari of falsely claiming its authorship. He has it reprinted as a work of Melone.[8] Bottrigari responds to this affront in his *Lettera di Federico Verdicelli*.[9]

1602. In *Il Melone*[10] Bottrigari sides with Nicola Vicentino and against Zarlino in Vicentino's famous quarrel with Vicente Lusitano about the chromatic and enharmonic genera. Drafted in 1591, this answers a query from Melone, but it was not published until after the latter's death. About this time Bottrigari also addresses a polemic pamphlet to Artusi, *Ant-Artusi*, not extant.

1603. Artusi dedicates the *Seconda parte dell'Artusi*[11] to Bottrigari, promising in it to defend Patrizi against the criticisms Bottrigari had made in his *Patricio*. The *seconda consideratione* is dedicated to this question, while the *prima consideratione* prints and responds to letters of L'Ottuso about Monteverdi's madrigals.

1604. Bottrigari replies in *Aletelogia di Leonardi Gallucio . . . per la difesa del M. I. sig. Cav. Hercole Bottrigaro, contra à quanto . . . ha scritto lo autore delle inconsiderationi musicali.*[12]

1605. Claudio Monteverdi answers Artusi briefly in the preface to *Il quinto libro de' madrigali a cinque voci.*[13]

1606? *Discorso musicale di Antonio Braccino da Todi*, not extant, is known from citations in the items under 1607 and 1608. Artusi is assumed to be the author.

1607. Giulio Cesare Monteverdi, 'Dichiaratione della Lettera stampata nel Quinto libro de suoi madrigali'—a gloss upon Claudio Monteverdi's remarks of 1605 by Claudio's brother, is printed in *Scherzi musicali a tre voci, raccolti da Giulio Cesare Monteverde suo fratello.*[14]

1608. *Discorso secondo musicale di Antonio Braccino da Todi per la dichiaratione della*

[8] *Il Desiderio . . . dialogo di Annibale Meloni* (Milan: Stampatori archiepiscopali, 1601).

[9] *Lettera di Federico Verdicelli . . . in difesa del Sign. Cav. Hercole Bottrigaro* (12 July 1601), Bologna, Civico Museo Bibliografico Musicale, MS I-68.

[10] Bottrigari, *Il Melone, discorso armonico . . . et Il Melone secondo, considerationi musicali . . . sopra un discorso di M. Gandolfo Sigonio* (Ferrara: Vittorio Baldini, 1602; facs. edn., Bologna: Forni, 1969).

[11] *Seconda parte dell'Artusi overo delle imperfettioni della moderna musica* (Venice: Giacomo Vincenti, 1603; facs. edn., Bologna: Forni, 1969).

[12] Bologna, Civico Museo Bibliografico Musicale, MS B-43.

[13] Venice: Ricciardo Amadino, 1605; the preface is translated in the essay that follows.

[14] Venice: Ricciardo Amadino, 1607. The 'Dichiaratione' is trans. in Oliver Strunk, *Source Readings in Music History* (New York: Norton, 1950), 405–12.

lettera posta ne' Scherzi musicali del Sig. Claudio Monteverde.[15] Here Artusi, if, indeed, he is the author of this pamphlet, finally names Monteverdi as the composer of the madrigals criticized in 1600 and answers him directly.

In the context of this three-way exchange, the quarrel with Monteverdi seems to have been at first incidental to the dispute with Bottrigari and probably would never have reached print if it had not been provoked by Bottrigari. But after L'Ottuso's letters, it moved to the foreground. Although echoes of the Artusi—Monteverdi dispute continued to resonate during the next half-century, the printed exchange between the principals ended in 1608. One of the echoes is the quarrel between Marco Scacchi, on one side, and Romano Michele Romano in Rome and Paul Siefert in Danzig, on the other. This time it is a partisan of the new music who is the critic. The main document from the standpoint of Italian music is published and discussed in Essay 4.

The following essay was first published in *The Monteverdi Companion*, ed. Denis Arnold and Nigel Fortune (London: Faber and Faber, 1968), 133–66; with minor revisions, it appeared in *The New Monteverdi Companion*, ed. Arnold and Fortune (London: Faber and Faber, 1985), 127–58.

THE debt music history owes to Giovanni Maria Artusi is only grudgingly recognized. Yet it is a great one, for he focused attention on one of the deepest crises in musical composition and stimulated the composer who most squarely confronted it to clarify his position. Without Claudio Monteverdi's letter in the fifth book of madrigals and his brother's glosses upon it in the *Scherzi musicali* (1607), Monteverdi's youthful creative thrust would have left a blunter mark in history. His stylistic profile without Artusi's criticism would be set less boldly in relief.

If the controversy between Artusi and Monteverdi gives us a valuable commentary upon music history in the making, it also affected the course of musical evolution. Claudio and his brother Giulio Cesare, by publishing their manifestos for the new or second practice, held up a banner for others to rally around. Their slogans echoed for half a century in the prefaces and pamphlets of the avant garde. Nor is this the only significance of the controversy; it also gives us a glimpse into the way composers thought about certain points of technique, how they justified them, what precedents they recognized, and how they viewed the act of composition itself.

What are the real issues of this debate? In one sense it was the usual battle of the generations. Monteverdi rebelled against the strictures of his masters; Artusi, a generation older, stood by the standards of composition taught by Gioseffo Zarlino, among whose followers he was one of the most eminent. He expected dissonances to be introduced according to the rules

[15] Venice: Giacomo Vincenti, 1608; facs. edn., Milan: n.p., 1924; repr. Milan: Bollettino Bibliografico Musicale, 1934; facs. edn., Bologna: Forni, 1968.

of counterpoint, and he insisted upon unity of modality within a piece.
These conventions had been challenged already in the middle of the
sixteenth century, and Artusi's offensive—or rather counter-offensive—was
only one of a chain of attacks and counter-attacks that can be traced back to
the debate between Nicola Vicentino and Vicente Lusitano in 1551. Artusi
was not an arch-conservative through and through. His own books on
counterpoint relaxed unnecessarily strict rules that were often honoured in
the breach. He recognized, as Zarlino did not, that dissonances were of
primary importance in composition and devoted a whole volume to them.
He was one of the first to take a strong position in favour of equal
temperament as a standard tuning for instrumental music. Yet it grieved
him to see counterpoint, which had reached a point of ultimate refinement
and control, become a prey to caprice and expediency. He honestly believed
that the patiently erected structure was under siege.

In another sense it was a battle between two contemporary points of
view. On one side were those like Monteverdi who accepted the advances
of concerted instrumental music, improvised counterpoint, ornamented
singing, the rhythms of dance music, and the enlarged vocabulary of
chromaticism blended with the diatonic. On the other side were those
like Artusi who felt that these innovations, mainly products of relatively
unschooled musicians, corrupted a pure, noble, and learned art. In one
camp were those who held to a single standard of counterpoint; in the other
those who followed a double standard, one for everyday sacred compositions and another for compositions on texts expressing violent passions.
From a long view, neither side won an absolute victory. The strict standards backed by Artusi returned by the mid-seventeenth century in a
modified form, and the modifications represented concessions to the other
side.

Artusi printed and analysed in his dialogue of 1600 nine examples from
two madrigals of Monteverdi that he knew from manuscript copies. He
withheld both the composer's name and the texts. The dialogue is divided
into two *ragionamenti* or discourses, of which the first, dealing with tuning,
was probably Artusi's main pretext for publishing the book. The second
dealt with the anonymous composer's madrigals.[16] Artusi saw no reason
to print the words, because he did not recognize a double standard of

---

[16] *L'Artusi, overo delle imperfettioni della moderna musica* (Venice: Giacomo Vincenti, 1600). The first
ragionamento takes issue with Ercole Bottrigari's conclusions about tuning and concerted instrumental
groupings set forth in *Il Desiderio* (Venice: Ricciardo Amadino, 1594). A part of the second *ragionamento*
is translated in Strunk, *Source Readings in Music History*, 393–404. Artusi had started the ball rolling
with his 'Opinione intorno alli conserti musicali' in *Seconda parte dell'arte del contraponto nella quale si
tratta dell'utile et uso delle dissonanze* (Venice: Giacomo Vincenti, 1589), bk. ii, ch. 17.

contrapuntal correctness. To omit them also helped conceal the authorship of the madrigals. Although Artusi knew the name of the composer, he refrained from revealing it, because in view of his criticism to do so would have been indelicate. To soften the blow further the author expressed his opinion through one of the interlocutors, a fictitious musician named Vario, who converses with a cultivated amateur named Luca.

Three years after this dialogue appeared Artusi, having received letters from a defender of the anonymous composer who signs himself 'L'Ottuso Academico', published a second book. In the first part of this he answers his correspondent's letters. In the *Considerationi* that follow he defends Francesco Patrizi's statements about Greek music against Ercole Bottrigari's criticisms.[17] Although now the discussion of the anonymous madrigals deals largely with the question of text expression, Artusi again omits texts when he prints examples by the anonymous composer and by L'Ottuso. The composer's identity was not made known in print until Monteverdi answered Artusi in the famous letter that opens the fifth book of madrigals of 1605. Of the madrigals criticized in the 1600 dialogue, *Anima mia, perdona* was not published until 1603 in the fourth book of madrigals and *Cruda Amarilli* and *O Mirtillo* not until 1605 in the fifth book. In addition to these, also under discussion in the 1603 book are *Era l'anima mia* and the second part of *Ecco Silvio*, both from the fifth book.

Throughout the controversy the treatment of dissonances was the most bitterly contested territory. The dissonant effects Artusi objected to in Monteverdi's madrigals are of three kinds: (i) those caused by the application of ornaments to a consonant framework; (ii) those which, though accepted by usage in improvised counterpoint and instrumental music, were outside the norms of the severe style; (iii) those outside these two categories that could be justified only in terms of the expressive demands of the text. The text, of course, was the principal motivating force behind all three kinds of dissonances. But it was possible to talk about the first two without the text, and this is what Artusi does in his first critique, even though some of his examples could not be explained adequately without the text.

Each of the examples cited by Artusi in the 1600 book violates one or more rules of the strict style as taught by Zarlino and Artusi in their

---

[17] *Seconda parte dell'Artusi, overo delle imperfettioni della moderna musica* (Venice: Giacomo Vincenti, 1603); Francesco Patrizi, *Della poetica, la deca istoriale* (Ferrara: V. Baldini, 1586), ed. Danielo Aguzzi Barbagli, i (Florence: Istituto nazionale di studi sul Rinascimento, 1969); Bottrigari, *Il Patricio, overo de' tetracordi armonici di Aristosseno* (Bologna: Vittorio Benacci, 1593). By 1603 Artusi and Bottrigari had exchanged a number of acrimonious pamphlets and letters, both printed and manuscript. The urge to respond to Bottrigari may have provided a stronger motive for the 1603 book than continuing the criticism of Monteverdi.

Ex. 3.1. Monteverdi, *Cruda Amarilli*, bars 12–14

counterpoint books.[18] Luca, who plays the advocate for Monteverdi, pleads that modern composers excuse these lapses by various pretexts. The defences Luca timidly brings up are very revealing of the thinking of the time.

The composer in Ex. 3.1 is charged by Vario with failing to accord the upper parts with the bass. Luca argues that the example should be regarded as 'accented' singing: that is, it is a written example of an improvisational practice. Vario protests that no author has yet spoken of accented music or defined what accents are. Actually, Lodovico Zacconi had spoken of these at length and defined them as follows:

The graces (*vaghezze*) and accents (*accenti*) are made by splitting and breaking the note-values when in a bar or half-bar is added a number of notes that have the property of being rapidly performed. These give so much pleasure and delight that it appears to us that we are hearing so many well-trained birds which capture our hearts and render us very happy with their singing.[19]

For example, when a part has two semibreves or minims, particularly separated by a skip, the singer may fill the time- or pitch-interval with shorter notes.

[18] Gioseffo Zarlino, *Le istitutioni harmoniche* (Venice, 1558), pt. iii; Artusi, *L'arte del contraponto ridotta in tavole* (Venice: Giacomo Vincenti et Ricciardo Amadino, 1586); *Seconda parte dell'arte del contraponto* (1589); *L'arte del contraponto . . . novamente ristampata, & di molte nuove aggiunte, dall'auttore arrichite* (Venice: Giacomo Vincenti, 1598).

[19] Lodovico Zacconi, *Prattica di musica* (Venice: Girolamo Polo, 1596), bk. i, ch. 66, fo. 58ʳ. All the translations in this chapter are mine.

However, he should know that these notes are accompanied by certain accents caused by certain retardations and sustainings of the voice, which are accomplished by taking away a particle from one value and assigning it to another.[20]

Zacconi gives the following illustration:

Ex. 3.2

Girolamo dalla Casa, another exponent of florid singing, inserts the semiquaver runs shown in Ex. 3.3.

Ex. 3.3. Cipriano de Rore, *Tanto mi piacque*, with diminutions from Dalla Casa, *Il vero modo di diminuir* (Venice: Angelo Gardano, 1584), ii. 48

If Monteverdi's passage in Ex. 3.1 is reduced to a hypothetical simpler framework (Ex. 3.4) and Zacconi's suggested *accenti* and runs similar to Dalla Casa's are applied, we arrive at a version close to Monteverdi's and just as faulty from Artusi's point of view (Ex. 3.5).

Ex. 3.4

---

[20] Ibid., bk. i, ch. 63, fo. 56ʳ. The ensuing example is at fo. 56ᵛ.

Ex. 3.5

Ex. 3.6. Monteverdi, *Cruda Amarilli*, bars 35–8

Luca finds the effect of the *accenti* attractive. Compositions embellished by such ornaments 'when played by various instruments or sung by singers skilled in this kind of accented music full of substitutions (*suppositi*) yield a not displeasing harmony at which I marvel'.[21]

Vario's answer is doctrinaire, as expected. Composers and singers who use these portamentos, delays, and turns, while they may avoid offensive sounds by instinct or deceive the ear by the quickness of their embellishments, corrupt the good old rules with their mannerisms.

Another ornamental figure lies at the basis of the dissonances in Ex. 3.6 which are quoted by Artusi. A hypothetical simple version is shown in Ex. 3.7. Christoph Bernhard, in a manuscript treatise of around 1660, shows

---

[21] *L'Artusi*, fo. 41ᵛ.

Ex. 3.7. Reduction of Ex. 3.6

Ex. 3.8. Bernhard, *Tractatus compositionis augmentatus*, example of *quaesitio notae*

how a similar passage can be embellished by means of the figure he calls
quaesitio notae (searching note; see Ex. 3.8).[22]

Only some of Monteverdi's licences can be passed as *accenti*. Luca suggests
another defence for others:

> These musicians observe their rule that the part making the dissonance with the
> lowest part should have a harmonic correspondence with the tenor, and that it [the
> first] accord with every other part, while the lowest part also should accord with
> every other part.[23]

A situation governed by this rule would arise in *contrapunto a mente* if a
bass and a higher voice were improvising against a *cantus firmus* in the
tenor. The two improvisers would be obliged to accord with the tenor but
not necessarily with each other. Tinctoris states as a rule that in singing
super librum, that is, over a plainchant book, the part-singer needs to
observe the laws of consonance with respect to the tenor part alone, while

---

[22] Christoph Bernhard, *Tractatus compositionis augmentatus*, ch. 33, printed in Joseph Müller-Blattau,
Die Kompositionslehre Heinrich Schützens (2nd edn., Kassel: Bärenreiter, 1963), 81–2; trans. in Walter
Hilse, 'The Treatises of Christoph Bernhard', *Music Forum*, 3 (1973), 1–196.

[23] *L'Artusi*, fo. 43ʳ.

in *res facta*, that is, written counterpoint, all parts must have regard to one another. It is laudable, he says, when all the parts accord with one another even in improvised counterpoint.[24] But this will happen only by accident or through rehearsal. In the sixteenth century it was customary to have the bass sing the *cantus firmus*. To judge by the profusion of manuals or portions of them dedicated to the art of improvised counterpoint towards the end of that century and the beginning of the next, it was a widespread practice, particularly in the principal chapel and cathedral choirs.[25]

Adriano Banchieri recalls with pleasure the wonderful effect, peculiar charm, and very tasteful sensation of the *contrapunti a mente*, with their unexpected consecutive fifths and octaves, the dissonant encounters, and extravagant turns:

In Rome in the Chapel of our Lord, in the Holy Mansion of Loreto and in countless other chapels when they sing *contrapunto alla mente* on a bass, no one knows what his companion is going to sing, but together through certain observances agreed among themselves they give a most tasteful sensation to the hearing. It can be stated as a general maxim that even if a hundred various voices (so to speak) were singing consonantly over a bass, all would agree, and those dissonances, fifths, octaves, extravagances, and clashes are all graces that make up the true effect of *contrapunto alla mente*.[26]

So impressed was Banchieri with the possibilities of this effect that he made up a set of ten instructions for counterfeiting such counterpoints in writing. The trick, he shows, is to write each of the parts against the bass independently of the others.

Monteverdi accepts into written composition some of the fortuitous clashes that occur when parts are moving independently around some common focus. One of the passages Vario points to as following the relaxed rules of harmonic correspondence between parts is bars 41–2 of *Cruda Amarilli*. Ex. 3.9 divides the texture into two groups, each of which corresponds harmonically with the tenor, but parts of opposing groups may clash with each other. The composer takes advantage of the tolerance for free mixtures of intervals acquired through improvised music to introduce a variety of rhetorical effects. This device is particularly fitting to illustrate the word 'fugace' ('elusive'), as it affords at once smooth and independent

[24] Johannes Tinctoris, *Liber de arte contrapuncti*, bk. ii, ch. 20, in Edmond de Coussemaker, *Scriptores de musica medii aevi*, iv (Paris, 1876), 129; in *Johannis Tinctoris Opera theoretica*, ed. Albert Seay (Corpus scriptorum de musica, 22; American Institute of Musicology, 1975), ii. 110.

[25] See Ernest T. Ferand, 'Improvised Vocal Counterpoint in the Late Renaissance and Early Baroque', *Annales musicologiques*, 4 (1956), 129–74.

[26] Adriano Banchieri, *Cartella musicale nel canto figurato, fermo & contrapunto . . . novamente in questa terza impressione ridotta dall'antica alla moderna pratica* (Venice: Giacomo Vincenti, 1614), 230.

Ex. 3.9. Monteverdi, *Cruda Amarilli*, bars 41–2

voice movement. The diminished fifth and seventh on the word 'fera' ('fierce') serve both the musical function of providing a climactic cadence and heightening the feeling of the word.

Luca makes another significant remark about how musicians became receptive to the chance combinations that arise from rapidly and independently moving parts. In answering Vario's objection that in bars 42–3 some of the quavers do not correspond either to the bass or tenor, Luca says this licence is derived 'from perceiving that in instruments these [quavers] do not much offend the ear because of the quickness of movement'.[27]

Vincenzo Galilei, in his manuscript treatise on counterpoint (1589–91), made precisely this observation about rapidly moving parts, which he found 'more appropriate for instruments than for voices'.[28]

Whenever two or more parts move against one another gracefully according to the decorum of the art of counterpoint, whatever dissonance occurs among them not only will be tolerated by the sense, but it will take delight in it.[29]

Although it was customary, he said, to alternate consonance and dissonance in writing such runs, he declined to make a hard-and-fast rule, showing

[27] *L'Artusi*, fo. 43ᵛ.

[28] Vincenzo Galilei, *Il primo libro della prattica del contrapunto intorno all'uso delle consonanze*, Florence, Biblioteca Nazionale Centrale, MSS Galilei 1, fo. 78ʳ; ed. in Frieder Rempp, *Die Kontrapunkttraktate Vincenzo Galileis* (Cologne: Arno Volk, 1980), 40. See Palisca, 'Vincenzo Galilei's Counterpoint Treatise', Essay 2, p. 43.

[29] Palisca, 'Vincenzo Galilei's Counterpoint Treatise', Essay 2, p. 43, quoted from *Discorso intorno all'uso delle dissonanze*, MSS Galilei 1, fo. 143ʳ; ed. Rempp, 152.

Ex. 3.10

rather that as many as three dissonances may occur in succession with impunity. By coincidence, his example uses the very same progression as Monteverdi does in bars 42–3 of *Cruda Amarilli* between the two uppermost parts and the bass (Ex. 3.10).[30]

Up to now I have been reviewing some of the arguments on behalf of Monteverdi adduced by Luca in the second discourse of Artusi's dialogue of 1600. In 1603, as we saw, Artusi published a defence of his criticism of Monteverdi in reply to letters from L'Ottuso Accademico. This book begins with the text of a letter Artusi purportedly wrote to L'Ottuso in response to one from him of 1599. In his letter Artusi quotes selectively from L'Ottuso's reply, which, though not dated, is obviously subsequent to Artusi's dialogue of 1600, as it counters some points made there.

The mystery of L'Ottuso's identity has not been satisfactorily solved. Emil Vogel and others before him[31] simply assumed that he was Monteverdi, and later writers have generally followed suit. Several circumstances, however, militate against this assumption. Monteverdi begins his foreword to *Il quinto libro de' madrigali* (1605) with the remark, 'be not surprised that I am giving these madrigals to the press without first replying to the objections that Artusi made against some very minute portions of them'. He could not have made such a plea if his reply had already appeared in print under the name L'Ottuso. There is no resemblance between L'Ottuso's letter and Monteverdi's style of writing. Further, Artusi prints (fos. 50ᵛ–51ʳ) fourteen breve-bars taken from five-part madrigals of L'Ottuso—'passaggi fatti dall'Ottuso ne suoi Madrigali'—and these cannot be reconciled with any

[30] *Discorso intorno all'uso delle dissonanze*, fo. 126ʳ.

[31] See Emil Vogel, 'Claudio Monteverdi', *Vierteljahrsschrift für Musikwissenschaft*, 3 (1887), 315. On p. 332 Vogel cites the authority of Zaccaria Tevo, *Il musico testore* (Venice: Antonio Bortoli, 1706), 175, to support the attribution of the letters to Monteverdi. Gaetano Gaspari (died 1881), in his manuscript notes appended to his own copy of the *Seconda parte dell'Artusi* now in Bologna, Civico Museo Bibliografico Musicale, also expressed the opinion that L'Ottuso was Monteverdi. This copy, which was the one used in this study, bears the signature of the official censor at the end of the *Considerationi*, 54, and the note that the author should be required to place his name and surname and native city on the title page. All the more personally offensive passages, including the entire sarcastic letter of dedication addressed to Bottrigari and the letter to the reader, are struck out in this copy with a single stroke of the pen.

known works of Monteverdi. Besides, when Monteverdi is referred to in the correspondence it is always as 'Signor Etc.', not as L'Ottuso.

If L'Ottuso is not Monteverdi, who is he? Several possibilities need to be examined.

1. L'Ottuso is a straw man contrived by Artusi to be knocked down as he refutes objections made to his earlier critique of Monteverdi.

2. L'Ottuso is Ercole Bottrigari, to whom the book is dedicated and against whose *Patricio* half of it is directed.

3. L'Ottuso is a composer and academician probably from Ferrara or Mantua.

Is L'Ottuso Artusi's creation? Just as Artusi invented the interlocutors Vario and Luca to argue the merits of the questions discussed in the 1600 dialogue, it is reasonable that he would invent an opponent against whom he could debate in the first person about Monteverdi's modernisms. L'Ottuso writes garrulously and redundantly like Artusi himself. He cites many classical and modern authors and has a command of the calculations of proportions every theorist, but not necessarily every composer, had to know. He makes a moderately good case for Monteverdi, something Artusi was perfectly capable of doing, because he understood the modernists even if he disagreed with them. It is even conceivable that Artusi might have gone to such lengths as fabricating excerpts from non-existent madrigals, which he claimed were sent to him from L'Ottuso's academy. If L'Ottuso's letter of 1599 was not faked later, why did Artusi not produce it in the dialogue of 1600, when it would have made a good pretext for attacking the modernist point of view in the first place? The dedication in Venice on 20 November 1600 shows that he had ample time to do so. The possibility that L'Ottuso was an invention of Artusi is, therefore, not to be excluded.[32]

May L'Ottuso be Bottrigari, to whom the 1603 book is dedicated? The whole second part of the book is a defence of statements about music, particularly on the Greek tunings, made by Francesco Patrizi in his *Della poetica, la deca istoriale* (1586), against the objections of Bottrigari in his *Il Patricio, overo de' tetracordi armonici di Aristosseno* (1593).[33] At the same time Artusi answers a pamphlet by Bottrigari entitled *Ant-Artusi*.[34] The possibility that L'Ottuso is Bottrigari is made unlikely by the fact that Bottrigari

---

[32] John Harper, in 'Frescobaldi's Early *Inganni* and their Background', *Proceedings of the Royal Musical Association*, 105 (1978–9), 11, has raised the possibility that Artusi concealed his own name in the similar sounding 'Ottuso' as an *inganno*.

[33] See above, n. 17.

[34] This pamphlet was mentioned by Artusi in his letter dedicating the *Seconda parte dell'Artusi* to Bottrigari.

treats him as a real person. In his *Aletelogia*, an answer to Artusi's book of 1603, Bottrigari says he will not refute what Artusi writes against L'Ottuso in his ninth 'Inconsideratione', because the academician is wise and capable and will defend himself with sagacity and valour.[35] Bottrigari may have known his identity, having lived a long time in Ferrara and now in Artusi's own city of Bologna.

The most likely possibility is that L'Ottuso was a composer active in Ferrara or Mantua. Artusi introduces the first quotation from L'Ottuso's letter with the words:

Finding myself in Ferrara in the year 1599, I was given a letter without proper name but with the signature 'L'Ottuso Academico'. Later from a good source I had the information that this was a man of much authority and that he was very much a musician.[36]

The pseudonym, meaning 'the obtuse one', fits the current style of academic names, which were often teasingly self-derogatory, like 'L'Ebbro' (the drunken one), 'L'Incruscato' (the crusty one, Giovanni Bardi's name in the Alterati), 'L'Affannato' (the breathless one, Marco da Gagliano's name in the Elevati and Scipione Gonzaga's in the Invaghiti), 'Lo Smemorato' (the forgetful one), and so on. As to which academy he may have belonged there is no clue. The Accademia degli Intrepidi of Ferrara, to which Monteverdi dedicated his fourth book of madrigals, was founded in 1600,[37] too late for L'Ottuso to have acquired his academic name in it by 1599. Another Ferrarese academy, the Accademia dei Parteni, had as one of its councillors the composer Count Alfonso Fontanella and as its musical censors Count Alfonso Fogliani and Luigi Putti.[38] Fontanella, a man of culture and an accomplished composer, had the necessary qualifications to be L'Ottuso, but Anthony Newcomb finds the letters published by Artusi 'too hysterical, too learned . . . and too witless to be connected with the urbane, mildly cynical style of Fontanelli', and he could not locate any of the excerpts from L'Ottuso's madrigals quoted in the second letter among Fontanella's surviving works. However, he has not excluded altogether the possibility that Fontanella was the writer of the letters.[39] Another good candidate is

---

[35] Bottrigari, *Aletelogia di Leonardo Gallucio ai benigni, e sinceri lettori, lettera apologetica D.M.I.S.C.H.B.* (1604), Bologna, Civico Museo Bibliografico Musicale, MS B-43, p. 72.

[36] *Seconda parte dell'Artusi*, 5.

[37] Stuart Reiner, 'Preparations in Parma', *Music Review*, 25 (1964), 289 n. 78.

[38] Anthony Newcomb, 'Carlo Gesualdo and a Musical Correspondence of 1594', *Musical Quarterly*, 54 (1968), 412.

[39] Newcomb, 'Alfonso Fontanelli and the Ancestry of the *seconda pratica* Madrigal', in Robert L. Marshall (ed.), *Studies in Renaissance and Baroque Music in Honor of Arthur Mendel* (Kassel: Bärenreiter, 1974), 67–8.

the Ferrarese composer Antonio Goretti, at whose salon Artusi's dialogists Vario and Luca are represented as hearing Monteverdi's not yet published madrigals.[40]

Stuart Reiner, in a review of the first edition of *The Monteverdi Companion*,[41] proposed that L'Ottuso may have been Giulio Cesare Monteverdi. This is an interesting suggestion and would merit further exploration if their styles of writing and thinking were not so diverse. Giulio Cesare speaks in generalities and with a certain touch of sophistry; L'Ottuso is very direct, concrete, cites his sources precisely, is innovative in his theoretical ideas, and extremely well read, citing not only numerous composers but poets such as Guarini and Tasso (to whom he refers as 'nostro', suggesting a Ferrarese connection), Ficino's *Compendium in Timaeum*, and the Pseudo-Aristotle *Problems*, and he refers to 'Monsignore Zarlino' rather than, as Giulio Cesare does, to 'Reverendo Zerlino'.

There was an academician L'Ottuso active as a court poet later in the century, but he is not likely as Monteverdi's supporter. A sacred play, *L'Ave Maria addolorata*, by him has a dedication to the Holy Roman Emperor Ferdinand III (reigned 1636–57) and signed 'L'Incognito Ottuso'.[42]

Although Artusi's credibility on this subject is naturally suspect, it should be recalled that he claims in his last discourse, written under the pseudonym Antonio Braccino da Todi, that the whole quarrel began because a number of friendly and civil letters Artusi wrote to Monteverdi remained unanswered, and instead Monteverdi replied through a third person (obviously meaning L'Ottuso).[43] It is clear, in any case, that Artusi never pretended that L'Ottuso was Monteverdi or that he was calling the composer a blockhead.

Whoever he was, L'Ottuso finally brought the debate around to the main point—why the new harmonic effects were necessary. He is quoted as saying in his letter of 1599:

[40] There is a possibility, though not a strong one, that the correspondent was a member of an academy called 'degli Ottusi'. If he had been a member of such an academy, 'Accademico Ottuso' would have been more normal usage than 'L'Ottuso Accademico'. There were two academies so named. One was the Accademia degli Ottusi in Bologna, of which, unfortunately, nothing is known; see Michele Maylender, *Storia delle accademie d'Italia* (Bologna, 1926–30), iii. 173. The Accademia degli Ottusi of Spoleto seems to go no further back than 1610 (ibid. iv. 176).

[41] *Journal of the American Musicological Society*, 23 (1970), 344–6.

[42] Vienna, Österreichische Nationalbibliothek, MS Pal. Vind. 13278. According to Maylender, *Storia*, iii. 202–4, there had been two academies called 'Incogniti' in Italy in the 16th c., one in Naples between 1546 and 1548 and another in Turin, instituted in 1585 but short-lived. The Ottuso discovered by Reiner in the Roman Accademia degli Umoristi, the dramatist Girolamo Rocco, may be the same person as the Vienna poet.

[43] *Discorso secondo musicale di Antonio Braccino da Todi* (Venice: Giacomo Vincenti, 1608; repr. Bologna: Forni, 1968), 6.

The purpose of this new movement of the parts (*modulatione*) is to discover through its novelty a new consensus (*concenti*) and new affections, and this without departing in any way from good reason, even if it leaves behind somehow the ancient traditions of some excellent composers.[44]

New affections call for new harmonic combinations to express them. This is the crux of the matter.

Artusi's retort deals in semantics. He first defines 'concento': 'it is a mixture of low and high notes intermediated in such a way that when sounded they produce an infinite sweetness to the ear'.[45] There are only four ways of mediating the interval between a low and high sound, through the arithmetic, geometric, harmonic, and counter-harmonic divisions. None of these will divide a seventh, one of the new combinations defended by L'Ottuso, consonantly. Therefore the new combinations are not *concenti*. Indeed no new *concenti* are possible, because the number of consonances is limited. So no new affections can be expressed by them.

L'Ottuso's second letter, written a month after Artusi's reply, is printed in full by Artusi.[46] L'Ottuso, not intimidated by Artusi's sophistry, insists that if Artusi can find something in Signor Etc.'s madrigals to complain about, it must come from the progression of the parts (*modulatione*), the consensus (*concenti*) resulting from it, or from the lines (*arie*) assigned to the various voices. If he finds these unusual and new, they are so because they must express new affections. The central argument is in this passage of L'Ottuso's letter:

It is therefore true that the new progression of the parts (*modulatione*) makes a new consensus (*concento*) and a new affection, and not (as you say) new confusion and discord. But Your Lordship himself admits in his [letter] that there is a new air (*aria*), a new stimulation to the ear, which, struck by the quickness and tardiness of movement, is affected now harshly, now sweetly according to the air that [Signor] Etc. has given to the parts. What is this, then, if not new part-movement (*modulatione*) full of new affection, imitating the nature of the verse and justly representing the true meaning of the poet? And if it appears that this somehow contradicts the authority of the very learned Monsignor Zarlino of reverent memory in the Second Part of the *Istitutioni harmoniche*, nevertheless he himself confesses at the end of the [twelfth] chapter that from this movement of the parts (*modulatione*) is born melody (*melodia*).[47]

The major barrier to communication between the two writers now becomes apparent. Artusi follows the terminology of Zarlino, while L'Ottuso uses such terms as 'modulatione', 'concento', and 'aria' loosely, in the

---

[44] *Seconda parte dell'Artusi*, 5.   [45] Ibid. 6.
[46] Ibid. 13−21.   [47] Ibid. 14.

manner of the current musical jargon. By *modulatione* Zarlino meant the movement from pitch to pitch through various intervals by one or more parts, with or without measured rhythm. *Modulatione*, properly speaking, that is *modulatione propria*, is the movement of two or more parts meeting in consonances through measured rhythm. This kind of *modulatione* produces *harmonia*.[48] *Harmonia*, according to Zarlino, can be of several kinds: *propria*, a mixture of two or more moving lines of low and high sounds that strikes the ear smoothly; *non propria*, a mixture of low and high sounds without any change of pitch; *perfetta*, in which the outer voices are mediated by one or more inner parts; *imperfetta*, when the outer two parts are not so mediated. When the parts meet in consonances, this is called *concento*. *Harmonia propria* has more power to move the passions than *harmonia non propria*, but it does not acquire its full power except through rhythm and text. 'Therefore from these three things joined together, that is *harmonia propria*, rhythm (*rithmo*), and text (*oratione*), arise (as Plato would have it) *melodia*.[49] *Melodia*, then, is not melody but the synthesis of the musical, textual, and expressive content of a composition. This usage of *melodia* not only clarifies what L'Ottuso wants to say in the excerpt quoted above but is also, as we shall see, a key to Monteverdi's preface.

So the difficulty was that L'Ottuso, though he had read Zarlino, had garbled his terms. Properly translated into Zarlinian, what he was saying is this. Monteverdi was striving for a *harmonia*, which when combined with the other two elements of Plato's triad, rhythm and text, would produce a *melodia* expressive of a particular text. When this text expressed new and violent passions, the *modulatione* that made up the *harmonia* had to be new to produce a new *melodia*.

The contradiction that bothered Artusi now becomes evident. Only mixtures of several lines that strike the ear smoothly can be considered *harmonia propria*. Monteverdi's mixtures sometimes did not. Moreover, the *modulatione* was sometimes faulty by Zarlino's criteria; it used intervals not accepted into vocal music. So Artusi could say that Monteverdi's new *melodia* was no *melodia* at all, because it violated the standards of good *modulatione* and *harmonia propria*.

The usages to which Artusi took exception may be considered in two categories, then: irregularities of 'modulation' or melody-writing, and irregularities of 'harmony' or vertical combination.

---

[48] See Zarlino, *Istitutioni*, Pt. ii, ch. 14, p. 81.

[49] Ibid., ch. 12, p. 80. Artusi summarizes these definitions, paraphrasing Zarlino (*Seconda parte dell'Artusi*, 24 ff.). Melody in the sense of a line that an individual part makes as it is 'modulated' is called 'aria'.

Artusi objected to the following interval because it passes from a diatonic note to a chromatic one and is therefore unnatural to the voice, which, unlike instruments, is limited to a small number of consonant and dissonant intervals, through which it passes from one consonance to another:[50]

Ex. 3.11

This interval is made up of one tone (A–B) and two semitones (B–C and A–G♯). A 9:8 tone added to two 16:15 semitones results in an interval in the ratio 32:25. Artusi is assuming the syntonic diatonic tuning of Ptolemy advocated by Zarlino as the only possible tuning for voices singing unaccompanied. The interval C–G♯ is therefore a most dissonant interval. It is neither a major nor a minor third, and Artusi defies his correspondent to tell him what it is.

Whereas L'Ottuso should have challenged Artusi's assumption of the syntonic diatonic tuning, by then proved unserviceable by several authors,[51] he replies feebly: 'It is a new voice progression (*modulatione*) for the sake of finding through its novelty a new consensus (*concento*) and a new affection.'[52]

The interval occurs twice in the madrigal under discussion in these pages, *Era l'anima mia* (Book V)—at bars 28–9 in the quintus part at the words 'Deh perchè ti consumi?' ('Say, why do you waste yourself?') (Ex. 3.12) and at bars 58–9 in the tenor at the words 'Non mori tu, mor'io', ('Don't die yourself, I shall die').

Although L'Ottuso calls it new, he goes on to defend it by precedents (an inconsistency Artusi was quick to point out). Cipriano de Rore uses it in *Poi che m'invita amore* at the words 'dolce mia vita'[53] and Giaches de Wert in *Misera, non credea* at the word 'essangue' (bars 79–84)[54] (Ex. 3.13).

---

[50] This example appears in Artusi (p. 9) as follows:

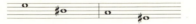

I have assumed a soprano clef.

[51] Cf. Vincenzo Galilei, in *Dialogo della musica antica et della moderna* (Florence: G. Marescotti, 1581), and Giovanni Battista Benedetti, in *Diversarum speculationum mathematicorum & phisicorum liber* (Turin: apud Haeredem Nicolai Bevilaquae, 1585). See Palisca, 'Scientific Empiricism in Musical Thought', below, Essay 8, pp. 222–3.

[52] *Seconda parte dell'Artusi*, 15.

[53] *Le vive fiamme* (Venice: G. Scotto, 1565). L'Ottuso quotes (p. 15) a fragment of the soprano. See Cipriano de Rore, *Opera omnia*, ed. Bernhard Meier, v (American Institute of Musicology, 1971), 79, bar 38.

[54] *Ottavo libro de' madrigali a cinque voci* (Venice: Angelo Gardano, 1586); L'Ottuso quotes (p. 15) fragments of the soprano, tenor, and alto. See *Vier Madrigale von Mantuaner Komponisten*, ed. Denis

Ex. 3.12. Monteverdi, *Era l'anima mia*, bars 28–9

Ex. 3.13. Giaches de Wert, *Misera non credea*, bars 79–84

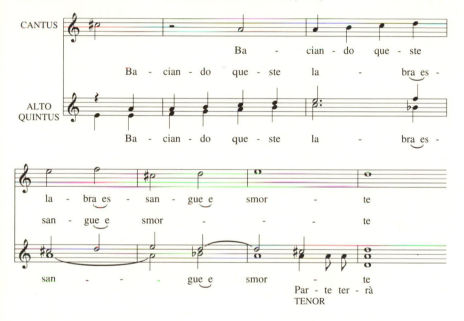

Another usage that Artusi criticizes and L'Ottuso defends is that of following a sharpened note by a descending interval and a flattened note by a rising one. Artusi does not cite any examples in Monteverdi; but many can be found.[55] All *the moderni* are doing it, says L'Ottuso, 'most of all those who have embraced this new second practice' (*questa nuova seconda pratica*).[56] This is the first time the expression 'seconda pratica' appears in the controversy, and it is introduced without fanfare, as if the term were

Arnold (Das Chorwerk, 80; Wolfenbüttel: Möseler, 1961), 10; also see Giaches de Wert, *Opera omnia*, viii, ed. Carol MacClintock (American Institute of Musicology, 1968), 32, bars 21–2.

[55] For example, in the fourth book: *Anima mia, perdona*, bars 38 ff., second part, bar 17; *Luci serene e chiare*, bars 31, 34–5; *Voi pur da me partite*; *Ohimè, se tanto amate*, bar 6, flat rising, etc.

[56] *Seconda parte dell'Artusi*, 16.

Ex. 3.14. Giaches de Wert, *Misera non credea*, bars 86–7

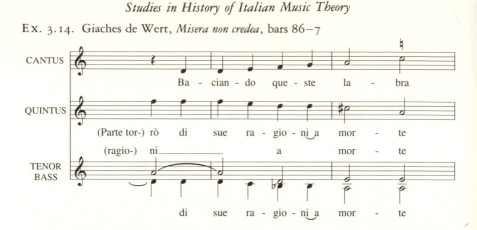

already current in oral if not written discussions. The particular examples cited by L'Ottuso[57] are: the beginning of Marenzio's *Dura legge*[58] and *S'io parto*;[59] and Wert's *Misera, non credea* at the words 'parte tornò'.[60] In *S'io parto*[61] the step Bb–C is used constantly, as is to be expected in any G minor piece. In Wert's madrigal (see Ex. 3.14) the progression to the dominant of D minor is entirely fitting to the modern minor mode (bars 86–7). But it does not belong in the first or second mode, and Artusi expected a composition to remain within the steps of a mode and its plagal form. In this he was a loyal follower of Zarlino, who denounced inflections and chromaticism in vocal music.

The issue of modal purity and unity had already come up in the dialogue of 1600, when Artusi singled out *O Mirtillo* for attack because it seemed to begin in one mode and end in another.[62] Then in his letter to L'Ottuso, Artusi criticized *Cruda Amarilli* for having more cadences in the twelfth mode (C plagal) than in the mode of its closing or opening, namely the seventh (G authentic). L'Ottuso's answer is weak. Everybody knows, he says, 'that a mode is determined from the first and last notes and not from the median cadences'.[63] Giulio Cesare Monteverdi's gloss on his brother's letter is similarly naïve in replying to the first attack. He justifies the disunity of mode in *O Mirtillo* on the precedents of the mixed modes of

[57] Ibid. 18; Artusi prints only fragments of the offending parts.

[58] Marenzio, *Il nono libro de madrigali a 5* (Venice: Gardano, 1599).

[59] Marenzio, *Il sesto libro de madrigali a 5* (Venice: Gardano, 1594); in Luca Marenzio, *Sämtliche Werke*, ed. Alfred Einstein, ii (Publikationen älterer Musik, 6; Leipzig, 1931), 103.

[60] Wert, *Opera omnia*, viii. 32, bar 24.

[61] Printed in *Masterpieces of Music before 1750*, ed. Carl Parrish and John F. Ohl (New York: Norton, 1951), 102.

[62] *L'Artusi*, fo. 48ᵛ.

[63] *Seconda parte dell'Artusi*, 21.

plainchant and the mixtures of modes in compositions of Josquin, Willaert, Rore, and Alessandro Striggio the elder.[64] The latter's *Nasce la pena mia*[65] is cited as being built upon four modes.

Artusi had reason to be shocked at this mixed bag of examples, which left him wondering if the commentator understood what mixed modes were. He replied for the traditionalists forcefully through 'Braccino da Todi' in 1608:

> Now for the mixture of tones or modes, which the commentator seems to reproach Artusi for not knowing. What it is, how many kinds there are, what is rational and what is irrational, I shall tell you. If Monteverdi wished to write a composition in a single mode (*Tono*) such as the first, he could not, because perforce there would be a mixture of modes. For when a composer constructs a piece in the first mode, he must keep to the following order. The tenor should proceed or 'modulate' by way of the notes of the first natural mode or whichever mode he intends to construct it in . . . and the bass by way of its collateral [the plagal mode]. The cantus corresponds and 'modulates' an octave higher and by the same steps [and mode] as the tenor. The contralto regularly corresponds to the bass, but an octave higher. So all vocal compositions are mixtures of the authentic and plagal. But the mixtures of Monteverdi are not regular like these, but irregular. If he sets out to give one form to his composition, he ends up giving it another, because he exceeds the bounds of mixture. Therefore one may say that he lumps the pumpkins in with the lanterns.[66]

Modal unity was of some moment to Artusi, because he, like Zarlino and Glareanus before him, believed that each mode had its special character. In his dialogue of 1600 Artusi had assigned an ethos to each of the modes and urged the composer to choose one suited to the subject of a composition and stick to it.[67]

Giulio Cesare's reply did not come to terms with the issue, because he lacked either the courage or conviction to proclaim the end of the tyranny of the modes. Galilei had already prepared their demise when he exposed the false humanism of the modal theorists in 1581[68] and again ten years later. In his counterpoint treatise he asserted that modality had become more a matter for the eye than the ear, for no one now paid any attention to the internal cadences:

---

[64] 'Dichiaratione della lettera stampata nel quinto libro de suoi madrigali', in G. Francesco Malipiero, *Claudio Monteverdi* (Milan: Fratelli Treves, 1929), 83–4; trans. in Strunk, *Source Readings*, 411–12. Also see *Claudio Monteverdi: Lettere, dediche, e prefazioni*, ed. Domenico De' Paoli (Rome: De Santis, 1973), 393–407.

[65] Striggio, *Il primo libro de madrigali a 6* (Venice: G. Scotto, 1560).

[66] *Discorso secondo musicale*, 11–12.

[67] *L'Artusi*, fo. 68ᵛ.

[68] One of the main points of the *Dialogo* was that the ecclesiastical modes had none of the virtues claimed for them by Glareanus and Zarlino.

The best and most famous contrapuntists have used cadences on any step at all [of the mode] in their vocal compositions. Moreover . . . the sure identification of the mode is derived from the last note in the bass. That this is true is obvious every time this last note is hidden from the sight of the person studying the piece . . . With the eyes, therefore, and not with the ears, do modern practitioners know the modes of their pieces . . . Moreover, take any modern vocal piece in whatever mode and remove or add one or two notes at the end to make it terminate in other notes than the previous ones (without going to extremes, though), and practitioners today will say that there has been a mutation of mode . . . And when Zarlino too would wish to persuade me again of the simplicities he writes, saying that among our modes one has a quiet nature, another deprecatory, others querulous, excited, lascivious, cheerful, somnolent, tranquil, or infuriated, and others yet different natures and characters, and finally that the modes as practitioners use them today have the same capacities as those he mentioned the ancient modes possessed, I would answer, convinced by experience, which teaches us the contrary, that these are all tales intended to confuse dunderheads. If our practice retains the smallest part of these aptitudes it does not derive them from the mode or the final note or the harmonic and arithmetic divisions but from the way contrapuntists make the parts progress in any of the modes according to what suits them best.[69]

It is usual to compose a sonnet, he continues, so that

each quatrain and tercet, indeed each particular verse, is of a different mode from the rest. Whoever does differently is taken for a satrap and is accused of indolence and of lacking inventiveness. The ancients sang a history, an action of a hero and an entire book in one same tone (*Tono*), but the goal of the ancients was to make men moderate and virtuous, and that of the moderns is to amuse them, if not to make them effeminate.[70]

Galilei's objective in criticizing the loose modality practised by composers in his time was the opposite of Artusi's. Galilei wanted to see modality abandoned in favour of tonal unity based on pitch level, on the model of the ancient Greeks. Monteverdi was heading pragmatically in the same direction, though unencumbered by Galilei's theoretical bias. To judge by Giulio Cesare's reply, which must have had his approval, Claudio could not yet foresee the theoretical implications of his creative impulses.

The controversy had begun around the use of dissonance. Luca's rationalizations for its free employment fit only those combinations that seem to come about casually as a by-product of independent part-movement. But more characteristic of Monteverdi's style are dissonances deliberately planted in exposed situations. Some of the exposed dissonances illustrated in Artusi's eighth and ninth examples, both from *Anima mia, perdona*,[71] are the result of suspension. But the suspended note, instead of being held, is

---

[69] *Il primo libro della prattica del contrapunto*, fo. 100^{r-v}; ed. Rempp, 70–1.
[70] Ibid., fo. 101^r; ed. Rempp, 72.   [71] See Strunk, *Source Readings*, 395.

Ex. 3.15. Monteverdi, *Anima mia, perdona*, bars 59–62

sounded again. Artusi fails to make this clear, because he omits bar 59 of the second part of this madrigal in the second of his examples; the repetition of the suspended C in the alto in bar 60 can be seen in Ex. 3.15. This repetition violated the regular suspension usage as analysed in Artusi's own counterpoint text, where one of the notes of a suspension is regarded as the 'patient' (*paziente*) and the other as the 'agent' (*agente*). The 'patient' remains stationary as it suffers the 'agent' causing the dissonance to move and strike against it.[72]

The reasons traditionally given for tolerating the suspension depend on this absorption of the shock of the dissonance by the sustained voice. Franchino Gaffurio speaks of the hidden and dulled nature of this dissonance.[73] Zarlino finds such a dissonance tolerable

because in singing the syncopated semibreve the voice holds firm, and a certain suspension is heard (*si ode quasi una sospensione*), a taciturnity that is noticed amidst the percussions that produce the tones and make them distinguishable from one another in time. So the ear barely notices this dissonance, not being sufficiently stimulated by it to comprehend it fully.[74]

Monteverdi's seventh in bar 60 of Ex. 3.15 does not crouch behind the consonances but steps out to be noticed. As Galilei put it, when a composer uses dissonances in this manner he does not expect them to

blend in harmony with wonderful effect; but rather that the sense become satisfied with them, not because they harmonize . . . but because of the gentle mixture of the sweet and the strong, which . . . affect our ears not unlike the way in which taste receives satisfaction from both sugar and vinegar.[75]

---

[72] Artusi, *Seconda parte dell'Arte del contraponto*, bk. ii, ch. 1, pp. 27 ff.

[73] *Practica musicae* (Milan: Guillaume Le Signerre [G. Pietro da Lomazzo], 1496), bk. iii, ch. 4: 'est item et latens discordia in contrapuncto praeter sincopatam scilicet inter plures cantilenae partes concordes continetur et obtunditur.'

[74] Zarlino, *Istitutioni*, pt. iii, ch. 42, p. 197; Eng. trans. from Zarlino, *The Art of Counterpoint*, trans. Guy A. Marco and Claude V. Palisca (New Haven, Conn.: Yale University Press, 1968; repr. New York: Da Capo, 1983), 97.

[75] Quoted above, Essay 2, pp. 39–40.

Even more prominent, of course, is the seventh in the top part in bar 61, which is not sounded in the previous bar. L'Ottuso admits that he can offer no theoretical demonstration to justify these usages. Yet he is convinced they are admissible, not only on grounds of precedent but also by virtue of the context or as a poetic licence. He is not driven, as Artusi implied, to call a dissonance a consonance—he realizes that a dissonance would always be a dissonance:

> but by circumstance (*per accidente*) it can well be otherwise, for there is no dissonant interval which is in itself one that by circumstance cannot be made good with reference to the accompaniments among which it is placed . . . As an accent, as a deception, or indeed as a dissonance, though sweetened by the accompaniment of the other parts, it [a seventh] will undoubtedly not only have a good effect but, being something new, will give greater delight to the ear than would the supposed octave. And since you desire a proof, you will draw it very easily from this: you allow an excellent poet the metaphor purposefully used; similarly the seventh is taken in place of the octave.[76]

The octave is understood or 'supposed' (*supposta*), but the seventh is heard in its stead. As the poet metaphorically takes one word for another, the composer takes one note for another. For example, Marenzio, 'who was not in the habit of staying within the narrow prescriptions of music theory', used the seventh above the bass in two of the madrigals of his ninth book of five-part madrigals:[77] in *E so come in un punto* at the words 'per le guancie' and 'ascoso langue', and in *Così nel mio parlar*[78] at the words 'maggior durezze', and in the second part at 'da i colpi mortali'. The last of these is in Ex. 3.16. The word 'colpi' ('blows') is accompanied by a second and seventh above the bass instead of a third and octave. Like the figure of speech in which a word with stronger and richer associations replaces the normal one, the composer, L'Ottuso would have us believe, substitutes a sharp dissonance for the normal consonance. This notion has great potential, as Bernhard shows when he classifies many irregular uses of dissonance as rhetorical figures. But L'Ottuso fails to develop the thought. Nevertheless, he is one of the very few Italian writers who associates musical licences with rhetorical figures.

[76] *Seconda parte dell'Artusi*, 16. Angelo Berardi paraphrased this passage in his *Miscellanea musicale* (Bologna, 1689), pt. ii, ch. 12, p. 39: 'the moderns use the bare seventh (*settima nuda*) as a deception (*inganno*) and accent (*accento*), or as a dissonance, yes, but sweetened by the accompaniment of the other parts, as something new that produces a new affection in the ear'. He then cites the madrigals of Marenzio named by L'Ottuso.

[77] *Il nono libro de madrigali a 5* (Venice, 1599).

[78] Printed in Einstein, 'Dante im Madrigal', *Archiv für Musikwissenschaft*, 3 (1921), 414–20. From the four places in these two madrigals cited, Artusi prints (p. 17) the two voice-parts that form the seventh.

Ex. 3.16. Marenzio, *Cosi nel mio parlar*, bars

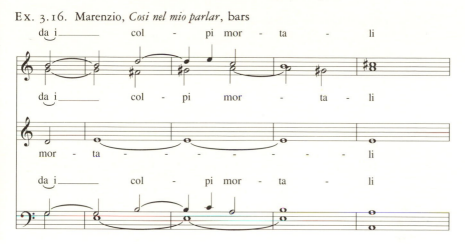

The two principal sources for Monteverdi's free treatment of dissonance that emerge from Artusi's dialogue and the letters of L'Ottuso are the impromptu practices of singers and the pioneering efforts of Rore and his followers, and they are corroborated by Zacconi in the second part of his *Prattica di musica*, published in 1622. If someone were to ask him, he writes, whence came the practice of placing dissonances on the down-beat in the manner found throughout Monteverdi's works,

I would say that he took it from the second part of the motet of Cipriano Bora [i.e. Rore] *O altitudo divitiarum*, which uses this arrangement of notes. The first minim [see bar 94 of Ex. 3.17] is made dissonant as an affectation (*per affetto*), thereby making the second minim awaited by the melody so much the better. Or shall we say that, although he [Monteverdi] may have taken this practice from the forenamed composer, he was not moved entirely by this but by that everyday habit singers have today of performing things with the most grateful affectations (*affetti*), possibly to make themselves as pleasing as they can to listeners.[79]

Throughout his replies, Artusi insists upon the rules, because, he says, they are based on nature, demonstration, and the models of excellent composers. Although L'Ottuso too has recourse to the example of excellent composers, he challenges the principle of imitation. Every good painter, sculptor, poet, or orator seeks to imitate the ancients and particularly the excellent ones, but there are also those who esteem invention more than imitation. Indeed, in music invention is much more esteemed than imitation,

[79] *Prattica di musica seconda parte* (Venice: Girolamo Polo, 1622), bk. ii, ch. 10, p. 63. Zacconi quotes of the alto and quintus parts the second half of bar 93 and the first half of 94. The motet is published in Rore, *Opera omnia*, ed. Meier, i (1959), 122.

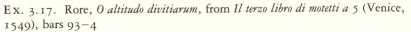

EX. 3.17. Rore, *O altitudo divitiarum*, from *Il terzo libro di motetti a 5* (Venice, 1549), bars 93–4

because only through invention can musical art advance. Signor Etc. (Monteverdi) is one of those dedicated to invention. *Era l'anima mia*, for example, in whose opening, staying for four bars on the chord of D minor, Artusi found nothing new, but rather a reminiscence of the *giustiniana*,[80] L'Ottuso defends as full of new harmonic progressions, elegant passages from plagal to authentic, ascents after accidental flats and descents after sharps, substitutions of unexpected notes for the expected, and other artful devices. 'If Your Lordship considered the madrigals of Signor Etc.', he pleaded, 'you will find them full of such flowers, embellished with such terse modulation, far from the common, indeed full of judicious deceptions.'[81]

So much of the effect of these licences depends on subtle nuances and emphases that, in L'Ottuso's opinion, compositions indulging in them, in order to be judged fairly, had to be sung by specially gifted musicians.

You must remember that the singer is the soul of music, and it is he who, in sum, represents the true meaning of the composer to us. In this representation, according to the variety of the subject, the voice is sometimes reinforced, at other times sweetened. For this reason you have to hear this manner of clever composition sung by singers who are out of the ordinary. Your Lordship's grounds [for criticism] would then cease to exist, in that the harshness of these madrigals would be covered in such a way that the dissonances would not be heard.[82]

For Artusi L'Ottuso relied too much on deluding the ear and the judgement with deceptions, suppositions, and artifices that have no basis in reality.

All those things that the modern confounders call suppositions, flowers (*fioretti*), deceptions, accents, and artifices, which are against the good rules, the student knows

---

[80] A type of villanella common in Venice. Similarly, Artusi asks if the first eight bars, which he quotes, of *Ma se con la pietà*, the second part of *Ecco Silvio* in the fifth book, is the beginning of a *giustiniana* or a *spifarata mantovana*: *Seconda parte dell'Artusi*, 5.

[81] Ibid. 19.

[82] Ibid. 19–20.

for false, false suppositions against the nature of the thing, false deceptions, false flowers, false artifices, false accents, and never true things and true suppositions.[83]

Modern composers take too much refuge in the deficiencies of the senses. In their ambition to sway the emotions they resort to means that are unnatural and therefore cannot stimulate a natural process like moving the affections, for like responds to like. The only new effects that come across are those the singers make when they turn the head slowly, arch their eyebrows, roll their eyes, twist their shoulders, let themselves go as if they want to die, and their many other metamorphoses, the likes of which Ovid never imagined. Indeed they make these grimaces just when they arrive at those dissonances that offend the sense to show what others ought to be doing. But instead of being moved, [the listeners] are ruffled by the bitterness and discontent they feel, and, turning their heads, depart dissatisfied.[84]

The following concise and eloquent statement, printed in the fifth book of madrigals (1605), is the only public reply Claudio Monteverdi made to Artusi's criticisms.

Studious Readers:
Be not surprised that I am giving these madrigals to the press without first replying to the objections that Artusi made against some very minute portions of them. Being in the service of this Serene Highness of Mantua, I am not master of the time I would require. Nevertheless I wrote a reply to let it be known that I do not do things by chance, and as soon as it is rewritten it will see the light with the title in front, *Seconda pratica overo perfettione della moderna musica*. Some will wonder at this, not believing that there is any other practice than that taught by Zerlino [*sic*]. But let them be assured concerning consonances and dissonances that there is a different way of considering them from that already determined which defends the modern manner of composition with the assent of the reason and the senses. I wanted to say this both so that the expression *Seconda pratica* would not be appropriated by others and so that men of intellect might meanwhile consider other second thoughts concerning harmony. And have faith that the modern composer builds on foundations of truth.
    Live happily.[85]

This is a statement full of promise. Monteverdi, though confident of his musical instinct, recognized the need for a theoretical rationalization of his new way of dealing with dissonances if it was to be generally accepted.[86]

---

[83] Ibid. 47.

[84] Ibid. 40–1.

[85] Italian text in Malipiero, *Monteverdi*, 71–2, and De' Paoli, *Monteverdi: Lettere*, 391–2.

[86] Monteverdi was apparently unaware of Galilei's counterpoint treatise, which for polyphonic music at least presents a new set of rules and considerations about consonance and dissonance on the basis of the works of some of the composers Giulio Cesare Monteverdi names as founders of the *seconda pratica*. See Palisca, 'Vincenzo Galilei's Counterpoint Treatise', above, Essay 2.

Like his predecessors Zarlino and Francisco de Salinas, he aimed to appeal to both the reason and the senses. The letter does not imply, as has sometimes been suggested, that Monteverdi considered the rules of the First Practice a theory, while the Second was a mere practice. He obviously knew the difference between *musica theorica* and *musica practica*. Zarlino's *Istitutioni* is a union of both, but its part iii, which deals with the use of consonances and dissonances in counterpoint, is essentially a *musica practica*. Monteverdi promised to replace it with a second and different *musica practica*.[87]

Giulio Cesare Monteverdi's commentary on his brother's letter, published in the *Scherzi musicali* (1607), is one of the most important manifestos in the history of music. As with most manifestos it is richer in slogans than in original aesthetic ideas. But it does illuminate some of Claudio's remarks, even if we cannot assume that he would have stood behind every word of it.

From the first paragraph we learn that Monteverdi's letter of 1605 was answered by a discourse printed under the name of Antonio Braccino da Todi. No copy of this is extant, but its existence is further corroborated by the title of the discourse published under the same name in 1608, *Discorso secondo musicale di Antonio Braccino da Todi per la dichiaratione della lettera posta ne Scherzi musicali del Sig. Claudio Monteverde*. The author of these discourses has always been assumed to be Artusi, and there is no reason to contest this attribution. The explanation for Artusi's hiding behind a pseudonym is probably that here for the first time he names the composer whose madrigals he attacked and out of delicacy wished to remain anonymous, as before he kept the composer anonymous.

The principal contribution of Giulio Cesare's commentary is that he informs us of the *seconda pratica*'s pedigree, both in practice and philosophy. He names Rore the founder and lists the composers who developed it before his brother,[88] and he aligns it with the famous dictum of Plato, which put the text ahead of the other two components of music, 'harmony' and rhythm. Giulio Cesare and, we may assume, Claudio, conceived the second practice as a revival of Plato's ideal music. It renewed or revived this lost art through 'our notation', that is, the mensural notation used in polyphonic

---

[87] This numbering of the 'practices' is obviously short in hindsight, as Artusi points out in the *Discorso secondo musicale*, 15; but the latter's suggestion of calling it the third or fourth practice, depending on whether that of the Greeks and Romans is considered the first or the first and second, is not much better.

[88] These are Marc'Antonio Ingegneri, Marenzio, Wert, Luzzasco Luzzaschi, Jacopo Peri, Giulio Caccini, and the 'Heroic School' of gentlemen-composers, which includes Carlo Gesualdo, Prince of Venosa, Emilio de' Cavalieri, Fontanella, 'the Count of the Camerata' (i.e. Bardi), Cavaliere Turchi, and Tommaso Pecci.

music. Both Zarlino and Artusi had quoted the relevant passage from the *Republic*, but neither had emphasized the order Plato gave to the three elements. One writer who did call attention to the priority of the text was Giulio Caccini,[89] who significantly figured among those Giulio Cesare named as developers of the Second Practice.

Caccini was not the first to note this side of Plato's definition. Johannes Ott pointed to it briefly in a foreword to his masses of 1539,[90] and Bishop Jacopo Sadoleto commented upon it at length in a sweeping condemnation of the polyphonic music of his time in his *De liberis recte instituendis* ('Concerning the Proper Education of Boys') in 1533. A humanist churchman who as cardinal was a member of the pontifical commission for the reform of the church and the Council of Trent, he appealed to musicians to restore the verbal message to its sovereignty among the components of music. Elaborating on the famous Platonian passage in his dialogue, Sadoleto has the father, Jacopus, tell his son Paulus:

If we inquire into what style is to be maintained in music, I believe that we should bear all the following in mind. A chorus consists of three elements, the sense of the words, the rhythm (which we call number), and tone. The words are the first and most important of the three as being the very basis and foundation of the others. By themselves the words have no mean influence upon the mind, whether to persuade or restrain. Accommodated to rhythm (*numerus*) and metre (*modus*) they penetrate much more deeply. If in addition they are given a melodic setting, they take possession of the inner feelings and of the whole man.[91]

Sadoleto missed this persuasiveness and feeling in the vocal music of his day, which he characterized as consisting of nothing but variation and patterns of notes. The music with text that he heard served only the sense of hearing, and this made the mind a slave of the body.

Giulio Cesare proclaims that the Second Practice has restored the supremacy of the text, subordinating 'harmony' and leading to the perfection of 'melody'. Without perhaps intending to, he gave a new twist to Plato's words. He assigned to the word 'harmony' a modern meaning, while

---

[89] In his foreword to *Le nuove musiche* (Florence: Marescotti, 1602); ed. and trans. H. Wiley Hitchcock in Recent Researches in the Music of the Baroque Era, 9 (Madison, Wis.: A-R Editions, 1970), 43.

[90] Cf. Strunk, *Source Readings*, 256, note k.

[91] Jacopo Sadoleto, *De liberis recte instituendis liber* (Venice: Ioannes et fratres de Sabio, 1533), fo. 42ᵛ: 'Quod si quaeratur qui modus sit in musicis tenendus, haec ego omnia attendenda esse puto: cum constet chorus ex tribus, sententia, rhythmo (hic enim numerus nobis est) & uoce, primum quidem omnium & potissimum sententiam esse, utpote quae si sedes & fundamentum reliquorum, & per se ipsa ualeat non minimum ad suadendum animo uel dissuadendum: numeris autem modisque contorta penetret multo acrius: si uero etiam cantu & uoce fuerit modulata, iam omnis intus sensus & hominem totum possideat.'

attempting to cling to the ancient concept of 'melody'. Zarlino had already planted the seed for this confusion, when he said (as we saw above) 'from proper harmony (*harmonia propria*), rhythm (*rithmo*), and text (*oratione*) arise (as Plato would have it) melody (*melodia*)'.[92]

The confusion resulted from the scant comprehension of Greek music on the part of the early translators of Plato. The translation most current in Italy was the Latin of Marsilio Ficino. Plato's phrase is rendered 'melodia ex tribus constare, oratione, harmonia, rhythmus'.[93] And later 'atqui harmonia et rhythmus orationem sequi debent'.[94]

In the original Greek, however, we read that *melos* ('song') consists of three things, *logos* ('the word', or 'that by which the inward thought is expressed'), *harmonia* ('agreement' or 'relation of sounds'), and *rhythmos* ('time' or 'rhythm'). Plato was saying simply that a song consists of a text, an agreeable arrangement of intervals, and measured time; and of these the text is the leader.

But Giulio Cesare, and L'Ottuso with him, are saying that a modern polyphonic composition, like the ancient song or *melos*, should subordinate to the text (its meaning and rhythm) the arrangement of notes both successive and simultaneous (broadening of the concept of *harmonia*) and rhythm (now broadened to include tempo, metre, and rhythm). This results in the perfection of 'melody', that is, expressive composition. He is not saying, as has sometimes been inferred, that melody in the sense of tune or monody should now take precedence over counterpoint or harmony. Melody in this sense is not even in question.[95]

The recognition that Monteverdi gave to the existence of two practices and their definition by Giulio Cesare were of resonant importance. Hardly a theoretical book was published after 1608 that did not help to confirm this dichotomy. It should be recalled, however, that the Monteverdi brothers underscored a dualism that already existed in both the music and the

---

[92] Zarlino, *Istitutioni*, pt. ii, ch. 12, p. 80; see above, pp. 70–1.

[93] *Republic* 398C. Plato, *Opera*, trans. Marsilio Ficino (Venice: Bernardinus de Choris de Cremona and Simon de Luere, 1491), fo. 201ʳ.

[94] *Republic* 398D.

[95] Artusi quite rightly, if unduly harshly, scolded Giulio Cesare for distorting Plato's meaning: 'Plato does not treat nor ever did, nor had he any thought of treating of modern melodies or music, but I believe, rather, that he discussed those melodies that flourished in his time. It was possible to say then that the text had greater force than the harmony or rhythm, because that history, tale, or whatever it may have been was recited to the sound of a single instrument . . . But the melodies of Monteverdi of which the commentator writes are not similar to those used in the time of Plato; they are deformed. In those [of the ancients] the text was stirring, in these, if anything, the harmony; in those the text was intelligible, in these the harmony; then they worked many effects, now none . . . There is no conformity or resemblance between the melody used in the time of Plato and that of our day. It is too diverse, too different. The quoted passage is out of the seminary, out of context, a chimera, malapropos' (*Discorso secondo musicale*, 9).

literature about it from the middle of the sixteenth century. The *musica nova* and *musica reservata* of the 1540s and 1550s broke the ground for the new direction that Giulio Cesare dates back to the madrigals of Rore.[96] Galilei, in his counterpoint treatise, contrasted the composers who followed the rules—the *osservatori*—and those who, like the painters Michelangelo and Raphael, were guided only by their own judgement based on both reason and sense.[97]

Girolamo Diruta in 1609[98] and Adriano Banchieri in 1614 distinguished between the *contrapunto osservato* and the modern freer *contrapunto commune*. The *osservato*, Banchieri notes, was explained both as to theory and practice by Zarlino, Artusi, and other writers, but of the *contrapunto misto* or *commune* writers had not produced a single rule or precept for accommodating the affections. Nor does he consider the subject one that could be written about.[99] The writer who most faithfully communicates both the language and spirit of the Monteverdi brothers is Marco Scacchi. He synthesizes the ideas of the 1605, 1607, and 1638 prefaces in a single system of style classification. While the *musica antica*, Scacchi asserts, maintained the same style for all serious subjects, whether meant for sacred or secular functions, modern music employs two practices and three styles. In the First Practice the composer is guided by the principle *ut harmonia sit domina orationis* ('that harmony be the mistress of the text'). In the Second Practice he obeys the rule *ut oratio sit domina harmoniae* ('that the text be the mistress of the

[96] See Palisca, 'A Clarification of *Musica reservata* in Jean Taisnier's *Astrologiae*, 1559', below, Essay 9.

[97] *Discorso intorno all'uso delle dissonanze*, fo. 142ᵛ; ed. Rempp, 151: 'The greatness and majesty that is contained in that Canzone which begins *Hor ch'el cielo, et la Terra, e'l vento tace* [*Li madrigali cromatici a 5*, book i (Venice, repr. 1562)], the loveliness and grace of *Anchor che col partire* [*Il primo libro de madrigali a 4* (Ferrara, 1550)], the varied sweetness and unusual sonority of *Cantai mentre ch'io arsi del mio foco* [*Li madrigali cromatici*], the sombreness of *Come havran fin le dolorose tempre* [*Primo libro a 5*, 1550] expressed with so much artfulness without any affectation: Cipriano did not learn the art of turning out such works as these in the books written about the rules of counterpoint, but it rested entirely on his own judgement.'

[98] *Seconda parte del Transilvano dialogo* (Venice: Giacomo Vincenti, 1609; repr. Bologna: Forni, 1969), bk. ii, p. 3.

[99] Adriano Banchieri, *Cartella musicale*, 161 ff. Already in an earlier publication, *Conclusioni nel suono dell'organo* (Bologna, 1609), 58–9, Banchieri had complained that the authors on counterpoint never gave 'any rule or precept that would show how in practice to imitate the affections when setting any kind of words [to music], whether Latin or vernacular, and in particular words signifying pain, passions, sighing, tears, laughter, question, error, and similar circumstances . . . There is no doubt that music, so far as harmony (*harmonia*) is concerned, must be subject to the words, since the words are those that express the thought.' Galilei in 1591 made a similar complaint: 'In the variety of books which are in print today written on the subject of the art of modern counterpoint, which I have read diligently many times, I have never been able to know two very principal things. One of these pertains to the soul of harmony, which is the meaning of the words; and the other pertains to the body, which is the diversity of successive sounds and notes by which the parts proceed. Regarding the soul, no one so far as I know, as I have said, has yet taught the way to accompany the words, or rather the thoughts behind them, with notes' (*Discorso intorno all'uso delle dissonanze*, fo. 105ᵛ; ed. Rempp, 77).

harmony').[100] Scacchi's three styles of music are indebted to the letter that precedes the *Madrigali guerrieri, et amorosi* (Venice, 1638). Here Monteverdi states, 'the music of grand princes is used in their royal chambers in three manners to please their delicate tastes, namely [music for] the theatre, for the chamber, and for the dance'.[101]

Scacchi built upon this base a broader scheme of classification. The three styles of the modern or second practice are the church style (*ecclesiasticus*), the chamber style (*cubicularis*), and the theatrical style (*scenicus seu theatralis*). These categories break down into further divisions, as shown in the following chart:[102]

Ecclesiasticus	*Cubicularis*	*Scenicus seu theatralis*
1. 4 to 8 voices, no organ	1. Madrigals *da tavolino* (*a cappella*)	1. *Stile semplice recitativo* (without gestures)
2. Polychoral with organ	2. Madrigals with basso continuo	2. *Stile recitativo* (with gestures)
3. *In concerto* (with instruments)	3. Compositions for voices and instruments	
4. Motets in modern style in *stile misto* (recitative with florid passages and arias)		

Scacchi's style system underwent further development at the hands of Christoph Bernhard,[103] who partly reconciled it with the terminology of Diruta and Banchieri:

---

[100] Marco Scacchi, *Breve discorso sopra la musica moderna* (Warsaw: Peter Elert, 1649), sigs. C3ᵛ–C4ᵛ; ed. Palisca in 'Marco Scacchi's Defence of Modern Music (1649)', below, Essay 4. This pamphlet is essentially a commentary on Giulio Cesare's 'Dichiaratione' in response to an opponent of the modern style, namely Romano Micheli. Scacchi comments on the Artusi–Monteverdi feud also in his *Cribrum musicum* (Venice: Alessandro Vincenti, 1643).

[101] Malipiero, *Monteverdi*, 91.

[102] In this chart I have incorporated into the classification presented in the *Breve discorso* the more detailed division of church music Scacchi makes in a letter to Christoph Werner, published in Erich Katz, *Die musikalischen Stilbegriffe des 17. Jahrhunderts* (Inaugural diss., University of Freiburg im Breisgau, 1926), 83–7. This classification of church music is adopted by Berardi, a pupil of Scacchi, in his *Ragionamenti musicali* (Bologna: Giacomo Monti, 1681), 134.

[103] *Tractatus compositionis augmentatus*, chs. 3 and 35, pp. 42–3 and 82–3; trans. Hilse, 34–5, 110–11.

Contrapunctus gravis or *stylus antiquus* or *a capella* or *ecclesiasticus* (*Harmonia Orationis Domina*)	*Contrapunctus luxurians* or *stylus modernus*
	1. *Communis* (*Oratio* as well as *Harmonia Domina*)
	2. *Comicus* or *theatralis* or *recitativus* or *oratorius* (*Oratio Harmoniae Domina absolutissima*)

Thus the slogans of Giulio Cesare Monteverdi still ring in the treatises and pamphlets of the mid-seventeenth century. The ripple started by Artusi's first stone reaches ever wider circles as the controversy over the two styles is stirred up in Rome, Danzig, Warsaw, and Hamburg, among other places. In Rome Romano Micheli takes up Artusi's role as defender of the First Practice, while Marco Scacchi challenges him from Warsaw.[104] Their quarrel grows out of a local difference between the composers Paul Seyfert and Kaspar Förster the Elder in Danzig. Then, as Scacchi gathers testimonials for his point of view throughout Germany and Poland, many of the other musical centres of northern Europe are drawn into the fray. In the heat of these debates were tempered and forged the rules of the neo-severe style of the late seventeenth century.

---

[104] See my articles 'Micheli, Romano', and 'Scacchi, Marco', in *MGG* ix (1961), 273–4, and xi (1963), 1466–9, respectively, and 'Scacchi, Marco', in *The New Grove Dictionary of Music and Musicians*, ed. Stanley Sadie, 20 vols. (London, 1980) (hereafter *New Grove*), xvi. 542–4.

❧ 4 ❧

Marco Scacchi's Defence of Modern Music (1649)

This essay was first published in *Words and Music: The Scholar's View, A Medley of Problems and Solutions Compiled in Honor of A. Tillman Merritt By Sundry Hands*, edited by Laurence Berman (Cambridge, Mass.: Department of Music, Harvard University, 1972), 189–235. Only the English translation of Marco Scacchi's *Breve discorso sopra la musica moderna* was published in that book. Here I have added the original Italian text, because the small book in which it was published is extremely rare and has not been reprinted. The text was edited from the copy in Rome, Biblioteca Nazionale, 69.8B.22, collated with that in Tübingen, formerly Berlin, Preußische Staatsbibliothek. The only emendations made were to conform with modern practice, namely to distinguish *u* and *v*, substitute *i* for *j*, *y*, or *ij*, *z* and *zz* for *t* and *tt* followed by a vowel, *et* for &, suppress *h* in words like 'havere', separate or unite words such as 'a gli', and normalize accents and apostrophes. The original capitalization was maintained except for adding capitalization at the beginning of a sentence. I have introduced paragraphing, which is entirely lacking in the original.

I first read Scacchi's 'Brief Discourse' in the Biblioteca Nazionale in Rome in April 1952. My mention of it and of Scacchi's first book of masses of 1633, whose locations were previously unknown,[1] in the article 'Scacchi' in *MGG* xi (1963), 1466–9, excited the interest of scholars in Poland, where Sacchi was a subject of research because of his activity as a choirmaster in Warsaw and through his polemics with Paul Siefert. Mirosław Perz of Warsaw subsequently wrote on the masses of Scacchi, and Zygmunt Szweykowski of Cracow on his theories of style and his defence of modern music.[2]

Scacchi appreciated what eluded many later music historians, that the first half of the seventeenth century was not dominated by a 'baroque' style but enjoyed a plurality of styles. Inspired by writings of the Monteverdi brothers, Claudio and

[1] François-Joseph Fétis, in *Biographie universelle des musiciens* (Brussels: Lerowt, 1835–44), vii. 424–5, appears to have read the *Breve discorso* but erroneously dates it 1647.
[2] M. Perz, 'Missarum quattuor vocibus liber primus Marci Scacchii Romani', *Pagine*, [2] (1974), 217–37; Z. Szweykowski, 'Poglądy Scacchiego na muzykę, jako sztukę' [Scacchi's conception of music as art], *Pagine*, [1] (1972), 17–28; id., 'Stile imbastardito i stile rappresentativo w systemie teoretycznym Marka Scacchiego', *Muzyka*, 19/1 (1974), 11; and id., *Musica moderna w ujęciu Marka Scacchiego: z dziejów teorii muzyki w XVII wieku* [*Musica moderna* as conceived by Marco Scacchi: a historical study of 17th-c. music theory] (Cracow: Polskie Wydawn. Muzyczne, 1977). For a biography and bibliography of Scacchi, see my article in *New Grove*, xvi. 542–4.

Giulio Cesare, Scacchi devised a broad classification, dividing the coexisting styles into church, chamber, and theatre. Within the first two categories he recognized two practices, the first, in which counterpoint and harmony prevailed over the text, and the second, in which the text governed the counterpoint and harmony. Moreover, within each of the broad divisions, there were particular styles suited to diverse functions; for example, there was a recitative style appropriate to the theatre and another appropriate to sacred motets. The composer chose a style according to the genre he set out to compose, whether a canzonetta, arietta, madrigal, motet, mass, psalm, or theatrical work.

Scacchi's ideas were grounded in his own experience as a composer of both sacred and secular music in which he practised both the strict contrapuntal style and the freer basso-continuo and recitative idioms. He deplored the tendency of some modern composers to contaminate the strict polyphonic style with the looser textures permitted in the concerted idiom. He was equally critical of those who would have banned the modern idiom from the church.

NEITHER Artusi nor Monteverdi had the last word in the celebrated controversy over the *seconda pratica*. Barely had the modernist cause won ascendancy in Italy than the battleground shifted north to Danzig.

The Danzig phase grew out of a quarrel between the organist and the choirmaster at the Marienkirche. In 1625 Paul Siefert, the organist, and Kaspar Förster, the choirmaster, competed for the choirmaster's job. Siefert was then organist at the Marienkirche, while Förster was cantor at the Gymnasium. The town council awarded the position to Förster. In carrying out his duties Förster tended to perform music by a large variety of composers, including Italians, but rarely his own. Siefert, a prolific composer himself, saw his compositions passed by and wrote numerous complaints to the council charging Förster with various degrees of incompetence. Some of Siefert's letters and Förster's replies, which extended into 1637, have been published by Max Seiffert.[3]

Rumbles of the quarrel reached Warsaw, where a younger cousin of Förster, also named Kaspar Förster, was in the royal choir. The choirmaster was Marco Scacchi, who had ascended to the post in 1628 under Zygmunt III and remained in it through the reign of Władysław IV, after whose death he left for Italy in 1649. Scacchi seized the opportunity to help the Danzig Förster when what seemed to him a poor book of psalms was brought out by Siefert in 1640.[4] He was also eager to defend his countrymen against some slanderous statements Siefert had made during the controversy about Italian music. Siefert had apparently assailed the Italians for abandoning the true church style and letting the art of counter-

---

[3] 'Paul Siefert', *Vierteljahrsschrift für Musikwissenschaft*, 7 (1891), 397–428.
[4] *Psalmen Davids, nach francösischer Melodey* (Danzig: G. Rhetius, 1640).

point decline. He had charged that no one in Italy any longer knew how to compose anything but comedies, *ariettes*, *bergamasques*, *passacaglie*, and similar trifles. Scacchi answered these charges and wrote a detailed critique of the psalms under the title *Cribrum musicum ad triticum Syferticum* (Musical Sieve for the Syfert Wheat, 1643),[5] dedicated to the Danzig Förster. In it Scacchi detected 151 errors in Siefert's compositions. Among the faults were failure to maintain the mode, parallel fifths and octaves, incorrect fugal answers, and misuse of the concertato idiom. Scacchi was offended most by Siefert's tendency to mingle several styles in a single piece.

In 1645 Romano Micheli, a notorious musical reactionary, entered the fray by sending Scacchi and Siefert copies of his *Canoni musicali composti sopra le vocali di più parole* as samples of the refinement and skill still possessed by Italian contrapuntists. Siefert congratulated Micheli politely in a letter of February 1647.[6] Scacchi, far from grateful for Micheli's backing, launched a bitter attack on Micheli's decadent pursuit of puzzle canons and similar artifices. Scacchi's pamphlet against Micheli has not survived.

In the *Breve discorso sopra la musica moderna* translated below Scacchi sums up his position with respect to both Siefert and Micheli. A pamphlet of sixteen folios printed in Warsaw, it defends the modern Italian concerted style against its opponents, foreign and native, and deplores the canon-making tourneys of certain choirmasters and counterpoint teachers. It is not entirely polemical in content, however. Taken as a whole, it articulates a musical philosophy that had no better advocate in the seventeenth century.

The theorists of the Renaissance tended to view their art as having attained a state of consummation and culmination after which there could be only decadence or imitation. By contrast, Scacchi accepted change as a fact of musical progress. Composers must always seek new ways and new sounds. Yet this is no argument for casting out the old. The best of the older techniques should be preserved alongside the new. Granted the resulting plurality of styles, it becomes necessary to define the various manners of composition and to distinguish the functions to which each is most appropriate.

Scacchi developed the prototype of a classification of styles that in various forms was to be propagated by authors better known to posterity than he, namely, Angelo Berardi, Christoph Bernhard, Johann Joseph Fux, and

---

[5] Marco Scacchi, *Cribrum musicum ad triticum Syferticum* (Venice: Alessandro Vincenti, 1643). I am indebted to the Universitätsbibliothek, Tübingen, for the use of its copy of the very rare *Cribrum musicum* of Scacchi (formerly in the Preußische Staatsbibliothek, Berlin), which I consulted through a microfilm supplied by the Deutsches musikgeschichtliches Archiv, Kassel.

[6] Joseph Surzynski, 'Ueber alte polnische Kirchenkomponisten und deren Werke', *Kirchenmusikalisches Jahrbuch*, 5 (1890), 77.

TABLE 4.1. *Marco Scacchi's classification of styles*

Stylus Ecclesiasticus (Church)	*Stylus Cubicularis* (Chamber)	*Stylus Scenicus seu Theatralis* (Stage or Theatre)
1. 4 to 8 voices, no organ 2. Polychoral with organ 3. *In concerto* (with instruments) 4. Motets in modern style in *stile misto* (including *stile recitativo imbastardito*)	1. Madrigals *da tavolino* (*a cappella*) 2. Madrigals with continuo 3. Compositions for voices and instruments	1. *Stile semplice recitativo* (without gestures) 2. *Stile recitativo* (with gestures)

Johann Mattheson. If Scacchi rarely receives credit for the system, it is partly because he never elaborated it in one definitive statement. It was probably his intention to accomplish such elaboration in a comprehensive work. Indeed, the *Breve discorso*, he says, is only a sketch of a large treatise he aimed to write. Such a book, if written, has not survived. However, it is possible to piece together an outline of Scacchi's style system from the *Breve discorso* and his letter of around 1648 to Christoph Werner;[7] see Table 4.1.

The composer operates in these categories either according to the first practice or the second practice, as Claudio Monteverdi called them. Scacchi adopts Giulio Cesare Monteverdi's neat antithesis to define the two practices. The first follows the principle *ut harmonia sit domina orationis*; the second, *ut oratio sit domina harmoniae*. Scacchi carries over the Latin from his *Cribrum musicum* whenever he refers to these two principles.

Christoph Bernhard was the first to develop Scacchi's classification system. A native of Danzig, he knew Scacchi's writings probably through Christoph Werner, choirmaster of St Catherine's there and occasional substitute for the aging Förster at the Marienkirche. Bernhard took over the basic distinction between first and second practice, which he called *contrapunctus gravis* (or *stylus antiquus*, *a cappella* or *ecclesiasticus*) and *contrapunctus luxurians* (or *stylus modernus*). He refined Scacchi's system by distinguishing under the *luxurians* on the one hand the common style (*communis*), in which the text shares the lordship with the harmony, and on the other hand the theatrical style (*stylus comicus* or *theatralis*, also called *recitativus* or *oratorius*), in which the text is the absolute mistress (*domina absolutissima*) of the harmony. Bernhard's system has the advantage of recognizing that the

---

[7] Hamburg, Staatsbibliothek, MS ND. VI 5573; published in Erich Katz, *Die musikalischen Stilbegriffe des 17. Jahrhunderts* (Inaugural diss., University of Freiburg im Breisgau, 1926), 83–9. The first two columns are from Werner's letter, the last from the *Breve discorso*, below, pp. 109–10.

first and second practices were equally applicable to both church and chamber music but that only the second practice was appropriate to the theatre.[8]

Angelo Berardi remained more faithful than Bernhard to Scacchi's system. Berardi studied with Scacchi after the latter's return to Italy from Warsaw. His main contribution was to apply the categories to more recent composers whom he names as exemplary in the various styles. Under the category of concerted madrigal with basso continuo, for example, he names Monteverdi, Mazzocchi, Scacchi, and Savioni, and he extends the category to *cantate concertate*, exponents of which are Caprioli, Carissimi, Tenaglia, Luigi Rossi, Celani, and Pacieri. Among the church compositions of Scacchi's third category (*in concerto*) he lists those of Sarti, Scacchi, and Cossonio; for the fourth category (*concertini alla moderna*, as Berardi calls them), he names compositions of Carissimi, Bicilli, Melani, and Corsi Celano.[9]

Johann Joseph Fux was indebted to Berardi on many points of contrapuntal technique and through him to Scacchi for the analysis of styles. Stylistic distinctions figure quite critically in Fux's method of teaching composition in the *Gradus ad Parnassum*. He recognized the division into church, chamber, and theatrical style, but he treated the first two only cursorily. The church style he divided into *a cappella* unaccompanied, *a cappella* accompanied by organ and instruments, and mixed style.[10]

It was Johann Mattheson who paid Scacchi the greatest homage by giving him credit for the classification on which the entire tenth chapter of the first part of *Der vollkommene Capellmeister* is based.[11] He also quoted two of Scacchi's madrigals to illustrate the category of continuo madrigal.[12]

Mattheson introduces Scacchi's contribution with these words:

Marco Scacchi was a famous Italian composer of his time and for thirty years choirmaster for two kings in Poland, Zygmunt I [*sic*] and Władysław IV, the first of whom reigned also over Sweden. In an unpublished manuscript book found in the Hamburg Public Library in St Johann and addressed to

---

[8] Christoph Bernhard, *Tractatus compositionis augmentatus*; printed in Joseph Müller-Blattau, *Die Kompositionslehre Heinrich Schützens in der Fassung seines Schülers Christoph Bernhard*, 2nd edn. (Kassel: Bärenreiter, 1963), 40–131.

[9] Angelo Berardi, *Ragionamenti musicali* (Bologna: Giacomo Monti, 1681), 133–6.

[10] Johann Joseph Fux, *Gradus ad Parnassum* (Vienna: Johann Peter van Ghelen, 1725), Exercitium V, Lectio VII, pp. 242–3.

[11] Johann Mattheson, *Der vollkommene Capellmeister* (Hamburg: Christian Herold, 1739), pt. i, ch. 10, pp. 68–93. See C. Palisca, 'The Genesis of Mattheson's Style Classification', in George Buelow and Hans Joachim Marx (eds.), *New Mattheson Studies* (Cambridge: Cambridge University Press, 1983), 409–23.

[12] Mattheson, *Der vollkommene Capellmeister*, pt. i, ch. 10, §§ 61–2, pp. 80–2.

Christian Werner, then cantor in Danzig, he affirms that all musical styles [*Schreib-Arten*] should rightly and necessarily be divided into three classes, namely, the church, theatrical, and chamber styles. No other principal manner can or must be recognized [he says], although these three styles could well be elaborated and considered under various sub-styles [*Neben-Arten*].[13]

Mattheson proceeds in the next twenty-four pages to elaborate a modern classification plan that is based not only on Scacchi's main threefold division but also frequently on his subgroupings.

Scacchi could speak of the many current styles of composition from firsthand experience. He published in 1633 a book of four-voice masses in the unaccompanied *a cappella* style and in 1634 a book of concerted madrigals for five voices; he left in manuscript a number of sacred concerti. He is also said to have composed at least one oratorio, *S. Cecilia,* and several operas, including *Le Nozze d'Amore e Psiche.*

The *Breve discorso* offers no musical examples. Fortunately, Scacchi illustrated some of his stylistic categories in an appendix to the *Cribrum musicum.* As models of both the new and old styles, they were meant to educate Siefert's consciousness of stylistic purity. First are several movements in *stylo antiquo* from his 1633 mass collection. He then gives two four-voice continuo madrigals, a five-voice motet with continuo, and a four-voice motet. A collection of forty-nine canons, mostly by Polish composers and Italians resident in Poland, follows under the rubric *Xenia apollinea.* Finally there is an example by Scacchi in mixed recitative style. Of these I have provided below transcriptions of the two continuo madrigals and the example in mixed recitative style, together with a translation of the commentary that accompanies the examples.

[13] Ibid., § 4, pp. 68–9.

Marco Scacchi, *Breve discorso sopra la musica moderna*

[Sig. A1ʳ] BREVE / DISCORSO / Sopra la / MVSICA MODERNA, / DI / MARCO SCACCHI ROMANO / Maestro di Capp: del Sereniβimo & Potentiβimo / GIOVANNI CASIMIRO / Rè di Polonia & Suetia, &c. &c./ IN VARSAVIA, / Per Pietro Elert, Stamp. di sua Maestà, nell'An. 1649.[14]

[A2ʳ] Al Prudente Lettore

Con mia non poca meraviglia, ho letto alcune scritture in dispregio della Musica moderna, e di chi anco la professa; dovriano prezzare questi tali quel nobile precetto d'Orazio.

> *Nec tua laudabis studia, haud aliena repraehendes.*[15]

Poichè dir solamente parole contro a' fatti d'altri. *Nil agit exemplum, litem quod lite resolvit.*[16] Lascino pure, ch'il Mondo sia giudice senza tante loro censure:[17] onde ho notato in una di dette scritture queste parole; come l'arte della Musica buona si perde, e che si dovria seguitare il Palestina, et dar di bando a questa Musica moderna, etc.[18] In un'altra poi si leggono le seguenti parole. Che in questa professione già sono molt'anni che in . . . non si studia, et è dominata dall'invidia, et dalla imperizia.[19]

Parole in vero non ben riflesse; Però dirò quel tanto, che appartiene alla Professione. Dico, che questi tali non considerano, che per la Musica moder[A2ᵛ]na è necessario consumare moltissimi anni avanti, che si possa arrivare a sapere in pieno i suoi effetti; forse credono che la Musica moderna sia fondata su l'arena, o priva di Regole, et sue considerazioni? Ma falla di certo chi a ciò, s'induce, e si mostrarà poco addottrinata nella Professione; e mi scusino, che loro non si rendono molto capaci di adoperare questa 2. prattica Musicale, la quale tira al suo fine, che è di rapire gl'Ascoltanti, con esprimere l'orazione in altra maniera; che non hanno fatto i nostri primi Professori antichi, ben che per altro devono essere per ogni merito in grandissima venerazione; e se questi Oppositori della Musica moderna si pavoneggiano perchè professano d'intendere i studi antichi, non hanno di chè; perchè al presente ancora si ritrovano quelli, che esercitano questa Musica, li quali sono versati ne gl'antichi studi; et hanno anco questo talento in avantaggio di più, che possiedono lo stile moderno, il quale porta in sè (quasi) un Chaos di variazioni, et di osservazioni per seguitare la

---

[14] I know of only two copies of this essay: Rome, Biblioteca Nazionale, 69.8B.22, and that in Tübingen, Universitätsbibliothek, formerly in Berlin, Preußische Staatsbibliothek. The latter is available on microfilm from Kassel, Deutsches musikgeschichtliches Archiv, catalogue no. 1/930.

[15] *Epist.* i. 18. 39; trans. H. Rushton Fairclough, *Horace: Satires, Epistles and Ars Poetica* (Cambridge, Mass.: Harvard University Press, 1961), 370–1: 'you will neither praise your own tastes, nor find fault with those of others . . .'. Scacchi's 'haud aliena repraehendes' has been corrected.

[16] Horace, *Sat.* ii. 3. 103; trans. ibid. 161–3: 'Useless is an instance which solves puzzle by puzzle.'

Marco Scacchi, *Brief Discourse on Modern Music*

[Sig. A1ʳ] *Brief Discourse on Modern Music by Marco Scacchi of Rome, Choir-master of the Most Serene and Most Mighty John Casimir, King of Poland and Sweden, etc.* In Warsaw, by Pietro Elert, Printer to His Majesty, in the year 1649. [Signatures A–D in fours. Signature D4 is blank.][14]

[Sig. A2ʳ] Prudent Reader:

With no little surprise I have read some writings scornful of modern music and also of those who practise it. These [authors] should take to heart that noble precept of Horace: 'Nec tua laudabis studia aut aliena reprendes.'[15] For to say only contrary words about what others have done: 'Nil agit exemplum, litem quod lite resolvit.'[16] Let the world be the judge without all their censures.[17] In one of these scripts I read these words: the good art of music is being lost; one should follow Palestrina and banish this modern music; and so on.[18] In another we read the following words: 'In this profession for many years now in . . . [undisclosed place] no one studies, and it [the profession] is dominated by envy and ignorance.'[19]

These truly are words little meditated upon. Yet I shall say this about our profession. Such types do not realize that before someone can fully know modern music {A2ᵛ} and its effects he has to spend many years. Maybe they think that modern music is founded on sand, devoid of rules and principles. But whoever induces himself to believe this is making a mistake and shows himself to lack instruction in the profession. It explains why such [musicians] do not turn out to be very able in this second musical practice, which has as its end to ravish listeners by expressing a text in a way different from what our first ancient masters did, who otherwise have every right to be greatly venerated. If these opponents of modern music parade themselves like peacocks, claiming to understand the ancient studies, they have nothing to boast about, because many who now practise this [modern] music are also versed in the ancient studies, and they have in

[17] From 'For to say nothing . . .' to '. . . all their censures' Scacchi parrots Giulio Cesare Monteverdi, 'Dichiaratione della lettera stampata nel Quinto libro de suoi madregali', in Claudio Monteverdi, *Scherzi musicali a tre voci* (1607, 1632), repr. in *Tutte le opere di Claudio Monteverdi*, ed. Gian Francesco Malipiero (Asolo: G. F. Malipiero, 1929; repr. Vienna: Universal Edition, 1954–68), x. 69, and in Gian Francesco Malipiero, *Claudio Monteverdi* (Milan: Fratelli Treves, 1930), 72–85. The passage in the 'Dichiaratione' reads: 'che per dir solamente parole contro a fatti d'altri. 'Nil agit exemplum litem quod lite resolvit.' Et lasci all'hora che il mondo sia poi giudice . . .' (Malipiero, *Claudio Monteverdi*, 76).
[18] Scacchi attributed to Paul Siefert the charges that musical composition had deteriorated in Italy and that composers there no longer knew the harmonic fundamentals; see *Lettera per maggiore informazione a chi leggerà il mio Cribrum* (Warsaw: Nella stamperia regia, 29 agosto 1644)—manuscript copy dated Rome, 22 Sept. 1745, in Bologna, Civico Museo Bibliografico Musicale, MS E-50 (hereafter cited as Bologna, MS E-50), p. 252.
[19] The author of this remark is unknown.

Dottrina di Platone:[20] e considerando quel particolare, che ha scritto quell'oppositore, cioè, che è dominata dall'invidia.

Non so in vero a chi si deve attribuire questo titolo, o a' Virtuosi moderni, overo a chi opponendogli, gli vuol [A3^r] dar norma per non dir' accusa; poichè in investigando il ristretto vero di questo negozio, ritrovo che questi tali non vorrebbero, che i Musici d'oggi, e forse gl'avvenire ancora, inventassero più avanti, di quello, che non è stato concesso a loro medisimi di potere, nè pur capire, non che tal volta imitare, e questo è assai chiaro; perchè biasimano, e vilipendono quello, ch'eglino non intendono, cioè, che cosa sia Musica moderna, poichè se l'intendessero, in luogo di vilipenderla, con dirne ogni male, la lodarebbero, et procurarebbero d'essere seguaci di sì nobile stile, quale è abbracciato quasi per tutte le parti del mondo; e sanno pure questi Signori che Iddio non ha ancora limitato l'intelletto umano a segno tale, che non possa operare anco più avanti, di quello che hanno operato gl'Antichi Professori, e questi tali, pare a me, che vorebbero impedire il corso dell'intelletto umano, quale viene largamente dotato da sua Divina Maestà per inventare cose nuove per sua maggior gloria.

Dichino di grazia, se il Colombo non avesse cercato con l'intelletto di passare le Colonne d'Hercole con la navigazione, avrebbe egli ritrovato un nuovo Mondo? E pure, è noto ad ogn'uno, che quando proponeva con le Raggioni demostrative questo suo sublime pensiero, era [A3^v] tenuto per pazzo, et il tutto procedeva, che quei tali, a cui referiva la sua impresa, non erano ancora capaci di quel tanto, che dimostrava, e pure al secolo presente il genere umano gli deve tant'obligo, quanto vale un Mondo nuovo. Ora così dico della Musica moderna, che se alcuno avesse proposto a nostri Antecessori, come l'arte della Musica si puole adoperare differentemente di quello che essi ci hanno insegnato l'avrebbero tenuto per Uomo di poco sapere, e questo non si può negare al tempo presente, poichè l'udito lo giudica, come quello, dal quale la Musica ha ricevuto, et riceve giornalmente maggior perfezzione; onde dico, sì come il Colombo ha fatto vedere in suo genere quello che non hanno saputo investigare i primi suoi Inventori della navigazione così la nostra Musica moderna fa oggi sentire, quello che non hanno sentito i primi nostri Maestri, nè meno gl'è stato concesso d'investigare, quel tanto, che hanno ritrovato i Musici moderni per esprimere l'orazione; e di ragione il mondo deve aver tant'obligo a' Compositori moderni, quanto importa la finezza della dilettazione Armonica, in rapresentare con nuovi accompagnamenti musicali le parole; e le opinioni

[20] Plato's assertion that harmony and rhythm should always follow the text and not the reverse is in *Republic* 398D.

addition the advantage of possessing the modern style. This style can boast an almost chaotic variety of techniques and observations that follow the doctrines of Plato.[20]

Consider the statement written by a certain opponent that modern music 'is dominated by envy'. I do not know truly to whom to attribute this distinction, whether to the modern virtuosi or, indeed, to those who by opposing them wish [A3ʳ] to judge them, if not to accuse them. When I examine the real dimensions of this question, I find that these [critics] would rather not see the musicians of today or even of the future invent anything more advanced than that which has been conceded them to know how to do, or even understand, or occasionally imitate. And this is very clear, because they censure and disparage what they do not understand, namely, what modern music is. For, if they understood it, instead of disparaging it and speaking badly of it, they would praise it and take steps to become followers of so noble a style, embraced by almost every part of the world. These gentlemen surely know that God has not put any such limits on the human intellect as that it cannot operate in advance of the way the ancient masters operated. These [gentlemen], in my opinion, would impede the course of the human intellect, which has been generously endowed by His Divine Majesty with the capacity to invent new things for His greater glory.

Let them please tell me, if Columbus had not sought with his intellect to pass beyond the Pillars of Hercules through navigation, would he have found a new world? Yet everyone knows that when he proposed this sublime thought and backed it by logical demonstration, [A3ᵛ] he was thought mad. This was because those to whom he reported his project did not yet have the capacity for what he was demonstrating. In our century mankind owes him as great a debt as a new world is worth. So I am saying of modern music that if someone had proposed to our predecessors how our musical art might be used differently from the way they taught us, he would have been deemed a man of little wisdom. But at present such a person could not be repudiated, since the hearing judges him as one from whom music has received, and daily receives, greater perfection. Therefore, I say that just as Columbus made evident in his field things that the first inventors of navigation were not able to investigate, so our modern music lets us hear today what our first masters did not hear, nor were they even privileged to investigate what modern musicians have discovered about expressing a text. The world has reason to be indebted to modern composers in the measure that they have brought finesse of harmonic delight to the representation of words with their new musical accomd'alcuni non possono abbattere per terra quello che viene approvato (quasi) da [A4^r] tutto il mondo per buono, mentre però non adduchino Ragioni sufficienti, con la confirmazione dell'udito per distruggere la Musica moderna; altrimente bisognarebbe confessare che tutti generalmente avessero il senso ottuso, eccetto gl'Oppositori di essa; finalmente se non avessero investigato i Professori di tutte le scienze, et arte tanto liberali, come mecaniche, ogni cosa sarebbe priva de tanti benefici, che continuamente riceviamo, per utilità nostra commune, e se altramente fosse, si potrebbe dire. *Tenebrae factae sunt*, sopra degl'intelletti. Dove che con investigare cose nuove, veniamo (oltre quello che ho detto) a rendere grazie a sua Divina Maestà dei benefici, che quotidianamente veniamo a ricevere, per mezzo della speculativa, et dell'atto prattico.

Me dichiaro però, che questo presente discorso, è un'abbozzo di quel' tanto, che sarò per mostrare in altra stampa, quanto s'ingannino gl'Oppositori della Musica moderna.[21] Dico per tanto, che se alcun Professore Armonico moderno ha trascorso troppo avanti, con pigliarsi una insoportabil licenzia nelle sue Cantilene, dovriano loro tacciar quello in particolare, e non tutti in generale con dispregiare tanti onorati, e ben fondati Professori della Musica moderna.

Per quanto pu[A4^v]blico per vigore di questo breve discorso, di voler provare a questi Signori Oppositori, che l'arte della Musica oggi dì è arrivata quasi al sommo della perfezzione, mediante i fondamenti di questa 2. Prattica Musicale, e vice versa mostrarò quanto siano di discapito alla Musica quelli, che attendono per il più a fabricare Cantilene in Canoni, senza aver riguardo all'Arte della soave Armonia, conforme più distesamente lo dinotarò nell'ultimo di queste carte; Pregoti benigno Lettore à leggere con favorevole attenzione questi pochi fogli, che spero, approverai il mio sentimento, e vivi felice.

[B1^r]   Breve Discorso
                    Sopra la Musica moderna

Sono state molte, e varie l'opinioni de gl'Antichi, di dove abbia avuto

---

[21] This longer treatise either was never written or is lost. It may be to this promised treatise that Heinrich Schütz referred in the preface to his *Geistliche Chormusik* of 1648. There he counsels musicians to find the right road to counterpoint by studying the excellent works of many composers, both Italians and others, whether written in the old or concertato styles. Then he says: 'In regard to this I still entertain the hope, indeed I have already reports that a musician well known to me, highly accomplished both in theory and practice, will soon bring to light an entire treatise. This could be very salutary and profitable, especially for us Germans' (Heinrich Schütz, *Neue Ausgabe sämtlicher Werke*, v [Kassel: Bärenreiter, 1955], p. vii). Both Erich H. Müller, editor of Schütz's *Gesammelte Briefe und Schriften* (Regensburg: Gustav Bosse, 1931), 342, and Joseph Müller-Blattau, *Die kompositionslehre Heinrich Schützens*, 2, were of the opinion that this was a reference to Christoph Bernhard's treatise.

paniments. The opinions of certain people cannot run to the ground what is approved as good by almost [A4ʳ] the whole world, unless, when they demolish modern music, they adduce sufficient reasons and the confirmation of the ear. Otherwise, we should have to conclude that people generally, apart from the opponents of modern music, have an obtuse sense of hearing. Finally, if the masters of all the sciences and arts, both liberal and mechanical, had not investigated them, we should be deprived of the many benefits of every kind that we continually receive for our common use. If things were otherwise, it could be said of intelligent men: *Tenebrae factae sunt.* By investigating new things we gain not only what I have said, but we can render thanks to His Divine Majesty for the benefits that we receive daily by means of speculative thought and practical acts.

I must confess that my present discourse is only a sketch of a future publication in which I wish to demonstrate how much the opponents of modern music deceive themselves.[21] This much I shall say: if any practitioner of modern harmony has run too far ahead by taking some intolerable licence in his vocal compositions, we should impugn him specifically and not disparage all the many honoured and well-grounded masters of modern music in general.

[A4ᵛ] I am publishing this brief discourse to prove to these gentlemen opponents that musical art today has reached nearly the summit of perfection through the foundations of this second musical practice and to demonstrate on the other hand how much damage to music is being done by those who pay more attention to fabricating canons in their compositions than to creating smooth harmony, as I shall note at greater length at the end of these pages.

I beg you, kind reader, to read these few sheets with favourable attention, and I hope that you will approve of my sentiments. And farewell.

[B1ʳ]
Brief Discourse
on Modern Music

There have been many and varied opinions on the part of the ancients concerning the origins of music. Some said that it was discovered in the

---

However, Bruno Grusnick, 'Bernhard, Christoph', *MGG* i (1949–51), 1786–7, has shown that Bernhard could not have written the treatise before 1657 and suggested that Schütz was referring to Scacchi. In his second letter (dated 1648) on the Scacchi–Siefert controversy Schütz refers to our author as 'the most excellent gentleman Scacchi, a man not only very learned in theory but also very well versed in practice . . .'. (Müller, 188). At the end of the letter he urges that 'Mr Marcus Scacchi complete and publish the treatise on the art of counterpoint that he promised in his book, for it would certainly greatly profit our German nation first of all and would bring immortal fame to himself and glory to his name' (Müller, 190). In his *Lettera per maggiore informazione* Scacchi did, indeed, promise 'to bring forth a brief treatise on the rules of counterpoint' (Bologna, MS E-50, p. 258).

origine la Musica. Alcuni hanno detto essere stata ritrovata dal canto de gl'Ucelli; altri, dal fischio del vento, il quale osservato, quando passava il di lui soffio per una canna forata, si sentiva il suono; altri asseriscono, che dal rumor del Acqua del Nilo, che fa in alcuni luoghi; altri vogliono, che sia stata inventata dal percuotere de' Martelli sopra dell'Ancudine.

Ma nella scrittura sacra leggesi, che Tubal figliolo di Lamech fosse egli il primo inventore, in conformità di che, nella Prattica del Finck si leggono queste pa[B1ᵛ]role: Si Iosepho, ac sacris Litteris nulla fides adhibenda est, Tubal filius Lamech inventor eius praecipuus, et antiquitate primus, ante Diluvium duabus Tabulis, latentia scilicet, et marmorea, Posteris eam reliquit inscriptam, ut sine ignis, sive aqua mundus puniretur, alterutra columnarum non aboleretur. Marmor enim non liquescit, lateres vero humore non resolvuntur; idem etiam Cytharae, et Organorum usum tradidisse;[22] altri vogliano che sia stato Pitagora; Plinio l'attribuisce ad Amphione d'Etiopia, creduto figlio di Giove,[23] che però nella Bucolica cantò il Poeta.

> *Io canto ciò ch'Amphione solea*
> *Cantar, chiamando a' pascoli l'armento.*[24]

E Statio nel primo della Thebaide scrive, come dice il Garzoni,

> *Dirò, come Amphion condusse i Monti*
> *A le Mura di Thebe col suo canto*
> *E i Tirii Monti si li fecer vicini*[25]

Li Greci vogliono, che sia stato Dyonisio; et altri Zeto, et Amphione fratelli; Solino tiene, che sia venuta da Candia;[26] Polibio l'attri[B2ᵛ]buisce a gl'Arcadi;[27] Diodoro a Mercurio:[28] di modo che sono molte le opinioni circa l'origine, e l'Inventori della Musica, Non dimeno la maggior parte e quasi tutti concludono, che l'abbiamo da Dio, datore d'ogni Arte, e

---

[22] Hermann Finck, *Practica musica* (Wittenberg: Haeredes Georgii Rhaw, 1556), sig. A1ᵛ. The quotation, incorrectly rendered in Scacchi, has been made to conform to the printed treatise. 'If Josephus and the scriptures are to be trusted, Tubal [i.e., Jubal] son of Lamech, its [music's] chief and oldest inventor, left it to posterity inscribed on two tablets, one of brick and the other of marble, before the flood, so that whether the world were punished by fire or by water, one of the columns should not be destroyed. For marble does not melt and brick is not dissolved by liquid. He is also said to have transmitted the use of the harp and the organ.' Genesis 4:21 credits Jubal as 'pater canentium cithara et organo' (the father of all such as handle the harp and organ).

[23] Pliny, *Natural History*, vii. 56. 204.

[24] Vergil, *Eclogues*, ii. 23–4; trans. H. Rushton Fairclough, *Vergil*, i (Cambridge, Mass.: Harvard University Press, 1947), 11: 'canto, quae solitus, si quando armenta vocabat, / Amphion Dircaeus in Actaeo Aracyntho' (I sing as Amphion of Dirce used to sing, / when calling home the herds on Attic Aracynthus).

song of birds; others in the whistling of the wind, having observed that a sound is heard when the wind blows through a perforated cane. Others assert that it was found in the roar that the waters of the Nile make in certain places; others would have it that it was invented by striking hammers on an anvil.

But in the sacred scriptures we read that Tubal, son of Lamech, was the first inventor of music; so we read in the *Practica* of Finck:

[B1ᵛ] Si Iosepho ac Sacris literis ulla fides adhibenda est, Tubal filius Lamech inuentor eius praecipuus, & antiquitate primus ante diluuium duabus tabulis, lateritia scilicet, & marmorea posteris eam reliquit inscriptam, ut siue igni siue aqua mundus puniretur, alterutra columnarum non aboleretur. Marmor enim non liquescit, Lateres uerò humore non resoluuntur. Idem etiam dicitur cytharae, & organorum usum tradidisse.[22]

Others would have it that Pythagoras was the inventor of music. Pliny attributes it to Amphion of Ethiopia, believed to be the son of Jupiter,[23] as the poet sang in the *Bucolics*:

> Io canto ciò ch'Amphione solea
> Cantar, chiamando a' pascoli l'armento.[24]

And Statius, in the first of the *Thebaid*, writes, according to Garzoni,

> Dirò, come Amphion condusse i Monti
> A le Mura di Thebe col suo canto
> E i Tirii Monti si li fecer vicini.[25]

The Greeks think that it was Dionysus; others, that it was the brothers Zetus and Amphion. Solinus holds that it came from Crete.[26] Polybius attributes [B2ʳ] it to the Arcadians,[27] Diodorus to Mercury.[28] Thus the

---

[25] Publius Papinius Statius (*c.* AD 40–*c.*96), *Thebaid*, i. 9–10; trans. J. H. Mozley, *Statius*, i (New York, 1928), 340–1: 'quo carmine muris/ iusserit Amphion Tyrios accedere montes' (Far backward runs the story, should I . . . relate with what song Amphion bade the Tyrian mountains move to form a city's walls . . .).

[26] Gaius Julius Solinus, *The Excellent and Pleasant Worke: Collectanea rerum memorabilium*, trans. Arthur Golding (London, 1587; facs. edn., Gainesville, Fla.: Scholars Facsimiles and Reprints, 1955), ch. 15, sig. L1ᵛ.

[27] Polybius, *The Histories*, iv. 20–1. Polybius does not say that the Arcadians invented music but that they introduced it early as an important component of their society. Scacchi's misinterpretation seems to derive from Pedro Cerone, *El Melopeo y maestro* (Naples: Juan Bautista Gargano y Lucrecio Nucci, 1613), bk. ii, ch. 17, p. 226, where Cerone says 'Polibyo en el 4. lib. quiere fuessen inuentores de la Musica los Arcadios'. Most of the other citations in this section seem to have been culled from Cerone.

[28] Diodorus of Sicily, i. 16; trans. C. H. Oldfather, *Diodorus of Sicily*, i (New York: G. P. Putnam's Sons, 1933; London: W. Heinemann, 1933), 53: 'he [Hermes] was the first also to observe the orderly arrangement of the stars and the harmony of the musical sounds and their nature . . . He also made a lyre and gave it three strings, imitating the seasons of the year . . .'. See Cerone, bk. ii, ch. 17, p. 226.

Virtù, come affermano moltissimi Autori, e sentenze scritturali, e particolarmente nella Prattica del detto Finck si leggono queste parole. Verisimilius tamen est, Deum ipsum ei Musicam tradidisse;[29] e di questa opinione furono i Gentili, come testifica il medesimo Autore. Idem [dice] sensisse videntur gentiles homines, Nam cum origine ad Deos referri vult.[30] Il Boroaldo nell'orazione fatta in esporre le questioni Tusculane,[31] et Orazio Flacco l'attribuisce ad una origine Divina, dicendo; Cuius origo coelestis memoratur, ipsiusque ratione mundum esse compositum pithagorici vulgaverunt;[32] Dunque diremo, che la Musica ci sia stata data per Privilegio particolare da sua Divina Maestà; dubbio non è, che quando il sommo Motore la {B2ᵛ} pone nelle mani delle sue Creature, acciò quest'Arte fosse posta in opera per laudare il suo santissimo Nome, fu ella nel comparire alla luce assai povera, per maggiormente mostrare la sua grandezza con il beneficio dei secoli, essendo che sua Divina Maestà opera tutto al contrario di quello che sogliono operare gl'uomini, perchè è proprio di Dio, quando vuol mostrare la sua omnipotenza di dar principio con cose picciole, per farle poi maggiori; ma l'uomo nel dar principio a suoi pensieri, s'immagina cose grandi, le quali poi nel ultimo si risolvono bene spesso in veruna sostanza.

Onde replico, che la Musica nel nascere, nacque povera, e poi con i secoli s'è talmente arrichita, che si può dire, essere arrivata al giorno presente quasi ad un'ottima perfezzione che però si vede chiaramente, che sua Divina M[aestà] particolarmente la protegge, et augumenta, come cosa di suo infinito sapere, e per l'utile grande, che se ne cava, come cantò quel Nobil Poeta.

{B3ʳ}   Musica Dei donum optime,
          Trahit homines, trahit Deos.
          Musica truces mollit animos,
          Tristesque mentes erigit
          Musica, vel ipsos Arbores,
          Et horridas movet feras.[33]

Onde considerando quel Salmo. Cantate Domino canticum novum, quia mirabilia fecit,[34] etc. ritrovo, come sua Divina Maestà vuole, che se gli cantino canti nuovi per il debito, che gl'abbiamo dei benefici nuovi che quotidianamente riceviamo, e questo coseglio, egli medesimo l'ordinò alla Sinagoga, benchè per altro Iddio sapesse, che gl'Ebrei sapevano cantare, e

---

[29] Finck, *Practica musica*, sig. A1ᵛ. The quotation has been edited to conform to the printed edition.
[30] Ibid. Scacchi omitted the words 'Homerus . . . Musicae'.
[31] Filippo Beroaldo, ed. with commentary, Cicero, *Tusculanae disputationes* (Bologna, 1496).
[32] Not found in the writings of Horace.

opinions about the origin and inventors of music are many. Nevertheless, the majority—indeed, almost all—conclude it comes from God, giver of every art and virtue, as very many authors and the words of the Bible affirm. In the *Practica* of Finck we read these words: 'Verisimilius tamen est Deum ipsum ei Musicam tradidisse.'[29] The Gentiles were of this opinion, as the same author testifies: 'Idem sensisse videntur gentiles homines. Nam cum Homerus Apollinem Cythara canentem fingit, proculdubio Musicae originem ad Deos referri vult.'[30] Beroaldo, in the oration made in exposition of the *Quaestiones tusculanae*[31] and Horace, attributes it to a divine origin, saying: 'Cuius origo coelestis memoratur, ipsiusque ratione mundum esse compositum pithagorici vulgaverunt . . .'.[32] Therefore, we shall say that music was given to us as a special privilege by His Divine Majesty. The Supreme Mover [B2ᵛ] placed this art in the hands of his creatures to be put in operation for the praise of His most holy Name. There is no doubt that He let it be very poor when it first saw the light, so that He could show His greatness through the benefits of the centuries to come. For His Divine Majesty operates in a manner contrary to that which men are accustomed to, because it is characteristic of God when he wants to show His omnipotence to begin with little things and then to make them bigger. But when man sets out to think, he imagines grand things, which then eventually are often resolved into something less substantial.

Therefore, I reply, music in its infancy was born poor and was so enriched in the course of the centuries that one may say it has arrived in the present day almost at an optimal perfection. So it is clear that His Divine Majesty protects and augments it, particularly as a product of His infinite wisdom and as a thing of great utility. As that noble poet sang:

[B3ʳ]
        Musica Dei donum optimi,
        Trahit homines, trahit Deos.
        Musica truces mollit animos,
        Tristesque mentes erigit,
        Musica, vel ipsas Arbores,
        Et horridas movet feras.[33]

Considering the psalm, *Cantate Domino canticum novum, quia mirabilia fecit*,[34] etc., I find that His Divine Majesty wished to have sung to Him

---

[33] This Neo-Latin poem was frequently set to music by northern composers, including Lasso. See Winfried Kirsch, '"Musica Dei donum optimi": Zu einigen Weltlichen Motetten des 16. Jahrhunderts', in Wilhelm Stauder, Ursula Aarburg, and Peter Cahn (eds.), *Helmuth Osthoff zu seinem siebzigsten Geburtstag* (Tutzing: Hans Schneider, 1969), 105–28. The following corrections have been made in the Latin text: optime/optimi; Tristeque/Tristesque; ipsos/ipsas. I am indebted to Bonnie Blackburn for this information.

[34] Vulgate Ps. 96.

comporre canti, come ce lo manifesta, chiaramente Mosè, il quale compose il canto di Debora, della buona Anna, del Re Ezechia etc. conforme dice il Gueguara nel suo Oratorio cap. xxxiv.[35]

Dunque bisogna confessare, che le cantilene nuove sono grate a sua Divina Maestà, e questo è chiaro, poichè non gustava il canto vecchio de [B3ᵛ] gl'Ebrei, ma sì bene cantilene nuove; leggo ancora, che molti Pontefici, et alcuni santi hanno sempre studiato, di ritrovare cose nuove, poichè non erano contenti delle antiche; Perciò Gregorio il magno inventò le sette lettere Musicale, che sono, A, B, C, D, E, F, G.[36] Ignazio martire inventò l'Antifone, come si raccoglie da questi versi.

Antiphonas dedit ad Psalmos Ignatius aptas,
Monte prout quodam de super audierat[37]

Damaso Papa ordinò, che si cantassero a vicenda i versetti dei Salmi nel choro, e v'aggiunse il Gloria Patri etc.[38] l'istesso Pontefice nell'Anno di N[ostro] S[ignore] 366. compose, et inventò le intonazioni dei Salmi, e di molt'inni;[39] Gregorio nominato da me, ordinò che si cantasse l'introito, il Kyrie, Alleluia nella Messa grande, et aggiunse quattro toni, chiamandoli laterali, o vero collaterali. Vitiliano Papa circa gl'anni di N[ostro] S[ignore] 658. comandò, che si suonasse l'Organo nella Chiesa Romana con il canto asieme, come si legge nei scritti di [B4ʳ] Monsignor Durante: Vintilianus cantum Romanum instituit (dice) et Organo concordavit. Leone secondo di nazione Siciliana, il quale fu dottissimo nella Musica, ne gl'anni di N[ostro] S[ignore] 682 (conforme scrive il Cerone) compose il canto dei Salmi, cioè ritrovò le loro Salmodie, et riformò gl'inni, et anco accomodò l'intonazioni conforme s'usa al presente,[40] e nella sua istoria si leggono queste parole: Leo secundus Pontifex Maximus Siculus, humanis et Divinis litteris, Graece et Latine doctus, musicis [*sic*] etiam eruditus fuit: ipse enim sacros hymnos et Psalmos in Ecclesia ad concentum meliorem reduxit, etc.[41]

---

[35] Antonio de Guevara, *Libro llamado oratorio de religiosos: y exercicio de virtuosos* (Valladolid: J. de Villaquiran, 1542). The biblical references are to Judges 5 (Deborah), 1 Kings 2 (Hannah), and Isaiah 38: 10–20 (Hezechiah).

[36] The source of this is Cerone, *El Melopeo y maestro*, bk. ii, ch. 35, p. 256, where he says: 'El bienauenturado Papa Gregorio primero deste nombre, cerca los años de nuestra Salud 598, inuentò las *siete letras* sobre las posiciones griegas; como oyendia las vsamos en la mano musical.'

[37] Scacchi has 'Antiphonas'. The author of the verses has not been identified.

[38] The source is again Cerone, bk. ii, ch. 29, p. 241: 'Pero despues Papa Damas Español, (diuidiendo el Choro en dos alas) ordenò que se cantassen alternatiuamente por versos, en toda la Yglesia vniuersalmente; aunque ya esto en algunas yglesias particulares se vsaua, por la noticia que diò dello S. Ignacio Obispo de Antiochia, en los años de nuestra saluacion 106.' Cerone's source is Gulielmus Durandus, *Rationale divinorum officiorum* (Antwerp: Vidua & haeredes Ioan. Stelsii, 1570), bk. v, ch. 2, pp. 217–18: 'Ipse autem Damasus instituit, vt chori in duas partes diuisi psalmos canerent alternatim: & dicuntur psal. alternatim ad notandum aeternam sanctorum, ad bene operandum exhortationem.'

new songs for the debt that we owe Him for the new benefits that we receive each day. Indeed He himself ordered that this be done in the synagogue, for God knew that the Hebrews were able to sing and to compose songs, as is manifested clearly by Moses, who composed the Song of Deborah, of good Hannah, of King Hezechiah, and so on. Guevara in his *Oratorio*, chapter 34, says as much.[35]

Therefore, it must be acknowledged that new songs are pleasing to His Divine Majesty, and this is clear, since He did not relish the old chants of [B3ᵛ] the Hebrews, but rather new songs. I read also that many pontiffs and some of the saints always studied to find new things, because they were not content with the ancient. So Gregory the Great invented the seven musical letters: A, B, C, D, E, F, G.[36] Ignatius the Martyr invented the antiphon, as we gather from these verses:

> Antiphonas dedit ad Psalmos Ignatius aptas,
> Monte prout quodam de super audierat.[37]

Pope Damasus ordered that the choir sing the verses of the psalms in alternation [antiphonally], and he added the Gloria Patri, and so on.[38] The same pontiff in the year AD 366 composed and invented the intonations of the psalms and of many hymns.[39] The Gregory mentioned before ordered that the Introit, Kyrie, and Alleluia be sung in the high mass and added four modes, calling them lateral or collateral. Pope Vitalian around the year AD 658 ordered that the organ be played in the Roman church with the chant, as we read in the writings of [B4ʳ] Monsignor Durante: 'Vintilianus cantum Romanum instituit et Organo concordavit.' Leo II, a Sicilian very learned in music, in the year AD 682 (according to what Cerone writes) composed the chant of the psalms, that is, discovered the psalmodies [psalm tones], and reformed the hymns. He also arranged the intonations in the way they are used at present.[40] In his biography we read these words:

Leo Secundus Pontifex Maximus Siculus, humanis & divinis literis, Graece & Latine doctus, musices etiam eruditus fuit: ipse enim sacros hymnos & psalmos in Ecclesia ad concentum meliorem reduxit, etc.[41]

[39] Cerone, bk. ii, ch. 35, p. 256: 'Papa Damaso Portugues, que gouernò la Yglesia Romana cerca los años del Señor 366, compuso las *intonaciones de los Salmos, y muchas arias ò tonadas de los Hymnos.'*

[40] Ibid. 257: 'Este mesmo Pontifice [Gregorio I], por quanto escriue Platina, ordenò se cantassen por punto *los Introitos, los Kyries, el Alleluia,* y otras cosas que al presente se cantan en los sacrificios. Despues Vitaliano Papa, cerca los años 658, acomodò el canto y ordenò *los Organos en la Yglesia Romana.* Y esto (como dixe) sabemos por relacion de Monseñor Durante: el qual dize assi: *Vitalianus cantum romanum instituit, & Organo concordauit.* Mas Leon Segundo de nacion Siciliano, persona muy inteligente en la facultad de la Musica, cerca los años de nuestra Saluacion de 682, *reformò el canto de los Salmos y de los Hymnos*; es a saber, acomodò las intonaciones del modo que se cantan agora.'

[41] This quotation is copied out of Cerone, bk. ii, ch. 35, p. 257, who cites B. Platina, *De vitis pontificium Romanorum.*

Finalmente la santità di Papa Urbano VIII riformò con nuovo stile gl'inni; l'istesso Pontefice ha composto molti carmi in lingua Latina, li quali furono positi in Musica dal Sig: Gio: Girolamo Kapsperger, et dall'istesso mandati in luce,[42] le quali composizioni sono state cantate per le Chiese, et Oratori di Roma. Quanto poi sia delettabile il canto [B4ᵛ] nuovo, lo vediamo nell'Apocalisse quando san Gioanni dice d'aver veduto alcuni animali, che cantavano un cantico nuovo al Signore;[43] e molte altre auttorità potrei addurre a questo proposito, le quali per brevità tralascio.

Ora passiamo avanti: Dicami l'Oppositore dell'Armonia moderna, che maggior nuovità puole apportare all'Arte della musica, quanto che li stili variati, li quali rendono nuovo concento?[44] e per quanto si dilatano li fondamenti, che io possiedo nell'Arte Armonica, non vedo questa necessità, di ridurre la Musica sotto di un solo stile del Palestina (benchè per altro sia di tanta virtù, e stima l'Autore) poichè può essere ella ricchissima di tante varietà, con il campo dei stili diferenti, la quale si fa mirabile, quasi per tutto il mondo, e già si sa, ch'il fine della Musica è il dilettare, e sopra questo tutti gl'onorati Theorici, e Prattici si sono affaticati in dimostrare questa scuola della dilettazione; dunque se queste Cantilene moderne, in quanto [C1ʳ] allo stile dilettano più, che non fanno l'antiche, non mi pare, che si debbiano abbandonare, essendo che la moderna prattica ha il suo Tribunale, così ben fondato, che ella non teme d'essere oppressa da poco numero d'alcuni Oppositori, mentre che li sarà concesso di stendere le sue ragioni con il consentimento dall'udito principale istromento per giudicare la Musica, poichè da esso abbiamo raccolto il buono, et il perfetto nell'Arte Armonica come ho detto, poichè l'esperienza è Maestra di tutte le cose, e la ragione sola, Nullius est valoris, se non l'approva il senso, in questa nostra Musica.

E se bene questi Oppositori dicono, che nella Chiesa si canta nelle cantilene lo stile recitativo, dove non si scorge differenza alcuna dal Teatro, alla Casa di Dio; oltrechè si cantano Ariette, e Barzelette a guisa di serenate etc.[45] rispondo, che fa di bisogno intendere, che cosa sia stile recitativo; però si deve sapere, che lo stile recitativo, si distingue in due [C1ᵛ] modi; uno è semplice rappresentativo, il quale è quello, che si accompagna col gesto su Teatri; il secondo si chiama imbastardito; id est stile mischio, il quale va qualche volta rappresentando l'orazione con lo stile recitativo,

---

[42] *Poematia et carmina composita à Maffaeo Barberino olim S. R. E. Card. nunc autem Urbano Octavo P. O. M. musicus modis aptata à Jo. Hieronymo Kapsperger Nobili Germano. Volumen primum* (Rome: Soldi, 1624), ii (Rome: Masotti, 1633).

[43] Rev. 14: 1–3.

[44] This question was debated in the controversy between Claudio Monteverdi and Giovanni Maria Artusi. An anonymous writer who wrote to Artusi over the signature 'l'Ottuso Accademico' defended

Finally, His Holiness Pope Urban VIII reformed the hymns with a new style. The same pontiff composed many songs in the Latin language, and they were set to music by Sig. Gio. Girolamo Kapsperger, who had them printed.[42] These compositions were sung in the churches and oratories of Rome. How delightful is new song [B4ᵛ] we remark in the Apocalypse when St John says he saw some animals singing a new song to the Lord.[43] I could adduce many other authorities apropos of this, but for brevity's sake I pass over them.

Now let us move on. The opponent of modern harmony asks me: What increased novelty can the new varied styles, which produce a new sonority, bring to the art of music?[44] As long as the foundations of the harmonic art that I possess are broadening, I do not see the necessity of reducing music to a single style of Palestrina, however full of qualities and esteem he has as a composer. For the art of music could be rich with so many varieties of different styles composed almost throughout the world that it would be a marvel. We already know that the aim of music is to delight. All honoured theorists and practitioners have laboured to demonstrate this goal of delectation. Therefore, if these modern compositions, in so far as regards [C1ʳ] style, give greater pleasure than the ancient, it does not seem to me to be a case for abandoning them. The case for modern practice is so well founded that it has no fear of being resisted by a certain small number of opponents, so long as it is granted the opportunity of laying out its reasons with the corroboration of the hearing, the principal instrument for judging music. For with the ear we have gathered the good and perfect in the harmonic art, as I said, since experience in this music of ours is the mistress of all things. And reason alone *nullius est valoris* [is worthless] if the sense does not approve.

These opponents say that the recitative style is sung in compositions in church in such a way that you cannot tell the House of God from the theatre. Besides [they say], *ariette* and *barzelette* in the form of *serenate* are sung there.[45] To this I reply that we have to understand what recitative style is. In recitative style are distinguished two [C1ᵛ] manners. One is the simple representational type, which is the one that is accompanied by acting in the theatre. The second is called hybrid, that is, mixed style, which will go on for a while representing the text in the recitative style and

the new harmonies of Monteverdi as intended to produce new *concenti* and thereby to move people to new affections. Artusi replied that no new *concenti* or consonant harmonies, as he understood the word, were possible; therefore there could ensue no new expressive powers. See above, Essay 3, 'The Artusi–Monteverdi Controversy'.

[45] In his *Lettera per maggiore informazione* Scacchi quotes Siefert as saying that Italians know only how to compose 'commedie Barzelette, Ariette, Bergamasche, Passacagli, etc.' (Bologna, MS E-50, p. 252).

et in un subito varia con passaggi, e con altra modulazione; dove che in quello teatrale non si concede, perchè come ho detto, è semplice rappresentativo, ma quello che usano i moderni nella Chiesa alcuna volta, secondo l'occasione, e' il luogo, che lo ricerca, et anco l'orazione, è un modular variato a differenza del rappresentativo, cioè non è in tutto, e per tutto lo stile, che s'usa nei Teatri.

E questi tali fanno come li Diffidenti della Religione Cattolica, poichè pigliano un passo della scrittura, che fa per loro, et in quello solo si fondano, senza servirsi dell'altre infinite auttorità, che si ritrovano nei libri sacri per dichiarazione, o modificazione di quella. Dicono che nella Chiesa si canta lo stile recitativo, ma non considerano che [C2r] non è il vero rappresentativo; oltrechè non osservano la variazione della modulazione, il ponere delle consonanze, e dissonanze differentemente, il che non hanno fatto i nostri Antecessori, et anco le variazioni delle cantilene; et altre invenzioni, le quali sono ben' note a loro stessi.

Circa poi il cantare Ariette, etc. in Chiesa; mi dichino di grazia; gl'Inni non sono tante canzoni, o vero laudi, che si cantano a sua Divina Maestà, alla Gloriosa Vergine, et anco a' Santi? Se così è, perchè non sarà lecito al giudizioso Compositore Armonico, di trovare un'aria nuova, la quale si accommodi all'orazione? Dunque queste chiamansi Ariette, e Barzelette? Non vediamo, che nel canto fermo ogn'Inno ha la sua aria separata? E che altro sono li falsibordoni, se non arie imbastardite?

Per tanto si acquietono questi tali, poichè la ragione domina ogni cosa, Et qui bene distinguit, bene decernit; e benchè siano Arie, non sono però quelle che s'usano nelle serenate, et ancorchè fussero si[C2v]mili in altra maniera però, le tesse il giudizioso Compositore moderno nelle sue cantilene, e se bene molte volte il Musico moderno piglia per soggetto della sua Messa un'Aria commune, questa non è invenzione moderna, essendo che anco gl'Antichi l'hanno usate, come se ne vedono piene le stampe; et si deve anco considerare, come ho detto, che quell'Aria viene trattata dal moderno Compositore con variati contrapunti, et altre invenzioni, che in luogo di biasmo, debbiamo per ogni modo lodarle; oltrechè, sì come la Chiesa usa la prosa, et il verso, così ancora il giudizioso Compositore usa l'Arie per il verso, et il serio per la prosa.

Stupisco però di cotesti Signori, che dicono, che la Musica moderna si sia ridotta a tal termine, che sia necessario bandirla, come scrisse Girolamo santo in una Epist[ola] agli Efesi, dove si leggono queste parole. In Ecclesia theatrales moduli non audiuntur, et cantica.[46] Non posso finire di

---

[46] St Jerome, *Commentariorum in Epistolam ad Ephesios Libri tres*, bk. iii, ch. 5, 652D; ed. J. P. Migne, *Patrologiae cursus completus*, ser. 1, vol. xxvi (Paris: Migne, 1845), col. 528: 'Audiant haec

then, all of a sudden, will be varied with *passaggi* and other melodic effects. In the theatrical, on the other hand, these are not permitted, because, as I said, it is simple representational recitative. What the moderns sometimes use in church, according to the demands of the occasion, the place, and also the text, is a varied kind of vocal line as opposed to the representational recitative. Thus it is not altogether the same style as is used in theatres.

These [opponents] do the same as the diffidents of the Catholic religion. They pluck some passage out of the scriptures which is in their favour, founding everything on that without using any of the other countless authorities found in the sacred books by way of exposition or modification. They say that the recitative style is sung in church, but they do not consider that [C2ʳ] it is not the true representational style. Besides, they do not notice the variety of melody, the placement of consonances and dissonances, which is different from what our predecessors did, or the variations upon the chants and other devices that are well known to them.

As for singing *ariette* and so forth in the church, pray tell me, are not hymns so many songs or lauds that are sung to His Divine Majesty, to the Glorious Virgin, and to the saints? If this is so, why should it not be legitimate for a judicious composer to find a new air that will suit the text? Should such airs be called *ariette* and *barzelette*? In plainchant does not each hymn have its own tune? And what are the *falsibordoni* if not hybrid airs?

So these opponents can calm themselves down. Reason dominates everything: *Et qui bene distinguit, bene decernit.* Although they are airs, they are not those that are used in *serenate*, even if they [C2ᵛ] resemble them; the judicious modern composer weaves them into his compositions in a different way. If often the modern musician takes as a subject of a mass one of the common airs, this is not a modern invention, since the ancients used them, as may be seen in the prints which are full of them. Also to be considered, as I said, is that an air is treated by a modern composer with varied counterpoints and other inventions, which, far from being open to blame, should be in every way praised. Moreover, just as the Church employs prose and verse, so the judicious composer uses airs for the verse and the severe [style] for the prose.

I am amazed, however, at those gentlemen who say that modern music has reached such a pass that it is necessary to banish it, as St Jerome wrote in a letter to the Ephesians, where we read these words: *In Ecclesia theatrales moduli non audiuntur, et cantica.*[46] I cannot cease to wonder at the injury

---

adolescentuli: audiant hi quibus psallendi in ecclesia officium est, Deo non voce, sed corde cantandum: nec in tragoedorum modum gutture et fauce; dulci medicamine colliniendas, ut in ecclesia theatrales moduli audiantur et cantica, sed in timore, in opere, in scientia Scripturarum.'

maravigliarmi di tal aggravio, che [C3ʳ] si fa alla Musica moderna, essendo che, in ogni proposizione, si ricerca la sua distinzione; vero è, che Girolamo santo prohibisce la Musica theatrale, nella Chiesa santa, perchè li Greci in quel tempo cantavano semplicemente lo stile recitativo rappresentativo, e l'accompagnavano con gesti indecenti al virtuoso Cantore della Chiesa santa, che movevano a riso gli Uditori; cosa, che non si puole approvare al tempo presente, perchè se l'onorato Cantore canta in qualche Cantilena alcune pause di stile recitativo, non lo gestisce però, ne tam poco muove a riso, come presuppongono gli Oppositori di questa (dirrò) quasi Divina scuola moderna, poichè rapisce l'animo de gl'uomini, e si rende ammirabile tra l'altre Arti liberali.

E benchè questi tali dicono assai, son sicuro però, che quando si venisse alla prova, ogni lor proposizione restarebbe svanita; e sì come i discorsi dei Pittori non dilettano la vista, ma sì bene l'atto prattico in rappresentare una vaga Pittu[C3ᵛ]ra, così la Musica moderna non si pasce di discorsi solamente, essendo che si tratta dell'atto pratico, con attendere al canto per dilettazione dell'Udito, e non alla prosa, come hanno fatto tanti insigni Virtuosi di questa nobile Arte Armonica; e conforme è lecito ad ogni altra Arte liberale, d'avanzarsi con ritrovare nuove invenzioni, e stili, perchè non sarà concesso alla Musica di fare il medesimo essendo ella tutta immersa nella dilettazione; sanno pure, che sempre più è lodabile l'invenzione, che l'imitazione; dunque perchè cercare di privarla di quelle condizioni, delle quali può essere Capace, et ampliamente copiosa di tante varietà? E che sia il vero; ecco i frutti, e la ricchezza della Musica moderna, ritrovati con sudori da Maestri di tal Arte.

La Musica antica consiste in una prattica sola, e quasi in un medesimo stile, di adoperare le consonanze, e dissonanze; Ma la Moderna consiste in due pratiche, et in tre stili, cioè, stili di Chiesa, di Camera, e' di Teatro; [C4ʳ] le prattiche sono: la prima è, Ut Harmonia sit Domina orationis; la seconda, ut Oratio sit Domina harmoniae;[47] et ogn'uno di questi tre stili portano in se grandissime variazioni, novità, et invenzioni di non ordinaria considerazione.

E si deve, avvertire, che li moderni intendono in questa nuova Musica, in quanto allo stile, et al adoperare le consonanze, e dissonanze differente- mente dalla prima prattica, che sia quella, che versa intorno alla perfezzione della melodia, e per questo si chiama seconda prattica, a differenza della prima mossi da queste parole di Platone; Nonnè est Musica quae circa

---

[47] Here Scacchi paraphrases Giulio Cesare Monteverdi (Malipiero, *Claudio Monteverdi*, 74), who stated that his brother's intention was 'di far che l'oratione sia padrona del armonia e' non serva' (to

[C3ʳ] done to modern music. In every proposition a distinction is sought. It is true that St Jerome prohibits theatrical music in the church, because the Greeks of that time sang simply representational recitative style and accompanied it with gestures which would be indecent in a virtuous church singer and which roused the listeners to laughter. This is something that we should not approve of at the present time. When an honourable singer performs passages of recitative style in a [sacred] composition, he does not act it out; nor does he move anyone to laughter, as the opponents presuppose about this almost divine modern school. I shall call it so, because it ravishes the soul of men and renders itself admirable among the liberal arts.

Although these opponents have a great deal to say, I am sure that, should it come down to a proof, every proposition of theirs would dissolve. Just as the speeches of painters do not delight the eye, but rather their practical act of representing a beautiful picture, [C3ᵛ] so modern music is not nourished by discourses only, because it is a matter of a practical act. It must attend not to prose but to song for the delectation of the ear, such as many notable virtuosi of this noble harmonic art have produced. If every other liberal art is permitted to advance by discovering new inventions and styles, why should not the same be conceded to music, since it is entirely dedicated to giving pleasure? They well know that invention is always more praiseworthy than imitation. Then, why seek to deprive music of those conditions and of the abundant variety of which it is capable? And in witness of this, consider the fruits and the richness of modern music, discovered with sweat by the masters of this art.

Ancient music consists in one practice only and almost in one and the same style of employing consonances and dissonances. But the modern consists of two practices and three styles, that is, the church, chamber, and theatre styles. [C4ʳ] The practices are: the first, which is *ut Harmonia sit Domina Orationis*, and the second, which is *ut Oratio sit Domina Harmoniae*.[47] Each of these three styles contains very great variations, novelties, and inventions of extraordinary dimension.

It must be noted that the moderns understand such things as style and the use of consonances and dissonances in their music differently from the way they are understood in the first practice. The second practice revolves around the perfection of song, motivated by the words of Plato: 'Nonnè et

compose so that the text would be the mistress of the harmony and not the servant). This clarified Claudio Monteverdi's concept of *seconda pratica*, which he said superseded the *prima pratica*, whose rules 'pongono l'armonia signore del oratione' (75–6; make the harmony the lord of the text). Scacchi renders the phrases in Latin, because he had previously used them in his *Cribrum musicum*, 132–3.

perfectionem melodiae versatur?[48] poichè con quietanza della ragione, e dal senso, si difendono le composizioni moderne; con quietanza della ragione, perciò che appogierassi sopra le consonanze, e dissonanze della Matematica; sopra il comando dell'Orazione, Signora principale dell'Arte, nella perfezzione della Melodia considerata, come c'insegna Platone nel [C4ᵛ] terzo de R[e] P[ublica][49] e perciò è chiamata seconda pratica; con quietanza del senso, perchè il composto d'orazione commandante di Rithmo, et Armonia serviente a lei; serviente, perchè non vale il composto solo a perfezzionare la melodia, come dice Giulio Monteverde in una sua lettera,[50] il quale seguita, e dice: muovono le affezzioni dell'animo conforme descrive Platone: Sola enim Melodia non omnibus quotcunque distrahunt animum retrahens, contrahit in se ipsum.[51]

E non l'Armonia sola sia pure perfetta quando si vuole; e questa scuola l'intese molto bene Cipriano, Marenzio, Luscasco, il Fontanella, Monteverde, et altri celebri Virtuosi Armonici; e benchè l'Artusi abbia scritto dell'imperfezzione della Musica moderna,[52] bisogna sapere, che egli si fonda sopra della prima Pratica musicale, ut Harmonia sit Domina Orationis, come ho detto; ma li moderni si fondano sopra la seconda pratica, ut Oratio sit Domina harmoniae.

Tal che essendo differente [D1ʳ] nell'opinione non è maraviglia, se anco li scritti sono differenti; però procurino pure li Signori Virtuosi Armonici con il campo di questa seconda pratica musicale di superare, et avanzare d'invenzioni gli nostri Antichi, et anco gl'effetti, che faceva la primiera Musica, come la descrive Aulogelio nelle notte Attiche;[53] che spero che gl'Oppositori di essa un' giorno s'avvedranno della loro sinistra opinione, et in luogo di biasmarla, cercaranno d'intenderla, con esser studiosi seguaci di questo sì leggiadro stile: e se disinganino pure con dire, che li studi buoni della Musica si perdono con questo stile moderno, perchè non si può essercitar bene la moderna Musica senza qualche capacità delle vere Regole Antiche; oltrechè bisogna considerare, che sono molti i geni dei studiosi di quest'Arte Armonica, cioè chi attende ai studi Antichi, altri a seguitar il Dottissimo Palestina, et altri a differenti stili; sicchè, sè ogn'uno dovesse attendere ad un' solo stile, e ad una [D1ᵛ] sola scuola, la Musica si riddurebbe povera, e senza varietà di stili; oltrechè sarebbe mendica d'invenzioni, con discapito della dilettazione, fine principale dell'Arte della Musica, et anco restarebbe destrutta quella gran dottrina di Platone, della

---

[48] *Gorgias*, 449D: 'Does not music also turn on the perfection of melody?' Scacchi cites the Latin translation of Marsilio Ficino, but incorrectly: 'Nonnè est Musica, quae circa perfectionem melodiae versatur.' The same place was cited by Giulio Cesare Monteverdi (Malipiero, *Claudio Monteverdi*, 79).

[49] *Republic*, 398D.

Musica quae circa melodiae perfectionem [versatur]?'[48] For modern compositions are supported by the assent jointly of the reason and the senses. [I say] with the assent of the reason, because [this music] depends upon the consonances and dissonances [as defined by] mathematics and upon the command of the text, principal mistress of the art. This art aspires to the perfection of song, as Plato teaches us in [C4ᵛ] the third [book] of the *Republic*.[49] With the consent of the senses, because the composite of the commanding text, rhythm, and harmony are subservient to them. I say subservient, because this composite is not enough for the perfection of song, as Giulio Monteverdi says in a letter of his.[50] As he goes on to say, these [components] move the affections of the soul, in keeping with Plato's description: 'Sola enim Melodia non omnibus quotcunque distrahunt animum retrahens, contrahit in se ipsum.'[51]

Harmony alone is also not sufficient, however perfect it may be. And this principle was well understood by Cipriano, Marenzio, Luzzasco, Fontanella, Monteverdi, and other celebrated harmonic virtuosi. Although Artusi wrote concerning the imperfection of modern music,[52] it is necessary to consider that he founds his beliefs on the first practice, *ut Harmonia sit Domina Orationis*, as I said. But the moderns build on the second practice, *ut Oratio sit Domina harmoniae*.

That they should differ [D1ʳ] in their opinions is not anything to marvel at, since their writings are also different. However, let the harmonic gentlemen-virtuosi, with the range of this second musical practice, attempt to surpass and advance beyond the inventions of our ancients, and even to surpass the effects that the first music achieved, as it is described by Aulus Gellius in the *Attic Nights*.[53] I hope the opponents of modern music will one day realize the inadequacy of their opinion and instead of censuring this music try to understand it by becoming studious followers of its gracious style. When they delude themselves by saying that the good musical studies are lost on the modern style, [let them remember] that modern music cannot be put into practice without some ability in the old rules. Besides, it is necessary to consider that there are many bright spirits among the scholars of harmonic art who attend to the ancient studies, and others who follow the very learned Palestrina, and still others who follow other styles. If everyone were compelled to pursue the same style and [D1ᵛ] one school, music would be reduced to poverty and left without variety of

[50] Malipiero, *Claudio Monteverdi*, 81.

[51] Marsilio Ficino, *Compendium in Timaeum*, xxx. The statement is not Plato's but Ficino's.

[52] Giovanni Maria Artusi, *L'Artusi, overo delle imperfettioni della moderna musica* (Venice, 1600).

[53] i. 11. 1–4; iv. 13; xvi. 19.

quale si è servito anco un'Oppositore di questo stile moderno, per difendere vn' suo Canone composto sopra le vocali, Pater et Filius etc.,[54] benchè abbia preteso d'intendere detta scuola, ma finalmente s'è ingannato, come lo dimostrano le mie considerazioni,[55] fra le quali, una delle principali, che faccio contro questi Oppositori, è, che alcuni vogliono fare, dirò la scimia dei moderni, con servirsi dell'auttorità di Platone, e quando si viene all'atto pratico, quello, che pretendono d'intendere, non l'intendono; e quel poco, che in effetto intendono, non lo vogliono intendere, perchè non fabricano le loro Cantilene con la quietanza del senso.

[D2ʳ] Ora per il presente discorso publico a tutti gl'Oppositori della Musica moderna, come dichiaro oltre le brevi ragioni della presente scrittura di provare con la ragione, e con il senso assieme.

1. Che questo stile moderno diletta più, et è meglio, che non è l'antico.

2. Che questa seconda pratica non può destruggere la prima, nè meno pretende di far ciò, perchè il suo fine è differente da essa, che però si nomina seconda pratica, e non altrimente Teorica.[56]

3. Che il benefizio di questa moderna pratica, l'Arte Armonica s'è grandemente arrichita.

4. Che abandonandosi questo stile moderno, si verebbe a distruggere una gran parte della Musica, et anco si redurebbe nella sua primiera povertà.

5. Che l'Arte del modulare ritrovato da' moderni, ha superato quello de' nostri primi Maestri.

[D2ᵛ] 6. Che li studi dei Canoni, et altre semili [*sic*] Cantilene, le quali attendano solamente all'invenzione senza aver riguardo all'Armonia, rendono per il più confusione ai Studiosi della Musica, et anco si viene a distruggere il fine d'essa, per secondare l'obbligo nel quale è fondata la Cantilena.

7. Come ad un'Oppositore di questo stile moderno voglio provare, che in quel suo libro intitolato Vaghe, et Arteficiose cantilene, stampate

---

[54] In his broadside, *Canoni musicali* (Rome: L. Grignani, 1645), Romano Micheli published a canon on the words 'Pater, et Filius, et Spiritus Sanctus, et hi tres unum sunt'. It is set for three choruses, each of three voices, to symbolize the Trinity. When a 'musico peritissimo' of Rome suggested that Micheli could add a fourth part, Micheli answered in his *Virtuosa risposta* (Rome: L. Grignani, 1645), fo. 1ʳ, that according to the doctrine of Plato the harmony should follow the text and not the contrary. Therefore, a judicious composer would make the number of parts conform to the sense of the words. To show that he could add a fourth part Micheli appended a 'Canon for four voices composed on the vowels by Romano Micheli, in which there is no imitation or any curiosity in honour of those sacred words because it is sung in four parts'. He again referred to his canon 'Pater, et Filius' in *Avviso inviato . . . insieme col foglio reale del Canone musicale Fons Signatus* (Rome: L. Grignani, 1650), where he says, 'I wished my canon to represent the Holy Trinity under obscure symbols and hieroglyphics, so that it would not be understood except by intelligent musicians' (sigs. A2ᵛ–A3ʳ).

styles. Besides, it would become beggarly in inventions to the damage of its ability to please, which is the principal end of the art of music.

It would result also in the destruction of that great doctrine of Plato, which an opponent of this modern style has used to defend a canon of his composed on the vowels of *Pater et Filius*, etc.[54] Although he has pretended to understand this school, in the end he has deceived himself, as my considerations have shown him.[55] One of my main points against these opponents is that certain composers want to ape the moderns by leaning upon the authority of Plato, but when they come to the practical act, they [show they] do not understand what they pretend to understand. The little that they do in effect understand, they do not want to understand, because they do not fashion their vocal compositions with the assent of the senses.

[D2^r] Now with the present discourse I make public to all opponents of modern music my intention to prove, with both the reason and the senses, beyond the brief arguments given in this present essay, the following [points]:

1. That this modern style is more pleasing and better than the ancient.

2. That this second practice cannot destroy the first; nor does it claim to do so, because its end is different, and therefore it is called the second practice and not [the second] theory.[56]

3. That through the benefits of this modern practice harmonic art has been greatly enriched.

4. That abandoning this modern style would result in the destruction of a large part of music and would reduce it to its primitive poverty.

5. That the art of melody discovered by the moderns has surpassed that of our first masters.

[D2^v] 6. That the study of canons and similar pieces which aim only at invention, without regard for harmony, yields, at best, confusion in students of music. Besides, in order to observe the condition [*obbligo*] on which a piece is based, one is compelled to negate the end of music.

7. I wish to prove to an opponent of this modern style that in his book

[55] This essay is lost, but Scacchi referred to it previously in his letter to Christoph Werner as 'Consideratione canonum R. D. Romani Michaelis Romani' (Katz, *Die musikalischen Stilbegriffe*, 85). The letter to Werner is of around 1648. The 'Consideratione' can be dated through a reference by Micheli in *Avviso inviato* (1650), in which he recalls that 'a musician in the year 1647 without cause had printed in *partibus* [privately] a pamphlet and had it distributed in Rome and various other kingdoms. In it he seeks to charge that I am not the inventor of the method of composing musical canons on the vowels of various words but that this is an ancient invention and used by many . . .' (A1^v).

[56] This statement, a commentary upon Giulio Cesare Monteverdi (Malipiero, *Claudio Monteverdi*, 78), implies that while theory remains always the same, practices change. This conception is based on the dichotomy between *musica theorica* and *musica practica* traditional in pre-Baroque music theory. See above, Essay 3, 'The Artusi–Monteverdi Controversy'.

in Venezia,[57] non v'è alcuna vaghezza rispetto le Cantilene moderne; se-condariamente, che in luogo d'artificio, si ritrova qualche disordine contro la formazione del Tono, materia principale d'intendere, per quelli par-ticolarmente che vogliono riformare gl'altri, et anco vogliono usurpare l'invenzioni altrui, cosa in vero, che non pretendono di fare li moderni.

8. Et per conclusione di questa mia breve scrittura, starò aspettando le ragioni, che [D3ʳ] produranno gl'Oppositori contro il presente discorso, e della Musica moderna per potere mediante l'aiuto di sua Divina Maestà, provargli con la ragione, e col senso assieme, quanto s'ingannano nella loro opinione; e mentre che non daranno alla luce i loro fondamenti, per abbattere quello, che brevemente s'è detto per diffesa di questa seconda pratica Musicale, con la ragione appoggiata al senso, debba con ogni fondamento restare nel suo essere la Musica presente, con essere abbracciata, agumentata, e' seguitata da nobili intelletti dei virtuosi moderni, per ridurla, ad una somma perfezzione. Dichiarandomi, che di tutto quello, ho detto in queste carte, m'intendo di distinguere ogni cosa, quando farà il bisogno: protestandomi però, che non intendo, che si debba, abbandonare la Musica antica, per abbraciare la nuova; ma che restino in piedi et agumentate ambedue, cioè l'antica per [D3ᵛ] Messe, Inni, et altre semili {*sic*} Cantilene da Cappella; la moderna per concerti, et per il metro volgare, et altre simili Cantilene; riservandomi in un'altra occasione di dimostrare ogni cosa distintamente per far capace, come ho detto, chi biasima la Musica moderna.[58]

Fine

---

[57] Romano Micheli, *Musica vaga et artificiosa* (Venice: G. Vincenti, 1615).
[58] Once again Scacchi refers to a more extended but probably never completed treatise.

entitled *Vaghe, & arteficiose cantilene*, printed in Venice,[57] there is no beauty [*vaghezza*] that can compare to modern pieces. Secondly, that instead of artfulness [*artificio*] we find a disorder contrary to the nature of the mode, a principal consideration, particularly for those who wish to reform others and to usurp the inventions of others—something, indeed, that the moderns do not pretend to do.

8. In concluding this brief essay, I shall await the arguments that [D3ʳ] opponents will produce against this present discourse and against modern music, so that with the help of His Divine Majesty I can prove by reason and sensation together how much they deceive themselves in their opinion. Until they reveal their grounds in reason and sensation for attacking what I briefly have adduced in defence of this second musical practice, the present music has every reason to continue to exist. It should be embraced, augmented, and pursued by noble intellects and modern virtuosi, so that it may be led to a summit of perfection. I declare that I intend to clarify everything I have said in these pages when the need arises. I want to make plain, however, that I do not intend that ancient music should be abandoned to embrace the new. Rather, let the two both stand and be augmented, namely, the ancient for [D3ᵛ] masses, hymns, and similar pieces *a cappella,* the modern for concerti and vernacular poetry, and similar pieces. I shall reserve for another time the task of demonstrating everything distinctly to give a chance, as I said, to those who disparage modern music.[58]

The End.

APPENDIX

The following three compositions, with the commentary that accompanies them, are drawn from Scacchi's *Cribrum musicum*, 169–84, 245–8. They are included here to illustrate some of the categories of secular style discussed in the *Breve discorso*.

Madrigalia a 4 Voc.

Madrigalia sequentia consulto sine nimia alacritate, que alias hodie Italis in eiusmodi cantionum generibus imprimis approbatur, componere volui, siquidem satis scio, stylum illum nimis alacrem atque affectatum ab omnibus aeque comprehendi non posse. Quod si quoque talia a me desideras, habebis, simul ac mihi otium ad haec absolvenda datur, typis impressa duo volumina, unum continens Motetas 5. Voc. alterum Madrigalia 4. Voc. Interim haec sufficiant.

Madrigals for Four Voices

I wished to compose the following madrigals purposely without the excessive liveliness which sometimes is approved in this kind of songs and printed, since I well know that this too lively and affected style cannot be equally understood by everyone. If you wish to have such songs from me, you will have them as soon as I have time to complete and have printed two volumes, one containing motets for five voices, the other madrigals for four voices. Meanwhile let these suffice.

See Examples 4.1 and 4.2.

[p. 184] Dictum est supra, in stylo hoc recentiori orationem esse dominam, et non ancillam, ipsius harmoniae, recentiorumque compositiones considerandas esse non quoad verba tantum, set et cumprimis quoad ipsum loquendi modum, qui iuxta diversas animi affectiones subinde variatur; (haec enim sunt quasi concatenata, et in oratione continentur:) nam in animi affectionibus (secundum maius et minus) ad exprimendum verborum sensum et loquendi modum tam consonantias quam dissonantias modo differente a stylo antiquo coordinare solent. Id ipsum et ego secutus, de industria extra chordas Toni principium in alto constitui. Solent quoque colligationem notularum, non sine

It was stated above that in this recent style the text is the mistress and not the servant of the harmony and that the compositions of the moderns should be considered not so much with respect to the words as particularly the very manner of speaking, which changes frequently in the diverse affections of the soul (these are almost as if in a chain, and they are contained in the text). For in the affections of the soul they [modern composers] are accustomed to arrange the consonances and dissonances differently (more or less) from the ancient style to express the meaning of words and the manner of speaking. I, too, following this method, constituted the beginning of the alto [of *Ah dolente partita*] outside

gratia, ob certas causas facere peculiari modo, qui apud antiquiores non fuit in usu.

the steps of the mode. They are also accustomed to making runs of notes in a particular way not used by the ancients that is not without grace for certain purposes.

See Example 4.3.

[p. 248] Stylus iste, quem recitativum vocant, et qui quaedam peculiaris est species musices, ad hoc inventus est, ut quis harmonice loqui possit: seu, est quaedam locutio harmonica: vel quo quis canendo loquitur et loquendo canit. Modum autem cantandi negligere videtur, campum sibi liberum constituens divagari per nudas falsas chordas, quae ad exprimendum quemlibet affectum sunt valde idoneae. Si tempus talis inventionis spectemus, puto non excedere 42. annorum spatia, ut ex impressis operibus colligere fas est, et praesertim ex Euridice Julii Caccini Romani. Marcus a Galiano in sua Daphne in epistola ad Lectorem asserit Iacobum Perum in musicis suo tempore satis celebrem fuisse, qui primo cantando recitaret. Alii vero existimant, huiusmodi stylum apud priscos Graecos originem duxisse, quo in suis tragaediis et fabulis ipsi usi sunt: quod si ampliorem notitiam de hiis habere cupis, legas supra citatos authores.

This style, which is called recitative and is a rather special species of music, was invented so that one could speak melodically [*harmonicè*]. It is a kind of melodic speech [*locutio harmonica*], through which one speaks singing and sings speaking. It is a way of singing carelessly, as it were, allowing oneself the liberty of wandering through naked dissonances which are particularly appropriate for expressing any affection. If we look into the time of its invention, I believe that it was not before forty-two years ago, as may be gathered from printed works, notably the *Euridice* of Giulio Caccini Romano. Marco da Gagliano, in his letter to the reader in *Dafne*, claims that Jacopo Peri was very celebrated in the music of his time and was the first to recite singing. Others, however, believe the origins of this sort of style can be traced to the ancient Greeks, who used it in their tragedies and fables [*fabulis*]. If you desire fuller information concerning this, read the authors cited above.

In demonstrando modum componendi diversas cantilenas, ut sunt octavae (quod est certum genus poematis) coloratae, ariettae, madrigalia, sonetti, lamentationes, et aliae huiusmodi, quae diversimode et considerantur et cantantur, cum variatis accentibus, exclamationibus, gutturis repercussionibus, trillis, gruppis, (uti loquuntur) reiteratis respirationibus, vocis inflexionibus obliquis, extensis, vim reassumentibus, fractis, et aliis pluribus modis, quibus cantus redditur non datur certa et determinata regula,

No certain and determinate rule is given to demonstrate the ways of composing various songs, such as *ottave* (which is a category of poem), *colorate*, *ariette*, madrigals, sonnets, lamentations, and the like, which are considered and sung differently, with various accents, exclamations, repercussions in the throat, trills, *groppi* (as they are called), with repeated respirations, sliding and protracted inflections of the voice, increasing its force, breaking the voice, and many other manners in which a song is

quoniam haec omnia admirabili modo quodam elegantissimus, suavissimus, et maxime patheticus, citius, et commodius viva voce quam ex scriptura cognoscuntur ac discuntur, et proinde nolui fuse de illis agere.

performed. For all of these, which add in a wonderful way something very elegant, very smooth, and exceedingly moving, are known and learned more quickly and conveniently *viva voce* than through writing. So I did not want to deal with them at length.

prei non sa - prei se più bel - la o più ca - no - -

Non sa - prei non sa - prei se più bel - la o più ca -

Non sa - prei non sa - prei se più bel - la o più ca -

ra. Per l'o - rec - chie n'al - let -

no - ra. Per l'o - rec - chie n'al - let - ta

no - ra. Per l'o - rec - chie n'al - let - ta E

Per l'o - rec - chie n'al - let - ta E per

ta n'al - let - ta per l'o - rec - chie n'al - let -

Per l'o - rec - chie n'al - let - ta

per gli oc - chi in - a - mo - ra.

gli oc - chi in - a - mo - ra. Per l'o - rec - chie n'al - let -

126

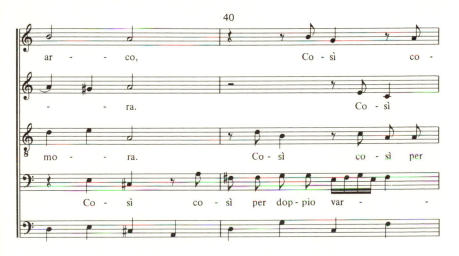

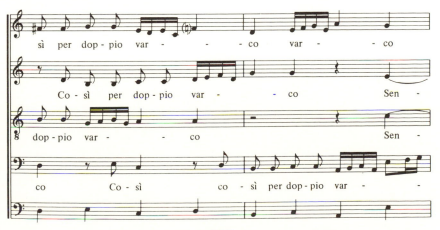

Sen - za o - pra fa - - ce od ar - co,

- za o - pra fa - - ce od ar - co, A la

- za o - pra fa - ce od ar - - co, A la

- co Sen - za o - pra fa - ce od ar - co,

roc - - ca del co - - re

roc - - ca del co - - re

S'a - pre la stra-da in - si - di -

A la roc - - - ca del

A la roc - - - ca del

o - so A-mo - - re. S'a - pre la stra-da in - si - di - o - so A -

A la roc - - - - ca
mo - - re. A la roc -
mo - re. S'a - pre la stra - da in - si - di - o - so A - mo - - re.
mo - - re. S'a - pre la stra - da in - si - di -

del co - re S'a - pre la stra - da in - si - di -
ca del co - re S'a - pre la stra - da in - si - di -
A la roc - - - -
o - so A - mo - - re.

o - so A - mo - - re.
o - so A - mo - - re.
ca del co - - re S'a - pre la
S'a - pre la stra - da in - si - di -

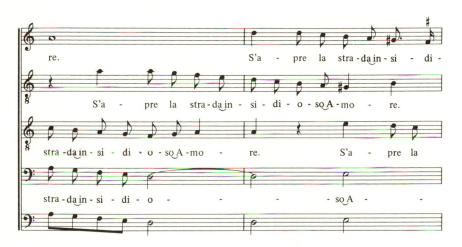

Ex. 4.2. Scacchi, *Cribrum musicum*, 177–84 (text by G. B. Guarini)

ne - vi, ohi - mè, le vi - ve ro - se

ohi - mè, le vi - ve ro - se che

15

Ei ru - bi - ne e l'o - stro e l'o - ro

per - le e l'o - stro e l'o - ro

Do - ve, do - ve son hor do - ve son

Do - ve, do - ve son hor do - ve son

hor ch'io pur di lo - ro Vo per que - ste cer -

hor ch'io pur di lo - ro Vo per que - ste cer -

20

can - do om - bre do - glio - - - se?

can - do om - bre do - glio - - - se?

ci - de e sol - ve. Spa - ri - to è'l mio bel

ci - de e sol - ve. Spa - ri - to è'l mio bel

40

sol ap - pe - na ap - par - so E la bel - tà ce -

sol ap - pe - na ap - par - so

le - ste e fu - mo e pol - ve.

Spa - ri - to è'l mio bel sol ap - pe - na ap -

Spa - ri - to è'l mio bel so - le spa - ri - to è'l mio bel

par - so Spa - ri - to è'l mio bel so - le spa - ri - to è'l mio bel

45

so - le ap - pe - na ap - par - so Spa - ri - to è'l mio bel - so - le ap - pe - na ap -

so - le ap - pe - na ap - par - so E la bel - tà ce -

par - so   Spa - ri - to è 'l mio bel so - le Spa -

le -   ste e fu - mo e pol -   ve.   Spa -

50

ri - to è 'l mio bel sol è 'l mio bel sol ap - pe - na ap - par - so

ri - to è 'l mio bel sol è 'l mio bel sol ap - pe - na ap - par - so

E la bel - tà   ce - le - ste, e la bel -

E la bel - tà   ce - le - ste, e la bel -

tà   ce - le -   -   -   -   -

tà   ce - le -   -   -   -   -

55

- ste e fu - mo e pol -   ve.

- ste e fu - mo e pol -   ve.

The Musica *of Erasmus of Höritz*

This article was first published in 1966 in *Aspects of Medieval and Renaissance Music: A Birthday Offering to Gustave Reese*, edited by Jan LaRue (New York: Norton, 1966), 628–48.

I first came across the treatise that is the subject of this essay in the spring of 1961 while leafing quite systematically through the unordered handwritten catalogue (No. 336) of the Regina collection of the Biblioteca Apostolica Vaticana. The name of the author, given in the catalogue as Erasmus Horicius Germanus,[1] was at that time unfamiliar to me. But once I looked at the manuscript, I was convinced that it was an important work that had been unjustly ignored by historians of music theory. Coincidentally, I was then preparing the article on Bartolomé Ramos de Pareja for *Die Musik in Geschichte und Gegenwart* (x (1962), cols. 1909–12) and had requested a film of the treatise that had been attributed to Ramos in Berlin, Deutsche Staatsbibliothek, MS Mus. theor. 1310. As soon as I saw the film, I recognized in the Berlin manuscript the hand, style, and thought of Erasmus of Höritz's treatise in the Vatican Library. I was able in the 'Ramos' article to rectify the misattribution. The task of coming to terms with the contents of the Vatican treatise and comparing it with the Berlin manuscript and the treatise of Erasmus published by Theodor Kroyer would have to wait for another moment. An invitation to contribute to the *Birthday Offering* to Gustave Reese offered me an opportunity.

Ironically, the work of Erasmus of Höritz that had previously received the most attention was this very treatise in Berlin, because it was attributed to Ramos. It was cited by Hugo Riemann and Johannes Wolf (see below nn. 14–15), though mostly to cast doubt on Ramos's authorship. But next to the Vatican treatise, it is an imperfect and less comprehensive work. For this reason my essay deals with the Vatican treatise.

Since the publication of my article, relatively little additional notice has been taken of Erasmus of Höritz. In my *Humanism in Italian Renaissance Musical Thought* (283–4), I dealt briefly with its place in the history of the revival of the Greek tonoi and presented in facsimile his table of the Greek tonoi from the Vatican manuscript, fo. 48^{r-v}. Mark Lindley, in his chapter 'Stimmung und Temperatur', for volume 6 of the Geschichte der Musiktheorie, *Hören, Messen und Rechnen in der frühen Neuzeit* (Darmstadt: Wissenschaftliche Buchgesellschaft, 1987), 120–1,

---

[1] The catalogue entry reads: 'Erasmi Horicij Germani de Musica libri viii. ad N. [*sic*] Grimanum Cardinalem S. Marci. Cod. ex pap. fol. C.S. 114.'

commented briefly on the 'equal' or geometric division of the $9:8$ whole tone and gave the upper half of the diagram of it from *Musica*, fo. 66ᵛ (see below, Pl. 5.2). By omitting the numerical calculations in the lower part of the diagram, Lindley gives the impression that Erasmus was making this division by geometry. Although a footnote (121 n. 24) corrects this impression, it is misleading, because it simplifies Erasmus's process as one of multiplying the string-lengths of the two pitches between which a mean is sought and then taking the square root of the product to get the geometric mean. The circuitous process by which Erasmus divides the tone into two minor semitones on either side of a Pythagorean comma cannot be dismissed so easily, because, unlike the simple process of taking the square root of the product of the two string-lengths, Erasmus is searching for a more satisfactory method by arriving at a very much expanded value for $9:8$.

Igor Popovic, in an unpublished paper, has justified Erasmus's use of large-number ratios, such as the eleven-digit terms in which the $9:8$ ratio is expressed for the purpose of finding the ratio that is its square root.[2] Popovic compares this expansion of a ratio to the use of a large number of decimal places in modern computation to achieve finer precision. The large-number ratio that Erasmus arrives at is equivalent to $9:8$, but the ratio that is the square root of this proportion in its simplest terms has a denominator that is a function of the square root of two, consequently not a whole number but an approximation. The large number, like a generous number of decimal places, permits a sharper approximation, taking some of the curse off the irrational number's impreciseness.

MARIN MERSENNE closed a brief review of current books on music in 1644 with this note about an obscure author:[3]

To these I add Erasmus Horicius Germanus, who offered a musical book to Cardinal Grimani which, if it is not yet published, would merit seeing the light. Although he follows the opinion of Boethius and others who still did not use the major and minor semitones, and he knows only the major tones, nevertheless he is worthy of being read. Certainly admirable is what he communicates concerning the proportions in the Third Book.

Since Mersenne saw only a recently penned copy, he would probably have been surprised to know that the treatise dated from the first decade of the sixteenth century. Its existence had been called to his attention by Nicolas-Claude Peiresc of Aix. Peiresc procured in 1635 a copy of what he believed was the original manuscript owned by Jacques Golius, an orientalist and professor at the University of Leiden. The copy was intended for

---

[2] Igor Popovic, 'The *Musica Erasmi Horitii Germani*: Mathematics and Speculative Theory of Music in the Renaissance: A Case Study', unpublished directed studies paper, Yale University, 1988.

[3] Marin Mersenne, *Cogitata physico-mathematica, in quibus tam naturae quam artis effectus admirandi certissimis demonstrationibus explicantur* (Paris: Sumptibus A. Bertier, 1644), *Harmoniae liber iv*, 367: 'His autem addo Erasmum Horicium Germanum, qui Musicum opus Grimanno Cardinali nuncupauit, cuius liber, si nondum sit editus, meretur lucem: quamquam enim Boetii, & aliorum mentem sequatur, qui nondum tonis maioribus & minoribus, nostrisque semitoniis maioribus & minoribus vtebantur, & solos tonos maiores agnoscat, lectu tamen dignus est, quippe praeclara tradit de proportionibus libro 3. propositionibus 27.'

Giovanni Battista Doni of Rome, who was holding up the printing of his *Compendio del trattato de' generi e de' modi della musica* (Rome, 1635) pending its arrival.[4] Peiresc, knowing Mersenne's deep interest in music theory, invited Mersenne to scan the treatise as it passed through Paris on the way from Leiden to Aix in December of that year, cautioning him, however, not to keep it or mention it in his 'grand ouvraige' (*Harmonie universelle*, 1636–7), lest Doni be offended.[5] As soon as he saw it, Mersenne advised Peiresc to have another copy drafted so that it might be available for more leisurely study. Mersenne eventually received such a copy and kept it for at least several years. He thought highly enough of the Erasmus treatise to recommend its reading to Johann Albert Ban, though he insisted it contained 'nothing or little that is new'.[6] Peiresc also recommended the volume to Pierre Gassendi, saying he did not wish to dispatch the copy made for Mersenne until Gassendi had had a chance to see it.[7]

In contrast to the eager curiosity and urgent correspondence it awakened in 1635 and 1636, the *Musica* of Erasmus of Höritz has been shrouded in virtual silence since that time. Of the lexicographers, only Johann Walther[8] recognized Erasmus. He owed his knowledge of him to a citation in Gerhard Johann Vossius's *De quatuor artibus popularibus*[9] of the praise bestowed on the book by Mersenne.

The *Musica* of Erasmus of Höritz exists in an undated manuscript of 114 folios, the very copy presented to Cardinal Domenico Grimani, in the Vatican Library, Regina collection, Latinus 1245.[10] Markings on the front

---

[4] Letter from Peiresc in Aix to Monsieur de Fontenay Bouchard at the court of Cardinal Barberini in Rome, 31 Oct. 1635, in *Lettres de Peiresc*, ed. Phillippe Tamizey de Larroque, iv (Paris: Imprimerie nationale, 1893), 148–9. Cf. also Mersenne, *Correspondance*, ed. Cornélis de Waard, v (Paris: Éditions du CNRS, 1959), 397.

[5] Peiresc in Aix to Mersenne, 4 Nov. 1635, ibid. v. 458. Cf. also v. 397, 461, 465, 499, 506, 547; vi (1960), 7, 69, 217.

[6] Mersenne in Paris to André Rivet in Leiden, 23 Jan. 1638, ibid. vii (1962), 34.

[7] Peiresc in Aix to Gassendi in Digne, 9 Jan. 1636, ibid. vi. 7.

[8] *Musicalisches Lexicon* (Leipzig: W. Deer, 1732); facs. edn. Richard Schaal (Kassel: Bärenreiter, 1953), 318.

[9] Vossius, *De quatuor artibus popularibus* (Amsterdam: J. Blaev, 1650), ch. 22, 'De musicis partibus, generibus; ac praecipuis ejus, quos habemus, scriptoribus', 97.

[10] The codex contains 114 paper folios measuring 19.3 by 27.3 cm. The writing begins on fo. 1ᵛ in red ink with the dedication: 'Reuerendissimo germanie Principi Dominico grimanno Cardinali S. Marci Ac patriarche Aquileijensi/ Erasmus Horicius germanus Philosophie et medicine doctor patrono suo humillime se Commendat.' The undated letter of dedication follows and continues through fo. 2ʳ. Fo. 2ᵛ is blank, and on fo. 3ʳ appears the title in green ink: 'Musica Erasmi Horicij Germani pro Rᵐᵒ Cardinali Dominico Grimanno Tituli. S. Marci Ac patriarche Aquilejensij in Germanie principe.' Then a subtitle begins in red ink, describing the general contents: 'Librum hunc nostrum musice in octo partiales libellos propter Huiusmodi Claritatem diuidere . . .'. A preamble follows on fo. 3ᵛ and 4ʳ, where book i begins. The treatise ends on fo. 114ʳ with these words: 'et non erit Labor aliquis si priores numeros Calculatos bene inspexeris. et Cum hijs finem huic Libro nostro dabimus.' Throughout the manuscript the scribe has employed initial capital letters quite indiscriminately, and punctuation is

flyleaf and on the first folios reveal a partial pedigree of the book's owners. On fo. 1^v appears 'liber D. Grimani Car^{lis} S. Marci'. The first front flyleaf is marked: 'Ex libris M. Meibomius', and at the bottom of fo. 2^r is written 'ex Biblioth^a Regia Rom:', that is, the library of Queen Christine of Sweden. This manuscript may also be the 'original' that served as the basis for the copy made for Doni, since Jacques Golius, like Marcus Meibom, lived in Holland. The first owner, Cardinal Grimani, collector of many precious Greek and Latin manuscripts, inscriptions, and other antiquities, died in Rome in 1523. Many of his books went to the Library of Sant'Antonio di Castello in Venice, which he founded. This library later burned, and the salvaged books were dispersed. Our manuscript must have found its way to Holland, where it was eventually acquired by Meibom, possibly from Golius. Meibom, who often had to dispose of his books to raise money, must have sold it to the library of Queen Christine. He served her for a while, and it was to her that he dedicated his *Antiquae musicae auctores septem* (Amsterdam, 1652).[11] On the Queen's death in 1689, her library was inherited by her friend Cardinal Decio Azzolini, who himself died later that year. Azzolini's nephew, elected Pope Alexander VIII the same year, bought the Queen's codices with his own funds and presented them to the Vatican Library.

Erasmus of Höritz has not been entirely unknown, thanks to Theodor Kroyer, who published in 1918 a brief manuscript treatise of thirty-seven folios entitled *Musica speculativa per magistrum Erasmum Heritium lecta. 1498* from a codex in Munich.[12] Its contents parallel the Vatican treatise at many

erratic, consisting of occasional periods, colons, and virgules. Otherwise the manuscript is clearly written in a humanist secretarial hand and contains very few errors in spite of the profusion of diagrams and numerical calculations.

The Vatican MS is not the only surviving copy of the *Musica* of Erasmus. One copy, as we have seen, was made in 1635 from an 'original', perhaps the Vatican MS, then owned by Jacques Golius of Leiden. Peiresc had this copy made through the courtesy of Claude Saumaise of Leiden for G. B. Doni, and it was sent to Doni in December 1635 at the Barberini palace in Rome. Before it was dispatched, a copy of this copy was made by Peiresc's scribe Bouis for Mersenne's use. Margaret Murata has identified the copy of the Erasmus treatise made for Doni as Biblioteca Apostolica Vatticana, MS Barberini latinus 351 (letter to me of 23 Jan. 1978). Later, in June 1636, Saumaise requested a copy of the treatise, and Peiresc asked Jacques Dupuy to borrow Mersenne's copy to have it recopied. Thus there were surely two copies, and perhaps a third made between 1635 and 1636.

I am indebted to four students of my pro-Seminar at Yale University in the spring of 1964 who together transcribed and translated about one-fourth of the *Musica*: John G. Brawley, Jr., Raymond Erickson, Martha Maas, and Barbara M. Tabak. Without their help I could not have finished this article in time for inclusion in the Reese Festschrift.

[11] Meibom made no mention of Erasmus of Höritz in his book. By coincidence Isaac Vossius, son of Gerhard, was the custodian of the library of the Queen when Gerhard Vossius published his book mentioning Erasmus: A. Wilmart, *Codices reginenses latini*, i (Vatican City, 1937), p. viii.

[12] Munich, Universitätsbibliothek, Codex 752, ed. in Kroyer, 'Die *Musica speculativa* des Magister Erasmus Heritius', in *Festschrift zum 50. Geburtstag Adolf Sandberger* (Munich: F. Zierfuss, 1918), 65–120.

points, but in a compendious form. On the other hand, the most original aspects of the *Musica* are missing. Kroyer has suggested that the Munich treatise, which is in a hand different from that of the Vatican manuscript, is a compilation of lecture notes. If so, it is nevertheless organized in Erasmus's typical style, and his characteristic terminology and method are faithfully preserved.[13]

Still another treatise, one that has not until recently been connected with Erasmus of Höritz, may now be securely attributed to him: Berlin, Deutsche Staatsbibliothek, MS Mus. theor. 1310. It was once believed to be by Bartolomé Ramos de Pareja, but both Hugo Riemann and Johannes Wolf doubted that he could have been its author. Riemann found in it no trace of Ramos's theoretical innovations,[14] and Wolf reasoned that if the Berlin treatise had been written by Ramos before the *Musica practica* (Bologna, 1482), he would have mentioned it there; if afterwards, the manuscript would have contained some discussion of his reforms of the solmization system and the tuning of the imperfect consonances.[15] I first suggested the attribution to Erasmus in 1962,[16] after Dr. Karl-Heinz Köhler, Director of the Musikabteilung of the Deutsche Staatsbibliothek, courteously provided me a microfilm of the manuscript. The treatise begins on fo. 4[r]: 'Hunc nostrum Librum Musice in duos partiales Libros diuidemus de modis musicis sensualiter deprehensis: secundus Rationis investigationem Clare docebit.'[17] Hence it may be known as *Liber musicae*. The codex contains 86 folios (the first three are blank), written mainly by the same hand as the Vatican manuscript. The contents and mode of presentation are similar to the Vatican treatise, but the organization of the work is radically different in many respects. Each, moreover, contains material not in the other. The *Liber musicae*, for example, goes beyond the scope of theoretical music into rules for solmization and discant. The *Musica*, on the other hand, is more

---

[13] In the same MS 752 and in the same but smaller and hastier hand there are on fos. 95 to 114: 'Annotationes in Musicen magistri Joannis de muris per magistrum Andream Perlachium accuratae traditae.' Andreas Perlach or Perlacher received his doctorate of medicine at the University of Vienna in 1530 and lectured on mathematics there from 1515 to 1549, when he became Rector. Cf. Joseph Ritter von Aschbach, *Die wiener Universität und ihre Humanisten im Zeitalter Kaiser Maximilians I*, vol. ii of *Geschichte der wiener Universität im ersten Jahrhunderte ihres Bestehens* (Vienna: W. Braumüller, 1877), 339.

[14] H. Riemann, *History of Music Theory*, trans. (from the 2nd. German edn., 1920) by Raymond Haggh (Lincoln, Nebr.: University of Nebraska Press, 1962), 280 n. 1.

[15] *Musica practica Bartolomei Rami de Pareia*, ed. Johannes Wolf (Publikationen der internationalen Musikgesellschaft, Beihefte, 2; Leipzig: Breitkopf und Härtel, 1901), p. xv.

[16] 'Ramos', in *MGG* x (1962), 1910. See the page from the manuscript reproduced there.

[17] It ends on fo. 86[r]: 'Et hoc facto finem librj imponimus.' Fétis, who described the manuscript in his article on Ramos in *Biographie universelle*, vii. 179, believed it was written in the last years of the 15th c. According to Fétis, the MS was purchased in Catania, Sicily on 3 Dec. 1817 by Johann Christian Niemeyer. He ceded it to Georg Poelchau, whose rich library was acquired by Frederick William IV of Prussia.

detailed and explicit in its demonstrations. The question of whether it represents an earlier or later working will not be considered here. One important feature of the Berlin MS is that besides the principal, fair hand of the Vatican MS, there appears another hand in marginal notes, calculations, and corrections, and throughout the section from folios 14^r to 21^v. This hand is hasty and employs many abbreviations, while the principal hand uses them sparingly. The last six lines of fo. 21^v are repeated by the principal hand on fo. 22^r, suggesting that the section 14^r–21^v was inserted to replace a previously copied version later rejected. The revision is probably in the hand of the author. Thus the Berlin treatise, probably partly autograph, represents a less finished work than the Vatican treatise.

Erasmus of Höritz emerges as one of the German humanists of the early sixteenth century most articulate on musical matters. His biography, while still full of lacunae, is fortunately not as vacant as the musical dictionaries until recently have been silent about him.[18] All evidence points to Höritz as his place of origin. It is a small town in what was then south-west Bohemia, since made famous by its passion plays, and now called Hořice because it is within the boundaries of Czechoslovakia. It is on the road from the Czech town of Český Krumlov, which is eight miles to the north-east, to the Austrian border, which is about the same distance to the south-west. The nearest cities are Budweis (now České Budějovice) and Linz. Since, in spite of these facts, he considered himself a German in a generic sense, it is appropriate to call him Erasmus of Höritz.

At the head of his dedication of the *Musica*, Erasmus assumes the title of Doctor of Philosophy and Medicine. Records show that he matriculated at numerous universities, as was the custom of students and scholars at the time. The first was Ingolstadt, on 14 May 1484 as Erasmus de Heritz.[19] Next he was at Erfurt, where he matriculated as Erasmus de Erytz de Bohemia on St Michael's Day (29 September) in 1486.[20] Two years later in May he registered at Cologne in the faculty of arts as Herasmus Herics and eventually received the degree of Magister (Doctor) there.[21] In the autumn of 1494 he signed at the University of Cracow: 'Magister Erasmus de

---

[18] See my articles on him: 'Horicius, Erasmus' in *MGG*, Supplement, xvi (1979), 732–3; and 'Horicius, Erasmus', in *New Grove*, viii. 696.

[19] Kroyer, 'Die *Musica speculativa*', 70.

[20] Gerhard Pietzsch, 'Zur Pflege der Musik an den deutschen Universitäten im Osten bis zur Mitte des 16. Jahrhunderts', *Archiv für Musikforschung*, 1 (1936), 433. See also Nan Cooke Carpenter, *Music in the Medieval and Renaissance Universities* (Norman, Okla.: University of Oklahoma Press, 1958), 225, 244, 281.

[21] Pietzsch, 'Zur Pflege der Musik', 433: 'Herasmus Herics; art.; iuravit et solvit. Herijchs L., 1488 Dec. 10 determinavit sub m. Everh. de Amersfordia.'

Hericz universitatis Coloniensis'.[22] In his matriculation at Tübingen in 1499 as Erasmus Hericius ex Bohemia he is also designated a Magister of Cologne. At Vienna he is entered in the registry on Easter Sunday, 14 April 1501, among the 'Ungarum nacio', students of Hungarian nationality. The record reads: 'Erasmus Ericius mathematicus de Horitz nihil dedit', the last words indicating that he did not pay the usual tax.[23] He later taught there but had certainly left well before 1514, as may be gathered from these words written by Thomas Resch (Velocianus) in a letter addressed to the famous mathematician Georg Tannstetter, known also as Collimitius, and published in Tannstetter's edition of the *Tabulae Eclypsium* of Georg Peuerbach (Vienna, 1514):

Truly, again and again I have myself wished to have with me both you and [Johann] Stabius of Styria, Rosinus,[24] [Johannes] Angelus, [Erasmus] Ericius, noble mathematicians, shining with much splendour of letters, so that the renowned and very precious studies of mathematics, for a while now shamefully and savagely neglected, might through them have endured and breathed and have been preserved in our German countries by the excellent and almighty God.[25]

Of those mentioned, Johannes Angelus of Bavaria had died already in 1512. Tannstetter himself left the teaching of mathematics for medicine and university administrative posts after 1510, when he was appointed physician to Emperor Maximilian.[26] The impression given by Resch, who was Dean of the arts faculty in 1504, 1508, and 1513, is that mathematical studies suffered a decline. This may have given Erasmus a motive for going elsewhere. Tannstetter, later recalling better times, said 'Johannes Eperies and Erasmus Ericius, very distinguished men, at this same time taught mathematics with the admiration of many'.[27]

A manuscript from the Kloster Tegernsee near Munich, dated 1510, confers upon a certain Magister Erasmus the degree of Bachelor of Theology and Canonic Law ('sacrae theologiae et jurispontifici bacalaureus magister Erasmus'). This may well be our Erasmus.[28] Another side of his activity is

---

[22] Ibid. Cf. also *Album studiosorum universitatis cracoviensis*, ed. Adam Churiel, ii [1490–1551] (Cracow: Typis Universitatis Jagellonicae, 1892), 35.

[23] Institut für Österreichische Geschichtsforschung, *Die Matrikel der Universität Wien*, ii [1451–1518] (Graz: Hermann Böhlhaus Nachf., 1959), 294.

[24] Rosinus or Stefan Rösel, like Erasmus, also came to Vienna from the University of Cracow in 1501: Rudolph Kink, *Geschichte der kaiserlichen Universität zu Wien* (Vienna: C. Gerold and Sohn, 1854), i. 208.

[25] The Latin original is in Pietzsch, 'Zur Pflege der Musik', 433.

[26] Aschbach, *Geschichte der wiener Universität*, 272.

[27] Pietzsch, 'Zur Pflege der Musik', 433.

[28] Munich, Bayerische Staatsbibliothek, MS Clm. 18635, cited by Kroyer, 'Die *Musica speculativa*', 71 n. 2, and Pietzsch, 'Zur Pflege der Musik', 433.

probably represented by some astronomical speculations marked 'Annotatio M. Erasmi', dealing mainly with Ptolemy's *Almagest*, a work Horicius claims in his *Musica* to have corrected.[29] Kroyer found these among notes taken at lectures of various professors, and specifically in a series marked 'Inchoauit 1 Nov. a. 1544'. If Erasmus was about 20 when he matriculated at Ingolstadt in 1484, he would at this time have been 80, so the glosses were probably taken down second-hand.

The dedication (Pl. 5.1) of the *Musica* to Cardinal Grimani, whom he calls his patron, suggests that Erasmus took the road to Italy after leaving Vienna. His critical remarks about both Greek and Latin authorities, among them Aristotle, Ptolemy, and Boethius, and his progressive views concerning scientific investigation strongly hint at a connection with the University of Padua. Padua was either within or close to areas of the Cardinal's jurisdiction under a number of his appointments.[30] Erasmus cites three of Grimani's titles: cardinal of San Marco, patriarch of Aquileia, and prince in Germany. Domenico Grimani, himself a scholar, received a Doctor of Arts at Padua on 23 October 1487 and remained there until 1489, when he was chosen to be one of four ambassadors to escort Emperor Frederick III to north Italy at the time of the armistice between the Emperor and Matthias Corvinus of Hungary. As a reward for this service,

---

[29] Kroyer, 'Die *Musica speculativa*', 71; *Musica*, fo. 66ʳ. Florence, Bibl. Medicea Laurenziana, MS Ashburnham 1417 (*olim* 1341) preserves by our Erasmus a treatise identified on the spine of an 18th- or 19th-c. binding as 'Tractatus de Spera' by Horicius Germanus. The MS consists of 211 numbered pages, with the incipit (p. 1): 'Reuerendissimo Cardinale [*sic*] Dominico Grimano Tituli Sancti Marci Ac patriarche Aquileensi Erasmus Horicius Germanus Artium et Medicine doctor et Mathematicus principi ac patrono suo Humillime se Commendat.' What appears to be the title occurs on p. 3: 'Viaticus motuum planetarum Erasmi Horicij Germani . . . In quinque partiales partitur Libellos.' Ptolemy's *Almagest* is frequently mentioned in the text. The explicit on p. 211 is: 'sed mitto nobilissima scientiarum secreta que plus quam aurea sunt et penitus incorruptibilior Ampe hoc benigniter Ab Erasmo tuo. et vale.' The hand is the same as in the Vatican and Berlin MSS of his music treatises.

[30] No Erasmus is listed in the *Acta graduum academicorum ab anno 1501* [ad annum 1525], ed. Elda Martellozzo Forin (Padua, 1969). However Dr Ernst Kurz of Kempten/Allgäu, a physician who has been compiling biographies of illustrious men of Höritz, has called my attention (in a letter of 28 June 1989) to the following entries in the Acta graduum of 1503: 'iun. 30, hora 12. Gracie amore Dei d. Rasini Theutonici in med.' and '1503 iul. 7 In loco solito examinum. Mag. Rasini in med. Privatum examen et doctoratus in facultate med. d. mag. Rasini Porsetiz ex Horiz—approbati—nem. discr., coram d. vicario ultrascripto, sub rectoratu ultrascripti, sub promotoribus suis dominis magistris Ioanne de Aquila, Hieronimo de Verona, Gabriele Zerbo qui dedit insignia, Petro Trapolino et Symone Estensi. Testes: d. Dominicus Seo civis Patavus chyrurgicus; d. Hieronymus ex Salpurgo, d. Guilielmus Nobilis ex Eib Padue studentes.' It is probable that Erasmus, not finding employment as a mathematician or astronomer, decided to become a physician. This is supported by his identifying himself as a doctor of medicine in the Vatican music treatise and in his astronomical treatise in Florence, Biblioteca Medicea Larenziana, MS Ashburnham 1417. See above, n. 29. For further information on Erasmus's education and on the village of Höritz, see Ernst Kurz, 'Erasmus von Höritz, ein Humanist aus dem Böhmerwald', in *Der Kreis Krummau an der Moldau, die Heimat Adalbert Stifters*, ed. Rupert Essl (Krummau a. M: Selbstverlag des Heimatkreises, 1983), 224–7, and 'Geschichte des Marktes Höritz im Böhmerwald', ibid. 430–3.

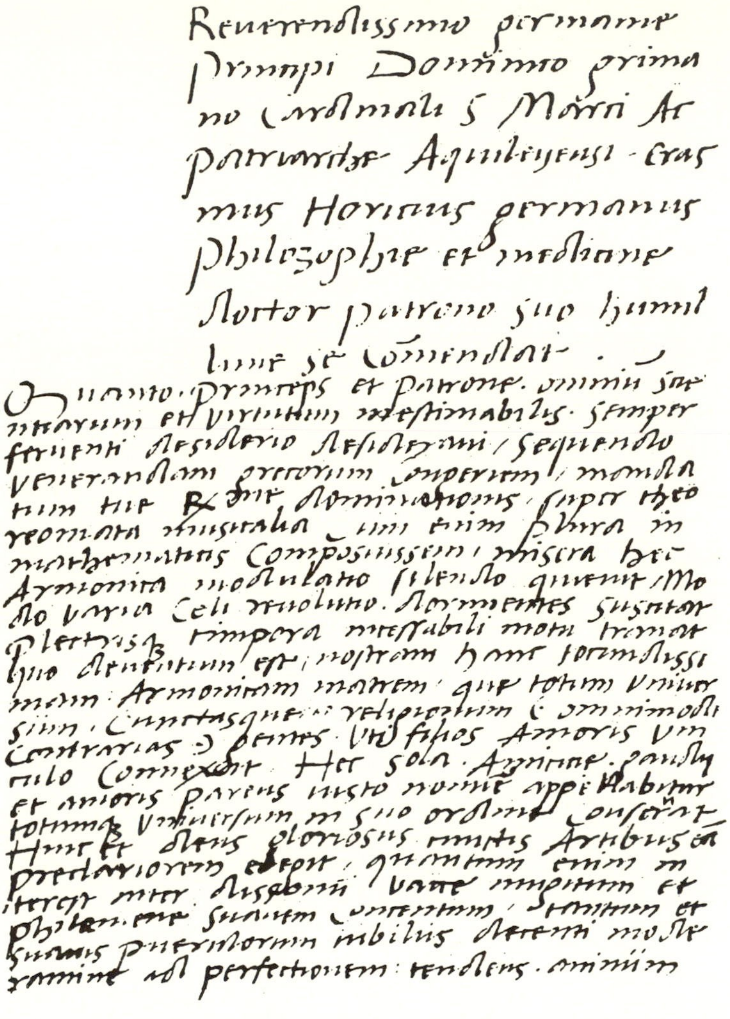

PL. 5.1. Dedication of Erasmus of Höritz, *Musica*, to Cardinal Domenico Grimani. Rome, Vatican Library, MS Regina lat. 1245, fo. 1ᵛ

Frederick made Grimani a knight, and this probably accounts for the title of 'Prince in Germany'.[31] After entering the Roman court in 1491, Grimani advanced rapidly, being promoted to cardinal by Alexander VI on 20 September 1493. He was made patriarch of Aquileia (north-east of Venice)

[31] Mario E. Cosenza, *Biographical and Bibliographical Dictionary of the Italian Humanists and of the World of Classical Scholarship in Italy, 1300–1800* (2nd edn., Boston: G. K. Hall, 1962), ii. Cosenza's information is taken mainly from Pio Paschini, *Domenico Grimani, Cardinale di S. Marco* (Rome: Edizioni di 'Storia e Letteratura', 1943).

on 13 September 1497, but because of local political pressure he resigned in 1517. He was named cardinal of San Marco on 25 December 1503, a title he retained throughout his life, though he gave up the administrative duties connected with it in 1508.[32]

The year 1504, consequently, is the earliest possible date for the *Musica*, since by then the Cardinal had earned all the titles attributed to him by Erasmus. The year of Grimani's resignation as patriarch of Aquileia, 1517, would be the latest possible date for the treatise. But since Grimani continued to accumulate titles, it is plausible that Erasmus, in his desire to flatter his patron, would have cited those he currently held: on 22 September 1508 named Episcopus Albanensis; on 3 June 1509 transferred to Episcopus Tusculanensis; on 20 January 1511 transferred to Episcopus Portuensis et S. Rufinae, which he kept until his death; and on 29 May 1514, in addition, named Bishop of Urbino.[33] Between 4 March 1507 and 1512 he was also head of the Abbey of S. Maria delle Carceri at Este in the diocese of Padua.[34] He was mainly absent from the Curia during the papacy of Leo X (1513–21), with whom he was not on good terms.[35] Domenico Grimani died on 27 August 1523. The years of highest probability for the completion of the *Musica* of Erasmus, then, are between 1504 and 1508; of secondary probability are the years 1508–14. Of little probability, however, are the years 1514–17, since Bishop of Urbino is too significant a title to overlook.

The *Musica* of Erasmus belongs to the category of *musica theorica*. Following the tradition of the *De institutione musica* of Boethius, it covers the musical part of the university curriculum in the four mathematical disciplines or quadrivium. Like many other university-centred theorists, Erasmus is a conservative on matters affecting musical practice. Apparently unaware of the controversy raging around Ramos de Pareja's advocacy of the just tuning of imperfect consonances, Erasmus stands by the time-honoured Pythagorean division of the diatonic tetrachord into two 9/8 tones and a semitone in the ratio 256/243. He tries to reconcile this with the modern chromatic system, which he recognizes has resulted from widespread employment of *musica ficta* and modal transposition. Another sign of his conservatism is that he fails to apply his very sophisticated techniques of geometry and

---

[32] Conrad Eubel (ed.), *Hierarchia catholica medii aevi sive summorum pontificum, S.R.E. Cardinalium ecclesiarum antistitum series*, ii (Regensburg: Sumptibus et typis librariae Regensbergiana, 1910), 22. His first title was Cardinal of S. Nicola inter Imagines: ibid., iii (Regensburg, 1910), 76, and briefly he was archbishop of Nicosia in Cyprus in 1495 (ibid., ii. 224).

[33] Ibid., ii. 60, 62–3, 103, 224; iii. 61, 63, 65, 73, 76, 127.

[34] Cosenza, *Biographical and Bibliographical Dictionary*, ii.

[35] Pio Paschini, 'Domenico Grimani,' in *Enciclopedia cattolica*, iv. 1168.

calculation to certain practical problems, such as tempered tuning, that were awaiting solutions at the very moment his methods offered a ready path. If Erasmus shuns the innovations of the more practically oriented theorists such as Ramos and Spataro, he is nevertheless dissatisfied with the way the classic problems of music theory were treated in the past. His quarrel with his predecessors lies mainly in the area of methodology. It is in this sphere that he makes his principal contribution, though the novelty of his method often spills over into the matter demonstrated.

The method of Erasmus is that of natural science. He first observes as accurately as possible with the senses the phenomenon under study. Then, as the astronomer does, he investigates by means of geometry and mathematics the causes behind the effects noted through the senses. This, he was fond of repeating, was the method of the ancient Greeks in all the sciences. For example:

It is immediately clear to the ear that there is no difference between the consonance of the diapason and the just diapente and diatessaron taken together. From *ut* to *sol*, that is from Gamma-*ut* to *d sol re*, a fifth, and from *d sol re* to *g sol re ut*, a fourth, is nothing other than the diapason. For this [diapason] is composed of the extreme terms from both, and all three [terms] are combined in a way imperceptible to the sense. In so far as the sense can grasp them, these things are plainly known. There remains only to confirm this by means of geometrical and arithmetical demonstrations and to investigate the truth concerning the doubt that exists between the sense and the intellect.[36]

If the senses know with certainty that an octave is the sum of a fifth and a fourth, only mathematical analysis will reveal the cause of this: that the three terms 2, 3, 4 are such that the extremes are in the ratio 2/1, and that the two ratios 3/2 and 4/3 'added' (multiplied) produce the ratio of the octave.

Of the two large treatises of Erasmus, the organization of the one in Berlin follows most faithfully the method of proceeding from sense-perception to rationalization. It devotes the first book of 19 pages, divided into 6 *canones*, to the sensory aspect, and the remaining 147 pages in 4 parts and 64 propositions to mathematical analysis. The same method, more subtly applied, is fundamental to the organization of the Vatican treatise. Here

---

[36] *Musica,* fo. 54ʳ. 'Per auditum enim id clarum modo est inter diapason consonantiam nihil esse differentiae ad diapente et diatessaron iustas simul nihil aliud est de ut ad sol de Gamma-ut ad d sol re quinta, vel diapente, et de d sol re ad g sol re ut diatessaron, consonantia quam diapason, quoniam haec extremorum terminorum composita est ex duabus et omnes tres ad sensum inperceptibiliter. Quantum sensus videlicet capere potest iam cognitae sunt. Restat modo istud geometricis ac Aritmeticis demonstrationis [*sic*] confirmare et de dubio quod inter sensum et intellectum est investigare veritatem.' (I have normalized the spelling and added punctuation.)

books i, ii, iv, and v deal with knowledge derived from sense perception, while books iii, vi, vii, and viii apply mathematical demonstrations to the phenomena discovered.

The *Musica* is divided into eight books. In book i (fos. 4^r–6^v), Erasmus defines and demonstrates the *voces*, that is the solmization syllables *ut*, *re*, etc.; the *litterae*, namely the alphabetical letters, A, B, C, etc. designating the steps of the octave; and finally the *claves*, which are the twenty steps of the gamut identified by joining the appropriate letters and syllables, such as Gamma-ut, A-re, etc.

Book ii (fos. 6^v–10^r) proceeds to the definition of the intervals (*modi*), the conventional classification of consonances into perfect and imperfect and a consideration of the usefulness of combinations of them, such as the fifth plus major third.

Book iii (fos. 10^v–38^r) begins to depart from the traditional procedures of musical treatises of this time. It is divided into twenty-seven propositions, derived mainly from Euclid's *Elements*, each of which demonstrates some geometrical method useful for the study of the ratios of musical intervals. Erasmus shows how to 'add' (multiply) and 'subtract' (divide) proportions. He proves, for example, that in a geometric progression the ratio of the extremes is a product of all the intermediary proportions. He shows how to reduce fractions to their simplest terms, and how to manipulate irrational fractions or surds. All these operations, he holds, are necessary to the proper study of consonances and dissonances.

Book iv (fos. 39^r–42^r) returns to categories known to sense perception, specifically the three genera of the Greeks, whose differences are considered from an aural and affective standpoint.

Book v (42^v–48^v) extends this discussion to systems of tetrachords used in Greek and Latin (medieval) music. Here Erasmus gives an account of the Greek *tonoi* and attempts to distinguish them from the Western modes.

After this empirical exploration of musical systems, Erasmus is ready to apply the operations taught in book iii to problems related to the material presented in books iv and v. Book vi takes up problems relating to the diatonic system in thirty-nine propositions (fos. 49^r–93^v), while book vii (fos.94^r–99^v) extends this to the chromatic and enharmonic systems, but only briefly, in four propositions, because Erasmus saw limited application for these genera in his own time.

The eighth and last book in thirteen propositions (fos. 100^r–114^r) demonstrates by geometric constructions and numerical calculations some divisions of the monochord for the three genera.

Only a few of the original contributions of the treatise can be considered here, because of limitations of space. Surely the most characteristic is the exhaustive application of the theorems of Euclid's *Elements*. It is this comprehensive geometrical work rather than the summary arithmetical and musical books of Boethius that serves Erasmus as his starting-point and model. Good humanist that he was, Erasmus goes back to the Greek sources of the doctrines of Boethius. He thus communicates to musical readers an important fruit of the revival of interest in ancient texts.

Euclid's *Elements*, the first mathematical book of any importance to be printed, was published in 1482 in a Latin translation by the thirteenth-century mathematician Johannes Campanus.[37] This is the translation that Erasmus specifically cites several times because of its commentary (for example, fo. 41^r). Erasmus's division into propositions, some with corollaries, his manner of stating them, the style of his demonstrations and of the diagrams: these are all modelled on Euclid, and the Latin terminology is that of Campanus. But Erasmus does not merely parody or slavishly imitate the ancient geometer. He avoids repeating any of the proofs of Euclid, presenting rather proofs of purely musical or musically relevant propositions. Where a step is sufficiently demonstrated by Euclid, Erasmus is content to cite book and proposition, and pass on.[38]

A striking example of the freshness of thinking often encountered in the *Musica* is Erasmus's insistence upon exploiting irrational as well as rational proportions. The Boethians dismissed the possibility of dividing equally superparticular intervals such as the octave (2/1), the fifth (3/2), or the whole tone (9/8).[39] Each of these ratios lacks a square root expressible in integers that would provide a mean proportional between two string-lengths. Since irrational numbers are condemned because of their impreciseness by the philosophers influenced by the Pythagoreans, they were neglected throughout the Middle Ages.[40] Erasmus declares:

In this matter all the philosophers proclaim loudly, following Boethian dictates, stated hypothetically in his *Musica*, that no superparticular proportion can be

---

[37] *Praeclarissimus liber elementorum Euclidis perspicacissimi in artem Geometrie* (Augsburg: Erhard Ratdolt, 1482).

[38] The books of Euclid most frequently cited are those dealing with proportions, namely v, vii, and viii. Among the most used propositions are v. 15: 'parts have the same ratio as the same multiples of them taken in corresponding order'; vii. 18: 'If two numbers by multiplying any number make certain numbers, the numbers so produced will have the same ratio as the multipliers'; and viii. 2: 'To find numbers in continued proportion, as many as may be prescribed, and the least that are in a given ratio.' These translations are from T. L. Heath, *The Thirteen Books of Euclid's Elements* (Cambridge: Cambridge University Press, 1908). Frequently used are also books i, ii, iii, and x. It may be assumed that Erasmus had at his command the entire corpus of Greek geometrical doctrine preserved by Euclid.

[39] Boethius, *De institutione musica*, iii. 2, and iii. 11.

[40] It must be acknowledged that Erasmus too betrays a certain horror of irrational numbers, for he expresses them as integers whose roots must be found.

divided equally. This is very false, as we shall demonstrate here . . . Once the proportion of the whole has been found, any part of it will be obtained, and the half quite readily . . . We affirm generally that any proportion, rational or irrational, of any genus, can be divided into any number of parts.[41]

These remarks serve to introduce a demonstration of the division of the 9/8 tone into two equal parts by discovering the geometric mean between 8 and 9. In book ii, proposition 3, he showed:

the geometric mean is obtained when such a series of three terms is given that the proportion of the first to the second is the same as that of the second to the third. For example, in the three terms *a*, *b*, *c*, which are continuous proportionals, and where $a:b = b:c$, I say *b* is the geometric mean.[42]

He also showed there that if *a* and *c* are given, to find *b*, multiply *a* by *c* and take the square root of the product. Or $b = \sqrt{ac}$. He gave the example: $a = 2, c = 8$; then $b = \sqrt{16}$ or 4.[43] Now in book vi, he applies the method to a number of irrational proportions, and in proposition 17 specifically to the ratio 9/8.

Following a method, established in earlier propositions, of representing the value of a ratio by a single straight line, he proceeds as follows (see Pl. 5.2):

As in the figure let the whole [line] *AB* be the sesquioctave proportion divided at point *C*, so that *AC* is a minor semitone.

By i. 2 [Euclid] I cut off from point *B* the equal of *AC*, which is *BD*. The remainder, *CD*, will be the difference between the tone and two minor semitones.

If you add the mean of this to both *AC* and *DB* by means of the doctrine often given already [in preceding propositions] the whole known *AB* results, the half of which proportion is what is sought.

In lines, with numbers, this would be as follows.

Let *F* be half of the proportion *CD*, which, expressed by lines, is *G:H*, or in numbers 531441:524288 [the major semitone minus the minor semitone, or $2187/2048 \div 256/243$].

Let *LM:PQ* and *MN:QR* be two minor semitones. Since they are known [both being 256/243], their sum will be known, namely the proportion *LN:PR*, which is 65536:59049 [i.e. $(256/243)^2$] composed of two equal and known proportions.

If you add to these the proportion *G:H*, which will be *KL:OP*, the total will be

---

[41] Bk. vi, prop. 17, fos. 65ᵛ−66ʳ: 'In hac re omnes philosophi clamitant, boetiana dicta sequentes, eam scilicet hipotesim in musica sua, scilicet nullam superparticularem proportionem in aequa dividi posse, quod falsissimum est, ut in hoc loco demonstrabimus . . . Et cum proportio totius iam inventa sit, dabitur eius quotacumque pars, et facilius dimidium . . . Et dicimus universaliter quod omnis proportio tam rationalis quam surda cuiuscumque generis sit potest dividi in quodlibet [*sic*] partes.'

[42] Ibid., fo. 50ᵛ: 'Medietas geometrica ex proportione accipitur, scilicet, quando tribus terminis propositis eadem est proportio primi ad secundum, sicut secundi ad tertium. Ut sint tres termini, a, b, c, continue proportionales ita quod proportio a ad b sit sicut b ad c. Dico b esse medium geometricum.'

[43] Ibid., fo. 51ʳ.

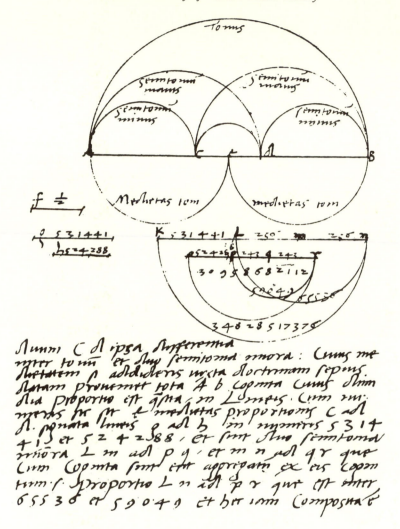

PL. 5.2. Geometric division of the 9:8 whole tone, from Erasmus of Höritz, *Musica*, Vatican Library, MS Regina lat. 1245, fo. 66ᵛ

KN:OR, composed of three known proportions. Since this total itself is known by v. 15 [of Euclid], its mean proportion will be given. [The total proportion, that is, *KN:OR*] is 34,828,517,376:30,958,682,112. The half of this [that is, the square root] is what is sought, or in the first figure either *AE* or *EB*.[44]

[44] Ibid., fos. 66ʳ–67ʳ: 'Ut in exemplo sit tota AB proportio sesquioctava divisa in puncto C ita ut AC sit semitonium minus. Et per secundam primi a puncto B accipio aequalem ei quae sit BD. Erit residuum CD ipsa differentia inter tonum et duo semitonia minora. Cuius medietatem, si addideris iuxta doctrinam saepius datam, proveniet tota AB cognita, cuius dimidia proportio est quaesita. In

Erasmus does not proceed to compute the square root. He may have felt that this was a purely arithmetical problem not requiring demonstration, particularly for a student of the quadrivium. Certainly, throughout his treatise he shows little regard for the musician unschooled in mathematics. He also seems little aware of the practical applicability of his theorems. Having found a method for obtaining mean semitones, Erasmus does not apply it to derive a chromatic note which would divide equally the whole tone between two diatonic steps. Between G and A, for example, this would give a note that would serve equally well G♯ and A♭, as found in the monochord of Heinrich Schreiber (Grammateus), who still deserves credit for this innovation.[45] Schreiber, however, according to J. M. Barbour, derives the mean semitone by a geometrical construction rather than by computation.[46] It must be noted with some disappointment that Erasmus never departs from the Pythagorean minor semitone, 256/243.

Indifference to musical practice is also betrayed in the exhaustive application of geometric division to consonant intervals. Erasmus divides the octave equally to get two equal tritones in the proportion $\sqrt{144/72}$.[47] While this falls within the chromatic scale, the products of several of his other divisions—of the fourth, fifth, and minor third[48]—are purely theoretical entities. The demonstrations do lead, however, to some useful corollaries, such as the determination of the excess of the ditone over the semiditone. Similarly, though we are apt to dismiss the eightfold multiplication of the ratio 9/8 to produce a whole-tone scale of eight steps[49] as an idle exercise, it does serve to prove that six such tones exceed the octave by a Pythagorean comma, or that five such tones added to two minor semitones make an octave.[50]

While books iii, vi, and vii use geometrical methods for calculating

lineis cum numeris sic. Sit F medietas proportionis C ad D, signata lineis G ad H, in numeris 531441 et 524288. Et sint duo semitonia minora LM ad PQ, et MN ad QR. Quae cum cognita sint, erit aggregatum ex eis cognitum, scilicet proportio LN ad PR, quae est inter 65536 et 59049. Et haec iam composita est ex duabus proportionibus aequalibus et cognitis. Quibus si adieceris proportionem G ad H, quae sit KL ad OP, erit tota KN ad OR composita ex tribus proportionibus cognitis. Et ipsa cognita hinc per decimaquintam proportio quinti, eius media proportio cognita dabitur, quae est inter 34828517376 et 30958682112. Cuius medietas est quaesitum et est in prima figuratione AE vel EB.'

[45] Heinrich Schreiber, *Ayn new kunstlich Buech* (Nuremberg: Stüchs, 1518). Cf. J. Murray Barbour, *Tuning and Temperament* (2nd edn., East Lansing, Mich.: Michigan State College Press, 1953), 139. Schreiber attended three of the same universities as Erasmus: Erfurt, Cracow, and Vienna, but about ten years later. The two may have known each other in Vienna, where Schreiber studied under Collimitius around 1510; Pietzsch, 'Zur Pflege der Musik', 444.

[46] Concerning this construction, see also below, n. 57 and the surrounding text.

[47] Bk. vi, prop. 13, fos. 61ᵛ–62ʳ.

[48] Bk. vi, props. 14–16, fos. 62ᵛ–65ʳ.

[49] Bk. vi, prop. 26, fos. 77ʳ–79ʳ.

[50] Bk. vi, prop. 33, fos. 86ʳ–87ʳ.

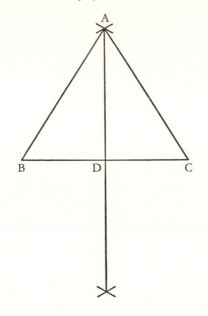

F<small>IG</small>. 5.1

interval-ratios, the first part of book viii applies geometrical constructions to the division of strings without using numbers. The problem Erasmus attacks here is the very real one faced by every musician or instrument-maker who wishes to divide a given string or a pipe into a certain number of equal parts. The classic method of dividing the monochord taught by Boethius and many of his successors requires the division of the string into two parts to get the octave, into three parts for the fifth, into four parts for the fourth, and into nine parts for the whole tone 9/8.

The division into two parts is easily done, Erasmus shows (see Fig. 5.1). Upon a given length, *BC*, as a base, a triangle with two equal sides is constructed and a perpendicular is dropped upon this length from the opposite angle *A*, by Euclid i. 1. This, by Euclid i. 6, divides the length into two equal parts, *BD* and *DC*.[51]

The division of a given length into three equal parts is considerably more difficult. First, around the given length *AB* is constructed an equilateral triangle (see Fig. 5.2). This is done by bisecting *AB* at *C*, by Euclid i. 10. With *C* as a centre, the circle of which *AB* is a diameter is described. *AD* and *AE* are then drawn equal to the semi-diameter *AC*, and *D* and *E* are

---

[51] Bk. viii, prop. 1, fo. 100ʳ⁻ᵛ. This method is equivalent to Euclid i. 10.

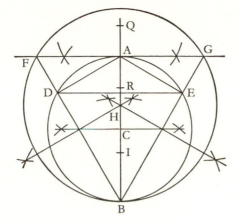

F IG. 5.2

joined. Then a perpendicular is drawn to *AB* at *A*. (Although he does not say so, Erasmus obviously meant this to be done by Euclid i. 11: on *AB* extended find points *Q* and *R* equidistant from *A* and construct an equilateral triangle as in Fig. 5.1. Then drop a perpendicular through *AB* at *A*.) This line, by Euclid iii. 18, will be a tangent. *BD* is now drawn and extended to *F*, and similarly *BE* to *G*. We now have an equilateral triangle *FBG* around the given line *AB*.[52]

About this equilateral triangle a circle is circumscribed, by Euclid iv. 5.[53] (Euclid here shows that if *FB* and *GB* are bisected, perpendiculars at the midpoints will meet in the centre of the circle.) The semi-diameter of this circle is *BH*, and the line *AB* is a diameter and a half.[54] If now *HI* is measured off on *AB* equal to *AH*, the given length *AB* is divided by points *H* and *I* into three equal parts.

The division into nine equal parts, Erasmus shows,[55] can be accomplished by repeating the process just described for each of the parts, *AH*, *HI*, and *IB*.

Another way to accomplish the ninefold division is by the construction that divides a line into any number of equal parts.[56] This is described

[52] Bk. viii, prop. 2, fo. 101[r–v]. I have combined the figures of propositions 2, 3, and 4, fos. 101[r], 101[v], and 102[r], into a single figure, somewhat as Erasmus does in his *Liber musicae*, Berlin MS Mus. theor. 1310, part iv, prop. 2, fo. 77[r].

[53] Bk. viii, prop. 4, fo. 102[r].

[54] This is proved in Erasmus viii. 3 by means of Euclid iv. 5, i. 16, i. 5, iii. 3, and i. 4.

[55] Bk. viii, prop. 6, fos. 103[v]–104[r].

[56] A different solution of this problem is presented in Mersenne, *Harmonie universelle* (1636–7), First Book of Instruments, trans. Roger E. Chapman in Mersenne, *Harmonie universelle: The Books on Instruments* (The Hague: Martinus Nijhoff, 1957), prop. x, pp. 39–41.

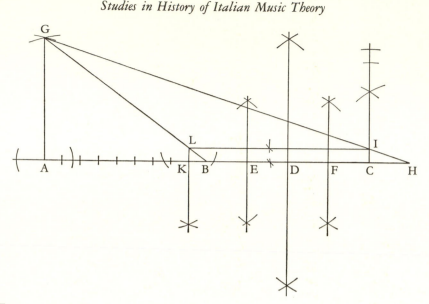

FIG. 5.3

in book viii, proposition 5, of which the special case of nine parts is elaborated very briefly in proposition 6. Here I shall combine the two demonstrations into one, using the figure of proposition 6, with the lettering slightly altered.

The line *AB* of Fig. 5.3 is that which we wish to divide. It is extended by the addition of *BC*, equal to *AB*. *BC* is bisected at *D*. Then *DC* and *BD* are bisected at *F* and *E*. *BC* is thus divided into four equal parts. The line *AC* is now extended to *H* by the addition of a part equal to *FC*, which is 1/8 of the whole line *AC*. A perpendicular at *A* of any length is drawn to *G*, and *GB* and *GH* are drawn. At point *C* a perpendicular is raised as far as *I* on line *GH*. A line parallel to *AH* is extended to *L* on line *GB*. (This may be done by Euclid i. 31 and i. 23, though Erasmus omits mention of these constructions.) From *L* a perpendicular is drawn to line *AH*, by Euclid i. 12, and this will be *LK*. Since, by Euclid i. 29, and i. 34, *LI* = *KC*, then *CH*:*AH* = *KB*:*AB*.[57] Also, since *CH* is the ninth part of *AH*, *KB* will be the ninth part of *AB*, and *AB*:*AK* = 9/8.

It may appear strange that in this section on geometric constructions Erasmus overlooks one of the most useful—that for finding the mean

[57] The proof of this last step is rather extended in prop. 5, fos. 102ᵛ–103ᵛ, and depends on Euclid i. 32, vi. 4, and v. 11.

proportional between two lines. This construction, based on Euclid vi. 9 and vi. 13, was already published in a musical book by Jacques Lefèvre d'Étaples in 1496.[58] Erasmus did not omit it out of ignorance, for he cited the basic proposition of Euclid in his book vi, proposition 3, which deals with the finding of geometric means, though he erroneously refers to Euclid vi. 13 as vi. 16. Why he failed to describe the construction in book viii can be easily explained. This book develops the division of the monochord according to the Pythagorean tuning, and for this no mean proportional needs to be found.

The *Musica* of Erasmus is not so oblivious of contemporary practices as this adherence to the Pythagorean tuning suggests. Like others in his time, he sought to come to terms with the proliferation of *musica ficta*. Erasmus recognizes two systems or *scalae* of 'real' music: that 'of the six modes', I, II, III, IV, VII, and VIII, which spans the range from Gamma-ut to EE-la, analogous to our *G* to *e″*; and the system 'of modes V and VI', which goes from Gamma-ut to EE-fa, or from our *G* to *eb″*. These two systems, found also in other German theorists of this time, seem to have been postulated in imitation of the Greek greater perfect and lesser perfect systems respectively, of which they are extensions. The system of modes V and VI, for example, in its three lowest conjunct tetrachords from *B* to *d′*, is identical to the synemmenon system of the Greeks. This is extended upwards by two conjunct tetrachords from *e′* to *d″*, to which is added a note *eb″* at the top. The notes *A* and *G* are similarly added at the bottom (see Fig. 5.4).[59]

G   A   B   c   d   e   f   g   a   bb   c′   d′   e′   f′   g′   a′   bb″   c″   d″   e″

FIG. 5.4

To these two fundamental systems Erasmus adds two more, both branches from the *scala quinti et sexti toni*. These he calls *scala ficta* and *scala ficta universalis*. They both require an additional tone *F* below Gamma-ut, but

---

[58] *Musica libris demonstrata quatuor* (Paris: Johann Higman & Wolfgang Hopyl, 1496), book iii, ch. 35, sig. g6ᵛ. In the edition of 1552 (Paris: Gulielmus Cavellat), this occurs on fo. 29ᵛ. For a facsimile of Lefèvre's demonstration, see Mark Lindley, *Lutes, viols and Temperaments* (Cambridge: Cambridge University Press, 1984), 24.

[59] *Musica*, bk. vi, prop. 28, fos. 79ᵛ–80ᵛ. Erasmus presents his scales in several charts which show the pitches descending from top to bottom. For each step are given string-length, solmization syllable, and *clavis*. In my simplified figures 4, 5, and 6, the scales are shown in terms of a standard modern alphabetical notation ascending from left to right. All tetrachords, which are marked by brackets, are formed of the ratios 9/8–9/8–256/243.

they proceed at the other extremity like the *scala quinti et sexti toni* to EE-fa (or *eb″*).[60]

The *scala ficta* contains three conjunct tetrachords from *A* to *c′* and two more conjunct tetrachords from *d′* to *c″*, with extra tones *d″* and *eb″* at the top and *G* and *F* at the bottom. All the tetrachords are sung *la−sol−fa−mi* descending and are figured 9/8, 9/8, 256/243, producing in the *scala ficta* an equivalent of the *Eb* major scale from *eb″* down to *Bb*, with *A*, *G*, *F* added at the bottom (see Fig. 5.5).

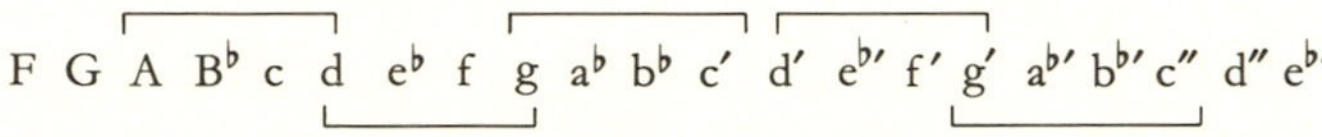

F G A B♭ c d e♭ f g a♭ b♭ c′ d′ e♭′ f′ g′ a♭′ b♭′ c″ d″ e♭″

FIG. 5.5

Whereas the *scala ficta* provides a path for mutations from the *scala quinti et sexti toni*, the *scala ficta universalis* permits mutations from the *scala ficta*. Thus *bb*, which is *sol* in the *ficta* tetrachord *c″−bb′−ab′−g′*, becomes *la* in the *universalis* tetrachord *bb′−ab′−gb′−f′*. Similarly, *eb*, which is *fa* in the tetrachord *g−f−eb−d* of the *ficta* system, now becomes *la* in the tetrachord *eb′−db−cb−bb* of the *universalis* (see Fig. 5.6). A by-product of this last system, then, is to provide 'a minor semitone between any *claves*', that is, between any two diatonic steps.[61] It should be observed, however, that this is a minor semitone only when the fictitious note is used as a flat; employing the fictitious note as a sharp, as in the succession *d−db−d*, produces a major semitone, 2187/2048.

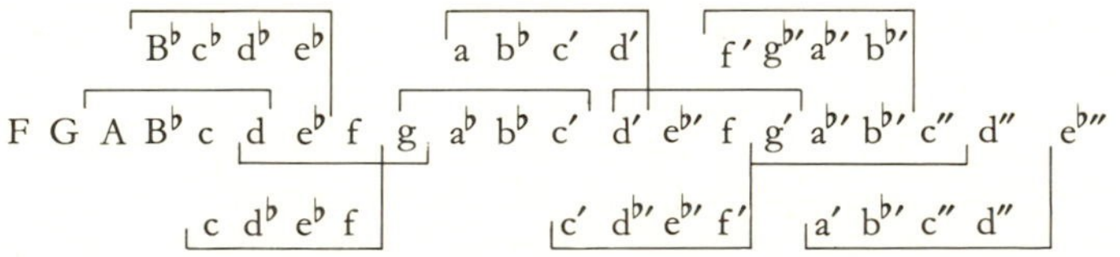

FIG. 5.6

[60] Bk. vi, prop. 24, fo. 81ᵛ. The string-length 2304, which in the *scala quinti et sexti toni* represented dd-la or our *d″*, now represents cc-la, or our *c″*. However, it would be wrong to see these scales as transpositions upwards by a whole tone of the scales of modes V and VI simply because cc-la has moved from 2592 to 2304. The string-lengths do not represent absolute pitch but are merely numbers found convenient for computing relative pitch-distances.

[61] Bk. vi, prop. 30, fo. 82ʳ.

166

Throughout these systems Erasmus has ignored the tradition established by Hermannus Contractus in the eleventh century of constructing tetrachords by ascending tone—semitone—tone. He prefers to form them, like the Greeks, by descending tone—tone—semitone. This is in keeping with his evident desire to form the *scala quinti et sexti toni* on the model of the ancient synemmenon system.[62] The *scala ficta* then becomes a modern counterpart of a Greek *tonos*, since it transposes the *scala quinti et sexti toni* down a whole tone. For the *ficta* tone of disjunction, between *c'* and *d'*, is a whole tone lower than that of the *scala quinti et sexti toni*, between *d'* and *e'*. Erasmus knew that the system of Greek *tonoi* was a means for transposing a single scale to various levels. However imperfectly he understood other aspects of the *tonoi*, he must have incorporated this simple parallel quite consciously.

These few samples of his thought show how Erasmus of Höritz confronted the perennial challenge faced by Renaissance theory: to point the way to 'the ancient music reduced to the modern practice'. The theoretical doctrine that reached Erasmus, rooted in ancient thought but fitted to medieval Western music, was neither true to the Greek writings nor congruent with the musical systems in use. Returning to ancient sources, Erasmus sought to restore the perennial laws of harmonics and at the same time to correct them, make them more accessible, and render their application easier. But, like his predecessors, he played the game of grafting convenient aspects of Greek theory to modern practice. So he found it expedient to revive the *tonoi* and the tetrachordal method of constructing scales. As a reconciliation of ancient theory and modern practice, his solutions were neither more nor less successful than parallel attempts by Glareanus or Vicentino. Perhaps less relevant than theirs to the contemporary musical situation, his were better founded in classical learning and objective facts.

It is not possible at this time to assess the influence his theory may have had on musical thought in his time. Echoes of his doctrines appear in Rhaw, Ornithoparcus, Spangenberg, and Bogentanz, to cite a few of his own countrymen. Whether this resonance is owed to Erasmus or to a common doctrine that he happened to expound, his unpublished work was not a solitary flash. It bears witness to the fertile soil existing in Germany for the flowering of music theory enjoyed there in the first half of the sixteenth century.

---

[62] This does not apply to the Berlin treatise, however, where the *scala quinti et sexti toni* is represented on fo. 62ᵛ as proceeding from F-ut to e-mi with *B♭* throughout. The Vatican treatise uses *B♮* in the lowest tetrachord, as shown in Fig. 5.4, in keeping with Greek practice.

6

*Boethius in the Renaissance**

This paper was prepared for the conference 'Musical Theory and Its Sources: Antiquity and the Middle Ages', held at the University of Notre Dame 30 April to 2 May 1987. It was first published in *Music Theory and Its Sources: Antiquity and the Middle Ages*, edited by André Barbera (Notre Dame, Ind., 1990), 259–80.

BOETHIUS as a music theorist was both revered and maligned in the Renaissance, mostly for the wrong reasons. He was cast in the alien role of musical law-giver to a culture dedicated to polyphony, a kind of music he never knew. His teachings were expected to be relevant to the training of musicians who would go on to sing, play, and write counterpoint. Already in the early Middle Ages Guido of Arezzo had set Boethius aside as a foundation for current musical practice, this in constrast to the earlier authors of *Musica enchiriadis* and *Scolica enchiriadis*, who somewhat incongruously bolstered elementary practical instruction with Boethian theory. Throughout the Middle Ages, the treatise of Boethius was copied and recopied, but musicians did not read it with attention, because, apart from the division of the monochord, they could not connect it with their everyday concerns. He was read, to be sure, in the universities within the context of the liberal arts curriculum, as a guide to one of the mathematical arts of the quadrivium. But this was not an educational path musicians often took.

Despite this and the prevailing anti-medievalism, Boethius enjoyed a revival in the Renaissance. The revival took two forms. In the fifteenth century his instructions were advanced as the eternal foundation for any music theory, including a theory of modern practice. Also as early as the fifteenth century, but more characteristically in the sixteenth, his music treatise opened a window to the music and theory of the ancient Greeks.

Both aspects of the Boethian revival are exemplified in the *Ritus canendi*

---

of Johannes Legrense Gallicus de Namur (*c.*1415–73), written between 1458 and 1464.[1] The treatise may be dated through mention of the pontificate of Pius II in the preface. Although he was trained as a musician in the north[2] and studied at the University of Padua, he did not encounter Boethius until he 'heard' him in the school of Vittorino da Feltre in Mantua, where he himself later taught. Gallicus' orientation towards Boethius was in some ways sharply different from his predecessors', and this may be owed partly to humanist tendencies of Vittorino, who possessed in his library the famous codex Venice, Biblioteca Nazionale Marciana, gr. Cl. VI. 10, containing the musical treatises of Aristides Quintilianus, Bacchius Senior, Ptolemy, Porphyry's commentary on the latter, the Bellermann anonymi, and the hymns attributed to Mesomedes. Whether Vittorino, who knew Greek, studied any of these is not known, but Gallicus reveals a critical reading of Boethius coupled with a respect for his authority not as a theorist but as transmitter of the learning of the ancient Greeks. Early in the *Ritus canendi*, Gallicus makes a rather startling reference to 'that Music, which the so often mentioned Boethius turned into Latin from the Greek' ('ea namque musica, quam totiens allegatus Boethius de Graeco vertit in latinum'),[3] early recognition of the fact that Boethius was not truly the author of that theory.

I shall give only a few examples of Gallicus' new historicism. He attributes the observation of the blacksmiths' hammers not to Pythagoras, as stated by Boethius, but to Jubal.[4] He deals with the tetrachord historically, tracing its development in Greece, and credits 'the Greek philosophers' with originating the concept. The most striking departure from the conventional interpretation of Boethius is his recognition of the distinction between the Greek 'tropes' and the modern 'modes'. He begins the ninth chapter of his third book with a description of the tropes according to Boethius:

Boethius, in the fourth book, mentioned above, of his Music, Chapter 14, defines tropes, tones, or modes with these words: *Tropes*, he said, *are constitutions different in all their steps by lowness and height* [*of pitch*]. Do you want to see how many this is? Look carefully at the figures of the constitutions. If you consider the matter rightly, the first is lower by a tone than the second, and the second similarly higher by a tone, and so on for each following one. If they are compared with each other in this way, one exceeds the preceding or is followed by another that is a tone

---

[1] Johannes Gallicus, *Ritus canendi*, ed. Albert Seay (Colorado Springs, Colo.: Colorado College Music Press, 1981), Pars prima, 1. 6.

[2] Ibid., Praefatio, 16: 'Gallia namque me genuit et fecit cantorem.'

[3] Ibid. 1. 4. 13 (p. 11).

[4] Ibid. 1. 10. 13 (p. 20).

or minor semitone away. From this we gather that the tropes, whether Greek or Latin, whether secular or ecclesiastical, are not, nor ever were, anything but constitutions, and a constitution, according to the definition of Boethius, is nothing but a joining of consonances.[5]

Gallicus provided a diagram of this system, in the borders of which he wrote:

These Greek tropes and modes shown, which they also called tones, expressed in Greek letters and made clear by the Latin letters, are rather put together by art than founded in nature: they differ only in location, and on the whole appear alike. In Boethius, however, diverse signs differentiate them, and the measurements [of their string-lengths] were dissimilar, I believe, in all. Now our Latin tropes are certainly created by nature totally unlike one another, though arranged in a single system.[6]

In the diagram (Pl. 6.1) Gallicus represented the identity of the double-octave scales by designating all their constituent steps as A to A.

In giving this objective account of the tropes as described by Boethius, Gallicus was well in advance of a number of his successors, including Gaffurio and Glareanus, who continued to confuse them with the church modes. For example, Glareanus, in his edition of 1546 of the music treatise of Boethius,[7] in the diagram of the modes, writes alongside the Hypermixolydian 'Acutissimus Tetrardus', and labels the Mixolydian 'Plagis Tetrardi', and so on down to 'Plagis Proti' for the Hypodorian. However, the modes do rise correctly Tone, Tone, Semitone, Tone, Tone, Semitone, Tone, and not, as in the 1492 edition and in Gallicus, Tone, Semitone, Tone, etc. as the A to A scale ascends.

In the next generation, Gaffurio's attitude towards Boethius was ambivalent. He seems eager never to contradict him; yet he furnished an abundance of contradictory evidence that he neither fully accepted or rejected.

---

[5] Ibid. 3. 9. 2 (p. 70). 'Boetius in allegato superius quarto suae musicae libro, capitulo necnon eodem quartodecimo, tropos, tonos sive modos diffinit in haec verba: *Sunt*, ait, *tropi constitutiones in totis vocum ordinibus vel gravitate vel acumine differentes*. Vis videre quot ita sit? Figuras illas de constitutionibus diligenter aspice. Prima namque gravior est uno tono secunda, si rem iuste discurreris, et secunda tono similiter altior magis acuta, sicque de singulis subsequentibus. In hunc modum ad invicem comparatis, quae se semper uno tono superant aut minori semitonio, seque praecedunt et subsequuntur. Ex quo quidem colligimus nil esse vel umquam fuisse tropos tam Graecos quam Latinos, tamque seculares quam ecclesiasticos nisi constitutiones illas nilque rursum aliud constitutio quam consonantiarum iuxta Boetii diffinitionem coniunctio.'

[6] Ibid. 3. 10; the inscription is missing in Seay's edn. 'Hi tropi modique Graeci, / Quos et vocavere tonos, / Expressi Graecis litteris / Ac declarati Latinis / Arte magis compositi, / Quam [a] natura conditi, / Solis locis hic differunt / Totique parent similes. / Quos tamen in Boetio / Notae diversae variant / Et mensurae dissimiles / Erant, opinor, omnibus, / Nam tropi nostri Latini / Sunt a natura geniti, / Certe toti dissimiles / Quamquam simul colligati.'

[7] Boethius, *Opera, quae extant omnia* (Basle: Henricus Petrus, 1546), 4. 15, p. 1159.

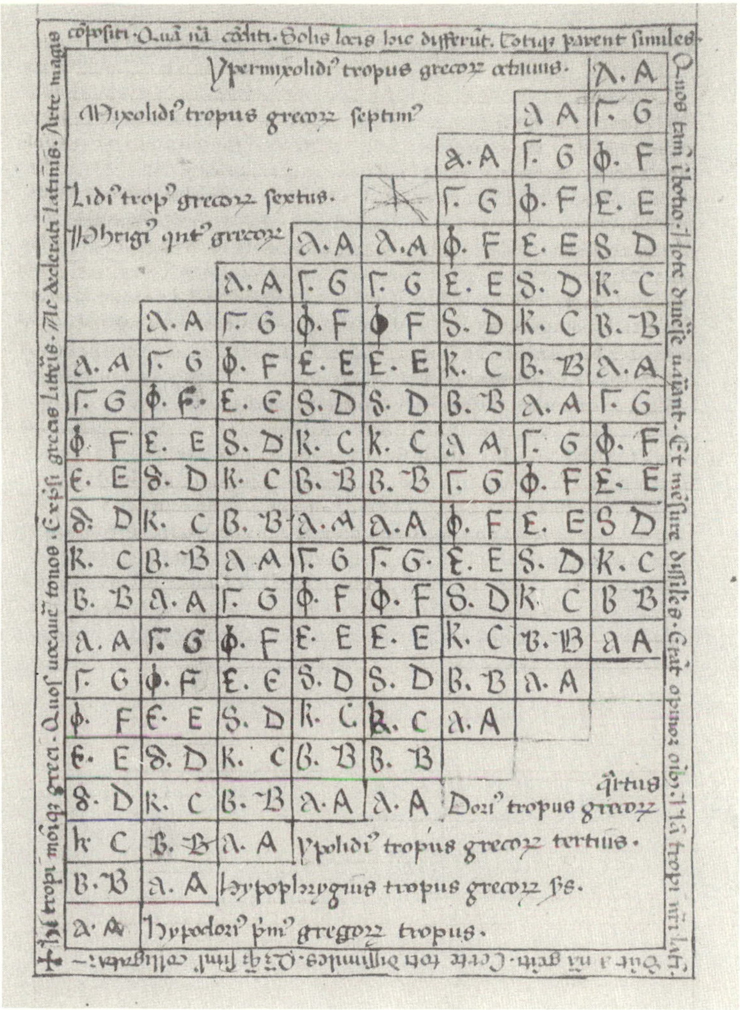

PL. 6.1. The system of Greek tropes, from J. Gallicus, *Ritus canendi*, bk. iii,
ch. 10. London, British Library, Add. MS 22315, fo. 26ʳ

Gaffurio's *Theoricum opus musice discipline* of 1480 consisted in great part of
paraphrases of Boethius.[8] With the revision of 1492 under the title *Theorica
musice*, a quantity of material from Bacchius, pseudo-Plutarch, Themistius,
Plato, Aristotle, and other Greek authors was introduced to supplement
Boethius, but when these authors disagreed, Gaffurio was reluctant to

---

[8] Franchino Gaffurio, *Theoricum opus musice discipline* (Naples: Francesco di Dino, 8 Oct. 1480).

decide who was correct.[9] The *De harmonia musicorum instrumentorum opus* of 1518[10] is anchored in Ptolemy and Bryennius, but on some major issues, such as the division of the monochord, Gaffurio remained loyal to Boethius, and this got him into a dispute with followers of Ramos de Pareja, notably Giovanni Spataro.[11]

Although many authors passed over Boethius in silence, Nicola Vicentino, who had a passion for completeness, after spending sixteen short chapters of his first book—only six out of 146 folios—on certain chapters of Boethius that he deemed most necessary and difficult, sent the reader to Boethius himself for the rest, but not before adding an 'Epilogue of the things spoken of as well as the things not spoken of in the five books of the Music of Boethius'.[12] It is interesting particularly to see what Vicentino in 1555 did not consider necessary to review. In the first book of Boethius he listed: the antiquity, excellence, and effects of music, whether cosmic, human, or instrumental; the elements of music; the species of inequality; the five genres of proportions; what sound, interval, and consonance are; the weakness of the judgement of the senses; the various ways that Pythagoras experienced the musical proportions; what is the continuous and the discrete voice; how we hear; the orders of the Theorem, that is, the three genera of tetrachord; of who added to the strings; the disputes among Plato, Nicomachus, Ptolemy, Aristoxenus, and others; what a musician and singer are.

Then, from the second book, he felt that he could pass over: how the Pythagoreans considered philosophy to rest in the differences of quantity; why the multiplex genre proceeds to the others; square numbers; numbers that generate consonances; the geometric and arithmetic means; conjunct

---

[9] Gaffurio, *Theorica musice* (Milan: Filippo Mantegazza, 15 Dec. 1492; repr. Milan: La Musica Moderna, 1934; repr. Monuments of Music and Music Literature in Facsimile, second series, no. 21, New York: Broude Brothers, [1967]). See Walter K. Kreyszig, 'Franchino Gaffurio's *Theorica musice* (1492): Edition, Translation, and Study of Sources', Ph.D. diss. (Yale University, 1989) and Franchino Gaffurio, *The Theory of Music*, trans. with introduction and notes, by Walter Kreyszig, ed. Claude V. Palisca (New Haven, Conn.: Yale University Press, 1993). Kreyszig's commentary is scheduled for publication by Wilhelm Braumüller, Vienna, under the title *Franchino Gaffurio's Theorica musice (1492): A Study of the Sources* in the series Musica Mediaevalis Europea occidentalis, ed. Walter Pass.

[10] Gaffurio, *De harmonia musicorum instrumentorum opus* (Milan: Gottardo Ponzio, 27 Nov. 1518; repr. Monuments of Music and Music Literature in Facsimile, second series, no. 97, New York: Broude Brothers, 1979), trans. with an introduction by Clement A. Miller (Musicological Studies and Documents, 33; n.p.: American Institute of Musicology, 1977).

[11] See C. V. Palisca, *Humanism in Italian Renaissance Musical Thought* (New Haven, Conn.: Yale University Press, 1985), 191–225.

[12] Nicola Vicentino, *L'antica musica ridotta alla moderna prattica* (Rome: Antonio Barre, 1555; repr. Documenta musicologica, 17, ed. Edward E. Lowinsky, Basle: Bärenreiter, 1959), Libro della theorica musicale, i. 16, fo. 6ʳ: 'Epilogo si delle cose dette come anchora delle non dette nelli cinque Libri della Musica di Boetio.'

and disjunct means; the consonances according to Nicomachus, Eubulides, and others.

From the third book Vicentino left out: how Philolaus divided the tone; that the tone is more than eight commas but less than nine; that apotome means major semitone.

From the fourth book Vicentino overlooked: the differences of stable steps; discrete quantity; the names of the notes in Greek and Latin letters; the division of the regular monochord in the diatonic and other genera.

From the fifth book (Vicentino does not give the book number) he mentions omitting: Ptolemy's opinion concerning differences of tones (because this would be included in the *Prattica*); unison, equisone, consone, and discordant pitches; the division of the tone; the genera according to Aristoxenus; dense and non-dense, intense, and relaxed steps in all the three genera. Vicentino justified this table of exclusions by the statement: 'We have omitted all these things because they are not of any use today in our practice.'[13]

Vicentino's attitude towards the content of Boethius' treatise is all the more appalling because it is expressed in a book that purports to adapt ancient music, which is the subject of Boethius' treatise, to modern practice: *L'antica musica ridotta alla moderna prattica*. At the same time the list is evidence that Vicentino was familiar with all the contents of Boethius (or, at least, with the Table of Contents). But if not Boethius, whom did he follow? He had no translations of Ptolemy, Aristoxenus, Nicomachus, Bryennius, or Aristides Quintilianus. Only Euclid, Cleonides, and pseudo-Plutarch had been published in translation.[14] It is not only ancient music that is reduced in this book to the modern practice; knowledge of ancient theory is reduced to a minimum.

With Francisco de Salinas we have a very different case. He knew a great deal about ancient music and read (or rather, had read to him, because he was blind) almost all the Greek authors from the original Greek. From this perspective he could place Boethius in a historical context. He says of him:

Boethius is entirely Pythagorean, and in his two books concerning arithmetic and in the first four books concerning music he followed Nicomachus and set forth the position of the Pythagoreans; in the fifth, however, he promised the opinions of others on matters concerning which the ancient authors disagreed. Here, with subtle judgement, he would have led us to a middle course, but he left it incomplete, whether because death intervened or because he was preoccupied with

[13] Ibid., fo. 6ᵛ: 'Hauiamo lasciato a dire tutte queste cose per non ci essere hoggi utile alcuno alla nostra prattica . . .'.

[14] M. Rika Maniates is preparing a translation of Vicentino's book for the Yale Music Theory Translation Series, in which Vicentino's sources will be studied in detail.

other adversities. For, had he fulfilled his plan, perhaps he might have relieved us of these labours.[15]

It is strange that in speaking of the fifth book Salinas did not mention Boethius' dependence therein on the first book of Ptolemy, because Salinas knew Ptolemy well. Indeed, Salinas, who leaned on Ptolemy more than on any other ancient author, implied that, had Boethius completed his summary of Ptolemy, Salinas's own work would have been rendered unnecessary. There is an element of ceremonious tribute in this, because a little later Salinas accused Boethius of confusing the tonoi and the modes.[16]

Salinas marked a turn in the Renaissance reception of Boethius, who was then no longer the prime authority on *musica theorica*; others more ancient had taken his place. Boethius was now perceived as a transmitter rather than originator of theoretical precepts. He was also not infallible. Nevertheless, Salinas was wrong to charge Boethius with mixing up the modes and the *tonoi*, even if it must be acknowledged that Boethius did little to make the distinction clear, particularly by the looseness of his terminology.

The first scholar to point out that Ptolemy did not add the eighth 'mode' or *tonos* imputed to him by Boethius was Girolamo Mei. Mei made plain that Ptolemy considered the Hypermixolydian futile and superfluous, reporting Ptolemy's arguments against exceeding the number seven.[17]

Despite the declining valorization in the Renaissance of the theoretical system of Boethius, the last decades of the sixteenth century witnessed the drafting of the first vernacular translations of this work, both into Italian. Neither one of them, unfortunately, was ever published.

The earlier of the translations, which were independent of each other, was by Giorgio Bartoli, descendant of a prominent and ancient Florentine family. He completed the Boethius translation in 1579. He was already dead when in 1584 his only known book was published, *Degli elementi del parlar toscano* (Florence: Giunti, 1584), with a letter of dedication from Cosimo Bartoli to Lorenzo Giacomini. Giorgio Bartoli had served as amanuensis to Giacomini, a fact that may be gathered from sixty letters written

---

[15] Francisco de Salinas, *De musica libri septem* (Salamanca: Mathias Gastius, 1577; repr. Documenta musicologica, 13, ed. Macario Santiago Kastner, Kassel: Bärenreiter, 1958), i. 18, p. 73: 'Boëtius autem totus Pythagoricus est, & in libris duobus de Arithmetica, & quatuor primis de Musica Nicomachum secutus, Pythagoraeorum tantùm positiones exposuit: quintum autem, in quo promiserat se aliorum opiniones, in quibus veteres autores sententiarum diuersitate discordant, in medium adducturum, & de his subtile iudicium facturum, imperfectum reliquit, aut morte, aut alijs calamitatibus praeoccupatus: quod si re praestitisset, fortasse nos his laboribus liberasset.'

[16] Ibid., iv. 12, p. 198, speaking of Boethius, *De institutione musica*, 4. 15.

[17] Girolamo Mei, *De modis musicis antiquorum*, Biblioteca Apostolica Vaticana, MS Vat. lat 5323, bk. ii, pp. 90–1, ed. as *De modis* by Tsugami Eisuke (Tokyo: Keiso Shobo, 1991), 65. The passage is quoted and translated in Palisca, *Humanism*, 312–13.

by Giorgio Bartoli to Giacomini preserved in the Biblioteca Riccardiana.[18] They are valuable for their reports on literary and theatrical activities in Florence. Giorgio Bartoli was the copyist of the set of letters from Girolamo Mei to Vincenzo Galilei and Giovanni Bardi preserved in the Regina collection of the Vatican Library.[19] The copy may have been made for Giacomini, who had an intense interest in ancient music, but Bartoli may also have made it for his own use. The Boethius translation attests to a sympathetic understanding of ancient music theory, which may have been cultivated through Bartoli's contacts with Galilei and Bardi. The years 1578 to 1581 were the most productive of writings by those associated with Bardi's Camerata, which Bartoli may have attended. Bardi's own Discourse, addressed to Caccini,[20] the drafting of Galilei's *Dialogo della musica antica et della moderna*, published in 1581,[21] as well as the Boethius translation fell in those years.

Bartoli's autograph of the translation is in the Biblioteca Nazionale Centrale of Florence in MS Magl. XIX. 75,[22] followed by the table of notation.

The other translation is by Ercole Bottrigari. There are two copies in Bologna, one in the Civico Museo Bibliografico Musicale, MS B-43, the other in Bologna, Biblioteca Universitaria, MS 326, Busta I, 1. I used the University copy. They are both in the hand of Bottrigari and have nearly identical title-pages and colophons.[23] A Proemio by Bottrigari precedes the

---

[18] Florence, Biblioteca Riccardiana, MS 2438.

[19] Vatican City, Biblioteca Apostolica Vaticana, MS Reg. lat. 2021.

[20] A new edition and translation of *Discorso mandato a Giulio Caccini detto Romano sopra la musica antica, e 'l cantar bene* by Giovanni Bardi is in C. V. Palisca, *The Camerata Fiorentina: Documentary Studies and Translations* (New Haven, Conn.: Yale University Press, 1989), 78–131.

[21] Vincenzo Galilei, *Dialogo della musica antica et della moderna* (Florence: Giorgio Marescotti, 1581; repr. Monuments of Music and Music Literature in Facsimile, second series, no. 20, New York: Broude Brothers, [1967]).

[22] The title, in Bartoli's hand, at the top of the first folio reads: 'DE LA MVSICA DI BOETHIO LIBRO PRIMO', after which ch. 1 immediately follows. An added preliminary leaf in an unknown hand gives the following information: 'No. 579 / Della Musica di Boetio, di Giorgio / Bartoli / originale / Del Sen.^re Carlo di Tommaso Strozzi / 1670.' The manuscript consists of 156 folios, and after ch. 18 of bk. v, on fo. 156^v, the translator wrote 'Finito à di 17 di Marzo 1579'. It is a fair copy, but fo. 105^{r–v} contains a draft of part of iv. 3, which is recopied almost verbatim on fos. 106^r–107^r.

[23] The title-page in the University copy reads: 'I CINQVE LIBRI/ DI MVSICA/ Di Anitio Manlio Severino Boetio/ dallo Ill:^e Sig:^e Cavaliere/ Hercole Bottrigaro/ tradutti in parlare/ Italiano./ In Bologna MDIIIC.' At the end (Univ., fol. 90^r; Civ. Mus., p. 194) Bottrigari wrote (following the Civico Museo copy; spelling and abbreviations vary slightly in the University copy): 'Fù dato fine alla Traduttione in parlare Italiano di questi cinque libri di Musica di Boethio da me Herc.^e Bottrigaro à hore 3 5/6 (secondo che mostra il mio Horol.° da Tauola) della ns. il dì 21 di Novemb. 1597, in Bolo.ª.' He also gave the date and time he finished each of the other books (bk. i was finished on 17 Oct. 1597). On fo. 90^v of the University copy (Civ. Mus., p. 195) are added tables of Ptolemy's own tetrachord divisions (from *Harm.* i. 15) as an appendix to Boethius v. 19, numbered v. 18 in Bottrigari. This addition is dated 22 Nov. 1597 in both copies.

translation. Here he states that in the preface to his translation into Italian of Euclid's *Division of the Monochord* and his *Harmonic Institution* (now attributed to Cleonides), works that he particularly admired, he promised to translate also the 'Harmonic Fragments' of Aristoxenus and Ptolemy, the 'fragmentary Isagoge Armonica' of Alypius, the synopsis of Psellus, the *Introduction* of Gaudentius, all that concerns music in the writings of Martianus Capella, Censorinus, Cassiodorus, Fogliano, and other Latin authors. After completing these, he said he would turn to the five books of the 'Instituzione Musicale' of Boethius. Having, in fact, finished the other translations, and, besides, section 19 of the *Problems* of Aristotle, he resolved now to do the Boethius. None of the translations of the Greek authors he mentioned survives, though there exists one of Aristotle's *De audibilibus* as well as corrections to Gogava's translations of Aristoxenus and Ptolemy.[24] At first, Bottrigari confesses, he was bothered by the many unnecessary repetitions and the prolixity of the Boethius treatise, but he ended up admiring the 'beautiful order' (*bell'Ordine*) of the work as a whole.

Both Bartoli's and Bottrigari's translations are generally reliable and fluent. At times they are very similar, but Bottrigari does not give evidence of knowing Bartoli's translation. Bartoli based his translation on the Venetian edition of 1492, as is apparent from the table of notation of iv. 3 and the diagrams.[25] However, the diagram of the *tonoi* in iv. 15 is corrected to show them rising Tone, Tone, Semitone, Tone, Tone, Semitone, Tone, instead of the 1492 edition's incorrect Tone, Semitone, Tone, Tone, Semitone, Tone, Tone. Galilei pointed out this error in 1581.[26] Bottrigari did not follow the printed editions but seems to have made a collation from various sources, about which his preface is silent.

I shall compare Bartoli's and Bottrigari's versions of two chapters that I believe present particular challenges to a translator. The first is book i, ch. 12, concerning the motion of the voice (see Table 6.1). Bottrigari's rendition is clearly superior. Bartoli goes astray in lines 8–9 at the phrase 'et l'espedire i sensi et esprimere i parlari continuamente opera l'impeto de la voce'—'and the impetus of the voice operates continually to convey the meanings and to express the speeches'. It is not clear to me what that

[24] 'Dell'oggetto dell'vdito overo delle cose udibili, Libbro Frammentato di Aristotile tradutto in Lingua Italiana Dal Molto Illustre Signore Cavaliere Hercole Bottrigari', dated 14 Jan. 1606, Bologna, Biblioteca Universitaria, MS lat. 326, no. 6. The corrections to the Gogava is in a copy of Gogava's collection, *Aristoxeni musici antiquiss. harmonicorum elementorum libri iii* . . . (Venice: Vincenzo Valgrisio, 1562), Bologna, Civico Museo Bibliografico Musicale, MS A-1. Concerning these works, see Palisca, *Humanism*, 157–60.

[25] Boethius, *Opera* (Venice: Giovanni e Gregorio de Gregori, 18 Aug. 1492), fo. 194ʳ; Bartoli, fo. 107ʳ.

[26] Galilei, *Dialogo*, 59.

means. Bottrigari renders the idea well: 'e nella spedizione de sensi, e nella espressione de ragionamenti lo impeto della voce continuata fà la sua operazione'—'and the impetus of the continuous voice accomplishes its operation in the conveyance of the meanings and in the expression of the thoughts'.

In the definition of the diastematic voice, lines 10 to 14, Bartoli again stumbles: 'et è la voce pju tarda et per le varietà cantabili fa un intervallo, non di taciturnità, ma piu tosto di sospesa et tarda cantilena' (and this is the slower voice and through singable variety makes an interval, not of silence, but rather of suspended and sluggish song). Again the meaning is obscure. Bottrigari is more transparent: 'Tarda ancora è essa voce, e per cantar variatamente fà certi intervalli non tacendo: ma sospendendo, e più tosto impigrendo la cantilena' (This voice is also sluggish, and through varied singing makes certain intervals, not keeping silent but suspending and rather making the song lazy). Bartoli, though he was a literary critic, also fails to catch the reference to the genre of heroic poetry, speaking instead of poems of heroes.

I might cite here Calvin Bower's translation of the key sentences, since it captures the spirit of the original. For the first passage, lines 8–9, Bower has: 'and the impulse of continuous voice is occupied with pronouncing and giving meanings to the words'. For the second passage, lines 11 to 14: 'This particular voice is more deliberate, and by measuring out differences of pitch it produces a certain interval, not of silence, but of sustained and drawn out song.'[27]

Chapter 14 of book iv[28] (see Table 6.2) is one of the most crucial and difficult in the entire treatise and was a stumbling block to most of the medieval and early Renaissance readers of Boethius. Although both translators were hampered by a faulty text, their Italian versions are as accurate as the text permitted. The difficulties that exist in the Latin text are reflected without distortion in the Italian. Anyone reading these translations would gather from them a configuration of modes, tropes, or tones that consists of transpositions of systems containing an octave, octave-plus-fourth, or double-octave at levels separated by tone, tone, semitone, and so on for the rest. The diagram given in Bartoli for chapter 15 (Pl. 6.2) agrees with this conception of the tropes, although it adds the spurious eighth, Hypermixolydian, mode, not mentioned in this chapter. The arches enclos-

[27] Boethius, *Fundamentals of Music*, trans. Calvin M. Bower, ed. Claude V. Palisca (Music Theory Translation Series; New Haven, Conn.: Yale University Press, 1989), 20.

[28] In Friedlein the table of Greek notational signs after ch. 3 is numbered as ch. 4, whereas in the 1492 and 1546 editions and in the Bartoli and Bottrigari translations this is not a separate chapter. Thus Friedlein's chapter numbers after the third are one greater than the older editions.

TABLE 6.1. *Translations of Boethius, i. 12*

Friedlein text:	Bartoli:	Bottrigari:
1 De divisione vocum earumque explanatione.	[15ᵛ] De la divisione de le voci et loro dichiarazione C	[16ᵛ] Della divisione delle voci, e della dichiarazione di quelle.
2 XII. Sed de his hactenus. Nunc vocum differentias	XII Ma di queste cose insino à qui, ora raccogliamo	Cap. 12. Ma non più di questo: raccontiamo ora le differentie delle voci;
3 colligamus. Omnis vox aut συνεχης est, quae continua,	le differenze de le voci, pero che ogni voce e ò sineches cio è continua;	imperòche ogni voce o è [syneches] la quale è detta continuata,
4 aut διαστηματικη, quae dicitur cum intervallo suspensa.	ò diastematica, la quale è detta sospesa con intervallo:	ò diasematica la quale è detta sospesa con [17ᵛ] intervallo.
5 Et continua quidem est, qua loquentes vel prosam orationem	continua è quella con la quale parlando ò	Et continovata è quella; con la quale quando si parla over che si
6 legentes verba percurrimus. Festinat enim tunc vox	leggendo la prosa scorriamo le parole; peroche allora la voce si	legge una prosa trascorriamo le parole: imperòche allora la voce si sollecita
7 non haerere in acutis et gravibus sonis, sed quam velocissime	affretta non fermarsi ne' suoni acuti e gravi, ma quanto piu velocemente	di non fermarsi ne' suoni acuti, e gravi ma di scorrere velocemente
8 verba percurrere, expediendisque sensibus exprimendisque	puo scorer le parole et l'espedire i sensi et esprimere	le parole; e nella spedizione de sensi, e nella espressione de
9 sermonibus continuae vocis impetus operatur.	i parlari continuamente opera l'impeto de la voce:	ragionamenti lo impeto della voce continuata fà la sua operazione.

10	Διαστηματικη autem est ea, quam canendo suspendimus,	Diastematica è quella la quale cantando sospendiamo,	Diastematica è quella; la qual teniamo sospesa in cantando,
11	in qua non potius sermonibus sed modulis inservimus,	ne la quale non piu tosto à parlari, ma al canto serviamo;	et in lei non serviamo piuttosto al ragionamento: ma alla cantilena.
12	estque vox ipsa tardior et per modulandas varietates quoddam	et è la voce piu tarda et per le varietà cantabili	Tarda ancora è essa voce, e per cantar variatamente
13	faciens intervallum, non taciturnitatis sed suspensae	fa un intervallo, non di taciturnità, ma piu tosto di sospesa	fa certi intervalli non tacendo: ma sospendendo, e più tosto
14	ac tardae potius cantilenae. His, ut Albinus autumat, additur	et tarda cantilena. à queste sicome afferma Albino si aggiugne	impigrendo la cantilena. A questi (come dice Albino) si aggiunge
15	tertia differentia, quae medias voces possit includere,	la terza differenza la quale include le voci mezzane, quando	la terza differenza: la quale possa contenere le mezze voci;
16	cum scilicet heroum poema legimus neque continuo cursu,	cio è leggiamo i poemi de gli Eroi, ne con corso continuo come la prosa,	allora cioè che noi leggiamo i Poemi Eroici, non con corso continovato,
17	ut prosam, neque suspenso segnioríque modo vocis, ut	ne con modo di voce sospeso et tardo come il	come la Prosa ne con modo sospeso e pigro come
18	canticum.	cantico.	il Canto.

TABLE 6.2. *Translations of Boethius, iv. 14*

Friedlein text:	Bartoli:	Bottrigari:
[341]		
17 De modorum exordiis, in quo dispositio notarum per	[133ᵛ] De principii de modi et disposizion de le note di	[76ᵛ] De Principi de Tuoni et dell'Ordine delle Note per Tutti i Tuoni,
18 singulos modos ac voces.	ciascun modo et suono	e per tutte le Uoci
19 XV. Ex diapason igitur consonantiae speciebus existunt,	CAP XIIII. De le spezie dunque de la consonanza nascono quelli	Cap. 14. Delle specie adunque della consonantia Diapason nascono
20 qui appellantur modi, quos eosdem tropos vel tonos nominant.	che sono chiamati modi, i quali anco nominano Tropi, ò tuoni.	i nominati modi: che anco sono detti Tropi, over Tuoni:
21 Sunt autem tropi constitutiones in totis vocum ordinibus	et sono constituzioni negli ordini de le voci, li quali constituzioni	et i Tropi sono costituzioni in tutti gli ordini delle voci diverse
22 vel gravitate vel acumine differentes. Constitutio	differiscono di gravità et di acutezza. et la constituzione	o per gravitade, o per acutezza: et la costituzione
23 vero est plenum veluti modulationis corpus ex consonantiarum	è quasi corpo pieno di modulazione composto di	è siccome in un intiero corpo di modulazione:
24 coniunctione consistens quale est vel diapason	congiunzion di consonanze, quale è la diapason ò la diapente, et	composto di conjiungimento di consonantie, quale è la Diapente,
25 vel diapason et diatessaron vel bis diapason. Est enim	diatessaron, o vero la bisdiapason peroche è constituzione di diapason	ò la Diatessaron, ò la Bisdiapason. et la Diapente è una

[342]

1	constitutio a proslambanomeno in mesen ceteris	da la proslamvanomenon à la mese, connumerate	costituzione da Proslambanomenos à Meson, comprese
2	quae sunt mediae vocibus adnumeratis, vel a mese rursus	l'altre voci che sono in mezzo: et da la mese	le altre voci; che sono trameze overo da Mese ancora
3	in neten hyperboleon cum vocibus interiectis, vel ab hypate	à la nete iperboleon con le voci interposte et da la ipate	à Nete hyperboleon insieme con le voci proposte. overo da Hypate
4	meson in neten diezeugmenon cum his, quas extremae	meson à la nete diezeugmenon con quelle che racchiuggono le voci	Meson à Nete hyperboleon con le voci; che ricercaua [?]
5	voces medias claudunt. Synemmenon vero constitutio ea	estreme. Ma la constitutione di diapason diatessaron è quella che	nel mezzo l'estreme. La Diapason Diatessaron è quella costituzione,
6	est, quae a proslambanomeno in neten synemmenon cum	è da la proslamvanomeno à la nete sinemmenon	che è da Proslambanomenos à Nete synemmenon, insieme con le voci,
7	his, quae mediae interiectae sunt, constat. Bis diapason	con le voci interposte. Ma la bisdiapason	che sono tramezze. La Bisdiapason si ha in considerazione principiandosi

TABLE 6.2. *Continued*

Friedlein text:	Bartoli:	Bottrigari:
8 autem a proslambanomeno in neten hyperboleon cum his,	è considerata da la proslamvanomenos à la nete iperboleon con le interposte. queste	da Proslambanomenos sino à Nete hyperboleon con quelle voci
9 quae in medio sunt interpositae, consideratur. Has igitur		che sono loro in mezzo. Se qualcuno adunque farà tutte queste
10 constitutiones si quis totas faciat acutiores, vel in gravius	costituzioni adunque se alcuno farà pju acute,	costituzioni più acute; o tutte le farà più gravi
11 totas remittat secundum supradictas diapason consonantiae	ò vero più gravi secondo le spezie sopradette de	conforme alle sopradette specie della consonantia
12 species, efficiet modos. VII. quorum nomina sunt haec:	la diapason farà i sette modi, de quali questi sono i nomi.	Diapason: formarà i sette modi i nomi de quali sono questi.
13 hypodorius, hypophrygius, hypolydius, dorius, phrygius,	Ipodorio, Ipofrigio, Ipolidio, Dorio, Frigio,	Hypodorio, Hypofrigio, Hypolidio, Dorio, Frigio,
14 lydius, mixolydius. Horum vero sic ordo procedit. Sit in	Lidio, Mixolidio. et l'ordine di questi cosi procede. Sia nel	Hypolidio, Lidio, Missolidio. Et l'ordine loro è tale. Se nel genere
15 diatonico genere vocum ordo dispositus a proslambanomeno	genere diatonico disposto l'ordine [134ʳ] de le voci da la proslamvanomeno	diatonico l'ordine delle voci da Proslambanomenos
16 in neten hyperboleon atque hic sit hypodorius modus.	à la nete iperboleon, et questo sia il modo ipodorio.	a Nete hyperboleon: et questo sia il Modo Hypodorio.

17	Si quis igitur proslambanomenon in acumen intendat tono	se alcuno acutirà la proslamvanomeno per un tuono: et medesimamente	Se qualcuno inacutirà per un Tuono la Proslambanomenos et per un'
18	hypatenque hypaton eodem tono adtenuet ceterasque	l'hipate ipaton per l'istesso tuono et gli altri tuoni farà più acuti,	altro Tuono la Hypate hypaton e faccia più acuti tutti gli altri suoni:
19	omnes tono faciat acutiores, acutior totus ordo proveniet,	tutto l'ordine diverà più acuta che fusse prima	tutto l'ordine diventerà più acuto che non era prima
20	quam fuit priusquam toni susciperet intentionem. Erit	che ricevesse l'acutezza del tuono. Sarà	che gli fusse inacutito per un Tuono[.] Tutta
21	igitur tota constitutio acutior effecta hypophrygius modus.	adunque tutta la constitutione fatta piu acuta modo Ipofrigio.	questa costitutione adunque fatta più acuta farà il modo Hypofrigio.
22	Quod si in hypophrygio toni rursus intentionem voces	Et se nel ipofrigio le voci riceverano di nuovo acutezza	Et se di nuovo le voci pigliaranno acutezza quel modo Hypofrigio per un
23	acceperint, hypolydii modulatio nascetur. At si hypolydium	di tuono nascera la modulazione del Ipolidio. Ma se alcuno	Tuono, la cantilena sarà del modo Hypolidio: et se l'Hypolidio si acutirà
24	quis semitonio intendat, dorium faciet. Et in aliis quidem	acutira per semituono l'Ipolidio farà il Dorio, et negli	per un Semituono, nascerà il Dorio[.] [77'] Et il procedere
25	similis est in acumen intentionemque processus, quorum	altri e simile progresso ne l'acutezza.	verso l'acutezza è simile negli altri (Modi). La intelligentia de quali,
26	non ut intelligentia solum ratio conprehendatur, verum	L'intelligenza de la quali cose accioche non solo da la ragione sia compresa,	accioche si abbia non solamente con ragione, ma che si possa conoscere
27	oculis quoque forma possit agnosci, ab antiquis tradita	ma ancora la forma possa esser conosciuta	ancora con gli occhi la forma data da Musici antichi:

TABLE 6.2. *Continued*

Friedlein text:	Bartoli:	Bottrigari:
[343]		
1 musicis descriptio subponenda est. Sed quoniam per singulos	con gli occhi si dee porre la descrizione	qui sotto si ha da puonere la descrizione. Ma perciòche in ciascun
2 modos a veteribus musicis unaquaeque vox diversis	data da gli antichi musici. Ma perche ciascuna	modo fù da Musici antichi segnata ogni voce con diversi caratteri:
3 notulis insignita est, descriptio prius notularum videtur	è da i musici notata per ciascun modo con diversi segni,	pare che sia da esser posta prima la descrizione di esse Noticelle:
4 esse ponenda, ut his primum per se cognitis in modorum	pare che sia prima da porsi la descrizion de segni, accioche conosciuti	accioche conosciute primieramente queste da per loro,
5 descriptione facilis possit esse dispectio.	questi pju facile sia la considerazione ne la descrizion de modi.	possa alla vista riuscir facile la descrizione de Modi[.]

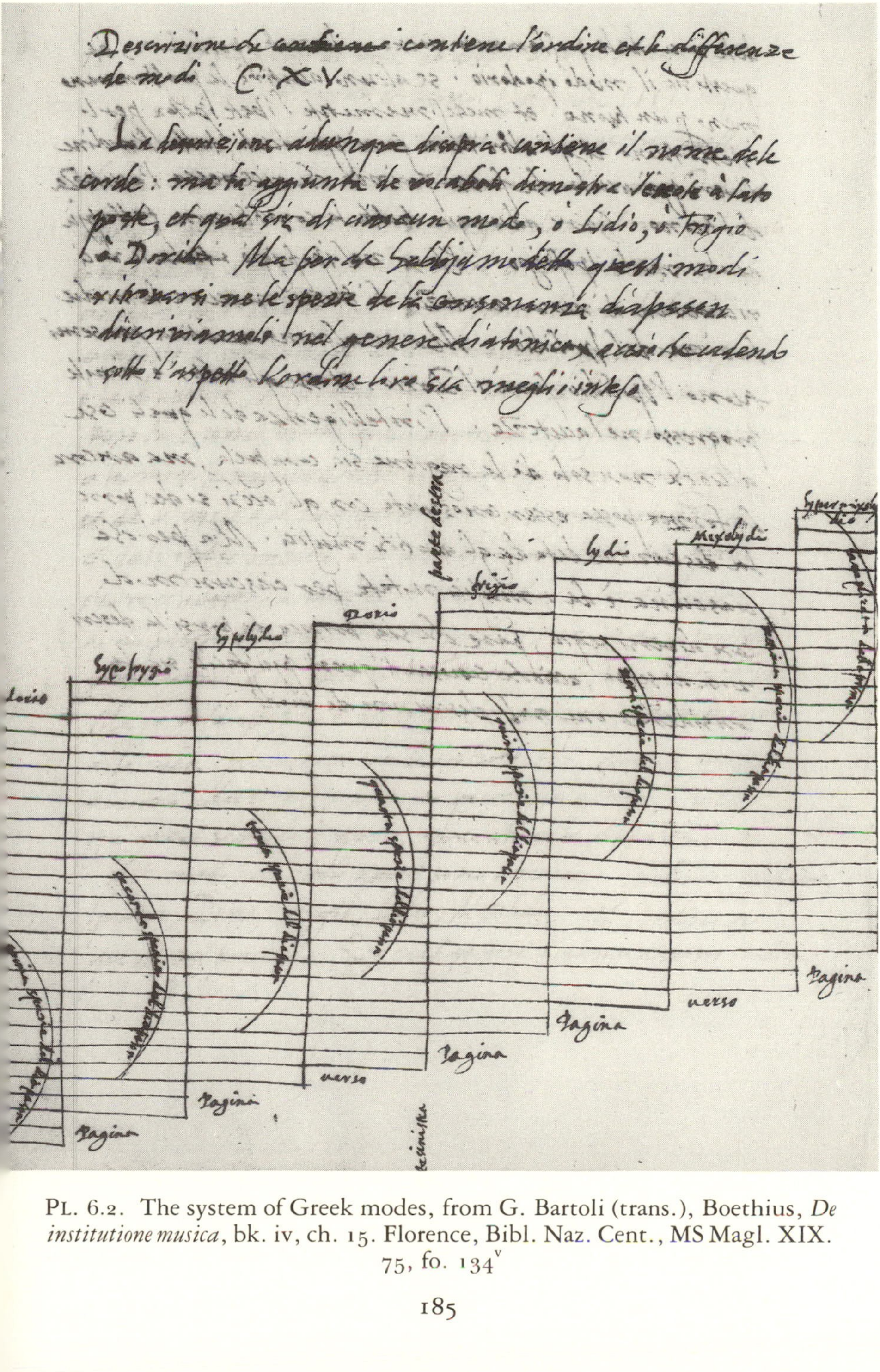

PL. 6.2. The system of Greek modes, from G. Bartoli (trans.), Boethius, *De institutione musica*, bk. iv, ch. 15. Florence, Bibl. Naz. Cent., MS Magl. XIX. 75, fo. 134ᵛ

ing the species of octave are meaningless, because they simply mark off twelve semitones without showing the placement of the semitones among the whole tones. Bottrigari, in both the Bologna University and Civico Museo copies, drew the vertical lines but never completed the diagram. Bottrigari was incredulous about this system, as he shows by his comments in the preface, referring to several places in which he hypothesizes that Boethius perhaps did not have a chance to revise his writing.

[1ᵛ] Come quando egli ordina la descrizione dell'ordine de Tuoni ò Modi nel Genere Diatonico, facendoli [2ʳ] ascender tutti indifferentemente nel loro proprio sistema per Semituono, Tuono, e Tuono. Così non vengono essi ad essere uno istesso e solo systema diverso in acutezza di suono solamente dal principio loro? Et ei pur conforme a' Musici Greci confessa nel 15. et 14. cap. antecedente che ciascun systema di sette Modi ò Tuoni sono tra loro diversi per quella diversità, che è tra Diapason, et Diapason: Ma di questo avendo io, come hò teste accennato, lungamente discorso altrove, siccome di essa divisione del Tuono, in due Semituoni hò fatto in questa mia traduzione al suo luogo annotazione, per ora non ve ne dirò Cortesissimi Lettori cosa alcuna altra:

For example, when he arranges the description of the order of the *tonoi* or modes in the diatonic genus, making them all ascend without any difference in their proper system by semitone, tone, and tone. Thus do they not end up being the same one and only system different only in height of pitch from the beginning? Yet he, in keeping with the Greek musicians, confesses in the 15th and 14th chapters previously that each system of seven modes or *tonoi* is different, just as the diapasons are different from each other. But since, as I mentioned, I discussed this at length elsewhere, as also concerning the division of the tone into two semitones, I have made an annotation in this translation in the proper place, and for now, courteous reader, I shall not say anything more.[29]

Perhaps it is because he could not believe Boethius' words that Bottrigari failed to finish the diagram for chapter 15. Bartoli, unburdened by the bias of modern musicians, gives as good a representation of the system as may be found anywhere at this date (apart from Mei's *De modis musicis*), anticipating in this respect Galilei's *Dialogo* of 1581.

Comparing the translations on some smaller points, I should point to the following:

The first sentence, Friedlein 341. 19–20, is faulty in both versions for diverse reasons. Bartoli leaves out the word 'diapason' in 'De le spezie dunque de la consonanza [diapason]'. Bottrigari says 'nascono i nominati

---

[29] Actually no annotations appear in these places in the translations in the University copy.

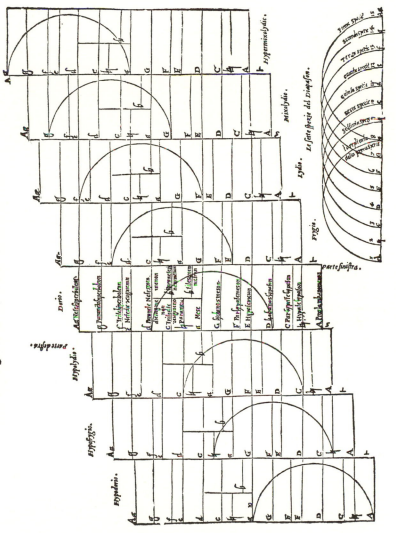

PL. 6.3. Demonstration of the eight *toni* according to Boethius, from V. Galilei, *Dialogo* (Florence, 1581), p. 58

modi' (arise the modes named), when the meaning is 'nascono quelli che sono chiamati modi' (arise those things which are called modes), as Bartoli has it. Both translators fail to render correctly the conjunctions of consonances mentioned in Friedlein 341. 23–5. Here Boethius names the systems that are subject to transposition in the *tonoi*, namely the diapason, diapason-plus-diatessaron, and bisdiapason. Bartoli says 'composto di congiunzion di consonanze, quale è la diapason, ò la diapente, et diatessaron, o vero la bisdiapason', when he should have said 'congiunzion di consonanze, quale è la diapason, la diapason et diatessaron, overo la bisdiapason'. Similarly, Bottrigari says 'conjiungimento di consonantie, quale è la Diapente, ò la Diatessaron, ò la Bisdiapason'. This error stems from the 1492 edition or manuscripts having a similar reading. In the next sentence, Friedlein 341. 25 to 342. 1, Bottrigari makes a slip and says 'Diapente' instead of 'Diapason' in describing the system between proslambanomenos and mese.

But these are small matters. Either Italian version would be suitable for publication today with some good editing.

Why should Bartoli and Bottrigari have translated the Boethius work for the first time in the last quarter of the sixteenth century at the very moment when musicians were losing interest in classical music theory? One answer, of course, is that competence in Latin was no longer possessed by musicians generally, nor even by persons deeply interested in music theory. Although church musicians still studied Latin, those who were trained outside the church did not necessarily learn it. Vincenzo Galilei is an example. His papers show that he had Valgulio's Proem to the Latin translation of pseudo-Plutarch, *De musica*, and the Plutarch translation itself as well as Gogava's translation of Aristoxenus rendered into Italian for him.[30] The Boethius also may have been prepared by Bartoli partly for Galilei's use. The diagram of the modes of Boethius in the *Dialogo* (Pl. 6.3) resembles that of Bartoli.

The principal reason for these late translations, I believe, is that Boethius was now seen as a resource for the study of Greek music theory and practice and no longer as the gospel for music theory generally. Before, much of Boethius was an embarrassment to music theorists, because they could not understand large parts of it, and many parts they could understand disagreed with what they believed. Now these confrontations and prejudices could be cast aside and the text studied for what it revealed about Greek musical thought.

---

[30] These translations are in Florence, Biblioteca Nazionale Centrale, MSS Galilei 7 and 8.

❧ *7* ☙

Aristoxenus Redeemed in the Renaissance

This essay was presented in the form of a paper at the Study Session 'Ancient Greek Elements in Later Musical Traditions' at the fifteenth Congress of the International Musicological Society in Madrid, 10 April 1992.

O F the Greek authors on music, Aristoxenus was the least read in the early Renaissance. Ptolemy, Aristides Quintilianus, Bacchius, pseudo-Plutarch, Bryennius, and even the anonymi of Bellermann were translated into Latin in the fifteenth century. But Aristoxenus was not translated until the middle of the sixteenth century and received little attention from music theorists until the 1580s and 1590s.

There were several reasons for the delay in recognizing the importance of this pioneer of Greek harmonics. Manuscripts containing the *Harmonic Elements* were scarce in the fifteenth century, but they became quite plentiful in the sixteenth century, thanks to Greek scribes in Italy, such as Bartholomaeus de Zanettis and Ioannes Honorios, who produced numerous copies.[1] A more important reason is that the most frequently read ancient author on music, Boethius, and authors influenced by him, such as Gaffurio, expressed a low opinion of Aristoxenus' approach to harmonic science, because they regarded music as a discipline subordinate to mathematics and defined the relations between pitches as numerical ratios, whereas Aristoxenus, although himself a mathematician, aimed to divorce the musical discipline from mathematical considerations.

Franchino Gaffurio, in preparation for writing his *Theorica musice* (1492) and *De harmonia musicorum instrumentorum opus*, finished in 1500 but not published until 1518, thoroughly absorbed Boethius' arithmetical and musical treatises and read in translation Ptolemy, Aristides Quintilianus, Bacchius, and Bryennius, but what he learnt through them of Aristoxenus was often accompanied by a negative commentary. In *De harmonia*, Gaffurio

---

[1] See Thomas J. Mathiesen, *Ancient Greek Music Theory: A Catalogue Raisonné of Manuscripts* (Munich: Henle, 1988), RISM B XI, p. xxv and *passim*.

reports from Ptolemy Aristoxenus' divisions of the tetrachord in the three genera—diatonic, chromatic, and enharmonic.[2] These are transmitted faithfully, except that by Aristoxenus' reckoning the consonant fourth would have contained thirty equal units, whereas Ptolemy doubles that number to avoid fractional parts. Gaffurio correctly states that Aristoxenus divided the whole tone into two, three, and four equal parts, calling these respectively 'semitones', 'soft chromatic dieses', and 'enharmonic dieses'. But after setting forth his six divisions of the tetrachord, Gaffurio lists the 'errors' of Aristoxenus: (i) he divided the whole tone into two equal semitones, which is impossible, because a sesquioctave proportion cannot be divided into equally proportional parts; (ii) he represented intervals as simple numbers [of parts or units] instead of ratios; (iii) the difference between corresponding steps in two of his chromatic tetrachords (the soft and the hemiolic) was only a twenty-fourth part of a whole tone, too small to be perceived by the ear; he also made the two lower intervals in the chromatic equal in size, whereas the lowest interval should be smaller. These purported errors had been pointed out by Ptolemy (*Harm.* i. 12) and Bryennius (*Harm.* ii. 2), on whom Gaffurio depended and whom he did not challenge.

That Aristoxenus was not without some advocates among Gaffurio's contemporaries is witnessed by the latter's reference to the theories on proportions of Philippus Bustus of Milan, physician, mathematician, 'very sharp philosopher', and 'adherent of Aristoxenus' (*Aristoxeno adhaerens*).[3]

What Gaffurio could not have known is that much of the doctrine transmitted without objection by Ptolemy, Aristides, Bryennius, and Bacchius originated with Aristoxenus. To give just one example, Gaffurio ascribes to Aristides and Bacchius the distinction between the continuous movement of the voice in speech and the discrete notes of song (*De harm.* i. 2), but the distinction is first found in Aristoxenus.

The first modern defender of Aristoxenus, Carlo Valgulio, in his proem to his translation of Plutarch's *De musica* (1507),[4] gives no evidence of having known the *Harmonic Elements*. The only passages by Aristoxenus that Valgulio quotes directly are fragments from the rhythmics and other writings embedded in Porphyry's commentaries on Ptolemy's *Harmonics*

---

[2] Franchino Gaffurio, *De harmonia musicorum instrumentorum opus* (Milan: Gottardo Ponzio, 1518), trans. Clement A. Miller (Musicological Studies and Documents, 33; Neuhausen-Stuttgart: Hänssler, American Institute of Musicology, 1977), bk. ii, ch. 16.

[3] Gaffurio, *De harmonia*, bk. ii, ch. 38, trans. Miller, 146.

[4] Carlo Valgulio, *Prooemium in musicam Plutarchi ad Titum Pyrrhinum* (Brescia: G. A. de Gandino detto de Caeguli, 1507); repr. and trans. in Palisca, *The Florentine Camerata: Documentary Studies and Translations* (New Haven, Conn.: Yale University Press, 1989), 21–44.

or in pseudo-Plutarch's treatise. We know that Valgulio had access to Porphyry's commentaries as well as Ptolemy's *Harmonics* because there is a record of his borrowing from the Vatican Library a manuscript containing them that is now Vaticanus graecus 186, which he returned on 26 September 1498.[5]

Valgulio became convinced, partly through reading excerpts quoted by Porphyry, that Ptolemy and the Pythagoreans had unjustly attacked Aristoxenus for dividing the whole tone into two equal parts. Such a division was possible, Valgulio believed, because an interval is a quality, not a quantity. He adduced the opinion of Panaetius (again in a fragment from Porphyry) in support of the contention that intervals are not magnitudes but qualities. Although Valgulio admitted that a sesquioctave ratio cannot be divided into two equal ratios of whole numbers, a string, he argued, is a continuous magnitude that can be cut into an infinite number of spaces or parts, and among them would be the distances that would yield equal semitones. In adducing this fact in the defence of Aristoxenus, however, Valgulio resorted to measurement of quantity, albeit continuous rather than discrete quantity, when Aristoxenus carefully avoided introducing either geometric or arithmetic magnitudes into his analysis of intervallic and melodic phenomena. Galilei was to point out this incompatibility of approaches.

Despite the bad press that Aristoxenus received at the hands of Boethius, Gaffurio, and others, there appears to have been an undercurrent of enthusiasm for his theories among musicians who were struggling with the problems of tuning instruments and also among some theorists. In an undated set of definitions and tables concerning intervals and the genera that Giovanni del Lago prepared for Girolamo Molino, his Venetian patron, Del Lago cites Aristoxenus by name several times and once refers to the 'secundo libro delli *Harmonici elementi*'.[6] But the calculation of the sizes of intervals of 'Aristoxenus et practici', compared side by side with those according to the Pythagoreans,[7] obviously depends on Ptolemy and could have been derived from Gaffurio's chapter on the tetrachord divisions of Aristoxenus (*De harm.* ii. 16), which is based on Ptolemy; or Del Lago could have extracted the information from Boethius, *De inst. mus.* v. 16, which is based on Ptolemy's *Harmonica* i. 12. In Del Lago's table, the

---

[5] See Palisca, *Humanism in Italian Renaissance Musical Thought* (New Haven, Conn.: Yale University Press, 1985), 3.

[6] *A Correspondence of Renaissance Musicians*, ed. Bonnie J. Blackburn, Edward E. Lowinsky, and Clement A. Miller (Oxford: Clarendon Press, 1991), 899.

[7] Ibid. 905–7.

semitone is given the value of 12, the whole tone 24, the ditone 48, and the fourth 60. Assigning these integers to the fractional values used by Aristoxenus is consistent with Ptolemy and Boethius. Del Lago does not take any position on the two ways—Pythagorean ratios or Aristoxenian parts—of describing the sizes of intervals, but the fact that he links the preferences of Aristoxenus with practitioners suggests that musicians were seeking simpler units of measurement than the opaque magnitudes of ratios.

Edward Lowinsky once suggested that Adrian Willaert wanted to teach singers a lesson about the equal-tempered tuning of Aristoxenus when he composed the famous chromatic work, *Quidnam ebrietas*, which seems to end on a seventh but actually closes on an octave, provided the proper alterations are made by the singers.[8] The Aristoxenus connection, as Lowinsky noted, was first proposed by Giovanni Maria Artusi in 1600. 'I hold it for certain', proclaimed Artusi, 'that Messer Adriano followed the opinion of Aristoxenus, who divided the tone into two equal parts, that is, into two semitones, which you see observed in lutes and viols.'[9] Artusi shows that only if musicians divide the whole tone into two equal parts, and make six whole tones equal to an octave, is it possible to perform the composition in such a way that the parts meet in well-tuned consonances. Angelo Berardi agreed with this interpretation.[10]

It might have been expected that the publication of Vitruvius' *De architectura* would have spurred interest in Aristoxenus, since his extensive chapter (bk. v, ch. 4) on music is based on this ancient writer. But there is no evidence that the early editions, beginning with that of Sulpitius (Rome, *c.*1486), then Fra Giocondo (Florence: Junta, 1522), and Philander (Rome, 1544), or the Italian translation by Cesare Cesariano (Como: Birovano, 1521) had any influence on musical thought. However, the commentary and Italian translation of Daniello Barbaro (Venice: Francesco Marcolini, 1556), did help to propagate the Vitruvius work among musical

---

[8] Edward E. Lowinsky, 'Adrian Willaert's Chromatic "Duo" Reexamined', *Tijdschrift voor Muziek-wetenschap*, 18 (1956–9), 1–36, repr. in *Music in the Culture of the Renaissance and Other Essays*, ed. Bonnie J. Blackburn (Chicago and London: University of Chicago Press, 1989), ii. 681–98.

[9] *L'Artusi overo delle imperfettioni della moderna musica* (Venice: G. Vincenti, 1600), Rag. i, fo. 25ʳ: 'Tengo per fermo, che M. Adriano habbi seguitata la opinione di Aristosseno, il quale diuideua il Tuono in due parti eguali, cioè in due Semituoni, il che vedete osseruato ne' Lauti, et nelle Viole . . .'.

[10] *Miscellanea musicale*, 59–61, quoted in Lowinsky, *Music in the Culture*, ii. 708. In another composition that may be by Willaert, the canon *Qui boyt et ne reboyt*, Lowinsky sees a *canon per tonos* in which the music is repeated on successively higher pitches a whole tone apart, ending on the starting-note, something that is possible only with equal tones. See 'Music in Titian's *Bacchanal of the Andrians*: Origin and History of the *Canon per tonos*', in David Rosand (ed.), *Titian: His World and His Legacy* (New York: Columbia University Press, 1982), 191–282, repr. in *Music in the Culture*, i. 289–350.

readers. But Barbaro in his commentary could not resist noting that Aristoxenus' methodology was questionable. 'Aristoxenus is rebuked, for he does not use numbers to define the steps that will yield the ratios, but takes the difference between the [pitches], in such a way that he theorizes not about the steps but their differences, which is not judicious. He thinks he knows the difference between pitches, which he neither measures nor discovers their quantity, leaving everything to the judgement of the ear.'[11] Barbaro then goes on to define the various species of tetrachords in terms of numerical ratios, which is altogether contrary to Aristoxenus' method.

The most important event for the *fortuna* of Aristoxenus was the publication of the Latin translation of his *Harmonic Elements* by Antonio Gogava in 1562 in a collection of translations that included also the *Harmonics* of Ptolemy.[12] In the preface to the collection Gogava credits Zarlino with giving him the impetus to translate this work. The translation was probably completed too late for Zarlino to use in his *Istitutioni harmoniche* of 1558, but he had ample time to read it before publishing his *Dimostrationi harmoniche* in 1571. Yet Aristoxenus is mentioned only in connection with his division of the whole tone into two equal parts, which Zarlino rejects,[13] although he shows that a whole tone can be divided into equal halves by geometric means, as previously demonstrated by Jacques Lefèvre d'Étaples and Lodovico Fogliano. It was only after Vincenzo Galilei introduced Aristoxenus into the controversy about tuning that Zarlino took the latter seriously, and we find him cited prominently in the *Sopplimenti musicali* of 1588.

Although Gogava's translation is notoriously faulty, it was serviceable and introduced Vincenzo Galilei to the thought of Aristoxenus. Indeed Galilei began an Italian translation of Gogava's Latin, but then abandoned it and had someone else more competent make such a translation, which survives among his papers in the Biblioteca Nazionale Centrale in Florence.[14]

Like Gaffurio, Galilei in his *Dialogo* of 1581 reviews the points made by Ptolemy against Aristoxenus (i. 9, 12 and ii. 9, 11). But unlike Gaffurio,

---

[11] Vitruvius, trans. Daniello Barbaro, 1567 edn., 231–2: 'è ripreso Aristoxeno, il quale non usa numeri nel notare le uoci per raccore le proportioni, ma piglia la loro differenza nel mezo, di modo, che egli pone la speculatione non nelle uoci, ma in quello, in che elle sono differenti, cosa non bene considerata, credendosi egli sapere la differenza di quelle uoci, delle quali egli nè misura, nè grandezza ritruoua, dando il tutto al giudicio delle orecchie.'

[12] *Aristoxeni . . . harmonicorum elementorum libri iii . . . Cl. Ptolemaei harmonicorum . . . lib. iii. Aristoteli de objecto auditus*, trans. Antonio Gogava (Venice: V. Valgrisio, 1562).

[13] Gioseffo Zarlino, *Dimostrationi harmoniche* (Venice: Francesco dei Franceschi Sense, 1571), Rag. iii, Proposta 11, p. 165.

[14] See Palisca, *Humanism*, 154.

Galilei sets out to defend Aristoxenus, whom he praises as 'truly one of the most judicious and learned musicians that the world has ever known'.[15] In i. 9, Ptolemy seems to attribute to Aristoxenus (actually to Aristoxenians) a division of a string in equal parts to get equal intervals, when, according to Galilei, Aristoxenus knew very well that he was dividing 'the quality of sound in equal parts, and not the quantity of the line, string, or space—operating like a musician with a sounding body and not as a pure mathematician with continuous quantity'.[16]

The semitone of Aristoxenus, as Galilei interprets his division, was smaller than the half of a 9:8 tone, and his diatessaron was similarly of his own design. Thus in the system of Aristoxenus, as on the lute, the fifths are diminished and the fourths augmented with respect to those whose ratios are 3:2 and 4:3. Apart from the octave, Galilei maintained, none of the consonances is sung in its true ratio, yet listeners accept them 'as perfect and are entirely satisfied with them (having never heard the true intervals) . . . I tell you, besides, that the fifth is generally heard with greater pleasure in the size that Aristoxenus gives it, than in its true sesquialter ratio.'[17] In fact, the sesquialter fifth sounded harsh to Galilei, while the Aristoxenian fifth, which he used in tuning the lute, had a grace and certain softness and languidity that suited the current taste.

Zarlino finally utilized the translation of Gogava in his *Sopplimenti musicali* of 1588,[18] though in his citations he ostentatiously gave Aristoxenus' still unpublished Greek text. Zarlino devotes several chapters to the tetrachord divisions of Aristoxenus (iv. 13–18), but in setting forth the number of parts contained in each interval of the tetrachords, he shows that he followed Ptolemy's exposition and not the original text of Aristoxenus. In these tetrachords the tone is alternately divided into equal halves, thirds, and fourths. Zarlino, aware that Aristoxenus was reputed to be an 'huomo di buona dottrina', expresses disbelief that he should have claimed to divide the 9:8 tone into two or more proportional equal parts, which everyone knew could not be done with rational numbers. For Zarlino was convinced, unlike his pupils Galilei and Artusi, that when Aristoxenus derived the tone by subtracting a fourth from a fifth, these intervals were presumed to be in their true ratios of 4:3 and 3:2, and therefore the tone was 9:8.

[15] Vincenzo Galilei, *Dialogo della musica antica et della moderna* (Florence: G. Marescotti, 1581), 54.
[16] Galilei, *Dialogo*, 53: 'sapeua Aristosseno, d'hauere à distribuire in parti vguali la qualità del suono, & non la quantità della linea, corda, & spatio: operando allhora come Musico intorno al corpo sonoro, & non come semplice Matematico intorno la continua quantità.'
[17] Ibid. 55. Actually, the difference between the equal-tempered fifth of 700 cents and the pure fifth of 702 cents is hardly noticeable.
[18] Gioseffo Zarlino, *Sopplimenti musicali* (Venice: Francesco de' Franceschi Sanese, 1588).

From this misunderstanding stems the incredibly tangled account that he gives of the theories of Aristoxenus, whom, out of respect for authority, he feels obliged to treat sympathetically. It cannot be said that Zarlino used Gogava's translation of Aristoxenus to any advantage either to his own position or to an appreciation of what Aristoxenus really stood for.

Aristoxenus received unexpected attention from the Platonic philosopher Francesco Patrizi. In his *Della poetica, la deca istoriale* (1586),[19] Patrizi permitted himself an unfortunate digression on the tonal systems of the ancient Greeks in which he gave an account of some of the tetrachord divisions of Aristoxenus. He based this on the author now known as Cleonides, whom he calls Euclid, a common attribution. After correctly stating that the diatessaron is divided into thirty equal parts or twelfths of a tone and reporting the number of parts in each of the three intervals of the tetrachord, such as in the enharmonic 3, 3, and 24 parts, he then represents these parts as segments of strings and this in a completely erroneous way. The prose is correct, but the diagrams superfluous and misleading. To make matters worse, Ercole Bottrigari, usually a dependable classicist and mathematician, corrected his application of the part-numbers to strings, inferring the ratios 40/39, 39/38, and 19/15 for the three intervals making up the tetrachord,[20] when it truly consists of two equal quarter-tones and a ditone equivalent to four of the latter, a ratio in pitch distances of $1:1:4$. Neither Patrizi nor Bottrigari could comprehend a system in which numbers represented not string-lengths, but audible pitch-distances.

The most enthusiastic champion of Aristoxenus besides Galilei was, surprising as it may seem, Giovanni Maria Artusi, who is so often dismissed as an arch-conservative and thrown in the dustbin of music history. Artusi believed that Willaert assumed the Aristoxenian division of the tone into two equal semitones when he wrote his enigmatic *Quidnam ebrietas*. In reflecting about this piece Artusi makes a comment that would have upset his teacher Zarlino, who steadfastly believed that the tuning employed in vocal music was the Ptolemaic syntonic diatonic. Artusi's interlocutor Vario ventures to state: 'Let the moderns say what they want, but not everybody will say that the tuning that is sung or played is the syntonic of Ptolemy, but a good part of them will maintain that it is that of

[19] Francesco Patrizi, *Della poetica, la deca istoriale* (Ferrara: Vittorio Baldini, 1586). Critical edn. by Danilo Aguzzi Barbagli (Florence: Istituto Nazionale di Studi sul Rinascimento, 1969), i, bk. vi, 345 ff.
[20] Ercole Bottrigari, *Il Patricio overo de' tetracordi armonici di Aristosseno* (Bologna: Vittorio Benacci, 1593; repr. Bologna: Forni, 1969), 45–56.

Aristoxenus, of which Messer Adriano gives evidence with this piece . . .'.[21]
Later, Artusi's Vario is even more emphatic about the inadequacy of
the syntonic tuning of Ptolemy: 'so many absurdities arise, that it is
stupefying; imperfections are not lacking; they rain down in sevens'.[22] The
discussion between Vario and Luca then turns to *musica ficta* and transposition. To permit the kind of transposition being practised at this time,
Vario proposes that the octave be divided 'without ratios into equal parts,
the semitone being half a tone, as Aristoxenus did. Then, I think, a good
artist will, with all convenience and without imperfection, make this
transposition up or down as he wants.'[23] It will then be possible to place a
sharp or flat anywhere, dividing any whole tone into two equal semitones.

Artusi sets forth Aristoxenus' famous proof (*Elem. harm.* ii. 56) that the
fourth consists of two and a half tones.[24] This is more an interpretation
than a translation of the passage, but the proof is on the whole interpreted
faithfully for the first time in western history, with the addition of a
diagram and a musical example on which points are marked by alphabetical
letters (see Fig. 7.1), a feature missing in both the manuscripts and the
Gogava translation.[25] Artusi does not show how he obtained the two
ditones *AC* and *DB*, which Aristoxenus says should be determined 'by
means of concords'.[26] The theorem proves not only that the fourth is made
up of two and one half tones, but that these tones are equal, and that the
fourth comprises five equal semitones.

Artusi defends Aristoxenus as 'a very significant and shrewd man, but he
never let himself assume what ratios intervals should have, understanding
very well how many imperfections result from assigning [proportional]
forms to them'.[27] Artusi reviews the ancient objections of Ptolemy to the

---

[21] *Imperfettioni*, fo. 25ʳ: 'Dicano pur li Moderni quanto uogliono, che non tutti diranno, che questa
sia la spetie Syntona, che si Canta, ò Suona, dico di quella di Tolomeo, ma bona parte tenirà che sia
quella d'Aristosseno, di che ce ne fa fede M. Adriano con questo Canto . . .'.

[22] Ibid., fo. 33ᵛ: 'sono tanti gli assurdi che ne nascono, che è vn stupore; non ci mancano
imperfettioni; ci piouono à sette à sette.'

[23] Ibid., fo. 31ᵛ: 'Tengo bene per possibile io, che senza proportioni bisognerà diuidere il Tuono in
parti eguali, e 'l Semituono per la metà del Tuono, come faceua Aristosseno, & all'hora crederò, che con
ogni commodità & senza imperfettione si farà questa trasportatione, & nel graue, & nello acuto à voglia
sua il buono Artefice.'

[24] Ibid., fos. 31ᵛ–32ᵛ.

[25] On the evidence of a quotation in Latin of a passage from the *Harmonic Elements*, it appears that
Artusi used the Gogava translation. Compare to Gogava, 27 the following: 'Maximum ergo, & in
summa Flagitiosum est peccatum, referre ad Instrumentum rei Harmonice naturam' (Artusi, fo. 36ᵛ;
Aristoxenus, *Elem. harm.* ii. 41).

[26] Artusi, fo. 35ʳ: 'per consonantiam'. Andrew Barker, *Greek Musical Writings, ii: Harmonic and
Acoustic Theory* (Cambridge: Cambridge University Press, 1989), 169 n. 114, shows how this may be
done.

[27] Artusi, fo. 34ᵛ: 'vn'huomo molto segnalato, e molto accorto; non si lasciò mai intendere di che
proportione fossero gl'interualli, conoscendo molto bene tante imperfettioni, che dallo assignar le forme
loro nasceuano.'

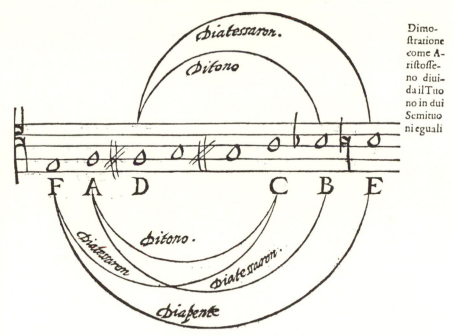

Dimo-
ſtratione
come A-
riſtoſſe-
no diui-
da il Tuo
no in dui
Semituo
ni eguali

PL. 7.1. Aristoxenian demonstration of the division of the tone into two equal semitones, from G. M. Artusi, *L'Artusi overo delle imperfettioni della moderna musica* (Venice, 1600), bk. i, p. 32

method of Aristoxenus, rehearsed by Boethius and Gaffurio, but he answers each one. To the contention that the tone cannot be divided into two equal semitones, Artusi replies that Aristoxenus did not choose a 9:8 tone but an interval that was the difference between a fifth and a fourth, whose sizes he did not define, and since these were irrational, this whole tone was also numerically irrational.[28] The point that Artusi makes concerning the indeterminacy of the sizes of the fourth and fifth is an important one, because a number of modern commentators on this theorem have maintained that Aristoxenus began with a fourth in the proportion 4:3, which invalidates his theorem.[29] Like Valgulio and Galilei, Artusi argues that Aristoxenus was a mathematician and knew that it was not possible to divide 9:8 into two rational equal proportions. Similarly, Aristoxenus' detractors questioned that an octave contains six tones, for it is well known, says Artusi, that 9:8 taken six times 'falls short of an octave'. Artusi slipped

---

[28] Artusi notes, *Imperfettioni*, fo. 34ᵛ, that some mathematicians, namely Michel Stifelio and Nicolò Tartaglia, maintained that it was possible to find such a ratio with 'certain and determinate numbers'.

[29] Most recently Malcolm Litchfield, 'Aristoxenus and Empiricism: A Reevaluation Based on his Theories', *Journal of Music Theory*, 32 (1988), 51–73, at 62–5.

here, because, as pseudo-Euclid proves (*Sectio canonis* 9), six sesquioctaval tones are greater than a duple proportion. But Artusi points out that the tones of Aristoxenus resulted from dividing the octave into twelve equal parts, and that six of these, each of which was of a size that could not be described through rational numbers, did constitute an octave.

Artusi calls upon Aristides Quintilianus, who, he says, compared the division of the diapason into six tones to the division of the hexameter into six spondaic feet.[30] The hexameter line is divided into two unequal parts, one of two and a half feet, the other of three and a half, analogous to the division of the octave into a fourth (two tones and a half) and a fifth (three tones and a half). Thus Aristoxenus' opponents were very wrong to challenge him, and their injudicious opposition should reflect glory on him rather than shame.

Artusi further argues that Aristoxenus was misunderstood by those who maintained that he made the sense of hearing the sole judge in the discipline of harmonics, excluding the reason. Aristoxenus himself pointed out in his second book that deliberations concerning harmonics required both sense and reason.[31]

Artusi adduced the authority of Aristoxenus in another controversial issue, the identity of the genera employed in polyphonic music, debated by Nicola Vicentino and Vicente Lusitano in 1551. Although Artusi did not subscribe to Vicentino's arguments, he agreed with the conclusion, that the genus used in modern music was neither diatonic, nor chromatic, nor enharmonic, but a mixture of the three. Artusi refers to the statement by Aristoxenus that a melody might be either diatonic, chromatic, or enharmonic, or a mixture of these.[32]

The champions and defenders of Aristoxenus in the Renaissance turn out to be strange bedfellows: a literary humanist—Carlo Valgulio—who had no access to his original writings but whose reading of Porphyry made him suspect that Ptolemy dealt with Aristoxenus unjustly; then there was Zarlino's least faithful pupil, Vincenzo Galilei; and finally Zarlino's most devoted pupil, Giovanni Maria Artusi. These supporters of Aristoxenus had in common the perception that he rejected all attempts to define the sizes

---

[30] Francisco de Salinas, *De musica libri septem* (Salamanca: Mathias Gastias, 1577; repr. Documenta musicologica, 13, ed. Macario Santiago Kastner, Kassel: Bärenreiter, 1958), iv. 22, p. 213, refers to such a passage in Aristides' bk. iii, but I have not been able to locate it. Salinas based his discussion of the tetrachord divisions of Aristoxenus on Ptolemy's account of them. Salinas dismissed Aristoxenus' divisions as useless for the construction of his 'perfect instrument', though he considered his 'diatonum contentum' the same as the temperament used in lutes and viols; v. 24, p. 214.

[31] Artusi refers to the famous statement in ii. 32 that through the hearing we appraise the magnitudes of intervals and through reason we investigate their function.

[32] Aristoxenus, *Elem. harm.* ii. 44; Artusi, *Imperfettioni*, fo. 37ʳ.

of the consonances or the steps of the tetrachord by means of numerical ratios or proportional string-lengths. Those who pursued phenomenological and empirical investigations of sound found in Aristoxenus the support of an ancient authority. Those who would solve the problems of instrumental tuning by dividing the octave into equal semitones also leaned on this support, but perhaps less legitimately, because Aristoxenus did not set out to tune a chromatic cithara capable of intertonal modulation.[33]

[33] Since, it is said, he advocated thirteen tonoi a semitone apart, a system of equal semitones would have permitted modulation by other than intervals of fourths and fifths. But this is a less likely reason for his turning to purely aural determination of the size of consonances than the Pythagorean comma's rearing of its ugly head whenever one tried to extend a tuning system beyond the perfect fourth.

❦ 8 ❧

Scientific Empiricism in Musical Thought

This essay is an expanded version of a lecture presented at Swarthmore College on 28 February 1960 in the series 'Seventeenth-Century Science and the Arts', sponsored by the William J. Cooper Foundation. It was published in Hedley Howell Rhys (ed.), *Seventeenth Century Science and the Arts* (Princeton, NJ: Princeton University Press, 1961), 91–137.

In the course of research for Essay 9 on Jean Taisnier, I realized how little of the information, insights, and discoveries revealed in Lynn Thorndike's *A History of Magic and Experimental Science*[1] and similar books was known to historians of music. When I was invited to participate in the series of lectures at Swarthmore, I seized the opportunity to follow up some leads that I had encountered while working on Taisnier. I became particularly interested in the writings of Girolamo Fracastoro and Giovanni Battista Benedetti.[2] The work of both these men was well known to historians of science, but their writings on acoustic problems were never discussed in the standard sources, scientific or musicological.[3] Fracastoro was remembered principally for his verse-treatise on syphilis, while Benedetti was recognized as one of the most important forerunners of Galileo in the field of mechanics.[4] Earlier, during the research for my dissertation,[5] I had read Vincenzo Galilei's shorter treatises on the diapason and unison, in which he reported experiments that he had made with various sounding bodies, and I was struck by how they anticipated

---

[1] Lynn Thorndike, *A History of Magic and Experimental Science*, 8 vols (New York: Macmillan, 1923–58; Columbia University Press, 1964–66).

[2] Taisnier plagiarized Benedetti's *Demonstratio proportionum motuum localium contra Aristotelem et omnes philosophos* (Venice, 1554) in his *Opusculum perpetua memoria dignissimum de natura magnetis* (Cologne: J. Birckmann, 1562).

[3] Coincidentally, the same year as my lecture at Swarthmore, Clifford Truesdell published translations and interpretations of several of the same key passages from Fracastoro and Benedetti as I presented and discussed in my lecture. See Truesdell, *The Rational Mechanics of Flexible or Elastic Bodies, 1638–1788*, in Leonhard Euler, *Opera omnia*, series 2, vol. xi (Zurich: Orell Fussli, 1960), 22 ff. So far as I know, Truesdell's study was first acknowledged in a musicological work in Burdette Lamar Green, 'The Harmonic Series from Mersenne to Rameau: An Historical Study of Circumstances Leading to its Recognition and Application to Music', Ph.D. diss. (Ohio State University, 1969). The time-lag was getting shorter!

[4] As late as 1966, the article 'Benedetti, Giovanni Battista' in *Dizionario biografico degli italiani*, viii (Rome: Istituto della Enciclopedia italiana, 1966), 259–65 by V. Cappelletti makes no mention of Benedetti's investigations of sound.

[5] Palisca, 'The Beginnings of Baroque Music: Its Roots in Sixteenth Century Theory and Polemics', Ph.D. diss. (Harvard University, 1953).

Galileo's later investigations.[6] This connection between father and son was never mentioned in the Galileo literature. There was obviously a knowledge-gap between historians of science and historians of music in our time. But even more remarkable is that there was also such a gap in the sixteenth and seventeenth centuries, when science and music were much more closely allied and when many scientists were musicians and some musicians dabbled in science.

Several strands in the link between music and science in the sixteenth and seventeenth centuries first touched upon in this essay were subsequently investigated by other scholars: Fracastoro's theory of sympathetic resonance, Benedetti's theory of consonance, early advocates of equal temperament, the influence of a certain Benedetti (whom I probably incorrectly identified as Giovanni Battista Benedetti) on Mei's attitude towards scientific method, Mei's influence in turn on Galilei's experimental projects, the discovery by Vincenzo Galilei of the true ratios of weights stretching strings in the production of consonances, the rejection by Galilei of Pythagorean numerology, and the gradual progress in the understanding of the phenomenon of harmonic partials in the vibration of a string and the eventual reinforcement of the theories of Rameau as a result. My interpretations of the sources on these points were challenged by some and supported by others. I also followed up on several of these topics in later publications. In this introduction I wish to review these developments.

Sigalia Dostrovsky, in her Princeton dissertation of 1969, pushed more deeply into the search for understanding the mechanics of the vibrating string.[7] She abridged and refined her account in a fundamental article in the *Archive for History of Exact Sciences* (1975)[8] and, together with John T. Cannon, reviewed her findings for a musicological audience in the new multi-volume Geschichte der Musiktheorie sponsored by the Staatliche Institut für Musikforschung in Berlin.[9]

Stillman Drake, starting from my findings concerning the discoveries of Benedetti, Vincenzo Galilei, and Galileo, proposed that their testing of mathematical theories could be recognized as the beginnings of experiment in physics.[10] Drake stated in 1970 that 'the fountainhead of Renaissance music was . . . at least partly responsible for the emergence not of experimental science alone, but of a whole new approach to theoretical science that we now know as mathematical physics'.[11] Not all historians of science went along with bold statements such as this:

The first conscious experiments to test a preexisting mathematical theory were probably the musical experiments of Benedetti and Vincenzo Galilei. They were extended into mechanics by Galileo, whose pupils Castelli and Torricelli carried them on over into hydraulics and phenomena of air pressure, refined by Pascal and

[6] Ibid. 60–7.
[7] Sigalia Dostrovsky, 'The Origins of Vibration Theory: The Scientific Revolution and the Nature of Music', Ph.D. diss. in physics (Princeton University, 1969).
[8] Sigalia Dostrovsky, 'Early Vibration Theory: Physics and Music in the Seventeenth Century', *Archive for History of Exact Sciences*, 14 (1975), 169–218.
[9] Sigalia Dostrovsky and John T. Cannon, 'Entstehung der musikalischen Akustik (1600–1750)' in Carl Dahlhaus *et al.*, *Hören, Messen und Rechnen in der frühen Neuzeit* (Geschichte der Musiktheorie, ed. Frieder Zaminer, 7; Darmstadt: Wissenschaftliche Buchgesellschaft, 1989).
[10] Stillman Drake, 'Renaissance Music and Experimental Science', *Journal of the History of Ideas*, 31 (1970), 483–500.
[11] Ibid. 500.

Boyle . . . Boyle's law is said to have been the first scientific law to be experimentally discovered. Yet Vincenzo Galilei's discovery that the weights required for producing tensions corresponding to given pitches are as the inverse squares of lengths must have been empirical. In any event, the manipulation of physical equipment set up to test a mathematical law had come much earlier than Newton, even earlier than Galileo; and it came because of the conflict between numerology and physics in the field of music.[12]

A more cautious reaction came from D. P. Walker, who dismissed the experiments of the Galileis as 'thought experiments' and sought to minimize the differences between Zarlino and V. Galilei that I considered quite fundamental.[13] Walker also challenged Vincenzo's statement that the ratio of the volumes of two pipes that sound an octave should be the string-ratio, 2:1, cubed, that is, 8:1. This, Galilei believed, was the ratio that determined the octave in pipes, not 2:1, the ratio of the lengths of the pipes. 'Here it is evident that Galilei did not do any experiments,' Walker wrote, 'since the pitch of a pipe is a function of its length and not of its cubic capacity.'[14] I have already replied to this assertion in my introduction to the edition of Vincenzo's scientific essays.[15] To be sure, the pitch of a pipe depends roughly on its length, but to produce a good tone throughout the pitch range—as Galilei and Mersenne knew from experience or experiment and organ-builders by tradition and practice—not only the length but also the diameter of a pipe must be doubled to get an octave, resulting in the cubing of the volume. Mersenne demonstrated that the volumes of two pipes an octave apart should be approximately in the ratio of 8:1.[16]

In a paper read in the symposium 'Music and Science in the Age of Galileo' at the University of Calgary on 28 April 1989, I took up again the question 'Was Galileo's Father an Experimental Scientist?'[17] There I dealt with one particular experiment that Vincenzo described in his 'Discorso particolare intorno alla diversità delle forme del diapason'. In this instance Galilei deliberately designed an experiment to test the hypothesis that two strings of unlike material stretched on a lute and tuned to a unison will not yield unisons when stopped at the frets on the fingerboard. In preparation for that symposium, I set out to replicate Galilei's experiment and obtained results that supported his contention.

---

[12] Ibid. 499.

[13] D. P. Walker, *Studies in Musical Science in the Late Renaissance* (London: The Warburg Institute, University of London; Leiden: E. J. Brill, 1978), 14–33.

[14] Ibid. 24.

[15] Palisca, *The Florentine Camerata: Documentary Studies and Translations* (New Haven, Conn.: Yale University Press, 1989), 159.

[16] Marin Mersenne, *Harmonie universelle* (Paris: S. Cramoisy, 1636–7; repr. Paris: Centre National de la Recherche Scientifique, 1963), bk. vi, prop. 14, p. 335. Francis Bacon was also aware that the volume of the pipes was the important dimension, for he stated: 'The just and measured proportion of the air percussed, towards the baseness or trebleness of tones, is one of the greatest secrets in the contemplation of sounds . . . It may be found out in the proportion of the winding [stretching] of strings; in the proportion of the distance of frets; and in the proportion of the concave of pipes, & c., but most commodiously in the last of these' (*Sylva sylvarum*, London: J. H. for William Lee, 1627, Century II, §183–4 in *Works*, ed. J. Spedding, R. L. Ellis, and D. D. Heath (London, 1857–9, repr., New York: Garrett, 1988), quoted in Dostrovsky and Cannon, 'Entstehung der musikalischen Akustik (1600–1750)', 19 n. 19). For a history of the scaling of pipe-lengths and diameters, see Green, 'The Harmonic Series', 266–73.

[17] Victor Coelho (ed.), *Music and Science in the Age of Galileo* (Dordrecht: Kluwer Academic Publishers, 1992), 143–51.

One of the scholars who attended the Calgary symposium but who had been sceptical of Galilei's 'experiments', H. Floris Cohen of Holland, appears to have been won over by this paper. Although he acknowledged that Walker's and my attempts to link musical science with the other sciences 'was the original inspiration' for his book, *Quantifying Music*,[18] this synthetic and comprehensive history makes notably original contributions, particularly in the attention given to Simon Stevin, Isaac Beeckman, and Christiaan Huygens as well as in its reinterpretation of the roles of Benedetti, Vincenzo and Galileo Galilei, Descartes, and Mersenne in the promulgation of the coincidence theory of consonance. This theory, first hinted at by Benedetti, holds that the degree of consonance varies directly with the frequency of the meeting-points of vibrations of two pitches. Cohen does not give Benedetti sufficient credit, however, when he says that Benedetti seems not to have realized the power of his theory to explain the physical origin of consonance. This may be because he did not have access to the beginning of Benedetti's letter, (which I did not quote in the essay below), where Benedetti clearly stated his belief that consonance depended on the concurrence of vibrations. Benedetti introduces his subject as follows:

Nec alienum mihi videtur a proposito instituto, speculari modum generationis ipsarum simplicium consonantiarum; qui quidem modus fit ex quadam aequatione percussionum, seu aequali concursu undarum aeris, vel conterminatione earum.	It does not seem to me foreign to my plan to speculate concerning the generation of these simple consonances, which surely are produced by a certain equality of percussions, or the equal concurrence of the waves of the air, or the coincidence of their terminations.
Nam, nulli dubium est, quin unisonus sit prima principalis audituque amicissima nec non magis propria consonantia; et si intelligatur, ut punctus in linea, vel unitas in numero, quam immediate sequitur diapason, ei simillima, post hanc vero diapente, caeteraeque. Videamus igitur ordinem concursus percussionum terminorum, seu undarum aeris, unde sonus generatur.[19]	Now there is no doubt that the unison is the first principal consonance and the friendliest to the ear as well as the most proper consonance, if it is understood the way the point is to a line, or unity to number, after which immediately follows the diapason, very similar to it, after which the diapente, and then the others. Let us see therefore the order of the concurrence of the terminations of the percussions or waves of the air, from which sound is generated.

---

[18] H. F. Cohen, *Quantifying Music: The Science of Music at the First Stage of the Scientific Revolution, 1580–1650* (Dordrecht: D. Reidel, 1984), p. xiii.

[19] G. B. Benedetti, *Diversarum speculationum mathematicarum et physicarum liber* (Turin: Apud haeredem Nicolai Bevilaque, 1585), 283.

Benedetti intended to present an 'order' or scale of decreasing degree of consonance, and it is for this reason that he multiplied the terms of the ratio to indicate the distance from the unison, $1:1$. The octave $2:1$ or $2 \times 1 = 2$ is second. The fifth $3:2$ or $3 \times 2 = 6$ is third, and the fourth $4:3$ or $4 \times 3 = 12$ is fourth in the series, and so on. Walker and Cohen, relying on my incomplete quotation of Benedetti, misinterpreted his closing remarks to mean that he delighted in the 'proportion' (as they translate *analogia* in my quotation on p. 306 below) exhibited by these numbers, such as 12 (for the fourth) to 6 (for the fifth), giving $2:1$. 'Benedetti's only concern', Cohen states, 'was to demonstrate that the ratios of the consonant intervals are also to be found in the proportions of their products . . . But this is just empty number speculation, devoid of any physical or musical significance.'[20] Although Benedetti may have admired this proportionality, his purpose in presenting the scale of numbers was to show that consonance decreases in proportion with the size of the product of the ratios.

Another issue that arose from my essay concerns the identity of the 'Benedetti' that Girolamo Mei said he heard lecture in Rome. I suggested in the original version of note 48 to my essay below that he might have been the same as Giovanni Battista Benedetti. This has been quite rightly contested. In a letter to Piero Vettori of the last of August 1560 (British Library, Add. MS 10268, fos. 214^r–215^r), Mei reported hearing a 'Benedetti', about 30 to 34 years of age, lecture on Aristotle's *De coelo* and *De generatione animalium* in Rome during the academic year 1559–60 but had missed him reading the *Physics* that winter. There he described him as a Spanish 'reformed priest' and praised his command of languages, fluency, acumen, and independence of mind.[21] G. B. Benedetti, however, had to employ his pupil Francesco Maria Vialardo to put his thoughts into Latin, and there is no evidence that he was ever a priest. The Spanish connection is there, though, because G. B. Benedetti's father is said to have been a physician from Valencia who settled in Venice.[22] But his lack of Latin and Greek would have made him unqualified in Mei's eyes to read and comment on Aristotle's works, as Mei reported to have heard his 'Benedetti' do. No Benedetti appears in any of the official lists of professors that year. However, my identification of Mei's Benedetti with our author was accepted by Stillman Drake in his article on him in *Dictionary of Scientific Biography*.[23]

It has been gratifying to observe how this essay has aroused in the past twenty years not only some constructive debate but also helped bridge the gap between history of science and music.

I N any discussion of science in the seventeenth century, among the names that inevitably arise are those of Galileo Galilei, Marin Mersenne, René

[20] Cohen, *Quantifying Music*, 76–7.

[21] For the text of the portion of the letter dealing with Benedetti, see Donatella Restani, *L'itinerario di Girolamo Mei* (Florence: Olschki, 1990), 37.

[22] Anon., 'Clarorum virorum elogia', Paris, Bibliothèque nationale, MS Dupuy no. 348, fo. 168^r. This collection of notes on illustrious persons, mostly Italians, is addressed to Jacobus Augustus Thuanus (Jacques Auguste de Thou), from whose *Historiarum sui temporis ab anno 1543 usque ad annum 1607 pars v* (Frankfurt, 1625–8), lib. 99, these facts about Benedetti are reported by Thorndike, *History of Magic*, vi. 373.

[23] Stillman Drake, 'Benedetti, Giovanni Battista', in *Dictionary of Scientific Biography*, ed. Charles Coulton Gillispie (New York: Scribner's, 1970), i. 604–9.

Descartes, Johannes Kepler, and Christiaan Huygens. It is no mere coincidence that these as well as other less renowned scientists—for example, Athanasius Kircher and John Wallis—were all trained musicians and authors on musical subjects. Kepler,[24] Kircher,[25] Mersenne,[26] and Christiaan Huygens[27] wrote important treatises on music; Galileo considered several fundamental musical questions in his scientific writings and was not only a lutenist himself, but a son, brother, and father of musicians, in short, a member of a musical dynasty. This preoccupation of scientists with music was no coincidence, because music until the seventeenth century was a branch of science and held a place among the four mathematical disciplines of the quadrivium beside arithmetic, geometry, and astronomy.

Strictly speaking, only theoretical music occupied this exalted place among the exact sciences, and until the Renaissance this aspect of music remained rather aloof from the world of practical musicianship. In the later Middle Ages especially, musicians tended to evolve their own rules without recourse to the traditional doctrine of musical science. In the Renaissance the mythical union of musical practice and theory that humanists ascribed to the Greeks inspired musicians to subject musical practice once again to the precepts of musical science.[28] But no sooner was a relatively satisfactory synthesis achieved, than musical art and science began to go their separate ways again.

The separation of musical art from science was an event of considerable importance for the future development of composition and musical practice in the seventeenth century. It pays to dwell upon this critical moment, towards the end of the sixteenth century, when the quadrivium exploded from its inner stresses and expanding constituents, and the two disciplines, musical art and musical science, began to acquire their separate modern identities.

[24] Johannes Kepler (1571–1630) dealt comprehensively with music in bks. iii and v of his *Harmonices mundi libri v* (Linz: Godfried Tampach, 1619).

[25] The most important writings on music are in Athanasius Kircher's *Musurgia universalis* (Rome: F. Corbelletti, 1650).

[26] The works on music by Marin Mersenne (1588–1648) are numerous; the most comprehensive is *Harmonie universelle*. Concerning others, see Hellmut Ludwig, *Marin Mersenne und seine Musiklehre* (Halle/Saale: Buchhandlung des Waisenhauses, 1935).

[27] Christiaan Huygens (1629–95), the son of the lutenist, composer, and musical theorist Constantijn Huygens (1596–1687), made notable contributions to theoretical music, especially in the field of temperament. His *Œuvres complètes* (The Hague: Martinus Nijhoff, 1940), x. 1–173, contain manuscript writings on music, including an early French version as well as the Latin version of the *Novus cyclus harmonicus*. See Cohen, *Quantifying Music*, 209–30.

[28] Wylie Sypher has observed this same tendency in the visual arts: 'The Renaissance artist, unlike the medieval artisan-builder-sculptor-craftsman, was often a doctrinaire scientist, attempting to impose upon his aesthetic world a unity, a closed system of ratios' (*Four Stages of Renaissance Style* (Garden City, NY: Doubleday, 1955), 58).

Meanwhile, it is important to keep in mind in analysing music's relationship to science that music, unique among the arts, is at the opening of the scientific age inseparable from science. It is not surprising under these circumstances that the areas of musical thought most affected by the scientific revolution were those bordering on the fields of science that underwent the greatest transformation. These, it will be recalled from Professor Toulmin's lecture, were astronomy and dynamics.[29] Astronomy, music's sister-science in the quadrivium, had until the middle of the sixteenth century bolstered the idea that earthly music contained in microcosm the divine harmony of the universe; but now there was growing evidence that the universe was not a harmony at all. In the field of dynamics the studies of the nature of vibration and of sound likewise upset many of the widely held notions of number symbolism and of the way music affects the senses and the mind.

In considering the impact of the new cosmology and physics on music, we shall discover, as Professor Bush did in literature,[30] that there is usually a considerable time-lag between the discovery and its manifestations in artistic products. We have seen that the reactions in literature to a new discovery were often delayed a generation at least. This is no less true with music. The scientific discoveries that were most important in determining the trends of early Baroque music were made not in the seventeenth century but in the sixteenth. Similarly, the most significant acoustical discoveries of the seventeenth century did not begin to bear fruit in musical practice until the eighteenth century. Let us review a classic case of the interrelations between music and science in this period.

The work of Jean-Philippe Rameau is surely the best example of the delayed application of seventeenth-century discoveries, scientific method, and Cartesian rationalism to musical problems. Rameau's greatest contribution was probably his application of scientific method to the investigation of harmonic practice. He treated the collected musical production of his immediate predecessors and contemporaries as a body of empirical evidence, to which he added his own trials with tonal materials. From this collection of facts he derived the general laws that govern the movement of chords over a fundamental bass or root progression. As Newton had synthesized in his laws of motion a great number of observations of different movements made by himself and others, so Rameau drew from his observations of the movements of chords and melodies the fundamental laws that governed all

[29] Stephen Toulmin, 'Seventeenth Century Science and the Arts', in Rhys (ed.), *Seventeenth Century Science and the Arts*, 3–28.
[30] Douglas Bush, 'Science and Literature', ibid. 29–62.

such movements. Modern textbooks of harmony still use the concepts that Rameau first presented—the progression of chord-roots, the generation of a chord by its root, the invertibility of chords, the functional names of tonic, dominant, subdominant, dominant seventh, and so on. Apart from its important theoretical value, the practical result of Rameau's theory, like that of any clarification of syntax, was to encourage the simplification of musical language, particularly harmonic style. This became an important feature of the musical classicism of the later eighteenth century.

But Rameau was too faithful a disciple of his countryman Descartes to be satisfied with this purely empirical theory. He wished to enclose his natural laws within a rationally developed scheme of arithmetical and geometrical progressions. To be true to the Cartesian tradition, this system had to issue from a single self-evident principle.[31] This principle he found in the first six divisions of a single string, those made, that is, by dividing the string successively into halves, thirds, fourths, fifths, and sixths. The result could be represented by the series 1, 1/2, 1/3, 1/4, 1/5, 1/6. By manipulating these ratios in a number of ways, Rameau attempted to rationalize the laws he had previously induced from musical facts. Never completely successful in this attempt, he kept revising his numerical progressions, falling into ever greater inconsistencies and errors. D'Alembert, a true geometrician, in making a compendium of Rameau's theories that would be comprehensible to musicians, found it expedient to throw out all Rameau's numerical speculations, keeping only the very sound laws of harmony that the composer had induced from his rich practical experience.[32]

The strongest support for his theory became known to Rameau only after he had completed his first major treatise. This came not from the realm of geometry but from physical science, from the discovery of the overtones present in individual string and pipe tones. These overtones coincided with the tones produced by the first five divisions of the string and thus provided an even more natural and convincing first principle for his system than these. Moreover, it proved beyond doubt that chords are generated by fundamental bass tones. Rameau learned of the phenomenon from the

---

[31] 'Music is a science which ought to have certain rules; these rules ought to be derived from a self-evident principle; and this principle can scarcely be known to us without the help of mathematics' (*Traité de l'harmonie réduite à ses principes naturels* (Paris: Ballard, 1722), trans. in Oliver Strunk, *Source Readings in Music History* (New York: Norton, 1950), 566; for a complete translation of this treatise see Rameau, *Treatise on Harmony*, trans. with an introduction and notes by Philip Gossett (New York: Dover, 1971)). For a detailed survey of the theories of Rameau, see Joan Ferris, 'The Evolution of Rameau's Harmonic Theories', *Journal of Music Theory*, 3 (1959), 231–56.

[32] Jean Le Rond d'Alembert, *Élémens de musique, theorique et pratique suivant les principes de M. Rameau* (Paris: David l'aîné, 1752).

papers of Joseph Sauveur,[33] and exploited its implications in his second treatise, *Nouveau système de musique théorique*, of 1726. Sauveur's almost definitive statement and explanation of the principle in his paper to the French Academy of Sciences, however, came only after a century and a half of investigation along two different lines: the study of the multiple sounds produced simultaneously by strings, pipes, and bells, and the study of sympathetic vibration.

Both lines of investigation are already documented in Aristotle's *Problems* on physics. There he suggests that the low tone contains its upper octave,[34] but not the reverse; he notes that as the tone produced by a vibrating string becomes weaker, the higher octave seems to sound.[35] He also observes that when a high string of a lyre that has been sounding is stopped, the string of the octave below seems to resound.[36] Aristotle gives no satisfactory explanation of either phenomenon.

The first modern 'breakthrough' came with Girolamo Fracastoro's explanation of sympathetic vibration of unison strings in his *De sympathia et antipathia rerum* (Venice, 1546).[37] Here Fracastoro showed that two strings of equal length stretched to the same tension will be susceptible to each other's vibrations. Fracastoro conceived of sound as a succession of condensations and rarefactions (*addensatio et rarefactio*) of the air. Thus the impulse or compression given to the air by the first string as it moves from its stationary position will be communicated to the second string. When the first string then returns to its position, rarefying the air, the second will also if it is of the same tension. Otherwise, it will impede the motion of the air produced by the first string (evidently because it takes a longer or lesser time for its rarefaction–condensation cycle). So it will cease to move. Mersenne cited Fracastoro's explanation[38] and applied it to the sympathetic vibration of strings which were not in unison but in simple ratios to each other.[39]

---

[33] 'Système général des intervalles des sons', in *Histoire de l'Academie Royale des Sciences*, Année 1701; *Mémoires*, 2nd edn. (Paris: Charles-Etienne Hocherau, 1719), sect. ix, 'Des sons harmoniques', 349–56.

[34] *Problemata*, xix. 918ª8.

[35] Ibid., xix. 921ᵇ42.

[36] Ibid., xix. 919ᵇ24; 921ᵇ42.

[37] *De sympathia et antipathia rerum liber unus*, ch. 11, *Opera omnia*, 2nd edn. (Venice: Giunta, 1574), 66–7. See also ch. 4 for his general theory of sound.

[38] Marin Mersenne, *Harmonicorum libri* (Paris: Guillaume Baudry, 1635), bk. iv, prop. 27, pp. 65–8.

[39] Descartes reported observing this kind of sympathetic vibration in his *Musicae compendium* (Utrecht: Gisbertus à Zijll & Theodorus ab Ackersdijck, 1650; repr. New York: Broude Bros., 1968), 12; ed. in *Œuvres*, x. 97: '. . . in nervis testudinis, ex quibus dum aliquis pulsatur, qui illo 8ª. vel quinta a cutiores sunt, sponte tremunt & resonant, graviores non ita . . .'. But his explanation of the phenomenon is insufficient; nor is Beeckman's, quoted ibid. 52, any better. V. Galilei cited Fracastoro's *De sympathia* in *Dialogo*, 88, but on a different subject.

The second line of investigation, that of the multiple sounds of a single tone, made no headway until Mersenne and his circle began to inquire into them. Mersenne first noted the presence of a plurality of tones in the vibration of a single string in the early 1620s. Later he recognized that what he heard were the upper octave, twelfth, fifteenth, seventeenth, and twentieth.[40] When he queried his scientific friends, as he was accustomed to do, for an explanation of the phenomenon, they put forward different theories. Isaac Beeckman suggested that the thickness of the string must have been uneven and caused the particles of air around it to vibrate at different rates.[41] Descartes put forward the theory that in sounding bells some parts vibrate faster than others.[42] None of these reasons satisfied Mersenne, and he acknowledged that this was the most difficult problem he had encountered in his study of sound.

It was only when the two lines of research were united into a single experiment by John Wallis that the true cause was discovered. In 1673 William Noble of Merton College, Oxford, and Thomas Pigot, of Wadham College, Oxford, showed experimentally that when strings tuned at the octave, twelfth, or seventeenth below a previously sounding string vibrated sympathetically, they produced unisons to the sounding string by vibrating in aliquot parts. This was shown by placing paper riders on the sympathetic strings at the points where, if the string were stopped, unisons would be produced. The paper riders remained still, showing that the strings were vibrating in parts. A few years later, Wallis applied this knowledge to the study of the vibration of a single string and observed that a clear and multiple sound would occur only when the points of no vibration (called nodes) were not disturbed by plucking at these points.[43] Thus partial

---

[40] In *Quaestiones celeberrimae in Genesim* (Paris: sumptibus Sebastiani Cramoisy, 1623), ch. 4, Quaest. 57, Art. 3, col. 1560, Mersenne tells of hearing a string emit several tones at once, as if it were simultaneously vibrating in a number of ways, but the tones were too confused and fleeting to be identified. In the 'Fourth Book on Instruments' of the *Harmonie universelle*, prop. 9, however, he identifies the component sounds, saying that he has experienced more than a hundred times that when a single string is struck there are sounded, besides the natural pitch of the string, five other tones: the upper octave, twelfth, fifteenth, seventeenth, and twentieth, giving the series C c g c' e' a'. In the *Harmonicorum libri*, bk. i, ch. 33, p. 54, he claims to have detected also the twenty-third (d').

In his *Compendium*, 14, Descartes had already remarked that the octave is always somehow present in any tone: 'existimo nullum sonum audiri, quin huius octava acutior auribus quodammodo videatur resonare.' Lloyd P. Farrar has dealt comprehensively with the history of the phenomenon of overtones in his Master's thesis, 'The Concept of Overtones in Scientific and Musical Thought (Descartes to Rameau)', University of Illinois, 1956. More recent studies are Green, 'The Harmonic Series from Mersenne to Rameau', Dostrovsky, 'Early Vibration Theory', and Dostrovsky and Cannon, 'Entstehung der musikalischen Akustik'.

[41] Letter of 30 May 1633, in Mersenne, *Correspondance* (Paris: Presses Universitaires de France, 1946), iii. 403.

[42] Letter of 25 Feb. 1630, in Mersenne, *Correspondance*, ii (1936), 397.

[43] *Philosophical Transactions*, xii (Apr. 1677), 839–42. See also A. Wolf, *A History of Science, Technology, and Philosophy in the 16th and 17th Centuries* (New York: Harper Brothers, 1959), i. 283–5.

vibration was shown to be characteristic of single sounds and to be the cause of overtones.

The history of the investigation of the overtone series presents a striking example of the concurrent labour of scientists and musicians in the search for an explanation of a mysterious phenomenon. Without the persistent inquiries of Mersenne, a trained musician gifted with an acute ear, the problem would probably have gone unrecognized for some time. Similarly, it was another man learned in music, John Wallis,[44] who recognized how the experiments in sympathetic vibration made by his colleagues of the Royal Society were relevant to the problem of the overtones. Finally, it was a Frenchman, Sauveur, interested in methods of tempering instruments, who transmitted the theory to our musical theorist Rameau.

The theory of Rameau, then, is a good illustration of the slowness with which scientific facts were absorbed into artistic theories once music had been separated from science. Therefore, if we are to observe scientific developments that influenced the course of musical history in the seventeenth century, we must seek them in the preceding period. There, because of the closer rapport between music and science, we shall find that the problems subjected to scientific, or at least objective, investigation were not the most fundamental, but were those that demanded solution for practical reasons. In the seventeenth century, the age of the emergence of instrumental music, it was natural that attention should be focused on the components and characteristics of the tones of pipes and strings; and in the preceding period, during which composers broke the bounds of the diatonic, modal, and consonant vocal idiom, it was characteristic that scientific discussion should be concentrated on the nature of the consonances and dissonances and their changed relationships in the new chromatic spectrum.

When Claudio Monteverdi replied to the critic Giovanni Maria Artusi in a famous declaration of faith printed in the fifth book of madrigals in 1605, Monteverdi acknowledged that his manner of using dissonances was the crucial issue in the controversy about the new and old styles. The established considerations for the use of consonances and dissonances as taught by Zarlino,[45] he said, were now superseded by a second scheme, and this constituted a *seconda pratica*. This modern manner of composition, he added, was founded on truths supportable by both reason and sensation. What he implied was that the products of the new practice were not a

---

[44] Wallis edited the Greek texts of the *Harmonics* of Ptolemy, the commentaries upon them by Porphyry, and the *Harmonics* of Manuel Bryennius.

[45] Gioseffo Zarlino, *Le istitutioni harmoniche* (Venice, 1558).

haphazard harvest of men who sow and toil without design. But, he emphasized, neither were they products of a new theory. For theory in the old sense of a musical science dictating to practice was dead, or at least stagnant. Monteverdi promised to write a treatise about the new practice, but he never did so.

It was a discouraging task for anyone to undertake. The older system had collapsed and it would take years of experience with the expanded resources before a new one could be erected. And no new system appeared until that of Rameau. The scientific revolution played a part in the demise of the old system as well as in the foundation of the new.

To appreciate the change in attitude towards consonance and dissonance fostered by the discoveries in the nature of sound, it is necessary to understand the traditional explanations of them. The identity of the purest consonances with the simplest ratios was observed very early in the history of science. If the ratios of the principal consonances did not actually inspire Pythagorean numerology, they were certainly among its strongest pillars. The consonances recognized by the ancients were the octave, produced by string-lengths in the ratio of $2:1$, the fifth, by $3:2$, and the fourth, by $4:3$. Medieval polyphony accorded at least practical recognition to consonances outside the sacred precinct of the first four numbers. It was therefore the task of the theorists of the fifteenth and sixteenth centuries to find a justification for the major and minor thirds and sixths. The most eloquent spokesman, if not the author, of the new numerology was Gioseffo Zarlino (1517-90). He extended the realm of consonance to combinations produced by the ratios within the first six numbers, the *senarius* or *senario*. He took great pains to show that within the frame of the Neo-Pythagorean and Neoplatonic ideology the number six was quite as sacred as the number four. It was the first perfect number, which means that it is the sum of all the whole numbers of which it is a multiple: $1 + 2 + 3 = 1 \times 2 \times 3 = 6$. The number six possessed many other metaphysical virtues that Zarlino enumerated. The enlarged sacred precinct now included the previously excluded major third ($5:4$), minor third ($6:5$), and major sixth ($5:3$). Zarlino also contingently admitted the minor sixth, although its ratio ($8:5$) was outside the first six numbers.[46]

Οὐδὲν χωρὶς ἐμοῦ, 'nothing without me', that is, proportion, was the motto on Zarlino's personal device, which shows a cube inscribed by various lines that intersect to form the ratios of the consonances (see Pl.

[46] Ibid., pt. i, chs. 14-16.

PL. 8.1. Zarlino's personal device, from G. M. Artusi, *Impresa del molto Rev. M. Gioseffo Zarlino . . . dichiarata* (Bologna, 1604)

8.1).[47] Below the cube is the legend, ἀεὶ ὁ αὐτός, 'always the same', which indicates the permanence and universality of this system of proportions.

The 'sounding numbers' of the *senario* constituted in Zarlino's mind a divinely ordained natural sphere within which the musician could operate

[47] Giovanni Maria Artusi, *Impresa del molto Rev. M. Gioseffo Zarlino . . . dichiarata* (Bologna: G. B. Bellagamba, 1604). Contrary to what one reads in most sources, including the articles on Artusi in *MGG* i (1951), col. 748, and in *Baker's Biographical Dictionary* (5th edn.; 1958), this is not an attack on Zarlino but a eulogy in the form of an explanation of his personal device printed after Zarlino's death by his most loyal pupil.

freely to produce the main fabric of his compositions. Outside the safe sanctuary of the *senario* was the wilderness of dissonances, some of which could be brought into a composition under certain restrictive conditions to embellish and underscore the effect of the consonances. In his monumental *Harmonic Institutions* of 1558, Zarlino developed the rules of composition based on these premisses. The treatise's mathematical underpinning and theological overtones won it the acclaim of both the pseudo-scientific and religious. Although Zarlino had merely summed up the polyphonic practice of his immediate predecessors, the imprimatur he gave to this particular practice tended to discourage experiments in the use of the illicit intervals. Many were of the opinion that musical composition had at last reached perfection of method. Little, indeed, was added to the theory of strict counterpoint during the next century and a half.

But during the one hundred years after Zarlino's text was published, the premisses upon which his theory rested were undermined by a number of scientific discoveries, demonstrations, and hypotheses. The first wedges to pry musical theory loose from its numerological foundations were already driven in the sixteenth century.

The cause of consonance, or at least its formal cause in the terminology of Aristotelian analysis, was generally stated to be the *numerus sonorus* or harmonic number. Until the sixteenth century no attempt had been made to study the process whereby a numerical ratio became a pleasing sensory experience. It sufficed to believe that the soul, which was considered a harmony of diverse elements, should be pleased by a similar harmony in the sounding numbers.

Perhaps the first to investigate the mechanics of the production of consonances was Giovanni Battista Benedetti. He was born in Venice in 1530 and died in Turin in 1590. Between 1558 and 1566 he was a lecturer in mathematics in Parma under the patronage of Duke Ottavio Farnese. It was here that he probably met the composer Cipriano de Rore, who was choirmaster to the duke between May 1561 and early 1563, when he succeeded Willaert as *maestro di cappella* at St Mark's in Venice. In 1567 Benedetti moved to Turin, where he was court mathematician for the dukes of Savoy and lecturer at the university.[48]

Benedetti worked on a great variety of geometrical, mathematical, astronomical, and mechanical problems, including the acceleration of falling

---

[48] Giovanni Bordiga, 'Giovanni Battista Benedetti, filosofo e matematico veneziano del secolo XVI', in *Atti del Reale Istituto Veneto di Scienze, Lettere ed Arti*, 85, pt. 2 (1925–6), 585–754. Concerning the Benedetti Mei heard lecture on Aristotle in Rome during the academic year 1559–60, see my prefatory note to this essay.

bodies, where his studies anticipated those of Galileo. He was also an amateur musician and composer and was interested in the problem of tuning instruments. In his major work, *Diversarum speculationum mathematicarum & physicorum liber*, 1585, several questions concerning sound and music are considered. The most interesting discussions to us are those in two undated letters addressed to Cipriano de Rore printed in this book. They were probably written around 1563.[49]

In the second of these letters Benedetti inquires—possibly for the first time—into the relation between the sensation of pitch and consonance and rates of vibration. In introducing this subject he says he wishes to speculate about the way the simple consonances are generated. They arise, he says, from a certain equalization of percussion (*aequatione percussionum*), or from an equal concurrence of air waves (*aequali concursu undarum aeris*), or from the coincidence of their terminations (*conterminatione earum*). The unison, he continues, is the first and most agreeable consonance, and after it comes the diapason or octave, then the fifth. Now, these preferences may be shown to be the result of the 'order of agreement of the terminations of the percussions of the air waves, by which the sound is generated'.[50]

In the unison the air waves agree perfectly without any interference (*intersectio*) or fractioning (*fractio*). This may be demonstrated by dividing the string of a monochord into two equal parts. He then continues:

---

[49] *Diversarum speculationum mathematicarum & physicorum liber* (Turin: apud Haeredem Nicolai Bevilaquae, 1585). The last part of this work, headed 'Physica, et Mathematica Responsa', contains replies of which he had kept copies to queries by various persons on topics in physics, astronomy, geometry, mathematics, and music. Manuscript copies of the letters, some with annotations in Benedetti's hand, were in MS LXXXIII. N. II. 50 and CXIV. N. III. 27 of the Biblioteca Nazionale of Turin, but were destroyed by fire; see Bordiga, 'G. B. Benedetti', 613, and Benedetti, 'Ad lectorem', in *Diversarum*, 204. The two letters on music are under the heading, 'De intervallis musicis', and are both addressed to 'Cypriano Rore Musico celeberrimo', but they give no indication of date or place. The first letter (277–8) demonstrates with the aid of seven three-part examples in score how false intervals are produced through the introduction of chromatic alterations in a diatonic system. The second letter, headed 'De eodem subiecto. Ad eundem', 279–83, presents further examples and considers several modes of temperament that aim to circumvent this difficulty. Finally, there is the section on the cause of consonance. The two letters have been reprinted by Josef Reiss in 'Jo. Bapt. Benedictus, *De intervallis musicis*', *Zeitschrift für Musikwissenschaft*, 7 (1924–5), 13–20, but with hardly any comment. They are summarized in Bordiga, 'G. B. Benedetti', 724–6, though again without any appreciation for the importance of Benedetti's theory of consonance.

By a number of known facts the period during which the letters might have been written may be narrowed down to the two years between 1562 and 1564. The positive boundary dates are 1558, the date of Zarlino's *Istitutioni harmoniche*, mentioned in the second letter (p. 281), and 1565, the year Rore died. Benedetti probably became acquainted with the composer when Rore came to Parma in 1561 to take the post of *maestro di cappella* to Duke Ottavio Farnese. In 1563 Rore became *maestro di cappella* at San Marco in Venice, returning to Parma in 1564. The period of Rore's absence from Parma—1563 to 1564—therefore seems the most likely for the two letters.

[50] 'Videamur igitur ordinem concursus percussionum terminorum, seu undarum aeris, unde sonus generatur' (p. 283).

Sed cum ponticulus ita diviserit chordam, ut relicta sit eius tertia pars ab uno latere, ab alio vero, duae tertiae, tunc maior pars, dupla erit minori, et sonabunt ipsam diapason consonantiam, percussiones vero terminorum ipsius, tali proportione se invicem habebunt, ut in qualibet secunda percussione minoris portionis ipsius chordae, maior percutiet, seu concurret cum minori, eodem temporis instanti, cum nemo sit qui nesciat, quod quo longior est chorda, etiam tardius moveatur, quare cum longior dupla sit breviori, et eiusdem intensionis tam una quam altera, tunc eo tempore, quo longior unum intervallum tremoris perfecerit, brevior duo intervalla conficiet.

Cum autem ponticulus ita diviserit chordam, ut ab uno latere relinquantur duae quintae partes, ab alio vero tres quintae, ex quibus partibus generatur consonantia diapente; tunc clarè patet, quod eadem proportione tardius erit unum intervallum tremoris maioris portionis, uno intervallo tremoris minoris portionis, quam maior portio habet ad minorem; hoc est tempus maioris intervalli ad tempus minoris erit sesquialterum; quare non convenient simul, nisi perfectis tribus intervallis minoris portionis, et duobus maioris; ita quod eadem proportio erit numeri intervallorum minoris portionis ad intervalla maioris, quae longitudinis maioris portionis ad longitudinem minoris; unde

But when the bridge so divides the string that a third of it remains on one side and two-thirds on the other, then the larger part is twice the smaller and the two will sound the consonance of the octave. The percussions of the boundary-tones of this octave will have between them such a proportion that in every second percussion of the minor portion of this string, the larger will percuss or concur with the minor at the same instant of time. For everyone knows that the longer the string, the more slowly it is moved. Therefore, since the longer part is twice the shorter, and they are both of the same tension, in the time that the longer completes one period of vibration, the shorter completes two.

Now if the bridge so divides the string that two-fifths remain on one side and three-fifths on the other, the consonance of the fifth will be generated. It is clear that a single period of vibration of the larger portion will take more time than one period of the smaller portion by the same proportion as exists between the major portion and the minor. That is, the ratio of the duration of the major portion to that of the minor will be sesquialtera. Therefore they will not convene at one instant until three periods of the minor portion and two of the major have been completed. It follows that the ratio between the number of periods of the minor portion and that of the major will be the same as the ratio between the lengths of the two portions.

productum numeri portionis
minoris ipsius chordae in
numerum intervallorum motus
ipsius portionis, aequale erit
producto numeri portionis
maioris in numerum
intervallorum ipsius maioris
portionis; quae quidem producta
ita se habebunt, ut in diapason,
sit binarius numerus; in diapente
verò senarius; in diatessaron
duodenarius, in hexachordo maiori
quindenarius; in ditono
vicenarius, in semiditono
tricenarius, demum in hexachordo
minori quadragenarius; qui quidem
numeri non absque mira ili
analogia conveniunt invicem.

Therefore the product of the
number of the minor portion of
the same string and the number of
periods of the same minor portion
will be equal to the product of
the number of the major portion
and the number of periods of the
same major portion. These
products will be therefore: for
the diapason, 2; for the
fifth, 6; for the fourth, 12; for
the major sixth, 15; for the
ditone [major third], 20; for the
semiditone [minor third], 30;
finally, for the minor
sixth, 40. These numbers agree
among themselves in a wonderful
way.

This passage contains several statements of primary importance in the history of acoustics. First, Benedetti states the law that the ratio of the frequencies of two strings varies inversely with their lengths, the tension being equal. He does not show how he arrived at this conclusion or how he managed to compare the rates of vibration. Only in the seventeenth century was the truth of his observation adequately demonstrated. Secondly, Benedetti shows that the concordance of intervals depends on the coincidence of the terminations of vibration-cycles. These moments of no vibration will concur every two vibrations of the shorter string in an octave, every three of the shorter string against one of the longer in a twelfth, and so on. Thirdly, Benedetti arrives at an index of the degree of agreement in a consonance by multiplying the two terms of its ratio. He is thus able to express the standing of each of the consonances in a descending scale of concordance.[51]

Benedetti's discovery was potentially a fatal blow to number symbolism. When consonance is understood as the frequent concurrence of the termination points of vibrations, the distinction between consonance and dissonance becomes one of relative frequency of concordance. There is no sudden falling off of this agreement of waves when the bounds of the

---

[51] This system is the ancestor of a number of later attempts at grading intervals, from the grades of suavity of Leonhard Euler in *Tentamen novae theoriae musicae* (St Petersburg: Typographia Academiae scientiarum, 1739) to Paul Hindemith's classes of chord intensity in his *Craft of Musical Composition* (New York: Associated Music Publishers, 1942), i. My contention that Benedetti has set up a graded scale of concordance has been challenged by D. P. Walker in *Studies in Musical Science in the Late Renaissance*, 31 n. 16. I respond to this in my prefatory note to the present essay.

mystic number six are overstepped. Nor is any clear boundary discernible anywhere in the infinite series of musical intervals. Moreover, if one were to pursue Benedetti's scale of concordance beyond the so-called consonances to the dissonances, one would have to recognize that the number for the diminished fifth ($7:5$)—35—is between that of the minor third, 30, and that of the minor sixth, 40. This puts the diminished fifth, rejected by Zarlino, ahead of the minor sixth, which, though outside the *senario* (because of its ratio, $8:5$), he somehow rationalized into his system. While Benedetti failed to draw these obvious conclusions from his ranking of the consonances, his scepticism of the exclusiveness of the *senario*, revealed in another demonstration (to which we shall come presently), leads one to believe he was aware of these implications of his theory.

Benedetti's voice found few echoes in the intellectual void of the reigning Pythagoreanism. But his point of view gained momentum during the next hundred years, and by the middle of the seventeenth century it held the field, at least among progressive musicians.

One of the earliest supporters of the empiricist view was Galileo's father, Vincenzo Galilei (*c.*1520–91), a renowned lutenist and musical theorist. Galilei laid aside all numerological grounds for the classification of consonance and dissonance. He worked out a new ranking on the basis of pure sense experience and artistic usage. The octave, fifth, thirds, and sixths came first; only then followed the fourth, which was subject to restrictions in composition. Then came the augmented fourth and diminished fifth in a category intermediate between the dissonances and imperfect consonances.

In the second and third decades of the seventeenth century the question of the ranking of consonances became the subject of a lively debate between Marin Mersenne and René Descartes. It was Isaac Beeckman, rector of the college of Dordrecht, who in 1618 had shown Descartes a demonstration of the correspondence between the wave motions of consonances. Though his explanation was almost identical to Benedetti's, Beeckman had probably arrived at it independently, as so often happens in scientific research.[52] Mersenne accepted this as proof that the relative pleasingness of consonances was caused by the concurrence of the 'returns' of vibrations. Descartes, however, remained sceptical of this as an explanation of the subjective reaction of a listener to the various consonances. In a letter to Mersenne of 18 December 1629, Descartes wrote: 'As for your manner of determining

---

[52] See Descartes, *Œuvres*, x (1908), 57, and Mersenne, *Correspondance*, i. 606. In a letter to Mersenne of 13 Jan. 1631, Descartes presents a diagram that shows the concurrence of the vibrations of a tone with its upper octave, twelfth, eleventh, and tenth, and the mutual concurrence of the other tones among themselves: Mersenne, *Correspondance*, iii. 26.

the goodness of consonances, . . . it is too subtle, if I dare say, to be distinguished by the ear, without which it is impossible to judge the goodness of any consonance, and if we judge by reason, this reason must always consider the capacity of the ear.'[53]

In a subsequent letter, in the middle of January 1630, Descartes added: 'All this calculation serves only to show which consonances are simpler, or, if you wish, the sweetest or most perfect, but not for that the most pleasing.'[54] For the fifth is generally regarded as more agreeable than the twelfth, although in the twelfth the frequency of concurrence is twice that of the fifth. Finally, on 13 January 1631 Descartes concluded:

Concerning the sweetness of consonance, there are two things to be distinguished, that is, what makes them simpler and more concordant (*accordantes*) and what makes them more pleasing (*agréables*) to the ear.

Now, as for what renders them more pleasing, this depends on the places where they are employed, and there are places where even the diminished fifths and other dissonances are more pleasing than the consonances, so it is not possible to determine absolutely that one consonance is more pleasing than another. One may say, surely, that the thirds and sixths are generally more pleasing than the fourth, that in gay compositions the major thirds and sixths are more pleasing than the minor, and the contrary in sad compositions, etc., since there are more opportunities to use them pleasingly.

But we can say absolutely which consonances are simplest and most concordant, because this depends only on whether their tones unite better and approach more closely the nature of the unison. So we can say absolutely that the fourth is more concordant than the major third, even though ordinarily it is not more pleasing, in the same way that senna (*la casse*) is sweeter than olives, but not more pleasing to our taste.[55]

Descartes's distinction between concordance or simplicity and pleasing-ness recognizes the separation of objective and subjective that will be a recurrent theme in our study. To leave to the scientist the investigation of acoustical truths and to the musician the manipulation of sonorous combinations seems to us today only common sense; yet this simple rule gained acceptance only after many battles. Mersenne, after resisting Descartes's conclusions for a time, finally resolved the question in the *Harmonie universelle* in the manner put to him by his correspondent Descartes.[56]

Yet on this question neither Descartes nor Mersenne ventured so far into pure empiricism as did Christiaan Huygens. Huygens contemplated the extension of the range of consonance to include the dubious ratios involving the number seven: the tritone or augmented fourth (10:7) and the dim-

---

[53] Ibid., ii. 338.   [54] Ibid., ii. 371.
[55] Ibid., iii. 24–5.   [56] 'Traitez des consonances', bk. i, prop. 19, p. 66.

inished fifth (7:5). At least he saw no reason for excluding them. Huygens compared the status of these intervals in his time to that of the thirds and sixths in ancient times. The latter intervals were regarded as dissonances then only because of their relative unfamiliarity. Just as these became recognized consonances, so would the augmented fourth and diminished fifth in time be welcomed among them.[57] Not long after, indeed, the forms of the dominant seventh chord, which contain these dubious intervals, became recognized harmonic entities that needed no special preparation.

Let us now return to the letters from Benedetti to Rore printed in the *Diverse Speculations* of 1585. We have already considered the last part of the second letter. In the scientist's first letter and in the first part of the second Benedetti's purpose was to show the composer why a system of equal temperament was a necessity for modern music. The importance of what Benedetti has to say on this subject does not lie in any new facts presented but in his scientific attitude towards a question which was rife with prejudices. The two tunings that had received theoretical sanction up to now, the Pythagorean, sponsored by Boethius and his followers, and the syntonic diatonic of Ptolemy, advocated by Giovanni Spataro, Lodovico Fogliano, and Zarlino,[58] were both originally devised for purely melodic music, such as that of a voice singing alone, or in unison with other voices or instruments. When either of these tunings was used in polyphonic music, many difficulties arose because of their unequal tones or semitones, or their harsh-sounding consonances on certain steps of the scale. From earliest times instrument-builders and tuners compensated for these shortcomings by tempering the consonances by ear. Theorists after post-classical times, however, generally evaded the problem. But the coalescence of theory and practice in the Renaissance made coming to terms with this issue imperative. Thus the problem of tuning became the subject of the most heated musical controversies in the fifteenth and sixteenth centuries. Musically minded scientists and scientifically minded musicians were at the head of those who faced the new challenge.

[57] Huygens, *Nouveau cycle harmonique*, in *Œuvres*, xx. 162–4.
[58] Spataro in *Errori de Franchino Gafurio* (Bologna: Benedictus Hectoris, 1521), pt. iv, Error 26, had already suggested that the syntonic diatonic of Ptolemy would remove many of the faults inherent in the Pythagorean tuning, and in pt. v, Err. 16, stated that this syntonic was in fact the tuning used by practical musicians. Spataro's teacher Bartolomé Ramos de Pareja, in his *Musica practica* (Bologna, 1482), had broken the ground for the acceptance of justly tuned thirds and sixths. Later Lodovico Fogliano took up the advocacy of the Ptolemaic syntonic tuning in *Musica theorica* (Venice: Io. Antonius & fratres de Sabio, 1529). See my articles, 'L. Fogliano' and 'Ramos de Pareja', in *MGG* and my *Humanism in Italian Renaissance Musical Thought* (New Haven, Conn.: Yale University Press, 1985), 234–44.

It is in this context that Benedetti wrote to Rore. He wanted to prove that whenever a composer writes certain intervallic progressions or introduces chromatic steps in a part, singers or players cannot maintain the true intervals without causing the pitch to rise or fall by a minute amount. He supported his contention with a number of examples: seven one-measure, three-part progressions in the first letter and two longer examples in the second letter. The second of the longer examples repeats four times a two-measure progression containing one chromatic alteration. If the theoretically true tuning of the consonances is maintained through the common tones that link one interval with the next, the pitch will fall one syntonic comma during each statement, totalling at the end of Benedetti's example nearly a full semitone (or, more precisely, 88 per cent of an equal-tempered semitone). The first three and one-half measures of his example are given in Ex. 8.1. The ratios which appear in my example stand for the intervals named by Benedetti in the text of his letter.[59]

Ex. 8.1

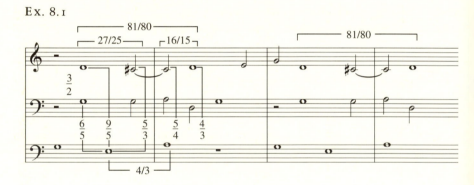

Benedetti's proof may be stated as follows:

$$3/2 \times 6/5 = 9/5$$
$$9/5 \div 5/3 = 27/25$$

[59] *Diversarum speculationum . . . liber*, 280: 'in prima cellula discedens bassus à quinta cum superiori, & ab unisono cum tenore discedens ad tertiam minorem cum ipso tenore, facit cum superiori septimam maiorem, quae est ut .9. ad .5. superquadripartiensquintas scilicet, à qua discedens postea superius, ut faciat cum basso sextam maiorem, descendit per semitonium maius, à qua sexta maiori descendens bassus, & ascendens per quartam, efficit cum dicto superiori tertiam maiorem, à qua discedens superius ut efficiat quartam cum ipso basso (qui quidem bassus transit in tenorem) ascendit per semitonium minus, differens à semitonio maiori per unum comma, unde cantilena remanet depressa per unum comma, cum deinde idem faciat inter tertiam, & quartam cellulam, per aliud comma descendit, & sic toties facere posset, ut postremo valde deprimatur cantilena à primo phthongo.'

Therefore the soprano descends 27/25, a large semitone.

$$5/3 \div 4/3 = 5/4$$
$$4/3 \div 5/4 = 16/15$$

Therefore the soprano in the second measure ascends 16/15, a small semitone.

$$27/25 \div 16/15 = 81/80, \text{ a syntonic comma}$$

Therefore in the first two measures the pitch has fallen a syntonic comma.

Benedetti noted that Rore had made such a departure from a diatonic mode when he introduced semitone motion at the words 'Les yeulx en pleurs' in the chanson *Hellas comment voules-vous* (1550).[60] If we follow Benedetti's method and divide the ratios over the common tones to get the sizes of the semitones, the succession of semitones in the soprano part is 16:15, 25:24, 16:15. Multiplying these ratios, we get for the total descent of the soprano part a minor third in the ratio 32:27. This is one syntonic comma smaller than the true minor third, 6:5. Therefore, the pitch will have risen one syntonic comma, 81:80, or 22 per cent of an equal-tempered semitone, between the G of the tenor and the same G in the alto a bar later. Since the passage sung here by the soprano is heard in three other voices, the pitch will have risen at the end of the section on the words 'Les yeulx en pleurs'—nearly a semitone (Ex. 8.2).

Ex. 8.2

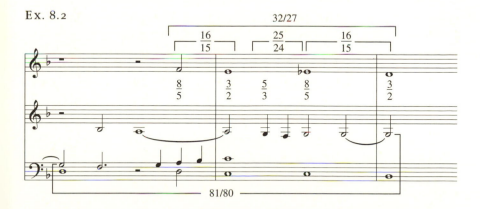

[60] Ibid. 278. The chanson is published in *The Madrigals of Cipriano de Rore for Three and Four Voices*, ed. Gertrude Parker Smith (Northampton, Mass.: Smith College, 1943), 84–9, and in Rore, *Opera omnia*, ed. Bernhard Meier, viii (Neuhausen-Stuttgart: Hänssler, 1977), 41–3. It was first printed in *Il primo libro de madrigali a 4 voci* (Ferrara: Buglhat & Hucher, 1550).

Benedetti further shows that purely diatonic music is not free from such pitfalls. In the perfectly innocuous progression of the first two measures of Ex. 8.3, the pitch rises one syntonic comma if the true fourth and fifth are used over the alto's common tone D in the first measure and the true fifth and minor third in the following measure over the alto's E. By the ninth measure the pitch has risen four syntonic commas.[61]

Ex. 8.3

In the first two cases the cause of the difficulty is an inequality of semitones, in the third case an inequality of whole tones. The solution to the problem is obviously equal semitones and tones, or what is called equal temperament. The demonstration also proves, as Benedetti states at the beginning of this letter, that a composition need not end in the tone in which it began, that this in fact is almost an impossibility. Thus one of the cardinal rules of the orthodox theory is nullified.

In the above examples, the performance will continue on an even keel only if the true intervals of the *senario* recommended by Zarlino are abandoned through judicious adjustments by the singers. A system of temperament thus becomes a necessity. Temperament was already tolerated in the tuning of the lute and keyboard instruments, but whether it should be countenanced in purely vocal music was a burning issue at this time. It was the issue, in fact, that most clearly divided the Neoplatonists like Zarlino from the empiricists in the decades preceding the seventeenth century. Benedetti probably addressed his letter to Rore because he knew that this composer would be responsive to his ideas, for Rore was the

[61] Ibid. 279: 'in prima figura, ubi superius à .g. primae cellulae ad .g. secundae, interest unum comma, eo quod progrediens superius in prima cellula ipsius cantilenae à quarta ad quintam cum tenore, ascendit per tonum sesquioctavum, à prima cellula deinde ad secundam, tenor ascendit similiter per tonum sesquioctavum cum transeat à quinta ad quartam, quod facit cum superiori, in secunda cellula postea, cum superius descendat à maiori sexta ad quintam, quod facit cum bassu, seu à quarta ad tertiam minorem, quod facit cum tenore, tunc descendit per tonum sesquinonum, ita quod non revertitur ad eundem phthongum, ubi prius erat in prima cellula, sed reperitur per unum comma altius, quod quidem comma est differentia inter tonum sesquioctavum & sesquinonum, ut alias tibi demonstravi.'

recognized leader of the avant garde of his generation and was conspicuous in his use of harmonies outside the immediate range of the traditional diatonic church modes.

Zarlino's opposition to temperament for vocal music grows out of his rationalistic classification of consonances. Since he rejected the ratios outside the *senario*, the only acceptable tuning was that first described by the Greek theorist Didymus and later modified and named syntonic diatonic by Ptolemy. Nearly all the consonances between the tones of a diatonic scale tuned to this system are in their simplest ratios and will sound true to the ear. Such a system is also called just intonation. Zarlino admitted that certain instruments that had to be played in a number of keys (harpsichords, organs, lutes, fretted viols) could not do without temperament in some form. But voices and instruments with flexible tuning were free of this necessity. His argument is typically mystic:

If it were true that in voices as well as in instruments we only hear consonances and intervals out of their natural proportions, there would follow that those born of the true harmonic numbers would never find realization in fact but would exist always potentially. These potentialities would be wasted and frustrated, for any natural potentiality which is not reduced to action at some time is without any utility in nature. And yet we see that God and Nature never do anything in vain. Therefore it is necessary to say that this potential is at some time reduced to action.[62]

This defence of just intonation reminds one of Kepler's reply to a question that must have seemed to his contemporaries, if not to us, altogether theoretical: Is the planet Jupiter inhabited? It must be so, said he, and, moreover, some day we shall fly there, for what good will it do to have four moons coursing about Jupiter if there is no one on that planet to watch them?[63] Neither Kepler nor Zarlino had yet given up the notion that all of nature exists simply for the benefit of man.

A more thorough refutation of Zarlino's position than Benedetti's was undertaken by Vincenzo Galilei in his *Dialogo della musica antica et della moderna*.[64] Galilei had been a pupil of Zarlino in Venice around 1564, having been sent there by his humanist patron Count Giovanni Bardi to acquire a mastery of theoretical music. As a popular lute-player and singer, Galilei used to frequent the Count's home, where an academy, later known as the 'Camerata', was accustomed to meeting. Upon his return from his study with Zarlino, Galilei taught his master's doctrine for a while to the noblemen of Bardi's circle. But after a period he became dissatisfied

---

[62] *Istitutioni harmoniche*, bk. ii, ch. 45.
[63] Thorndike, *History of Magic*, vii. 13.
[64] Florence: G. Marescotti, 1581.

with certain of Zarlino's solutions to important theoretical questions, and, encouraged in this opposition by another humanist, Girolamo Mei, Galilei became Zarlino's most outspoken and severest critic.

In the first pages of the *Dialogue*, Galilei disposes of both the syntonic diatonic of Ptolemy and the diatonic ditoniaion—so-called Pythagorean tuning—advocated by the Boethians. He shows that in the syntonic tuning not only are the consonances formed between the natural tones of the diatonic scale and such tones as Bb, F♯, and C♯ not in their true ratios, but certain combinations within the diatonic system itself also do not conform to these true ratios.[65] One example will suffice: the minor third, D–F. The first four tones of the syntonic diatonic scale are separated by the following intervals:[66]

C	D	E	F
major tone	minor tone	major semitone	
9/8	10/9	16/15	

To get the ratio of D–F we multiply 10/9 by 16/15, which is 160/135, or 32/27. This is smaller than the minor third (6:5) by a syntonic comma (81:80).[67] Thus the syntonic tuning is shown to be inadequate even apart from the difficulties introduced by the use of simultaneous consonances or chromaticism.

Zarlino's tenacious adherence to the syntonic tuning as the basis for the ideal medium of vocal music in the ensuing controversy shows that this loyalty was merely a symptom of a deeper credulity, of a philosophic nature. It was at this that Galilei directed his subsequent attacks. He aimed to reveal the fallacy, for example, of the premiss that some intervals were natural because they had simple ratios, while others were unnatural. 'Whether we sing the fifth in the 3:2 ratio or not', Galilei argued, 'is of no more importance to Nature than that a crow or a raven lives three hundred or four hundred years and a man only fifty or sixty.'[68] 'Among the musical intervals', he declared in another place, 'those contained outside the *senario* are as natural as those within it. The third contained in the 81:64 ratio is as natural as that in the 5:4 ratio. For the seventh to be dissonant in the

---

[65] Ibid. 4 ff.

[66] Zarlino, *Istitutioni*, Bk. ii, ch. 39.

[67] Galilei, *Dialogo*, 10.

[68] *Discorso intorno all'opere di messer Gioseffo Zarlino da Chioggia* (Florence: G. Marescotti, 1589), 116–17.

9:5 ratio is as natural as for the octave to be consonant in the 2:1 ratio.'[69] In short, Zarlino was mistaken in imputing a universal harmony to nature.

It is obvious that Galilei was not inclined either towards the idols of the tribe or the theatre; but neither would he fall before those of the market-place. He was critical of contemporary theorists who manipulated concepts to construct rigid rules, when the objects of their legislation had no precise definition or any real existence apart from sensation. They pretended to speak about the things themselves, he complained, when in truth they were talking about mere words. Such was their categorical prohibition of parallel fifths. Some parallel fifths sound well, Galilei objected; only the musical ear can be the judge. The musician, Galilei insisted, deals in a subjective realm in which the sense has sufficient powers unaided by the reason. 'For the senses apprehend precisely differences in forms, colours, flavours, odours, and sounds. They know moreover the heavy from the light, the harsh and hard from the soft and tender, and other superficial accidents. But the qualities and intrinsic virtues of things, with respect to whether they are hot or cold, humid or dry, only the intellect has the faculty of judging, through becoming convinced by experiment and not simply by the sense through the medium of the diversity of forms and colours or other circumstances . . .'.[70] This statement, written in 1589, while it seems to adumbrate the theory of primary and secondary qualities of Francis Bacon, Galileo, and Thomas Hobbes, only expressed what was already in the air. Ludovico Vives and Bernardino Telesio, among the philosophers Galilei may have known, had both revived this distinction of the ancient sceptics. For Telesio, however, the primary active qualities or forces were simply hot and cold, while Galilei went back to the four primary qualities of Aristotle: hot, cold, dry, and moist.[71] To isolate more specifically the source of Galilei's scientific orientation is difficult. The ancient atomists and sceptics were being widely read and commented on. As the musical preceptor of Giovanni Bardi's academy, the 'Camerata', Galilei was in close contact with the prevailing intellectual currents. According to Pietro Bardi, the academy heard 'discourses and instructions in poetry, astrology, and other sciences', as well as being entertained with music.[72]

[69] Ibid. 92–3.
[70] 'Discorso intorno all'uso delle dissonanze' (1589–91), Florence, Biblioteca Nazionale Centrale, MS Gal. 1, fo. 120ᵛ, ed. Frieder Rempp in *Die Kontrapunkttraktate Vincenzo Galileis* (Cologne: Arno Volk, 1980), 104.
[71] *De generatione et corruptione*, ii. 2. 329ᴮ. Aristotle, however, does not speak of colours, flavours, odours, and sounds, except to say that whiteness, blackness, sweetness, bitterness, and similar perceptible contrarieties do not constitute basic elements.
[72] Pietro de' Bardi, Conte di Vernio, 'Lettera a G. B. Doni sull'origine del melodramma' (1634), in Angelo Solerti, *Le origini del melodramma* (Torino: Bocca, 1903), 143–4.

Two important influences on Galilei may be indicated, however. The first was the Greek philosopher of the Peripatetic School, Aristoxenus of Tarentum.[73] Neglected by medieval and early Renaissance musical theorists because he was the *bête noire* of Boethius, he became known to musicians through Antonio Gogava's (however inadequate) Latin translation of his *Harmonics*, published in 1562. Ironically, the translation had been made for Zarlino, who evidently received it too late to put it to use in his *Harmonic Institutions*. Unlike Plato, Aristotle, and Ptolemy, Aristoxenus was not concerned with fitting musical facts into a rational system; he aimed only to set down musical and acoustical observations and laws as they were gathered from sense experience. He recommended an empirical tuning approximating equal temperament. Serious consideration of equal temperament in theoretical writings begins characteristically with the discovery of this Greek authority who could be cited in its behalf. The Aristoxenian tuning was considered by Galilei the most practicable of the Greek systems for modern instruments.

Another important influence on Galilei's thought was the Florentine humanist Girolamo Mei, who resided in Rome. By the time Galilei first consulted him, in 1572, Mei had read every available ancient Greek and Latin source on Greek music. He communicated much of his data and conclusions to Galilei during the next nine years.[74] Mei's revelations persuaded Galilei that his former teacher Zarlino and other contemporary theorists had misinterpreted Greek music. It was for a clarification of some points concerning this music that Galilei had first approached Mei. But in the course of their exchanges Mei succeeded in changing Galilei's entire philosophy, as the latter shows in his *Dialogo*.

Mei emphasized in his letters the necessity for distinguishing artistic from scientific facts:

The science of music goes about diligently investigating and considering all the qualities and properties of the constitutions, systems, and orders of musical tones, whether these are simple qualities or comparative, like the consonances, and this for no other purpose than to come to know the truth itself, the perfect goal of all speculation, and as a by-product the false. It then lets art exploit as it sees fit without any limitation those tones about which science has learned the truth.[75]

<hr/>

[73] Galilei left among his papers a translation of Aristoxenus into Italian, in Florence, Biblioteca Nazionale Centrale, MS Gal. 8.

[74] The extant letters from Mei to Galilei are printed in C. Palisca, *Girolamo Mei, Letters on Ancient and Modern Music* (American Institute of Musicology, 1960; 2nd edn., Neuhausen-Stuttgart: Hänssler, 1977). The letter of May 1572 is trans. in Palisca, *The Florentine Camerata*, 56–77.

[75] Letter of 8 May 1572, in Palisca, *Mei*, 103, trans. in Palisca, *The Florentine Camerata*, 65.

The tendency in the Renaissance had been to base artistic rules on presumed scientific or metaphysical facts. Mei understood that this was a violation of the independent subjective nature of artistic procedures.

On one occasion, seeing that his correspondent clung to Zarlino's *senario* theory and to just intonation, Mei suggested to Galilei that he try a simple experiment to prove whether voices sang the supposedly natural intervals. Mei wrote:

Stretch out over a lute (the larger it is, the more obvious will be what we wish to prove to the ear) two . . . strings of equal length and width, and measure out the frets under them accurately according to the distribution of the intervals in each of the two species of tuning—the syntonic [just intonation] and ditonic [Pythagorean]—and then, taking the notes of the tetrachord one by one by means of the frets of each string, observe which of the two strings gives the notes that correspond to what is sung today. Thus without any further doubt the answer will result clear to anyone, even if what I have often fancied on my own more as a matter of opinion than judgment is not proved true.[76]

It is likely that Galilei went ahead to make this simple experiment, because he was soon convinced that the syntonic was not the tuning in use, but that neither was it what Mei had 'fancied'. That year, 1578, Galilei sent his first discourse to Zarlino under a pseudonym, to begin the polemic that was to last more than eleven years.[77] The climax of the controversy was the publication in 1581 of the *Dialogo* already mentioned, one of the most influential treatises of the late sixteenth century and probably the one that gave the greatest impetus to progressive musical techniques.

Once the seed of scepticism had been planted in Galilei's mind, its roots spread to every region of his thought. He worked out a new empirical theory of counterpoint that was based entirely on facts gathered from the practice of his contemporaries and predecessors. Before the Baroque as we know it really began, he had proclaimed many of its ideals in his treatise on counterpoint—which remained, however, in manuscript.[78]

Towards the end of his life Galilei applied the experimental method to a problem that had come up in the polemic with Zarlino: to what degree were the numerical relationships usually associated with intervals on the basis of string-division truly bound up with the physical cause of these intervals? The tradition for the numbers assigned to the consonances was,

[76] Letter of 17 Jan. 1578, ibid. 67, 140.
[77] This 'Discorso', sent to Zarlino on 7 June 1578, is mentioned in Zarlino's *Sopplimenti musicali*, in *Opere* (Venice: F. de Franceschi Senese, 1588–9), iii. 5–6, and in Galilei's *Discorso* of 1589, 14–17, but it has not itself survived.
[78] See above, Essay 2.

as we have seen, a very old one, but Galilei had resolved to question even such venerable concepts. That the ratios of $2:1$ produced the octave, $3:2$ the fifth, and so on, was supposed to have been observed by Pythagoras in the weights of hammers at a blacksmith shop. In Galilei's last published work, a discourse refuting certain points made in Zarlino's *Supplements* of 1588, Vincenzo shows (as his son Galileo and Mersenne were later to do again) that these ratios produce the consonances usually associated with them only when their terms represent pipe- or string-lengths, and other factors are equal. It was generally believed at this time that the same ratios would also produce these consonances when they expressed relative weights of hammers, weights attached to strings, or the volume enclosed in bells or glasses. In the woodcut published in Franchino Gaffurio's *Theorica musice* (1492), the same numbers, 4, 6, 8, 9, 12, 16, appear in each picture, implying that they would always produce the same intervals, for example, *A E a b e a'* (see Pl. 8.2). Galilei seems to have been the first to upset this doctrine, which was so plainly false that in 1627 Mersenne was to exclaim: 'I am certainly astonished that Macrobius, Boethius, and other ancients, and after them Zarlino and Cerone, were so negligent that they did not make a single experiment to discover the truth and disabuse the world.'[79]

About thirty years earlier, in his *Discorso* of 1589, Galilei had declared: 'In connection with [the theories of Pythagoras] I wish to point out two false opinions of which men have been persuaded by various writings and which I myself shared until I ascertained the truth by means of experiment, the teacher of all things.'[80] Contrary to common belief, he explained, two weights in the ratio of $2:1$ attached to two strings in the manner shown in Gaffurio's woodcut (Pl. 8.2) will not give the octave. The two weights must be in the ratio of $4:1$ to produce the octave, $9:4$ for the fifth and $16:9$ for the fourth. Pythagoras plucking the strings marked 12 and 8 in the woodcut (lower left) would get the irrational interval equivalent to string-lengths in the ratio $\sqrt{3}:\sqrt{2}$!

The second false opinion Galilei wished to correct was a consequence of the first. Since the pure octaves, fifths, fourths, and thirds were produced by string-lengths in superparticular ratios (of the class $(n + 1)/n$), and the compounds of these intervals (double octave, twelfth, etc.) by multiple ratios within the *senario*—$3:1$, $4:1$, $5:1$, $6:1$—the Pythagoreans and Boethians recognized only these two classes of ratios as productive of consonance. But now Galilei could show that ratios outside these two

---

[79] *Traité de l'harmonie universelle* (Paris: Guillaume Baudry, 1627), 447, quoted in Hellmut Ludwig, *M. Mersenne*, 54.
[80] *Discorso*, 103–4.

PL. 8.2. Discovery of the ratios of the consonances from F. Gaffurio,
Theorica musice (Milan, 1492)

classes could also produce consonances, as 9:4 and 16:9, when they
represent string tension.

Galilei did not pursue this line of reasoning further in the printed
discourse. However, he developed his theory more fully in two manuscript
essays whose contents are unknown to historians of both science and
music.[81]

---

[81] The Italian text and translation of these two essays are published in my *The Florentine Camerata*,
180–207.

In an essay entitled 'A Particular Discourse concerning the Diversity of the Ratios of the Octave', probably of 1589–90, Galilei reported on some experiments he had made with strings of different materials, with weights, coins, and pipes.[82] The octave, Galilei demonstrated, may be obtained through three different ratios, 2:1 in terms of string-lengths, which corresponds, he said, to linear measurement, 4:1 in terms of weights attached to strings, which is analogous to area or surface measurements, and 8:1 in terms of volumes of concave bodies like organ pipes, which corresponds to cubic measurements. In a second essay, 'A Particular Discourse concerning the Unison', of about the same date, Galilei noted the results of testing strings of various materials.[83] He found that to produce a true unison two strings had to be made of the same material, of the same thickness, length, and quality, and stretched to the same tension. If any of these factors was absent, the unison would be only approximate. Moreover, he discovered that if a lute were strung with two strings, one of steel and one of gut, and these were stretched to the best possible unison, the tones produced by stopping the strings at the various frets would no longer be in unison.[84]

What was the significance of these discoveries for the musician? First, he had to revise his fundamental concepts about musical sounds. The legendary sonorous or harmonic numbers had no real existence, Galilei showed. The sonorous number, which is referred to everywhere in the preceding literature as the material cause of sound, was a myth. It confused the corporeal—the vibrating body—with the incorporeal, the abstract numbers measuring the divisions of the body. Numbers, properly used, he emphasized, must refer to a particular dimension, of line, surface, or volume. And if numbers are properly applied, the octave or fifth cannot be said to have only one ratio, but a certain ratio according to stated conditions. It was therefore not true, as Zarlino had stated,[85] that the natural form of the octave is the duple ratio and can be none other, for the duple ratio can be found in dissonant intervals, as between two coins, when it will produce a tritone, or between the volumes of two pipes, when a major third approximately in the

---

[82] 'Discorso particolare intorno alla diversità delle forme del Diapason', Florence, Biblioteca Nazionale Centrale, MS Gal. 3, fos. 44ʳ–54ᵛ. The essay may be dated through a mention of the printed *Discorso* of 1589 on fo. 45ʳ. See my *Florentine Camerata*, 156 n. 20.

[83] 'Discorso particolare intorno all'Unisono', MS Gal. 3, fos. 55ʳ–61ᵛ, ed. and trans. in *The Florentine Camerata*, 198–207.

[84] Ibid. 203–4 (fo. 59ʳ–59ᵛ). I repeated this experiment and obtained a similar result, as reported in my paper 'Was Galileo's Father an Experimental Scientist?', in Victor Coelho (ed.), *Music and Science in the Age of Galileo*.

[85] *Istitutioni harmoniche*, pt. i, ch. 13.

'intense' tuning of Aristoxenus will result.[86] All his observations proved that numbers were significant only when applied to certain material relationships in sounding bodies, but meaningless as abstractions invoked to support this or that theory.

Moreover it is futile, Galilei showed, to try to prove the superiority of one or another tuning system on mathematical grounds. The ear has no regard for systems; it operates on a purely subjective level that eludes quantitative measurement. The large major thirds used in the lute tuning do not seem objectionable because of the mellow quality of the gut strings, but those same thirds in the harpsichord's steel strings are less tolerable because of the sharper sound of such strings.[87] The only interval whose tuning is really critical is the octave, which the ear cannot stand imperfectly tuned. The other intervals are usually found in some deviation from the true ratios. The ear tolerates these small deviations because it cannot detect smaller differences than one-ninth of a tone. Numbers, Galilei emphasized, are discrete quantities, while the intervals found by a viola-player as he moves his finger down the fingerboard are points in a continuum that contains many 'minimal little particles, almost like atoms', as he put it.[88] This infinity of points could yield an infinity of consonances and an even greater infinity of dissonances.

One may well ask at this point what effect Galilei's experiments, made in isolation and recorded in inaccessible manuscripts, could have had either on the course of music or of science. First, Galilei is only one of several whose thoughts were running in this direction at this time, though he was probably the most influential. Secondly, the essays were probably communicated to a group of musicians and humanists, since both discourses were written in reply to objections of certain 'Aristoxenian friends' mentioned in them. The objections had probably arisen from the *Dialogo* of 1581 and the *Discorso* of 1589.[89] Moreover, the published writings of Galilei were known to succeeding scientists. Mersenne in *La Vérité des sciences* (1625) recognized Vincenzo Galilei's priority in the discovery of the laws governing strings, pipes, and bells.[90] Mersenne clarified some aspects of these, such as the role of specific gravity and weight in determining the

---

[86] 'Discorso particolare intorno alla diuersità delle forme del Diapason', ed. and trans. in *The Florentine Camerata*, 188–91 (fos. 49ᵛ–50ᵛ).

[87] Galilei had already made this observation in *Dialogo*, 47–8.

[88] 'Discorso . . . delle forme del Diapason', in *The Florentine Camerata*, 196–7 (fo. 54ᵛ).

[89] The unnamed Aristoxenians are referred to in *Discorso*, 104, 116, and more obliquely in 'Discorso . . . intorno all'Unisono', in *The Florentine Camerata*, 202–3 (fo. 58ᵛ).

[90] Mersenne, *La Vérité des sciences* (Paris: T. Du Bray, 1625), 616. Cf. Mersenne, *Correspondance*, i. 203.

pitch of a string, but the essential concepts in what are known in acoustics as Mersenne's Laws he owed to Galilei.

There is a further link between Vincenzo Galilei and later scientific studies of sound. This link is Vincenzo's son, Galileo. Obvious though it seems, it has been consistently overlooked by biographers and historians of science and music. Vincenzo's books and manuscripts passed to Galileo in 1591 on the father's death. Moreover, during the period the experiments described above were being carried out, Galileo lived mainly at his father's home in Florence. In 1585 Galileo had abandoned his medical studies at Pisa and returned to Florence, there to remain until he took the post of lecturer in mathematics at Pisa in 1589.[91] While at home Galileo must have become aware of and perhaps even involved in his father's experiments, for the very problems his father treated appeared prominently in the *Dialogues concerning Two New Sciences*.[92]

Someone might suggest, though, that the influence proceeded in the opposite direction: from son to father. But this seems unlikely for a number of reasons. Galileo while in Florence was preoccupied with mathematics, an interest which had prompted his leaving medicine. There is no trace of experiments in the area of acoustics by Galileo at this time. In fact, the earliest study showing any trace of experimental method is the *De motu*, a manuscript prepared between 1589 and 1592 in Pisa. In this essay Galileo challenged a number of Aristotelian solutions to classic problems of motion.[93] On the other hand, the possibility that the father may have encouraged an empirical direction in the young mathematician is not to be excluded.

While the possibility of such an influence is only conjectural, it is a striking fact that Galileo, in the section on the consonances in the *Dialogues concerning Two New Sciences*, repeats in the conversation between the two interlocutors, Sagredo and Salviati, the thought process that is documented in the discourses of Vincenzo Galilei. In the following passage Sagredo sums up the doubts Vincenzo had expressed upon the definitiveness of the ratios assigned to the consonances:

For a long time I was perplexed about the ratios of the consonances, since the explanations commonly adduced from the writings of authors learned in music did

---

[91] The appointment was conferred in July, and Galileo gave his inaugural lecture on 12 Nov. Cf. Antonio Favaro, 'Serie settima di scampoli Galileiani', in *Atti e memorie della Reale Accademia di scienze lettere ed arti in Padova*, NS 8 (1892), 55.

[92] *Discorsi e dimostrazioni matematiche intorno à due nuove scienze* (1st edn.; Leiden: Elsevirius, 1638), in *Opere*, Edizione Nazionale (Florence: G. Barbèra), viii (1898), 139 ff.

[93] Raffaele Giacomelli, *Galileo Galilei Giovane e il suo 'De motu'* (Pisa: Domus Galileana, 1949), 19 ff.

not strike me as sufficiently conclusive. They tell us that the diapason, i.e. the octave, is contained in the duple ratio, the diapente, which we call the fifth, in the sesquialtera [3:2] etc.; because if a string is stretched on the monochord and sounded, and afterwards a bridge is placed in the middle and the half-string is sounded, an octave will be heard between the two. If the bridge is placed at one-third the length of the string, then, plucking first the open string and afterwards two-thirds of its length, the fifth is sounded. For this reason they say that the octave is contained in the ratio of two to one and the fifth in the ratio of three to two. This explanation, I repeat, did not impress me as sufficient to justify the determination of the duple and sesquialteral ratios as the natural ratios of the octave and fifth; and my reason for thinking so is as follows. There are three ways to raise the pitch of a string: first, by shortening it; second, by tightening or stretching it; third, by making it thinner. If we maintain the tension and thickness of the string constant, we obtain the octave by shortening it to one-half, i.e. by sounding first the open string and then one-half of it. But if we keep the length and thickness constant and we wish to produce the octave by stretching, it will not suffice to double the weight attached to the string; it must be quadrupled. If the string was first stretched by a weight of one pound, four will be required to raise it to the octave . . .

Granted these very true observations, I could see no reason why those wise philosophers should have established the duple ratio rather than the quadruple as that of the octave, or why for a fifth they should have chosen the sesquialtera [3:2] rather than the dupla sesquiquarta [9:4].[94]

Up to this point Galileo has reproduced the arguments found in his father's discourses. But now Galileo departs from this line of reasoning to announce that he has discovered real grounds for a constant numerical relationship between the tones of a consonance or of any other interval. This constant relationship is the ratio between the two frequencies of vibration. Such a ratio, he shows, is the inverse of that given by the string-lengths. This, as we have seen, was already suggested by Benedetti, who gave no proof for it. Then Beeckman in 1614–15 demonstrated the rule geometrically, and finally Niccolò Aggiunti, a pupil of Galileo, recorded a proof for the fact in 1634, four years before the publication of Galileo's *Dialogues*.[95] With the Pythagorean ratios reinstated, a new cycle of number theories could begin and did in fact.

Meanwhile, the empirical trends had transformed the face of seventeenth-century music. Some composers still wrote in a laboured polyphonic style, but the dominant fashion now was the accompanied monody and the concertato medium for few voices. Seconds and sevenths, dissonances previously used with great restraint, were now introduced freely for expressive

---

[94] *Opere*, viii. 143–4 (my translation).
[95] Cf. Mersenne, *Correspondance*, ii. 234–5.

reasons, while the augmented fourths and diminished fifths were treated almost like consonances, both melodically and harmonically. Few composers any longer respected the diatonic modes, which Zarlino had sought to keep pure of foreign tones. Chromaticism had become rampant in the last decades of the sixteenth century and was now the backbone of almost every piece that sought to express the more intense passions.

It would be wrong to conclude from this exposition that the sensualism and freedom of early Baroque music can be ascribed mainly to the liberalizing force of scientific investigation. The empirical attitude operated on two levels. On the objective level of the observation of nature, with which I have been primarily concerned, the studies of the nature of consonance and of sound engendered an enlightened approach to some ancient problems of musical composition, performance, and instrumental tuning. But empiricism was also at work on the practical level of artistic effort. Whether influenced by scientists or not, musicians have always experimented with new resources. Such experimentation was particularly intense from around 1550 to 1650. The urge to abandon the rigorous methods of old and try the new probably had its origin in the same humanistic ferment that produced the scientific revolution. Science cannot therefore be held responsible for the empirical tendencies of musical practice, because both depended on a common cause.

Scientific thought did reveal, however, the falseness of some of the premises on which existing rationalizations of artistic procedures had rested. Musicians exposed and inclined to this new thought were liberated by it from some of the superfluous strictures of the older practice. In an age that admired reason and suspected the senses, it was not enough to find a new path through artistic experimentation; it was important to prove the fallacy of the old and to justify the new by adequate theoretical concepts. To cite one example: in 1533, about fifty years before Galilei upset Zarlino's system, Giovanni Maria Lanfranco recommended a keyboard tuning that approximated equal temperament.[96] But not until the seventeenth century did written music really exploit the possibilities of such a keyboard. The new solutions had to be openly debated and endorsed by common consent before composers generally had courage to imitate the isolated experimenters. In a society in which the composer depended directly upon the consumer, many forces tended to preserve and canonize established practice and to discourage change—fear of open criticism, respect for the traditions and authorities of the church, the layman's eternal

---

[96] *Scintille di musica* (Brescia: Lodovico Britannico, 1533).

resistance to the unfamiliar. By creating a favourable climate for experiment and for the acceptance of new ideas, the scientific revolution greatly encouraged and accelerated a direction that musical art had already taken.

Finally, the new acoustics replaced the elaborate conglomeration of myth, scholastic dogma, mysticism, and numerology, which was the foundation of the older musical theory, with a far less monumental but more permanent and resistant base. Unlike the old metaphysics, this new science recognized the musician's prerogative. While it taught him to understand the raw material he received from nature, it left him free to employ it according to his needs and to frame his operating rules according to purely aesthetic motives.

PART II

Studies in the History of Italian Music

9

A *Clarification of* Musica reservata *in Jean Taisnier's* Astrologiae, *1559*

This essay was first published in *Acta musicologica*, 31 (1959), 133–61, on the quadricentennial of Jean Taisnier's *Astrologiae*, the little book whose dedication contained the text that is commented upon here. But my own involvement with *musica reservata* goes back to my doctoral dissertation of 1954.[1] There I analysed the known occurrences and purported occurrences of the term and came to the conclusion that it was not capable of precise definition and therefore did not lend itself to scholarly usage. I thought it prudent then to drop it as a label for any aesthetic movement. I communicated my analysis of the sources and conclusions in a paper delivered at the Midwest Chapter of the American Musicological Society at Indiana University, Bloomington, 15 May 1954.[2]

Upon encountering in Lynn Thorndike's *A History of Magic and Experimental Science*[3] the passage in which Taisnier railed against what he called *musica nova* or *musica reservata*, I saw that his statement, which had not been brought into the discussion of the term, called for a re-examination of the question. Taisnier came closest of any of the users of the term to a definition. He also broadened its scope to include criteria of chromaticism, rhythmic organization, variety of constructive devices, improvised counterpoint, pride in originality and individual accomplishment, revival of older ideals, and instrumentation, all of which were consistent with musical trends in the last half of the sixteenth century and with a number of the other usages. This led me to suggest that the music to which he objected was unstable, unpredictable, and manneristic. The notion of a mannerist style at the end of the Renaissance had achieved some acceptance among art historians but was not yet recognized by music historians. Robert E. Wolf had proposed it as a label for the experimental and expressionistic music of the last decades of the sixteenth century.[4]

[1] 'The Beginnings of Baroque Music: Its Roots in Sixteenth Century Theory and Polemics', Ph.D. diss. (Harvard University, 1954), 227–34.
[2] 'Musica Reservata and Osservata: A Critical Review', Abstract in *Journal of the American Musicological Society*, 7 (1954), 168–9.
[3] Lynn Thorndike, *A History of Magic and Experimental Science* (New York: Macmillan, 1923–58).
[4] Robert E. Wolf, 'The Aesthetic Problem of the Renaissance', *Revue belge de musicologie*, 9 (1955), 83–102.

Perhaps no more than a coincidence, around the time that my article was published, Helmut Hucke drew parallels between mannerism as a recurrent phenomenon in music and the arts and *musica reservata*.[5] Hucke went back for inspiration to an article by Leo Schrade of 1934 that called attention to the importance of *maniera* or style-consciousness in the arts of the sixteenth century and specifically music of the post-Josquin period.[6] Hucke saw the opportunity of fruitfully linking the deliberate cultivation of various manners and the stylistic consciousness that the references to *musica reservata* suggested. Basing his view of *musica reservata* on points made by Bernhard Meier in his review of the problem,[7] Hucke identified four areas of correspondence between aspects of *musica reservata* and manneristic phenomena in music: (i) the cultivation of music for connoisseurs, (ii) the pursuit of learned contrapuntal devices, (iii) the introduction of chromatic and enharmonic steps, and (iv) the exploitation of irregularities in musical composition (such as unusual cadences, mixture of modes, licences for rhetorical effect). Although not based on any critical examination of the sources,[8] Hucke's imaginative spin-off was a sensible move in the direction of viewing *musica reservata* as a natural product of the dynamics of musical change and clashing cultural environments.

The most ambitious venture at integrating the various usages of the term after mine was that of Henry W. Kaufmann in his book on Nicola Vicentino. In his fourth and final chapter, '*Reservata*—A Problem of Musical Mannerism',[9] he took up the idea of linking the two concepts in a new synthesis that was grounded in art-critical theory about Mannerism. He made good use of the passage from Taisnier as well as the previously known references to the term. He examined the manneristic character of *musica reservata* under eight headings: (i) *reservata* as a reversion to earlier style-periods, (ii) the conversion of this revival into a 'new' style, (iii) the definition of the 'new' style in terms of deviations from the normal practices, (iv) justification of these deviations by necessity to express the text, (v) humanistically inspired experiments and new and ingenious methods of composition, (vi) return in this context to the chromatic and enharmonic genera, (vii) the assumption for these experiments of an élite of initiated listeners, and (viii) the expectation by these listeners of virtuoso performance. Perhaps he pressed a little too hard at times to make these points fit into the known occurences of the term.

Edward Lowinsky, who as much as anyone inspired the original wave of interest in *musica reservata* with his chapter on it in *Secret Chromatic Art in the Netherlands Motet*,[10] continued to utilize the concept in his historical criticism. Particularly

---

[5] 'Das Problem des Manierismus in der Musik', *Literaturwissenschaftliches Jahrbuch*, im Auftrage der Görres-Gesellschaft, NS 2 (Berlin: Duncker & Hublot, 1961), 219–38.

[6] Leo Schrade, 'Von der "Maniera" der Komposition in der Musik des 16. Jahrhunderts', *Zeitschrift für Musikwissenschaft*, 16 (1934), 3–20, 98–117, 152–70. Schrade avoided the term 'mannerism' because it had derogatory connotations.

[7] 'Reservata-Probleme, Ein Bericht', *Acta musicologica*, 30 (1958), 77–89.

[8] Indeed, Hucke accepts Meier's uncritical adoption of Lowinsky's interpretation of Vicentino as a ground for broadening the scope of *musica reservata* to include chromaticism and enharmonicism and the idea of music for an élite.

[9] *The Life and Works of Nicola Vicentino (1511–c.1576)* (American Institute of Musicology, 1966), 175–224.

[10] New York: Columbia University Press, 1946; repr. New York: Russel & Russel, 1967.

notable are his interpretations of several works of Lasso[11] and Rore[12] in terms of this concept. He clung tenaciously to his controversial interpretation of the passage from Vicentino's *L'antica musica ridotta alla moderna pratica*[13] and listed the numerous scholars who 'accepted' his interpretation, namely Charles van den Borren, Alfred Einstein, Helmut Federhofer, Gustave Reese, Knud Jeppesen, Wolfgang Boetticher, and H. H. Eggebrecht.[14] He did not acknowledge the fact that Kaufmann, a specialist in Vicentino, denied that Vicentino knew the term, although Kaufmann recognized that Vicentino certainly thought of his chromatic and enharmonic music as most suitable for princes and other initiates, just as in ancient times these genera were reserved for private entertainments of lords and princes and to sing the praises of great public figures and heroes.

Most music historians in recent times have treated the term with circumspection.[15] Bernhard Meier concludes his admirably objective article on the term (1976) in the *Handwörterbuch der musikalischen Terminologie*[16] with the opinion that it leaves a great deal of room for speculation and arbitrary assignments of meaning but is not a term subject to any precise and stable definition. With this I should agree.

THE fascination the term *musica reservata* has held for scholars from its first discovery increases as each new source unveils a new layer of meaning, adding to the mystery rather than resolving it. As Alfred Einstein aptly put it: 'this term has been haunting the history of sixteenth-century music, but like a true ghost it has not been possible to nail it down.'[17]

Does it signify music expressive of a text or highly ornate music, erudite music or music restrained in its use of contrapuntal and mensural complexities, music for princely chambers or for secret pious gatherings, solo music or ensemble music, chromatic music or music with flowing uninterrupted rhythm, a new style or a neglected older one? All these in the past have been put forward as meanings of *musica reservata*, and all but a few rest on documented usages in the sixteenth century. How can a single

[11] 'Humanism in the Music of the Renaissance', in *Medieval and Renaissance Studies*, 9, *Proceedings of the Southeastern Institute of Medieval and Renaissance Studies, Summer, 1978*, ed. Frank Tirro (Durham, NC, 1982), repr. in Lowinsky, *Music in the Culture of the Renaissance & Other Essays*, 202–9, on *Tityre, tu patulae, Bestia curvafia pulices*, and *Dulci sub umbra*.

[12] The motet *Beati omnes* is analysed as a specimen of *musica reservata* in 'Rore's New Year's Gift for Albrecht V of Bavaria', in Lowinsky, *Music in the Culture of the Renaissance*, 636–43.

[13] See below, 267 and n. 103.

[14] 'Humanism in the Music of the Renaissance', in *Music in the Culture of the Renaissance*, 202 n. 111, where he gives the bibliographical references.

[15] For example, Howard M. Brown in *Music in the Renaissance* (Englewood Cliffs, NJ, 1976), 306; Albert Dunning, 'Musica reservata', *New Grove*, xii. 825–7; Bernhard Meier, 'Musica reservata', *MGG*, ix. (1961), 946–9.

[16] Ed. Hans H. Eggebrecht (Wiesbaden: Franz Steiner). Meier comprehends in his article, as is customary in the *Handwörterbuch*, related terms, such as the adjectival use of *reservato, reconditus, secretus, osservato*, and the like.

[17] *The Italian Madrigal* (Princeton, NJ: Princeton University Press, 1949), i. 225.

term have denoted or connoted so many different and often contradictory qualities?

The answer is that the expression had a much broader meaning than any hitherto known source by itself reveals, if we can trust Jean Taisnier, mathematician, astrologer, and musician, a prolific and encyclopaedic author who flourished in the middle of the sixteenth century. He tells us in two works printed in 1559 and 1562 that *musica reservata* is a name for a new style then emerging. In the publication of 1559 he goes on to give a detailed if somewhat obscure description of the properties of this style. The mystery of *musica reservata* lifts as Taisnier, in a remarkably concise passage, furnishes the clues that tie together much of the heterogeneous known evidence.

But Taisnier has been called a charlatan and a plagiarist.[18] Should we trust his authority in the field of music when his boast of having written a musical manual has never been substantiated? The facts of his life, which was rich in professional musical experience, should allay our doubts.

Jean Taisnier (Hannoniensis) was born in the town of Ath on 2 September 1508, the son of Thomas Taisnier and Catherine de L'Issue.[19] He studied in the College of Ath and in 1531 was attending the University of Louvain, from which he claimed to have obtained the degree of Doctor of Civil and Canon Law. Shortly afterwards he joined the chapel of Emperor Charles V as a singer. In 1535 he took part in the expedition to Tunis[20] and was rewarded for his services with a prebend in Leuze. 1538 found him in Toledo with the emperor, 1541 in Valladolid, and, later that year, Algiers. He refers to himself in 1542 as a *maître d'école des enfants* of the chapel of the emperor, then resident in Madrid.[21] Between 1546 and 1547 he held the chair of mathematics in Rome and, in 1547 and 1548, in Ferrara, where he published a book on terrestrial and celestial measurements.[22] He also

[18] Jules Dewert, 'Jean Taisnier, d'Ath', in Cercle royale archéologique d'Ath et de la région, *Annales*, 1 (1912), 1–36. Cf. especially 18–19.

[19] Ibid. 4–6.

[20] Edmond Vander Straeten, *La Musique aux Pays-Bas avant le XIXᵉ siècle* (Brussels: Van Tright, 1867–88), vii. 316, gives documentary evidence.

[21] Ibid., vii. 356. This post is not to be confused with that of *maître des enfants*, occupied at this time by Cornelius Canis. The text of a letter, dated 3 Mar. 1542, to Queen Marie of Hungary in which Taisnier gives himself this title is printed ibid., iii. 152. Another document that names him 'mᵉ d'escole des enffans de la chappelle* is printed in Vander Straeten, *La Musique aux Pays-Bas*, vii. 356.

[22] *Opera nuova molto vtile, et necessaria à tutti architettori, geometri . . . astronomi* (Ferrara: Giovanni de Buglhat & Antonio Hucher, 1548). Isidore Plaisant, a chronicler of the 16th c., in a *mémoire* published in *Revue d'histoire et d'archéologie*, 4 (1864), 303, states: 'Vers cette époque Ferrare et Rome décernèrent encore, l'une après l'autre, leur chaire de mathématiques à Jean Taisnier, d'Ath, qui avait visité une grande partie de notre globe. Ses leçons étaient suivies avec empressement, et il vit toujours autour de lui un concours de gens avides de s'approprier une partie de ses vastes connaissances.'

claimed to have taught mathematics in Florence, Bologna, Padua, and Palermo.[23] In 1549 he was in the service of Pietro Tagliania, Archbishop of Terra Nova and Cardinal of Palermo. He took with him there ten singers and two young sopranists from Flanders. For two years he filled the post of choirmaster and gave mathematics lessons. In 1551 he was in Trápani, Sicily, and later he set out from Naples on the expedition to Reggio Calabria. In 1552 he directed the musicians maintained by Cardinal Francisco de Mendoza in Rome and accompanied him on a trip to the Low Countries, visiting Florence, Venice, Trent, and Malines. Between 1553 and the abdication of Charles V in 1555, Taisnier may have been in charge once again of the emperor's young singers. From 1555 to 1557 he apparently headed a gymnasium or college in Lessines, teaching the children Greek, Latin, Spanish, French, and other languages as well as music. His last known post was that of musical director for Johann Gebhard, Archbishop of Cologne, which he held from 1558 to 1562.[24] He must have died soon after. Taisnier, it is evident from this career, satisfactorily met the standards of more than one profession, having held demanding positions as a choirmaster, mathematician, and teacher of languages.

Although it is known that Taisnier borrowed much of his material for publication from other authors[25] and dabbled in the pseudo-sciences of astrology and palm-reading, there is no reason to mistrust him as a musical observer. One so boastful as he was of his own accomplishments may be expected to exaggerate the virtues of what he praises and the evils of what he blames, but in the field of music, it must be acknowledged, he was on familiar ground. He claims, indeed, in the letter of dedication to Johannes Jacob Fugger, dated March 1562, in the *Opus mathematicum*, to have completed at least part of a book on music. He names it among several treatises he still wishes to bring out:

There will remain, furthermore, for me to bring to light, when at last they are completed, our Books concerning the Theory and Practice of Music, which (as I hope) will not be disagreeable to musicians. These will treat the new (which they

---

[23] Cf. Dewert, 'J. Taisnier', 9–10; Taisnier, *Opusculum perpetua memoria dignissimum, de natura magnetis et eius effectibus* (Cologne: I. Birckmann, 1562), 16.

[24] All this information is based on statements by Taisnier in his *Opus mathematicum octo libros complectens* (Cologne: I. Birckmann & W. Richwin, 1562). Cf. Dewert, 'J. Taisnier', 13–15. In addition, the records of the University of Cologne contain the following entry: '1558 Dez. 17 immatr.: d. Joh. Taisnier, Hannoniensis, u. iur. dr., Ferrarie promotus, i. et. s.'—quoted by Gerhard Pietzsch, 'Zur Pflege der Musik an den deutschen Universitäten bis zur Mitte des 16. Jahrhunderts', *Archiv für Musikforschung*, 5 (1940), 82. According to Johann Walther, *Musikalisches Lexicon* (Leipzig: W. Deer, 1732), 594, Taisnier died towards the end of the century at a very advanced age, but the epitaph given there is undated.

[25] On this point cf. Thorndike, *History of Magic and Experimental Science*, v. (1941), 580.

call *reservata*) and the old music, and finally they will contain (without boasting) all those things which are considered as belonging to the perfection of music.[26]

The treatise on music is mentioned also in the *Astrologiae iudiciariae ysagogica*[27] within the quotation that is the subject of the present article. There, with reference to the chromatic and enharmonic genera, Taisnier states that he has 'sufficiently discussed' their difficulty 'in our book concerning music', and later, referring to some musical instruments, he notes: 'we have discussed [them] with pictures in our book on music.' While certain portions of the treatise must therefore have been finished by 1559, it was still not nearly complete in 1562.[28] The other two unfinished projects named by Taisnier in his dedication of 1562 have also never been found: *De hierarchiis angulorum* and *Librum mathematicum de diversis fabricis & instrumentorum astronomicorum geometricorumque usibus*.

The only two extant discussions of music by Taisnier are those that occur in the *Astrologiae* and in a small book on the utility of the mathematical disciplines.[29] It is with the first of these, from the *Astrologiae*,[30] that we are concerned in this article. The passage has been reprinted twice in modern times, first by Edmond Vander Straeten,[31] and more recently by Lynn Thorndike,[32] who had no knowledge of Vander Straeten's quotation. The section on music is in the 'Epistola dedicatoria', at the end of a praise and discussion of the utility of the four mathematical disciplines. It reads as follows:

[26] Fo. 2ᵛ: 'Demum plura & maiora successu temporis, volente Deo, scripturus sum, vtpote Hierarchiis Angulorum, Librumque: Mathematicum de diuersis Fabricis & instrumentorum Astronomicorum, Geometricorumque vsibus. Supererit etiam, vt tandem his absolutis, Libros nostros de Theorica & Praxi Musicae in lucem prodam, qui (vt spero) Musicis non erunt ingrati. De noua enim (quam reservatam volunt) & veteri Musica tractabunt, & tandem (salua arrogantia) ea continebunt, quae ad totius Musicae perfectionem spectare videntur.'

[27] *Astrologiae iudiciariae ysagogica et totius divinatricis artis encomia cum nonnullis Hebrahami Iudẹi et Lucẹ Gaurici dictis . . . In epistola dedicatoria quatuor mathematicae quantitates cum earum laudibus & utilitate notantur* (Cologne: apud haeredes Arnoldum Birckmanni, 1559).

[28] *Opus mathematicum*, fo. 3ʳ.

[29] *De mathematicae quattuor quantitatum utilitate libellus* (n.p., n.d.).

[30] Only after this article was submitted for publication did I notice that Dr Nan Cooke Carpenter, in her recently published *Music in the Medieval and Renaissance Universities* (Norman, Okla.: University of Oklahoma Press, 1958) has reprinted this passage from the *Astrologiae* from Thorndike's book in her footnote 87, p. 248. Otherwise she would have received more prominent mention here for having restored this statement by Taisnier to circulation among musical scholars. However, it must be added that she makes only a passing comment about the link between *reservata* and chromaticism and then drops the subject.

[31] *La Musique aux Pays-Bas*, iii. 236–7.

[32] *A History of Magic*, v. 583 n. 13. It is through this quotation that I was first led to the present study of Taisnier. Only later did I realize that Vander Straeten had presented a fuller and more faithful transcription of this passage.

Superest ultima et quarta Mathesaeos quantitas Musica, quae animos à quovis irae motu revocans, in consonam multitudinem proportionum suarum, in quadam aequalitate vocum conciliat, per cuius harmonias, gratia contemplationis, ad divinarum scientiarum studia, non mediocriter iuvantur, animique à curis liberantur, et quadam interna laetitia ad exultationem in Deum mentes humanae provocantur, immo et equos (teste Alpharabio) in bellis musicales concentus incitant, Delphines, Syrenes, caeteraque animalia, laetificant. Omitto quod asserunt Poetae Orphaeum sua lyra saxa movisse, et haec est quantitas quae in sonorum concordantiis sistens, ad auditum transfertur, quae humanis delectationibus convenit, de qua Boëthius libro primo Musicae habundè tractavit dicens, quantitatem vocum, sub una concordantia et consonantia coniungi, et in sua numerali proportione deduci. Estque Musica, Theorica, Practica, et Poetica, mundana, humana, et instrumentalis, choralis, et figurata, antiqua, et moderna, ab aliquibus nova dicta sive reservata, qui arbitrabantur impositionem [*sic*] unius aut alterius dioesis [*sic*] aut diaschismatis in cantilena, aut motteto, diatonicum Musices genus, in chromaticum verti, differentiam Diatonici à Chromatico et Enarmonico [*sic*] penitus ignorantes, quorum difficultatem in nostro libro Musicae satis exposui: Novumque quid ubi excogitare nituntur, suarum cantilennarum [*sic*] tonos, quae in Musicae principiis sistunt, praetermittentes, magnum errorem committunt, notarum ligaturas, valores, in modo, tempore, et prolatione negligentes, contrapuncta [modulantes], ut aiunt (vulgaris est locutio; Musica enim sermonis elegantia non modulatur) harmoniosa, fluentia, currentia, per minimam, ad semiminimam, ad fugam, reiterata, in modo perfecto, et imperfecto per hemiola majus et minus, per sesquialtera, sesquitertia, sesquiquarta, etc. Item contrapunctum 3, 4, 5, 6, 7 partium extemporaneum, à diversis cantoribus modulandum, pro praedecessorum documentis in mentem revocent, demum fiant cantores Poëtae, opus absolutum praedecessorum exemplo provocati, in sui memoriam et posteritatis usum linquentes, instrumentis musicalibus alternis vicibus indulgeant, utpote fistulis rectis, et obliquis, Monochordo, Claviciterio, Virginali, Clavicordio, Clavicembalo, Lyrae, lutinae sive testitudini, Cytharae, Psalterio, portativo positivo, Regali, Organo, Vtri, Claretae, Tubae, cymbalis, Tympano, Cytharae Hieronymi, Timpano eiusdem, Psalterio decacordo, tubae Hieronymi, Organo Hieronymi, fistulae Hieronymi, aliisque propemodum innumeris, quorum sigillatim in libro nostro Musices mentionem fecimus. Et haec etiam de Musica tandem sufficiant.[33]

Because Taisnier's statements require extensive elucidation and commentary, we shall present our translation piecemeal, interspersing it with explanatory discussion. The aim will be not only to illuminate obscurities but also to locate Taisnier's point of view in the musical actualities and ideologies of his time.

Taisnier begins with the traditional *encomium musicae*:

There remains, finally, the last and fourth mathematical entity, music, which, restraining the soul from any angry agitation, unites in a certain equality of voices

---

[33] *Astrologiae*, 14–16: copy used was Paris, Bibliothèque nationale, Rés. V. 2230.

through consonance the multitude of its proportions. Through its harmonies the study of theology is furthered not a little by the help given to contemplation, and souls are freed of cares, and human minds are stimulated by a certain interior joy to exult in God. Musical harmonies, indeed, even incite horses to war (according to Alpharabius), delight Dolphins, Sirens, and other animals. I pass over the poets' claim that Orpheus moved rocks with his lyre. This, then, is the entity that, residing in the concordance of sounds, is transferred to the hearing and conforms with human pleasures, concerning which Boethius copiously treated in his first book on music, saying that a quantity of tones is joined under a concordance and consonance and that this derives from its numerical proportion.

The four *quantitates*[34] are the four mathematical disciplines of the quadrivium: astronomy, geometry, arithmetic, and music. Taisnier immediately betrays his position among sixteenth-century humanists when he subordinates music to mathematics. Theoretical music was for him still a subject in the curriculum of studies for which the texts of Boethius served as the principal guides. Although Taisnier, in his *Opus mathematicum*,[35] claims to have read Euclid and Ptolemy, though not specifically on music, his opening eulogy smacks strongly of Boethius and reflects the Neoplatonic outlook of the first quarter of the sixteenth century.

The purpose of music is to restore the harmony of the soul. Through contemplating the harmony of proportionate musical sounds the mind is liberated from its cares and affections and turns towards divine thoughts. The pleasure and benefit we derive from music, according to this view, spring from its resolution of opposite forces and its tempering of diversity into a concordant unity. In his opening statements, Taisnier sums up the musical philosophy of a passing generation, which held the suppression of discord, whether psychological or acoustical, and the attainment of a harmonious equilibrium as the supreme goal. The so-called *ars perfecta*[36] of Josquin des Prez and his contemporaries fulfilled this purpose and undoubtedly served both Taisnier and Glareanus as a standard of excellence. Taisnier had little sympathy, as we shall see, for the rising school of composers who aimed to stir up the passions and whose 'cupiditas rerum novarum'—to borrow Glareanus's phrase—led them into the constantly

---

[34] Boethius (*De institutione musica*, i. 1. 21) speaks of *quattuor matheseos disciplinae*, rather than, as Taisnier always prefers, of *quantitates*.

[35] Bk. i, ch. 2, p. 9.

[36] Henricus Glareanus, *Dodekachordon* (Basle: H. Petri, 1547), 241: 'perfectae artis, cui . . . nihil addi potest'. Cf. also Leo Schrade, *Monteverdi* (New York: Norton, 1950), 24 ff. It is interesting to note that the only modern musical authors in Taisnier's list of writers consulted (*Opus math.*, bk. i, ch. 2, p. 9) are Glareanus and Jacob Stapulensis (Jacques Lefèvre d'Étaples), author of *Arithmetica et musica* (Paris: J. Higman & W. Hopyl, 1496) and *Musica libris quatuor demonstrata* (Paris: Gulielmus Cavellat, 1551).

varying effects and mannerisms that upset the serene balance achieved by their predecessors.

Music, then, is [divided into] [i] theoretical, practical, and poetic; [ii] universal, human, and instrumental; [iii] choral [plainchant] and figured; [iv] ancient and modern—called new or *reservata* by some who have held that the application of one or the other diesis or diaschisma in a secular song or motet turns the diatonic genre into the chromatic.

Taisnier presents here four classifications of music. The first three are all in some sense traditional. The fourth is the most interesting to us, not only because it equates new and *reservata* but also because it represents a new departure in the classification of music.

The oldest of these categorizations, the second, is taken from Boethius[37] and remained the standard division of *musica theorica* as late as Glareanus.[38] This is complemented by Taisnier's third division—*choralis, figuralis*—the standard subdivision of *musica practica* in the early sixteenth century.[39] More up to date is Taisnier's first categorization, the threefold division *theorica—practica—poetica*, which, however, is substantially a revival of Aristides Quintilianus' classification.[40] It appeared already in the *Rudimenta musicae planae* of Nicolaus Listenius[41] and more definitively in his *Musica* of 1537.[42]

We come finally to Taisnier's fourth division, which classifies music according to its 'newness' or 'antiquity'. Here we have an anticipation of the seventeenth-century distinctions, *stile moderno* and *stile antico*, which, like Taisnier's, are not so much chronological layers as designations for two simultaneously practised modes of composition. To draw a line between one generation of composers and another by calling one group *antichi* and another *viventi*, as did Giovanni Maria Lanfranco;[43] or *veteres* and *recentiores* as did Hermann Finck;[44] or *antichi* (from Ockeghem to Senfl), *vecchi* (from

---

[37] *De institutione musica*, i. 2.

[38] *Dodekachordon*, bk. i, ch. 1.

[39] e.g. Georg Rhaw, *Enchiridion utriusque musicae practicae* (Wittenberg: G. Rhaw, 1538; facs., ed. Hans Albrecht, Kassel & Basle: Bärenreiter, 1951).

[40] *De musica libri iii*, i. 5: (i) pertaining to the theory of music, (ii) to its exercise, (iii) to its execution. See the translation by Thomas J. Mathiesen in *On Music in Three Books* (New Haven, Conn.: Yale University Press, 1983), 76–7.

[41] Wittenberg: G. Rhaw, 1533. Cf. W. Gurlitt, 'Der Begriff der sortisatio in der deutschen Kompositionslehre des 16. Jahrhunderts', *Tijdschrift der Vereeniging voor Nederlandsche Muziekgeschiedenis*, 16 (1942), 194–211.

[42] Wittenberg: G. Rhaw, 1537; facs. of 1549 edn., ed. Georg Schünemann, Berlin: Martin Breslauer, 1927.

[43] Giovanni Maria Lanfranco, *Scintille di musica* (Brescia: Lodovico Britannico, 1533), fo. 2^r.

[44] *Practica musica* (Wittenberg: G. Rhaw, 1556), bk. v.

Willaert to Palestrina), and *moderni*, as did Lodovico Zacconi[45]—this was a common practice. Taisnier's distinction between new and old does not belong with these; it separates rather two coexistent styles, as we might today set off progressive 'new' music from what is merely contemporary. The progressive music, Taisnier further informs us, was called by some of its partisans *musica reservata*.

As to Taisnier's own preferences among the new and old, it becomes clear in his next sentence that he is on the side of conservatism. Like many another philosopher, critic, or amateur who lives in the periphery of musical development, Taisnier admires most the music that was in vogue during his youth, and now at 51 rails against the new styles with grumbling disfavour.

Before going on to examine what characterized this new music for Taisnier, it is worth recalling the position of the *musica nuova* at this time. The conflict between the supporters of the new and traditional styles goes back at least to the 1530s. The complaints of Johannes Stomius against the new trends in 1536, for example, bear a striking resemblance to those of Taisnier:

> Now, to single out those who call their music (so please God) new, as it were, while they wrap up every kind of composition with such a disorder of steps and signs . . . so that there is need for some Delian swimmer rather than more learned persons . . . neither do they rest on any mathematical reason, nor is the sense soothed by sweetness of sound.[46]

From 1540 the term *musica nuova* or similar expressions appear frequently on title-pages, especially of the group of composers around Willaert.[47] In 1540 there is the *Musica nova accommodata per cantar et sonar*,[48] containing compositions by Willaert, Giulio Segni, Girolamo Parabosco, and others. The collection of Adrian Willaert himself, called *Musica nova*, contains motets and madrigals probably composed in the 1540s, although it is dated 1559.[49] In 1546 Willaert's pupil Don Nicola Vicentino issued in Venice the *Madrigali a 5 voci per theorica et pratica composti al nuovo modo dal celeberrimo suo maestro ritrovato*, that is, in the new manner discovered by

---

[45] *Prattica di musica* (Venice: Bart. Carampello, 1596), pt. i, bk. i, ch. 9.

[46] From 'Conclusio epitomes' of his *Prima ad musicen instructio* (Augsburg: Ulhardus, 1536); original Latin quoted in Hans Unger, *Die Beziehungen zwischen Musik und Rhetorik im 16.–18. Jahrhundert* (Würzburg: Konrad Triltsch, 1941; repr., Hildesheim: Olms, 1969), 27.

[47] Zacconi, *Prattica*, bk. i, ch. 10, fo. 7ᵛ, recalls that Willaert and Cipriano de Rore, 'quei Vecchi nella professione si intelligenti, et dotti, s'incominciò a ritrouarsi altri nuoui, et vaghi effetti'.

[48] Venice: al segno del Pozzo.

[49] Armen Carapetyan, 'The *Musica Nova* of Adriano Willaert', *Journal of Renaissance and Baroque Music*, 1 (1946), 205, asserts that 'the theoretical substructure of the *Musica Nova* is decidedly formed of progressive elements'.

Willaert. The books of madrigals that began to be published in 1542 by Cipriano de Rore,[50] another Willaert pupil, bearing such labels as *chromatici* or *a note nere*, represent another aspect of the new manner.

The most outspoken critic of the *musica nova* in mid-century was Ghiselin Danckerts, who for this reason can often be called upon to elaborate certain points only touched by Taisnier. Danckerts lamented the tendency of the new composers to claim Willaert, whose polished style he admired, as their leader, for he could detect few of his virtues in their products. 'The joke is that these novel composers say without any deliberation that they compose in this way to imitate the manner of M. Adriano Willaert, by them called *nuova*, although it is very old and because of the disorders and errors we have discussed is repudiated by learned and expert composers.'[51] Danckerts analyses their blunders at length: they fail to observe the correct endings of the modes; they use always the same consonances and proceed continuously note against note; they abuse uncomfortable intervals; their music is lugubrious and disconsolate and lacking the beautiful lines and artful counterpoint of Willaert. We shall meet some of these grievances again in Taisnier's quotation.

The sponsors of the *musica nova* or *reservata*, Taisnier informs us, upheld the theory that the introduction of either the diesis or the diaschisma renders a composition chromatic. This, in fact, was Vicentino's contention in his debate with Vicente Lusitano in 1551. The major semitone, he held, was the earmark of the chromatic genus. Since the major semitone, as distinguished from the diatonic minor semitone, was everywhere being used when the natural steps of the mode were altered, Vicentino argued that the music of his day was not purely diatonic but mixed with the chromatic. Such an inference was very much resented by those who chastely clung to the ideal of modal purity, among them Lusitano, Danckerts, and Zarlino.

The difference in terminology between Taisnier, who speaks of diesis and diaschisma, and Vicentino, who employs the terms major and minor semi-

---

[50] The earliest extant edition under the title *Primo libro de madregali cromatici a 5 voci*, however, is of 1544 (Venice: A. Gardane).

[51] *Sopra una differentia musicale*, Rome, Biblioteca Casanatense, MS 2880, pt. iii, ch. 2, p. 96: 'Il bello è che questi musici Compositori novelli, dicono, senza consideratione alcuna: che compongono di questa sorte: per imitare la maniera di M. Adriano Willart, da loro chiamata nuova (benche vechissima) et dalli Dotti et esperti compositori, per causa delli sudetti considerati disordini et errori ripudiati sia.' P. J. De Bruijn dates this treatise as of 1559–60 in 'Ghisilinus Danckerts, zanger van de pauselijke Cappella van 1538 tot 1565', *Tijdschrift voor Muziekwetenschap*, 17 (1951), 147. The Casanatense manuscript is a faithful copy made by Giuseppe Baini of the fair copy in Rome, Biblioteca Vallicelliana, MS R56, no. 33. Two apparently autograph drafts are also in the Vallicelliana, MS R56, nos. 15 and 15b.

tone, needs explanation. The disagreement between Taisnier and Vicentino is only one aspect of the confusion that reigned at this time in the naming and measuring of semitones and microtones. Two principal theoretical systems existed side by side: that of the Boethians and that of the Ptolemaics.[52] Meanwhile, practising musicians discoursed in looser terms and usually said *diesis* when they meant semitone. In effect, both Taisnier and Vicentino were using the Boethian language but in reference to a medium—that of mixed genera—incompatible with the Boethian system, which cleanly separated them. It is helpful in this context to see the Boethian diatonic and chromatic[53] and the 'modern' mixed genera juxtaposed in diagrammatic form (Fig. 9.1). The diaschisma, a purely theoretical division, does not even belong in Boethius' chromatic. Taisnier must have used this term loosely for a 'diesis' of the enharmonic type, which results whenever both major and minor semitones alter the natural degrees, leaving gaps like those between *f♯* and *g♭* in the diagram in Fig. 9.1.

16 [They are] completely ignorant of the difference that exists between the diatonic on the one hand and the chromatic and enharmonic on the other, the difficulty of which [last two genera] I sufficiently discussed in my book concerning music.

Taisnier opposes calling all music that introduces the small intervals chromatic or enharmonic. He maintains, with Ghiselin Danckerts, that such music may still be diatonic. In justifying his verdict against Vicentino in the famous controversy, Danckerts had stated this position explicitly:

And thus I say that in any voice or part . . . where there is found a progression of four notes ascending or descending through three continuous intervals of a tetrachord, such a progression must be said to be in one of the three genera. The genre of a voice or part of a work should be judged according to the progression of the intervals, provided the tetrachord is complete and none of the three adjacent intervals is missing . . . For if any of its intervals is missing, it cannot truly be said that any genre is found there, but only one or two intervals of this or that genre, which are only parts of a genre.[54]

[52] Zarlino and Salinas favoured Ptolemy's syntonic diatonic, in which each tetrachord has the scheme: minor tone (10:9), major tone (9:8) and major semitone (16:15).
[53] *De institutione musica*, iv. 6.
[54] MS 2880, p. 43: 'Et cosi dico che in qual si voglia voce ò parte di qual si voglia Canto . . . ove si trouarà vn progresso di quattro note, ascendendo, ò, discendendo, per tre interualli continui in un Tetrachordo; si deue dire che tal progresso sia d'alcuno delli tre Generi sopradetti; et secondo il progresso delli interualli, si de giudicare di qual genere sia, tal voce ò parte di Canto, pur che 'l detto Tetrachordo sia intiero, et non gli manchi alcuno delli suoi tre interualli continui . . . Perche se a tal tetrachordo mancasse alcuno delli suoi interualli, non si potrebbe ueramente dire, che iui fosse alcun genere, ne spetie di genere, ma un interuallo solo (ouero due) di tale, ò di tal genere, quali sono parti di genere.'

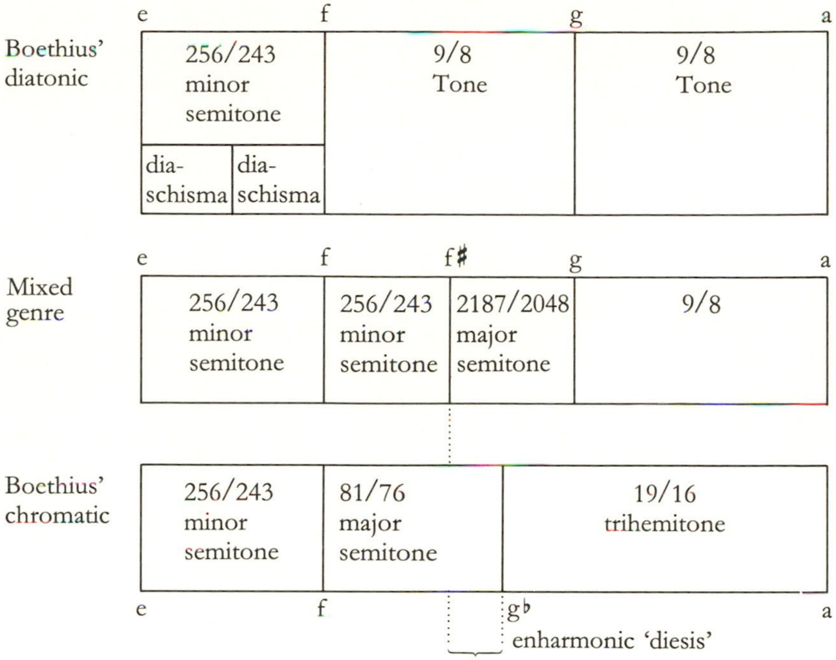

	e	f	g	a
Boethius' diatonic	256/243 minor semitone	9/8 Tone	9/8 Tone	
	dia-schisma | dia-schisma			

	e	f	f♯	g	a
Mixed genre	256/243 minor semitone	256/243 minor semitone	2187/2048 major semitone	9/8	

	e	f	g♭	a
Boethius' chromatic	256/243 minor semitone	81/76 major semitone	19/16 trihemitone	

enharmonic 'diesis'

FIG. 9.1

To belong to the chromatic genre the tetrachord must progress by minor semitone, major semitone, and trihemitone, and for the enharmonic by diesis, diesis, and ditone.[55] Danckerts, and with him obviously Taisnier, refused to recognize the modern version of the chromatic and enharmonic tetrachords. Advocated by Vicentino and adopted by many of his successors, these were dense with semitones or dieses throughout the tetrachords, not only in the lower portions, as their Greek counterparts.[56]

Taisnier adds that he has discussed the difficulty of the chromatic and enharmonic in his book. He obviously sides with those whom Danckerts

---

[55] This is how they are defined also by Vicente Lusitano, *Introduttione facilissima, et novissima, di canto fermo, figurato, contraponto semplice, et in concerto* (Venice: Francesco Rampazetto, 1561), fo. 22ᵛ.

[56] Cf. Vicentino, *L'antica musica ridotta alla moderna prattica* (Rome: Antonio Barre, 1555), bk. v; Francisco de Salinas, *De musica libri septem* (Salamanca: M. Gastius, 1577), bk. iii, ch. 2; Eucharius Hoffman, *Doctrina de tonis seu modis musicis* (Greifswald, 1582), quoted in Bernhard Meier, 'Ein weitere Quelle der Musica Reservata', *Die Musikforschung*, 8 (1955), 83; Giovanni Maria Artusi, *L'Artusi, ouero delle imperfettioni della moderna musica* (Venice: Giacomo Vincenti, 1600), fo. 18ʳ; Vincenzo Galilei, *Discorso intorno all'uso dell'enharmonio, et di chi fusse autore del cromatico*, Florence, Biblioteca Nazionale Centrale, MSS Galileiani 3, fo. 28ʳ, ed. Frieder Rempp, *Die Kontrapunkttraktate Vincenzo Galileis* (Cologne: Arno Volk, 1980), 176.

cited to support his case: 'the Pythagoreans and Platonists, the suceeding ancients and moderns, learned and excellent practical musicians, composers and singers', all of whom have always repudiated the two unused genera as 'fastidious, rough, and almost impracticable in singing'.[57]

18 And whenever they endeavour to contrive something new, disregarding in their compositions the modes that rest on the principles of music, they commit a great mistake;

Courting the chromatic, the composers of the *musica nova* flaunted their disregard for the proprieties of modal composition. The correct usage of the modes for Taisnier was undoubtedly that codified by Glareanus. A mode is chosen at the beginning of a composition and maintained throughout the work. Accidentals tending to establish a new mode are avoided. Only rarely, and then for very special circumstances, may one modulate from one mode to another. In direct opposition to this view, Vicentino affirmed the freedom of the composer to proceed from one mode to another within a composition according to the demands of the text, except when the responses of the office or mass required adherence to some mode. The composers of the new music, in fact, paid little heed to modal purity; rather, as Bernhard Meier has demonstrated, they sought out unusual modulations.[58]

20 neglecting the ligatures of notes, their values in *modus*, *tempus*, and prolation; [modulating], as they would have it (the expression is colloquial, for music, properly speaking, is not modulated), harmonious, flowing, running counterpoints in minims and semiminims, *ad fugam*, with repetitions, in perfect and imperfect *modus*, through major and minor hemiola, by sesquialtera, sesquitertia, sesquiquarta, etc.

In criticizing his contemporaries' rhythmic and notational practices, Taisnier betrays the nostalgia of an old man watching the intricate and difficult art he painstakingly learnt as a youth forsaken by pragmatic moderns in favour of unsophisticated, transparent methods. Ligatures, apart from a few *cum opposita proprietate*, had virtually disappeared from written music with the adoption of a tactus on smaller values. Theorists no

[57] *Astrologiae*, 20. Franchino Gaffurio, *Theorica musice* (Milan: P. Mantegatius, 1492), bk. v, ch. 2, is the obvious precedent for this opinion: 'Chromaticum tamen atque Enarmonicum genus ob quam in sui pronunciatione moliciem difficultatemque tenebant a musicis reiecta sunt. Diatonicum vero Pythagorici atque Platonici coeterique musici ob coaptatam eius productionem naturaliter disposita summo studio frequentare consueverunt.'
[58] 'The *Musica Reservata* of Adrianus Petit Coclico and its Relationship to Josquin', *Musica disciplina*, 10 (1956), 67–105.

longer probed their secrets at length, but, like Zarlino,[59] Luscinius,[60] or Coclico,[61] dutifully consecrated a meagre chapter to them, knowing full well that the pupil will scarcely use them.

The tendency to overlook the higher orders of metrical organization, mode and *tempus*, was another effect of the devalued tactus. For Lanfranco[62] the beat fell normally on the semibreve, while about a quarter of a century later Zarlino stated that the normal beat was on the minim. The indication, *alla breve*, originally signifying that the beat was shifted from the semibreve back to the breve, no longer meant that the beat was truly *alla breve*. In *alla breve* the beat was now on the minim. Its purpose was apparently to keep the number of flagged and black notes to a minimum. Separate syllables were now commonly given to semiminims, which even Zarlino considered inappropriate.[63]

Danckerts's views, which here again parallel those of Taisnier, add welcome detail to the latter's tight-lipped prose. Danckerts scolded those who entitled their works 'alla misura di breve' or 'delle note negre alla misura di breve' or 'chromatici', all terms for him most inappropriately applied. Writing in O or C, the new composers indicated minims when they wanted the length of semibreves 'and semiminims in place of minims, and for the semiminims *chrome*, and for the *chroma* the *semichroma*',[64] as if they were writing in subdupla proportion. Thus their measure was worth a semibreve and not, as the titles read, a breve. It is partly in this context, surely, that one should interpret Taisnier's comment about 'harmonious, flowing, running counterpoints in minims and semiminims'.

These words and the list of contrapuntal devices that follows remain problematic, however. Perhaps the most fruitful approach is to study Taisnier's list of devices—or to take his point of view, of abuses—in the light of the later theory of rhetorical figures. What were rejected as abuses by some, we know were eagerly embraced by others for their descriptive and figurative value. It is significant that from earliest times the figure was considered a *vitium* cleverly exploited.[65] Several of the *vitia* singled out

---

[59] *Le istitutioni harmoniche* (Venice, 1558), pt. iv, ch. 34. See the translation by Vered Cohen, ed. with an introduction by C. V. Palisca, under the title *Zarlino On the Modes* (New Haven, Conn.: Yale University Press, 1983), 99–102.

[60] *Musurgia, seu praxis musicae* (Strasburg: J. Schott, 1542), bk. ii, ch. 3.

[61] *Compendium musices* (Nuremberg: J. Montanus & U. Neuber, 1552), sig. F4.

[62] *Scintille*, 67.

[63] *Istitutioni*, pt. iv, ch. 33; trans. Vered, 97–9.

[64] MS 2880, p. 110.

[65] Quintilian, *Institutio oratoria*, ix. 3. 3–4: 'For every *figure* of this kind would be an error, if it were accidental and not deliberate. But as a rule such figures are defended by authority, age and usage, and not infrequently by some reason as well. Consequently, although they involve a divergence from direct

by Taisnier are, in fact, reckoned by later theorists among the figures: seminimum runs (a form of *hypotyposis*),[66] *fuga*, repetition, etc. Other devices, not particularly noted by the figure-theorists, such as change from duple to triple and hemiola, were used for the same purposes. Viewed from this slant, Taisnier's passage becomes an enumeration of mannerisms exploited by modernist composers to depict the sense of the text.

Semiminim runs on certain words, such as 'cantare', 'ardere', and 'gioia', constituted a stock-in-trade of the madrigalists. The technique, carried over into the motet, served to underline such words as 'laetitia', 'cordis', or 'spiritus'.

In 'ad fugam' Taisnier probably comprehended all forms of imitation: strict imitation (*fuga realis*), double imitation (*metalepsis*), inverse imitation (*hypallage*), partial imitation (*apocope*), imitation of paired or groups of voices (*mimesis*), and imitation involving only a few parts (*anaphora*). Here we are dealing with devices that serve chiefly a constructive purpose and are only occasionally used descriptively (as to suggest flight or a chase).

Taisnier probably did not so much object to the use of imitation as to the mixing of imitation with the 'harmonious' or the 'flowing, running' style. What he meant by *contrapuncta harmoniosa* is open to speculation, but it is not unlikely that by this he wished to describe the note-against-note declamatory style ridiculed by Danckerts[67] and fauxbourdon.[68] These last two techniques, innocuous in themselves, when introduced suddenly, frequently, and in alternation, as had become common, break up the texture in a way that undoubtedly drew frowns from conservatives like Taisnier.

Taisnier's objection to *reiterata* also marks him as a follower of an older school of theorists. Tinctoris, in his *Liber de arte contrapuncti*, states as a rule that in singing or composing over a plainchant *redictae* should be avoided as much as possible.[69] By this he meant that the statement of the same melodic pattern by a voice on the same or another tonal level has a poor

and simple language, they are to be regarded as excellences, provided always that they have some praiseworthy precedent to follow.' Trans. by H. E. Butler (Cambridge, Mass.: Harvard University Press, 1921–2).

[66] The terms in parentheses are those given to the figures by Joachim Burmeister in *Musica poetica* (Rostock: S. Myliander, 1606; facs., ed. Martin Ruhnke, Kassel and Basle: Bärenreiter, 1955), ch. 12, pp. 55 ff.

[67] This is the *noema* of Burmeister, who says of it: 'est harmoniae affectio, sive periodus cujus habitus voces conjunctas habet in eadem sonorum quantitate, aures, imo & pectora suaviter afficiens & mirifice demolcens [*sic*], si tempestivè introducitur' (59).

[68] Burmeister, *Musica poetica*, 65, recognizes this as a figure. A. Schmitz, in *Musikforschung*, 6 (1953), 59–60, has suggested that even before Josquin fauxbourdon may have been applied as an ornament for expressive reasons.

[69] Bk. iii, ch. 6, ed. Albert Seay in Corpus scriptorum de musica, 22 (American Institute of Musicology, 1975), 152–4.

effect. We know that Josquin was fond of such repetitions, especially involving two or more voices proceeding in similar rhythm (Burmeister's *analepsis*). Duplications of a passage in a single voice (*palillogia*) and sequential repetition (*auxesis*) were other reiterative devices constantly used to call attention to a particular word or phrase of text and for musical imagery.

The phrase, 'in perfect and imperfect *modus*, through major and minor hemiola, by sesquialtera, sesquitertia, sesquiquarta', must refer back to Taisnier's complaint that the modern musicians neglect the value of notes in *modus*, *tempus*, and prolation. This is to say, the moderns mix two kinds of *modus*, the two kinds of hemiola, and the various proportions indiscriminately. While metrical and tempo changes brought about by coloured notation and proportions were frequent in the music of the traditionalists, their sudden and frequent juxtaposition in the declamatory-style sections of the motets and madrigals of the new school invited the charge of excess. A usage such as that shown in Ex. 9.1, in a declamatory

Ex. 9.1

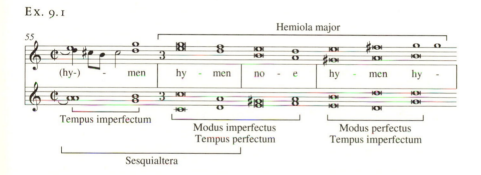

passage of the motet *Pronuba Juno* of Lasso,[70] conceivably transgressed the bounds of Taisnier's orthodoxy. Within a few measures we pass from *modus imperfectus* to *modus perfectus*, from *tempus imperfectum* to *perfectum* and back to *imperfectum*; a proportional change by sesquialtera overlaps a metrical transition from duple to triple through hemiola major. These changes, like the figures previously discussed, are prompted by the text, which here dictates a turn from the more severe duple to the lighter triple. Such a change had previously occurred in this motet at the words 'ad laetos thalamos carmina pangat hymen' ('Let Hymen compose songs to the delightful

[70] *Sämtliche Werke*, Neue Reihe, i, 6, mm. 55–9. This motet was printed in *Disieme livre de chansons à 4 parties d'Orlande de Lassus & autres* (Paris: A. le Roy and R. Ballard, 1570), but it is dated 1554–6 by Wolfgang Boetticher, *Orlando di Lasso und seine Zeit* (Kassel: Bärenreiter, 1958), i. 204.

marriage-chambers'), and now at the return of the same thought is called forth again.

Although rhythmic changes do not figure in the usual inventories of rhetorical devices, theoretical justification for freedom in temporal matters by reference to oratorical principles may be found in Vicentino's treatise:

> the movement of the measure should be changed to slower or faster according to the words . . . The experience of the orator teaches us to do this, for in his oration he speaks now loudly, now softly, now slowly, now quickly, and thus greatly moves the listeners; and this manner of changing the measure has great effect on the soul . . .[71]

To be sure, Vicentino is speaking here of a rubato performance rather than of a written-out change of tempo and measure. But his argument applies equally well to the notated temporal changes prescribed by hemiola and proportional signs.

24 Also they would call to mind through the models of their predecessors an extemporaneous counterpoint of 3, 4, 5, 6, 7 parts to be improvised by singers of different voices.

The predilection of singers for extemporaneous counterpoint and embellishment was the butt of many critiques and satires in the sixteenth century. Taisnier's passing jab allows two interpretations. On the one hand, he may be criticizing only the simultaneous improvisation by a number of singers against a cantus firmus. On the other hand, 'extemporaneous counterpoint' may be interpreted to cover also the improvised embellishment by three to seven solo singers of as many written parts.[72] It is difficult to imagine that Taisnier conceived of seven singers improvising simultaneously without such written parts before them.[73] Moreover, the practice of singing divisions over written parts was much more characteristic of the modernist taste than the *contrapunto a mente*.

Taisnier's phrase, 'pro praedecessorum documentis in mentem revocent', to denote the improvisers' source of inspiration, immediately brings Coclico to mind. Coclico's primary purpose in writing his *Compendium*, as he repeatedly emphasizes, was to revive (i) the art of ornate singing, and (ii) the practice of extemporaneous counterpoint. It is undoubtedly this twofold

---

[71] Vicentino, *L'antica musica*, bk. iv, ch. 42, fo. 94ᵛ.

[72] That they were soloists seems implied by the phrase: 'à diversis cantoribus modulandum'.

[73] This is nevertheless not to be ruled out altogether, since in 1574 there appeared in Venice a collection under the following title: *Li Introiti fondati sopra il canto fermo del basso con li versetti e Gloria patri con le risposte de contraponti, secondo l'ordine del Messal novo, per tutte le feste maggiori ed altre feste nell'anno a 4, a 5 ed a 6 voci*. Cf. Ernest Ferand, *Die Improvisation in der Musik* (Zurich: Rhein-Verlag, 1938), 212.

improvisatory art that he implies when in his preface he states: 'I wrote this compendium to restore to light that music which is commonly called *reservata*' (*musicam illam, quam vulgo reservatam iactitant, in lucem revocem*).[74] Taisnier understood that modern musicians wished to found their practice on examples of their predecessors. But obviously he did not mean their immediate predecessors, since the art they sought needed reviving. Thus Vicentino, Coclico, and Zacconi, among others of the new school, although they repudiated most older techniques, such as obscurities of notation, wished to preserve certain other older practices. One of these was improvisation. Why this needed reviving, especially in Germany, is evident if we read the opinions of some of Coclico's contemporaries.

The art of extempore counterpoint had behind it a long tradition. Most of the older manuals of counterpoint dealt as much with the improvised as with the written variety.[75] As late as 1477, Tinctoris granted the two equal recognition, although he found that the rules of the *contrapunctus scriptus* or *res facta* needed fuller treatment than those of the *absolute* or *mentaliter* variety, sung *super librum*.[76] Subsequent writers up to about 1550 are increasingly contemptuous of the improvised counterpoint. As the norms for the written counterpoint become more refined, the rudeness of the extemporized variety was increasingly exposed to unfavourable comparison. Moreover, the improvised technique seems to degenerate more and more into a species of fauxbourdon. Heinrich Faber (*c.*1548) dismisses improvisation as a 'ratio canendi non valde probatur eruditis' (a method of singing not much approved by the learned).[77] So frequent are the complaints against the improvising singers that Coclico feels compelled to defend this counterpoint against those who say it is full of 'poor and corrupt intervals' that 'offend the ear'. Josquin and Pierre de La Rue and their successors, who possessed most delicate ears, practised it, he recalls, 'and it is practised in the imperial, royal, princely, and pontifical chapels'.[78]

If we examine Coclico's illustrations of this practice, all in two parts, it becomes obvious that for him the *contrapunto a mente* was bound up with the art of elegant singing. His last examples[79] particularly are full of the runs and turns of melody taught in his chapter on embellished singing.

---

[74] Sig. A2ᵛ.

[75] Cf. Ferand, *Die Improvisation*; Palisca, 'Kontrapunkt' in *MGG*, vii. 1522–32; Manfred Bukofzer, 'Discantus', ibid., iii. 572.

[76] *Liber de arte contrapuncti*, especially bk. ii, ch. 20.

[77] Hof, Bibliothek des Gymnasiums, MS Paed. 3713, quoted in Gurlitt, 'Der Begriff der sortisatio', 207.

[78] *Compendium*, sig. I4ʳ.

[79] Ibid., sig. K4.

Vicentino also associates the two kinds of improvisation. Though he prefers counterpoint to be written if in more than four or five parts, he admits that the mental counterpoint 'is good to hear when the ensemble is well coordinated . . . and the sopranos make their *passaggi*, and likewise the contraltos and tenors, over the bass, which will have the cantus firmus . . .'.[80]

The second aspect of improvisation, that on written polyphonic parts, also suffered a period of decline just before the time of Coclico's book. Some of the *clausulae* or cadenzas presented by Coclico in his chapter on ornate singing he claims to have learned from Josquin, who apparently did not disdain putting them to use. Yet almost every serious writer on music around Coclico's time took a dim view of the practice. Especially significant are Juan Bermudo's words in condemnation of it, because he shows that the art of ornamenting parts was considered by some a thing of the past and no longer either necessary or desirable. He urges the performer 'not to make any melodic ornamentations, but to play the music as it was set down by the composer. If, perhaps, music in the older style needs such embellishments because of its clumsiness, the music of our day does not need them . . . The music of our day is so complex, so complete in its melodic line, that it is at one and the same time foundation and embellishment.'[81] Zarlino too was emphatic in his disapproval of *passaggi*, enjoining the singer not to imitate the exhibitionists who introduce wild and inappropriate diminutions but to adhere to the written text.[82] The generation brought up on the *ars perfecta*, highly trained in the proprieties of polyphonic writing, recoiled from a practice that compromised its ideals.

But the composer remained only briefly the lord of musical society. Coclico's manual ushered in the era of the coloratura singer. It was soon followed by those of Hermann Finck (1556), Girolamo dalla Casa (1584), Giovanni Bassano (1585), Riccardo Rognioni (1592), Lodovico Zacconi (1592), Luca Conforto (1593), Giovanni Bovicelli (1594), and finally and triumphantly, Giulio Caccini (1602). In contrast to the reluctance on the part of Zarlino and Bermudo to admit improvised divisions, this group of writers, mainly singers themselves, enthusiastically supported them.[83] The

---

[80] *L'antica musica*, bk. iv, ch. 23, fo. 83ʳ.

[81] *Declaracion de instrumentos musicales* (Ossuna: Juan de Leon, 1555; facs., ed. Macario S. Kastner, Kassel and Basle: Bärenreiter, 1957), bk. iv, ch. 43, trans. in Lowinsky, *Secret Chromatic Art*, 100.

[82] *Istitutioni*, pt. iii, ch. 45, trans. Marco–Palisca, 110.

[83] Lowinsky, who could not reconcile the art of embellishment with other known or assumed characteristics of *musica reservata*, failed to take into account the fact that the composers he quoted, Zarlino and Bermudo, expressed a declining viewpoint, while the *musica reservata*, although inspired by the past, was an ascendant movement. Cf. especially Bermudo's tirade against innovations in bk. iv, ch. 13.

musicians of his own generation, Coclico asserts, though trained primarily in composition by their predecessors, know also how to 'sing counterpoint extemporaneously over a chant, and they restore every precept and every power of singing as they suavely, ornately, and artfully sing in order to delight men and make them rejoice, and in this sweetness of the voice they excel the others by far . . .'.[84] Similarly, Vicentino, though he gave no detailed instructions for improvisation, encouraged the singer to 'imitate the text with the voice and use various manners of singing . . . and demonstrate that he is abundantly and richly endowed with many modes of singing, with a disposition for *gorgia* or for making divisions'.[85] Zacconi, ever the spokesman for 'modern' musicians, attributes much of the superiority of their music to the ability of the singers who decorate it:

> we may easily conclude that since the singers are those who, when they have good music before them, redouble its effectiveness, provided modern music is made with very good rules and sung by very good singers, masters of the beautiful accents and gracious manners, it will have much more power than the ancient music had, because the singers of those times did not pay any attention to anything but to sing well their notes without mistakes.[86]

Thus the art of embellishment, which Bermudo consigned to the grave as obsolete, is called forth by the modernists to lend charm to a music that had once again become simple enough to invite its graces. In opposing improvised counterpoint and—as we suppose—embellishments, Taisnier revealed good defensive instincts. It was from the impromptu sweet accents, mellifluous runs, and graces lavished by the skilled vocalist upon the superius of a madrigal or motet that the style of the seventeenth-century florid air was to issue; and improvising singers, like Vincenzo Galilei, Jacopo Peri, and Giulio Caccini, were to become the leaders of the monodic movement.

Finally, they would have singers become poets [i. e., creative musicians], and, stimulated by the example of the ancients, leave in memory of themselves and for the benefit of posterity the finished art-work.   26

Taisnier sees the modernists, not content with altering the work of others and inventing music extemporaneously, ready to usurp the field of the composer. Imitating the example of the ancients (that is, the school of

---

[84] *Compendium*, sig. V₄ᵛ.
[85] *L'antica musica*, bk. iv, ch. 42, fo. 94ʳ.
[86] *Prattica*, bk. i, ch. 12, fo. 8ʳ.

Josquin), these singers would leave their works behind in permanent form, as *opera absoluta*, to be enjoyed by present and posterity alike.

The meaning of the expression *opus absolutum* has been the subject of some discussion recently. There are those who would assign no special significance to it;[87] others who see in it an aspiration for the perfect art-work;[88] finally, those who interpret it simply as designating a composition free of a cantus firmus.[89] For an understanding of the expression it is necessary to go back to its probable author, Nicolaus Listenius. In his *Musica*, after explaining that music is made up of three aspects—*theorica*, *practica*, and *poetica*—he elaborates upon the last of these:[90]

Poetica, quae neque rei cognitione, neque solo exercitio contenta, sed aliquid post laborem relinquit operis, veluti cum à quopiam Musica aut Musicum carmen conscribitur, cuius finis est opus consumatum & effectum. Consistit enim in faciendo siue fabricando, hoc est in labore tali, qui post se etiam, artifice mortuo opus perfectum & absolutum relinquat. Unde Poeticus Musicus, qui in negotio aliquid relinquando versatur.	*Poetica* is that which strives neither for knowledge of things nor mere practice, but leaves behind some work after the labour. For example, when some music or musical song is written by someone, the goal of this action is the consummated and completed work. For it consists in making or fabricating something, that is, in a kind of labour that leaves behind itself, even after the artist dies, a perfect and completed work. Therefore the musical poet is he who is engaged in the occupation of leaving something behind.

---

[87] Bukofzer, foreword to facs. of Coclico, *Compendium musices* (Kassel & Basle: Bärenreiter, 1954).

[88] Paul Matzdorf, *Die 'Practica Musica' Hermann Fincks*, diss. (J. W. Goethe-Universität, Frankfurt a. Main, 1957), 51–6; and to a lesser extent, Heinrich Besseler, 'Erläuterung zu einer Vorführung ausgewählter Denkmäler aus der Musik des späten Mittelalters', *Bericht über die Freiburger Orgeltagung für deutsche Orgelkunst*, ed. W. Gurlitt (Augsburg, 1926), 152–4.

[89] Gurlitt, 'Die Kompositionslehre des deutschen 16. und 17. Jahrhunderts', *Kongreßbericht Bamberg* (Kassel & Basle: Bärenreiter, 1953), 103–13.

[90] Listenius, *Musica* (1549 edn.), sig. A3ᵛ. This conception of the *musicus poeticus* is even more forcefully expressed by a later champion of the new practices, Johann Andreas Herbst in *Musica poetica* (Nuremberg: J. Dümler, 1643), 1: 'Poëtica oder Melopoëtica fingit carmen musicum, à ποιεω, *effingo*: So da im *componi*ren bestehet, wie man nemlich einen newen Gesang oder wolklingende liebliche harmoniam setzen und machen soll, daher kompt Musicus Poëticus, oder *Compon*ist, welcher nicht allein Singen kan: Sondern welcher auch zugleich ein new *Opus* oder Werck an ihm selbsten zuverfertigen weiss, daher es auch von etlichen *Fabricatura* oder *Aedificium*, ein Baw genennet worden: Dann gleich wie ein Werckmeister oder Zimmermann, ein Hauss oder sonsten ein Gebäw, so von ihme verfertiget, hinter ihm verläst: Also auch und der gestalt kan ihme ein *Musicus Poëticus* Oder *Compon*ist, ein dergleichen *Musica*lisches Wercklein, welches mit grossem Fleiss, müh und arbeit, durch diese Kunst zusammen gebracht, zu seines Namens immerwährendem Gedächtnuss den Nachkömlingen hinderlassen.' Cf. also Gurlitt, 'Der Begriff der sortisatio', 202.

It is this new conception of the creative artist whose sole concern is with the masterwork that the new music wished to restore after a period of extreme obsequiousness towards Prince and Church. Such an ideal seems also to have been present in Coclico's mind when he stated that the second requirement of a good composer, after the ability to sing counterpoint extemporaneously, was a natural ardour for composition: 'ut ad componendum magno ducator desiderio, ac impetu quodam naturali ad compositionem pellatur, adeo ut nec cibus nec potus ei sapiat, ante absolutam cantilenam . . .' (Secondly, it is necessary that the composer be led by a great desire and be driven to composition by a certain natural impulse to such a degree that he forgoes the taste of either food or drink until the composition is finished . . .).[91]

In citing this last and important aspiration—to produce self-contained art-works that will live beyond the composer's own time—Taisnier once again shows a keen awareness of the ideals of the new school. For his part, he obviously regards such aims as presumptuous. He regrets the passing of the time when a composer was asked nothing more than to be a good craftsman who correctly and diligently wove his counterpoints and canons around a given subject to grace some particular occasion. But Taisnier is out of touch with the ideals of the new generation, for the natural *ingenium* is soon to play an increasingly prominent role as a desirable and necessary faculty for a creative musician.[92]

They indulge in the interchange between alternate musical instruments, namely [28] between vertical and transverse flutes, monochord, upright harpsichord, virginal, clavichord, spinet, hurdy-gurdy, lute or testudo, harp, psaltery, portative, positive, [30] regal, organ, bagpipe, clareta ('clear' trumpet), horn, cymbal, tympanum, cithara of Jerome, tympanum of Jerome, ten-string psaltery, tuba of Jerome, organ of Jerome, fistula of Jerome, and others nearly innumerable, which we have discussed with pictures in our book on music. And this, finally, is enough about music.

Taisnier's final count against the moderns is that they indulge in a constant interchange between different instruments. Here our author's own inspiration seems to have faltered, for, far from being consumed by creative fire and eschewing all food or drink before concluding his piece on music, he took time out to make an inventory of the instruments illustrated in one of the musical manuals popular in his day, Sebastian Virdung's *Musica getutscht*,[93] or, more likely, Ottmar Luscinius, *Musurgia seu praxis*

---

[91] *Compendium*, sig. L2ᵛ.

[92] It was not long before Juan Huarte was to investigate this faculty in his *Examen de ingenios para las sciencias* (Baeza: Juan Bautista de Montoya, 1575), especially ch. 8, which is on the arts.

[93] Basle, 1511; facs., ed. Leo Schrade, Kassel: Bärenreiter, 1931.

Musicae.[94] The roster is a curious conglomeration, completely out of touch with the instrumental practice of Taisnier's own time. It combines medieval instruments, such as the monochord and hurdy-gurdy, and instruments contemporaneously in use, such as virginal, harpsichord, and spinet, with legendary ones, like those called 'of Hieronymus'.

The latter class disturbed Vander Straeten, who conjectured that perhaps Hieronymus was an instrument-builder, a friend of Taisnier, whose atelier was hereby accorded some free publicity.[95] Hieronymus is, of course, St Jerome, and the instruments are those found represented in medieval manuscripts of his epistles.[96]

Did Taisnier mean to criticize the constantly changing variety of instruments and ensembles used by his contemporaries? If so, he hit upon a characteristic practice of the avant-garde circles, to judge by the ensembles described by Ercole Bottrigari. That all but the most perfect of such ensembles produced many offensive sounds is obvious from the seriousness with which the problems of tuning and of combining differently tuned instruments was tackled by various authors.[97] Gratiano Desiderio, in Bottrigari's dialogue,[98] tells of the displeasing confusion and discordance he experienced when he heard an ensemble consisting of a harpsichord, spinet, three lutes, many viols, many trombones, one straight and one curved cornett, two rebecs, several flutes, both vertical and transverse, a double harp, and a lira. Taisnier must have had frequent occasion in his travels to encounter such *concerti*. If so, he must have turned away from them not only for their cacophony but also for the sensual excess they exhibited.

Undoubtedly, many scholars will find other meanings in Taisnier's words than those presented in my lengthy glosses. The main lines of my interpretation were directed by the statements of Taisnier that are least ambiguous: (i) *musica reservata* is the new music; (ii) its advocates are the chromatic and enharmonic experimenters; (iii) the composers of *musica reservata* do not conform to the rules. As far as possible, I have guarded against being swayed

[94] Taisnier probably knew the Virdung through the Latin version of Luscinius (Strasburg: Johannes Scotus, 1536), since where Virdung names the instruments in German, Taisnier uses the Latin of Luscinius.

[95] *La Musique aux Pays-Bas*, iii. 237.

[96] The letter on music is in *Patrologia latina*, xxx. 214–15, Epist. XXIII ad Dardanum. It is regarded as spurious. For a discussion of the instruments and facsimiles of the illustrated manuscripts, cf. Reinhold Hammerstein, 'Instrumenta Hieronymi', *Archiv für Musikwissenschaft*, 16 (1959), 117–34. All the instruments named by Taisnier are pictured in Virdung, *Musica getutscht*, sigs. C3ʳ–D3ʳ, and in Luscinius, *Musurgia*, 29–33.

[97] Bottrigari, *Il Desiderio overo de' concerti di varij strumenti musicali* (Venice: R. Amadino, 1594); Artusi, *L'Artusi* (1600).

[98] *Il Desiderio*, 3.

by the voluminous literature on *musica reservata*, so full of misreadings, conflicting hypotheses, and imaginative exegesis. Yet this same literature is undeniably brightened by many sparks of deep insight. Now, indeed, it is time to re-examine some of the other known uses of the term and some of the older and recent hypotheses in the light of Taisnier's discussion. The sources and the problems they present, as well as the pertinent bibliography, have been adequately reviewed recently,[99] so there is little purpose in going over this ground again. Rather, I shall proceed on the basis of some of the main points made by Taisnier and attempt to correlate them with previously known sources.

Musica reservata as *Musica nova*

The identification of *musica reservata* with *musica nova* has been both advocated and attacked in the past. The opposing views have departed from the same evidence, namely that presented by two letters written by Dr Seld, Vice-Chancellor of the Holy Roman Empire. They are addressed to Duke Albert V of Bavaria, in whose behalf Seld was scouting for new singers and composers. In a letter dated 22 September 1555 Seld recommended Filippo de Monte as incontrovertibly the best composer in the whole land [England], especially in the new style and *musica reservata* ('new art und Musica reservata').[100]

Kurt Huber[101] interpreted the phrase as signifying the 'new style of musica reservata'. Van Crevel judiciously cautioned against jumping to such a conclusion, and subsequent commentators have heeded him only too conscientiously. Huber's interpretation, however, seems now to be vindicated by Taisnier's equation of the two styles.

Fortunately, another letter of Dr Seld strengthens the link between the new and *reservata* styles. On 28 April 1555 Seld reported again from Brussels. The alto singer Egidius Fux, after being found competent in a church audition, was taken to Seld's private home and there with other guests acquitted himself well singing 'a variety of *Reservata*—and to him unknown—music'. The structure of the sentence implies that the 'Reservatam [musicam]' was unknown to the singer, possibly because it was in

---

[99] Gustave Reese, *Music in the Renaissance* (New York: Norton, 1954), 511–17; Bernhard Meier, 'Reservata-Probleme, ein Bericht', *Acta musicologica*, 30 (1958), 77–89. See also Albert Dunning, 'Musica reservata', in *New Grove*, xii. 825–7.

[100] Quoted in Adolf Sandberger, *Beiträge zur Geschichte der bayerischen Hofkapelle unter Orlando di Lasso*, 2 vols. (Leipzig: Breitkopf und Härtel, 1953), i. 55; and in Marcus van Crevel, *Adrianus Petit Coclico* (The Hague: Martinus Nijhoff, 1940), 295.

[101] *Ivo de Vento* (Lindenberg i. Allgäu: J. A. Schwarz, 1918), 51.

a newer style.[102] Later in the same letter Dr Seld observes that the Choirmaster Cornelius Canis is leaving his post and is to be replaced by Nicolas Payen,[103] a devout and honorable priest with a good reputation in musical circles. 'And so *Musica reservata* will be much more in vogue than up to now.'[104] Cornelius Canis has been described as a composer who followed the style of Gombert, especially in the use of pervading imitation.[105] This would seem to mark him as a partisan of the old style, like his colleague Taisnier at the emperor's court. Thus all the qualifications of new and *reservata* applied by Seld support Taisnier's identification of the two styles.

Lasso, who has more than once entered the *musica reservata* discussion, aligned himself with the new music—'la nouvelle composition d'aulcuns d'Italie'—in the five motets included in his publication of Italian madrigals, villanelle, chansons, and motets.[106] The 'new music' in the collection includes the assiduously chromatic *Alma nemes* of Lasso and *Calami sonum ferentes* of Rore.[107] In his preface Lasso makes note of the fact that his patron, Sir Stefano Gentile, was an admirer of 'the music that here is called *osservata* and wishes that it should be plain to all and that it should please everyone'. Music in the *stile osservato*, the observed or strict style,[108] Lasso seems to intimate, was not easily understood by the public because of its contrapuntal 'tours de force'.[109] Now, in this collection, Lasso has made an effort to temper these erudite tendencies. Early in his career, then, Lasso

---

[102] 'Da wir allerlay Reservatam und ime unbekhante Musick gesungen, begind, das er der aller gewiss genug, also das er, wie die andern all sagn, sich neben ainem leden Altisten, so wir in der khay. Capell haben, wol vergeen möcht . . .' (Sandberger, *Beiträge*, iii. 300; Van Crevel, *Coclico*, 294). I have modified the translation in Reese, *Music in the Renaissance*, 512—'As we sang all sorts of *Reservata* and music unknown to him'—because 'Reservata' is there made to function as a neuter plural noun, while in the original both 'Reservatam' (adjective agreeing with *musicam*, which is implied) and 'ime unbekhante' modify 'Musik'.

[103] Coclico, *Compendium*, sig. B4ᵛ, significantly names Payen but not Canis among the kings of music 'qui vere sciunt cantilenas ornare, in ipsis omnes omnium affectus exprimere'.

[104] Sandberger, *Beiträge*, iii. 300; Van Crevel, *Coclico*, 294.

[105] Joseph Schmidt-Görg, 'Canis, Cornelius', in *Die Musik in Geschichte und Gegenwart*, ii. 750. Heinz Brandes, *Studien zur musikalischen Figurenlehre im 16. Jahrhundert* (Berlin: Triltsch & Huther, 1935), 73, states that he has compared a number of works of Canis and Payen and found Payen's 'viel klarer und strenger figürlich'.

[106] *Le quatorzieme livre . . . contenant dix huyct Chansons Italiennes, Six Chansons Françoises et six Motets faictz (à la nouvelle composition d'aulcuns d'Italie)* (Antwerp: Susato, 1555).

[107] Printed in Charles Burney, *A General History of Music*, ed. Frank Mercer (London: G. T. Foulis, 1935), ii. 255 (original edn. iii. 317). For a modern transcription, see Rore, *Opera omnia*, ed. B. Meier, vi. 108.

[108] This style (though the term *osservato* is not used) is described in Zarlino, *Istitutioni*, pt. iii, ch. 63, trans. Marco–Palisca, 215–20.

[109] V. Galilei, in his *Discorso intorno all'uso delle dissonanze* of 1589–91, Florence, Biblioteca Nazionale Centrale, MSS Galileiani 1, fo. 142ʳ (ed. Rempp, 151), noted that the public taste favoured the less 'observed' compositions, 'for no one cares to sing or hear any more those cantilene which go around under the name of *osservate* . . . perhaps because they are insipid . . .'.

embraced the ideals of the *musica nova* and so identified his position in the public mind with the *musica reservata*.[110]

Chromaticism

Taisnier, we saw, attributes the term *musica reservata* to the supporters of chromaticism. One of the few known statements on the *reservata* by a musical theorist supports Taisnier's attribution. It was recently discovered by Bernhard Meier in the *Doctrina de tonis* of Eucharius Hoffman.[111] This author, like Taisnier, points to the supporters of chromaticism as customary users of the term:[112]

Hodie vero [hoc genus chromaticum] a quibusdam in cantum revocatur, et ab iis Musica reservata appellatur, quod quasi reservata sit in quibusdam instrumentis musicis et in cantu non recepta seu usurpata.	Today, however, the chromatic genre is being restored by certain people to singing and by them this is called *musica reservata*, since it is almost reserved for certain musical instruments and is not accepted or practised in singing.

Leaving aside, for the moment, Hoffman's etymology, it is of considerable significance that two of the few musicians known to have employed the term both link it directly with chromaticism.

Hoffman's description of the modern chromatic tetrachord in an earlier passage[113] conforms with that presented by a number of other theorists, among them Francisco de Salinas, Galilei, and Artusi.[114] Their common source is Vicentino. The chromatic tetrachord consists for all of them of a series of semitones, alternately major and minor. This, we have seen, was also the gist of Taisnier's vague description of their theory.

A further source should be cited as a link between *musica reservata* and

---

[110] See below, 270. In another document, dated 1559, owed to Dr Seld, a specific composition of Lasso is described as *musica reservata*, a setting of *Tityre, tu patulae* from Vergil's first eclogue that was published in 1560. See Wolfgang Boetticher, 'Neue Lasso-Funde', *Die Musikforschung*, 8 (1955), 385–97. For a discussion of this work in terms of *musica reservata*, see Lowinsky, 'Humanism in the Music of the Renaissance', in *Music in the Culture of the Renaissance*, 154–218, esp. 202–4.

Meier quite rightly saw the connection between the conflict of the new and old styles and the *reservata* problem when he stated recently that one of the essentials for its solution is an understanding of 'die im späten 16. Jahrhundert schon klar bewußten (und bei Lasso recht oft schon absichtlich kontrastierten) Unterschiede "älteren" und "neueren" Stils innerhalb der niederländischen Musik' ('Reservata-Probleme', 89).

[111] Cf. Meier, 'Ein weitere Quelle', 53–5.
[112] Ibid.
[113] Ibid.
[114] Cf. above, n. 56.

chromaticism, although the two are not directly related in it. In an anonymous treatise dating from between 1559 and 1571 in which *musica reservata* is connected with the technique of avoiding the cadence,[115] the student is encouraged to use chromaticism. The fourth rule reads:[116]

Quartum: Mutationes generum,	Fourth: Mutations of genre,
ut ex diatonico in chromaticum,	as from diatonic into chromatic
seu ex tetrachordo disjuncto	or from the disjunct tetrachord
in conjunctum &	into the conjunct and the
contra, suaves sunt:	reverse, are smooth-sounding
etiam in monodia. Siquidem	even in monody. Indeed, such
mutationes, quas b molle	mutations, which are called 'by
vocant, si loco suo	*b molle*' when they are on this
fiant; non sinunt torpere	degree of the hexachord, do not
auditorem,	allow the listener to become
sed ad attendendum	numb but excite him with the
soni novitate excitant.	newness of the sound to pay
	closer attention.

This passage, and the entire treatise as well, are too short to permit us to define the author's stand with any certainty. From the work as a whole it appears that he is a humanist, learned in Greek and a reformer of church music (he begins: 'Nihil omnino praetermisit Ecclesia artificii in cantu.'). He must have held a post in the church of Besançon, since he cites some practices of the 'Ecclesia Bisuntina'. On the definition of the chromatic, he sides with Vicentino: 'majus [semitonium] hoc nusquam concinit, nec in usum usquam venit, nisi in Chromate.' The sure sign of the chromatic for him, therefore, is the major semitone. His counterpoint rules are eclectic and rudimentary, though they include the often cited but as often slighted remark about avoiding the cadence. The most original aspect of the treatise is the author's attempt to apply Greek principles of *melopoeia* and its terminology to polyphonic composition,[117] or, as he calls it, 'monodia', undoubtedly to distinguish solo part-music from choral plainchant. Without being a partisan of the new music (he is critical, in fact, of the *novatores* who introduce barbaric, effeminate, lascivious music into the church), the

[115] This was first noted by Helmuth Osthoff, *Die Niederländer und das deutsche Lied* (1400–1640) (Berlin: Junker & Dünnhaupt, 1938), 275 n. 54. The portion on counterpoint, which includes the passage in question, is printed in W. Baumker, 'Über den Kontrapunkt', *Monatshefte für Musikgeschichte*, 10 (1878), 63–5. The entire treatise, entitled *De musica*, is printed from a manuscript in the Acts of the Synod of Besançon of 1571 in Johann F. Schannat and Joseph Hartzheim (eds.), *Concilia Germaniae* (Cologne: J. W. Krakamp & haeredum Christiani Simonis, 1759–75), viii. 203–5. My reason for dating it after 1559 is that Zarlino is cited in one place. I am indebted to the Library of Louisiana State University for making a typescript of the treatise available to me from its copy of this rare ten-volume series.

[116] *De musica*, 208.

[117] Concerning this, cf. the discussion of figure-theory below, 274.

author seems to accept the premisses of the *musica reservata* and deserves greater attention in this context than he has received.

Vicentino's name, inevitably, has been prominent in this discussion. It is time now to bring up the question: Did this acknowledged leader of the chromaticists know the expression *musica reservata*?

If he knew it, he was wary of using it. A passage from Vicentino's *L'antica musica ridotta alla moderna prattica*,[118] brought into the *reservata* discussion by Edward Lowinsky[119] and recognized by most scholars as having a bearing on it, does not actually show that he had any such concept in mind. In this place, Vicentino, proud of having finally mastered the lost art of chromatic and enharmonic music, tells us that he and his specially trained musicians

a molti Signori e
gentilhuomini intender facciamo
la dolcezza di questa armonia, di
cui senza modo
invaghiti, si sono con ogni
esquisita diligenza per
impararla affaticati; perche
con effetto comprendono che (come
li scrittori antichi dimostrano)
era meritamente ad altro uso la
Cromatica & Enarmonica Musica
riserbata che la Diatonica,
perche questa in
feste publiche in luoghi communi
à uso delle vulgari orecchie si
cantaua: quelle fra li
privati sollazzi de Signori e
Principi, ad uso delle purgate
orecchie in lode di gran
personaggi et Heroi
s'adoperauano.

allow many lords and
gentlemen to hear the sweetness
of this harmony, with which they
have been so thoroughly
enchanted that they have laboured
with extraordinary diligence to
learn it, because they
effectively understand that (as
the ancient writers demonstrate)
the chromatic and enharmonic
music was rightly reserved for
other uses than the diatonic,
since the latter, intended for
the ears of common people, was
sung at popular festivals in
public places, while the former,
meant for discriminating ears,
was used at private
entertainments of lords and
princes to sing the praises of
great public figures and heroes.

Lowinsky translated the key portion of this passage:

they understand that (as the ancient writers demonstrate) the chromatic and enharmonic *musica reservata* had a different application from that of the diatonic . . .

Leo Schrade already pointed out the error in this translation.[120] Yet the

[118] Bk. ii, ch. 4, fo. 10ᵛ.
[119] *Secret Chromatic Art*, 55 ff.
[120] In a review of Lowinsky's book in *Journal of Renaissance and Baroque Music*, 1 (1946), 165–6. Reese, *Music in the Renaissance*, 513, prints a corrected translation. Knud Jeppesen, in reviewing Reese's book, argues once again for Lowinsky's interpretation, maintaining that both translations are defensible; *Musical Quarterly*, 41 (1955), 390.

quotation has been absorbed into the *reservata* literature with hardly any hesitation by almost every author who has contributed to it. Because of the many unjustified assumptions it has fostered (which would otherwise merit discussion here), it is important to dispose of it once again.

Lowinsky translated the compound verb, 'era . . . riserbata', as if 'riserbata' were an adjective modifying 'musica'. Vicentino was not speaking here of a kind of music called *musica riserbata* but of a kind of music that was already very specifically named chromatic and enharmonic. It is true that he considered this style of music reserved, for the moment at least, for people of taste. But to assume from this that Vicentino recognized a class of music called *reservata*, with all the connotations it held for others, is a venturesome leap, to say the least.

There is no need to invoke such a concept to appreciate the motivation for Vicentino's remark. He wished to justify his revival of the chromatic and enharmonic genera by the example of the ancients. Although Vicentino was not a scholar and may not himself have read the ancient writers even in translation, he undoubtedly heard them cited often enough in the humanistic circles of Ferrara, which included the learned Francesco Patrizi.

Vicentino's statement gathers ideas from various sources. It recalls the traditional classification of music, repeated by Aristotle and others: there were melodies of action and passion used in theatrical performances meant for the vulgar class of mechanics and labourers, and ethical melodies for singing to the lyre.[121] Athenaeus, centuries after Aristotle, lamented the decline of the latter type of music, recalling that 'in ancient times it was the acts of heroes and the praise of gods that the poets set to music'.[122] Plutarch (or pseudo-Plutarch), about a century later, also spoke nostalgically of this admirable practice. In a very ancient epoch, Plutarch reports, 'it is said that the Greeks did not even known the music of the theatre. All their science in this domain was consecrated to the cult of the gods and the education of the young . . . Music was confined to sacred places where it served in the cult of the divinity and the praise of heroes'.[123] In another passage[124] Plutarch states that the chromatic genre was never used by the tragic poets, but it was practised in the cithara (and therefore singing to the cithara) from the very beginning and along with it the enharmonic. In still another place[125] Plutarch laments the neglect 'of the most beautiful of

---

[121] *Politics*, viii. 7. 1342ª.
[122] *Deipnosophists*, xiv. 633. Eng. trans. by Charles B. Gulick (Cambridge, Mass.: Harvard University Press, 1937), vi. 417.
[123] *De musica*, 1140D–E.
[124] Ibid. 1137E.
[125] Ibid. 1145A.

the genres, that which the ancients practised because of its nobility'—the enharmonic. While he never explicitly states that the chromatic and enharmonic were reserved for the praise of gods and the deeds of heroes, it is easy to see how such a conclusion logically follows from his statements. The enharmonic and chromatic were the most ancient genera, and the most ancient music was consecrated or reserved for sacred uses and moral education.

Vicentino's thought is thus perfectly clear without introducing the concept of *music reservata*. We might as well impute the term to the Greeks as to Vicentino on the basis of the disputed quotation. Nevertheless, one must bow to Lowinsky's characteristically sound scholarly instincts in suspecting a link between *musica reservata* and chromaticism before any documents supporting the tie had been brought to light.

If we are inclined to sever connections between Vicentino and the expression *musica reservata*, to link Vicentino with Taisnier personally is tempting. Taisnier could not have failed to know of Vicentino's experiments, since both were in Ferrara in 1547 and 1548.[126] Between 1546 and 1549 Vicentino was choirmaster to Duke Ercole d'Este of Ferrara.[127] By 1549, according to Danckerts, Vicentino had already been working for fifteen years on the recovery of the neglected genres of music.[128] Vicentino himself claimed that he finally was able to restore to life the practice of the ancient genres 'at my age of forty in the holy year 1550 in the most happy pontificate of Pope Julius III'.[129] Taisnier should have had another opportunity to become acquainted with Vicentino's work in 1552 in Rome, when Vicentino was in the service of Cardinal Ippolito d'Este and Taisnier directed in that city the musicians of Cardinal Francisco de Mendoza.[130]

Musica reservata as Chamber Music

The thesis that *musica reservata* signifies some sort of chamber music as opposed to church music has rested mainly on Lowinsky's interpretation of the quotation from Vicentino. Although the quotation cannot be sustained as evidence on *reservata*, it is undeniable that Vicentino was one of the

---

[126] Title-page of Taisnier, *De compositione s. fabrica et usu sphaerae* (Ferrara: G. de Buglhat & A. Hucher, Mar. 1548), where he names himself 'in almo Ferrariensi gymnasio mathematices profess. publ. oratio hab. ipsis idibus novembr. a. D. 1547'. The *Opera nuova molto utile, et necessaria à tutti architettori, geometri* was issued in Ferrara in Apr. 1548 (same publishers).

[127] Einstein, *The Italian Madrigal*, i. 413.

[128] Biblioteca Casanatense, MS 2880, 9.

[129] *L'antica musica*, bk. ii, ch. 4, fo. 10ʳ.

[130] Dewert, 'Jean Taisnier', 14.

leaders of the music so called. His views are consequently of some relevance. Was Vicentino truly campaigning for a music dedicated, like the ancient chromatic and enharmonic, to the praise of heroes and great men and addressed exclusively to the ears of lords and princes? As an experimenter unpopular with the average musical amateur and suspected by his fellow musicians, Vicentino relied greatly on the support and patronage of the Este family. By citing the high regard and noble purposes reserved in ancient times for the chromatic and enharmonic, he managed to win the following of the Ferrarese nobility. If we may believe the claim Vicentino makes immediately after the passage quoted above, Prince Alfonso d'Este, his aunt, Sister Leonora Estense, and the Princesses Lucretia and Leonora all took up and mastered the new practice. It is not surprising that in his *apologia* for the resuscitated genera Vicentino should exploit these connections, defending his new practice before a hostile world by associating it with the noblest traditions of the present as well as of antiquity. He did not say his music should be reserved for the nobility; he wished, rather, by citing their support to have it become acceptable to all musicians. One need not read far into his book to be convinced that his goal was a sweeping reform of the entire 'modern practice', not merely one segment of it. Vicentino's treatise thus offers no convincing proof that either chromatic music or *musica reservata* was restricted to the private chamber.

Other sources, however, do support the belief that *musica reservata* applies mainly to chamber music. The audition of Egidius Fux reported by Seld in which *reservata* music was sung took place in a private chamber. The *musica nova* movement made its greatest gains in the field of secular chamber music. Even the sacred music that can be relied upon as representative of the *reservata*, Lasso's Penitential Psalms[131] and the motets of Coclico's collection[132]—chiefly settings of psalm texts—was intended mainly for private devotions. Taisnier includes both *cantilena* (secular song?) and *mottetus* in his statement but does not mention the mass. The evidence in support of the link to chamber music is not impressive. It may be said with assurance, however, that *musica reservata* fully participated in the secular tendencies of its age.

Musica reservata as Solo Music

The special character of *musica reservata*, apart from the newness of its techniques, seems to stem at least partly from its manner of performance—by

[131] By virtue of Quickelberg's famous statement; cf. below, 272.

[132] *Musica Reservata. Consolationes piae* (Nuremberg, 1552); ed. Martin Ruhnke in Das Erbe deutscher Musik, 62 (Lippstadt: Kistner & Siegel & Co., 1958).

soloists as opposed to chorus. Coclico, in his *Compendium*, is intent upon training the soloist rather than the choral singer in the ornate style. The anonymous of Besançon finds chromaticism especially effective in *monodia*, part-music for soloists. The collection of Raimundus Ballestra published in 1611, described by the composer as including *Musicalischen Symphonien und Harmonien, ausser Etlicher reservata*,[133] contains in addition to various symphonies (concerted vocal-instrumental works) and *harmoniae* (choral and polychoral works), several motets in which solo sections are contrasted with tutti sections.[134]

A document recently brought to light by Willene Clark[135] names Biagio Marini as a *Musico riservato* in the sense of special musician or soloist. This occurs in the final draft of the document, while the second draft states: 'Il Marino Havera il titulo di Maestro de concerti. sara musico riservato et che con il suo violino non sia messo in concerti grandi dove non potra esser ben sentito.' Marini was not to be used as a 'ripieno' player in the concerti grossi, but only as a soloist, either alone or in an ensemble 'of three or four parts'. One of the functions of such a soloist was improvisation.

Seld, who found Egidius Fux particularly qualified in singing *musica reservata*, emphasized Fux's ability 'at the art of ornamentation, which is excellent in this land [Belgium] but which otherwise is considered so absolutely bad'.[136]

To these we can now add Taisnier's disparagement of the 'flowing, running counterpoints in minims and semiminims', obviously an indictment of the florid style, written or improvised. Furthermore, the extempore counterpoint he describes is for 'diverse voices', suggesting that one voice sang to a part. Taisnier's statement thus joins the other documents in supporting the idea that *musica reservata* was florid music intended for soloists.

Text Expression

The hardiest interpretation in the entire *musica reservata* debate has been that which links it with the expressive tendencies of the mid-sixteenth

[133] Hellmut Federhofer, 'Eine neue Quelle der musica reservata', *Acta musicologica*, 24 (1952), 33.
[134] Ibid. 39. Federhofer links the most unusual motet in the collection, 'in laudem Serenissimi Archiducis Ferdinandi' to *musica reservata* because it stands out in its use of contrapuntal artifices and because it supports Lowinsky's theory of music for princes. Federhofer's choice does not strike me as a happy one, however.
[135] 'A Contribution to Sources of Musica Reservata', *Revue belge de musicologie*, 11 (1957), 27–33.
[136] '. . . die art des Colorirens, wie in diesem land gepreuhig, aber sonst warlich durchaus so treffenlich übel bestimpt'. Letter, 22 Sept. 1555, in Sandberger, *Beiträge*, i. 54.

century. It stands securely on the most lucid document found so far. In this, the preface to a sumptuous manuscript of Lasso's Penitential Psalms, the humanist Samuel Quickelberg states:

Thus the illustrious Prince [Albert] commissioned his very excellent musician Orlandus Lassus, more distinguished and polished than any our century has produced, to compose these psalms mostly for five voices. Lassus expressed these psalms so appropriately, in accommodating, according to necessity, the thoughts and words with lamenting and plaintive tones, in expressing the force of the individual affections, in placing the object almost alive before the eyes: that one is at a loss to say whether the sweetness of the affections more greatly enhanced the lamenting tones or the lamenting tones brought greater ornament to the sweetness of the affections. This genre of music they call *musica reservata*. In it, whether in other songs (*carminibus*) which are virtually innumerable, or in these, Orlandus has wonderfully demonstrated the outstanding quality of his genius to posterity.[137]

Whatever other connotations *reservata* may have had, Quickelberg's statement leaves no doubt that it denoted music that was graphically and vividly expressive of a text.

Concerning this aspect of the style Taisnier is silent. This is regrettable but not difficult to understand. The achievements of the *musica nova* in text-expression were its most positive assets. Taisnier, bent on deflating its propaganda, singled out those characteristics which would strike the conservative musician as faults. Besides, the principle of setting a text according to its affections was by now generally accepted. Unable to deny it, the critics of the 'modern' music concentrated their attacks on the extreme means some composers sought to carry it out. Zarlino is our best witness to this attitude when he attacks the chromaticists on these very grounds:

The chromaticists are of the opinion, finally, that any interval one pleases may be used in vocal composition despite the fact that its form or proportion may not be found among the harmonic numbers. They proceed on these grounds: that since the voice is capable of forming every interval, and it is necessary to imitate familiar speech in pronouncing words, as orators rightly do, it is not inappropriate that one should use those intervals which fittingly express the ideas contained in the words, with the accents and other things, in the manner that we pronounce them in speaking, so that they might move the affections. To these I reply that this is most

---

[137] Sandberger, ibid. i. 56 n. 2, first saw a tie through *musica reservata* between Seld's remarks and this statement of Quickelberg. A critical text of the original Latin is in Boetticher, *O. di Lasso*, 250. My translation differs from that in Reese, *Music in the Renaissance*, in a few details, one of which is of some consequence. In the original and in my translation the phrase, 'in aliis carminibus', is included in the genre of music called *reservata*, while in Reese the 'other works' are not in this genre. The present translation, aside from being more accurate syntactically, thus supports Taisnier's broad definition. Cf. also the translation into German by S. W. Dehn quoted in Van Crevel, *Coclico*, 300 n. 2.

inappropriate, for speaking in the familiar manner is one thing and speaking while modulating or singing is another. Never have I heard an orator (since they say it is necessary to imitate the orator so that music might move the affections) use such strange and crude intervals as these [chromaticists] use.[138]

In a later chapter of his treatise Zarlino urges the composer to suit the music to the word but to be careful 'that it does not offend'.[139] Taisnier would probably have agreed with Zarlino that the methods of the new composers did offend.

The Oratorical Figures

As we have seen, Taisnier's enumeration of the *vitia* of modern composers is virtually a catalogue of what Burmeister later called oratorical ornaments or figures in music. The relationship of *musica reservata* to rhetoric and oratory has been explored by several writers.[140] A most searching analysis of a selected number of works from Dufay to Josquin from the standpoint of figures as text-illustrations was recently made by Fritz Feldmann.[141] The evidence there presented shows that Josquin and his contemporaries consistently used certain devices to symbolize, suggest, or depict ideas in the text. Another study particularly relevant to this discussion is Bernhard Meier's analysis of the *Musica reservata* motets of Coclico.[142] Concentrating on a smaller number of *figurae*, Meier convincingly demonstrates that Coclico used in a consistent manner for their expressive or pictorial value these figures: *commixtio modorum*, fauxbourdon, *nota contra notam* passages, *suspirationes*, semiminim runs, *catabasis* or low vocal registers, cross-relations, chromatic modulations, and *redictae*. He also shows that this usage was common, though to a lesser degree, in the motets of Josquin des Prez.

It is significant that Taisnier, unappreciative though he seems of their expressive value, notes as abuses some of the very text-illustrative devices that the modern analyst finds striking: chromaticism, departure from the mode, minim and semiminim runs, note-against-note style—if this is what is meant by *contrapuncta harmoniosa*—repetitions, fugal style, hemiola, and changes of metre and tempo.

Musical treatises before that of Burmeister unfortunately do not treat the

---

[138] *Istitutioni*, pt. iii, ch. 80.
[139] Ibid., pt. iv, ch. 32.
[140] Brandes, *Studien zur musikalischen Figurenlehre*; Unger, *Die Beziehungen zwischen Musik und Rhetorik.*
[141] 'Untersuchungen zum Wort-Ton-Verhältnis in den Gloria-Credo-Sätzen von Dufay bis Josquin', *Musica disciplina*, 8 (1954), 141–71.
[142] 'The *Musica reservata* of Adrianus Petit Coclico'.

musical figures, so that we cannot know to what extent a conscious theory about them had evolved among musicians and musical pedagogues by the middle of the sixteenth century. This fact necessarily weakens any ties drawn between the figures and *musica reservata*, whether in this article or elsewhere. While we know musicians were thinking in rhetorical terms, theorists earlier than Burmeister have not been found who name figures.

It is therefore encouraging to encounter in a writer who mentions *musica reservata*, the anonymous of Besançon, an attempt to apply the idea of figures or ornaments of composition to music.[143] He limits himself to four *figurae*:[144]

Sciant ergo Musici, quatuor esse figuras in monodia. Prima Graecis dicta est πλοκή: Latinis copulatio. Sed vulgus nunc cantorum fugam nominat.

He now classifies the first figure, the fugue, into four types. Continuing then, he declares: 'Sunt aliae tres figurae melopaejas [*sic*] τονή, ἀγωγή, πέττεια.' But these remaining three figures, which are sometimes rendered in Latin *extensio*, *ductus*, and *pettia* respectively,[145] are only very briefly described. *Tonè* is the repetition of the same idea in different places, equal intervals apart (apparently the same as the later *auxesis*). *Agogè* is the linking together of successive tones, that is, conjunct motion. *Pettia* is the manner of proceeding by skip. He ends the discussion by saying that these last three figures are easy to use, even for a beginner. Like Taisnier, this author seems preoccupied with devices for themselves rather than with their expressive functions. Unlike Taisnier, though, he sees nothing wrong with repetition[146] or with the fugue in all its forms.

[143] Cf. above, n. 115. This source has so far been overlooked by historians of rhetoric in music.

[144] The terms for these four figures are taken from the names of the parts of *melopoeia* in Cleonides, *Introductio harmonica*, 14 (ed. Meibom, p. 22; Strunk, *Source Readings*, 45). They are given there in the following order: ἀγωγή (*ductus*), πλοκή (*nexus*), πεττεία (*pettia*), τονή (*extensio*). Except for the definition of ᾿αγωγή, which is derived from Cleonides, there is little connection between the ancient usage and that of the Besançon anonymous. All but τονή may be found also in Aristides Quintilianus, *De musica*, i. 12 (trans. Mathiesen, 92), where they comprise the three species of χρῆσις (Lat. *usus*) or manners of musical composition. The Besançon author's *pettia* is closer to Aristides than to Cleonides, which suggests that he knew both sources. The treatise of Cleonides was available in a Latin translation by Giorgio Valla (Venice: Sim. Papiensis, 1497).

[145] Marcus Meibom's translation of Euclid (actually Cleonides), *Introductio harmonica*, in *Antiquae musicae auctores septem* (Amsterdam: Ludovicus Elzevirius, 1652), 22. Cf. also his explanatory examples, 65.

[146] On the contrary, he takes the opportunity to praise its virtues: 'Ergo in monodia repetitio juvat. Sed quoniam in re musica varietas prima est, quae in similitudine delectat; quae vero sine varietate & sine modo aliquo novo atque inexpectato continuantur, satietatem pariunt: repeti licebit frequenter idem prorsus vocum systema: sed utique ex uno loco transpositum in alium, ne idem omnino canamus, sed aliud: & una cum similitudine, dissimilitudo agnoscatur.'

Rhythmic Devices

Taisnier is one of the few authors on *musica reservata* to have taken rhythmic devices into account. His comments add new significance to certain passages in Coclico's *Compendium* and to the Besançon treatise, the only other sources that mention rhythm. The statement about *musica reservata* in the counterpoint section of the anonymous tract has puzzled scholars because of the difficulty of integrating it into current theories. The rule in question reads:

Third: one should tend to make voices progressing in diverse and (as far as possible) contrary motion unite at last in perfect consonances and return to a certain mode. However, in a continuous rhythm you will avoid the cadence (*clausulam*) so that there might result what is called *musica reservata*.[147]

A continuous flow not interrupted by too frequent cadences would seem to be a characteristic of this music. While it must be admitted that not all music identifiable with the style possesses this quality of continuous flow, this characteristic cannot be dismissed as cavalierly as does Meier[148] simply because Lasso's penitential psalms have rather pronounced cadences. Avoidance of the cadence, especially on the final of the mode, not to mention on perfectt consonances, and the preservation of a continuous flow are quite typical of the music of the progressive composers, though admittedly not confined to them.[149] Taisnier's expression, 'contrapuncta fluentia', may refer to this very uninterrupted flow and to the rather breathless quality of much of the new music.

The simplification of rhythmic procedure that Taisnier deplores in the music of his contemporaries is reflected in the attitude of Coclico towards the older complexities. Coclico dismisses *modus perfectus* and *imperfectus* as practically useless and ligatures as rarely applied.[150] On the other hand, *proportio tripla*, *sesquialtera*, and *hemiola temporis* are singled out by Coclico as 'maxime in usu . . . apud Musicos'.[151] The latter two, it will be recalled, are also mentioned by Taisnier as favoured by the modernists.

Etymology

A few words should finally be said concerning the derivation of the term *musica reservata*. Taisnier is of no help here except in that he fortifies two

---

[147] Schannat and Hartzheim (eds.), *Concilia Germaniae*, viii. 208.
[148] 'Reservata-Probleme', 85 n. 57.
[149] Zarlino, for example, devotes a chapter (*Istitutioni*, pt. iii, ch. 54) and part of another (ch. 53) to the harmonic implications of avoiding the cadence.
[150] *Compendium*, sigs. F3^v–4^r.   [151] Ibid., sig. G2^r.

characteristics of its usage that have become apparent in other sources. First of all, the term is not a technical one; secondly, it was customary among the chromaticists.

Most of the writers who use the term introduce it cautiously, as if it were not generally accepted. Taisnier, in the *Opus mathematicum*, implies it is colloquial: 'nova enim (quam reservatam volunt)'. Similarly, Coclico speaks of the 'Musica quam vulgo reservatam jactitant'—the music commonly called *reservata*. The Besançon anonymous also uses the phrase 'quam vocant musicam reservatam', while Hoffman restricts the term to the chromaticists: 'ab iis Musica reservata appellatur'. Evidently the expression was not sufficiently respected by the scholarly and technical writers who, had they endorsed it, might have been our most dependable sources. Men like Gallus Dressler, Glareanus, Heinrich Faber, all of whom must have known the term, eschewed it tactfully.

Taisnier's positive association of the term with the chromaticists, strengthened by Hoffman's attribution, enhances the probability that this music was called *reservata* because it was first practised in secret and privately. A document not previously introduced into this discussion demonstrates how closely Vicentino guarded his secrets at first. Danckerts passes on this story related to him by some Roman singers:

Several of them also told me that many many times they had begged the said D. Nicola to reveal to them this science of his either for a premium, or out of friendship or courtesy, and to teach them these two genera, chromatic and enharmonic, and he always replied that until he obtains a post suitable to himself, as for example the chapel of the pope, in return for the fifteen years he says he consumed before acquiring this science, he did not wish to teach it to anyone or even to show any example of it, lest the long-awaited fruit and reward for his many vigils and labours be taken from him by others. It was told to me that such an intention was expressed in a public instrument drawn up by M. Felice de Romaulij, Notary of the Auditor of the Apostolic Chamber, in Rome on 25 October 1549, in which he promised to five or six in the service of the late Cardinal Ridolfi (who were lovers of music) that he would teach them to sing various *cantilene* composed by himself in the said genera, with, however, the condition and obligation *in forma camerae* that at the penalty of two hundred or three hundred scudi, none of them might teach the said unused genera to any person alive for ten years, more or less, or speak or write about them in such a way that the knowledge of them might be revealed. This document, with the names of the obligated parties, may be inspected more minutely in the Acts of the said Notary (in case I have erred in the amount of the penalty or the period of time).[152]

---

[152] Biblioteca Casanatense, MS 2880, p. 9. Cf. De Brujin, 'Ghisilinus Danckerts', 149–50 for the original text in Italian.

It is easy to understand how those outside such a group might come to regard this music as 'secret' and 'reserved' for the initiated and how sufficient fascination might come to surround it to invite imitations and counter-products like Coclico's *Musica reservata*. This, however, is mere conjecture.

As to Hoffman's etymology, Meier is quite right in doubting its authenticity.[153] Hoffman assumes that *musica reservata* was so called because it was 'almost reserved for certain musical instruments'. He seems to associate this style too narrowly with chromaticism. It is true that the small intervals and the modulations of the experimental music were regarded by many as unsuitable to the voice, and Vicentino's compositions in this idiom were apparently never sung without instrumental support.[154] Yet Hoffman's derivation strikes one as too naïvely simple.

While it is tempting to identify the term with the circle around Vicentino, it must be remembered that Vicentino did not employ the term in writing, nor has any Italian usage ever been found.[155] The one source in the Italian language, that concerning Marini, was written in Neuburg, Germany, probably by a German.[156] The term, moreover, comes from the Latin rather than Italian, for when it is used in German by Seld and Ballestra it is inflected in the Latin manner. If it ever had an Italian past, it was probably absorbed into the German musical vocabulary through Latin, which in the northern countries was still the official language for musical instruction in the grammar schools.

Conclusion

Can Taisnier finally guide us to a satisfactory solution of the *musica reservata* problem? He certainly makes possible a safer definition of the term than has been feasible up to now. *Musica reservata* is clearly the experimental style that arose as the classical technique of certain followers of Josquin des Prez disintegrated under the pressure of representing the text. It lacked the control of resources, restraint, and homogeneity, the obvious symmetries and neat demarcations of the classical style. It is, in short, Mannerism,

---

[153] 'Reservata-Probleme', 86.

[154] Vincenzo Galilei testifies that he heard Vicentino's music 'at various times and places on a number of occasions' and emphatically points out that 'never was this sort of music sung without the instrument I mentioned [the archicembalo]'; *Discorso intorno all'uso dell'enharmonio*, MSS Galileiani 3, fos. 9ᵛ–10ʳ (ed. Rempp, 166).

[155] The phrase 'composti con dotta arte et reservato ordine', in the title of Vincenzo Ruffo's *Opera nuova* of 1556, should be translated simply as 'composed with learned art and restrained orderliness'.

[156] On this point, cf. Clark, 'A Contribution', 28.

a name adopted from art history to designate what only comparatively recently has been recognized as a movement separate from the traditional sixteenth-century idiom.[157] Like its artistic and architectural counterparts, this music tends towards overstatement. It is full of restless activity, rapid changes of mood and texture, sharp colour contrasts, unresolved tensions and asymmetries, and clambering ornamentation.

In the opinion of a traditionalist like Taisnier, adventures by his contemporaries into these uncharted regions of musical expression were blemishes, irrational departures from the established code. Many of the techniques he criticized were not new—they had been employed by Josquin des Prez and his contemporaries and even his predecessors. For this reason they could be justified, as Taisnier knew, by the 'models of the ancients'.[158] But the mastery of contrapuntal resources had engendered a self-conscious purity of style, to which Taisnier, like many theorists, subscribed. The mannerists, whose motto was to let the poetic text dictate the rules, found the purists' strait precepts confining. The unity of mode Taisnier missed in their compositions had to be sacrificed if the music was to bend to the poet's every turn of mood and image. Chromaticism, a resource still only vaguely understood, lay temptingly before the musical poet groping for telling new effects. The mannerist resorted to frequent changes of texture: from chordal declamation and homophonic movement with running divisions he turned to strict or free imitation. He interrupted the even flow of counterpoint to underline a word or phrase through passage-work, repetition, or sequence. Triple time might be exchanged for duple, or long sustained notes suddenly break the established pulsation. Meanwhile the revived art of improvisation restored to the singer his or her right and duty to project a personal participation in the emotions of the composer, unleashing the fantasy and posing another threat to the polished, precalculated art that Taisnier admired. All this and more, perhaps, was evidently implied in 'the music they called *reservata*'.

Addenda

After the present article went to press, a microfilm arrived of Taisnier's short introduction to the quadrivium: *Ioa. Taisnier Hannonii poetae laureati*

---

[157] A good case for adopting this term is made by Wolf, 'The Aesthetic Problem of the Renaissance'.

[158] Galilei, in fact, justified some of the new dissonance practices by reference to pre-Willaert composers. Cf. Palisca, 'Vincenzo Galilei's Counterpoint Treatise', above, Essay 2.

illustriss. ac reverendis. Card. de Burgos Mathematici de mathematicae quattuor quantitatum utilitate libellus (8 fos., n.d., n.p.).[159] This little primer contains essentially the same statement about the new music as found in the *Astrologiae*. However the word *reservata* is not used to describe the *musica moderna*, only the term *nova*. Moreover, the tone of the attack on the modernists is much more incisive than that of 1559. It is therefore of prime importance to fix a date for this *Libellus*.

The best clue to its date lies in the title Taisnier bestows upon himself in this print: 'Mathematicus' of the Cardinal of Burgos. This patron was Cardinal Francisco de Mendoza y Bobadilla, whom Charles V had sent to Rome as his representative and who, upon the emperor's recommendation, was made cardinal by Pope Paul III on 19 December 1544. In 1550 Mendoza was given the additional titles of Bishop of Burgos and Cardinal of St Eusebius.[160] Cardinal de Mendoza was a humanist, an avid collector of ancient codices, and an active participant in the Counter-Reformation and the Council of Trent.[161] Taisnier entered his service as choirmaster in 1552 in Rome just as the cardinal was preparing for a trip to Flanders. Although Taisnier had by now resolved to abandon his public musical career, he was glad to have the chance to return home at the Cardinal's expense, as he tells us in *Opus mathematicum*.[162] On their way they spent several months in Florence and Venice, stopped briefly at Trent, and eventually arrived in Malines.[163] Taisnier undoubtedly gave lectures on mathematics, as was his custom, wherever they stopped. It was also his custom to have something published in each city in Italy where he taught for any length of time. Quite characteristically, he chose on this occasion to assume the title of 'mathematicus', more a reflection of his aspirations than of his real services to the cardinal, which must have been purely musical. Since the only known copies of the *Libellus* are now in Italy and there is no record of Taisnier's return with the cardinal after their trip, it seems likely that it was published there in 1552.

The passage that contains the only significant variants from the 1559 version merits quotation in full:[164]

---

[159] I am much indebted to Prof. Napoleone Fanti of the Biblioteca Musicale 'G. B. Martini' in Bologna for rushing this to me after attempts to get the film from another library were unsuccessful.

[160] Cf. Conrad Eubel (ed.), *Hierarchia catholica medii aevi sive summorum pontificum S. R. E. cardinalium antistitum series*, iii (Regensburg: Libraria Regensburgiana, 1910), 31.

[161] Cf. *Enciclopedia cattolica*, viii (Florence, 1952), 678–80.

[162] p. 406.

[163] Cf. also Vander Straeten, *La Musique aux Pays-Bas*, iii. 231–2.

[164] *De mathematicae quattuor quantitatum*, fo. 8^r.

Estque Musica . . . antiqua &
moderna ab aliquibus cantoristis
noua dicta qui arbitrantur
impositionem unius aut alterius
diesis aut diaschismatis
diatonicum musices genus in
Chromaticum illico uerti
differentiam diatonici à
Cromatico & Enarmonico
penitus ignorantes
quorum ignorantiam
in nostro libro
de Theorica &
practica musica iam typis
subijciendo latius promulgabo
interea tamen uelim ut saltem
notarum ligaturas & ualores
in modo tempore & prolatione
subdiscant & motetorum
madrigaliumque, ut uocant,
tonos desinantque
caprarum more lamentationem
eructare & discant è gutture
melodiam atque symphoniam
cantus formare &
gargarizare
diuersa contrapuncta,
ut aiunt, parcat lector si
uulgaris & familiaris
nimis sit loquutio,
harmoniosa fluentia currentia per
minimam & semiminimam ad fugam
reiterata in modo perfecto et
imperfecto (etc.) . . .

Music is . . . ancient and
modern, called new by some
cantoristae who hold that the
application of one or the other
diesis or diaschisma immediately
turns the diatonic genre of
music into the chromatic. [They
are] completely ignorant of the
difference between the diatonic,
chromatic, and enharmonic. We
shall reveal their ignorance
more widely in our book
concerning theoretical and
practical music now undergoing
printing. Meanwhile, however, I
wish that they would at least
learn the ligatures and values
in *modus*, *tempus* and prolation
and the modes of [their] motets
and madrigals, as they call
them, and that they cease to
belch the lamentation in the
manner of goats and learn to
form the melody and harmony of a
composition from the throat, and
[that they cease also] to gargle
diverse harmonious, flowing
counterpoints, as they call them
(the reader must excuse this
expression, for it is so very
common and familiar), by means
of the minim and semiminim, in
fugue, with repetitions, in
perfect and imperfect mode
(etc.) . . .

This earlier version of Taisnier's attack on the *musica nova* reinforces several points made in the main body of this article. First, it brings Taisnier into closer rapport with the controversy that took place in Rome between May and June 1551 around Vicentino and Lusitano. Such a lengthy and bitter digression in the short space devoted to music can only have been provoked by the controversy, which affected Taisnier deeply enough to make him want to write a book to expose the ignorance of the chromaticists. This, it should be recalled, had also been Danckerts's motive in starting his treatise.[165] The immediacy of the issue in his mind is detectable in his reference to certain 'cantoristae' who hold ('arbitrantur') the use of the dieses and diachismata to be chromatic. In 1559 he states that this opinion was held by some ('ab aliquibus arbitrabantur'). Secondly, the older version suggests that Taisnier did not know the term *reservata* in 1552, supporting the belief that the modernists acquired this label in the north. In Rome their music was known simply as *musica nova*, as both Taisnier and Danckerts demonstrate.

[165] See above, n. 51.

10

Ut oratoria musica:
The Rhetorical Basis of Musical Mannerism

This and the following essay, 'Towards an intrinsically Musical Definition of Mannerism in the Sixteenth Century', were originally invited contributions to conferences on mannerism. The first was published in *The Meaning of Mannerism*, edited by Franklin W. Robinson and Stephen G. Nichols, Jr. (Hanover, NH: University Press of New England, 1972), 37–65. This book collected the six papers read at the New England Renaissance Conference held at Dartmouth College, 3 and 4 October 1970. The other five papers were on aspects of literature, by James V. Mirollo and Thomas M. Greene, of art history, by Samuel Y. Edgerton, Jr., on book-making, by Ray Nash, and on the concept of mannerism as applied in art history, by Henri Zerner.

The debate about mannerism and *maniera* among art historians grew to a climax in the 1960s. Among music historians, on the other hand, discussion of the concept was most intense in the 1970s. I had suggested in my article on *musica reservata* of 1959 (Essay 9 in this collection) that the qualities in mid-sixteenth-century music found objectionable by Taisnier were manifestations of a conscious cultivation of compositional manners. Henry Kaufmann developed this connection between *musica reservata* and mannerism in an extended chapter in his book on Nicola Vicentino, who was central to the movement that Taisnier deplored.[1]

The significance of mannerism as a concept and a term in the history of music was the focus of a conference organized by the Accademia Nazionale di Santa Cecilia in Rome under the direction of Nino Pirrotta, 'Manierismo in arte e musica', in 1973. Fifteen papers from that conference were published in *Studi musicali*, 3 (1974), though not actually printed until 1977. The second of my two essays introduced here appeared in that issue (313–31). Most of the speakers came to the conference with their own ideas of how mannerism in music might be defined, if they were willing to acknowledge its existence at all. Although there were many expressions of agreement with what one or another speaker said, no consensus emerged from the discussions. Those who were sceptical at the outset still were when they left, and those who held strong opinions about the term did not seem to have been swayed by the views of others.

Several strong threads were revealed in the conference papers and discussions. Many spoke of the difficulty of transplanting a concept such as mannerism from

[1] *The Life and Works of Nicola Vicentino* (American Institute of Musicology, 1966), 175–224.

one field, namely art history, to music. Most were careful not to define musical mannerism by analogy to other arts. It was easier to see a relationship between literary mannerism and music than with its manifestations in the figurative arts. Most of the examples of musical mannerism introduced by the speakers were, in fact, settings of poetry that was itself manneristic. The qualities that stood out in these works were departures from what several speakers called the classical style of the sixteenth century, which some located in the music of Josquin des Prez, others in that of Adrian Willaert. In the minds of some, the audacity of composers endeavouring to express intensely passionate texts was better classified as *seconda pratica* than mannerism. Others, particularly Edward Lowinsky, preferred not to make such a distinction. This stemmed from his effort to find in music the characteristics that art historians have identified as manneristic, therefore manifestations of restlessness, discomfort, imbalance, diverse and contradictory conceits, devices that shattered the sense of continuity in a composition, erratic and twisted melodic lines, exaggerations of harmonic departures, and sharp contrasts.[2] Many of these means were the core of what Monteverdi later called the *seconda pratica*.

There was little enthusiasm for calling an entire period of music, between the Renaissance and Baroque, Mannerism. Most recognized in this period works that could be called manneristic and others that were anti-manneristic, and agreed that some composers created both kinds. Participants disagreed whether Gesualdo should be considered a mannerist, as Glenn Watkins proposed.[3] Lorenzo Bianconi put forward as mannerist Achille Falcone, in whose *Ah dolente partita* he perceived artifices, alienations, and exaggerations—but always within the classical Renaissance practice—just as John Shearman regarded mannerism not as a break with the classical style but an eruption within it.[4] Lowinsky excluded Arcadelt, Willaert, and Palestrina, whom he used to set in relief as mannerists Giulio Fiesco, Francesco Manara, Pietro Taglia, and Gesualdo. Paolo Fabbri cited works of Monteverdi, while Helmut Hucke pointed to some translations of Italian madrigals set by Hans Leo Hassler in 1596.[5]

Next to the rather tentative applications of the concept by the Santa Cecilia participants, Maria Rika Maniates is whole-hearted and all-embracing in her book, *Mannerism in Italian Music and Culture, 1530–1630*. She claims an entire century for the movement, as an epoch between Renaissance and Baroque, 'which transforms renaissance concepts of music into baroque doctrine'.[6] One of the most interesting and original aspects of the book is the demonstration that theories of

[2] Lowinsky, 'The Problem of Mannerism in Music: An Attempt at a Definition', *Studi musicali*, 3 (1974), 131–218, repr. in *Music in the Culture of the Renaissance and Other Essays*, ed. Bonnie J. Blackburn (Chicago and London: University of Chicago Press, 1989), 106–53.

[3] 'Carlo Gesualdo and the Delimitations of Late Mannerist Style', *Studi musicali*, 3 (1974), 55–74. Watkins devoted a chapter to this aspect of Gesualdo's music in *Gesualdo: The Man and his Music* (Chapel Hill, NC: University of North Carolina Press; London: Oxford University Press, 1973), 95–110.

[4] Bianconi, ' "Ah dolente partita": espressione ed artificio', *Studi musicali*, 3 (1974), 105–20; John Shearman, *Mannerism* (Harmondsworth: Penguin Books, 1967).

[5] Paolo Fabbri, 'Tasso, Guarini e il "divino Claudio": componenti manieristiche nella poetica di Monteverdi', *Studi musicali*, 3 (1974), 233–54; Helmut Hucke, 'H. L. Hasslers *Neue teusche Gesang* (1596) und das Problem des Manierismus in der Musik', ibid. 255–84.

[6] M. Rika Maniates, *Mannerism in Italian Music and Culture, 1530–1630* (Chapel Hill, NC: University of North Carolina Press, 1979), 177.

tuning, harmony, counterpoint, chromaticism, and expression contributed to the rise and practice of mannerism. She does not fail to grant *musica reservata* its place, surveying the entire repertory of occurrences of the term once again, but unfortunately not casting out the spurious citations.[7] Maniates has probably not converted many of the doubters, but her book is a monument to a modern historiographic movement that, so far as music history is concerned, has not succeeded in transplanting the art-historical juncture between Renaissance and Baroque.

MANNERISM as a term denoting a stage in late Renaissance musical style or a transition to the Baroque is enjoying a certain vogue in scholarly writings.[8] If it is not being embraced with the enthusiasm that the term *Baroque* was forty years ago, part of the reason is that we have become sceptical of all period-divisions and blanket descriptions of them.

While in fields other than music enthusiasm for the term is also tempered with scepticism, music critics have a special reason to be hesitant in accepting new terms and concepts for musical phenomena. Every new critical insight or interpretation affects not only how music is heard but also how it is performed.

A new interpretation of early music thus transcends description to become potentially prescription. If a particular piece of music needs to be heard or understood a certain way, the performance ought to facilitate that way of hearing and understanding it. Only the art of the theatre shares this feature with music, but stage directors feel less compulsion to restore early theatre to its original mode of performance and are therefore less affected by changes in critical understanding. Performing an early work of music with the media and practices of more recent music is judged rightly as a violation of its very nature and is consequently avoided. An analyst who introduces modern concepts into the interpretation of Renaissance music may be turning performers away from a faithful rendering of a piece as surely as if he counselled vibratos or animated crescendos where none were contemplated by the composer.

---

[7] Ibid. 260–74.

[8] Robert E. Wolf, 'The Aesthetic Problem of the Renaissance', *Revue belge de musicologie*, 9 (1955), 83–102, and 'Renaissance, Mannerism, Baroque; Three Styles, Three Periods', in *Le 'Baroque' musical*, Colloques de Wégimont, 4 (1957), also in *Les congrès et colloques de l'Université de Liège*, 27 (1964), 35–80. ed. Suzanne LeClerx-Lejeune (Paris: Les Belles Lettres, 1963), 35–80; Claude V. Palisca, 'A Clarification of *Musica reservata* in Jean Taisnier's *Astrologiae*, 1559', *Acta musicologica*, 21 (1959), 133–61 (above, Essay 9); Beekman C. Cannon, Alvin Johnson, and William G. Waite, *The Art of Music* (New York, 1960); Henry W. Kaufmann, *The Life and Works of Nicola Vicentino* (American Institute of Musicology, 1966); James Haar, 'Classicism and Mannerism in Sixteenth-Century Music', *The International Review of Music Aesthetics and Sociology*, 1 (1970), 55–67; Don Harran, '"Mannerism" in the Cinquecento Madrigal?', *Musical Quarterly*, 55 (1969), 521–44; Maria R. Maniates, 'Musical Mannerism: Effeteness or Virility?', *Musical Quarterly*, 57 (1971), 270–93.

With this wide responsibility, the music critic enjoys the opportunity, not shared by art and literary critics, to hear his interpretations tested in performance. An anachronism will often be more glaringly exposed in the hearing of it than through intellectual reflection.

For these reasons it is perhaps more important to the music historian than to the art or literary historian whether mannerism is a concept imposed on the creative products of the late sixteenth century retrospectively or a quality consciously put there by their creators. The music critic, having experienced in falsified performances of early music the pitfalls of interpreting it by a methodology and aesthetic standards of more recent times, will feel more comfortable with the term *mannerism* if it can be shown that mannerism was for a composer of the sixteenth century a conscious approach to his art. It is particularly apropos that this be shown in the case of mannerism, because if it is not conscious or even self-conscious, is it truly mannerism? To choose a manner or imitate one is a style-conscious act, whereas a personal musical style is the result of a multitude of decisions made quite independently of any concern for style.

If it could be shown that composers, musicians, and observers of the musical scene in the second half of the sixteenth century recognized the phenomenon that has come to be called mannerism, we should accept with greater confidence than we do now the existence of a mannerist period or style in the late Renaissance or early Baroque. It would also add to our understanding of the relation of music to the other arts and to culture in general, because it would permit us to draw parallels, not by analogy, but through organic connections. The uncanny coincidence of mannerism in several arts at approximately the same time could be accounted for, not through evoking some illusory *Zeitgeist*, but by observing the transmission of ideas and techniques.

Neither the word *manierismo* nor its equivalent occurred in mid-sixteenth-century writings about music. But critics were conscious of a new departure, which they called *musica nuova*, *nuova maniera*, or *musica reservata*. As is often the case, we learn more about a new trend from its detractors than from its advocates.

Here is what one critic says about the new manners of composition in 1559 in a short section on music in a book on judiciary astrology. The author is Jean Taisnier, mathematician, doctor of laws, and choirmaster. In a digression from astrology, he announces that he is writing a book on the four mathematical disciplines in which he will treat music, both old and new. Of the new music, which he says some call *musica reservata*, he gives this opinion:

And whenever they endeavour to contrive something new, disregarding in their compositions the modes that rest on the principles of music, they commit a great mistake; neglecting the ligatures of notes, their values in mode, *tempus* and prolation; [modulating], as they would have it (the expression is colloquial, for music, properly speaking, is not modulated), harmonious, flowing, running counterpoints in minims and semiminims, *ad fugam*, with repetitions, in perfect and imperfect *modus*, through major and minor hemiola, by sesquialtera, sesqui-tertia, sesquiquarta, etc.[9]

Here Taisnier recites a virtual catalogue of new manners: he notes the disregard for the limits of the modes of plainchant through chromatic intervals and alterations; he deplores the neglect of the proper proportions between shorter and longer notes, as through the sudden introduction of many notes of small value, such as semiminims in running passages of embellishment or counterpoint, and the changes from triple to duple metre and back; he complains of the abuse of fugue and its mixture with chordal declamatory passages and of repetitions, which were frowned upon in the idealized style of the textbooks.

Perceptive as Taisnier is about the properties of the new style, he shows no understanding of the motivation for the devices he enumerates, many being intended to imitate the meanings, feelings, and conceits of the texts set by the composers using them. To Taisnier the devices are distortions of the accepted and beautiful manner of writing (*bella maniera di comporre*) such as taught by Gioseffo Zarlino.[10]

Taisnier became acquainted with the new style in two of the several breeding grounds of musical innovation—Rome and Naples—in the 1550s. In Rome a controversy flared up between the innovators and the defenders of the reigning practice. It is reflected in Nicola Vicentino's book, *The Ancient Music Adapted to the Modern Practice* of 1555.[11] Vicentino, who probably provoked Taisnier's tirade, gives us a key to what impelled composers to adopt certain of the devices: he counsels the composer to change the rate of movement of notes as a good orator would do:

---

[9] *Astrologiae iudiciariae ysagogica* (Cologne, 1559), 14–16; trans. in Palisca, 'A Clarification of *Musica reservata*', above, Essay 9, 252.

[10] *Le istitutioni harmoniche* (Venice, 1558), Proemio, p. 2. Here Zarlino praises the 'ordine ragionevole di componere con elegante maniera' (the rational orderliness of composing with an elegant manner) of Willaert. Vicentino, in *L'antica musica ridotta alla moderna prattica* (Rome: Antonio Barre, 1555), bk. iv, ch. 29, fo. 86ʳ, speaks derisively of those who think that fashioning melodies on the solmization syllables suggested by the vowels of a text is a 'bella maniera di comporre', which is achieved rather by appropriately expressing the sense and feeling of a text. See Maniates, *Mannerism*, 232–50.

[11] An English translation under this title, with introduction and notes, by M. Rika Maniates of *L'antica musica ridotta alla moderna prattica* will be published soon in the Yale Music Theory Translation Series.

The movement of the measure should be changed to slower or faster according to the words . . . The experience of the orator teaches us to do this, for in his oration he speaks now loudly, now softly, now slowly, now quickly, and thus greatly moves the listeners; and this manner of changing measure has great effect on the soul.[12]

Ut oratoria musica would have been a fitting motto of musical mannerism. There is hardly an author on music in the last half of the sixteenth century who does not dip into Quintilian's *Institutio oratoria*. It was one of the first printed books containing a discussion of music (Rome, 1470). It spread the idea that music is closely allied to oratory and that, like oratory, it has the function of moving listeners to various passions. In the section *De musica* (i. 11) Quintilian pleads for music that excites generous feelings and calms disordered passions. In the section *De divisione affectuum et quomodo movendi sint* (vi. 2) he classifies the affections and shows how the modulation of the voice differs according to the emotional circumstances of the speaker or character represented in a comedy or tragedy.

Despite the obvious links between music and oratory, no elaborate application of rhetorical theory to music appeared until 1599, and then not in Italy but in Germany. This was *Hypomnematum musicae poeticae . . . synopsis* [Notes for a synopsis of musical poetics] of Joachim Burmeister (*c.*1564–1629).[13] An elementary manual in musical composition written from a

---

[12] Ibid., bk. iv, ch. 42, fo. 94ᵛ. Except where indicated otherwise, all translations in this essay are mine.

[13] *Hypomnematum musicae poeticae ex isagoge cuius & idem ipse auctor est, ad chorum gubernandum, cantumque componendum conscriptam, synopsis* (Rostock: Stephan Myliander, 1599). Burmeister published two considerably revised versions of this treatise: *Musica* αὐτοσχεδιαστικη *quae per aliquot accessiones in gratiam philomusorum quorundam ad tractatum de hypomnematibus musicae poeticae ejusdem auctoris* σπωράδιω *quondam exaratas, unum corpusculum concrevit, in quâ redditur ratio I. Formandi & componendi harmonias; II. Administrandi & regendi chorum; III. Canendi melodias modo hactenùs non usitatô* (Rostock: Christoph Reusner, 1601), and *Musica poetica: definitionibus et divisionibus breviter delineata, quibus in singulis capitibus sunt hypomnemata praeceptionum instar* συνοπτικῶσ *addita edita studiô & operâ M. Joachimi Burmeisteri, Lunaeburg. Scholae Rostoch. Collegae Classici* (Rostock: Stephan Myliander, 1606; facs. ed. Martin Ruhnke, Kassel: Bärenreiter, 1955). The latter is translated in Joachim Burmeister, *Musical Poetics*, trans., with introduction and notes, by Benito V. Rivera, ed. Claude V. Palisca (New Haven, Conn.: Yale University Press, 1993).

Other German authors had noted relationships between rhetorical principles and musical composition, but they had tended to be analogical, such as Georg Rhaw's comparison between the eight parts of an oration and the eight modes of music (*Enchiridion utriusque musicae practicae* (Wittenberg: G. Rhaw, 1538), ch. 4) and Sebald Heyden's between grammatical signs and the various signs used in musical notation (*De arte canendi* (Nuremberg: Johannes Petreius, 1540)). Of the early authors only Gallus Dressler describes the task of musical composition in rhetorical terms: cadences on various notes of the mode are like comma, accent, and period (*comma, virgula, periodus*); pauses are inserted in music for emphasis, as at the name Jesus Christ in a motet, but also for elegance and suavity (*Praecepta musicae poeticae* (MS 1563), Magdeburg, Landeshauptarchiv, ed. B. Engelke, *Geschichtsblätter für Stadt und Land Magdeburg*, 49–50 (1914–15), 213–50.)). Clemens non Papa excels in the use of three ornaments in particular—syncopation, *vicinae clausulae*, and fugues. Dressler speaks of the *exordium*, middle, and end of a composition. These and other examples of rhetorical terms and concepts applied to music are given in an anthology of quotations in Martin Ruhnke, *Joachim Burmeister: Ein Beitrag zur Musiklehre um 1600* (Kassel: Bärenreiter, 1955), 135–8.

rhetorical slant, its approach was natural to an author brought up in the Latin school of the Lüneburg Johanneum, which had as the core of its curriculum the study of the Latin language, syntax, and rhetoric. After receiving the degree of *Magister* at the University of Rostock, Burmeister became cantor of St Mary's, the university church, and teacher of Latin in the city's Collegium.

In the second (1601) edition of the book, under the title *Musica auto-schediastike*, Burmeister eulogizes music as a higher form of oratory:

In the art of oratory, in so far as it has power, that power resides not in the simple collection of simple words, in the proper measuring out of periods, and although they be plain, in their exquisite combination, which remains naked and always even and equal. Rather it resides in those things in which charm and elegance lie concealed in ornament and through words charged with wit, in periods enclosing a range of emphatic words. Thus also this art [music], beyond the naked mixture of perfect and imperfect consonances, offers to the sense through the intermingling of dissonances a combination that similarly cannot fail to touch the heart . . . So that these things may deserve greater confidence, a single example may be selected from among many in the works of Orlandus [that is, Orlando di Lasso] in the song *Deus qui sedes {super thronum}* for five voices.[14] He interpreted the text 'Laborem et dolorem, etc.' so artfully; indeed he so portrayed it that through these very contorted inflections of intervals he put before the eyes the meaning of the thing [itself]. Certainly the mere regular interweaving of consonances does not accomplish this feat (*artificium*); rather the labour of craft and the learned syntax are swept away by the majesty of gesture and ornament. By Hercules, not Apelles, with the most accurate skill of his art, not Demosthenes, not Cicero by the art of persuading, deflecting, moving, and orating, would have better placed the burden of trouble and lamentation before the eyes, moved the ears, implanted these [feelings] in the heart than Orlandus did with this harmonic art.[15]

Some years earlier (*c.*1560), the humanist Samuel Quickelberg (1529—68) also praised the power of Orlando di Lasso (1532—94) 'to place the object almost alive before the eyes' (*rem quasi actam ante oculos ponendo*),[16] echoing the phrase *sub oculos subiiciendis* with which Quintilian describes the aim of the metaphor.[17] Another contemporary, the musician Gallus Dressler, cited Lasso's 'suavity and his skill in applying harmony to the words aptly and appropriately through ornament'.[18]

[14] Orlando di Lasso, *Sacrae cantiones quinque vocum* (Nuremberg: Joh. Montanus & Ulrich Neuber, 1562); modern edn. in Orlando di Lasso, *Sämtliche Werke*, ed. Franz X. Haberl, xix (Leipzig: Breitkopf & Härtel, 1908), 12–14.

[15] Burmeister, *Musica autoschediastike*, sigs. A2ᵛ–3ʳ. For the Latin text, see Burmeister, *Musica poetica*, facs. edn., *Nachwort* by Martin Ruhnke.

[16] Adolf Sandberger, *Beiträge zur Geschichte der bayerischen Hofkapelle unter Orlando di Lasso* (Leipzig: Breitkopf & Härtel, 1894–5), i. 56 n. 2. My translation of the full passage is in 'A Clarification of *Musica reservata*', above, Essay 9, 270.

[17] *Inst. orat.* viii. 6. 19.

[18] *Praecepta musicae poeticae*, ch. 15, quoted in Ruhnke, *Joachim Burmeister*, 137.

Lasso was for Quickelberg a master of the music called *musica reservata* and for Burmeister the model of musical composition generally, just as Adrian Willaert had been the model of perfect counterpoint for Gioseffo Zarlino a generation earlier and Josquin des Prez for Henricus Glareanus some years before that. If Josquin represents a classical moment in the music of the sixteenth century, Lasso is the epitome of mannerism. Few composers were such masters of the artifices of the composer-orator, and it is to Burmeister's credit that he identifies many of them, though we owe him little thanks, perhaps, for baptizing them with such names as *parrhesia* and *pleonasmus*, which to the non-rhetorician are more suggestive of fearful contagions than means of harmonic persuasion. Yet, in so far as a thing does not fully exist as a concept until it has been given a name, even Burmeister's pseudo-rhetorical terminology is better than none, and it has the advantage of descending from a venerable tradition.[19]

In a remarkable section of his *Musica autoschediastike* of 1601, expanded in his *Musica poetica* (1606),[20] Burmeister shows how one may construct with oratorical effect a sacred vocal composition by taking as a model the motet of Lasso *In me transierunt*.[21] I know of no other place where an author of the sixteenth century takes us step by step through a work as Burmeister does here, and that within only a few years of the composer's death. In his analysis Burmeister shows that this motet is a quilt of rhetorical devices, and he identifies ten of them. Even so, he fails to note other devices that he names elsewhere in the treatises and overlooks some figures recognized by other authors.

The first step in the analysis of a composition, Burmeister instructs, is its division into periods, or 'affections'. He uses the terms *period* and *affection* interchangeably, for he defines musical affection (*affectio musica*) as 'a period in melody or harmony terminated by a cadence that moves and

---

[19] The fullest and best-illustrated discussions of the musical figures are in the first two versions of the treatise: *Hypomnematum musicae poeticae*, ch. 12, sigs. G2^r–I1^v, and *Musica autoschediastike*, ch. 12, sigs. G1^r–L4^r. In the first of these the musical examples are in a special letter notation; in the second version, in mensural notation. *Musica poetica*, ch. 12, pp. 60–70, omits most of the examples, and the definitions of the terms are abridged. Rivera provides transcriptions of these examples in an appendix to his translation (see n. 13 above). Burmeister names twenty-five figures altogether. Most of his terms are borrowed directly from the rhetorical treatises, particularly from Lucas Lossius, *Erotemata dialecticae et rhetoricae Philippi Melanchtonis et praeceptionum Erasmi Roterodami* (Frankfurt: Petrus Brub, 1552). See Ruhnke, *Joachim Burmeister*, 147–60. However, a number of the terms are of his own coinage, a process he defends by the authority of Quintilian (*Inst. Orat.* viii. 3), who cited the Greeks as not averse to forming new words rather than continuing to labour under the poverty of language (*Musica autoschediastike*, sigs. A3^v–4^r).

[20] Burmeister, *Musica autoschediastike*, sigs. L4^r–M1^r, end of ch. 12; *Musica poetica*, ch. 15, pp. 71–4; see the translation of the entire chapter in the appendix to this essay.

[21] *Sacrae cantiones quinque vocum* (Nuremberg, 1562); *Sämtliche Werke*, ix. 49–52.

affects the souls and hearts of men'.[22] According to Burmeister's system, the periods of a composition, like those of an oration, fall into three main sections: the *exordium*, or introduction; the *corpus carminis*, the body of the song; and the *finis*, or conclusion.

In me transierunt of Lasso falls into nine periods, according to Burmeister.[23]

They cover the following phrases of the text:

Exordium	1.	In me transierunt irae tuae,
Confirmatio	2.	et terrores tui
	3.	conturbaverunt me:
	4.	cor meum conturbatum est.
	5.	Dereliquit me virtus mea.
	6.	Dolor meus in conspectu meo semper.
	7.	Ne derelinquas me
	8.	Domine Deus meus;
Epilogue	9.	ne discesseris a me.

Burmeister now analyses each of the segments in terms of the rhetorico-musical figures it contains. In the examples that follow, figures pointed out in Burmeister's analysis or elsewhere in his treatises are given in boxes □, figures named by Burmeister in his treatises but not specifically related to this example are given in square brackets [ ], and figures not recognized by Burmeister are given in curly brackets { }.

Exordium. Period 1. *Bars 1 to 20 (Ex. 10.1)*

Burmeister identifies this passage as an *exordium* with double ornament, meaning that there are two figures present: *fuga realis* and *hypallage*. By *fuga*

---

[22] Burmeister, *Musica autoschediastike*, sig. O2ᵛ.

[23] An analysis more attentive to the musical structure would produce eleven divisions:

			Psalms
Exordium	1.	In me transierunt irae tuae,	87: 17a
Confirmatio	2.	et terrores tui	} 17b
	3.	conturbaverunt me:	
	4.	cor meum	} 37: 11a
	5.	conturbatum est.	
	6.	Dereliquit me virtus mea.	11b
	7.	Dolor meus	} 18b
	8.	in conspectu meo semper.	
	9.	Ne derelinquas me	} 22a
	10.	Domine Deus meus;	
Epilogue	11.	ne discesseris a me.	22b

The text is split into even smaller segments than Burmeister acknowledges, if the cadences in Lasso's motet are really taken as the criterion for defining periods, as Burmeister instructs. (In *Musica poetica*, ch. 5, he implies that a period, or affection, is a section between two cadences.) Whereas a composer of the early 16th c. would have observed the integrity of the half-verses, Lasso splits the verbal message of three and a half psalm verses into eleven segments, each of which carries its separate musical message and is composed in a different manner.

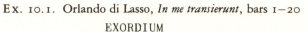

Ex. 10.1. Orlando di Lasso, *In me transierunt*, bars 1—20

realis is meant the texture in which every voice of a harmony after the first imitates the melody stated in the first voice through the same or similar intervals. Here the Altus imitates the Cantus by contrary motion (*hypallage*), except that the first note is transposed an octave down. This alteration of the subject gives this opening something of the character of a double fugue (*metalepsis*), particularly since the Bassus in bar 4 imitates the Altus exactly. The other voices have the subject in direct motion.

The *exordium* includes several figures that Burmeister points out as occurring in this motet, not in the analysis itself, but in other places in the treatise or in previous versions of the treatise. On the word 'irae' ('wrath') in the Cantus (bars 4–5) Lasso employs a *hypobole*, which Burmeister defines as a transgression of the lower limit of the ambitus of a mode, the mode in this case being Phrygian E to E.[24] Bars 4 to 7 of the Tenor 1 and Bassus are used to illustrate the *parrhesia* in *Musica autoschediastike*.[25] A *parrhesia* is defined as 'a mixture among other consonances of a single dissonance of the value of half a *tactus* [*tactus* = semibreve or a half-bar in the transcription]'.[26] The *parrhesia* is a special case of the *maius symblema*, a dissonance on the second part of a half-bar worth a minim, or half-note, of which there are numerous examples in this motet.[27]

Burmeister does not bother to point out the *syncopa*, or *syneresis*, a figure he describes as a dissonance in the beginning of a *tactus* that is bound to a sound that enters by syncopation in the preceding *tactus* and must be resolved (*dissoluta esse deberent*), in a consonance—the suspension of modern theory.[28] A more significant omission is the unorthodox leap of a minor sixth, frowned upon by the counterpoint rule books, with which the subject begins.

Oddly, Burmeister also says nothing about an important ornament occurring in bars 6–7, the evaded cadence. On the other hand, this device was recognized as a figure by Francis Bacon in 1605 in a passage apparently overlooked by musical scholars in the *Advancement of Learning*. Bacon's discussion of musical figures is worth quoting in full, as it seems quite independent of known Continental sources.

Is not the precept of a Musitian, to fall from a discord or harsh accord, vpon a concord, or sweete accord, alike true affection? Is not the Trope of Musicke, to auoyde or slyde from the close or Cadence, common with the Trope of Rhetoricke of deceyuing expectation? Is not the delight of the Quavering vppon a stoppe in Musique, the same with the playing of Light vppon the water?

Splendet tremulo sub Lumine Pontus

---

[24] Burmeister, *Musica poetica*, 64.

[25] Sig. L2^v.

[26] Burmeister, *Musica poetica*, 64.

[27] The *minus symblema*, of the value of less than a half-*tactus*, that is, a quarter-note or less, on the other hand, is not reputed to be an ornament or figure, Burmeister maintains, because it does not affect the hearing significantly (*Musica poetica*, 60).

[28] Ibid.

Are not the Organs of the senses of one kinde with the Organs of Reflexion, the Eye with a glasse, the Eare with a Caue or Straight determined and bounded? Neither are these onely similitudes, as men of narrowe observation may conceyue them to bee, but the same footsteppes of Nature, treading or printing vppon seuerall subiects or Matters.[29]

This plea for a comprehensive examination of the uniformity of nature is expanded in the *De dignitate et augmentis scientiarum libros ix* of 1623, and at the same time its language is clarified:

Tropus ille Musicus, *à clausulâ* aut *Cadentiâ* (quam vocant) cùm iam-iam *adesse videatur, placidè elabendi*; conuenit cum Tropo Rhetorico *Expectationem eludendi*. *Fidium sonus tremulus*, eandem affert auribus voluptatem, quam Lumen, Aquae aut Gemmae insiliens, Oculis . . .[30]

'To auoyde or slyde from the close or Cadence' and 'Cadentia . . . placidè elabendi' obviously refer to the deceptive or evaded cadence that Zarlino describes as 'fuggire la cadenza', and Thomas Morley as 'false closes'.[31] It is significant that an anonymous author in France, writing of musical figures somewhere between 1559 and 1571, singles out the evaded cadence as a favourite device of *musica reservata*.[32] Lasso and other masters of the new music depended greatly on the evaded cadence, which permitted them to break up their texts into short phrases for descriptive and affective emphasis, while maintaining harmonic continuity.

Bacon's expression 'Fidium sonus tremulus' in the Latin version helps us identify the 'Quavering vppon a stoppe in Musique' of the 1605 text as the vibrato, used at this time as an ornament in the playing of string instruments.

In *Sylva sylvarum*, published in 1627 after Bacon's death, the discussion of musical devices is integrated into section 113 of Century Two and is expanded at the end to include several more devices used by Lasso and his contemporaries. Now all the devices he mentioned earlier are included among the figures, or tropes, of musical rhetoric: vibrato, division (perhaps meaning diminutions of longer notes through trills and other ornaments), suspension, evaded cadence, fugue, and change from duple to triple and back:

---

[29] *The Tvvoo Bookes Of the Proficiencie and Aduancement of Learning diuine and humane* (London: Henrie Tomes, 1605), fos. 21ᵛ–22ʳ.

[30] *Opera Francisci baconis de Verulamio, tomus primus* (London: Ioannis Haviland, 1624), iii, ch. 1, p. 139.

[31] 'Being devised to shun a final end and go on with some other purpose' (Thomas Morley, ed. R. Alec Harman, *A Plain and Easy Introduction to Practical Music* (1597) (London: Dent, 1952), 111, 223).

[32] Anonymous, *De musica*, in Johann F. Schannat and Joseph Hartzheim (eds.), *Concilia Germaniae* (Cologne: J. W. Krakamp & haeredum Christiani Simonis, 1759–75), viii. 203–8. See Palisca, 'A Clarification of *Musica Reservata*', above, Essay 9, 275.

There be in *Musick* certaine *Figures*, or *Tropes*; almost agreeing with the *Figures* of *Rhetoricke*; And with the *Affections* of the *Minde* and other *Senses*: First, the *Diuision* and *Quauering* . . . [The passage omitted here is very close to the version of 1605.] The *Reports*, and *Fuges*, have an Agreement with the *Figures* in *Rhetorik* [*sic*], of *Repetition*, and *Traduction*. The *Tripla's*, and *Changing of Times*, haue an Agreement with the *Changes of Motions*; As when *Galliard Time*, and *Measure Time*, are in the *Medley* of one Dance.[33]

The progression of Bacon's thought from a recognition of the analogy between musical effects and the movements of the affections towards the identification of musical devices with the tropes, or figures, of rhetoric shows a growing awareness of the part musical artifices played in musical expression. Bacon's struggle for appropriate terms leads us to the conclusion that he arrived at this parallel of music and rhetoric through an independent observation of the ways of musical mannerism, which abounds in the Elizabethan and Jacobean madrigals, motets, and anthems.

Confirmatio. Period 2. Bars 20–6 (Ex. 10.2)

Burmeister likens the main body of the composition to the confirmation of an oration. The text of this central part of the work, he says, is impressed on the minds of the listeners in a manner similar to that of the confirming arguments of oratory.

The second period is adorned, Burmeister writes, with *hypotyposis*, *climax*, and *anadiplosis*. *Hypotyposis* 'is that ornament by which the significance of a text is so delineated that the music near the text is seen to acquire life'. Here is Quintilian's *sub oculis subiicere*. The syncopated repeated notes of 'et terrores tui' send a shiver through the voice parts like a spreading panic. At the same time the *climax*, a repetition of the same motive in stepwise progression in the Bassus, gives a sinking feeling. The texture of the four upper parts is subtly interwoven out of interlocking voice-pairs, each pair being immediately imitated by another, the technique called *anadiplosis*, which will be more clearly illustrated in the third period.

Period 3. Bars 26–32 (Ex. 10.3)

The parallel motion of bar 27 was considered out of style and cautioned against by Zarlino in 1558.[34] It was probably considered undesirable for the very reason it is effective here: it gives one the disconcerting feeling

---

[33] *Sylva sylvarum: or A naturall historie. In ten centuries* (London: J.H. for William Lee, 1627), 38.

[34] *Istitutioni*, pt. iii, ch. 45, trans. by Guy A. Marco and Claude V. Palisca in Zarlino, *The Art of Counterpoint, Part III of 'Le Istituzioni harmoniche', 1558* (New Haven, Conn.: Yale University Press, 1968), 194–5.

Ex. 10.2. Orlando di Lasso, *In me transierunt*, bars 20–6

AND YOUR TERRORS

Ex. 10.3. Orlando di Lasso, *In me transierunt*, bars 26–32

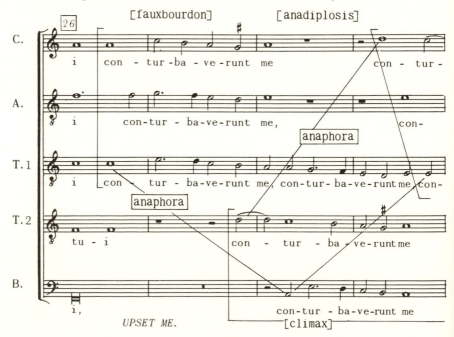

UPSET ME.

that the bottom has dropped out. Thus it illustrates perfectly the words 'conturbaverunt me' ('they upset me'). Burmeister elsewhere calls this figure *fauxbourdon*, the traditional name for the harmony of parallel sixths and thirds frequently improvised in the fifteenth century. As in period 2, the texture may be analysed as a set of interlocking imitations among several voice-groups (*anadiplosis*) in the succession Cantus–Altus–Tenor 1, Tenor 2–Bassus, Cantus–Tenor 1, Tenor 2–Bassus. Burmeister notes the presence of *anaphora*, or partial fugue, involving, that is, fewer than the full number of parts, in this case only two voice-pairs: Tenor 1–Bassus, bars 26–9; and Tenor 2–Cantus, bars 27–31.

Period 4. *Bars 32–45 (Ex. 10.4)*

Bar 33 introduces the most dramatic change in the piece. The movement slows down from a predominance of half-notes to the rhythm of the whole note (the semibreve, or unit of *tactus*).[35] The voices, alternating ties and attacks, produce a throbbing effect to represent the beating of the heart, a

---

[35] Some modern authors use the term *tactus* to signify the unit of measure, as in the German *Takt*. By *tactus* Burmeister means the beat, of which there are two to the bar. In ₵ the beat is on the semibreve, and there are two semibreves to the bar, totalling a breve, hence *misura alla breve*.

Ex. 10.4. Orlando di Lasso, *In me transierunt*, bars 32–41

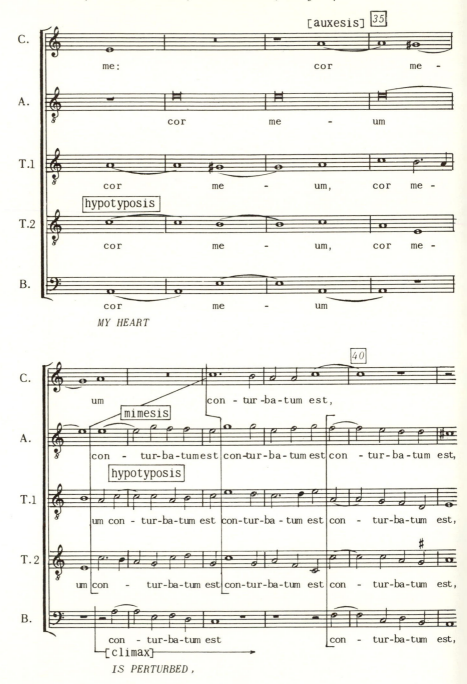

MY HEART

IS PERTURBED,

vivid *hypotyposis*. It is probably not incidental here that the rate of time-beating around 1560, when the semibreve was the unit of beat in ₵, was defined as the pulse of a man at rest. Thus the alternating voices are like the systole and diastole of the heart, to which Zarlino likened the down-beat and up-beat of the measure.[36] The 'cor meum' section also illustrates the device of *auxesis*, which Burmeister defines as occurring 'when a harmony made up only of consonances under one and the same text while being repeated once, twice, or three times or more, grows and rises'.[37] The 'cor meum' harmony rises an octave under the same text.

The phrase 'conturbatum est' ('is troubled'), which Burmeister seems to consider as part of the same period, literally disrupts the restful beating of the heart with its syncopations and contorted bass melody, descending by way of a *climax*, while the homophonic group of bars 36–8, Altus, Tenor 1 and 2, and Bassus, is answered through the device of *mimesis* by the highest four voices, then again by the lowest four.

Ex. 10.5. Orlando di Lasso, *In me transierunt*, bars 41–6

MY COURAGE DESERTS ME,

<hr>

[36] *The Art of Counterpoint*, 117.
[37] Burmeister, *Musica poetica*, 61.

Period 5. *Bars 41–6 (Ex. 10.5)*

The phrase 'dereliquit me virtus mea' ('my courage deserts me') introduces a new figure, *pathopoeia*, 'apt for arousing an affection, which is accomplished by introducing into the song semitones that do not belong to the mode or genus of the song'.[38] The F♯ in Tenor 1 of bar 41 is external to the Phrygian mode, as is the B♭ in Tenor 2 in bar 43. *Hypotyposis* is again present, as Burmeister notes, in the descending line of the Cantus and in the *hypobole* of the Bassus, which reaches below the modal ambitus in an image of despair.[39]

Period 6. *Bars 46–67 (Ex. 10.6)*

The only figure Burmeister identifies in this segment is the *fuga realis*, which begins at bar 52 in Tenor 2 at the words 'in conspectu meo semper' ('is continually before me'). The fugue subject is, indeed, ever before us, being repeated nine times in fifteen measures. But there are several other notable usages: half-step motion in the Cantus, inverted in the Tenor 2,

Ex. 10.6. Orlando di Lasso, *In me transierunt*, bars 46–67

---

[38] Ibid.

[39] Burmeister cites this passage as an example of the *hypobole* in his definition (ibid. 64).

[congeries]

C. in con-spec-tu me   o

[parembole]

A. me - us in con-spec - tu me-o sem-

T.1 us

fuga realis

T.2 us in con-spec - tu me - o

B. me - us in con-

IS CONTINUALLY BEFORE ME.

55

C. sem-per in con - spec - tu me - o

A. per, in con-spec-tu me - o sem-

T.1 in con-spec-tu me-o sem - per,

T.2 sem - per in con-

spec-tu me - o sem - per,

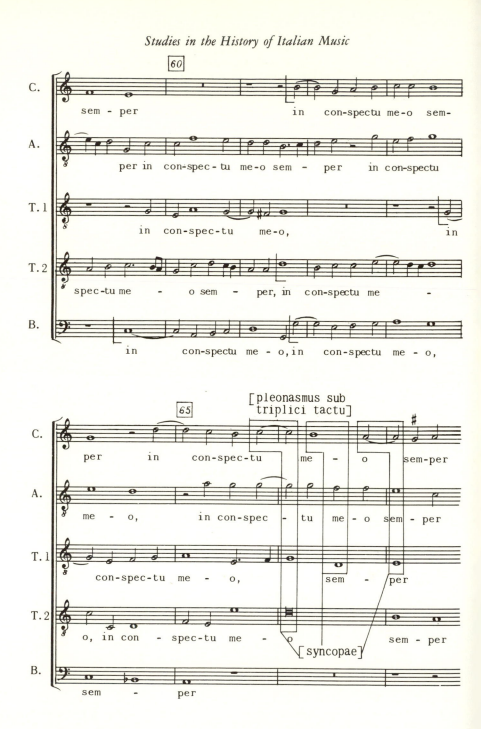

expresses the feeling of 'dolor meus', as does the *pathopoeia* through the added Bb in Tenor 1 and Bassus. *Congeries*, 'an accumulation of perfect and imperfect consonant intervals, the movement of which is permitted [by the rules of counterpoint]', lends a harmonic fullness and sweetness to bars 46–9 and 52–3.[40] At the end of the fugue, at bars 66–7, a figure that is the antithesis of *congeries*, an accumulation of dissonances over three beats (triple *pleonasmus*), brings the fugue to a close.[41]

Period 7. Bars 67–73 (Ex. 10.7)

After the *fuga realis* the sudden change to homophonic declamatory style (*noema*) is meant to attract the listener's attention to the plea 'ne derelinquas me' ('forsake me not'). The insecurity of the psalmist is characterized by the displacement of normal accents: the accented syllable *lin* of *derelinquas* falls almost every time on the second half of the beat. The pleading is made insistent with the use of *palillogia*, repetition of a melodic phrase at the original tonal level (bars 67–8 and 71–3 in the Bassus).

Period 8. Bars 73–7 (Ex. 10.8)

The displacement of the accented syllables persists in the *noema* on the words 'Domine Deus meus'. Only the Tenor 2 hits *Do* of *Domine* on the beat. This distortion of the normal metre insinuates in the listener again the uneasiness of the psalmist.

Epilogue. Period 9. Bars 78–87 (Ex. 10.9)

The close employs several rhetorical devices of repetition: the repetition of a motive in the Bassus a tone higher (*climax*, bars 78–80, 84–6); the corresponding repetition in the same place of a chordal section on the same text at a new level (*auxesis*); and the thrice-repeated sequence of notes in the Cantus, C–B–A–G#–A, in bars 81–2, 82–3, 86–7, the last time varied, which constitutes a *palillogia*. The composition seems to come to a close on bar 84 but is extended for a fuller close through four bars of *supplementum*. This Burmeister describes as 'the principal close, in which either the entire part-movement (*modulatio*) comes to a standstill or two voices or one holds fast while others scatter yet a small amount of melody . . . It is placed there so that it might penetrate the mind of the hearers more clearly by moving as the end approaches.'[42]

---

[40] Ibid. 65.

[41] The *pleonasmus* is defined as 'an abundance of harmony that in the formation of the cadence, particularly in its middle [i.e. between the preparation and the resolution], is made up of symblemas and syncopas, over two, three, or more half-bars' (ibid. 61).

[42] Ibid. 73.

Ex. 10.7. Orlando di Lasso, *In me transierunt*, bars 67–73

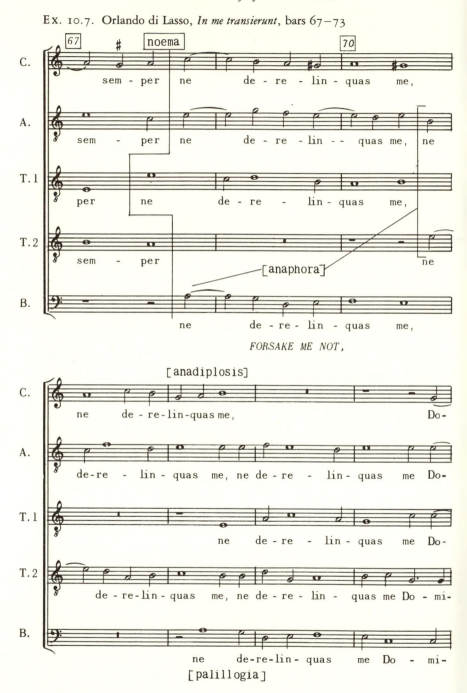

Ex. 10.8. Orlando di Lasso, *In me transierunt*, bars 73–7

This brings us to the end of Burmeister's analysis, which is given verbatim in translation in the appendix at the end of this essay. What is the significance of this analysis from the standpoint of mannerism?

Burmeister's purpose was to call attention to certain manners of composition so that young composers might imitate them. 'The separation of a song into affections is the division of the song into periods or affections for the sake of inquiring into the device (*artificium*) and for the sake of transforming it by imitation.'[43] A vocal composition is conceived as a collection of periods, each contrived by means of some artifice or more than one. Each period represents distinct affection through some manner inspired by the text.

However, not every device considered by Burmeister is expressive or has an expressive purpose. Many of them are simply constructive devices, artifices that grew out of a need to knit together the voices of a composition once the cantus firmus was abandoned as the main thread earlier in the century. The words *musica poetica* in Burmeister's title do not signify the art

---

[43] Ibid. 71.

Ex. 10.9. Orlando di Lasso, *In me transierunt*, bars 78   7

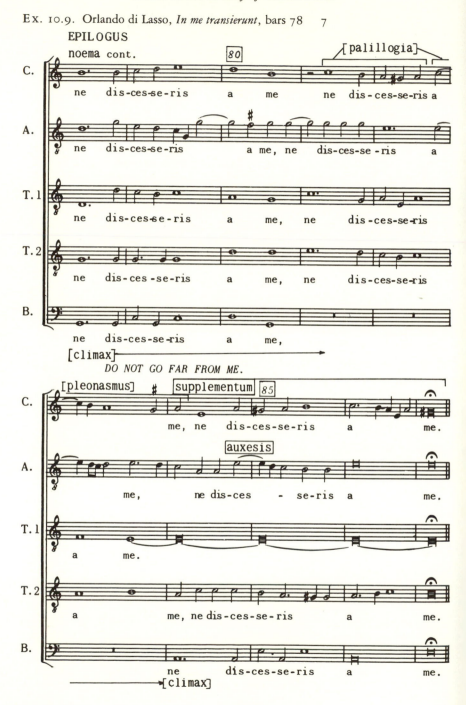

of poetic music or musical poetry, as some have inferred, but the art of 'making' musical compositions (from the Greek *poiein*): 'Musica poetica est ars quae *Melodias Harmonias* docet effingere et componere.'[44] *Fuga*, *mimesis*, *anadiplosis*, *hypallage*, and *anaphora* are various ways of interrelating the parts of a polyphonic composition. *Climax* and *auxesis* are means of achieving continuity. They are artfully disguised repetitions that permit the total sound to be renewed while details are being reused. The level of redundancy essential to musical coherence would be intolerable in prose, even in oratory. Consequently, music is a natural sanctuary for the rhetorical figures that involve repetition.[45]

Whether for reasons of artful construction or expression, a composition is strung out of devices or disparate manners of artful writing. The listener's attention at any moment is drawn to details, clever conceits that are integrated into the whole intellectually, not aurally as a flow of sound. There is less danger in music than in prose or poetry of losing continuity, because by its nature music moves on, impelled forward by the momentum of rhythm, the expectation of consonance after dissonance, the curve of the melodic line, and the march to the cadence. Laymen listening to *In me transierunt* may even be oblivious to the scattering effect of the succession of manners—particularly modern listeners, conditioned as they are by the variety of colours of instrumental music and accompanied vocal music. Many of the details must have escaped the notice of Lasso's contemporaries, too; this artful music was addressed more to singers, amateurs, and patrons than to church-going worshippers.

This music is for an in-group, one that understands Latin, is sensitive to the constructivist devices, recognizes the allusions, and enjoys mixed-media puns with words, sounds, and musical notation—it is, in a word, a *musica reservata*. It is not plain, transparent music, as Burmeister states in his preface to *Musica autoschediastike*, but elegant and artful. What Lorenzo Giacomini, a lover of music as well as a literary critic, said of Tasso applies as well to Lasso:

To consider first the beauty of style, he is not surpassed by any of the ancients or moderns in the choice of words—grave, sweet, harsh, sonorous, splendid, imperious—and in the loftiness and abundance of ornaments. And in those three

---

[44] Burmeister, *Musica autoschediastike*, sig. N2^r.

[45] Burmeister was able to borrow from rhetoric a number of the terms for figures of repetition: *anadiplosis*, in rhetoric the repetition of the last word of a period to initiate a new period, in music is the answering of one *mimesis* by another; *pallilogia*, in rhetoric the repetition of a word as opposed to a phrase, in music is a simple repetition of a series of pitches; *anaphora*, in rhetoric the repetition of the same word at the beginning of several periods, in music is the imitation of a musical subject in only some of the voice-parts.

[ornaments] to which the orator must particularly aim was he taught by the Master of all knowledge? Realizing that the Tuscan language, because it is sweeter than the Latin and less sonorous, needs a great boost of magnificence; recognizing that extreme clarity is but excessive ease of being immediately understood without giving the listener a chance to learn anything by himself, which, when joined by vulgarity and baseness, produces contempt and not pleasure in the alert listener, who disdains being treated as a child; with assiduous attention he banished from his poems loftiness, efficiency, and excellent grace, but not supreme clarity—not the clarity appropriate to that genre of speech, which, provided it reaches well the intellect, the end of all speech, avoids that excessive ease of being too quickly understood, and, departing from the customary, the humble and lowly, loves the new, the unused, the unexpected, the admirable, both in conceits and words. His words, interwoven with more artifice than in common speech, are adorned with a variety of figures apt for tempering that excessive clarity, such as interruptions, inversions, circumlocutions, hyperbole, irony, transpositions, and those that derive from the whole and the part, and the cause and effect. [His diction] thus is made to resemble not the winding, level, and muddy public alleys but the steep and rocky paths where the weak are exhausted and the unwary stumble. This manner of speaking—noble, rare, and remote from that understood by commoners—was assumed and followed by those famous sagas, which hence were told in a language other than that of usual speech . . . If we examine the conceits, we shall find them noble, vivid, apt for exciting the affections where and to the degree required, gracious, sharp, so that they have the power to keep the intellect of the listener alert and to stimulate him to press on.[46]

Like Tasso, Lasso avoids the transparent, plain, and uniform style of his predecessors and seeks constantly the unexpected, clever turns that inspire

---

[46] *Oratione in lode di Torquato Tasso* (Florence: F. Giunti, 1596), 14–17: '(per considerare primieramente la bellezza de lo stile) da nessuno de gli antichi e de' moderni riman vinto, ne la elezzione de le parole gravi, dolci, aspre, sonore, splendide, signoreggianti, e nel altezza e nel abondanza degli ornamenti, e in quei tre segnatamente, a' quali dover sempre avere la mira il dicitore, dal Maestro d'ogni dottrina fu insegnato? Egli considerando la Toscan favella come de la Latina più dolce cosò meno sonora grandi aiuti per la magnificenza ricercare, e conoscendo la estrema chiarezza, la quale altro non è, che soprabondante agevolezza di troppa subita intelligenza senza dare spazio al ascoltante d'imparare alcuna cosa da sè medesimo, aver congiunta seco viltà, e bassezza, e produrre dispregio e non aggradire al accorto uditore, ilquale si sdegna di esser fanciullescamente trattato, con sollecito studio procacciò a suoi poemi altezza, efficacia e leggiadra eccellente, ma non somma chiarezza; tale nondimeno, quale conviene a quella forma di parlare, che ben consegue la intelligenza fine d'ogni parlare ma sfugge quella soverchia agevolezza d'esser tosto inteso, et allontanandosi dal usitato, dal umile e dal abbietto, ama il nuovo, il disusato, l'inaspettato, l'ammirabile, sì ne' concetti sì ne le parole; le quali mentre fuor del vulgare uso artifiziosamente intreccia, e mentre le adorna di varie figure atte a temperare quell'eccesso di chiarezza, Troncamenti, Stravolgimenti, Circonscrizioni, Hiperbole, Ironie, Translazioni, e quelle che da luoghi del Tutto e de la Parte, de la Cagione e degli Effetti traggono origine, si rende simigliante non a le pubbliche stradechine e sdrucciolevoli o piane e fangose, ma a gli erti e sassosi sentieri, ove i più debili sogliono stancarsi, et i men cauti talor inciampare. La quale maniera di dire, nobile, peregrina e rimota da la vulgare intelligenza, fu amata e seguita da que' famosi saggi, i quali perciò furono detti in altra lingua lor proprio aver favellato . . . Ma se riguardiamo i Concetti, gli troverremo nobili vivi, atti ad eccitare affetti dove e quanto bisogna, graziosi, acuti, si che hanno forza di tenere desto l'Intelletto del uditore, e di sospingerlo a considerare più avanti.'

wonder and test the ingenuity of the listener to penetrate the thought and follow the thread of the music. In the lofty style of the late sixteenth-century motet and madrigal, as with the poetry of Tasso, the musician dons the toga of the orator and equips himself from the armoury of devices catalogued by Burmeister.

If musical mannerism was the product of the oratorical impulse of the mid-sixteenth century, it was also a cul-de-sac, because the means were not equal to the end, which was to move listeners the way an orator or preacher moves his audience. Mannerism was a stage on the way to fulfilling this aspiration. The true *stilus oratoricus* was the recitative style, which rewarded a renewed search for an adequate manner towards the end of the sixteenth century. In this, mannerism was a search, the Baroque a fulfilment.

APPENDIX

Here follows the entire analysis of *In me transierunt* of Lasso by Joachim Burmeister, as translated from *Musica poetica* (Rostock, 1606), ch. 15, pp. 73–4.[47]

This elegant and splendid composition, *In me transierunt*, by Orlandus Lasso is bounded by the Phrygian authentic mode.[48] The ambitus covers the entire system of steps, from *B* to *e"*.[49] The ambitus of the single voices is as follows: the Discantus, from *e'* to *e"*; the Tenor, from *e* to *e'*; the Bassus from *B* to *b*; the Altus from *b* to *b'*.[50] The basic temperament[51] is Orthian[52] or authentic. The interval of the fifth from E to ♮ [b] is manifested. Then, at the place where this fifth is divided into two equal parts, a *clausula affinalis* is introduced, as a full or *hexaphonos* (ἐχάφωνος) close [sixth to octave], which is usually formed there. The ambitus of the Altus and Bassus voices is plagal. Where cadences lead to a full close, that is, *triphonon* (τρεφωνῶυ [*sic*])[53] [third to octave], they are formed in a manner accepted through long use in this mode, with the ambitus of the lower voice mediated by a fourth, that of the higher voice by a fifth. Semitones appear in both their locations. The place of the lower semitone is the first interval of the authentic ambitus. The place of the higher semitone is plainly the same as the place of the lower, etc. The composition has its authentic and principal ending on *e*, which is the customary lowest sound of the ambitus of the tenor.[54] Secondly, it belongs to the diatonic genus of melody, since its intervals are formed mainly by tone, tone, and semitone. Thirdly, it belongs to the broken genus of antiphons[55] (*genus antiphonorum fractum*) [that is, the diminished or florid class of counterpoint]. For the notes are mixed with each other in unequal values. Fourthly, it has the quality of the diezeugmenon [that is, of the disjunct or hard b]. In the whole composition the disjunction of the tetrachords occurs between a and b.

[47] The footnotes give essential variants in the *Musica autoschediastike* (1601) and explain Burmeister's special analytical terminology.

[48] '. . . is in the diatonic genre, since the intervals employed proceed by tone and semitone. It is determined to be in the Phrygian authentic mode.'

[49] 'The system goes from A to e.'

[50] 'The Bassus from A to a; the Altus from a to a. The mediation of the Discant and Tenor is authentic.' In *Musica poetica*, Burmeister gives the conventional ranges of the modes rather than the actual ranges, which in this motet are: for the Cantus *e'* to *e"*, the Altus *g* to *a'*, Tenor 1 *d* to *e'*, Tenor 2 *c* to *e'*, and Bassus *E* to *c'*.

[51] Ch. 6, p. 41, explains that 'temperament' refers to the division of the octave into a fifth and fourth. When the *basis temperamenti* is a fifth, this is Orthian, when a fourth, it is *plagia*.

[52] Orthian, in the sense of 'high', from post-classical Latin *orthius*, meaning 'lofty' or 'high'.

[53] Rivera transliterates this as 'triphonal', signifying a cadence in which the major third is the penultimate interval in the structural voices. The terms *triphonos* and *hexaphonos* are defined in *Musica poetica*, ch. 5.

[54] The passage from here to the end of the paragraph is missing from *Musica autoschediastike*.

[55] Burmeister uses the term 'antiphon' for counterpoint, because it is more authentically classical than the vulgar Latin 'counterpoint'. He evidently contracted 'antiphonus' from the Greek 'phonos anti phonon', as 'contrapunctus' had been contracted from 'punctus contra punctum'.

Moreover, this composition may be divided conveniently into nine periods. The first contains the *exordium*, which is adorned with a double ornament, one of which is *fuga realis*, the other *hypallage*. The seven internal [periods] are the body of the composition and are equivalent to the *confirmatio* in an oration (if one may be permitted to compare thus one art to a cognate art). Of these [seven periods] the first is adorned with *hypotyposis*, *climax*, and *anadiplosis*. The second similarly, and, in addition, *anaphora* may be added. The third: *hypotyposis* and *mimesis*; the fourth in a similar way, and, besides, with *pathopoeia*; the fifth *fuga realis*; the sixth *anadiplosis* and *noema*; the seventh *noema* and *mimesis*. The last, that is, the ninth period, is like the *epilogue* in an oration. The composition has a principal close—arrived at through harmonies that are in keeping with the nature of the mode, to which the composition returns and is accustomed to touch again and again along with foreign harmonies—sometimes called the supplement of the final cadence, which bears very frequently the ornament *auxesis*.

11

Towards an intrinsically Musical Definition of Mannerism in the Sixteenth Century

On the origin of this essay, see the introduction to Essay 10.

THIS *convegno*, it might be said, is about a word in search of a concept. Scholars, quite rightly, prefer to put concepts into words. But having chosen the word, they often find that it has enriched or even unduly amplified the concept. Or the word may restrain a concept from reaching out to embrace what it ought logically to include.

'Mannerism' is such a word, richly overlaid with meanings; yet its inherent connotations limit our liberty to assign to it special meanings. To designate by it a style or period of art seems to me a contradiction, because 'mannerism' in common usage designates an abuse or lack of consistent style. At least in speaking about an art-work 'manner' is not the same as style, and 'mannerism' is even more removed from it. 'Mannerism', therefore, is inappropriate to describe a consistent, well-integrated, distinctive style. It implies, rather, an absence of genuine style.

On the other hand, it is a good term to describe a way of writing, representing, or composing that lacks consistency and integration of technique. A composer who throughout a piece or a particular repertoire uses a set of techniques quite homogeneously has a style rather than a manner or a set of mannerisms. But a composer who, consciously or not, seeks special and pronounced effects that differ in each piece or section of one—techniques that are not consistently identifiable as his own—such a composer does not possess a style so much as a set of manners. This is particularly true if a composer's vocabulary of devices is borrowed eclectically from different sources, such as from various other composers or historical periods. It seems appropriate to characterize a technique marked by such shifting, uncertain, or affected manners as mannerism.

I speak of composers rather than creative artists in general, because I am searching for a definition of mannerism in music that rests on musical facts and not analogies. For analogies cannot lead us to a definition. Simply to seek in music characteristics that determine mannerism in the other arts and to be satisfied with this process means ignoring whatever indigenous mannerist musical movements may have existed. Music history as a discipline must realize a definition of mannerism independent of the histories of other arts. Yet it ought not be in conflict with what mannerism is thought to be in the other arts. Such inconsistency would reduce our ability to communicate with historians of the other arts and render the task of historians of culture unnecessarily difficult.

Now 'mannerism', in the sense of a multifaceted style or wavering stylishness, can occur at any time in history, today as well as the fourteenth and sixteenth centuries. Mannerism with a small 'm' may be recognized whenever it occurs and be called by that name if the concept illuminates the phenomena it describes. On the other hand, to call an entire period of music history Mannerism is a mistake, in my opinion, because it glosses over the diversity of musical expression that every age has enjoyed. Even within the *œuvre* of a single composer there are mannerist pieces and others that are not.

By its nature mannerism is at least partly a conscious seeking after style or styles. Elsewhere I said: 'if it is not conscious or even self-conscious, is it truly mannerism? To choose a manner or imitate one is a style-conscious act, whereas a personal musical style is the result of a multitude of decisions made quite independently of any concern for style.'[1]

We should investigate the self-concept of the period or of composers that we are calling mannerist to see if there is some justification for the appellation in conscious creative practices. Confessions of aesthetic creed were rare in any period and particularly so in the sixteenth century; we have none by a Lasso or a Rore, or any major composer for the second half of the sixteenth century, as we have for the early seventeenth—for example Cavalieri, Peri, Caccini, Monteverdi, and Schütz. But for the earlier period we have the next best thing, statements by contemporaries and near-contemporaries.[2]

I shall summarize briefly some of the evidence I have found for the

---

[1] '*Ut oratoria musica*: The Rhetorical Basis of Musical Mannerism', above, Essay 10, 285. In the present paper I shall take the liberty of summarizing some points and citing a few musical examples and literary quotations from this article, since it is in a book not widely available.

[2] James Haar, in his paper at the Santa Cecilia conference, did cull from composers' prefaces and dedications a number of confessions of aesthetic purpose that are interesting in this context: 'Self-Consciousness About Style, Form and Genre in 16th-Century Music', *Studi musicali*, 3 (1974), 219–27.

recognition in the sixteenth century of the phenomenon of mannerism. My first texts are negative acknowledgements of its existence.

Ghiselin Danckerts, in defending his judgement in the debate between Lusitano and Vicentino, attacked certain practices of composers who wrote in the 'new manner' (*che compongono . . . alla nuova maniera*). Among these practices were the use of accidentals not merely to raise a note at a cadence or to avoid clashes called false relations or false consonances, but to achieve new melodic effects, destroying thereby the identity of the modes. He also complained of the abuse of note-against-note writing and the notational method called *a note nere*. According to Danckerts, the 'novel' composers justified these practices by claiming to follow Adrian Willaert:[3]

Il bello è che questi Musici compositori novelli dicono: senza consideratione alcuna che compongono di questa sorte per imitare la maniera di M. Adriano Willart, da loro chiamata nuova (benchè vecchissima et dalli Dotti et esperti compositori, per causa delli sudetti considerati disordini et errori repudiata sia) volendo essi cuoprire la crassa ignorantia et persuasion loro, sotto il scudo della profonda scientia del detto M. Adriano: le cui opere di canto figurato, e tra le altre la Messa di Mente tota: Il pater noster: Enixa est puerpera: ò salutaris hostia: Beata viscera: Petite camusette: Faulte d'argent: Sonnez mi don et infinite altre opere Musicali de la simil maniera da lui in diversi idiomi con mirabil osservation delli ordini de i tuoni predetti composte le quali se lasciamo qui per brevità sono degne di somma lode. si

The beautiful thing is that these novel musical composers say thoughtlessly that they compose in this way to imitate the manner of Mr Adrian Willaert, which they call new (although it is very, very old and repudiated by all the learned and expert composers because of the above-named deliberate disorders and errors). They wish to veil their crass ignorance and stubbornness under the shield of the profound science of the said Mr Adrian, whose works of polyphony, among others the Mass *Mente tota*, the *Pater noster*, *Enixa est puerpera*, *O salutaris hostia*, *Beata viscera*, *Petite camusette*, *Faulte d'argent*, *Sonnez mi donc*, and infinite musical works that deserve supreme praise, which I pass over for brevity's sake. They are composed by him in a similar manner in various styles with wonderful observation of the described

[3] Ghiselin Danckerts, *Sopra una differentia musicale*, pt. iii, ch. 2; Rome, Biblioteca Vallicelliana, MS R-56B, fo. 28[r–v]; Biblioteca Casanatense, MS 2880, pp. 96–8.

come ancho da molti eccellenti,
Dotti, Esperti, et lodati Musici
sono approbate: lodate: et
tenute per buone et eccellenti:
per la somma
bellezza d'aria,
et vaghezza di
armoniosa variatione, piene di
dotte et eccellenti
inventioni di Canoni, e
variate fughe et altre
artificiosissime imprese,
allegrissime: soavissime:
melodiosissime et con
maestrevole gravità
dilettevolissime a le orecchie
delli audienti et non sono come
li concetti della detta nuova
maniera composti da questi
compositori novelli,
meste, lugubri,
sconsolate et senza
aria bella alcuna;
le quali paiono in ogni passo,
tanto nel principio
nella fine: e nel mezzo:
quanto innanzi et
doppo il mezzo et per tutto 'l
canto sempre, una medesima cosa,
et un medesimo procedere di
consonantie senza variatione
alcuna: et senza assegnare la
determinata fine conveniente a
i suoi tuoni autentici ò
plagali, come se appartiene a
una bona compositione di Musico:
Onde paiono propriamente simile
al rumore, overo al bombilare
che fanno le api: quando
scacciate da i lor cupponi, et
avendo smarriti lor proprio et
natural nido, vanno errando in
frotta senza ordine in
perditione non sapendo ove
vadano. et oltra questi
disordini et errori, i detti
compositori novelli procedono

orders of the modes. For they
are approved, praised, and
held to be good and excellent
by many excellent, learned,
expert, and lauded musicians
because of the supreme beauty
of air, the charm of
harmonious variation—full of
learned and excellent
inventions of canons, and
various fugues, and other
most artful undertakings—
very cheerful, very smooth,
very melodious, and with
masterful gravity most
delightful to the ears of
listeners. And they are not
like the harmonies of this
said new manner composed by
these novel composers:
mournful, lugubrious,
disconsolate, and without
beautiful melody at all,
which appear to be always the
same song, the same thing,
and the same progression of
consonances without any
variation at all, whether in
the beginning, the end, or
the middle. [This they do]
without assigning a
determinate proper final to
the authentic or plagal
modes, as pertains to a good
composition by a musician. So
they seem truly comparable to
a noise or buzzing that the
bees make when, chased from
their honeycomb, they stray
from their natural haven and
go meandering in a swarm,
lost, without direction, not
knowing where they are going.
Besides these disorders and
errors, these said novel
composers proceed in their
songs so foolishly

ancho goffissimamente per	by leaping intervals very
intervalli di salti	uncomfortable for voices to
incommodissimi nel cantare	sing, without
delle voci de i lor canti,	any passage of nice runs
senza passaggio d'alcuna tirata	of seminimins or *crome*,
bella di semiminime o crome;	hewing always to the same
zappando sempre d'una maniera,	manner, in the guise of note
a guisa di nota contra nota,	against note, as if they were
come sogliono essere i canti	chants for lamentations
delle lamentationi: o de Morti.	or for the dead.

Danckerts recognized in this passage both a *maniera* of Willaert, abundant with artful devices, and a manner of his would-be imitators, modelled evidently on isolated and occasional mannerisms of Willaert, such as the homophonic passages in certain madrigals of the *Musica nova*.[4]

Jean Taisnier, choir director, mathematician, and astrologer, was another who criticized the practitioners of the *musica nuova* or *musica reservata*. He objected to their introduction of the chromatic diesis, which threw the modal system into disarray:[5]

Novumque quid ubi excogitare	And whenever they endeavour to
nituntur, suarum	contrive something new,
cantilenarum tonos,	disregarding in their
quae in Musicae principiis	compositions the modes that
sistunt, praetermittentes,	rest on the principles of
magnum errorem	music, they commit a great
committunt, notarum ligaturas,	mistake; neglecting the
valores, in modo, tempore, et	ligatures of notes, their
prolatione negligentes,	values in *modus*, *tempus* and
contrapuncta [modulantes],[6]	prolation; [modulating], as

[4] *Musica nova di Adriano Willaert* (Venice: Antonio Gardano, 1559), ed. H. Zenck and W. Gerstenberg in Willaert, *Opera omnia* (Rome: American Institute of Musicology), v (1957) and xiii (1966). Although published in 1559, the *Musica nova* almost certainly existed as a manuscript collection known as *La Pecorina* already in the early 1540s: see A. Carapetyan, 'The "Musica Nova" of Adrian Willaert', *Musica disciplina*, 1 (1946) (i.e. *Journal of Renaissance and Baroque Music*), 200–21; Edward E. Lowinsky, 'A Treatise on Text Underlay by a German Disciple of Francisco de Salinas', in *Festschrift H. Besseler* (Leipzig: VEB Deutscher Verlag für Musik, 1961), 231–57; Anthony Newcomb, 'Editions of Willaert's "Musica nova": New Evidence, New Speculations', *Journal of the American Musicological Society*, 26 (1973), 132–47.

[5] Jean Taisnier, *Astrologiae iudiciariae ysagogica et totius divinatricis artis encomia* (Cologne: A. Birckmann, 1559), 'Epistola dedicatoria'. The passage in question is quoted, translated into English, and analysed in my article 'A Clarification of *Musica reservata*', above, Essay 9.

[6] A present participial verb form is needed here to match the previous 'praetermittentes' and 'negligentes'. The phrase 'Musica enim sermonis elegantia non modulatur' suggests that the missing word is 'modulantes', which Taisnier, a linguistic purist, seems to challenge as being vulgar Latin. It was suggested at the Convegno of the Accademia Nazionale di Santa Cecilia in which this paper was presented that the 'vulgaris est locutio' applies to 'contrapuncta', a word that is often introduced apologetically as 'vulgar' Latin by Renaissance writers. But then 'Musica enim sermonis elegantia non modulatur' has no motivation.

ut aiunt (vulgaris	they would have it (the
est locutio:	expression is colloquial, for
Musica enim sermonis elegantia	music, properly speaking, is
non modulatur) harmoniosa,	not modulated), harmonious,
fluentia, currentia,	flowing, running
per minimam, ad	counterpoints in minims and
semiminimam, ad fugam,	semiminims, *ad fugam*, with
reiterata in modo perfecto, et	repetitions, in perfect and
imperfecto per	imperfect *modus*, through
hemiola majus et minus, per	major and minor hemiola, by
sesquialtera, sesquitertia,	sesquialtera, sesquitertia,
sesquiquarta, etc.	sesquiquarta, etc.

It is tempting to read into this passage a virtual catalogue of new manners: mutation of mode through chromatic intervals; the introduction of running passages, perhaps their juxtaposition with passages in slower motion; variation of metre; fugal as against declamatory texture; rhetorical repetitions. Taisnier's references are admittedly vague. It is not even absolutely clear whether he was for these devices or against them. But it certainly can be shown that they were practised in his time and in rather abrupt juxtaposition.

We may hear a number of them tumbling into one another in the motet of Lasso *Cum essem parvulus* (Ex. 11.1), composed in 1579 on the epistle of St Paul, 1 Cor., 13:11.[7] (Throughout this paper I shall use works of Lasso to illustrate my points not only because for me he is the greatest master of mannerism, but because his own contemporaries recognized him as exemplary in those techniques that I call mannerist. A further reason to draw upon his works for illustration is that some of his best examples are sacred motets, a genre that has been generally neglected in the study of mannerism in favour of the madrigal.)

Cum essem parvulus is a work in which texture and contrapuntal technique are completely subservient to the text. The phrase 'Cum essem parvulus' (When I was little) is set for the Cantus and Altus 1, to suggest the high voice of a child, and its motif is decorated with a semiminim run to evoke the diminutive movements of the child. Rather than compose afresh the reference to childhood each time it recurs, Lasso parallels the rhetorical repetition in St Paul with rhetorical musical repetition. The words 'loquebar' (I spoke), 'sapiebam' (I understood), and 'cogitabam' (I reasoned) are given to the lower voices, representing the voice of the

---

[7] F. X. Haberl, in the prefatory notes to Lasso, *Sämtliche Werke*, vol. xv, p. viii, states that this motet is inscribed 'August 1579' in Munich, Staatsbibliothek, MS 11. It was first published in *Motetta sex vocum* (Munich: Adam Berg, 1582) and is found in *Sämtliche Werke*, xv, as no. 570, pp. 72–3.

Ex. 11.1. Orlando di Lasso, *Cum essem parvulus, prima pars*

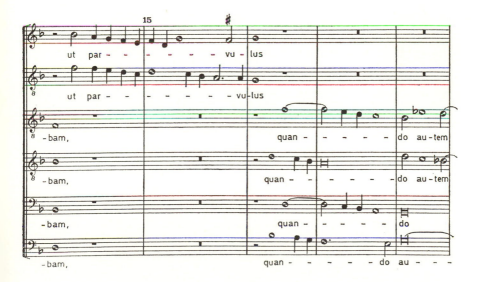

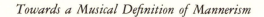

disciple. Until bar 16 the texture is almost entirely *nota contra notam*. Now follows an *ad fugam* section, the Altus 1–Bassus 1 pair imitating the Tenor–Bassus 2 pair. At the same time the idea of growth into maturity, 'quando autem factus sum vir', is suggested by the progressive expansion of the choir from two voices to six. The phrase 'evacuavi quae erant parvuli' (I set aside childish things), bar 22, combines with the childhood motif a new one for 'evacuavi'. A five-note motif surrounded by rests, it is perhaps a pun on the literal meaning 'evacuate'.

'Videmus nunc per speculum in aenigmate' (For now we see through a glass darkly), bar 28, issues from the mode by introducing in the Altus 1 an Eb on the word 'nunc'. The Eb is required again in the Bassus at 'in aenigmate', but the flat sign is cryptically omitted, perhaps as an enigmatic wink to the singer. The passage on the words 'tunc autem' (but then) build up towards the full-choir declamatory final section for the words 'facie ad faciem' (face to face). These words are repeated with emphasis through a change to triple metre by means of sesquialtera.

Taisnier could not, of course, have known this motet when he wrote his comments on the new style. I chose it because it packs into a short example all the devices he named. But he could have known motets, both by Lasso and others, that introduced these devices more sparsely, if none the less abruptly. The instability of texture, rhythm, and mode that are exhibited here must have offended his taste, nourished on the homogeneity and smooth contrapuntal flow of such a composer as Gombert.

Vicentino, whose campaign for chromatic music probably stimulated Taisnier's tirade, was an early defender of the oratorical style. He recognized in the unstable rhythmic pulse of the new music a striving to match the persuasiveness of oratory:[8]

il moto della	the movement of the
misura si dè muovere, secondo	measure should be changed to
le parole, più tardo et più	slower or faster according to
presto . . . et la esperienza,	the words . . . The
dell'Oratore l'insegna, che si	experience of the orator
vede il modo che tiene	teaches us to do this, for in
nell'Orazione, che ora dice	his oration he speaks now
forte, et ora piano, et più	loudly, now softly, now
tardo, et più presto, e con	slowly, now quickly, and thus
questo muove assai gl'oditori,	greatly moves the listeners;
et questo modo di muovere la	and this manner of changing
misura, fa effetto assai	measure has great effect on

[8] Nicola Vicentino, *L'antica musica ridotta alla moderna prattica* (Rome: Antonio Barre, 1555), bk. i, ch. 42, fo. 94ᵛ.

nell'animo, et per tal ragione	the soul. For this reason

nell'animo, et per tal ragione
si canterà la Musica alla
mente per imitar gli accenti,
et effetti delle parti
dell'orazione . . .

the soul. For this reason
music should be sung by
memory to imitate the accents
and effects of the parts of
speech . . .

Vincenzo Galilei turned in the course of his career from advocate to critic of some of the techniques of the mannerists. In the *Fronimo* (1568) he noted that the rule that tritones are to be avoided between the parts (that is, cross-relations)—by proceeding from an imperfect consonance to the nearest perfect consonance and by avoiding consecutive imperfect consonances of the same species—may be broken to 'imitate the words'.[9]

Patisce . . . eccezione ne
l'imitazione delle parole, come
bene lo manifestò
fra gl'altri eccelenti
musici in più luoghi
il famoso Adriano, et
particolarmente nel
principio di quella sua dotta
Canzone, che già compose
a sei voci, qual comincia.
Aspro core, et
selvaggio et cruda voglia,
dove passa più volte
(per esprimere con grazia tal
concetto) non solo dalla
Sesta maggiore alla Quinta ma
da una Terza maggior a l'altra
col movimento congiunto . . .

It suffers exception in the
imitation of the words, as
the famous Adriano
[Willaert], among other
excellent composers,
demonstrated in various
places and particularly in
the beginning of that learned
Canzone that he composed for
six voices, which starts, 'Aspro
core, e selvaggio e cruda
voglia', where he passes
several times (to express
with grace that idea) not
only from the major sixth to
the fifth but from a major
third to another by conjunct
motion . . .

The passage from the sonnet of Willaert published in the *Musica nova* is shown in Ex. 11.2.[10] Bars 2, 3, and 5 each contain the forbidden progression from major sixth to fifth between the Altus and Bassus, while bars 7, 8, and 10 contain the same progression between Cantus and Tenor. Parallel major thirds between the Bassus and Quintus in bars 2–3 and between the Quintus and Sextus in bars 7–8, produce highly audible false relations, while the prohibited movement from major third to fifth hardens the harmony in bars 5–6 between Bassus and Quintus.

[9] Vincenzo Galilei, *Fronimo, dialogo* (Venice: G. Scotto, 1568), 13. In the revised edn. of 1584 Galilei more correctly identified the piece as a sonnet.

[10] Adrian Willaert, *Opera omnia*, xiii, ed. Walter Gerstenberg (Rome: American Institute of Musicology, 1972), 54–60. In my example I have restored the original note-values to conform with my other transcriptions and with the contemporary references to note-values.

Ex. 11.2. Adrian Willaert, *Aspro core*, bars 1–10

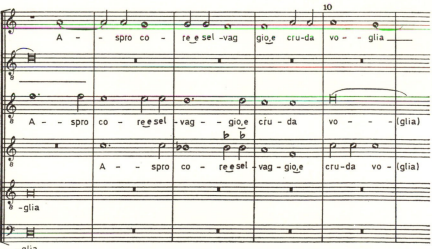

In his *Dialogo* (1581) Galilei cast aspersions on this very technique, mentioning the text 'Aspro core' but not Willaert's setting in particular, though the description fits the Willaert passage except for the absence in it of any seconds or sevenths:[11]

Dicono adunque, anzi tengono per fermo i nostri prattici Contrapuntisti, di avere espressi i concetti dell'animo in quella maniera che conviene, et di avere imitato le parole, tutta volta che nel mettere in musica un Sonetto, una Canzone, un Romanzo, un Madrigale, o altro; nel quale trovando verso che dica per modo d'essempio, Aspro core et selvaggio, et cruda voglia, che è il primo d'uno de' sonetti del Petrarca; averanno fatto tra le parti nel cantarlo, di molte settime, quarte, seconde, et seste maggiori, et cagionato con questi mezzi negli orecchi degli ascoltanti, un suono, rozzo, aspro, et poco grato . . . Altra volta diranno imitar le parole, quando tra quei lor concetti vene siano alcune che dichino fuggire, o volare; le quali profferiranno con velocità tale et con sì poca gratia, quanto basti ad alcuno imaginarsi; et intorno a quelle, che averanno detto, sparire, venir meno, morire o veramente spento; hanno fatto un'instante tacere le parti con violenza tale, che invece d'indurre alcuno di quelli affetti, hanno mosso gli uditori a riso, et altra volta a sdegno;	Our practising contrapuntists say, indeed they hold it for certain that they have expressed the ideas of the mind in the manner that is appropriate and have imitated the words every time that in setting a sonnet, a canzone, a romanzo, a madrigal, or other poem, when finding a verse that says, for example: 'Aspro core et selvaggio, et cruda voglia', which is the first line of a sonnet of Petrarch, they have sung among the parts many sevenths, fourths, seconds, and major sixths and by their means they have caused in the ears of the listeners a raw, harsh, and little grateful sound . . . Another time they will call it imitating the words when among their conceits there are some that say 'to flee' or 'fly', which they will declaim with such speed and with so little grace that it is enough to imagine it; and with words that mean 'disappear', 'faint', 'die', or 'extinguished', they have made the parts instantly be silent with such abruptness that instead of inducing any of those affections, they have moved the listeners to laughter and another time to

---

[11] Galilei, *Dialogo della musica antica, et della moderna* (Florence: G. Marescotti, 1581), 88–9.

tenendosi per ciò d'esser quasi	scorn, leading them to think
che burlati. Quando poi	they have been mocked. When
averanno detto, solo,	the text said 'alone', 'two',
due, o insieme;	or 'together', they have had
hanno fatto cantare un solo,	a single part sing, or two,
due, e tut'insieme con	or all together with uncommon
galanteria inusitata	elegance. Others in singing
hanno altri nel cantare questo	this particular verse of one
particolar verso d'una delle	of the *sestine* of Petrarch:
Sestine del Petrarca. Et	'Et col bue zoppo andrà
col bue zoppo andrà cacciando	cacciando Laura' have
Laura. profferitolo sotto	rendered this line with
le note a scosse,	quaking, undulating, and
a onde, et sincopando,	syncopating notes as if they
non altramente che se eglino	had the hiccups. And if the
avessero avuto il singhiozzo:	idea at hand (as at times
et facendo menzione il concetto	happens) was the roll of a
che egli hanno tra mano (come	drum, or the sound of
alle volte occorre) del romore	trumpets or a similar
del Tamburo, o del suono delle	instrument, they
Trombe, o d'altro strumento	have sought to represent to
tale, hanno cercato di	the hearing with their
rappresentare all'udito col	singing the sound of the
canto loro il suono di esso,	instrument without caring
senza fare stima alcuna, d'aver	that they pronounced these
pronunciate tali parole in qual	words in an unheard-of
si voglia maniera inusitata.	manner.

The passage cited by Galilei, it is believed, refers to Lasso's setting of *La ver' l'aurora che si dolce l'aure* (Ex. 11.3).[12]

Galilei went on to ridicule the use of black notes for the idea of dark and white notes for light, and the naïve descent to the depths of a vocal range for a line such as 'Nell'inferno discese in grembo a Pluto' (He descended into Hell, into the lap of Pluto) and asking singers to strain for their highest notes for 'Questi aspirò alle stelle' (This one aspired to the stars). To Galilei these attempts to express the verses missed the boat, because for him the real test was whether the listeners were moved to feel what the poet expressed.

Here, then, is the case against mannerism passionately argued. Not averse to using it himself on occasion, Galilei provided the best contemporary description we have of the mannerist approach.

---

[12] *Sämtliche Werke*, iv. 80. Oliver Strunk suggested this identification in *Source Readings in Music History* (New York: Norton, 1950), 316 n. 19.

Ex. 11.3. Orlando di Lasso, *La ver l'aurora che si dolce l'aura*, sixth part, bars 27–35

A later, but even more revealing testimony, this time a positive one, is that of a teacher of music and Latin in Rostock, Germany, a great admirer of Orlando di Lasso, Joachim Burmeister, who in 1599 published *Hypomnematum musicae poeticae . . . synopsis*[13] (Notes for a synopsis of musical poetics).

The central thesis of this book is that simple writing and speaking, whether in music or words, however harmonious and correct, lacks vigour. This force can come only from a mode of expression in which elegance, wit, and ornament are combined 'in periods enclosing a range of emphatic words'. Similarly in music the careful choice of artifices of composition appropriate to each phrase of text will place the subject before the listeners' consciousness and the feeling in their hearts. In the motet *Deus qui sedes (super thronum)* for five voices (Ex. 11.4),[14] Lasso, in Burmeister's judgement, 'interpreted the text "Laborem et dolorem, etc." so artfully; indeed he so portrayed it that through these very contorted inflections of intervals he put before the eyes the meaning of the thing [itself]. Certainly the mere regular interweaving of consonances does not accomplish this feat (*artificium*); rather the labour of craft and the learned syntax are swept away by the majesty of gesture and ornament.'[15]

In this book and in its revisions of 1601 and 1606 Burmeister developed a terminology derived from rhetoric for various technical devices and manners used in the composition of motets, particularly by Lasso and his contemporaries. He urged students of composition to study the manners of the great composers and to this end he instructed them how to classify and dissect a work into its component sections, periods, or affections, as he called them.

The analysis of a vocal composition is its examination according to a certain mode and the particular class of counterpoint to which it belongs [that is, *simplex*, *fractus*, or *coloratus*], and separating the song into its affections or periods, a determination of how the device by which each period unfolds may be considered and adopted for imitation.[16]

A vocal composition was conceived as a collection of periods, each based on a small segment of text, each contrived by means of some artifice or

---

[13] Rostock: Stephanus Myliander, 1599. The book was twice revised under the following titles: *Musica autoschediastike* (Rostock: C. Reusner, 1601); *Musica poetica* (Rostock: S. Myliander, 1606; facs., ed. Martin Ruhnke, Kassel and Basle: Bärenreiter, 1955).

[14] Lasso, *Sämtliche Werke*, xix. 12–14.

[15] Burmeister, *Musica autoschediastike*, sigs. A2ᵛ–A3ʳ. For the Latin text, see M. Ruhnke, *Nachwort* to the facs. edn. of *Musica poetica*.

[16] *Musica poetica*, ch. 15, p. 71: 'Analysis cantilenae est cantilenae ad certum Modum, certumque Antiphonorum Genus pertinentis, & in suas affectiones sive periodos, resolvendae, examen quo artificium, quo unaquaeque periodus scatet, considerari & ad imitandum assumi potest.'

Ex. 11.4. Orlando di Lasso, *Deus qui sedes*, bars 48–63

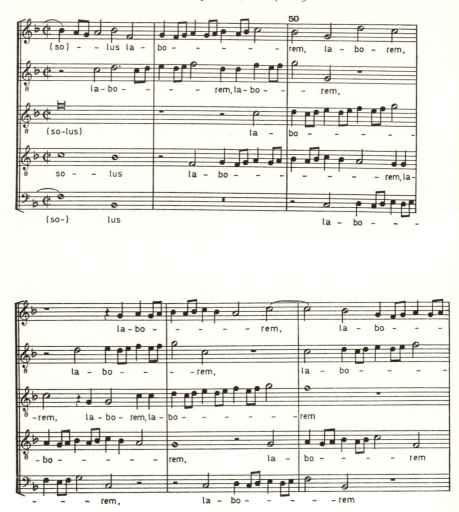

more than one. Through some manner inspired by a previous model, the composer made each distinct affection in the text manifest to the listener. Burmeister, indeed, defined *affectio musica* as 'a period in melody or harmony terminated by a cadence that moves and affects the souls and hearts of men'.[17] Although he recognized the importance of unifying a composition through a certain key mode, he concentrated upon the discrete techniques that were available to a composer appropriately to set particular phrases of text. A composition thus became a string of devices or disparate manners of artful writing. The listener's attention at any moment was drawn to details, clever conceits that he could integrate into a whole intellectually, if not aurally, as a flow of sound.

The repertory of rhetorical figures of music as enumerated by Burmeister and illustrated through citation of works by composers of the third quarter of the sixteenth century is well known.[18] Without inventorying his terms, some derived from Greek and Latin rhetoric, others coined by Burmeister himself, I would recall that they involve such devices as suspension, passing notes of more than normal duration, exceptionally high or low register of a voice, melodic sequence, fauxbourdon, various forms of polychoral or split-choir technique, word-painting, issuance from the mode, degree-inflection, contrast of imitative and homophonic texture, declamatory style, parallel motion, certain kinds of melodic and harmonic repetition, different types of fugue, and numerous others. Although Burmeister's list of figures is quite exhaustive, he did not name every musical device used in late sixteenth-century polyphony or recognized by other authors. For example, the evaded cadence and the change of metre, both noted only a few years later by Francis Bacon as musical figures or tropes, are absent. If we were compiling a list today, we would certainly add the false relation, melodic chromaticism, and the pedal point, for example.

While some of the rhetorical devices may partake of several functions, it is possible to distinguish three main categories:

1. *Constructive devices*. Fugue, imitation, repetition, declamatory style (*noema*), sequence, evaded cadence. These are mainly ways of organizing the motivic and melodic material to which the text is set. Although the material may reflect closely the nature of the text, the compositional method may depend more on factors such as position in the piece—beginning, middle, or end—the number of voices, or the need for contrast.

[17] *Musica autoschediastike*, sig. O2ᵛ: 'Affectio musica est in Melodia vel in Harmonia periodus clausula terminata, quae animos et corda hominum movet et afficit.'

[18] See M. Ruhnke, *Joachim Burmeister: Ein Beitrag zur Musiklehre um 1600* (Kassel: Bärenreiter, 1955), and above, Essay 10.

Certain texts, however, may demand a particular method or exclude certain modes of construction.

Although these were constructive devices, they were no longer the *sine qua non* of polyphonic music, as in the contrapuntal system of Zarlino. Rather, many of them had become a means of exhibiting skill and of giving the composition a learned, flowery eloquence. Descartes recognized this when he admitted in his *Compendium* of around 1618 that they led to *contrapuncta artificiosa* but hardly to the stirring of the passions:[19]

Sed etiam in medio cantilenae huius cadentiae fuga	However, in the midst of a vocal composition the evasion of such a cadence [one ending on an octave or fifth, preceded by a suspension]
non parvam affert delectationem, cum scilicet una pars velle videtur quiescere, alia autem ulterius procedit; atque hoc est genus figurae in Musica quales sunt figurae Rhetoricae oratione, cuius generis etiam sunt consequentia, imitatio, et similia, quae fiunt cum vel duae partes successive, hoc est, diversis temporibus plane idem canunt, vel plane contrarium, quod ultimum etiam simul facere possunt. Et quidem id in certis cantilenae partibus aliquando multum iuvat, quod autem attinet ad contrapuncta illa artificiosa, ut vocant; in quibus tale artificium ab initio ad finem perpetuo servatur, illa non magis arbitror ad Musicam pertinere quam Acrostica aut retrograda carmina ad Poëticam, quae ad motus animi excitandos est inventa, ut nostra Musica.	gives no little pleasure, as when a part seems to want to rest, while another proceeds onward. This is a kind of figure in music like the figures of rhetoric in oratory. Of this kind also are fugue, imitation, and the like. They occur when two voices sing successively, that is either the same melody at different times or the contrary melody, which last can be done at the same time also. This, indeed, sometimes is of much use in certain parts of compositions, for it leads to artful counterpoints, as they call them. But when this artifice is employed perpetually from beginning to end in a composition, I do not consider it to belong to music any more than acrostics or retrograde verses belong to poetics, which was invented for stirring the movements of the soul, like our music.

---

[19] René Descartes, *Musicae compendium* (Maastricht: Gisbertus à Zijll & Theodorus ab Ackersdijck, 1650), 55–6.

2. *Expressive, descriptive, or representational devices.* These are turns of melody, choices of intervals, melismas, chromaticism, harmonic effects, such as suspensions, minor or major chords, the sixth or fourth to the bass, false relations and dissonances, and rhythmic effects, such as syncopations. These may be imbedded within the constructive devices, or a constructive device may itself serve to illustrate an idea in the text, as fugue for flight.

3. *Technical virtuosity*: devices whose main object may have been to exhibit the composer's facility, cleverness, or mastery. These include esoteric kinds of fugues or canons, erudite allusions to other music, combinations of archaic and normal techniques, and hidden relationships. Many would be neither audible nor noticeable to the listener and would be intended as a challenge to the acuity of the composer's professional colleagues.

All these devices, to be sure, are the stock and trade of polyphonic writing. But when their purpose is to draw attention to themselves and through them to the text, then we have mannerism.

Burmeister, in a remarkable analysis of the motet *In me transierunt irae tuae* by Lasso,[20] showed that it was constructed of nine periods or affections, each based on one or more rhetorico-musical figures. I have considered this motet and his analysis of it in great detail elsewhere. Here I shall outline Burmeister's observations and give two brief examples of it before applying the method of Burmeister to another motet of Lasso, one that is even richer in rhetorical figures. It should be noted that Burmeister often failed to identify in his analysis of *In me transierunt* figures to which he had given a name earlier in the book.

Burmeister identifies the following periods and figures in *In me transierunt*:

Exordium

1. *In me transierunt irae tuae: fuga realis-hypallage* (fugue by contrary motion)

Confirmatio

2. *et terrores tui: anadiplosis* (multiple imitation by half-choirs), *hypotyposis* (text-expression and word-painting), *climax* (melodic sequence)—see Ex. 11.5

3. *conturbaverunt me: anaphora* (partial fugue)

4. *cor meum conturbatum est: hypotyposis* (word-painting), *mimesis* (simple imitation of a single voice by a voice-group)—see Ex. 11.6

---

[20] *Musica autoschediastike*, sigs. L4–M1, end of ch. 12; *Musica poetica*, ch. 15, pp. 71–4; see my English translation of the entire chapter in the appendix to Essay 10.

Ex. 11.5. Orlando di Lasso, *In me transierunt*, bars 20–6

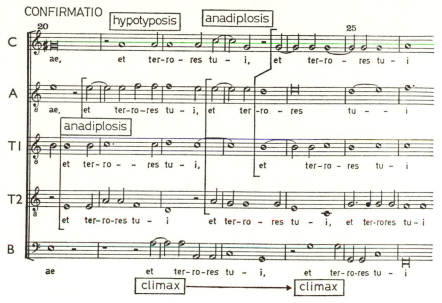

5. *Dereliquit me virtus mea: mimesis* (simple imitation of a single voice by a voice-group), *pathopoeia* (accidental note from outside the mode), *hypotyposis* (text-expression), *hypobole* (low register in a voice)

6. *Dolor meus in conspectu meo semper: fuga realis* (fugue)

7. *Ne derelinquas me: noema* (note-against-note declamatory style)

8. *Domine Deus meus: noema, mimesis*

Epilogus

9. *ne discesseris a me: auxesis* (harmonic repetition), *supplementum* (added close with one part holding a note)

The second period (Ex. 11.5) shows how the composer interwove a number of figures to set the words 'et terrores tui'. The voices enter in syncopation on secondary beats with the shuddering 'terrores' motif. Meanwhile there is a double *mimesis* or *anadiplosis* between voice-groups T.1—T.2—A. and A.—T.1—T.2—C., which adds force to the unsettling syncopated entrances. A *climax* or melodic sequence in the bass develops the rhythmic motif first announced in Tenor 2.

The most dramatic moment of the composition is reached with the words 'cor meum conturbatum est' (Ex. 11.6). Here the movement slows down to the pulse of the semibreve, the rate of which was likened

Ex. 11.6. Orlando di Lasso, *In me transierunt*, bars 31–41

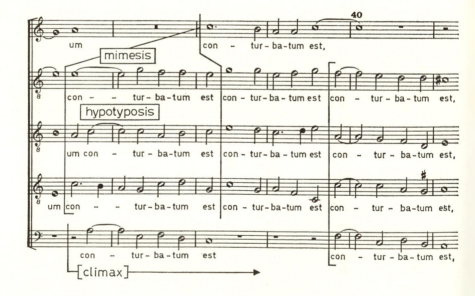

336

by a number of sixteenth-century authors to that of the human pulse. The voice-attacks on the syllables 'cor meum', alternating between the T.1—T.2—B. group and the Altus, simulate the systole and diastole of the heart, to which Zarlino likened the down-beats and up-beats of the measure.[21] The remainder of the example shows a *mimesis* at the words 'conturbatum est' and a *climax* not noted by Burmeister.

In me transierunt was published in Lasso's *Sacrae cantiones* in 1562;[22] twenty years later, in 1582, Lasso included in a collection of *Lectiones sacrae novem ex libris Hiob*[23] one of the most intensely manneristic of all his motets, *Diliges proximum tuum* for four voices, on a text from the epistles of St Paul to the Galatians, 5: 14–21.[24] Lasso broke up the text into even more minute parts than in the examples just studied; many of the musical periods set only one or two words. The following outline shows his division of the text:

(1) Diliges (2) proximum tuum (3) sicut te ipsum: (4) quodsi invicem mordetis, (5) videte ne ab invicem consumamini. (6) Dico autem in Christo: spiritu ambulate (7) et desideria carnis non perficietis. (8) Caro enim concupiscit (9) adversus spiritum; (10) spiritus autem (11) adversus carnem; (12) haec sibi invicem adversantur, (13) ut non, quaecumque vultis, (14) illa faciatis. (15) Quodsi spiritu ducimini (16) non estis sub lege. (17) Manifesta sunt autem opera carnis, quae sunt: (18) fornicatio, (19) immunditia, (20) impudicitia, (21) luxuria, (22) idolorum servitus, (23) venificia, (24) inimicitiae (25) contentiones, (26) aemulationes, (27) irae, rixae, dissensiones (28) sectae, (29) invidiae, (30) homicidia, (31) ebrietas, (32) comessationes, (33) et his similia, quae praedico vobis, (34) sic ut praedixi.

It is clear that Lasso divided his text not according to grammatical units as marked by punctuation signs, but according to affections, as Burmeister called them, groups of words each of which evoke a single idea, image, or feeling.

My aim is to focus attention particularly on periods 17 to 34, bars 55–106, but a quick review of the first sixteen periods will exhibit the variety of techniques Lasso calls into play:

1. bars 1–5, double fugue
2. bars 6–8, declamatory style (*noema*)
3. bars 8–11, fugue at the distance of a minim
4. bars 11–15, fugue by paired voices

---

[21] Gioseffo Zarlino, *Le istitutioni harmoniche* (Venice 1588), pt. iii, ch. 48, p. 207, trans. C. Palisca and Guy Marco as *The Art of Counterpoint* (New Haven, Conn.: Yale University Press, 1968; New York: Da Capo, 1983), 117.

[22] Nuremberg: J. Montanus & Ulrich Neuber.

[23] Munich: Adam Berg.

[24] *Sämtliche Werke*, i, no. 88, pp. 113–19.

5. bars 14–18, imitative duet
6. bars 18–23, fugue by contrary motion
7. bars 23–9, declamatory style, semitone motion outside the mode (*parrhesia*)
8–9. bars 29–35, imitative duet of lowest two voices, *hypotyposis* on the phrase 'For the flesh longs for that which is against the spirit'
10–11. bars 35–40, imitative duet of highest two voices, *hypotyposis* on 'the spirit, on the other hand, against the flesh'
12. bars 39–45, point of imitation
13. bars 44–8, point of imitation, three upper voices only
14. bars 48–51, imitative duet, soprano–tenor only
15. bars 50–3, imitative duet, alto–bass
16. bars 52–5, fugue

At period 17 (Ex. 11.7) begins the enumeration of the sins of the flesh: fornication, filth, immodesty, luxury, idolatry, sorcery, hostility, disputation, jealousy, anger, quarrelling, dissension, heresy, envy, homicide, drunkenness, and rioting. The section begins: 'Plain are the works of the flesh, which are . . .'. These words are set prominently in declamatory style (bars 55–61), ending on a D major chord. After a minim rest, the choir enters jarringly on a C major chord with the word 'fornication', bars 61–3. Three of the five chords in this declamatory passage are first-inversion chords, and the soprano's upward leaps span a major seventh, D–A–C♯, creating a false relation on the last two syllables. 'Immunditia' (filth) leads to an uncertain cadence. 'Impudicitia' (immodesty) and 'luxuria' are both set in a mock fauxbourdon style, 'luxury' illustrated besides by runs of semiminims. Lasso proceeds without transition from the E major chord in bar 69 to the D major chord of bar 70, which begins the passage 'idolorum servitus' (worship of idols) in a triple-time popular style of root-triads, ending with a false relation, perhaps to suggest false idols.

A diminished chord opens period 24, 'inimicitia' (bars 75–8). Two inner voices introduce an angry motif, framed by a tritone in the outer voices as they enter with the same motif. The alien sound of the tritone permeates this passage. For 'contentio' two half-choirs compete at the distance of a minim. The tritone is again exploited in 'aemulationes' (jealousy), while 'irae' brings back the motif of 'inimicitia'; the imitative duet of the upper two voices competes against the angry motif in contrary motion in the lower two voices.

Without stopping for a cadence, Lasso portrays 'rixae' with the pattern of

Ex. 11.7. Orlando di Lasso, *Diliges proximum, prima pars*, bars 56–106

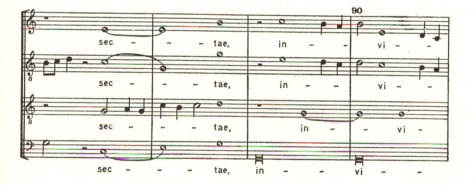

'irae'. 'Dissensiones' brings for the first time a succession of syncopations at the level of a semiminim, after which the voices break off one by one in a flourish of eighth-notes. The motif from 'inimicitia' returns for 'homicidia', the soprano now descending to its lowest note against a moribund cadence in which only the tenor moves, falling by a semitone. 'Ebrietas' is set in a staggering villanella style with the down-beat displaced by a minim. 'Comessationes' (rioting) displays in its steady motion in semiminims an early example of *stile concitato*. After an evasive move towards A minor, in bar 104, the cadence is avoided, and Lasso proceeds to a final cadence on D, the fifth degree of the mode. This weak close looks forward to the *secunda pars*, which is not half as interesting, being about such virtues as faith, goodness, and temperance.

Lasso marshalled almost all the *vitia* of counterpoint to portray the *vitia* of St Paul's homily. And he did so with breathtaking virtuosity. To make virtue of licence and brilliant display of combinatorial skill are two basic ingredients of mannerism. They are products of the tension between the desire to maintain a high order of contrapuntal craft and the impulse to match the images, ideas, and feelings of the text. On the one hand, the norms of polyphonic writing are demanding and restricting; on the other hand, only departures from them will draw attention to the individual qualities of a text. So figurative devices that are freakish or forbidden departures from the normal homogeneous style are discovered to have the power by their suggestiveness to evoke mental and affective reactions, at least in the most keen and initiated listeners. These figurative devices, like the oratorical figures, are really elements of language taken out of context. As Quintilian observed, 'every figure of this kind would be an error, if it were accidental and not deliberate'.[25] The manners that had developed in the motet, fauxbourdon hymn, falsobordone, psalm settings, madrigal, chanson, villanella, air, etc.—these are all exploited for their capacity to frame some particular thought. A composition becomes a chain of near-quotations, paraphrases, and often genuine parodies, a virtual gallery of manners. Correctly handled in their own terms, they appear out of ordinary musical context.

The mannerist composer was interested in projecting a text but not always in making the listener feel its emotional power. Indeed, the favoured texts often lacked emotional communicativeness and directness, depending rather on clever and involved images and rhetorical flourishes

---

[25] *Institutio oratoria* ix. 3. 3–4, trans. H. E. Butler (Cambridge, Mass.: Harvard University Press, 1921–2).

that hover around a subject concerning which the poet felt somewhat detached. The composer, in turn, set out to match the artifices of the poet and succeeded in stimulating the intellect more than the feelings.

Mannerism, therefore, must not be confused with the *seconda pratica*. Giulio Cesare Monteverdi rightly allied his brother Claudio with Rore and his followers. They were not mannerists, or at least they tried—not always successfully—to escape from the limitations of mannerism and to touch the feelings of listeners directly, without the mediation of the intellect. To this end they developed a vocabulary of dissonance, speech-like declamation, and exclamations, false relations, harmonic nuances, chromaticism, rhythmic contrasts, abrupt and dramatic changes of all kinds, and put them in the service of communicating the passions.

Galilei understood that there was a difference. He mercilessly denounced the mannerists for their graphic images and tricky conceits while championing the innovations of Rore and seeking to rediscover the power of ancient music. So such composers as Rore, Wert, Fiesco, Taglia, Luzzaschi, Monteverdi, Gesualdo, and Sigismondo d'India are better classed as *seconda pratica* composers than as mannerists. They wanted listeners to feel what they deeply felt. On the other hand, in much of their work Lasso, Marenzio, and Palestrina, for example, were truly mannerists. This is not to say that *seconda pratica* and mannerism never met. On the contrary, in many works of the men of both schools they were intertwined. But as mannerists they were more interested in playing upon the imagination of listeners and to astonish and amuse them while providing a vehicle for and amusing the performers.

Danckerts, Taisnier, Vicentino, Galilei, and Burmeister all bear witness to the awareness of the ends and means of mannerism in the sixteenth century. Its practitioners set out to represent and evoke through musical rhetoric the meaning, feeling, and images of a text. As Quintilian advised orators to vary their style according to the subject, Burmeister urged them to seek in exemplary compositions of the past models of compositional technique that fit the needs of individual segments of a text. The diverse manners had another object besides expression, as Burmeister implied; they gave the composition ornament and elegance. The clever coupling of text and musical device displayed the ingeniousness of the composer, as the fanciful juxtaposition of a motto and a graphic emblem in a device showed off the academician's erudition and wit. Virtuosity in the construction of varied musical textures as much as the power to delight with imagery was the test of the artful composer. A text was an obstacle course in which the

344

composer who surmounted each difficulty with ease and grace, often in competition with others who had set it before, won the acclaim of the singers and a few connoisseurs who alone could judge and appreciate the many clever images, in-jokes, and allusions.

12

Vincenzo Galilei and some Links between 'Pseudo-Monody' and Monody

This essay was first published under the above title in *Musical Quarterly*, 46 (1960), 344–60. I should note concerning this title that there is nothing really pseudonymous about the monody called 'pseudo-monody'. The label arose because 'monody' was thought to be a new genre of solo music brought about by a revolution in taste at approximately the time that recitative was invented. Caccini's airs and madrigals were considered to be monody, as was recitative. But verses sung to standard airs before 1600 were not. When a frottola was sung to lute accompaniment, this was 'pseudo-monody'. But a similar song by Caccini was monody. Vincenzo Galilei, in the passages quoted in this essay, recognized no such distinction, nor should we. The category 'monody' should include all these manifestations of solo song. Perhaps a polyphonic madrigal sung by a solo voice is a special case, but this is simply one of several possible arrangements that is no more 'pseudo' than when performed exclusively by instruments. The term 'pseudo-monody' is enclosed in quotation-marks in my title because it is a presumed but spurious category.

Galilei had no special term for the kind of solo music he was recommending in his treatises of 1589–91. Both he and Caccini had by then written settings for solo voice, Galilei on *terze rime* from Dante's *Inferno* and on the Lamentations of Jeremiah,[1] Caccini on madrigal texts.[2] Galilei cited as models the airs published by Petrucci early in the sixteenth century. In his mind there was no essential generic difference between these antique airs and those he would have written, save the greater emphasis he would have placed on expressing the affections and the freedom he would have felt to use more speech-like melody and chromatic, enharmonic, and non-harmonic effects.

Among the models Galilei named were the standard airs for singing poetry, such as the *romanesca* and *Ruggiero*. The debate about whether these were ostinato basses

---

[1] Letter, Pietro Bardi to G. B. Doni, Florence, 16 Dec. 1634, printed in Angelo Solerti, *Le origini del melodramma* (Turin: Fratelli Bocca, 1903), 143–5.

[2] In the foreword to *L'Euridice* (Florence: Giorgio Marescotti, 1600), Caccini claimed that he was composing songs in the new manner fifteen years earlier, and in the preface to *Le nuove musiche* (Florence: I Marescotti, 1601), ed. and trans. H. Wiley Hitchcock (Madison, Wis.: A-R Editions, 1970), 45, he named three madrigals that he composed and performed in Bardi's Camerata around that time.

or treble tunes continues. In his article 'Romanesca' in *MGG* (1963),[3] John M. Ward gives eight variants of the treble tune and one example of the bass, whereas Richard Hudson, in his article on the subject in *New Grove* (1980),[4] gives examples of the bass only. Whereas Ward defines *romanesca* as a widely distributed *aria per cantar*, a dance, and a theme for variations, Hudson calls it 'a musical scheme used particularly in Italy from about 1550 to 1650 for songs and instrumental variations', but his text emphasizes chordal patterns. Ward, in his article 'Ruggiero' (also 1963), defines the *Ruggiero* as a model for singing epic and other poetry and gives six examples of treble tunes and seven of basses. On the grounds that there is greater variation in the treble melodies and more consistency in the basses, Ward concludes that it was a bass-model.[5] Hudson, in his article 'Ruggiero' in *New Grove*,[6] goes to some length to show that it was a bass melody that supported a variety of discant tunes, though the bass also shows some variations. Nino Pirrotta, who drew everyone's attention to the unwritten tradition of the music of poet-singers, as recently as 1984 continued to maintain that 'bass patterns such as *passamezzo, romanesca, Ruggero*, and the like . . . were not melodies and yet were called arie because they dictated typical harmonic sequences and thus imparted to every melody built on them the air of having something in common'.[7]

Warren Kirkendale, in his study of the Aria di Fiorenza or *del Gran Duca*, also holds to the belief that the *romanesca* and *Ruggiero* are bass and harmonic progressions and puts the Aria di Fiorenza in the same category.[8] The numerous examples he published show that subsequent composers disregarded Cavalieri's upper parts and made variations on the bass, which in this case surely captures the essence of the music of the ballo, that is, its aria. Recently John Walter Hill has suggested that the Aria di Fiorenza may have had an earlier life as a polyphonic laude and points to a strambotto, *Sean fiume et fonti*, with a similar bass that may have had an earlier oral tradition.[9]

In a passage quoted in my present essay (p. 352), Galilei, who composed or arranged two of the earliest surviving specimens of these airs,[10] states unequivocally that the 'soprano' (probably in the sense of superius or treble) has the air in both the *romanesca* and *Ruggiero*, no matter what the accompaniment may have been.[11] This convinced me that the *romanesca, Ruggiero*, and similar standard airs were tunes for singing that were usually accompanied by simple triadic harmony in which the root of the chords was always in the bass, producing at once a standard

---

[3] Vol. xi. 778–9.

[4] Vol. xvi. 126–7.

[5] MGG xi. 1086–8.

[6] Vol. xvi. 323–4.

[7] 'Willaert and the *Canzone Villanesca*', originally in *Studi musicali*, 9 (1980), trans. Vanni Bartolozzi, in Pirrotta, *Music and Culture in Italy from the Middle Ages to the Baroque* (Cambridge, Mass.: Harvard University Press, 1984), 195.

[8] *L'Aria di Fiorenza, id est Il Ballo del Gran Duca* (Florence: Leo S. Olschki, 1972), 15–21.

[9] '*O che nuovo miracolo!*': A New Hypothesis about the *Aria di Fiorenza*', in Fabrizio della Seta and Franco Piperno (eds.), *In cantu et in sermone, for Nino Pirrotta on his 80th Birthday* (Florence: Leo S. Olschki; University of W. Australia Press, 1989), 283–322.

[10] These are in his unpublished 'Libro d'intavolatura di liuto' dated 1584, Florence, Biblioteca Nazionale Centrale, MSS Galileiani 6.

[11] Ward was evidently not convinced by this, since in his article in *MGG* xi (1963), 1088, he cites my present essay.

bass and a harmonic scheme. The two tunes have in common the fact that they were used for singing *ottave rime*, the poetic form of Ariosto's *Orlando furioso*, in which the line 'Ruggier, qual sempre fui, tal'esser voglio' (xliv. 61), may have given the tune its name.[12] Among the many settings of *ottave rime* using the *romanesca* tune is Monteverdi's *Ohimè dov'è il mio ben*, in which the pitches of the tune wander through the two voices, while the bass is decorated with diminutions.[13]

Galilei's advice to composers to model their songs on the antique airs rather than the more recent polyphonic madrigals found an echo in the work of Caccini. Caccini claimed to have learnt more from the conversations in Bardi's Camerata, in which Galilei's was a prominent voice, than from years of studying counterpoint. But he may have been steered in the direction of imitating the simple manner of the *villanelle alla napolitana* also by his teacher, the Neapolitan Scipione della Palla.[14] One or two of Palla's compositions survive in *Aeri raccolti . . . di diversi, dove si cantano sonetti, stanza, & terze rime* of 1577,[15] which offered a number of simple airs by Della Palla and others of the kind that could be adapted to a variety of poems.[16] The verses set here in this simple style are not the usual popular poetry but sonnets of Petrarch, Bembo, and Tansillo, and stanzas of Ariosto.[17] It was this elevation of poetic level more than the character of the melody and harmony that distinguished the new monodies from the 'pseudo' kind.

FOR a long time there was a tendency to dissociate seventeenth-century monody from earlier manifestations of solo singing, to regard it almost as the fruit of a miraculous conception in a body known as the Camerata. Advances in our knowledge of the second half of the sixteenth century, however, have revealed many subtle links between its music and the new style. Inevitably, the prestige of Vincenzo Galilei, the revolutionary hero of the Camerata legend, has suffered. Some would have him committed to the populous gallery of music history's exploded myths.[18] But before we allow

---

[12] Elena Ferrari Barassi suggests that the aria received its name from a Mastro or Masto Ruggiero of Naples, named in literary works as a famous singer. See her article 'A proposito di alcuni bassi ostinati del periodo rinascimentale e barocco', *Quadrivium*, 12/2 (*Festschrift* for F. Ghisi, 1971), 347–64. She insists that *Ruggiero* was a bass for improvising dances before it was a tune for reciting *ottava rima*.

[13] See Palisca, *Baroque Music* (3rd edn., Englewood Cliffs, NJ: Prentice Hall, 1991), 54–5, where Ex. 3-13 shows the relation between Monteverdi's music and the aria and bass of the *romanesca*. This madrigal was published in Monteverdi's Seventh Book (Venice, 1619), ed. G. F. Malipiero in *Tutte le opere* (Asolo, 1926; Vienna: Universal), vii. 152–9.

[14] The link to Neapolitan music is suggested by Nino Pirrotta in *Li due Orfei: da Poliziano a Monteverdi* (Rome: Edizioni RAI, 1969), 250. Caccini acknowledged in the preface to *Le nuove musiche* that some of the songs therein were 'musical studies I made after the noble manner of singing learned from my famous master Scipione del Palla', ed. and trans. Hitchcock, 43.

[15] Naples: Giuseppe Cacchio dell'Aquila, 1577.

[16] See Howard Mayer Brown, 'The Geography of Florentine Monody: Caccini at Home and Abroad', *Early Music*, 9 (1981), 147–68, esp. 147–52.

[17] Brown rightly points out in connection with these unassuming compositions, citing the present essay, that 'Vincenzo Galilei quite purposely and explicitly cited villottas, villanellas and canzonettas as models for the sort of monody he dreamed of'. Ibid. 152.

[18] Nino Pirrotta once said: 'Galileo's father cuts a poor figure as a theorist and has nothing, or next to nothing, original to say; nor does he ever face up to the real problem of how such a return (i.e. to ancient monody) was to be effected.' 'Temperaments and Tendencies in the Florentine Camerata', *Musical Quarterly*, 40 (1954), 172.

him to pass into this inglorious fate, we should take another look at this key figure.

It is true that the *Dialogo della musica antica et della moderna*,[19] on which Galilei's fame principally rests, fails to demonstrate how his ideal in music, the monody, was to be put into practice. The *Dialogo* was written in the heat of a controversy with Gioseffo Zarlino and under the spell of Girolamo Mei's fascinating discoveries concerning Greek music.[20] Partisanship on the one hand, and the enticement of unexplored fields on the other, temporarily distracted Galilei from the concrete problems of musical composition. In several essays that he completed shortly before he died in 1591, however, Galilei eventually made some very practical observations on composition in the new melodic idiom. These neglected manuscripts prove him to be one of the links in the very process of evolution, from the earlier improvised solo song to the monody, that his dialogue did so much to obscure.

Galilei's interest in vocal monody as a working art can be traced back to the period around 1570. Dating from about that time are the manuscript arrangements of favourite madrigals, villanelle, and similar pieces for solo voice and lute which he left in a copy of the *Fronimo* printed in 1568.[21] There we find in his hand thirteen melodies for bass or baritone—apparently Galilei's own voice-range. Twelve of them are provided with lute reductions of the four- and five-voice pieces from which they were taken. In all cases in which the original compositions could be consulted for comparison, the melodies given by Galilei turned out to be the original bass parts, with minor alterations. Evidently Galilei, who is said to have possessed a pleasant voice, entertained courtly circles and Bardi's Camerata by singing the bass part of well-known madrigals and part-songs while accompanying himself with a lute reduction of the original composition. The familiar music, thus enhanced by the familiar text, and heightened by the expressive accents of the voice, must have found greater favour than the bare instrumental reductions that are so numerous in the *Fronimo*. These so-called pseudo-monodies show that the experience of monody as a style of performance preceded Galilei's theoretical speculations. In the choice for arrangement of numerous pieces in homophonic villanella style, moreover,

---

[19] Florence: Giorgio Marescotti, 1581; facs., ed. Fabio Fano, Rome: Reale Accademia d'Italia, 1934.

[20] See C. Palisca, 'Girolamo Mei: Mentor to the Florentine Camerata', *Musical Quarterly*, 40 (1954), 1, and id., *G. Mei: Letters to V. Galilei and Giovanni Bardi* (American Institute of Musicology, 1960; rev. edn., Neuhausen-Stuttgart: Hänssler, 1977).

[21] These were briefly mentioned by Alfred Einstein in 'Galilei and the Instructive Duo', *Music and Letters*, 18 (1937), 360–8. The copy of *Fronimo* containing the manuscript, then in the Library of Baron Horace de Landau, is now in the Landau-Finaly memorial collection in the Biblioteca Nazionale Centrale in Florence. See below, Essay 13. A facsimile of one of the arrangements may be seen in *MGG* iv, pl. 54.

Galilei already displayed a decided partiality for uncomplicated harmony and a popular idiom. While his ardent espousal of the monodic principle awaited his contacts with Mei, the arrangements reveal a musical nature receptive to the new creed.

The next phase of Galilei's activity in behalf of the monody is well known and amply documented in the *Dialogo*. The theory of monody contained there was a musician's bowdlerization of a philologist's disquisitions, hastily compiled in a wave of enthusiasm over the novel ideals about Greek and modern music communicated by Girolamo Mei. The discussion remains on the plane of aesthetics, aloof from practical problems. Because of this the *Dialogo* could not, by itself, have put a composer on the path of modern expressive solo song, but it announced two important principles: (i) The emotional quality of a melody depends on the part of the range of a voice it uses—the high, medium, or low register—and on the tempo and metre; (ii) other independent parts should not be allowed to interfere with the voice, which expresses the text.

How these principles, so much exalted in the dialogue, were to be applied to modern music was a question Galilei left open in that work. In the essays referred to earlier there are finally some clues to the character of the monodic music Galilei advocated. The first of the essays is called *Discorso intorno all'uso dell'enharmonio, et di chi fusse autore del cromatico* (Discourse concerning the use of the enharmonic and regarding the originator of the chromatic).[22] The second essay is a short supplement to this and is entitled *Dubbi intorno a quanto io ho detto dell'uso dell'enharmonio con la solutione di essi*—'Doubts concerning what I have said about the use of the enharmonic with their solutions'.[23] These two brief works, which Galilei left unpolished when he died, were intended as supplements to his *Prattica del contrapunto*, a large-scale work in two books, completed by 1588 and twice rewritten before he died in 1591.[24] Galilei aimed to supplant Zarlino's contrapuntal theory, now obsolete by his standards, with a theoretical formulation of the harmonic practice of his own contemporaries. In the supplementary essays he sought to fill a need that became evident to him after he had finished the two books on counterpoint—a theory of chromatic and enharmonic music.

---

[22] Florence, Biblioteca Nazionale Centrale, MSS Galileiani, 3, fos. 3ʳ–34ᵛ, ed. Frieder Rempp, *Die Kontrapunkttraktate Vincenzo Galileis* (Cologne: Arno Volk, 1980), 163–80.

[23] MS Gal. 3, 63ʳ–68ʳ, ed. Rempp, 181–4.

[24] This treatise, or set of two treatises, found in several versions in MSS Gal. 1 and 2, is discussed in C. Palisca, 'Vincenzo Galilei's Counterpoint Treatise: A Code for the Seconda Pratica', above, Essay 2. In insertions to the second draft of bk. i (MS Gal. 1, fo. 75ᵛ; cf. Rempp edn., 37), and the second draft of bk. ii (Gal. 1, fos. 124ᵛ, 147ᵛ), both probably of 1590, Galilei promised that 'a discourse concerning the enharmonic and the invention of the chromatic genus' would follow the counterpoint treatise.

The chromatic and enharmonic, their history, and their use in modern music, are the main subject of the two essays. But a large part of the second discourse, the *Dubbi*, is devoted to the problems of melodic composition and accompaniment. Galilei sought a solution to these problems in the two sources most dear to Renaissance men: nature and Greek letters. To sing a simple melodic line was first of all the way of nature: when shepherds and workers in the fields were finished with their labours they turned for solace to the popular airs, which they sang to the strumming of some instrument. Many lessons could be learnt from these simple songs of the populace. A further model for modern music to emulate was provided by the odes and hymns sung to the cithara by the ancient poets. The imitation of nature and the imitation of the classics, two principles that dominated the literary discussions of the day, thus served Galilei as the fountainheads for his musical experiments.

The songs of the legendary Olympus, Galilei recalled, were said to have worked great wonders although they required only four strings, and for a long time poets were limited to four-string citharae. Galilei interpreted this to mean that a melody playable by such an instrument would have to be constructed out of four notes.[25] The secret of the Greek art, then, was limitation of means.

It is evident, finally, that using few notes is natural both in speaking and singing, since the end of one and the other is solely the expression of the states of the soul by means of words, which, when well expressed and understood by the listeners, generate in them whatever affections the musician cares to treat through this medium. Using many notes is artificial. This suits instruments, which are products of art, when playing alone; but not at all voices, which are produced by nature, whether they are singing alone or to the sound of some instrument. The latter kind of singing succeeds very well, provided one knows that part of the rules of counterpoint which is adequate for this end. And, if someone were to ask me, since it is natural for a man to be able to reach with his voice eight or ten notes without straining, whether therefore all notes outside the three or four used by Olympus were to be scorned—I would reply in this way. The three or four that Olympus used in one song were not apt for expressing all the passions and affections of the soul. The three or four notes that a tranquil soul seeks are not the same as those which suit the excited spirit, or one who is lamenting, or a lazy and somnolent one. For the tranquil soul seeks the middle notes; the querulous, the high; and the lazy and somnolent, the low. Thus, also, the latter will use slow metres; the tranquil the intermediate; and the excited the rapid. In this way the musician will tend to use now these and another time others, according to the affection he wants to represent and impress on the listeners.[26]

---

[25] Some scholars have proposed that the four-stringed cithara was capable of at least a six-note scale through stopping.

[26] *Dubbi*, MS Gal. 3, fo. 67^(r–v) (ed. Rempp, 181).

Galilei found that the popular airs sung by the people of his own time confirmed his theory of limited means.

As for his [Olympus] airs not requiring more than three or four strings or notes . . . still today many of our airs do not reach or extend beyond a compass of six notes, for example, the soprano parts of *Come t'haggio lasciato vita mia*, *Ti parti cor mio caro*, *La brunettina mia*, *La pastorella si leva per tempo*, the standard air for the *terza rima*, that of the *romanesca*, and a thousand others. The soprano of these, which is the part that principally provides the air, even when six or eight others are singing in harmony [*in consonanza*], does not extend beyond this number of notes.[27]

In a subsequent passage Galilei named two more popular airs of the many that fitted his description: 'l'aria della Girometta', and 'quella di Gianbrunaccio'.[28]

The airs listed by Galilei were among the most celebrated of his day and for many years afterwards. They were named repeatedly in the contemporary popular literature, and their texts often printed. The music, in most cases, can be found in collections of laude, villotte, and villanelle, or in intabulations.

Come t'haggio lasciato vita mia was published in *Il primo libro de villotte alla padoana intitolate Villotte del fiore* by Filippo Azzaiolo.[29] The melody has the range of a sixth (see Ex. 12.1). The lovely *Ti parti cor mio caro* was printed in the same collection and later in similar collections,[30] and it occurs also as a galliard in a collection of dances of 1551.[31] In different publications it is classed variously among 'due canzon nove', 'frottole', 'Villotte alla Padoana', and *canzone a ballo*, demonstrating the looseness with which these terms were applied.[32] The melody of this song (Ex. 12.2) also lies within a sixth.

---

[27] Ibid., fo. 64[r–v] (ed. Rempp, 181–2).

[28] Ibid., fo. 66[v] (ed. Rempp, 183).

[29] Venice: Antonio Gardano, 1557, p. 14. Also in Venice: Girolamo Scotto, 1560, p. 16. Transcribed in *Filippo Azzaiolo, Villotte del Fiore*, ed. Francesco Vatielli (Bologna: F. Bongiovanni, 1921), p. 6.

[30] Azzaiolo, 1557, p. 15. It is also in *Villotte alla padoana. Con alcune napolitane a 4 v.* (Venice: F. Rampazzetto, 1566), p. 38. Transcribed, from Azzaiolo, in *Azzaiolo*, ed. Vatielli, 15, and in his *Arte e vita musicale a Bologna* (Bologna: N. Zanichelli, 1927), 40. The song is quoted in Alessandro Striggio, *Cicalamento delle donne al bucato*, 1569, in a version *a 3*: see *Rivista musicale italiana*, 12 (1905), 833. The full text, with many variants, is in Andrea Calmo, *Lettere*, ed. Vittorio Rossi (Turin: Loescher, 1888), 423–5, where there is a bibliography of song-text collections containing the poem, among them prints of 1562, 1585, and 1588.

[31] *Intabolatura nova di varie sorti di balli da sonare per arpichordi, clauicembali, spinete, et manachordi* (Venice: A. Gardane, 1551), 8. Other instrumental arrangements in Giacomo Gorzanis, *Intabolatura di liuto* (Venice: A. Gardano, 1561), fo. 31[v] (printed in O. Chilesotti, *Lautenspieler des 16. Jahrhunderts* (Leipzig: Breitkopf und Härtel, 1891), 28), and in *Intavolatura di leuto da sonare e cantare*, Lucca, Biblioteca Comunale, MS 774. Its having been a dance-song is confirmed by Andrea Calmo's remark in a letter to 'Signora Cavriola' that he recalled dancing to its music; see *Lettere*, ed. Rossi, 293–4.

[32] Rossi gives the titles and whereabouts of these publications in Calmo, *Lettere*, 423–4.

EX. 12.1. *Come t'agio lasciato o vita mia*, from Azzaiolo, *Il primo libro di villotte alla Padoana*, 1557 (after Vatielli)

EX. 12.2. *Ti parti cor mio caro*, from Azzaiolo, 1557

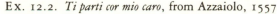

La brunettina mia is a frottola. Its text, once thought to be by Poliziano, is now attributed to Olimpo da Sassoferrato and identified with his poem *La pastorella mia*.[33] The song appeared in a number of the publications of Le Roy and Ballard in the years 1582 and 1585. My reconstruction (Ex. 12.3), omitting the missing contratenor, was put together from two of these publications.[34] The range here is again a sixth.

[33] See Alessandro Luzio, 'La Brunettina del Poliziano e Baldassare Olimpo da Sassoferrato', in *Nuova antologia*, 2nd ser., 23 (1880), 31–64. The full text is reprinted there, 36–9, from Olimpo's *Linguaccio* of 1523. The poem was also printed in *Canzone a ballo composte dal Magnifico Lorenzo de Medici*, etc. (Florence: B. Sermartelli, 1562).

[34] Superius: *Il primo libro dell'arie franzesi, italiche, & spagniuole, a 4 & 5 voci. Composte nouamente da Guglielmo Tessieri di Bretagna* (Paris: Le Roy & Ballard, 1582), fo. 36ʳ. Tenor and Bass: *Premier livre d'airs tant françois, italien qu'espagnol, reduitz en musique, à 4 & 5 parties par M. G. Tessier* (Paris: Le Roy & Ballard, 1585), fo. 36ʳ. Cf. François Lesure and Geneviève Thibault, *Bibliographie des éditions d'Adrian Le Roy et Robert Ballard* (Paris: Société française de musicologie, 1955), 213, 223. I am indebted to Dr John Ward for bringing these, as well as several of the other items, to my attention.

353

Ex. 12.3. *La brunettina mia*

The music of *La pastorella si leva per tempo* survives in collections of laudi printed in 1563[35] and 1609[36] and its text can be found in collections of popular poetry.[37] Serafino Razzi, in whose collections the song appears, set it to the words, 'Lo fratricello si leva per tempo'. When sung by nuns, this became 'La verginella si leva per tempo'.[38] The range of the soprano parts, once again, is that of a sixth.

Passing over the aria for the *terza rima* and of the *romanesca*, to which we shall return, we come to the *Girometta*, one of the most popular of all melodies in the late sixteenth and early seventeenth centuries. To a greater extent than the other songs, its tune was used to sing a variety of texts that followed the same poetic scheme. It is undoubtedly for this reason that Galilei referred to it as the 'aria della Girometta' rather than by its first line in the poem 'Noi siamo le tre sorelle', which is probably the prototype of its class.[39]

> Noi siamo le tre sorelle
> tutte tre polite, e belle
> tutte tre d'un gra, Girometta
> tutte tre d'un gra.

[35] Serafino Razzi, *Libro primo delle laudi spirituali* (Venice: F. Rampazetto, 1563), fo. 109ᵛ; repr. in Domenico Alaleona, 'Le laudi spirituali italiane nei secoli XVI e XVII e il loro rapporto coi canti profani', *Rivista musicale italiana*, 16 (1909), 33–4.

[36] Razzi, *Santuario di laudi overo rime spirituali* (Florence: B. Sermartelli & fratelli, 1609), 213.

[37] *Frottole composte da più autori, cioè La Pastorella si leva per tempo, Tu ti parti: o cuor mio caro* . . . (Florence, 1558); *Frottole composte da più autori, cioè Tu ti parti: o cuor mio caro— . . . La brunettina mia—La pastorella si leva per tempo* . . . (Florence, n.d.). It is interesting that three of the songs cited by Galilei should appear in the same collection. Concerning these prints see Luzio, 'La Brunettina', 41–2.

[38] Alaleona, 'Le laudi', 15.

[39] Complete text (from a print of 1587) in Severino Ferrari, 'Documenti per servire all'istoria della poesia semipopolare cittadina in Italia pei secoli XVI e XVII', *Il Propugnatore*, 13 (1880), 455–60.

Ex. 12.4. *Girometta*, from S. Razzi, *Santuario di laudi*, 1609 (after Alaleona)

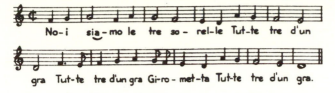

No-i sia-mo le tre so-rel-le Tut-te tre d'un

gra Tut-te tre d'un gra Gi-ro-met-ta Tut-te tre d'un gra.

Other poems sung to the same tune were: 'Chi t'ha fatto le belle scarpe',[40] and 'Chi t'ha fatto quella gunella'.[41] The *Girometta* melody can be found in a number of collections of laude.[42] The version given in Ex. 12.4 is that of Razzi, of 1609.[43]

Like several of the others, the *Girometta* tune served also as a dance piece. Ciro Spontone, a friend of Ercole Bottrigari, paid tribute to its versatility in his dialogue, *Il Botrigaro* (1589), recalling how in Bologna he had heard

the song 'Chi t'ha fatto quelle scarpette che ti stan si ben, Girometta?' sung by children, sung now to the lute, now to the viol, now to the harpsichord, or with the *pive* at a dance, and finally, as music for trombones, cornetts, cornemuses, played by excellent musicians at the railing of the Palazzo Maggiore on certain holidays to the very great satisfaction of the listening public.[44]

From time to time the *Girometta* received new texts, usually parodies of the prototype or spiritual texts adapted to its poetic scheme. But such a tune was not truly a melodic formula, like an aria for singing *terze rime*, *ottave rime*, or sonnets, which was intended by the composer to serve promiscuously a variety of poetic texts within a certain genre. It is significant that Galilei, who must have used many of the formulas in entertaining the Florentine nobility with verses sung to the lute, grouped together 'l'aria comune della terza rima, e quella della romanesca'. The latter tune was used to sing *ottave rime*.[45] Much more important is his revelation that these

---

[40] See ibid. 438.

[41] *Il terzo libro delle villotte del fiore alla padoana* (Venice: A. Gardano, 1569), 6.

[42] Razzi, 1563, 1609; Matteo Coferati, *Corona di sacre canzoni* (Florence: G. F. Barbetti, 1675; Eredi di F. Onofri, 1689; etc.). A version of the melody in the major mode is in Pietro Millioni, *Corona del 1°, 2° e 3° libro d'intavolatura di chitarra spagnola* (Turin, 1635), 61; facs. in Johannes Wolf, *Musikalische Schrifttafeln*, 2nd edn. (Bücheburg, Leipzig: Kistner & Siegel, 1927), pl. 65. An exhaustive bibliography on the *Girometta* is in Vittorio Santoli, *I canti popolari italiani* (Florence: G. C. Sansoni, 1940). See also Warren Kirkendale, 'Franceschina, Girometta, and their companions in a Madrigal *a diversi linguaggi* by Luca Marenzio and Orazio Vecchi', *Acta musicologica*, 44 (1972), 181–235.

[43] From Alaleona, 'Le laudi', 36.

[44] Quoted in Alessandro d'Ancona, *La poesia popolare italiana* (2nd edn., Leghorn: R. Giusti, 1906), 117.

[45] That *ottave rime* were sung to the *romanesca* was demonstrated by Einstein in 'Die Aria di Ruggiero', in *Sammelbände der Internationalen Musik-Gesellschaft*, 13 (1911–12), 444–54.

two, like the other melodies, were soprano airs: 'the *soprano* of these . . . principally provides the air, even when six or eight others are singing in harmony.'

If we compare this statement with one in the *Dialogo*, we may discern the crucial line that divided in Galilei's mind 'composed' contrapuntal music from popular monophonic music to which a harmonic accompaniment was improvised. In the *Dialogo* Galileo stated that in contrapuntal music 'the bass part is truly the one that gives the air' or movement to the composition.[46] Implied is the traditional method of piling up voices on a given *cantus firmus*, or the free invention of a contrapuntal fabric with reference to the lowest voice. In the homophonically conceived air, however, the bass relinquishes the helm to the soprano. Here the method is to compose a melody to fit a certain metrical and rhyming scheme in such a way that many stanzas may be sung to the same tune. If the occasion demands, one improvises a bass and chords below the tune, or one may have 'six or eight others singing in harmony', but this harmony is subservient to the tune.

Galilei's remarks throw new light on a controversial question: are such 'arias' as the *romanesca*, *Ruggiero*, and *terza rima* bass formulas or descant formulas? The term *aria* itself does not exclude either possibility. While it suggests something light, airy, and therefore high in pitch, *aria* has in reality a different derivation. This was already recognized by Ambros, who showed that the word *aer* as used in the phrase 'Aer de capituli' in Petrucci's fourth frottola book[47] does not connote *Luftgesang* but is a synonym for *modo*, the word used in the title of the collection that contains this *aer*: *Strambotti, ode, frottole, sonetti et modo da cantar versi latini e capituli*.[48] The early *arie* or *aere* were *modi da cantar versi*, manners of singing poetry—in short, melodic formulas. The *modo* was a melodic scheme that served the singer as a basis for the improvisation of a melody. The musical application of the word *aria* therefore derives from a secondary usage of the word, as meaning aspect or appearance, and thus manner or mode, and not from its primary usage as meaning atmosphere.[49]

[46] *Dialogo*, 76: 'che la parte graue sia veramente quella che dà l'aria (nel cantare in consonanza) alla Cantilena . . .'.

[47] *Strambotti, ode, frottole . . . libro quarto* (Venice: O. Petrucci, 1505), ed. in Rudolf Schwartz, Publikationen älterer Musik, 13; Leipzig: Breitkopf und Härtel, 1935), 99.

[48] *Geschichte der Musik*, iii (Breslau: Leuckart, 1868), 482.

[49] Further evidence for this etymology is collected in Hans H. Eggebrecht, 'Aus der Werkstatt des terminologischen Handwörterbuchs', in the Utrecht *Kongreßbericht*, 1952, 162–3. Zarlino compared the arias for singing verses to the Greek *nomoi* that Plutarch spoke about. Their *melos* 'consisted of a certain mode (*modo*) or *aria di cantare*, as we would say, such as the airs on which we now sing the sonnets or *canzoni* of Petrarch or the *rime* of Ariosto (*Istitutioni*, pt. iii, ch. 79, Marco–Palisca trans. 285–6).

Ex. 12.5. *Aria della Romanesca* scheme with typical harmonization and bass

While an aria can be a bass, if we accept this etymology, there is no reason to extend the term to basses that are not sung but over which a different melody is improvised. For the aria then ceases to be a mode of singing. Moreover, vocal improvisation over a bass was unlikely from a practical point of view. Set airs were used principally by poets and other amateurs. The best chapel-singers may have been capable of improvising parts over a bass, but amateurs, poets, and court-singers, who often had to have the tune composed for them, could not have been expected to improvise a melody over a given bass. What they could do was to improvise rhythmic variations and melodic embellishments on a melodic scheme to make it fit a particular text. That the *aria* or *modo* was the part sung is supported by an often-quoted passage from the *Cortegiano*:

Beautiful music, Messer Federico replied, it appears to me, is singing accurately and with a beautiful manner by the book; but much more it is singing to the viola, because in this manner the whole sweetness resides as if in a solo, and one notices and listens to the beautiful *modo* and *aria* with greater attention, since the ears are not occupied with more than a single voice . . .[50]

When a soloist sang to the viola da braccio or lute, the melody he sang was the *aria* or *modo*. When many singers performed in parts, it was the soprano, according to Galilei, who had the aria. But always the aria was a tune for singing, not a bass tune for contrapuntal improvisation like the *basse-danse* tenors.

It is natural, then, that Galilei should have referred to the *terza rima* and *romanesca* as soprano melodies. The *romanesca* melody Galilei had in mind undoubtedly followed the scheme given in the upper staff of Ex. 12.5. It could not have been the bass line encompassing a tenth, given below it, which has often been represented as the *Aria della Romanesca*. Once again, the melody is of narrow range—a mere fifth. This melodic outline can be traced in the treble of countless pieces labeled *romanesche*. Many of these use the standard bass given above, which probably evolved, as we shall see, from the nature of the harmony practised by the *improvvisatori*.

---

[50] Baldesar Castiglione, *Il Cortegiano*, ed. Vittorio Cian (Florence: G. C. Sansoni, 1894), bk. ii, ch. 13.

If we are to appreciate the significance of formulas like the *romanesca* in the development of solo song and in the continuity of this development from the sixteenth century through the seventeenth, it is essential to distinguish the aria, the thing sung, from the ground bass, which is a reduction of the typical accompanying bass to its simplest terms.[51] For that which Galilei speculated about, the composition of melodies on the model of the popular airs, was practised daily by the seventeenth-century monodists. Caccini's *Ahi dispietato amor*, an improvisation on the *romanesca* melodic scheme, is a classic example.[52] Melodies based on the *Ruggiero* scheme further illustrate this procedure. Here again one must not confuse the bass, which is often represented as the *aria di Ruggiero*, with the aria itself. A standard bass is found under many *Ruggiero* melodies, but it is not the aria. The true *aria di Ruggiero* is a discant tune, which, because of the many variations that have been made on it, cannot be isolated in its pristine state. Frequently the *Ruggiero* melody occurs in publications without accompaniment, as in Coferati's books of laudi of 1689 and 1710 under the title: *Aria dell'Ortolano, o Ruggieri, o Donne mi chiamano il maturo*.[53]

Although the *arie di romanesca* and *Ruggiero* must have been discant formulas, this did not prevent composers from writing pieces on the harmonic patterns derived from them and ignoring the melodies themselves. Sigismondo d'India conscientiously noted in his *Musiche* of 1609 whether it was the bass that he used or the air: 'Musica sopra il *Basso* della Romanesca', 'Musica sopra il *Basso* dell'aria di Genova', but 'Musica a due voci sopra *l'aria* di Ruggiero'. Other composers were less obliging: accordingly, we have pieces labelled *Aria di Romanesca*, for example, in which only the bass is discernible. To suffer its original tune to disappear

---

[51] The simplified *romanesca* bass as given in Otto Gombosi, 'Italia, patria del *basso ostinato*', in *Rassegna musicale*, 7 (1934), 25, cannot properly be called a melody or aria at all, but, as Gombosi rightly pointed out, is a skeleton for a bass theme. It is unfortunate that Alfred Einstein never corrected the impression given in his articles that the *romanesca* and *Ruggiero* were basses over which vocal upper parts were composed or sung ('Die Aria di Ruggiero', and 'Ancora sull'aria di *Ruggiero*', in *Rivista musicale italiana*, 41 (1937), 163–9). He well appreciated the melodic character of the *arie da cantar versi*, of which he printed an excellent example: Marchetto Cara's air for the sonnet *S'io sedo a l'ombra amor*, with its simple chordal lute accompaniment, in *The Italian Madrigal*, i. 101.

[52] *Le nuove musiche*, sig. Ci[v], ed. Hitchcock, 54. In this composition, as well as in other works mentioned in Einstein's article 'Die Aria di Ruggiero' as examples of *romanesca*-bass aria, nothing that can be called an aria is observable in the bass, while the melodic scheme illustrated in Ex. 12.4 appears very prominently in the treble. Another such example is Giovanni Stefani's *Eternita d'amore, aria della Romanesca* in *Affetti amorosi* (Venice: A. Vincenti, 1621), ed. in Chilesotti, Biblioteca di rarità musicali, iii. 15.

[53] Matteo Coferati, *Corona di sacre canzoni* (Florence: Eredi di F. Onofri, 1689), 223; 1710 edn., 275. See Alaleona, 'Le laudi', 26. Other monophonic versions of the *Ruggiero* may be seen in Dragan Plamenac, 'An Unknown Violin Tablature of the Early 17th Century', in *Papers of the American Musicological Society* (1941), 152.

while the bass and harmonic scheme persevere has always been the fate of a song that submits itself to constant variation, even in the jazz of our day.

How the standard arias acquired their standard basses becomes evident when we read Galilei's rules for the proper harmonization of melodies modelled on the popular airs. In the *Dialogo* Galilei had noted that whereas Greek choruses sang in unison, the instrumental accompaniments were not always in unison with the voices but often added simultaneous consonances.[54] A passage in Plato's *Laws* often adduced to support this view is cited by Galilei.[55] Plato recommended there that students of the lyre should be taught to accompany a singer only in the *proschorda* manner, never *synphonon*; that is, in unison, never in harmony. Galilei interpreted this passage in a special way. For him *proschorda* and *synphonon* represented two species of harmonic accompaniment. To play in unison did not mean merely to double on the instrument the melodic line of the voice, but should be interpreted to include another kind of accompaniment.

And this occurs when a soloist sings to an instrument in which are struck at the same time several strings disposed in such a way that they make various consonances among themselves, but in a manner uniform with the tones of the soloist, with which they thus become all of a single and one same sound, as happens in the airs I have mentioned above.[56]

Galilei demonstrated this method with a short example (Ex. 12.6). It is significant that both the melody and its harmonization are modelled on the popular songs—only the rationalization for the procedure is Hellenistic.

A harmonization of Galilei's tune that Plato would have repudiated is given in a second version (Ex. 12.7). Here 'the body of diverse consonances that the instrument causes is not perfectly adapted and united with the air of the singer'.[57] The second example introduces two first-inversion chords and twice the Eb harmony, which is not in the natural scale of the melody. If Galilei's interpretation of Plato will hardly stand the test of historical research, he has translated the spirit of Plato into modern terms. What Plato rejected was not so much richness of sound as artifice and virtuosity, the excesses that Galilei too wanted to see barred from vocal music.

To arrive at a simple but correct harmonization of a melody the appropriate rules of counterpoint were to be followed. 'Only that part of the

---

[54] *Dialogo*, 83.

[55] *Laws*, vii. 821D–E. MS Gal. 3, fo. 18ʳ (ed. Rempp, 170). D. P. Walker has discussed various interpretations of this passage in 'Musical Humanism in the early 16th and Early 17th Centuries', *Music Review*, 3 (1942), 61 n. 239, trans. in *Die musikalische Humanismus* (Kassel and Basle: Bärenreiter, 1949), 66 n. 239.

[56] *Dubbi*, MS Gal. 3, fos. 65ᵛ–66ʳ (ed. Rempp, 183).

[57] Ibid., fo. 66ʳ⁻ᵛ.

Ex. 12.6. 'Unisono' from *Dubbi*, MSS Gal. 3, fo. 66ʳ

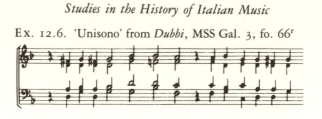

Ex. 12.7. 'Consonanza' from *Dubbi*, MSS Gal. 3, fo. 66ʳ

rules of counterpoint which is adequate for this end', however, was to be applied, because certain rules tended to preserve the independence of parts, which did not further the ends of the monodic style. For example, 'the law of modern contrapuntists that prohibits the use of two octaves or two fifths . . .', he declared, 'is a law truly contrary to every natural law of singing in such a case'. Galilei would have improved on the first harmonization (Ex. 12.6), he said, by making the fifth chord a B♭-chord—changing the bass to a B♭ and the alto to an F—in defiance of the prohibition of parallel perfect intervals.[58] It has often been pointed out, in fact, that parallel fifths are characteristic of the popular idiom in the sixteenth century. The chords of Galilei's first example otherwise came as close as one could to the unison because in them 'the three lower parts accord with the higher part in such a perfect way that it is as much as can be legitimately desired through the laws of modern counterpoint'.[59] The triad—the 'perfect harmony', as Zarlino called it—was the means for this perfect accord. It is used, in fact, to harmonize every note of the melody, the suspension at the cadence excepted.[60]

Thus Galilei's simple melodic style demanded the simplest means possible in the harmonization: triads in root position drawn from the natural scale in which the melody was composed. The bass should serve only to sustain the harmony; it need not avoid parallel motion with the melody. The inner

[58] Ibid., fos. 67ᵛ–68ʳ. Caccini noted in his preface to *Euridice* that he did not avoid parallel fifths and octaves in certain cases (Solerti, *Origini del melodramma*, 51).

[59] Ibid., fo. 66ᵛ.

[60] Galilei noted in his *Discorso intorno alle dissonanze*, MS Gal. 1, fo. 136ᵛ (ed. Rempp, 136), that in the oldest airs, such as those printed in Petrucci's collections, dissonances were used only at the cadence.

parts should follow the outline of the melody and avoid any progressions that would make them autonomous.

If we apply these principles to an analysis of the *romanesca* and *Ruggiero* in their typical harmonizations, we find that, given the melodic schemes, the basses are almost foregone conclusions. In the typical harmonization of the *romanesca*, for example (Ex. 12.5), only root triads are used. Parallel fifths are avoided but parallel motion towards perfect consonances is not.

Another quality in the popular airs that recommended itself to the modern composer was a certain characteristic movement which awakened a particular affection. To find in modern music an example of what the Greeks meant by a mutation of mode, one had to seek in popular music. The effect that the aulos-player was able to make on a Taorminian youth, when Pythagoras ordered the musician to change from an exciting to a quieting mode, 'is understandable if we compare the excited sound of the *romanesca* with the quiet one of the passemezzo'.[61] Galilei recognized in these dance-songs the very qualities that so endeared the characteristic dances to the Baroque composers—the striking directness with which they portrayed typical moods, and the sharp contrasts of affection they produced when juxtaposed.

To summarize, Galilei looked upon the popular airs as models of simplicity, naturalness, economy, and direct expression of text and mood, qualities he admired in Greek art. Modern composers needed to apply to the part that 'gave the air' the principles of Greek melody corroborated by the popular songs. In this way they might come nearer to the true goal of all music, the expression of the affections. The text-declamation of the popular airs was especially worthy of imitation because it approached that of common speech. Singing in the Greek manner, Galilei taught, 'has to be different from speaking only enough to distinguish it from speech'.[62] Composers could profitably imitate also the confined range of the airs and their attractive tunefulness and characteristic movement.

Some 'modern contrapuntists', whom Galilei did not name, had already approached the goal he envisioned in compositions that could be singled out 'for their great beauty of air', among them, *Pur viv'il bel costume, Si gioioso, Occhi miei che vedesti, Aspro core, Fuggi speme mia fuggi*.[63] Settings of *Pur viv'il bel costume, Si gioioso mi fann'i dolor miei*, and of the second part of *Aspro core (Vivo sol di speranza)* are significantly enough among the songs

---

[61] *Il primo libro della prattica del contrapunto*, MS Gal. 1, fo. 100ʳ (ed. Rempp, 71).

[62] *Dubbi*, MS Gal. 3, fo. 66ᵛ (ed. Rempp, 183). This idea was echoed by Jacopo Peri in the preface to *Euridice*. See Oliver Strunk, *Source Readings in Music History* (New York: Norton, 1950), 374.

[63] *Dubbi*, MS Gal. 3, fo. 66ᵛ (ed. Rempp, 183).

EX. 12.8. Galilei, *Pur viv'il bel costume*, MSS Gal. 6, fos. 18ᵛ–19ʳ

arranged for solo voice and lute in Galilei's lute-song manuscript,[64] and they are probably the compositions Galilei had in mind. These three are all homophonically conceived, and *Pur viv'il bel costume* (Ex. 12.8) illustrates especially well the harmonic style prescribed in the *Dubbi*. Compositions such as these gave Galilei reason to hope that a reawakening of melodic invention was already under way.

It has been a mistake, then, to seek the realization of Galilei's theories exclusively in the dry declamation of Jacopo Peri's *Euridice*. This represents but one facet of the renascence of melody Galilei foresaw. In the tuneful songs of Emilio de' Cavalieri's *Rappresentatione di anima et di corpo*, in the strophic airs of Monteverdi's *Orfeo*, in the ennobled *canzone alla villana*, the *romanesche*, and *Ruggieri* of the long series of collections led by Caccini's *Nuove musiche*—in these, rather, do we find embodied the ideals expressed in Galilei's last essays.

The true character of Galilei's reaction against polyphony, obscured by the controversial *Dialogo*, is thus revealed to us in these manuscripts. His revolt was not born simply of humanistic enthusiasm over an alleged Greek practice but principally of a devotion to the homophonic idiom of Italian

---

[64] MS Gal. 6, fos. 18ᵛ–19ʳ, 15ᵛ–16ʳ, and 5ᵛ–6ʳ respectively. The composers of *Pur viv'il bel costume* and *Si gioioso* have not been identified. The *Vivo sol di speranza* arranged by Galilei is by Giovan Domenico Nola, and it was also arranged by Bottegari in his lute-song book, Modena, Biblioteca Estense, MS Mus. C. 311, fo. 36ʳ. In the same manuscript, fos. 2ʳ, 10ᵛ, there is an *Occhi miei che vedeste* which may be the composition Galilei had in mind. The *Fuggi speme mia fuggi* by Alessandro Striggio intabulated in the *Fronimo* (1584), 139, is probably another of the compositions Galilei praised.

popular music. Like many of his countrymen, he found the artifices of counterpoint alien to his songful nature. He would have had the serious composers take over the popular forms of vocal music and embrace the creative technique of the *canzone alla villana*. In his counterpoint treatise, Galilei recalled the simplicity of the harmony in the 'arie' printed by Petrucci—meaning probably the frottole—and of 'yet other airs, older than these, which are sung and played daily, such as the *romanesca* and the *passamezzo*, considered however in their primitive simplicity and not adorned with the artifices of today'.[65] He also recalled how counterpoint had developed through the work of Ockeghem, Josquin, and Willaert into a complex but well-ordered art. Now he wished to see this art, which he believed had achieved a state of ultimate perfection, confined to purely instrumental music. For this it was admirably suited. Vocal music should return to the style of simple airs like the *romanesca* and *passamezzo* in their unadorned beauty. This style of vocal music, left after the days of Petrucci's prints to the cultivation of second-rate composers of villanelle and improvisers, should now engage the attention of worthy composers. No dilettante's fatuous dream of a new Arcadia, Galilei's plea for vocal monody was an affirmation of the continuity of the Italian tradition.

[65] *Discorso intorno all'uso delle dissonanze*, MS Gal. 1, fo. 136ʳ (ed. Rempp, 137).

❧ *13* ❧

Vincenzo Galilei's Arrangements for Voice and Lute

This essay was first published in *Essays in Musicology in Honor of Dragan Plamenac on his 70th Birthday*, edited by Gustave Reese and Robert J. Snow (Pittsburgh: University of Pittsburgh Press, 1969), 207–32 and is reprinted by permission of the publisher.

As a composer, lutenist, and singer, Galilei practised several kinds of accompanied solo vocal music. Although he did not categorize them in this way, they were (i) arrangements of polyphonic madrigals and part-songs for a single voice and lute, (ii) arias for singing poetry to the lute, and (iii) compositions for solo voice with instrumental accompaniment. The examples in the last category, his settings of verses from Dante's *Inferno* and of Lamentations of Jeremiah, do not survive. Of the other two categories we are fortunate in having a number of examples written in his own hand and preserved as personal appendices to two copies of his manual for intabulating for the lute, *Fronimo dialogo . . . nel quale si contengono le vere, et necessarie regole del intavolare la musica nel liuto* (Venice: Girolamo Scotto, 1568). Of the first category, there are twelve arrangements for bass voice and lute (counting second parts of madrigals as separate pieces). Of the second category, there are two arias for singing poetry: one for sonnets and one for capitoli.

This article describes these manuscript appendices, discusses their contents, provides an inventory with concordances, and presents a sample of the contents in transcription.

VINCENZO GALILEI is remembered chiefly as a theorist and polemicist. But in his daily professional activity these roles were subordinated to his work as a lutenist and composer. Indeed, his writings were most often stimulated by problems he met in musical practice. The dialogue called *Fronimo* (1568; 2nd edition, 1584)[1] undertakes to explain through a large

---

[1] The full title of the 1568 edn. is: *Fronimo dialogo . . . nel quale si contengono le vere, et necessarie regole del intavolare la musica nel liuto, posto nuovamente in luce & da ogni errore emendato* (Venice: Girolamo Scotto, 1568). An English translation and transcription of the 1584 edn. by Carol MacClintock has been published by the American Institute of Musicology in its series Musicological Studies and Documents, 39. For more information concerning the works cited in this and the next paragraph, see my articles, 'Galilei', in *MGG* iv. 1265–70 and in *New Grove*, vii. 96–8.

number of examples the rules for intabulating music for the lute. His *Dialogo della musica antica et della moderna* (1581) began as a disquisition on instrumental tuning, particularly on the differences between lute and keyboard tuning. His subsequent pamphlet, the *Discorso* (1589), grew out of his controversy with Gioseffo Zarlino on questions of tuning. The manuscript treatise on counterpoint, drafted during Galilei's last years (1589–91), reflects his recognition of the cleavage between the academic rules of composition as they were taught and as they were practised by leading composers, particularly in the instrumental field.

Documents are not lacking for Galilei's notable achievements as an arranger for the lute and as a composer. A book of intabulations of madrigals and *ricercari* (1563), two books of madrigals (1574 and 1587), a set of two-part counterpoints (1584), and many intabulations and original compositions in the two editions of *Fronimo*, 1568 and 1584, comprise the music printed in his lifetime. The largest collection of his compositions remains in manuscript and is still not available in transcription, apart from seventeen compositions edited by Fabio Fano and other selected pieces.[2] This is the 280-page book of lute intabulations, mainly of independent instrumental dances, preserved among the Galilei manuscripts in the Biblioteca Nazionale Centrale in Florence.

Perhaps the uniquely characteristic legacy of Galilei's vocation as a lutenist is in the two small collections of arrangements for lute and voice, airs, dances, and *romanesche* found at the back of two copies of the rare edition of *Fronimo* printed at Venice in 1568. The two copies, which must have belonged to Galilei, both contain manuscript appendices, mostly in his hand. One copy is in the Landau-Finaly collection at the Biblioteca Nazionale Centrale of Florence under the call-number Landau-Finaly MS Mus. 2, and is notable for its so-called 'pseudo-monodies'. It was first discovered by Alfred Einstein while it was still in the private library of Baron Horace de Landau. The other copy of *Fronimo* with a manuscript appendix is in the Biblioteca Riccardiana of Florence and bears the signature F.111.10431. The existence of this manuscript appendix, which contains only three pages of music, all of them instrumental, has not been previously reported in print.

My main purpose here is to draw attention to the arrangements for voice

---

[2] Fano, *La Camerata Fiorentina*, in Istituzioni e monumenti dell'arte musicale italiana, 4 (Milan: Ricordi, 1934). Further transcriptions are in Paolo Possiedi: 'Il manoscritto Galileiano "6" della Nazionale di Firenze', *Il Fronimo*, 30 (Jan. 1980), 5–13; 31 (Apr. 1980), 5–19; and Maria Therese Annoni, 'Ulteriori osservazioni sul manoscritto Galileiano "6" della Nazionale di Firenze', *Il Fronimo*, 69 (Oct. 1989), 22–32.

and lute in the Landau-Finaly copy of the *Fronimo* of 1568. The twelve songs with lute accompaniment thus preserved are precious remnants of a popular art of singing to the lute that has left only scant traces in Italy. A secondary purpose is to provide a description and inventory of the two little-known sources that are the subject of this article.

The Landau volume has only lately been accessible to the public. Until about 1948 it belonged to the library of Baron Horace de Landau. Its presence there is already recorded in the printed catalogue of 1885,[3] but no mention is made of the manuscript appendix, which was first reported by Alfred Einstein in 1937. At that time, because of limitations imposed by the owner upon his use of it, Einstein did not feel free to describe it in any detail.[4] The library then belonged to Mme Hugo Finaly, who in 1903 had inherited it from her uncle Horace de Landau (d. 1902). She continued to add to the collection, and her will expressed the wish that her son, Horace Finaly, should retain it for life, after which it was to be sold. Through the bequest of Horace Finaly—he died in New York on 19 May 1945—the *Fronimo* volume went, along with other precious items, to the City of Florence. These items now form the Horace Landau Memorial Collection in the keeping of the Biblioteca Nazionale Centrale.[5]

The first edition of *Fronimo* of 1568 is less well known than the much expanded and revised edition of 1584. Although there are seventeen copies of the later edition, according to the latest inventory in RISM, *Recueils imprimés*, only eight complete copies of the 1568 edition, and one that is incomplete, are known.[6] The manuscript supplement to the Landau-Finaly copy consists of twenty folios, on each page of which ten sets of six lines for tablature have been ruled by hand. With the exception of folios 14 and 20, all pages contain music, either in tablature or in mensural notation.

---

[3] *Catalogue des livres manuscrits et imprimés composant la bibliothèque de M. Horace de Landau-Finaly*, i (Florence, 1885), 522–3.

[4] 'Galilei and the Instructive Duo', *Music and Letters*, 18 (1937), 360–8.

[5] See Anita Mondolfo, 'La biblioteca Landau-Finaly', in *Studi di bibliografia in memoria di L. de Gregori* (Rome: Fratelli Palombi, 1949), 265–85. I first studied the manuscript in 1951, before it was catalogued, through the courtesy of Miss Mondolfo, who kindly permitted a film to be made of it at that time. The contents of the manuscript pages have since been described by Bianca Becherini in *Catalogo dei manoscritti musicali della Biblioteca Nazionale di Firenze* (Kassel: Bärenreiter, 1959), 132, no. 110. The inventory of the music there is not entirely accurate.

[6] The 1568 edn. is not listed in *Répertoire international des sources musicales* (hereafter abbreviated as RISM), *Recueils imprimés*, though it is in the volumes *Écrits imprimés concernant la musique*, i. 345, where ten copies, two of which are incomplete, are listed. Claudio Sartori included five of these copies in his inventory in *Bibliografia della musica strumentale italiana stampata in Italia fino al 1700* (Florence: Leo S. Olschki, 1952), 28–9, and in addition noted that there was once a copy in the Wolffheim collection, which is now in the Library of Congress.

Although the binding that combines into a single volume the printed book and its manuscript supplement is of comparatively recent date—probably from the nineteenth century—there is reason to believe that the two were united by Galilei himself. Even before the leaves of the appendix were trimmed and gilt-edged along with those of the *Fronimo*, they must have been cut to fit this volume (dimensions: 21.5 × 32 cm.), since the manuscript pages have normal margins all around. The Landau copy of *Fronimo*, moreover, has further traces of the author's handiwork: corrections in a faded red ink to two of the printed tablatures, those on pages 12 and 29. The hand cannot be identified, because the scribe aimed to imitate so far as possible the style of printed numbers; but the nature of the corrections suggests that the composer was responsible.

These circumstances might not be sufficient to persuade one that the book and manuscript belonged together, but for the existence of the parallel coupling in the copy of the same edition now at the Biblioteca Riccardiana. The 1568 *Fronimo* in the Riccardiana has hand-written corrections identical with those of the Landau copy, and, like it, contains appended twenty folios of paper ruled for tablature. They are uniform in size with the book and are bound with it, untrimmed, in a loose parchment folder. Only three pages of the Riccardiana copy contain tablatures, all but part of the third page in Galilei's hand. The other pages are ruled but contain no music. This copy too was probably Galilei's. He must have been in the habit of supplementing his personal copies of this book with additional arrangements and compositions. The purpose of including the additional pieces may have been to provide material either for performance or for use as illustrative pieces in teaching.

Another circumstance that suggests a link between the printed book and the Landau manuscript is the chronological proximity, as will be seen, of the material of the manuscript and of the publication. Five of the items in the manuscript (counting 'seconde parti' as separate items) occur in the printed book in slightly more literal transcriptions, suggesting that the manuscript grew out of the printed book.

Folios 1^r–6^v and 13^r–19^r follow a uniform scheme: the voice-part is on the left-hand page and the intabulated lute accompaniment on the one opposite, except for the page opposite 13^v, which is blank. Evidently this format was not contemplated when the extra sheets were first added to the book, for all twenty folios were originally ruled with six-line systems. When Galilei decided to use some of the left-hand pages for the vocal lines, he had to scratch out the lowest line of each six. The superfluous line still shows clearly in photographs.[7] The eleven pages in the middle (fos. 7^r–12^r) are filled with independent lute tablatures. All are *passamezzi* and *romanesche* save two, which are arrangements of popular songs. Folio 19^v was used to notate another arrangement of a part-song, and fo. 20 was left blank. Only one composer is identified in the manuscript: Giacomino, probably Bernardino Giacomini, for *Caro dolce ben mio*.

Close study of this layout of material reveals that the manuscript was incorrectly bound into the book. Folios 12^v and 1^r, containing respectively the voice- and the lute-parts of Palestrina's *Vestiva i colli*, should be facing one another. Folios 1 to 6 and 13 to 19 belong after fo. 12, and fos. 7 to 12 constitute the first six folios of the manuscript in its original state. Table 13.1 shows what the original sequence of numbers must have been. Galilei evidently put the first eleven pages (now fos. 7^r–12^r) to the use they were intended—lute tablatures. Then he decided to alternate voice-parts and intabulated accompaniments (fos. 12^v, 1^r–6^v, 13^r–19^r) and was forced to adapt the six-line tablature for five-line staves on the left-hand pages. He used up the verso of fo. 19 for an intabulation of a madrigal. Both sides of fo. 20 remained blank.

Except for two pages, the Landau manuscript is entirely autograph. This can be ascertained by comparing the notational mannerisms with those of the manuscript lute-book of 1584, and with a stray tablature in the volume containing a translation of the *Harmonics* of Aristoxenus.[8] The handwriting in the texts and titles also matches the hand in the manuscript treatises.[9] The tablatures on fos. 1^r and 2^r, however, are in a different hand, although the titles of the madrigals intabulated on those pages, *Vestiva i colli* and *Così le chiome mie*, are in Galilei's hand. That none of the other lute accompaniments are thus labelled suggests that Galilei may have marked the pages that were to receive the tablatures with the intention of filling them in later. Someone else did so, but less faithfully and skilfully than was Galilei's custom.

The Landau appendix appears to be approximately contemporary with the printed book. Every one of the vocal models that can be identified first appeared in print in some form earlier than 1569. For the eight items so identified, the first known publication dates, as may be seen from the table, are: two in 1555, one in 1560, one in 1561, two in 1566, one in 1568, and one in 1569. The single watermark that is visible throughout the

---

[7] Cf. facs. in *MGG* iv, pl. 54.

[8] Florence, Biblioteca Nazionale Centrale, MS Gal. 6. Facs. page in Fano, *La Camerata Fiorentina*, 96; MS Gal. 8, fo. 38^v.

[9] MSS Gal. 1 to 4.

manuscript pages belongs to papers represented by Zonghi's tables of Fabriano papers under numbers 897–906.[10] They are found in archive documents dated between 1527 and 1572. The closest in dimensions to that of our manuscript is no. 904, dated 1566.

The lute pieces are of little assistance in dating. Two of them, the *romanesca* on fo. 7^r and that on fo. 8^v, became respectively *Romanesca sesta* and *Romanesca quarta* in the MS lute-book of 1584, where they were used as subjects for variation. One such variation, of the *Romanesca sesta*, already appears on fos. 11^v–12^r of our manuscript. In each of the *romanesche*, the 1584 version has regular 2/2 barring, whereas the manuscript version is without bars. The printed versions also introduce some rhythmic or harmonic elaborations or simplifications. The lute pieces thus tell us only that our manuscript is earlier than 1584. All the circumstances considered, the most likely date seems to be *c.* 1570.

The compilation falls into the period of Galilei's career when he was engaged principally in teaching, playing, and composing for the lute. This was before he became engrossed in the study of ancient music. We know that his wife and family lived at Pisa in the 1570s, but he must have spent a great deal of time in Florence. He surely lived there from 1572 onward, although his family did not join him until 1574. During these years he was undoubtedly employed to entertain at the home of Giovanni Bardi, who was a lavish host, and at homes of other patrons. The 1584 edition of the *Fronimo*, for example, is dedicated by Galilei to 'my most honoured patron, Signore Jacopo Corsi'. It is known that Galilei sang as well as played, from a letter of Pietro Bardi, written many years later, relating that Galilei had sung his own monodic compositions at Bardi's house around 1582. It may be assumed, then, that he customarily sang to the lute popular songs, madrigals, and other vocal compositions, as well as poetry set to standard airs. All that remains of this part of his repertoire are the arrangements in the Landau copy and the airs in the Riccardiana copy of the *Fronimo* of 1568.

Although it is generally assumed that the singing of polyphonic compositions by a single voice to lute or other accompaniment was a widespread practice in sixteenth-century Italy, little evidence survives in the form of written arrangements. The printed arrangements of Bossinensis,[11]

---

[10] Aurelio Zonghi, 'Le marche principali delle carte fabrianesi dal 1298 al 1599', in *Zonghi's Watermarks* (Hilversum, 1953).

[11] Franciscus Bossinensis, *Tenori e contrabassi intabulati col sopran in canto figurato per cantar e sonar col lauto. Libro primo* (Venice: O. Petrucci, 1509); *Libro secondo* (1511). A similar collection is *Frottole de Misser Bartolomio Tromboncino et Misser Marcheto Carra con tenori et bassi tabulati et con soprano in canto figurato* (Rome: L. A. Giunta, 1520). An example from the second book of Bossinensis is transcribed

TABLE 13.1. *Contents of Landau-Finaly MS Mus. 2*

No.	Folio		Tuning	Text incipit or title	Composer and number of parts	Concordance and remarks
	Voice	Intabulation				
1		7r		Romanesca con 4 parti	[Galilei]	MS Gal. 6, 20r–v: 'Romanesca sesta'
2		7v		Pass'e mezzo	[Galilei]	
3		8r		Pass'e mezzo	[Galilei]	
4		8v		Romanesca con 4 parti	[Galilei]	MS Gal. 6, 77r–v: 'Romanesca 4a'
5		9r		A cas'un giono [*sic*] con la seconda parte	[popular song probably arranged by Galilei]	
6		9v–10r		Romanesca con 4 parti	[Galilei]	
7		10v–11r		Romanesca con 4 parti	[Galilei]	
8		11v–12r		Romanesca con 4 parti	[Galilei]	MS Gal. 6, 81v–82r: 'sopra la medesima [Romanesca 6a]'
9		12r		Bella man di valore		
10	12v	1r	A	Vestiva i colli	[Palestrina] a 5	RISM 1566³: *Desiderio*; *Fronimo* 1568, p. 15; *Fronimo* 1584, p. 47; Casimiri, *Opere*, ix. 117; lute part not autograph
11	1v	2r	A	[2da parte:] Cosi le chiome mie		
12	2v	3r	G	Fiera stella sel cielo ha forza in noi	[Lassus] a 5	Boetticher 1555a: *Il primo libro di madrigali a 5* (Venice: A. Gardano); *Fronimo* 1568, p. 129; *Sämtliche Werke*, ii. 50
13	3v	4r	G	(2da parte:) Ma tu prend'à diletto		

No.				Title	Composer	Source
14	4^v	5^r	D	Io son ferito ahi lasso	[Palestrina] a 5	RISM 1561^10: *Terzo libro delle Muse a 5*; *Fronimo 1568, p. 146
15	5^v	6^r	A	Vivo sol di speranza rimembrando [2da parte of *Aspro core*]	[Lassus]	Boetticher 1560β: *Primo libro di madrigali* (Venice: A. Gardano); *Bottegari MS, fo. 36^r, attr. to G. D. da Nola
16	6^v	13^r	A	Vatene o sonn'e mai		
17	13^v	missing	A	Madonna O felice quel giorno		Cf. Galanti, *Le Villanelle*, at 'O felice quel giorno'
18	14^v	15^r	A	Ancor chio possa dire	[A. Striggio] a 6	RISM 1591^10: *Melodia Olympica*, 1594^7, 1611^11; *Fronimo 1568, p. 153
19	15^v	16^r	G	Si gioioso mi fann'i dolor miej		
20	16^v	17^r	A	Se ben di sette stelle		
21	17^v	18^r	G	Dolce mi saria uscir d'affann'e pen e da martire	[G. Ferretti] a 5	*Il secondo libro delle canzoni alla Napolitana a 5* (Venice: G. Scotto, 1569, 2/1574, 3/1578, 4/1581) Partially printed *Musical Quarterly*, 46, p. 359
22	18^v	19^r	G	Pur viv'il bel costume		
23	19^v	19^v	G	Caro dolce ben mio à 4 del Giacomino	[Bernardino Giacomini?]	

* Intabulation varies.

Willaert,[12] and Verovio,[13] and the manuscript book of Cosimo Bottegari,[14] are among the few collections extant. To these, which give the voice part, should be added lute-books that include with the intabulations the texts to be sung.[15]

The Galilei arrangements differ in some important respects from other known collections of this kind. The arrangements of Bossinensis, Willaert, and Bottegari consist of single voice-parts for soprano, or occasionally tenor, with intabulated reductions of the remaining parts provided below the voice-part. Galilei's are bass parts accompanied by lute-reductions of all the parts. Pietro Bardi, in his letter of 1634, referred to Galilei as a tenor,[16] but at such a distance of years he could well have been mistaken, and these arrangements, clearly for a bass voice, were probably intended for Galilei himself. Their range is from F to d', though they are notated variously in tenor, baritone, and bass clefs.[17]

Galilei's choice of the bass part, since evidently this fit his range, was probably mainly a matter of convenience. But a deeper reason for preferring this part for at least some of the songs is suggested by a statement in his *Dialogo della musica antica et della moderna*. There he demonstrated that the bass voice was the one that gave a contrapuntal composition its 'air': '[C]he la parte grave sia veramente quella che dà l'aria (nel cantare in consonanza) alla Cantilena . . .'.[18] In the word *aria*, Galilei vaguely comprehended melodic and harmonic movement. By 'cantare in consonanza' he meant polyphonic singing in general, but he intended by this qualification to exclude any kind of melody-dominated music, such as popular songs,

along with the vocal model in Benvenuto Disertori, 'Contradiction tonale dans la transcription d'un "Strambotto" célèbre' in Jean Jacquot (ed.), *Le luth et sa musique* (Paris: CNRS, 1958), 39–40. Others may be seen in Oswald Körte, *Laute und Lautenmusik* (Leipzig: Breitkopf & Härtel, 1901), 158–61. The manuscript studied by Geneviève Thibault in 'Un manuscrit italien pour luth des premières années du XVIᵉ siècle', in *Le luth et sa musique*, 43–76, includes similar arrangements but omits the voice-part. Cf. the reconstructions, ibid. 67–76.

[12] *Intavolatura de li madrigali di Verdelotto da cantare et sonare nel lauto, intavolati per Messer Adriano* (Venice: O. Scotto, 1536; G. Scotto, 1540).

[13] Simone Verovio, *Ghirlanda di fioretti musicali* (Rome: [S. Verovio], 1589); *Diletto spirituale* (Rome: [S. Verovio], 1586).

[14] Modena, Biblioteca Estense, MS Mus. C.311. Cf. Carol MacClintock, 'A Court Musician's Songbook: Modena MS C.311', *Journal of the American Musicological Society*, 9 (1956), 177–92. This manuscript is ed. by MacClintock in *The Bottegari Lutebook* (Wellesley, Mass.: The Wellesley Edition, 1965).

[15] For example, Florence, Biblioteca Nazionale Centrale, MS Magl. XIX. 168, dated 10 May 1582; Magl. XIX. 109, late 16th c.

[16] Angelo Solerti, *Le origini del melodramma* (Turin: Fratelli Bocca, 1903), 145.

[17] The arrangements of Verovio, from which the singer chooses his voice-part out of the three parts on the left-hand page and a keyboard or lute reduction of the composition from the right-hand page, would produce for a bass about the same result as the arrangements of the Galilei manuscript.

[18] Florence: Giorgio Marescotti, 1581, p. 76.

which would not normally be sung polyphonically. In the imitative compositions of the manuscript—for example, *Vestiva i colli*, or *Ancor ch'io possa dire*—where the parts are of equal importance, the bass deserved precedence in Galilei's opinion, because it was the harmonic foundation. Galilei firmly opposed Zarlino's contention that the tenor was the part that governed a composition: 'It is to be understood that the lowest part, and not the tenor, as it pleases Zarlino, is that which reigns and governs and gives the air to the composition; and wherever the bass part does not vary its notes, the composition is not varied, or only little varied.'[19] The arrangement of the anonymous *ottava rima*, *Se ben di sette stelle* (transcribed in the musical appendix to this article), demonstrates how effective the bass part in a polyphonic texture is when it is set in relief by soloistic performance, because it is the part which moves, as Galilei implies, with greatest harmonic compulsion.

The singing by a solo voice to the accompaniment of instruments enjoyed a vogue at about this time, according to Vincenzo Giustiniani. He wrote of the practice in his *Discorso sopra la musica de' suoi tempi*, dated around 1628:

In the holy year of 1575 or slightly later there began a new manner of singing very different from the previous one, and this was continued for a number of years afterwards. This was the manner of singing with a solo voice over an instrument, as for example, that of a certain Neapolitan, Gio. Andrea and Sig. Giulio Cesare Brancacci and the Roman, Alessandro Merlo, who sang bass voices of twenty-two notes with a variety of *passaggi* new and grateful to the ears of all. These singers stimulated composers to write works to be sung by several voices as well as by a single one to the accompaniment of an instrument in imitation of these singers and also of a certain woman called Femia, but achieving greater invention and artfulness. There resulted various villanelle in a style intermediate between madrigals in contrapuntal style and villanelle.[20]

Giustiniani found two novel features in the new manner: the cult of the solo singer and the improvised passage-work. Solo singing itself was not novel, but its increasing use to render composed music, as opposed to that improvised over standard airs, constituted a new trend. Galilei's collection must be regarded as a product of the vogue observed by Giustiniani, although its music belongs to an intermediate category. It is neither composed for nor improvised by a solo voice but is adapted for solo performance from composed polyphonic music. Giustiniani's characterization

---

[19] *Il primo libro della prattica del contrapunto . . . intorno all'uso delle consonanze* (1589–91), Florence, Biblioteca Nazionale Centrale, MS Gal. 1, fo. 76ᵛ (ed. Rempp, 38). On this question see my article, 'Vincenzo Galilei and Some Links between "Pseudo-Monody" and Monody', above, Essay 12.

[20] Italian text printed in Solerti, *Le origini*, 106–7.

of the favoured style as falling between the madrigal and villanelle fits all but a few of Galilei's arrangements.

Years later, even after espousing the monodic principle proclaimed by Girolamo Mei,[21] Galilei continued to defend the performance of part-music by one voice with instrumental accompaniment, particularly when the music had a tuneful top voice. He wrote around 1591:[22]

per essempio nel cantare questa tale aria come t'haggio lasciato vita mia. dico che cantando il soprano di cotale aria sopre ad uno stromento che suoni tutte le sue parti, si domanda cantare proschorda; et il cantarne più si domanda cantare sinfone et in consonanza. et quante più parti canteranno nell'istesso tempo tostomeno sarà compresa tale aria dal senso, et opererà con meno efficacia negl'animi di quelli che l'ascoltano la sua natura: il qual soprano si può ancora cantare nella voce d'un tenore che torni bene.	For example in singing an air such as *Come t'haggio lasciato vita mia*, I say that when the soprano is sung to an instrument that plays all the parts, this is called singing *proschorda*; and to sing more parts is called *synphonon* or 'in harmony'. The greater the number of parts that sing at one time, the less will the air be grasped by the sense and the less efficaciously will its character work upon the souls of those who listen to it. It will also turn out well if such a soprano is sung by a tenor.

The compositions Galilei selected for transcription are about equally divided between those in imitative style (nos. 10–11, 12–13, 14, and 18) and those homophonically set (nos. 21, 22, 19, and 16). Two, nos. 20 and 15, are in a mixed style. The imitative compositions are favourite works of such well-known composers as Palestrina, Lasso, and Striggio. Among the homophonic songs, several are anonymous and are unknown outside this manuscript: *Vattene o sonn'e mai*, *Pur viv'il bel costume*,[23] and *Si gioioso mi fann'i dolor miei*.[24] One other song, *Se ben di sette stelle*,[25] has also not been

[21] See my *Girolamo Mei: Letters on Ancient and Modern Music* (Rome: American Institute of Musicology, 1960; 2nd edn., Neuhausen-Stuttgart: Hänssler, 1977).

[22] This statement was inserted in Galilei's essay, *Dubbi intorno a quanto io ho detto dell'uso dell'enharmonio con la solutione di essi*, Florence, Biblioteca Nazionale Centrale, MS Gal. 3, fo. 70ʳ⁻ᵛ, but subsequently it was crossed out and not used. The essay is from about 1591. The use of the words *proschorda* and *sinfone* points to an earlier discussion of Plato's criticism of certain accompaniments used by his contemporaries. See above, Essay 12, Ex. 12.1 for the song mentioned.

[23] No other compositions on these two texts have been found.

[24] Not based either on Vincenzo Ruffo's madrigal on this text in his *Primo libro di madrigali cromatici a 4 v.* (1556), or on Bernardo Lupacchino's setting in his *Il primo libro di madrigali a 5 v.* (1547).

[25] Not based on Bartolomeo Spontoni's madrigal on this text in his *Il primo libro di madrigali a 4 v.* (1558).

identified. It is probable that one of the criteria for selection was the melodiousness of the bass part. Other criteria may be inferred from Galilei's description of three compositions of the manuscript, in a short essay drafted in 1591, as possessing 'great beauty of air'. The three pieces are *Pur viv'il bel costume*, *Si gioioso mi fann' i dolor miei*, and *Vivo sol di speranza* (*seconda parte* of *Aspro core*).[26] By 'beauty of air' Galilei seems to have meant simplicity of texture, clarity of harmonic movement, and rhythmic vitality, as well as melodic distinctiveness in the leading voice.

The treatment of the original in Galilei's accompaniments ranges from almost absolute fidelity to the part-writing to a free chordal sketch. The key of the original is preserved in every one of the identifiable compositions. The importance of keeping the part-movement intact in a transcription for lute is repeatedly emphasized in the *Fronimo*. But this requirement was a stricture imposed upon instrumental transcriptions; it is not surprising that Galilei often departed from it in the accompaniments. At one extreme is the lute accompaniment for Striggio's *Ancor ch'io possa dire*. Except for the final measures, where Galilei has varied the harmony and bass, and for a few ornamental runs, this intabulation is a faithful transcription of the six-part madrigal. More typical is the free lute accompaniment for Lasso's sonnet *Fiera stella*. It is instructive to compare the opening measures of this with the original five-voice setting and with Galilei's faithful intabulation in the *Fronimo* (see Ex. 13.1).

The transcription printed in *Fronimo* is fussy in its preservation of the details of the original composition, extending even to attempts to reproduce the five-part texture. The manuscript accompaniment adheres less slavishly to the original. The harmony is almost always maintained, but it is no longer possible to trace Lasso's individual voice-parts. From the third bar on, Galilei even abandons the thread of the top part. In one place (b. 5) he chooses the C major chord over Lasso's C minor.

The loss of the top part of a composition in imitative texture as in *Fiera stella* may not seem serious; but the absence of the original top line in a homophonic song such as Giovanni Ferretti's *Dolce mi saria uscir d'affanno* does appear to violate a statement once made by Galilei, that in such songs the soprano has the 'air'.[27] In this song Galilei's accompaniment departs from the soprano melody as often as it preserves it—perhaps so as to detract less attention from the part that is sung. The one part in which Galilei respects the original in every detail, however, is the bass. This is true of all the arrangements, except at times when the bass has lengthy

---

[26] See above, Essay 12, p. 361.
[27] Above, p. 352.

pauses, and Galilei has borrowed a fragment of an interior part to fill the gaps. No ornamentation appears in the solo voice-parts, therefore, but one cannot exclude the possibility that the singer would have embellished them in the manner of the time, particularly where there are large skips.

The appendix to the Riccardiana *Fronimo* is of a much different character from the one just described. The collection of music is what dance-band musicians today would call 'fake-books'—musical notebooks in which they jot down standard tunes and their chords as guides to improvisation. Each piece in this manuscript consists of a single musical period. Today's tune collectors would call such a unit a 'chorus'; in the sixteenth century it would have been referred to as an 'aria' or air. The short span of the pieces

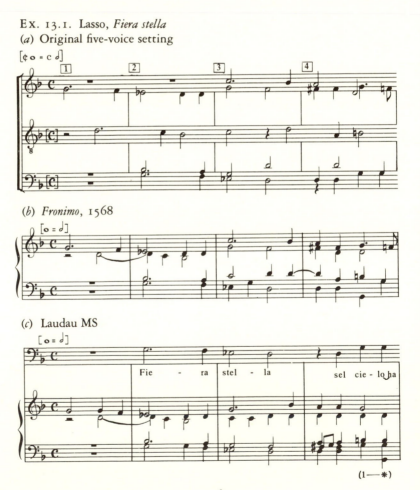

EX. 13.1. Lasso, *Fiera stella*
(*a*) Original five-voice setting

(*b*) *Fronimo*, 1568

(*c*) Laudau MS

Fie - ra stel - la   sel cie - lo ha

(1—*)

for - za in no -
i
sel cie - lo ha for - za in - no - i

* Tablature erroneously repeats these two beats, shifting
the barline a half value until corrected at measure 9.

here is in contrast to the instrumental compositions in the Landau manuscript, which are several periods long—for example, the *Romanesca con
quattro parti* on fo. 7^r, which utilizes the *romanesca* pattern of ten bars four
times over. In the first three pages of the Riccardiana fascicle—the only
pages utilized—Galilei notated nine pieces in tablature; a tenth incomplete
piece is in a different hand, which resembles the second hand of the Landau
manuscript. Each of the nine items by Galilei provides raw material for
improvisation or variation. The tenth item is itself a variation on the
passamezzo of no. 9. Another notable feature of the series of airs is that
they are all in the tonality of C, most of them minor, but nos. 1, 4, 5, and
8 are in major. This uniformity may have served to provide a standard
point of reference for transposition, which is easily effected on the lute by a
change in the tuning. In a number of the pieces the notation is more
explicit than what Galilei was accustomed to use. In all but nos. 4 and 5,
dots under the figures indicate the use of the index finger. In nos. 1, 2, and
8, dots are placed also after the figures in certain chords, evidently to

indicate immediate dampening. (In the transcription of no. 1 these latter dots are placed above or below the note.)

The numbers belong to several categories: standard tunes, dances, single variations of the standard patterns of the *romanesca* and *passamezzo antico*, and airs for the singing of poetry. The stock airs or tunes are no. 1, *Germini*, and no. 6, *Era di maggio*.[28] The variations on standard patterns are: no. 2, on the *romanesca*, and no. 9, on the *passamezzo antico*. No. 10 is a variation, unlabelled, of the *passamezzo* of no. 9. Dance airs are no. 3, a *gagliarda*; no. 7, another *gagliarda*; and no. 8, a *contrapasso*. The *passamezzo* is, of course, likewise a dance.

Perhaps the most valuable items in the group are the two airs for singing poetry. Such airs are not abundant in manuscripts and even less so in printed sources. No. 4 is an air for the singing of sonnets, and no. 5 an air for singing capitoli. The air for capitoli is identical with that for sonnets except for the omission of the third bar.

The collection is thus a small compendium of the diverse kinds of music a lute-player was expected to supply for social functions. To play for dancing and for theatrical performances, to improvise instrumental interludes, and to provide the accompaniment for poetic recitation: such were the lutenist's typical obligations in the service of his patrons.

---

[28] A variant of this melody, in mixed triple and common time, and repeating each phrase, is in Florence, Biblioteca Nazionale Centrale, Magliabecchi, XIX. 108. It is printed in Federico Ghisi, 'Alcune canzoni a ballo del primo cinquecento', in Horst Heussner (ed.), *Festschrift Hans Engel* (Kassel: Bärenreiter, 1964), 132. The text given there—'Era di Maggio, era la Primavera,/ Ch'ogn'albero produce il suo bel fiore'—fits the tune in the Galilei manuscript.

APPENDIX

*Thematic Index of Anonymous and Unidentified Compositions in the
Landau-Finaly MS Mus. 2*

(Except where indicated, note-values have been halved.
Barlines through the stave are those of the manuscript.)

No. 5. *A cas'un giorno con la seconda parte,* fo. 9ʳ

No. 9. *Bella man di valore,* fo. 12ʳ

No. 16. *Vattene o sonn'e maj,* fos. 6ᵛ, 13ʳ (see full transcription below)
No. 17. *Madonna O felice quel ginorno,* bass part only, fo. 13ᵛ (original note-values)

No. 19. *Si gioioso mi fann'i dolor miej,* fos. 15ᵛ, 16ʳ (see full transcription below)
No. 20. *Si ben di sette stelle,* fos. 16ᵛ–17ʳ (see full transcription below)
No. 22. *Pur viv'il bel costume,* fos. 18ᵛ–19ʳ

No. 23. *Caro dolce ben mio a 4 del Giacomino*, fo. 19ᵛ

Contents: *F. III.10431, Biblioteca Riccardiana*

Transcriptions

(All note-values have been halved. Bars through the stave are in the manuscript tablature; added barlines do not penetrate the stave. Added mensuration signs are in brackets. Where there is a conflict between the original sign and the modern time signature, the original is above the stave.)

Landau-Finaly MS

No. 16. *Vattene o sonn'e maj* (fos. 6ᵛ, 13ʳ)

no   o meste   lu - cj   pian - ge - te   si che'l   uostro pian - to ma -

don - n'error co - no - sch'e non in - gan - no

No. 19. *Si gioioso mi fann'i dolor miej* (fos. 15ᵛ, 16ʳ)

Si gio - io - so   mi fann'i   do - lor mie - j   don - na don -

na per a - mar uo - i che sempr'a -mand'ogn'hor morir uorre - j

che sempr'a-mand' ogn' hor mo - rir uor-re - j mo-rir uor-re-

j et fra me di-co po - i se tal gio - ia m'ar-

re-ca il mio mar-ti - re hor che fa-rà'l mo - ri - re hor

che fa - rà'l mo - ri - re hor che fa-rà'l mo - ri - re hor che

No. 20. *Se ben di sette stelle* (fos. 16$^\text{v}$–17$^\text{r}$)

stel - le ar - dent'e bel - le Ti cing' il

bion - do crin lie - ta co - ro - na.

Mentr'a di - por - to in questa part'en quel - le Vaj con la ua - ga

fi - glia di la - to - na Pur t'ac - ce - ser'il cor l'em -

Riccardiana *Fronimo*
No. 1 *Germini* (fo. 1ʳ)

No. 4. *Aria de sonetti* (fo. 1ᵛ)

No. 6. *Era di maggio* (fo. 1ᵛ)

❦ 14 ❦

Musical Asides in the Diplomatic Correspondence of Emilio de' Cavalieri

This essay was first published in *Musical Quarterly*, 49 (1963), 339–55. The thread that holds this piece together is the fascinating personality of Emilio de' Cavalieri, diplomat, administrator, impresario, composer, organist, teacher of singing, and choreographer. I recall first that he was a diplomat and administrator, because the correspondence studied here reveals him primarily in these roles, although our interest focuses on the light the letters throw on the musical life of Florence and Rome between 1590 and 1602. This was a very vital decade in the history of these musical centres, because it was the time when theatrical music was emerging from an accessory function to a dominant one. And Cavalieri was in the epicentre of this activity as a composer, organist, teacher of singing, choreographer, and impresario. As the administrator appointed by Grand Duke Ferdinand I of Tuscany to oversee the arts and spectacles, as the producer of the famous intermedi of 1589, as a composer of some of the early dramatic musical pastorals, and as a provider of music to two leading oratorio societies in Rome, he not only managed some of the most memorable events of those times but contributed to them as a creative artist.

The correspondence between Cavalieri and the secretaries of the Grand Duke of Tuscany studied here was very private and usually secret as well. Its main subject-matter was affairs of state, particularly relations between the Duchy and the papacy and individual cardinals. Music is very much a side issue and introduced usually as incidental gossip. Only occasionally does Cavalieri put on the hat of the overseer of arts and spectacles, as when he gives directions from Rome for the planning of future entertainments or when he reports about the building of a model of Jacopo della Porta's design for the Cappella dei Principi in S. Lorenzo and arranging its payment.

In the original publication of this article, the Italian texts of the letters were omitted to save space and because I then expected that a substantial anthology of the letters would be published by Warren Kirkendale, who by then had made a transcript of the most relevant among them. However, as I write nearly thirty years later, the Italian texts are still not published, though they are soon expected. Consequently I have given in the footnotes the original texts of those excerpts that I translated in my essay. Although I was tempted to modernize the punctuation and capitalization to make it more acceptable to readers of Italian, I decided to transmit them as faithfully as possible rather than tamper with these hasty, sometimes telegraphic, notes that Cavalieri wrote in the midst of his busy negotiations. The only editorial alterations are that the use of *u* and *v* are made to conform to modern practice, similarly *tia* and *tio* are emended to *zia* and *zio*, and *ij* to *i* or *ii*, essential apostrophes and diacritical marks are inserted (Cavalieri never used any accents), and abbreviations are tacitly expanded. Otherwise the original orthography is preserved, for its inconsistencies not only reveal the author's haste and lack of tranquillity but tell us something about his attitude towards the news he transmits.

Cavalieri's 'asides' have provided fuel for many scholars since I published them. They have sparked renewed interest in this man and his place in the history of music. Meanwhile, there is still no critical edition of his *Rappresentatione di anima et di corpo*, although there is a fine recording.[1] There have been several editions of Cavalieri's Lamentations, but only in 1990 did we get a scholarly edition, by Murray C. Bradshaw, who in an article, 'Cavalieri and Early Monody', has solved the puzzles of the two sets of Lamentations and several sets of responsories in the manuscript of the Biblioteca Vallicelliana.[2] One of the letters excerpted below helped Bradshaw to identify the second set of Lamentations as those done at Pisa in 1599.

The scholar who has contributed most extensively to Cavalieri studies is Warren Kirkendale, whose interest in him evidently began with a reading of these letters, which led him to further research on music and musicians at the court of Ferdinand I. He has recently finished a large documentary work covering the reign of the Medici dukes, with the texts of the letters mentioned below as well as many others.[3] Meanwhile, he has published brief biographies of Cavalieri that provide the main facts.[4]

'GIANNETTO DI PELLESTRINA died, and the Pope has given his position of composer to the chapel to Felice Anerio, to the disgust of the singers, because he does not measure up to the responsibility.'[5] This remark, written on 4 February 1594, two days after Palestrina's death, is

---

[1] Archiv Produktion, Deutsche Grammophon 2708 016, directed by Charles Mackerras, with Tatiana Troyanos as Anima and Hermann Prey as Corpo, based on a performing edition by Bernhard Paumgartner.

[2] *Journal of Musicology*, 9 (1991), 238–53. The edition by Bradshaw is published as Emilio de' Cavalieri, *The Lamentations and Responsories of 1599 and 1600 (Biblioteca Vallicelliana MS O 31)* in the series Early Sacred Monody, ed. M. Bradshaw, as Misc. 5, vol. iii of the American Institute of Musicology (Neuhausen-Stuttgart: Hänssler, 1990).

[3] The title announced by the publisher Leo S. Olschki is *The Musical Establishment at the Florentine Court during the Principate of the Medici (1543–1737)*.

[4] 'Emilio de' Cavalieri: A Roman Gentleman at the Florentine Court', in *Memorie e contributi alla musica dal medioevo all'età moderna offerti a Federico Ghisi, Quadrivium*, 12 (1971), 9–21, and 'Cavalieri', *Dizionario biografico degli italiani*. For a concise biography and consideration of his works, see also Palisca, 'Cavalieri', *New Grove*, iv. 20–3.

[5] Cavalieri to Marcello Accolti, Rome, 4 Feb. 1594, Florence, Archivio di Stato, Archivio Mediceo del Principato, Filza 3622 (hereafter ASF M.3622), fo. 114ʳ (my foliation): 'morì Gianneto di Pellestrina, et il Papa ha dato il suo luogo di compositor di cappella, a Felice anerio con disgusto de cantori, par non essere huomo de tal carico.'

among the precious asides that pepper the secret reports sent by Emilio de'
Cavalieri to the Tuscan court during his missions in Rome. In the form of
letters addressed to the secretaries of Duke Ferdinand I of the Medici, the
reports furnished news, sometimes several times a week, of the comings
and goings of ambassadors and visitors and of political, artistic, and social
affairs.

A large file of these letters in Cavalieri's hand is in Filza 3622 in the
section of the State Archives in Florence known as Archivio Mediceo
del Principato. It contains 144 complete letters, one undated note, one
detached postscript, and one note written on a letter addressed to himself.[6]
Almost all Cavalieri's letters in this folder are addressed to Marcello
Accolti, the Duke's secretary. The inclusive dates are 30 October 1587 and
1 February 1602, covering the period from just before his move from Rome
to Florence to six weeks before his death.[7]

The first evidence of a diplomatic assignment for Cavalieri appears in
documents of the fall of 1590. At this time he, together with Belisario
Vinta and Cipriano Saracinelli, were appointed to report upon and negotiate with members of the Sacred College in the conclave following the
death of Pope Sixtus V on 27 August 1590. Vinta had fulfilled similar
missions for Duke Francis and on Ferdinand's accession in 1587 was given
charge of foreign affairs. While Vinta was in Rome, Cavalieri stayed behind
to serve as an intermediary between the Duke and his Roman agents. The
conclave, which began on 7 September, led to the election of the Duke's
favoured candidate, Giovanni Battista Castagna, on 14 September as Urban

---

[6] A number of letters addressed to Cavalieri are also filed there. These are not replies but letters he
enclosed with his own and usually written by an agent who never signed his name for security reasons.
He can be identified as Cavaliere Pietro Paulo Azelio through the letter of 23 Nov. 1601, fo. 375.

[7] So far as I know, the contents of this folder had not been made known to musical scholars before
my paper, 'Musical Gossip in the Diplomatic Correspondence of Emilio de' Cavalieri', read at the
annual meeting of the American Musicological Society on 27 Dec. 1962 at Columbus, Ohio. The filza
is listed, however, in two recent publications: the catalogue, *Archivio Mediceo del Principato, inventario
sommario* (Rome: Ministerrio dell'Interno, 1951), 116; and Marcello del Piazzo, *Gli ambasciatori toscani
del Principato (1537–1737)* (Rome: Istituto Poligrafico dello Stato, 1953), 16. Other folders of official
correspondence contain further letters of Cavalieri pertaining to his missions in Rome, though their
presence is not indicated in the catalogue. I shall not include in this article any discussion of files such
as those of the Guardaroba that contain letters pertaining to Cavalieri's activities in Florence as artistic
administrator. Some of these are listed in Solerti, 'Laura Guidiccioni Lucchesini ed Emilio del
Cavaliere', in *Rivista musicale italiana*, 9 (1902), 817. Others were known to A. Cametti: cf. Nino
Pirrotta, 'Cavalieri', in *Enciclopedia dello spettacolo*, iii. 256. In 1962, about a year after my own limited
work on Filza 3622 and related folders, Warren Kirkendale made a much more extended search of the
archive for Cavalieri material and found altogether more than 300 letters by him, including those of
ASF M.3622. Since he planned to publish all musically relevant passages from these, together with
other documentary material on Cavalieri, the Italian texts were omitted in this article. Dr Kirkendale
has kindly supplied me with a list of the files he searched, to which I have to add only the fifty-eight
letters of Filza 3977 and the letters and minutes of letters to Cavalieri in Filze 19, 3976, and 3978.

VII. Since Urban VII's papacy lasted only thirteen days, almost all of which the Pope spent in bed, Vinta remained in Rome to be ready for the next conclave. This began on 6 October and, after fifty-eight days, ended with the election on 5 December of Nicolò Sfondrati, who, as Gregory XIV, turned out to be altogether inimical to the interests of Tuscany.[8] When about a year later Pope Gregory XIV became ill, it was Cavalieri who was dispatched to Rome around 4 September to prepare the ground for the next conclave. He apparently returned after a few days, only to make the trip again later in the month.

The duties of the agents in Rome were to send intelligence, to make known the Duke's preferences among the candidates to the cardinals who were his faithful supporters, and to try to win others over to his side. Having inherited from his brother Francis a duchy that was in economic decline, falling in world prestige, and poor in foreign alliances, Ferdinand was determined to raise Florence to its former glory and to extend its influence even beyond what it had been in the past. His policy rested on two principal cornerstones. He wished to see weakened the hold Spain had on the papacy and on Italy's southern principalities, and he aimed to strengthen the position of Henry IV of France, for Ferdinand regarded a balance of power between Spain and France as an essential condition to an independent Italy. The agents in Rome were particularly instructed to back candidates who would not bow to Philip II of Spain, but to do this without arousing the antagonism of the Spanish party, and to see that the cardinals who were dependent on the Duke carried out his strategy.[9] The instructions given to Cavalieri at the time of Gregory XIV's illness reveal the ruthlessness with which Ferdinand pursued this foreign policy.[10]

---

[8] Fifty-eight letters in Filza 3977 by Cavalieri to Vinta, dated 5 Sept. to 17 Nov. 1590, many partly in code, cover these last two conclaves. In addition, a large file of letters from Vinta, Cardinal Carafa, and Cardinal del Monte to Cavalieri, dated between 4 Oct. and 7 Dec. 1590, are in Filza 3976.

[9] The struggle between Philip II and Duke Ferdinand I for influence in the conclaves is documented in F. Petrucelli della Gattina, *Histoire diplomatique des conclaves*, ii (Paris: Lacroix, Verboeckhoven et Compagnie, 1864), 275 ff.

[10] Minutes in the hand of Accolti of a letter to Cavalieri dated 30 Sept. 1591, Filza 3978: 'Il Cavalier vinta ci lesse la lettera che gli scriveste da Staggia, et di poi ci ha letta la breve vostra scritta in Monterone, et con contento sentiamo che seguitaste il viaggio con salute. et subito arrivato in Roma vorremmo che con la vostra efficace et accorta maniera *ci guadegnaste dua Cardinali l'uno spinola con assicurarlo, che se ci vuole servire per davero ne i Conclavi che noi ci contentiamo che se l'Imperatore vuole che egli escluda Verona* che lo possa fare, et che possa anche *escludere un altro a sua fantasia, nominandocelo però hora et servendoci poi* in ogni altro conto a nostro modo, et a vostra piena sodisfattione, *et noi gli promettiamo et gliene daremo per mano vostra tutta quella sicurtà che egli sappia desiderare. una pensione di tre milia scudi l'anno durante sua vita, da cominciarsi a pagarglene subito che nel primo Conclave ci habbia dato effetivamente saggio di haverci servito, et di esser per continuar poi sempre, et quanto alla secretezza, certificatelo, che non lo saprà altri che voi, et che faremo anche che i pagamenti eschino da voi o da chi voi et egli vorrete d'una maniera che non si possa mai penetrare, che venghino da noi.*' (Emphasis is in original hand.)

Cavaliere Vinta read us the letter you wrote from Staggia[11] and then he read us your brief one written from Monterone[12] and we learnt with pleasure that you pursued your trip in good health. As soon as you arrive in Rome, we should like for you in your efficient and prudent manner to gain for us two cardinals. One is Spinola,[13] whom you should assure that, if he wishes to serve us truly in the conclaves, we would be content if, in case the Emperor wishes that he exclude Verona,[14] he may do so, and he may exclude one other according to his fancy, provided he name him to us now. Then on every other count he will serve us in our way and to our full satisfaction. We in turn promise him—and we shall give him by your hand every assurance that he may desire—a pension of 3,000 scudi a year during his lifetime, payable beginning immediately after the first conclave in which he has effectively given evidence of having served us and of continuing to do so for ever. As for secrecy, certify to him that no one besides you will know of it, that the payments will issue from you or from whomever you and he wish in such a way that it will not ever be possible to penetrate that the payments come from us.

An even more restrictive pact and only 2,000 scudi were to be offered to Cardinal Ottavio Paravicino, newly elevated 9 March 1591.

Cavalieri remained in Rome from the end of September to 6 October. Upon Gregory XIV's death on 15 October, Vinta was dispatched to Rome. The conclave lasted only two days, electing Giovanni Antonio Fachinetti (Innocent IX) of Bologna, with whom the Grand Duke, having predicted his election, had made a secret pact. As a reward to Cavalieri for his services, the Grand Duchess allowed his nephew Tiberio to have the honour of presenting to the new pope in her name an *organo di legno* 'to put in the chapel in which the vespers are sung'.[15] Innocent IX survived only sixty days, however, leaving the seat vacant again on 30 December 1591. This time the efforts of Cavalieri and Vinta, both again in Rome, were less successful, for the Duke's favoured candidate got one less vote than necessary. But the pope eventually elected, Ippolito Aldobrandini of Florence (Clement VIII), turned out to be an enemy of Spain and a friend of France, and he was to reign for thirteen years until 1605. So the Florentines won an ally for their world diplomacy.

Cavalieri did not enter the negotiations without personal political ambitions of his own. In a letter of 1 October 1590, from Florence, to Belisario Vinta in Rome, written during the reign of the sickly Urban VII, Cavalieri said:

[11] Staggia, apparently a stage for the Florence–Rome coach, is just north of Siena.

[12] This letter to Vinta, dated 28 Sept. 1591, is in Filza 829, fo. 315ʳ.

[13] Filippo Spinola, elevated on 12 Dec. 1583, upon the nomination of Emperor Rudolph II, was in the Spanish party. He died 20 Aug. 1593.

[14] i.e. Cardinal of Verona.

[15] Cavalieri to Ambassador Giovanni Niccolini, Florence, 9 Dec. 1591, ASF M.3622, fo. 20ʳ.

I know how much Your Lordship knows and how much you love me, and likewise Signor Cardinale dal Monte. He already knows my desire, which is to obtain a post as a secret gentleman of the chamber [*camerier segreto*], serving with rooms in the palace, or at least the governorship of Rimini . . .[16]

Vinta answered from Rome on 4 October: 'Should there come a pope who is amiable, I have no doubt, Your Lordship, that you and your brother will immediately be remembered and recommended . . . .'.[17]

When Clement VIII was elected, the Florentines began to claim their spoils. Giovanni Bardi was appointed *maestro di camera* to the new pope. As a reward to Cavalieri, the Duke recommended that Cavalieri's nephew, Tiberio, be assigned to the pope as a *cameriere segreto*.[18] Either Cavalieri had changed his mind about wanting the post himself, or the Duke was loath to let him go from his service.

Meanwhile, between the conclaves for Urban VII and Gregory XIV, Cavalieri found time to attend to his duties as director of entertainments at court, and even to compose. During the carnival of 1591 his *Satiro* and *La disperazione di Fileno* were produced.[19] After returning from the conclaves in 1591, Cavalieri was busy in March preparing the festivities for the double baptism of Princess Leonora and of Prince Cosimo.[20] The baptism took place around 23 April.[21]

In 1593 he went again to Rome for an extended stay. Fifty-one letters in Filza 3622, dated between 5 October 1593 and 25 March 1594, document this trip. The visit seems to have been made partly for personal reasons, since in the course of it he was arranging for the marriage of two of his three nieces—the third became a nun—and for the rental of his house. His natural son Valerio was now reaching school age and Cavalieri arranged to have him enter the Pages' School in Florence. One evening he had a modest *musicale* at his house.[22] That Cavalieri was a man of considerable means is

[16] Filza 3977: 'Io so quanto V. S. sa; et quanto mi ama; et similmente il Sig:ʳ Car:ˡᵉ dal Monte; di già sa il mio desiderio quale è di ottenere il luogo di camerier segreto servente con stanza in palazzo, o almeno, il Governo de Rimini.' A *cameriere segreto* is a member of the pope's personal staff.

[17] Filza 3976: 'Venga un' Papa, che ci sia amorevole, et non dubiti V. S., che ella, et il suo fratello gli saranno subito, et ricordati, et raccomandati . . .'.

[18] Minute of a letter from the Duke to Cavalieri, probably early 1592, Filza 19, fo. 183ʳ.

[19] Concerning these works, see Warren Kirkendale, 'L'opera in musica prima del Peri: le pastorali perdute di Laura Guidiccioni ed Emilio de' Cavalieri', in *Firenze e la Toscana dei Medici nell'Europa del '500*, ii: Musica e spettacolo, scienze dell'uomo e della natura (Florence: Olschki, 1983), 365–95.

[20] Letter, Florence, 31 Mar. 1592, to Accolti, Guardaroba, Filza 832, fo. 283, quoted in Solerti, 'Laura Guidiccioni', 818.

[21] Agostino Lapini, in his *Diario di Firenze*, noted the arrival of the Duke of Mantua and Virginio Orsini on 22 Apr. for the baptism: *Diario fiorentino di Agostino Lapini*, ed. Giuseppe O. Corrazzini (Florence: Sansoni, 1900), 327–8.

[22] Letter, Rome, 21 Nov. 1593, to Accolti, ASF M.3622 fo. 68ᵛ: 'Ier sera 20 [code number of Cosimo] fu in Casa mia; et avio con un poco di musichina con ogni modestia . . .'.

demonstrated particularly by the fact that to a suitor of one of his nieces he offered a dowry of 3,000 scudi.[23] He apparently went frequently to the Chiesa Nuova (Santa Maria in Vallicella), to which the Oratorio della Vallicella was attached, for he remarks that 'it is filled with prelates every morning'.[24] Besides attending to his personal affairs, Cavalieri must have been expected to send back intelligence and to carry on negotiations, for the letters were written at frequent intervals and many are partly coded.

Contrary to what has been believed, Cavalieri did not move to Rome in 1597, though he did make at least two separate visits that year. He is named in the records of the Oratorio del Crocifisso as having ordered payments made to Giovanni Maria Nanino as choirmaster and to others for singing, playing, copying, and tuning in connection with the music during Lent and Holy Week.[25] Cavalieri was therefore in Rome from around the end of carnival to Easter. He was again in Rome on 23 October, the date of the only letter sent from there that year in the file. He could not have stayed long on this visit, since in a letter of 20 September from Villegiano he states that he must go to Florence the next day, and a letter of 22 December is written from Florence.[26]

Cavalieri was in Rome again during the period from 18 December 1599 to 15 April 1600. The letters are less frequent, however, since he apparently was not on any state mission. On 18 December he offers to take back to Tuscany with him a singer whom he cannot send immediately because of the singer's holy-year duties. The next letter is dated 2 February 1600, and further letters are from 5 to 15 April 1600. It was during this period that Cavalieri saw his *Rappresentatione di anima et di corpo* produced at the Oratorio della Vallicella. He may also have supervised the music for Lent and Holy Week there, for in a letter to Accolti on 14 April, he excuses himself for having so little news, having done little visiting: 'I have attended to my house and to my devotions', he says.[27]

From Easter to November 1600 Cavalieri must have been busy in Florence with the preparations for the wedding of Maria de' Medici and Henry IV. His role in the entertainments will be discussed presently. After the festivities, Cavalieri left Florence for Rome, never to return. His position as director of music was given to Caccini. However, Cavalieri continued his political reporting from Rome, writing regularly about once

[23] Letter, Rome, 26 Nov. 1593, to Accolti, ASF M.3622, fo. 71ʳ.
[24] Letter, Rome, 9 Dec. 1593, to Vinta, ASF M.3622, fo. 81ᵛ.
[25] Domenico Alaleona, *Studi sulla storia dell'oratorio in Italia* (Turin: Bocca, 1908), 405. Concerning his activity at the Crocifisso, see also Bradshaw, 'Cavalieri and Early Monody'.
[26] To Accolti, ASF M.3622, fos. 154ʳ–156ʳ.
[27] ASF M.3622, fo. 182ᵛ: 'ho atteso, a Casa mia; et alle mie devozioni . . .'.

a week to Accolti or Vinta until shortly before his death. For a while in January 1601 he complained of illness, but appears to have at least partially recovered.[28] On 19 January he confesses to Accolti that he has been inactive musically: 'Although I have felt a desire for music, since being in Rome I have not heard anyone except a woman of the duke of Traietto. I also have not played anywhere, and from this you may judge the truth.'[29] In April he was still not feeling himself:

Believe me, I am not what I was once for many reasons. But health is the principal one, as I am little well. Then, I found my house half in ruin, and since I have been in Rome I have paid 12,000 scudi in debts. And, believe me, this has even taken all thoughts of music out of my head. For news I refer you to the enclosed letter. Your music must be better than this that we hear in Rome, because there has been only ordinary music.[30]

Cavalieri's complaints seem to have prompted a move at the Florentine court to invite him back with an offer of some position, but no definite offer seemed forthcoming. On 25 May he repeated to Accolti that he did not wish to return to Florence unless armed with a letter from the Grand Duchess that he could show to those who were ready to pay him discourtesies. He was particularly aggrieved by the fact that 'after having served the Grand Duke in so many crystalline matters', he should have been set aside for Giulio Romano.[31]

During the remainder of 1601 Cavalieri wrote regularly. When he had nothing to add he simply transmitted the unsigned reports of Cavaliere Pietro Paulo Azelio. There are three letters also in January 1602. The last letter by Cavalieri in the file is dated 1 February. There is no intimation in it of the illness that took his life on 11 March.

The letters of Cavalieri in Filza 3622 are particularly valuable for their insights and sidelights on the musical life of Florence and Rome. Roman by birth, Cavalieri never felt he received the credit he deserved from musical Florentines. Consequently, his reactions to events in Florence were almost always tinged with bitterness, particularly after he was superseded by Caccini. His references to musical events in Rome, though less numerous,

[28] Letters of 5 and 12 Jan. 1601, to Accolti, ASF M.3622, fos. 212r–215v.

[29] ASF M.3622, fos. 217v–218r: 'et se bene ho gusto di musica; doppo ch'io sono a Roma; non ho sentito nessuno; se non una donna del Duca di Traietto; et io non ho sonato in luogo veruno; et da questo giudicate il vero . . .'.

[30] Letter to Accolti, 21 Apr. 1601, ASF M.3622, fo. 257r: 'credi che io non sono più quel di prima, per molti rispetti; ma la sanità è la principale; che sto poco bene; poi haver ritrovata Casa mia, mezza rovinata; et ho pagato doppo sono in Roma D 12/m di debito; et creda che mi ha levato sino ai pensieri della musica del capo; delle nuove me rimetto all'inclusa; la lor musica dovrà esser molto meglio di queste di Roma; poichè non vi è stata musica se non molto ordinaria . . .'.

[31] Letter to Accolti, 25 May 1601, ASF M.3622, fo. 280v.

are more objective and reportorial, particularly since they were for the information of the Grand Duke and his secretaries.

Frequent references in the letters from Rome concern the soprano Vittoria Archilei, whose visits there coincided often—whether by accident or design—with Cavalieri's. These references are fortunate, since little has been known of her activities between the season of 1590, when she interpreted Cavalieri's *La disperazione di Fileno*, and 1602, when she is mentioned in the diary studied by Solerti.[32] She appears to have been a protegée of Cavalieri, both of them having been with Cardinal Ferdinand de' Medici in Rome before his succession to the Grand Duchy of Tuscany in 1587.[33] On 8 October 1593, Cavalieri notes that Vittoria is due in Rome shortly and that the Duke of Nivers 'is waiting with great desire to hear her'.[34] The letter of 18 January 1594 relates a whimsical incident that has the added novelty of being an anecdote about a saint. On the previous day there was a gathering in the room of a Messer Filippo, who must be Filippo Neri, the founder of the Oratory movement who was canonized on 12 May 1622, at this time a man of 82 and not altogether yet a saint:

Vittoria was in the room of Messer Filippo, and [Cardinal] Cusano was also present. She sang a Benedictus, but they wanted to hear *spagnole* and *galanterie* [popular songs]. There were many people there, and in the end Messer Filippo had a priest of the Vallicella dance. He did the *canario* and the *pedrolino*, and Vittoria said to me that he danced stupendously and must practise frequently. Messer Filippo then gave the benediction to several, notably to Vittoria, and so that she would remember him he gave her a good slap and made her promise to come back another time.[35]

Two circumstances particularly point to Neri as the Filippo of the story: the reference to the Vallicella, where he lived, and the presence of Cardinal Antonio Cusano, close associate of Neri during his last years. Vittoria was apparently on loan from Florence to the Grand Duke's nephew, Virginio

---

[32] For the most recent data cf. Emilia Zanetti, 'Archilei', in *Enciclopedia dello spettacolo*, i. 789; C. V. Palisca, 'Archilei', *MGG*, Supplement, xv (1973), 263–4, and *MGG*, 2nd edn., in press; and Kirkendale, 'Emilio de' Cavalieri', and id., 'Cavalieri', *Dizionario biografico degli italiani*.

[33] According to James Chater, 'Bianca Capello and Music', in Andrew Monogh *et al.* (eds.), *Renaissance Studies in Honor of Craig Hugh Smyth* (Florence: Giunti Barbèra, 1985), i. 569–79 at 574, Cavalieri was in the service of Giangiorgio Cesarini, a friend of Cardinal Ferdinand, but apparently not directly in Ferdinand's service.

[34] ASF M.3622, fos. 32^r–33^r: 'aspetta poi con molto desiderio Vittoria per sentirla . . .'.

[35] Letter to Accolti, ASF M.3622, fo. 112: 'Vittoria ieri stette in camera di Messer Filippo, dove fu Cusano; et cantò, un benedictus, ma volsero sentir spagnole, et galanterie, vi furno di molti; et in ultimo Messer Filippo fece ballare un prete della Vallicella, canario et da pedrolino; et mi dice Vittoria che stupendemente sichè deve esercitarsi, spesso; Messer Filippo poi dà la benedizione ad alcuni, et particolarmente a Vittoria, et perchè si ricordasse di lui; gli diede un bono schiaffo; et si fece promettere che ritornasse un altra volta . . .'.

Orsini, since Cavalieri notes on 11 February of the same year that with the permission of Don Virginio's wife Flavia, the soprano would sing on the 13th at a dinner given by Orazio Rucellai. Giovanni Francesco Aldobrandini was invited simply to hear her.[36] Vittoria was still in Rome on 7 March, when she put up jewels worth 250 scudi in a lottery at Don Virginio's.[37]

On 10 November 1600 Cavalieri reports that he has heard in Rome that both he and Vittoria have been removed by the Duke from their posts.[38] She must have been reinstated. The *Diario d'etichetta* records that on 1 October she had entertained in the Grand Duchess's room while Mons. Betuni, French Ambassador to the Pope, was visiting.[39] She was back in Rome in January 1602, when the Duke gave Cavalieri permission to have her sing at his house, but he declined the privilege, explaining that of his nieces only Laura liked music, and he and his natural son Valerio had heard her sufficiently. In the letter of 1 February Cavalieri reported that Cardinals Paravicino and Acquaviva went to see Cardinal del Monte's vineyard, and Antonio and Vittoria Archilei happened to be visiting also. The cardinals desired to hear her; so their instruments were sent for. Cavalieri tells that because she was 'in a wild mood and singing in a vaulted room, I certainly have never heard her in more beautiful voice. She gave so much satisfaction that Acquaviva said to me: "I for shame did not weep." Paravicino said he never thought such refinement was possible. They are both musicians.'[40]

Of the entertainments in Rome that Cavalieri describes, the most noteworthy is that given around 18 January 1601 by Marzio Colonna for the brother of the Viceroy of Naples. Many gentlewomen arrived after dinner, when there was a ball until two o'clock. Then a supper was served, and from three to seven in the morning a comedy was performed with five changes of scene and five intermedi and a ballo that Cavalieri says was 'fatto al modo mio', and indeed the entire production was 'nel modo di fiorenza', that is, modelled after the famous comedy and intermedi produced by Cavalieri in Florence in 1589.[41]

Among the numerous references to Florentine musicians and musical events, the most interesting are those that have to do with the musical pastorals, *Giuoco della cieca*, *Dafne*, and *Euridice*.

A letter dated Florence, 17 November 1598, provides fragments of information on the preparations for the revivals of Cavalieri's *Giuoco della*

[36] Letter to Accolti, ASF M.3622, fo. 119ʳ.
[37] Letter to Accolti, 8 Mar. 1594, M.3622, fo. 136ʳ.
[38] Letter to Accolti, M.3622, fo. 186ʳ.
[39] Vol. ii, 1589–1612, Guardaroba, Filza 2, p. 126.
[40] Letter to Accolti, ASF M.3622, fo. 402ʳ.
[41] Letter to Accolti, 19 Jan. 1601, ASF M.3622, fo. 216ʳ.

cieca and Jacopo Peri's *Dafne* early the following year.[42] Cavalieri was concerned because one of the singers had asked to resign. He dismisses the idea that Francesco Rasi could be tempted away from Mantua.[43] Then he says:

As for Il Zazzerino [Jacopo Peri], he is playing in the pastoral. Bad luck would have it that today his wife died, and he is most afflicted. However, in three days he should be in a condition to sing.

To save time, it seems to me that we should write a letter to Giugno,[44] and it should contain: 'His Highness is resolved that a pastoral should be done for Montalto; and he has written about it to Emilio, who has replied today that Duritio[45] is in poor health and his help will be lacking, as he has requested permission to resign, and there are other such things. So Emilio asked if His Highness would do him the favour of not giving him this burden this time. Should His Highness wish that the pastoral be done in any case, let Giugno tell me in behalf of Their Highnesses that this is their desire, exhorting me in every way that I do it, assuring me that he will facilitate costumes, stage-setting, and all the services. He should say that His Highness has ordered Giugno to satisfy me in all the things that will be needed and that I should request. His Highness should be assured that I shall not throw away his money.'[46]

---

[42] The *Giuoco della cieca*, with music by Cavalieri, was first performed on 29 Oct. 1595 in the Hall of Statues of the Pitti Palace. Peri's *Dafne* was first produced during the carnival of 1598 at Jacopo Corsi's house.

[43] This and an earlier letter furnish valuable information on the career of Francesco Rasi. On 16 Dec. 1593 Cavalieri warns the Duke's secretary concerning Rasi, then in the employ of the duke, 'che il Rasi, è deventato tanto buono, si de chitarrone come di cantante; che ne è fatto conferire stima in Roma. Don Verginio, et Montalto mi hanno pregato che con buona grazia di Sua Altezza ciascuno lo vorria al suo servizio . . .' (that he has become so good, both on the chitarrone and as a singer, that he has won esteem in Rome. Don Verginio and Montalto have each begged that with the good favour of His Highness he would like to have him in his service). Carlo Gesualdo, Prince of Venosa, also offered him a large salary. Cavalieri urged the Duke to raise his stipend from two to eight scudi a month, because 'oggi non vedo chi canti meglio di lui, et ancho sona bene affatto . . .' (today I do not see that there is anyone who sings better than he, and he also plays altogether well); ASF M.3622, fo. 83ᵛ. On 17 Nov. 1598 Cavalieri writes from Florence: 'Il Rasi riceve molte littere da ministri del Duca di Mantova; et in particolare una del Duca che lo richiamava con molte grate parole; il quale subito partì et è a Mantova . . .' (Rasi receives many letters from the ministers of the Duke of Mantua, and in particular one from the Duke himself that enticed him with many charming words. He immediately departed for Mantua); ASF M.3622, fo. 168ʳ. For the most recent information on Rasi, see Warren Kirkendale, 'Zur Biographie des ersten Orfeo, Francesco Rasi', in *Claudio Monteverdi: Festschrift Reinhold Hammerstein zum 70. Geburtstag* (Laaber: Laaber-Verlag, 1986), 297–335.

[44] Giugno handled costuming, decorations, stage sets, and the like.

[45] Duritio Isorelli or Usorelli della Viola, as he is named in the roll of court personnel of 1588 (Archivio mediceo, Depositeria generale, Filza 389, p. 17), was a protegé of Cavalieri. He had been an associate of Cavalieri at the Oratorio del Crocifisso in Rome: cf. Alaleona, *Studi*, 403, where he is listed as receiving six scudi for his services during Lent and Holy Week, 1584. He both played basso di viola bastarda and sang in the intermedi of 1589. He left Florence for Rome in 1599 and on 1 May of that year at the age of 55 was admitted into the Congregazione dell'Oratorio (ibid. 62–5).

[46] ASF M.3622, fo. 168ᵛ: 'Il Zazzerino faccio conto suona alla pastorale, ma per cattiva sorte, oggi se l'è morta la moglie; et stà afflittissimo, pure in tre giorni, dovrà ritornare in termine di cantare;

A me parria per più brevità; che si scrivesse una littera al Giugni; et contenesse; Sua Altezza è risoluto si faccia una pastorale a Montalto; et ne ha scritto a Emilio, il quale ha risposto; che per haver

Two pastorals are in question here, and they must be those performed respectively on 5 January[47] and 21 January 1599,[48] both in the Hall of Statues of the Pitti Palace. The first was the *Giuoco della cieca* or *Mosca cieca* of Cavalieri. The second was the *Dafne* of Peri and Corsi.

The first, in which Jacopo Peri was playing, was evidently already in rehearsal. The second had just been ordered by the Grand Duke to honour Cardinal Montalto. This cardinal, Alessandro Peretti Damasceni, great-grandnephew of Pope Sixtus V, was one of the richest prelates in Rome and a key to the outcome of many conclaves because he controlled about a score of votes. Already busy with the *Giuoco della cieca*, Cavalieri begged to be relieved of the task of producing another pastoral. Evidently the Duke acquiesced and asked Corsi to assume the task. Having produced the *Dafne* at his home at the preceding carnival, Corsi now undertook to present it at court on the occasion of Montalto's visit.

Peri must have sung in the *Dafne*, since Cavalieri implies that he was available. The death of his wife, who must have been the first of four, here established to have occurred on 17 November 1598, has not otherwise been recorded, nor is her name known. In 1599 he married Caterina di Niccolò Fortunati.[49] The other singers who performed in these pastorals have not been identified. Cavalieri mentions later in the letter that he has found someone to replace the contralto Duritio, and that this man, a Florentine, would accept the same remuneration, eight scudi a month.

On 5 April 1600, Cavalieri, still in Rome, returns to the subject of the two pastorals in a postscript to Lorenzo Usimbardi. He unburdens himself of his resentment of the Florentine public's coolness to his music and to his protégée Vittoria Archilei.

To hear it said that Portia and the *monacha* sing better than Vittoria, that the pastoral of Corsi pleased more than the *Cieca*, that Giulio Romano is the God of

oggi poca sanità esserle mancato l'aiuto di Durizio, il quale ha chiesto licenza; et altre cose simili; che le voglia far grazia, non le dar questo peso per questa volta; volendo Sua Altezza in ogni modo si faccia; che il Giugno, mi dica da parte di loro Altezze questo desiderio, esortandomi in ogni modo ch'io la facci; et che lui dove sarrà buono, mi facilitarà habiti, scena, et tutto il servizio; et che Sua Altezza ordini al Giugno che mi sodisfaccia in tutto quello vi sarrà necessario, et che chiederò; assicurando Sua Altezza che non gettarò la robba sua; . . .'.

[47] *Storia d'etichetta*, i, extracted in Jodoco del Badia (ed.), *Miscellanea fiorentina di erudizione e storia* (Florence: Landi, 1902), ii. 147: 'A dì 5 detto [genaio] sè li fece nel salone delle statue la pastorella in musica dal S. Emilio de' Cavalieri, che vi furono 60 gentildonne fiorentine.' Cf. also Solerti, *Gli albori del melodramma* (Milan, Palermo, Naples: Remo Sandron, 1904; repr. Hildesheim: Georg Olms, 1969), i. 61.

[48] *Storia d'etichetta*, i, in Del Badia, *Miscellanea*, ii. 148; Solerti, *Gli albori*, i. 61.

[49] Federico Ghisi, 'Peri' in *Die Musik in Geschichte und Gegenwart*, x. 1065. Concerning the performances of *Dafne*, see Tim Carter, *Jacopo Peri, 1561–1633: His Life and Works* (New York: Garland, 1989), i. 29–39.

Music, that the Lamentations were better this year in Pisa than the last—all this does not surprise me at all. Believe me, this is pure sugar after Rome. I have never seen or imagined such malignity, such trickery, and this in the most important things, and it has even reached the musicians. Their malice is such that I wonder if I am in Rome or in Turkey.[50]

Cavalieri sensed the tide turning against Romans like himself and Vittoria, who were brought in by Ferdinand I, as he observed Caccini, Antonio Naldi, and other Florentine musicians gaining favour. He may have been inclined to dismiss the possibility that Peri in *Dafne*, which was repeated perhaps with improvements during the carnival of 1600, had found a more expressive and dramatic monodic style than he himself had achieved in the *Cieca*. Prejudice, however, was undoubtedly strong from the first against Cavalieri, an outsider imposed on top of an existing hierarchy.[51]

Whether it was because of this prejudice against the *forestieri* or Cavalieri's own inefficiency arising from his frequent absences and the over-extension of his duties and interests, the Superintendent of the Arts evidently lost control of the musical situation during the preparations for the wedding celebrations of October 1600. Caccini's refusal to allow his singers to perform Peri's music, with the result that *Euridice* was a hybrid of two composers' thoughts and methods, the hero singing Peri and the heroine Caccini, was a sign of Cavalieri's inability to reconcile conflicting interests. A similar clash of motives that he was apparently unable to resolve occurred between the architect Bernardo Buontalenti and Ferdinand I's half-brother Don Giovanni de' Medici. Instead of the smoothly functioning team Cavalieri had led in the comedy and intermedi of 1589, for which a voluminous book of accounts bears witness to a triumph of efficient administration, the entertainments of the wedding of 1600 were in Cavalieri's opinion a disgrace, and he took refuge in Rome at the earliest opportunity, resolved never to return.

In his first letter from Rome he expressed satisfaction at the success of the banquet on 5 October, in which his *La contesa fra Giunone e Minerva* was sung. This, states Cavalieri, was universally admired. But 'the music of the

---

[50] ASF M.3622, fos. 178ᵛ–179ʳ: 'Il sentir dire; che la Porzia, et la monacha, canti meglio di Vittoria; la pastorale del Corsi, sia piacciuta più; della Cieca; che Giulio Romano sia il Dio della Musica; che siano state migliori le lamentazioni questo anno a Pisa; dell'anno passato, non mi maraviglio niente; et creda che è tutto Zucchero, alle cose di Roma; poichè non ho mai veduto, ne imaginatomi, tal malignità; et artifici; et questo è in cose principalissime; ma è arrivato ancho ne' musici; con tal malignità al parer mio, che sto a vedere; se io sono a Roma; o in Turchia . . .'.

[51] Cf. U. Rolandi, 'E. de' Cavalieri, il Granduca Ferdinando e l'Inferigno', in *Rivista musicale italiana*, 36 (1929), 32. A reconsideration of these pastorals is in Kirkendale, 'L'opera in musica prima del Peri'.

comedy I did', according to what the Cardinal of Florence and Cardinal Borromeo had heard from everyone, 'did not give satisfaction, the scenery not having been completed and also for other reasons'. This must refer to *Euridice*, since two of the court diarists call it the musical pastoral of Emilio de' Cavalieri, implying thereby that he was its musical director.[52] Concerning *Il rapimento di Cefalo* on 9 October, with music by Caccini and intermedi by Don Giovanni, Cavalieri wrote:

If only Signor Don Giovanni had been willing to listen to my opinion concerning the music of the comedy and to Bernardo's on matters concerning the machines, I believe everything would have been terminated and finished, and the music would have been proportionate to the place and to the theatre, and the money would have been spent with greater satisfaction to the listeners. Giulio Romano, too, would have had his satisfaction and been given something to do that he was capable of doing.[53]

Caccini's intimate style, Cavalieri implies, was not suitable to a theatre filled with 3,800 people. Alessandro Guidotti, acting as Cavalieri's spokesman, had said in the preface to the *Rappresentatione di anima et di corpo*:

Let the instruments be well played and be of a greater or lesser number according to the place or theatre or hall, which, to be proportionate to this style of recitation, should not hold more a thousand persons . . . for when staged in halls that are too large not everyone can hear the words, and so much music without the words being heard becomes boring, and the singer, compelled to force his voice, communicates less affection.[54]

---

[52] Cf. Solerti, *Musica, ballo e drammatica alla corte medicea dal 1600 al 1637* (Florence: Bemporad e figlio, 1905; repr. Bologna: Forni, 1969), 25. A further circumstance tying Cavalieri to the production is the probable presence in the cast of his pupils or members of his household: 'Giovannino del Sig. Emilio', who sang the prologue as 'Tragedia', and a 'Castrato del Sig. Emilio', who played both Venus and Proserpina, according to a libretto marked at a slightly later performance. Cf. my article 'The First Performance of *Euridice*', below, Essay 16.

[53] Filza 899, fos. 416ʳ–417ᵛ. The text of this letter was published in part by R. Gandolfi in 'Appunti di storia musicale', in *Rassegna nazionale*, 15/74 (1893), 304, and in its entirety by Solerti in 'Laura Guidiccioni', 819–20. Neither was sufficiently explicit about the musical works implied but not named in it. The date given by Gandolfi and Solerti and clearly written in Cavalieri's hand is 7 Oct. 1600. This date is questionable on several grounds. It is doubtful that Cavalieri, responsible for all the entertainments at court, would have been away at this crucial time. Besides, how could the cardinals have heard the reactions to the 6 Oct. performance and communicated them to Cavalieri in Rome in time for him to write about them the next day? He also speaks of the 9 Oct. performance as if it were a thing of the past. These doubts are confirmed by remarks in the final portion of the letter. There Cavalieri reports that because of an attack of erysipelas Signor Antonio Camaiani, who had planned to follow the Queen to France, did not go with her. He also reports that Cardinals of Florence and del Monte wished 'that the Queen before her departure from Tuscany had replied generally to the cardinals since if she replies from France they say it will be judged a French thought'. These remarks show that the Queen had already left. She embarked at Leghorn on 17 Oct. A clue to the probable date is given by the words: 'We are having the summer of St Martin's', that is, Indian Summer. St Martin's Day is 11 November. The letter was probably absentmindedly signed 7 Oct. for 7 Nov.

[54] Solerti, *Le origini del melodramma* (Turin: Bocca, 1903), 5–6.

The talents of Caccini, master of the florid chamber madrigal and aria, were not used to best advantage in a colossal show such as that of 9 October. Cavalieri's counsels had apparently little effect on Don Giovanni, who insisted on having his own way.

Cavalieri's dissatisfaction with the performances of 1600 is even more clearly expressed in a postscript to a letter of uncertain date in Filza 3622. The postscript, written on a separate folio, as Cavalieri often did when he wished the Duke not to see something he wrote to Accolti, has been detached from the letter itself. Although the archivist who arranged the correspondence, probably in the seventeenth century, marked it '1602' and placed it among the letters of that year, it appears to be from the period between November 1600 and January 1601 and probably belongs to the letter of 24 November 1600, which lacks the usual sealing folio.[55]

The postscript merits quoting in full:

I wish that what I write below not be heard by the Grand Duke.

In Rome one does not adulate. As many people of all ranks as I have spoken to have said to me: the things of moderate size did not succeed, and particularly the big production did not. [They say] that the music was tedious, that it seemed like the chanting of the passion. Marchese de Piano was particularly of this conviction. The feast of the banquet everybody praised as a thing of great beauty. Only there was a little confusion of people. Giovanni de' Bardi, a loyal servant of His Highness, asked me with amazement, how is it possible that His Highness had not made use of Bernardo [Buontalenti] and of me and failed to follow the example of the comedy of the wedding [of 1589] by having a comedy with intermedi, using il Guerrino [Guarini] also? For the few words that he composed lent honour to all the rest. And [he said] they should not have gone into tragic texts and objectionable subjects.[56] I merely listened and let him talk. To tell you the truth, I was pleased to hear that all the things in which I participated are said to have been done by Signor Don Giovanni, and those for which others were responsible and that did not succeed they say I did. I replied to this by giving an account of where I intervened. Then I defended the others by reasons such as the shortness of time and other factors, which are not acknowledged.

Whoever spends his money as His Highness has done this time should get satisfaction; and the servant should tie the ass where the master wishes, as I did. My only desire was that His Highness hear what is being said and that he know the truth in this matter: that he has thrown away the money he spent on the

---

[55] The reverse of the last page of the postscript (fo. 399ᵛ) bears the seal and address to Marcello Accolti. There are three letters lacking seals to which this might belong: 24 Nov. 1600, 4 May 1601, and 25 May 1601. Since in the letter Cavalieri mentions the *Rappresentatione* as having been performed 'this past carnival', and we know this occurred in Feb. 1600, the latest possible date of the letter is Jan. 1601. Because it seems to supply requested amplification of the letter dated 7 Oct. but probably of 7 Nov., the postscript is most likely a companion to the letter of 24 Nov.

[56] While 'tragic texts' can only mean *Euridice*, 'objectionable subjects' must refer to *Il rapimento di Cefalo*, which represents the Goddess Aurora's seduction of the unwilling mortal Cefalo.

comedies and also lost the reputation that Florence once had in such things; that this displeases Giovanni de' Bardi; and that by using Bernardo and myself he could have done wonders with less expense—and he had already tested us. To tell you the truth I am unburdening myself so that I can go to church afterwards.

The more these comedies became magnified by Bardella [Antonio Naldi] and Giulio [Caccini], and by others, and the more I was slighted, and also Bernardo, the more the miracles disappeared and they [the entertainments] appeared to foreigners as commonplace and struck people as tedious. Everyone says it lasted more than five hours, but it did not even reach three. If Milord the Archbishop should see this, it would not bother me. And once again I kiss your hand.

I forgot to say what the priests of the Vallicella told me, and this is great. Many prelates among those who came to Florence saw a *rappresentatione in musica* that I had done this carnival at their Oratorio, for which the expenditure was six scudi at the most. They say that they found it much more to their taste, because the music moved them to tears and laughter and pleased them greatly, unlike this music of Florence, which did not move them at all, unless to boredom and irritation. Pray to God that whoever will want to judge rightly will know my work. If I have had some detractors and so many disappointments—all in the service of the Grand Duke—nevertheless wisdom, diligence, and patience have surmounted them all.[57]

---

[57] ASF M.3622, fos. 398^r–399^r:

'Desidero che questo che le scrivo qui di sotto Sua Altezza non lo senti;

In Roma non si adula; et con quanti ho parlato di ogni grado di persona; tutti mi hanno detto; che le cose medie non sono riuscite; et in particolare la grande; et che le musiche sono state tediose; et che li è parso sentire cantar la passione; et in particolare è stato detto dal Marchese de Piano; di questa passione; la festa del Banchetto tutti approvano; per cosa bellissima; solo con un poco di confusione di gente; Giovanni de' Bardi; mi ha detto, maravigliandosi; il quale è servitore di cuore a Sua Altezza come è possibile; che Sua Altezza non si sia servito di Bernardo; et di me; et caminato, con l'esempio; della comedia delle nozze; et far una comedia; con intermedi; servendosi ancho del Guerrino; poichè quelle parole poche che lui ha fatte; portano l'honore di tutte; et non intrare; in parole tragiche; et soggetti da potervi opporre; Io sono stato ascoltatore; et lasciato dire; et ve dico la verità; io ho havuto gusto; in sentire; che tutte le cose che io vi sono intervenuto; dicono che siano state fatte dal Signore Don Giovanni; et quelle che sono proprie de' altri; et che non sono riuscite; dichino che le habbia fatte io; et in questo ho dato conto; dove io sono intervenuto; et difeso poi gli altri; per la brevità del tempo; et altre ragioni; che non sono acettate;

È dovere che chi spende il suo dinaro; si sodisfaccia come ha fatto Sua Altezza questa volta; et ancho che il servidore leghi l'asino dove vuole il padrone; come ho fatto io; quello solo che io desideravo; che Sua Altezza sentisse quello che si dice; et che conoscesse il vero di questo fatto; et che ha gettato via gli denari che si è speso nelle comedie; et ancho perso; la riputazione; che teneva Fiorenza in far cose simili; che questo dispiace a Giovanni de' Bardi; et che poteva; con servirsi di Bernardo; et di me; con meno spese; far fare gli miracoli; et di già ci haveva provati; ve dirrò il vero; mi sfogo; per poter poi andare alle chiese;

Et tanto piu è stato dal Bardella et Giulio; agrandito queste comedie; et da altri; et abbassato me; et Bernardo; tanto più sono spariti gli miracoli; et parso a forastieri cose ordinarie; et che li sia parso tediosa; tutti vogliono che durasse più di cinque hore; et non arrivò a tre; se questa la vedrà Monsignore Arcivescovo a me non darrà noia; et di novo le bagio le mani;

Mi era scordato dire; che questa è grande; che da quei preti della Vallicella mi hanno detto; che molti prelati; di quelli venuti a Fiorenza veddero una cotesta che io feci fare questo carnevale, di rapresentazione in musica; al loro oratorio; che si spese da D sei al più; et dicono; che ne riceverno altro gusto; poichè la musica li mosse a pianto et riso; et le diede gran gusto; et che questa musica di Firenze; non li mosse se non a tedio et fastidio; Laudato sia Dio; che chi vorrà giudicare rettamente; conoscerà l'opera mia; et che se bene ho havuto li sconciatori; et tanti disgusti; tutti in disservizio del Gran Duca; con tuttociò; il sapere; la diligenza; et la pazienza; ha superato ogni cosa.'

The brunt of the criticism here seems aimed at *Euridice*. Cavalieri acknowledges that he is being held responsible for its reputed failure. The main complaint against it is that the music was dull, resembling the chanting of the Passion. Here someone coined a simile that was to enjoy much currency as a drawing-room cliché in France to describe the music of Lully. Bardi, the host of the Camerata, far from being a champion of the revival of tragedy, as he is usually characterized, seems to have disapproved of the tragic theme of *Euridice* and to have preferred the old-fashioned formula of a comedy with intermedi.

If the undated postscript was truly part of the letter of 24 November, Cavalieri's feelings about Florentine musical affairs had reason by then to turn sour. In a letter to Accolti on 10 November 1600, Cavalieri begins: 'Everyone tells me that I have been discharged by His Highness and they are saying the same in Florence. I have already had several letters from Florence that treat me as if I were.'[58] He felt no great regret about losing the job of co-ordinator of music, now turned over to Caccini:

I should think that His Highness may put the music in charge of whom he pleases. For this man [Caccini] makes war on me. I do not care for the job at all. It is only a chore for me and a source of innumerable disappointments, and I do not know how to take them any longer. These two [Caccini and Naldi] have provoked me to the cudgel as much as they could, but I have given my arms back to St George.[59]

The following May, in a letter to Accolti, Cavalieri was still recalling the aggravations he had suffered in his job, while at the same time expressing doubts about Caccini's qualifications to take his place as director of music.

When I think of Bardella, of Giulio Romano, of the Model, and similar things, I ask myself if I am dreaming or imagining things. I have been here in Rome with Claudio da Correggio [Merulo] and now with Lucciasco[60] and everyone says in unison great things about me. That I, then, should have been set aside by Giulio Romano, who if he lived a hundred years could learn from me![61]

---

[58] Filza 3622, fo. 186r: 'Da tutti, mi vien detto; ch'io sono licenziato da Sua Altezza et ancho il simile si dice a Fiorenza; et di già ho havuto più littere da Fiorenza che mi trattano di ciò.'

[59] ASF M.3622, fo. 186r: 'crederei che Sua Altezza potesse dare il carico della musica, a chi piacesse a Sua Altezza poichè questo mi fa la guerra; la qual carica; io non la stimo nulla; non essendo per me se non briga; et cagione de infiniti disgusti; et io non sono più il caso; questi due; mi hanno provocato al bastone quanto mai hanno potuto; poichè che è loro ascendente; ma io ho reso le armi a San Giorgio . . .'.

[60] On 6 Apr. Cavalieri reported that Cardinal Aldobrandini arrived with great pomp, and 'he brought with him Luzzasco. They say he came for two months but he may well stay in Rome. I have not yet heard him play' ('Aldobrandino ha menato seco Luzzasco, dicono per due mesi; ma facilmente potria restare in Roma; io non lo ho ancho sentito sonare'). ASF M.3622, fo. 348r.

[61] Letter to Accolti, 25 May 1601, ASF M.3622, fo. 280v: 'et quando penso al Bardella; a Giulio Romano; al Modello, et cose simili; dico tra di me se io sogno; overo se, io vaneggio; et sono stato qui in Roma con Claudio da Correggio; et hora con Lucciasco et a una voce; tutti dicono gran cose di me; et che io poi, sia stato messo da parte per Giulio Romano; il quale se vivessi cento anni; potria inparare sempre da me . . .'.

To return to the letter of 10 November, Cavalieri goes on to confess that he was deeply hurt also by Ottavio Rinuccini's claims in his dedicatory letter to the Queen of France in the printed libretto of *Euridice*.[62] Cavalieri complains:

He acts, as you can see, as if he had been the inventor of this way of representing in music [*questo modo di rappresentare in Musica*], never before found or invented by anyone. He says that what difficulties this style presented were surmounted by the great science in music possessed by Jacopo Peri, that is il Zazzerino. I know that Rinuccini has gone head over heels into making everyone think he is more than most have been inclined to believe. It would please me if His Highness were aware of this, so that he would better know his sheep, who follow the principle: away with foreigners. I sense that with this publication he hopes to be employed by the Queen in France as a secretary or some other such fancy.[63] Indeed, I spoke to him about all this, for it seemed to me that he had done me wrong. Because this [style] was invented by me, and everyone knows this, and I find myself having said so in print.[64] Now whoever sees the libretto of the Ranocchino [little frog] will consider me a liar.[65]

Rinuccini indeed stated that the ancient manner of reciting in music had not been tried by anyone before he and Jacopo Corsi had decided to ask Peri to set *Dafne* in this manner.

When the printed score of Caccini's *Euridice* reached Cavalieri on 20 January, he immediately wrote to Accolti, who had probably asked his opinion of it. Cavalieri ignored the claims of priority made there, for he felt that anyone who compared Caccini's score with that of his own *Rappresentatione* could judge for himself the merits of the case.

I wrote last night. Having seen the print of Giulio Romano, I find nothing in it that annoys me. For my *rappresentatione*, which is printed, having been printed three and a half months earlier, settles all the contentions. And it will be

---

[62] English trans. in Oliver Strunk, *Source Readings in Music History* (New York: Norton, 1950), 367–9.

[63] Francesco Raccamadoro-Marelli, in *Ottavio Rinuccini* (Fabiano, 1900), 41, cites a document in which Ottavio confided to his brothers his hopes of being favoured by the Queen.

[64] He means the prefatory letters by Alessandro Guidotti in the edition of the *Rappresentatione*, where Guidotti acted as Cavalieri's spokesman.

[65] ASF M.3622, fo. 186ᵛ: 'tratta, come potrà vedere; che lui sia stato l'inventore; di questo modo di rappresentare in Musica; mai più da altri trovato nè inventato; et che per qualche difficoltà, che lui vi scorgeva, è venuta superata; dalla gran scienza sopra della Musica; da Jacopo Peri, cioè il Zazzarino; appresso a tutti so che si è data, la zappa sopra piedi; et fattosi conoscere; per quello che da molti non era tenuto in tal opinione; a me farria caro; che Sua Altezza lo sapesse; acciò meglio conoscesse le sue pecore; le quali sono, scaccia forestieri; sento che con questa stampa; spera di essere adoprato in Francia dalla Regina; per segretario, over altra sua chimera; Veramente; io ne ho parlato sopra di ciò, parendomi; che mi habia fatto torto; poichè questo è inventato da me; che ciascheduno lo sa; et io trovo haverlo publicato; Hora chi vede la stampa del Ranocchino; mi terrà per un bugiardo.'

recognized what is science and what is the difference between starlings and partridges.[66]

Jacopo Peri must have learnt of Cavalieri's annoyance at Rinuccini's claims, because when he wrote the preface to his score of *Euridice* a few weeks later—the dedication is signed 6 February 1600 (*ab incarnatione*, hence 1601)—he was careful to credit Cavalieri with being the first to use the modern manner of singing on the stage. He states there:

Although Signor Emilio del Cavaliere, before any other of whom I know, enabled us with marvellous invention to hear our kind of music upon the stage, none the less as early as 1594 it pleased the Signors Jacopo Corsi and Ottavio Rinuccini that I should employ it in another guise and should set to music the fable of *Dafne*, written by Signor Ottavio to make a simple trial of what the music of our age could do.[67]

Cavalieri does not help us solve the riddle of who 'invented' recitative. The solution may not be so simple as he imagined. Certainly his claim to priority in the introduction of sung dramatic dialogue—*rappresentar cantando*—rests on good grounds. But recitative is another matter.

Cavalieri does provide a more accurate chronology of the first monodic musical dramas in his letters than has been available. The dates of the dedicatory letters have been known, but such dates do not always indicate even approximately the publication dates. According to the last letter cited, the *Rappresentatione* appeared in print around 1 October, perhaps a few days before Rinuccini's dedicatory letter. Rinuccini's libretto must have been issued in time for the wedding guests to receive copies. Caccini's score appeared around 16 January 1601. The dedication of Peri's score was signed 6 February of the same year. There was too little time between Caccini's and his own score for Peri to have been influenced by his rival's setting, little of which had been performed publicly. On the other hand, Caccini had ample time to model the recitative portions of his setting upon Peri's. The letters and prefaces give the impression of claims and counter-claims. That they were precisely this is strongly suggested by the contentiousness and chronology documented in Cavalieri's letters.

---

[66] Letter to Accolti, 20 Jan. 1601, ASF M.3622, fo. 220ʳ: 'Scrissi iersera; et havendo veduta la stampa de Giulio Romano; non vi è cosa che mi dia noia; poichè la mia rapresentazione che si è stampata; essendo stampata; tre mesi e mezzo prima; chiarisce tutte le partite; et si cognoscerà; la scienza; et la differenza, che è da storni et starne . . .'.

[67] Strunk, *Source Readings*, 373.

15

The Alterati of Florence, Pioneers in the Theory of Dramatic Music

This essay was first published in *New Looks at Italian Opera: Essays in Honor of Donald J. Grout* (Ithaca, NY: Cornell University Press, 1968), 9–38. It is a reworking of a paper read at a meeting of the Greater New York Chapter of the American Musicological Society at the New York Public Library on 28 April 1962. The research in Florence in 1960–1 on which this essay was based was made possible by a fellowship from the John Simon Guggenheim Memorial Foundation.

I confined myself in this article to opinions about dramatic music exchanged among or promulgated by members of one Florentine academy, the Accademia degli Alterati. Similar conversations were surely carried on in other Florentine academies and circles as well as in such gatherings in other cities. Francesco Patrizi in Ferrara must have stimulated discussion of a whole range of questions about music in ancient drama. Angelo Ingegneri published in Ferrara in 1598 a treatise on how to perform plays that distilled wide experience and deep thought during a long career as stage director.[1] In the treatise he often points as a practical example to the tragedy with music *Edipo tiranno* that he staged at the Teatro Olimpico in Vicenza in 1585.[2] Although academies in which music was a central concern, as it was in the groups that met in the homes of Giovanni Bardi and Jacopo Corsi in Florence, were rather rare, there were academies in other cities that have been studied with regard to their musical interests or activities. The most famous is the Accademia Filarmonica of Verona, which was a focus of musical composition and performance.[3] The Accademia degli Unisoni in Perugia met to perform vocal and instrumental music and to hear discourses on various subjects, including music, and evidently Greek music theory as well.[4] The Academy of Domenico Venier in

---

[1] Angelo Ingegneri, *Della poesia rappresentativa e del modo di rappresentare le favole sceniche* (Ferrara: Vittorio Baldini, 1598).

[2] See Leo Schrade (ed.), *La Représentation d'Edipo Tiranno au Teatro Olimpico (Vicence 1585)* (Paris: Éditions du CNRS, 1960), 51–63 and id., 'L'*Edipo Tiranno* d'Andrea Gabrieli et la renaissance de la tragédie grecque' in *Musique et poésie au XVIe siècle* (Paris: Éditions du CNRS, 1954), 275–85.

[3] This was studied by G. Turrini, 'L'Accademia Filarmonica di Verona dalla fondazione (maggio 1543) al 1600 e il suo patrimonio musicale antico', *Atti dell'Accademia di Verona*, 5th ser., 18 (1941), 3–346.

[4] See Allan Atlas, 'The Accademia degli Unisoni: A Music Academy in Renaissance Perugia', in Edward H. Clinkscale and Claire Brook (eds.), *A Musical Offering: Essays in Honor of Martin Bernstein* (New York: Pendragon Press, 1977), 5–23.

mid-sixteenth-century Venice was mainly literary, but its promotion of Pietro Bembo's theories about vernacular literature has been shown to have had important implications for the history of the madrigal.[5] In the following century the topics that exercised the Alterati were taken up in the prefaces and letters of the Venetian librettists and in discussions in the Accademia degli Incogniti.[6] The Alterati remains unique among these academies in having left so many surviving documents, which permit us to reconstruct the discussions that have relevance to music.

Students of the subject of this essay should not fail to read Barbara Russano Hanning's *Of Poetry and Music's Power: Humanism and the Creation of Opera*, based on her Yale dissertation of 1969. She has probed more deeply than I did here into certain aspects of the writings of the Alterati that bear upon the early Florentine musical pastorals. She also singles out an author who belonged to a rival academy, the Accademia Fiorentina, Francesco Buonamici, who went over some of the same ground as Giacomini concerning the purgation of the passions and its physiology and psychology.[7]

I surveyed this subject more synthetically in my chapter 'Theory of Dramatic Music' in *Humanism in Italian Renaissance Musical Thought*.[8] There I contrasted the views of literary theorists who debated the place of music and the chorus in ancient tragedy, particularly Francesco Patrizi.

THE potent mixture of a brilliant musical life and flourishing literary academies in late sixteenth-century Florence was bound to fuse into an amalgam of unique and splendid properties. No wonder that the musical pastorals of Ottavio Rinuccini and Jacopo Peri emerged there between 1598 and 1600. Given the ingredients and the climate, the compound seems almost inevitable.

Yet early historians of opera, who knew little of the climate, looked for a catalyst. They thought they found it in the Camerata of Count Giovanni Bardi. But they were deceived. What they called the Camerata was really two different and separate, indeed even opposed, social and intellectual circles. One, Bardi's Camerata, was oriented towards talking about learned topics, listening to music, and perhaps amateur music-making. The later group, sponsored by Jacopo Corsi, was a kind of semi-professional musical and dramatic workshop, bent towards experimentation in theatrical productions. It was directly responsible for the first musical pastorals. The discussions in Bardi's Camerata undoubtedly stimulated the experiments

[5] See Martha Feldman, 'The Academy of Domenico Venier, Music's Literary Muse in Mid-Cinquecento Venice', *Renaissance Quarterly*, 54 (1991), 476–512.
[6] See Ellen Rosand, *Opera in Seventeenth-Century Venice: The Creation of a Genre* (Berkeley, Calif.: University of California Press, 1991), 34–65.
[7] Barbara Russano Hanning, *Of Poetry and Music's Power: Humanism and the Creation of Opera* (Ann Arbor, Mich.: UMI Research Press, 1980), 28–9.
[8] New Haven, Conn.: Yale University Press, 1985, 408–33.

and gave them direction. However, the process of cause and effect here, as in most historic events, is an elusive and complex one.

Nino Pirrotta has shown that the set of beliefs that is usually associated with the Camerata evolved mainly outside it and that Florence at this time seethed with conflicts of aesthetic principles and personalities.[9] Caccini and Peri were rivals, and so were their patrons Bardi and Corsi. Emilio de' Cavalieri, the boss of Florentine artistic enterprises under Grand Duke Ferdinand I, managed to alienate almost everyone, smooth diplomat though he was. The principal source of the ideology once attributed to Bardi and Galilei was actually in Rome in the person of an erudite classicist interested in ancient Greek musical theory—Girolamo Mei.[10] Furthermore, there were not only the Camerata and Corsi's workshop but four other academies interested in drama, and one of them, the Alterati, was full of musical amateurs. The overlapping of membership among all these groups, moreover, makes it hard to keep their contributions distinct. Of all the academies, the most poorly documented, because it was unofficial, is the Camerata. Besides the host Bardi, the only members of which we can be sure are Giulio Caccini, who acknowledged having frequented the circle and was the first to refer to it as the 'Camerata'; Vincenzo Galilei, a protegé of Bardi who wrote a dialogue to instruct certain members of the circle in music theory; and Pietro Strozzi, who with Bardi is one of the two interlocutors in the dialogue.[11]

By contrast to this informal academy, the official literary academies that were active in Florence in the second half of the sixteenth century are well documented. The one that contained the greatest number of musical amateurs was the Accademia degli Alterati. The records of this academy, from its first official meeting up to 23 January 1606, are preserved in the manuscript Ashburnham 558 of the Biblioteca Medicea Laurenziana of Florence. This is the 'Diario dell'Accademia degli Alterati' in three volumes, bound in two.[12] The Academy, according to the record, was founded on 17

---

[9] Nino Pirrotta, 'Temperaments and Tendencies in the Florentine Camerata', *Musical Quarterly*, 40 (1954), 169–89. See also above, Essay 14.

[10] See C. V. Palisca, *Girolamo Mei: Letters on Ancient and Modern Music to Vincenzo Galilei and Giovanni Bardi* (American Institute of Musicology, 1960; 2nd edn., Stuttgart: Hänssler, 1977).

[11] Giulio Caccini, 'Ai lettori', in *Le nuove musiche di Giulio Caccini detto Romano* (Florence: Marescotti, 1601/2), trans. in Oliver Strunk, *Source Readings in Music History* (New York: Norton, 1950), 378. Galilei, in his *Discorso intorno all'opere di messer Gioseffo Zarlino* (Florence: Marescotti, 1589), 51–2, says that it was mainly to instruct certain gentlemen with whom he was associated in some aspects of music theory that he wrote his *Dialogo della musica antica et della moderna* (Florence: Marescotti, 1581).

[12] Since the Diario is chronological, references to it will be by date rather than volume and folio. Dates are given in the Diario in Florentine style, which began the year on 25 March, *ab incarnatione*. I have converted these to the modern calendar. Members' names are recorded only through their academic pseudonyms. I have translated these to their proper names with the help of the list of members in

February 1568, Florentine style, or 1569 (all dates in this article will be converted to the modern calendar). Its founders were seven gentlemen, all but one already members of the Accademia Fiorentina. By 1571 it had twenty-one members and in that year acquired the name Alterati. The academic pseudonyms of the members are given in the Appendix following this article.

The significance of the name was explained by its first 'Reggente' or Regent, Giulio del Bene, in a discourse on the Academy's aims. It was dedicated, he said, to the 'alteration' or improvement of its members through the cultivation of elegant speech, good conduct, and a knowledge of all the arts and sciences.[13] Thus it had a broader base than the older Accademia Fiorentina or the younger Accademia della Crusca, which was modelled on the Alterati. Both these other academies were preoccupied with the study and spread of the Tuscan language and its literature.

The Alterati first met at the home of Tommaso del Nero. After his death on 3 August 1572, they used temporary quarters briefly before establishing their home in the palace of Giovanni Battista Strozzi the Younger, known as *il Cieco*. They ordinarily convened once or twice a week. Certain formalities through which their sessions were organized seem to have been original and peculiar to this academy. At the beginning of a regency—a term of six months—an amphora was formally opened with an oration. Into the amphora members were expected to drop original poems, essays, tragedies, comedies, translations, commentaries, and the like. At the end of a semester the accumulated writings were assigned to two censors and a defender, who prepared critiques of the works. The censures and defences were then heard to determine whether each composition itself should be read. If a vote was favourable, the tragedy, poem, or discourse was read and discussed, and the author often modified it on the basis of the Academy's review. This collective criticism constituted an important though small part of the work of the Academy.

From around 1571 it became the custom to focus discussions around a subject or subjects chosen for his term by the regent. For example, in June 1573, Baccio Neroni decreed that questions related to the *Poetics* of Aristotle

---

Domenico Maria Manni's history of the academy, *Memorie della fiorentina famosa Accademia degli Alterati* (Florence: Stecchi, 1748). The most extensive discussion of the Diario is Bernard Weinberg, 'The Accademia degli Alterati and Literary Taste from 1570 to 1600', *Italica*, 31 (1954), 207–14. Weinberg has also published extracts from the codex pertaining to literary matters in 'Argomenti di discussione letteraria nell'Accademia degli Alterati (1570–1600)', *Giornale storico della letteratura italiana*, 131 (1954), 175–94.

[13] Giulio del Bene, 'Del convivio delli Alterati', Florence, Biblioteca Nazionale Centrale, MS Magl. IX. 137, fo. 18ʳ. According to the Diario, this was delivered on 16 Feb. 1575.

would occupy the academicians during his regency. After January 1574 it became customary for two academicians to be assigned each time to take the pros and cons of a particular aspect of the topic. On 21 January 1574, the proposition that poetry may be defined as an imitation made with words was argued, Antonio degli Albizzi taking the affirmative and Alessandro Rinuccini the negative. Besides these prepared debates, there were prepared and impromptu lectures and discussions. Some of the prepared lectures and more of the extemporaneous ones were penalties imposed on academicians found guilty of such misconduct as failure to appear when scheduled to speak or late arrival. Mere absence was not considered sufficient cause for punishment.

No reigning philosophy can be attributed to the Alterati such as characterized the Accademia Platonica of the fifteenth century. There were certainly some Neoplatonists still around, but the dominant tone of the discourses that survive is anti-Platonic. A good index of the Alterati's temper is their attitude towards love. This was a favourite topic of earlier academies, particularly the relationship between earthly and divine love. The attitude of the Alterati towards love is pertinent to our interest in the Academy as a force in the development of attitudes towards music, because love is a key to the aesthetic theories of the early Renaissance. Through loving the beauty of earthly things and artistic products, it was believed, one rises by steps to the true love of the divine. One of the Alterati's leading thinkers, Lorenzo Giacomini de' Tebalducci Malespini, raised the question whether love was a suitable subject for academic discussion. Much of what the interlocutors of Plato's *Symposium* say about love and beauty, he declared, is either said in jest or is vain, sophistic, and plainly incredible. Giacomini proposed a more realistic view. He who is enamoured 'greatly loves and wishes well a beautiful person, and hoping to be loved in return, seeks with all means possible to attain this end as the most delightful thing and as a cause of many other delights'.[14] Love to Giacomini was simply one of the affections, along with such others as hate, anger, pleasure, and friendship. Thus stripped of such concepts dear to Platonists as desire for immortality, union with the divine, and intuition of divine beauty, love was admissible in academic forums only if investigated through natural

---

[14] 'Ragionamento d'amore', Florence, Biblioteca Riccardiana, MS 2437, fo. 3ᵛ: 'colui diciamo esser innamorato il quale grandemente ama et vuol bene à persona bella; et sperando essersi amato cerca con tutti i mezzi à lui possibili conseguire questo fine, come cosa dilettevolissima, et come cagione di molti altri diletti'. A somewhat edited version of this lecture is in *Prose fiorentine raccolte dallo Smarrito {Carlo Dati} accademico della Crusca* (Florence: Santi Franchi, 1716–45), pt. ii, vol. v (1730), 116–52. Quotations in these footnotes, on the contrary, preserve the archaic and inconsistent orthography of the original writers.

science and ethics. This changed outlook on love is an important sign of the philosophical orientation of the generation that founded the Alterati.

Some of the barriers that effectively excluded music from some of the earlier academies were now cut down. Giulio del Bene, in enumerating the liberal arts, takes music out of the quadrivium, in which it was a traditional partner of geometry, arithmetic, and astronomy, and places it beside the disciplines of the old trivium, grammar, dialectic, and rhetoric, to which he adds poetics.[15] He thus arrives at five liberal arts: grammar, rhetoric, music, poetics, and dialectics. Music, poetry, and rhetoric are further linked in that they all serve to move or express the affections. Del Bene betrays his dependence on Aristotle's *Politics* when he cites as the other uses of music its capacity to order and repose the soul and to provide pleasure and solace from workaday burdens. The tendency to look to Aristotle as the guide runs throughout the deliberations of the Academy. But there is also a pronounced desire to improve on Aristotle, to find solutions that better answered contemporary needs.

The Alterati's interest in music and its importance was not limited to the group's avowed concern with aesthetic principles. Many of the members themselves had noteworthy musical connections.

The man who deserves to be mentioned first is Giovanni Bardi. His attendance was recorded as early as 3 June 1574, when he improvised a sonnet, and he was a frequent participant from then on. Perhaps it was deemed wiser to have him in the group than not, for on 14 January 1573 the Diario reports that the regent, Cosimo Rucellai, failed to appear at a meeting and gave as his excuse that he had gone 'a far musica' at the house of Monsignor Bardi.[16] The Alterati present were so indignant, they resolved to stay away next time so that Rucellai would find himself alone. Bardi must have been initiated around December 1574, for on the thirtieth he was instructed to submit his academic pseudonym and *impresa*, or device. He adopted the name *il Puro* and a device showing a flask used for distilling brandy and the motto *Alterato, io raffino* (Altered, I refine).[17] All but the

---

[15] 'Del convivio delli Alterati', fos. 18ᵛ–19ʳ. We study the liberal arts, Del Bene says, 'à fine che noi possiamo, per la gramatica bene e correttamente ragionare, non havendo noi questo da natura, per la retorica persuadere, et tirare la volunta delli huomini dove ci pare, et per la musica imparare ad essere ordinati et composti bene nel animo nostro, et a movere gli affetti non meno che si faccia la retorica et per delettarsi et sollevarci dalle fatiche che nelle operatione humane ogni giorno supportiamo. et finalmente della poesia accio che possiamo descrivere et dimostrare col imitare lationi delli huomini quasi lidea delle virtu et de virtu de gli eccelenti huomini, et id il verso, nel quale é opinione che sia il parlare delli dei exprimere inoltre concetti et imitare gli affetti et i costumi altrui, e delettare et giovare l'uno laltro per questa cosi piacevole et bella arte.'

[16] This may be the earliest record of a meeting of the Camerata; Diario, vol. ii, fo. 3ᵛ.

[17] Giovanni Maria Mazzuchelli, *Gli scrittori d'Italia* (Brescia: Bossini, 1753–63), ii. 333.

earliest devices of the Alterati had some connection with wine, because the device of the Academy represented a vat for pressing wine heaped up with grapes bearing the motto *Quid non designat {ebrietas}* from Horace. Bardi was introduced, as was the custom, by another academician, whose oration in Bardi's behalf survives.

After praising Bardi's military and literary accomplishments, his great skill in Greek, Latin, and Tuscan, his understanding of mathematics, of both judicial and cosmic astrology, of many useful and liberal sciences, the anonymous orator finally extolled Bardi's dedication to poetry and music:

It is evident that everyone loves those things that are in keeping with and proportioned to his condition. For this reason the person of irate [temperament] desires contests, the Sanguine enjoys pleasing and cheerful things, the Melancholic loves solitude, and the Phlegmatic above all tranquillity and quiet. It is not surprising that our Signor Giovanni, altogether well proportioned in soul and body, has always borne a singular affection for the suave and delectable harmony of music, the art of the ancient Greeks, among whom flourished all the noble arts and virtues to such a degree that whoever was not versed and practised in music was looked upon as ill bred and vulgar. In music he has produced such artful compositions that he has surpassed many who pursue music as a profession.[18]

Another member, Piero del Nero, who had a keen interest in ancient music, was initiated on 12 February 1572. In 1602, he published Girolamo Mei's *Discorso sopra la musica antica e moderna*. This he dedicated to Baccio Valori, another of the Alterati.[19] The Del Nero family was prominent among the early members; the Academy met at first in the house of Tommaso del Nero.[20] Another member of the family who figures in the history of music is Nero del Nero, brother of Tommaso and twice regent of the Alterati. At his house in Rome early in the 1590s, Caccini sang some of the airs and madrigals which he had previously sung in Bardi's Camerata and which were later printed in *Le nuove musiche*.[21] Agostino del Nero, son of Tommaso, was an accomplished amateur singer and player and was also interested in ancient music. A long letter addressed to him on that subject by Girolamo Mei found its way to a later Alterato, Giovanni Battista Doni, who credited it with stimulating his researches into Greek music.[22]

[18] Florence, Biblioteca Medicea Laurenziana, MS Ashburnham 559, item 24. The reference to Bardi's compositions is interesting, because no music of his is known earlier than 'Lauro ohimè, lauro', printed in *Il lauro secco* (Ferrara: Baldini, 1582).

[19] Baccio and his son Filippo Valori are not listed as members by Manni, but Michele Maylender does include them in *Storia delle accademie d'Italia* (Bologna, 1926–30), i. 154–60.

[20] He was one of the founding members along with Giulio del Bene, Renato de Pazzi, Vincenzio Acciaiuoli, Lorenzo Corbinelli, Alessandro Canigiani, and Antonio degli Albizzi, according to Salvino Salvini, *Fasti consolari dell'Accademia Fiorentina* (Florence: Tartini, 1717), 203.

[21] Caccini, foreword to *Le nuove musiche*, trans. in Strunk, *Source Readings*, 379.

[22] Palisca, *Girolamo Mei*, 10. Francesco Nori, who delivered an oration on the death of Agostino at

Two Rinuccini brothers were Alterati. The older, Alessandro, was a noted poet and senator and three times regent of the Academy. He spoke on the choruses of the Greek drama in January 1575.[23] Ottavio, the librettist of *Euridice*, *Dafne*, and *Arianna*, was not proposed as a member until 28 March 1586, and was formally admitted on 4 September of that year.

One of the most scholarly members of the Academy was Lorenzo Giacomini. Although his main field was poetic theory, a manuscript attributed to him in the Riccardiana Library shows that he was learned also in ancient music. A translation of the musical section of Aristotle's *Problems* into Italian, it is the first known translation into the vernacular.[24] Giacomini may have been an amateur musician too, for Giorgio Bartoli, who often acted as his amanuensis and secretary, wrote him from Venice on 24 May 1572 that he had finally sent him his harpsichord.[25]

The only man honoured with nonresident membership during the Academy's first twenty years was Girolamo Mei. Although Florentine by birth and a founding member of the Accademia Fiorentina, he lived most of his life outside Florence. His writings on music and Tuscan prose and poetry circulated widely among the literary circles of his native city. Few spoke of the ancient drama without citing his authority. He was elected *in absentia* on 2 September 1585, and Piero del Nero was assigned the duty of advising him of this. Mei, then in his sixty-sixth year, replied on 20 September 1585, from Rome:

Most magnificent and worthy Sirs
If the favour with which Your Lordships have honoured my old age by desiring me with such amicable and universal affection to be of your number could alter that old age and make it regain the vigour of years gone by, I might then acquire the means to give you thanks, if not equal to my desire, at least sufficiently to succeed in persuading you of how much I consider myself obligated.[26]

---

the age of 21, praised his musical ability in *Delle lodi del Barone Agostino del Nero*, printed in *Prose fiorentine*, pt. i, vol. iv (1731), 58–92. He is not listed anywhere as a member, but he probably was one, since members' sons were admitted as soon as they came of age. On 1 June 1587 Agostino del Nero founded an academy, known as the Desiosi, said to have been interested in music and drama.

[23] This information is not found in the Diario, but in a letter dated 22 Jan. 1574/5 from Giorgio Bartoli to Lorenzo Giacomini in Biblioteca Riccardiana, MS 2438 bis, pt. iii, no. 60 (my numbering).

[24] Biblioteca Riccardiana, MS 1612. Since these words were written, a 15th-c. French translation of the musical section has surfaced in Chantilly, Musée Condé, MS 397, thanks to Paul Kristeller's *Iter italicum*, iii (London: The Warburg Institute; Leiden: E. J. Brill, 1983), 206.

[25] Biblioteca Riccardiana, MS 2438 bis, pt. iii, letter no. 24.

[26] Diario, iii, fo. 172^v: 'Molto m[a]g[nifici] S[ignori] miei oss[eruandissimi]. Se il fauor che le S[ignorie] V[ostre] hanno fatto onoratamj alla mia uecchiezza, hauendola io sì amoreuole e uniuersale affezione uoluta nel numero loro, potesse di piu così alterarla, che ella racquistando il uigor dell'età fuggita, ne conseguisse app[ropriato] modo da renderne lor grazie, se non pari al desiderio mio, almen tali, che mi riuscisser comportabilj a far conoscere quanto io me ne tengo lor obbligato . . .'.

He went on with similar rhetorical flowers, closing with regrets about the distance that would prevent him from enjoying 'the fruit of presence in a company after my own heart'. In replying, Vincenzo Martelli asked Mei to send some 'recent or older offspring of his noble genius' for their review.[27] Mei sent a tragedy, one of the four that he once acknowledged writing to test Aristotle's poetic theories. In the entry of the Diario for 11 August 1589 we read that Alessandro Rinuccini was sentenced for having been absent when he was due to lecture—to censure Mei's tragedy.

Another late entrant was Jacopo Corsi, harpsichordist, composer with Peri of Rinuccini's *Dafne*, and sponsor of Peri's and Rinuccini's *Euridice*. He was initiated on 4 September 1586.

Two men whose names have not previously been associated with music remain to be mentioned: Antonio degli Albizzi and Cosimo Rucellai, both among the earliest regents. They are credited in the *Diario* with pronouncing lessons on music.[28]

The only other members who can be connected with music are the poets whose verses were set by numerous composers. Most notable of these are Gabriello Chiabrera and Giovanni Battista Strozzi. The latter was author of the fourth intermezzo of the 1589 festivities produced by Emilio de' Cavalieri and directed by Giovanni Bardi. Prince Giovanni de' Medici, who staged Caccini's *Rapimento di Cefalo* in 1600, was another member.

Professional musicians are completely absent from the Academy's records, as is any trace of music-making. Perhaps the only occasions for music were the annual symposia held to celebrate the founding of the Alterati on the so-called 'Nativity' day, 17 February. This called for a sumptuous banquet. At the Riccardiana Library there is a large folded folio that documents this side of the Academy's activity. It is an itemized statement of expenses for one such annual feast: 'Spese fatte nel simposio'.[29] Some of the items listed below will give an indication of the academicians' taste for the good things of life, as well as of the degree of inflation of the lira over the years. The total expenditure was 205 lire, 3 soldi.

[27] Martelli's reply, along with Mei's letter, is in an appendix to the Diario, vol. iii, fos. 172ᵛ–173ᵛ.

[28] Albizzi was the author of a masque staged by Giovanni Bardi at the carnival of 1574 called *Mascherata del piacere e del sentimento* that cost the considerable sum of 4,000 scudi (Bartoli letters dated 20 and 27 Feb. 1573/4), Biblioteca Riccardiana, MS 2438 bis, pt. iii, nos. 57 and 51. Albizzi remained active as an amateur musician until his old age, which he spent in Kempten. See *Dizionario biografico degli italiani*, xi (Rome, 1960), 21–2.

[29] Biblioteca Riccardiana, MS 2471, fo. 98.

Expenses for the Symposium

10 lbs. grapes	1 lire	13 soldi	4 denari
150 prunes	3	15	
81 lbs. strawberries	1	26	8
48 large pears and others for cooking	2	18	8
peaches for the gelatin and others	4		
15 lbs. cake flour (*fior di farina*)	4	10	
6 legs of veal	4		
. . .			
1 bottle milk	1		
6 turkeys	27		
3 capons	15		
24 tortolotte [turtle-doves?]	20		
21 bottles red wine	25	10	
3 bottles greco di chianti	4	5	
78 lbs. snow [to cool the gelatin?]	7	16	
10 large 2-lb. candles	5	12	
. . .			

If the table was set, as I estimate, for about twenty-four people, the banquet enjoyed much better attendance by far than any of the weekly meetings, when an average of eight and sometimes only two turned up. Although music was probably an ornament to the banquets, it is never mentioned and no record of payments to professional musicians is preserved.

Lectures on music, orations in praise of it, and discussions of musical topics are recorded in the Diario at a number of points. The records are sketchy and uneven, however, and must contain only a partial accounting of the place music occupied in the Alterati's deliberations. On 19 November 1573, with only four present, Antonio degli Albizzi gave a lesson on music. The Diario tells no more about it and it cannot be traced among the papers of the Academy. This is unfortunate because his other contributions reveal a deep and independent thinker.[30] On 25 November 1574 Cosimo Rucellai delivered an oration in praise of music. He was the one who once was absent during his own regency to go to Bardi's 'to make music'. On 10 December 1574, an extemporaneous discussion was held on the proposition 'that music is better than conversation with friends'. Bernardo Davanzati took the affirmative and Carlo Rucellai the negative. The main significance of these items is that music should be on the agenda at all, as most of the literary academies ignored it.

[30] See Bernard Weinberg, *A History of Literary Criticism in the Italian Renaissance* (Chicago: University of Chicago Press, 1961), ii. 838 ff.

The most revealing and relevant statements about music are found in discourses on literary and philosophical topics. The definition of poetry and of its various genres and the nature of poetic creation were frequently recurring themes. What is said about poetry was either applied by the speaker himself to other arts or has such obvious general implications that these statements reveal better even than the musical writings of the period the basis of the changing artistic taste.

Several entire semesters were given over to poetic theory. The discussions were usually focused on specific areas, such as the theory of imitation, which occupied the period between December 1573 and February 1574. Sometimes the publication of a new commentary on Aristotle's *Poetics* or a new treatise on the subject occasioned the discussion.

Francesco Patrizi provided such a stimulus in 1584, two years before his *Poetics* was published. In June, Bardi returned from a trip to Mantua and Ferrara, where he had seen Patrizi, then working on his monumental treatise.[31] Bardi reported to the Academy on 12 June the titles of the parts and chapters of this work, and these were discussed. The first chapter of part ii, the 'Deca disputata', bears the title 'Del furore poetico', and it may have prompted Lorenzo Giacomini's lecture on 10 July on the question: 'Whether divine *furor* is the efficient cause of poetry and whether in the poet art is more important than nature.' Patrizi's fondness for the Platonic concept of divine madness was bound to incite opposition among the predominantly Aristotelian Alterati. Apparently, Giacomini revised his lecture after Patrizi's first two volumes appeared in 1586, for the version that has been published was delivered in 1587 under the title 'Del furor poetico'.[32]

Plato's theory[33] that poets composed during seizures of divine *furor* or madness was generally accepted by early Renaissance poetic theorists. Lorenzo Giacomini considered in his lecture all the arguments raised by Plato, Plutarch, Cicero, Seneca, and others in support of this theory and found them all insufficient. Giacomini asked if what these writers called *furor poeticus* was not rather 'an internal disposition that is often hidden from our knowledge'.[34]

The problem had come up on two previous occasions. On 28 January

---

[31] Francesco Patrizi, *Della poetica* (Ferrara: Baldini, 1586).

[32] 'Del furor poetico: Discorso fatto da L. G. Tebalducci Malespini nel Academia de gli Alterati nel anno 1587', in Giacomini, *Orationi e discorsi* (Florence: Sermartelli, 1597), 53–73. What appears to be an earlier version of this is in Biblioteca Nazionale Centrale, MS Magl. IX. 124, no. 21, fos. 168ʳ–186ᵛ.

[33] *Phaedrus* 244; *Ion* 533.

[34] P. 65: 'l'interna dispositione; la quale molte volte ci è ascosa'.

1584 Ruberto degli Albizzi was 'condemned' to defend the necessity of madness for the poet, while Francesco Guicciardini spoke against the proposition. Giovanni Battista Strozzi resolved the matter by redefining the term as 'a faculty and disposition to transform oneself into anything'. So understood, he concluded, *furor* was necessary to the poet. Alessandro Rinuccini agreed, but added that art too was necessary. Further back in the Diario we learn that on 18 March 1574 it was decided to argue the proposition that 'poetry derives from *furor*, not art', and eleven days later Baccio Neroni lectured on this topic. The Alterati evidently had been searching for a new determination of the roles of inspiration and art in the creation of poetry.

Although declining to recognize divine *furor*, Giacomini acknowledges that the poet must be gifted with several natural qualities: *ingegno*, *giudicio*, *docilità*, and *memoria* (genius, judgement, docility, and memory). A unique natural combination of all these gives the poet the capacity to enter into an affection through 'a concentration of the imagination' (*la fissa imaginazione*). In this state he composes not artificially and coldly but almost from the heart. For a genuine affection awakens the conceits that will express it and move others to the same affection. Thus what some regard as *furor* comes from the poet's capacity to transform himself into one possessed of a certain affection. After the poet has composed in the heat of a simulated affection, he must resort to judgement to correct the fruits of this rapt state, removing inappropriate conceits after examining his work as if it were that of another.

The affections are crucial to Giacomini's conception of the creative process. Once they were considered pertinent mainly to the arts of rhetoric and oratory. But in the last quarter of the sixteenth century, theorizing about the affections burgeoned in every area of criticism and philosophy. A symptom of this preoccupation is the naming of one of the masques of the carnival of 1574 *Gli affetti*.[35] The agenda of the Alterati reflect this obsession with the passions. On 28 February 1572 the question was 'whether the movement of the affections is outside the art of rhetoric', Tommaso del Nero taking the affirmative, Lorenzo Gabrielli the negative. The next five meetings were all on the passions in oratory. Years later the subject came up again (March 1584), with poetry now contrasted with rhetoric in their power to move the affections. Giacomini showed that poetry had greater means for moving the passions, while rhetoric was more apt for persuading.

[35] Bartoli, letters dated 20 and 27 Feb. 1573/4, Biblioteca Riccardiana, MS 2438 bis, pt. iii, nos. 57 and 51.

It was on the question of the purgation of the affections in tragedy that poetics and musical aesthetics met in the Alterati's deliberations. This link was already established by Aristotle. In speaking of music in the *Politics* he observed that certain melodies cured persons seized with a form of madness as if they had undergone a purgative treatment.[36] He added that he would explain more fully what he meant by this catharsis of the passions in his treatise on poetics. But either the section is lost or he failed to keep his promise, for catharsis is not clearly explained there. Indeed, it is barely mentioned in the definition of tragedy: 'Tragedy is an imitation of an action . . . through pity and fear affecting the proper catharsis, or purgation, of these emotions.'[37] Commentators have had to elucidate this application of the term *catharsis* through Aristotle's views on music.

The nature of purgation in tragedy was probed in several sessions of the Alterati. On 22 December 1583 Filippo Strozzi defended the proposition 'that tragedy through pity and fear purges us of the same passions', while Giulio del Bene took the negative side. Giacomini made a formal exposition on the subject in 1586 in a discourse entitled 'De la purgatione de la tragedia' that is rich in implications for music.[38]

Giacomini recognizes at the outset that several interpretations of what Aristotle meant by catharsis are possible. Tragedy purges compassion and fear by making men experience these same passions; or it purges not the passions represented on the stage but the opposite; or it shows us the vanity of things acquired through good fortune and therefore moderates love, desire, hope, and joy. Giacomini finds no substance in the last two. Catharsis, clinically speaking, denotes a medication that moves humours of the body that fail to move on their own. Such medications are homeopathic, that is, similar to the humours being purged. For example rhubarb, aloe, and black hellebore are used because they have a natural affinity to the choleric, phlegmatic, and melancholic humours. Consequently, catharsis of an affection is brought about by the representation of a similar affection. In experiencing the passion of the protagonist on stage the spectator is relieved of his own.

To drive this point home, Giacomini examines the nature and mechanics of the affections. He defines an affection as 'a spiritual movement or operation of the mind in which it is attracted or repelled by an object it has

---

[36] *Politics*, viii. 7. 1342ª.

[37] *Poetics*, vi. 2. 1449ᵇ.

[38] Giacomini, *Orationi*, 29–52, reprinted in *Prose fiorentine*, pt. ii, vol. iv (1729), 212–50. Baxter Hathaway has recently recognized this essay as one of major importance in the history of the interpretation of the concept of purgation: *The Age of Criticism: The Late Renaissance in Italy* (Ithaca, NY: Cornell University Press, 1962), 251–60.

come to know'.[39] He declines to agree either with Aristotle, who said the seat of the affections is the heart, or with Galen, who located it in the brain, for Giacomini regards its central place as immaterial. People vary in their disposition towards particular affections, depending on the balance and diversity of spirits in their bodies. An abundance of agile and thin spirits disposes a person towards joyous affections, while many torpid and impure vapours prepare the way for sorrow and fear. When the soul is in a sad affection, a great quantity of spirits evaporates and rises to the head. The vapours go particularly to the anterior part of the head, stimulating the seat of fantasy. Condensation of these vapours causes the face to contract and tears to flow. This contraction in turn affects the quality of the voice. Giacomini's elaboration of this last point has particular significance for musical aesthetics.

From the same cause arise cries of lamentation, expelled by Nature through a natural instinct without our awareness to remove thus the bad disposition that afflicts the sensitive part of the soul, contracting it and weighting it down, and especially the heart, which, full of spirits and heat, suffers most. Therefore the heart moves to shake off its pain and expand and liberate itself of anguish. The lungs and other organs of the voice are set in motion and emit shrieks and groans if not impeded by the intellect. In this way the soul, weighted down by sorrow, lightens itself and gives birth to sad conceits and liberates the passionateness that was in it. Having delivered itself of these, the soul remains free and unburdened. So, even if it should want to cry some more, it cannot, because the vapours that filled the head and are the substance of tears have been consumed. They remain scarce until the mind returns to its original disposition because of some internal alteration of the vapours, or through some active qualities, sad imaginings, or an external incident.[40]

This process, Giacomini explains, produces a natural cure. The principle of catharsis, which Aristotle probably meant to apply metaphorically to describe the effect of a tragic stage action, is reduced by Giacomini to

---

[39] Giacomini, *Orationi*, 38: 'altro non è affetto che seguitamento o fuga del anima di alcuna cosa appressa da lei, o come convenevole, o come disconvenevole'.

[40] Ibid. 39–40: 'Da la medesima cagione derivano le voci lamentevoli per naturale instinto senza nostro accorgimento da la Natura procacciate; per rimuovere cioè la mala dispositione, che affligge ristringendo & aggravando la parte sensitiva, e 'l cuore principalmente, che come pieno di spiriti, e di calore, piu patisce. onde per scuotere il dolore, e per allargarsi, e liberarsi dal affanno, si muoue, e muouesi il polmone, e gli altri organi de la voce, e fansi strida, e gemiti, se dal intelletto non sono impediti. Per queste vie l'anima gravida di mestizia si sgrava, e partorisce i dolorosi concetti, e gli appassionamenti, che erano in lei, i quali partoriti, resta libera, e scarica, si che quando il bramasse, piu non potrebbe piagnere, essendo consumati quei vapori materia del pianto, che riempievano il capo, fino a che o per altra interna alterazione di vapori, o da qualità attive, o per trista imaginatione o per accidente esterno non ritorna a la primiera disposizione.'

mechanical terms. The mechanics of the affections as analysed by Giacomini bear a strong resemblance to those later described by Descartes.[41]

Now Giacomini applies his theory to music. As a point of departure, he cites Aristotle's classification of songs into moral, active, and enthusiastic.[42] Aristotle's view that all these kinds of music should be cultivated appealed to Giacomini more than that of Plato, who allowed only ethical music. For ethical music was not capable of effecting purgation, because melodies analogous to the ancient Dorian, an ethical mode, were not suited to this purpose. Rather, most apt to achieve purgation was music like the ancient Phrygian and Mixolydian tunes and those of the aulos, which were not used in the moral training of youth.

From harmonies that serve to waken the affections like the Phrygian and Mixolydian, which had the property of making the soul contracted and somewhat saddened, and from purgative songs that are in keeping with these modes, persons who are quickly moved to sorrow, pity, and fear, as well as people in general, receive a purgation, alleviation, and relief that not only is not injurious but is delightfully salutary.[43]

Affections, then, are not evil in themselves, as Cicero implied, but quite useful. Only when passions are uncontrolled and misguided, Giacomini argues, are they evil perturbations.

Giacomini reflected in his thinking an important trend in contemporary music. No longer did the composer seek only to soothe and moderate emotions for ethical ends, but he aimed to move listeners to the strongest passions, perhaps thereby to purge them. The passions could be evoked only through vivid conceits and by exploiting the more exciting instrumental and vocal effects, melodic successions, and harmonies. The better a composer learned to sustain an affection, the more thoroughly could he induce purgation through a simulated passion.

The main purpose of Giacomini's essay was not, however, to deal with music but to illuminate the process of purgation in tragedy. By inducing pity and fear in the spectators, tragedy purged them of these emotions. This, he maintains, is what Aristotle meant in the *Poetics*. The most enlightened commentators, he says, are of this opinion, including Giovanni

---

[41] René Descartes, *Les Passions de l'âme* (Paris: le Gras, 1649).

[42] *Politics*, viii. 7. 1341[b].

[43] Giacomini, *Orationi*, 42: 'tanto coloro, i quali sono gagliardamente volti a la mestizia, a la compassione, & al timore, quanto universalmente tutti gli huomini, ricevon da le armonie che vagliono a destare affetti, quale è la Frigia, e la Mixolidia, di cui era proprio render l'anima ristretta, e per poco addolorata, e da canzoni purganti conformi a le armonie, ricever dico, purgatione, sfogamento, & allegiamento non dannoso, anzi salutevole con diletto.'

della Casa[44] and Girolamo Mei. Concerning the latter, he addresses the Alterati: 'You must add the opinion of this fellow academician, whose authority among you and among scholarly men in general is rightfully greatly esteemed. Mei, I say, understands purgation in the tragedy in this sense.'[45] The reference is probably to Mei's *De modis musicis antiquorum* (1573), of which the fourth book contains an extended commentary on the phenomenon of catharsis and its musical and medical significance.[46]

Having resolved the main issue of his essay, Giacomini now considers the elements in tragedy that aim at pleasure. Here are adumbrated many of the ingredients that were compounded into the Roman and Venetian operas of the seventeenth century. Tragedy delights the spectator, he states, by means of the following (my numbering):

(i) by teaching him about the action represented, for learning is naturally enjoyable; (ii) the marvellous, which shows incredible things actually happening; (iii) the recognition of things imitated; (iv) the loftiness of the conceits, the beauty of the metaphors; (v) the sweetness of the verse; (vi) the sweetness of the music; (vii) the festiveness of the dance; (viii) the magnificence of the apparatus or machinery and the sumptuousness of the regal costumes; (ix) the artfulness of the poet's arrangement of the plot— through digressions, recognitions, and reversals of fortune. (x) There are also pleasures accessory to the cathartic process. Since compassion is a virtuous act, we are happy in feeling virtuous. Fearful adventures cause pleasure by making us realize we are free of them. We delight in knowing kings and princes suffer calamities, because this shows that material possessions are no help in achieving virtue and immortality, the only true goals, which are accessible to all.[47]

These pleasures more than compensate for the small discomfort caused by the spectacle of painful, though unreal, objects. It is evident, Giacomini concludes, that the four goals assigned by Aristotle to music—purgation, moral training, relaxation of the mind, and aesthetic contemplation—should also be considered the ends of tragedy.

Although fundamentally a commentary upon Aristotle's *Poetics* in the

[44] Giovanni della Casa, *Il Galateo ovvero de' costumi*, trans. R. S. Pine-Coffin (Penguin edn., 1958), 41.

[45] Giacomini, *Orationi*, 44: 'Aggiugnete il giudicio di Academico vostro la cui autorità appresso voi, & appresso gli huomini scienziati è meritamente di molta stima, il Mei dico, che in questo sentimento prende la purgazione de la Tragedia.'

[46] Rome, Vatican Library, MS Vat. lat. 5323, bk. iv, 35 ff. There is evidence that Giacomini was already reading this and other writings of Mei in 1577. See below, nn. 55 and 56. The fourth book is available in two editions: Donatella Restani, *L'Itinerario di Girolamo Mei: dalla 'Poetica' alla Musica con un'appendice di testi* (Florence: Leo S. Olschki, 1990), 103–49; Girolamo Mei, *De modis*, ed. Tsugami Eisuke (Tokyo: Keiso Shobo, 1991). [47] Giacomini, *Orationi*, 46–7.

light of the philosopher's remarks about music in the *Politics*, Giacomini's essay is less a faithful elucidation of the text than a document of the prevailing taste. This was a taste that demanded of the stage not true tragedy but a mixed genre that added to the emotionally purgative experience a feast of the senses and the mind.[48]

The form of the tragedy was also a subject of discussion at the Alterati. On 29 May 1580 the Diario relates that the academy

argued about many things concerning tragedy, and it was resolved that to tragedy are appropriate the line of eleven syllables without rhyme, not excluding the use of seven syllables for certain purposes; and for the chorus one should compose *canzonette*. That the style in a tragedy should be magnificent and forceful. That the persons of the tragedy should be sought in history from as close to our times as possible, and failing to find these some action about a historical personage should be made up.[49]

Ottavio Rinuccini, who was not yet a member, did not follow this prescription, for in *Dafne*, *Euridice*, and *Arianna*, eleven- and seven-syllable lines are mixed in various rhyme schemes for the speeches of the characters, while the choruses only occasionally have the strict strophic forms and uniform lines and rhymes of canzonets. As regards subject-matter, the Alterati were well in advance of the earliest opera librettists, who relied upon Greek mythology, Roman history, and medieval romance to the exclusion of anything more contemporary.

Several other discussions betray a preoccupation with modern rather than ancient practice. On 30 December 1582, Torquato Malaspina contended that tragedy must have a happy ending, while Francesco Bonciani took the opposite view. On 13 April 1589 Marcello Adriani maintained that prologues should be linked to the action of the drama. Giacomini disagreed, explaining that in modern times they are detached from the play. Both Bonciani and the Regent seemed to side with Giacomini. Whether the tragedy should be divided into five parts came under examination on 28 January 1584, with Giulio del Bene taking the affirmative and Marcello Adriani the negative. Carlo Rucellai and the current regent, Alessandro Rinuccini, supported the five-act division.

---

[48] Francesco Bonciani, another accademico Alterato, in two discourses on imitation addressed to the Accademia Fiorentina in 1578, concentrated on the art of the masque, which he said was particularly popular 'in our times and in our city'. Visual ornament, he said, was more essential here than Aristotle conceded in the *Poetics*. Bonciani dwelt on the *meraviglia* (wonder) aroused by imitating—he clung to the word tenaciously—false and unlikely things, such as manlike gods; virtues, arts, sciences, or cities represented as human beings; and the personification of animals, plants, stones, and even the elements (Biblioteca Riccardiana, MS 2237, fos. 96ʳ–138ʳ). The attribution to Bonciani was made by Bernard Weinberg in 'Nuove attribuzioni di manoscritti di critica letteraria del Cinquecento', *Rinascimento*, 3 (1952), 249–50. [49] Italian text in Weinberg, 'Argomenti', 183.

In this connection it should be recalled that Guarini's *tragi-commedia pastorale Il pastor fido*, completed in 1585 and published in 1590, is in five acts, mixes lines of seven and eleven syllables in blank verse, and uses rhymed stanzas for choruses, as the Alterati recommended. Guarini's poem was read to the Academy before publication, and their opinion was to have been communicated to the poet by Matteo Botti. So Leonardo Salviati reported to Guarini in a letter of 8 October 1586, in which he added that from talking to five or six of the Alterati he gathered that *Il pastor fido* left them quite confused though full of admiration.[50] Rinuccini's *Euridice*, on the other hand, lacks the five-act division, being rather in six scenes; Striggio's later *Orfeo* does have the five acts.

The function of the chorus in the tragedy and the character of its music came up at least once in the discussions of the Alterati. Although the Diario is silent on these matters, there is evidence in a letter from Giorgio Bartoli to Lorenzo Giacomini. On 23 January 1575, according to Bartoli, Alessandro Rinuccini read a paper on the choruses of the tragedies and comedies. Bartoli, a member of the Accademia Fiorentina but not the Alterati, may have attended as an alternate for Giacomini, for he reported that 'the purpose for which he [Rinuccini] argued choruses were introduced in the tragedies was to leave the actors free to negotiate among themselves'.[51] The question had come up earlier in Bartoli's correspondence with Giacomini, when the latter was in Ancona taking part in a performance of the tragedy *Orbecche*. The author is not named, but what is said fits Giraldi Cinthio's tragedy of that name. Bartoli suggests that one chorus in the play should represent citizens coming to the palace on various business errands, and these should sit quietly except to make speeches. Another chorus of young people should enter singing and dancing, and he added: 'I believe these may sing anything they like, although it would be better to sing something related to the story of the tragedy, as Aristotle prefers, so that the entire tragedy would be as much as possible a single action.'[52] Two weeks later he revised his opinion. The chorus is important

[50] Salviati's letter is printed in Vittorio Rossi, *Battista Guarini ed Il pastor fido: Studio biografico-critico con documenti inediti* (Turin: E. Loescher, 1886), 299–300.

[51] Bartoli, undated letter of around the end of Jan. 1575, Biblioteca Riccardiana, MS 2438 bis, pt. iii, no. 37: 'il fine per il quale disse che si introduceva il coro ne le tragedie cio è per dare agio à gli istrioni di negoziare'. He had written in the letter dated 22 Jan. 1574/5, no. 60: 'Domani legge ne l'accademia il Rinucino, intendo che trattera de' cori de le tragedie e comedie.'

[52] Bartoli, letter dated 26 Dec. 1573, Biblioteca Riccardiana, MS 2438 bis, pt. iii, no. 11, fo. 1ᵛ: 'pero penso che questi possino cantare qualunque cosa vogliono, benche sia meglio cantar cose appartenenti à la favola de la tragedia, come vuole Aristotile, per fare quanto è possibile che sia tutta la tragedia una azzione'.

because it serves as an audience for those who relate messages. Some of the chorus members make individual speeches, while others sing.

Those who sing music, I should think, could imitate those who go around the city making feasts and masquerades, and one member may sing alone as well as many together and dance at the same time. And I do not believe it would be out of place if they sang interpolated songs, as Aristotle calls them,[53] although he does not sanction these but prefers that they sing things pertaining to the tragedy to make it so far as possible a single action . . . The ancient choruses, I believe, were performed in the following manner. A single person sang to the accompaniment of an instrument, reciting one verse. Then the others responded with the same air, their voices tuned in consonance. He who sang alone was called the Master of the Chorus, I believe. This is the procedure followed in singing litanies, but the music is not the same.[54]

Bartoli's argument provides some justification for the mixture of styles displayed in the *Euridice* scores of Peri and Caccini and in Monteverdi's *Orfeo*, where songs in villanella style are introduced amidst passages of severe recitative. Since such choral songs would be natural to participants in carnival feasts and masquerades, this kind of writing preserves verisimilitude by not demanding of the simple people represented in the chorus a music more sophisticated than they would ordinarily sing in real life. Bartoli also suggests a humanistic pretext for the method used both in the intermedi and the early musical pastorals of having one member of a group, such as a single shepherd, sing a strophe, followed by the entire group singing the same air, but in harmony, to one or more strophes, with perhaps further alternation between soloists and chorus in subsequent strophes.

As for the non-choral parts of a tragedy, Bartoli was not sure how much of the poetry of the dramatic roles was sung in ancient times. He believed that at least some of it was, as he wrote to Giacomini on 9 November

---

[53] *Poetics*, xix. 7. 1456ª.

[54] Bartoli, letter dated 9 Jan. 1573/4, MS 2438 bis, pt. iii, no. 16, fo. 2ʳ: 'quegli che cantano in Musica crederei che potessino imitar coloro che vanno per la cità facendo feste et mascherate et che possi cantare et un solo et molti et ballare ancora. et non mi par inconveniente che cantino framessi come chiama Aristotile benche non gli accetti, ma vorebbe che cantassero cose appartenenti à la tragedia per farla una azzione quanto piu è possibile . . . Il canto de cori antichi credo che fusse in questo modo cantava un solo accompagnato dal suono et diceva un verso, poj gli altri tutti rispondevano con la medesima aria con le voci accordate. et quello che cantava solo credo che si chiamasse maestro del coro. tal ordine si tiene in cantar le letanie, ma la musica non è la medesima.' Bartoli's implication that some interventions of the chorus are part of the action and should be spoken by individuals while others are choral songs anticipates interpretations of later commentators on Aristotle: Alessandro Piccolomini (Venice, 1575) and Antonio Riccoboni (Padua, 1587) and the theories of Angelo Ingegneri, *Della poesia rappresentativa & del modo di rappresentare le favole sceniche* (Ferrara, 1598). See the quotations and discussion in Donald Jay Grout, 'The Chorus in Early Opera', in Anna Amalie Abert and Wilhelm Pfannkuch (eds.), *Festschrift Friedrich Blume* (Kassel: Bärenreiter, 1963), 151–61.

1577. Giacomini had apparently asked Bartoli his opinion of Girolamo Mei's theories concerning the music of the tragedy.[55] Mei believed, as many in Florence knew, that the ancient practice was to sing both the choral and solo parts of the tragedies.[56] Bartoli replied that though he admired Mei's learning and partook of his distrust of secondary sources, he was not entirely convinced.

I believe that what he told you is the truth, particularly concerning ancient music and also about the manner of reciting speeches and dialogue in the tragedies. But perhaps this was not done universally, and what is more important it is not acceptable as the most perfect manner [of performance] if we follow the doctrine of Aristotle, for in the *Rhetorics* he gives tacit precepts . . . cautioning that speeches should not be made rhythmic, so that the listener would not become preoccupied with the voice of the speaker, as happened with the public crier who wished to communicate nothing when he chanted in this way. Now the theatres were built so that a great multitude of people could hear, and not everyone had the capacity to speak to large numbers, no more than Isocrates, but a naturally strong chest was required, which could be augmented by exercise. In short, that someone should have used a song-like delivery when reciting poems as well as speeches, this may stand; whether this is the best way is open to question.[57]

Bartoli's scepticism was not unusual. Most literary critics assumed that only the choruses were sung.

What kind of poetry should be set to music, and in what manner, ought

[55] Some notes, probably in Giacomini's hand, on the back of Bartoli's letter of 2 Nov. 1577 in Biblioteca Riccardiana, MS 2438 bis, pt. iii, no. 5, seem to be jottings of questions Giacomini intended to ask Bartoli concerning Mei's views: how the voice is produced; whether music is necessary to comedy and tragedy; whether the acute accent had the same effect in music [as in speech]; whether there are shorts and longs in the Tuscan language; if in Tuscan verse only this pleases; and two other questions that are not fully decipherable pertaining to purgation and the monochord. These questions suggest that Giacomini was reading not only Mei's *De modis musicis antiquorum* but also his treatise *Del verso toscano*, of which there are copies in Biblioteca Riccardiana, MSS 2597 and 2598, and Paris, Bibliothèque Nationale, lat. 7209[3].

[56] This theory was expounded mainly in bk. iv of *De modis musicis antiquorum*, which Mei sent to Piero Vettori in 1573, encouraging him to pass it around his circle, which included Giacomini. It may have been Giacomini's interest in Mei's writings that prompted Bartoli to copy six of the letters Mei wrote to Galilei and Bardi between 1572 and 1581. Bartoli apparently made these copies—the only ones extant—which are in the Vatican Library, MS Regina lat. 2021, between 1578 and 1582. See the addenda in Palisca, *Girolamo Mei* (1960 edn., insert, addendum to p. 82; 1977 edn., p. 206, addendum to p. 82).

[57] Bartoli, letter, 9 Nov. 1577, Biblioteca Riccardiana, MS 2438 bis, pt. iii, no. 19: 'Credo che dica il vero di quanto v'ha detto et massime de la Musica antica. et ancora del modo del recitar l'orazioni e parlare ne le tragedie ma forse non era fatto universalmente: et quello che è pju importante non acettabile per modo perfetto per la dottrina d'Aristotile, poiche ne la Retorica da tasiti precetti . . . advertendo di non far l'orazione numerosa accioche l'uditore non vadi a preocupando la voce del dicitore come avviene del banditore per il che non voleva dir niente quando ci diceva tali cose. et à la moltitudine si riparava con far i Teatri accioche tutti sentissero. et à la moltitudine ogniuno non era atto à parlare come ne anche Isocrate. ma bisognava forza di petto per natura, et per esercizio s'acquistava l'augumento. Insomma che qualcuno usasse pronunziare à modo di canto cosi il recittar li poemi come anche l'orazioni puo stare, ma è da advertire se è l'ottimo in tal modo facendo.'

to have been a vital subject for an academy strong in literary men who were sensitive to music. Yet all that has survived along these lines is an interesting comment by Giovanni Bardi in a lecture, 'In difesa dell'Ariosto', delivered to the Alterati on 24 February 1583. Bardi defended Ariosto's *Orlando furioso* against the criticism made by Francesco Bonciani in the Accademia Fiorentina, to which they both belonged. One of the proofs of the poem's excellence, Bardi said, was its popularity. This in turn was largely explained by the aptness of Ariosto's verses for musical setting. Ariosto's poem is sung in taverns and barber shops as well as by people of learning and nobility and has been set to music by professional musicians like Domenico da Nola. Poetry is written in verse to make it singable. 'Those verses will be best that have the best rhythm and the best sound. Consequently, they will be the most musical, hence the most singable.'[58] Bardi's other remarks in this lecture leaned heavily on Aristotle. Yet he was conscious of a standard apart from rules, measured by sensuous appeal and *sensus communis*.

These excerpts from the records and papers of the Alterati help us to reconstruct the intellectual environment out of which the early musical pastorals emerged. The treatises, discourses, and letters of Mei, Bardi, and Galilei, read against the background of surviving music, strike the scholar as iconoclastic. But it is evident from what survives of the discussions of the Alterati that the ideas circulating in Bardi's Camerata were equally at home at Giovanni Battista Strozzi's, that indeed they were characteristic of the milieu of humanist musical amateurs. Though amateurs of music, Bardi, Giacomini, and other leading Alterati cannot be dismissed as fatuous dilettantes. Some of them possessed a knowledge of the classics that later only professors of Greek and Latin could match. The humanist amateurs who first experimented with the musical pastoral were not innocent, chartless adventurers who discovered music drama while seeking to revive Greek tragedy. Rinuccini and his circle were too steeped in the classics to believe that *Dafne* or *Euridice* realized a rebirth of ancient tragedy, though they were conscious of certain parallels between these and the ancient tragedies and comedies. If any misunderstanding of Greek drama was a factor in the experiments, it was that inherent in the theory proposed by Mei, that the tragedies were sung in their entirety. To this, as we have seen, not everyone subscribed. The other classicistic features of the musical pastorals were mainly already familiar on the Florentine stage.

---

[58] Quoted and translated in Weinberg, *A History*, ii. 985.

The desire to imitate the ancients was still a powerful motive, but no longer the foremost one. The ancients were read as much in search of justification for prevailing trends as to find solutions and models to imitate. Aristotle, the most explicit of the philosophers about artistic matters and also the most sympathetic, bolstered the humanists' confidence in the rightness of what they were doing. As they interpreted the *Poetics* and *Rhetorics*, the proper goal of the creative artist was to move the affections through the imitation of human actions and feelings. This demanded of the artist not so much a divine madness through which to seize the heavenly harmony and truth as the exercise of the imagination. The artist must awaken in himself the emotional state he wants to express and to call forth the images and forms that will awaken it in others. The late sixteenth-century interpreters of Aristotle understood enough of the cultural context of his thought to know that the ancient genres and standards could not be transplanted into the modern world. Recent traditions and possibilities demanded new solutions. The knowledge that many differences of opinion existed among the classical authors also forced the humanists to recognize their own freedom and responsibility to make a choice. This choice, moreover, was not entirely rational. It could not help being influenced by the tastes of a leisure class that cared more for visible and audible marvels than for good drama. The battery of classical citations deployed in the academic discourses defended a pragmatic eclecticism. A head full of classical poetics but an ear to the ground was at this moment a good recipe for public success.

APPENDIX

The pseudonyms, dates, and principal occupations of the members of the Alterati mentioned in this article are listed below in alphabetical order.

Adriani, Marcello, *il Torbido* (1562–1604), professor of classics.

Albizzi, Antonio degli, *il Vario* (1547–1626), after 1576 mainly in Rome and Germany in service of Cardinal Andreas of Augsburg.

Bardi, Giovanni, *il Puro* (1534–1612), admitted 30 June 1574, poet, amateur composer, patron. (Florentine usage includes *de'* before Bardi, meaning 'of the family of the' in the name. Elsewhere, the particle is spelled *dei*, or is omitted, as has been the practice throughout this book.)

Bardi, Pietro, *l'Avvinato* (before 1570–after 1643), son of Giovanni, admitted 22 July 1599, one of leaders of Accademia della Crusca.

Bonciani, Francesco, for two years *il Dubbioso*, later *l'Aspro*, admitted 4 August 1572, literary critic, Archbishop of Pisa.

Chiabrera, Gabriello (1538–1612), poet.

Corsi, Jacopo (1561–1604), patron, amateur musician.

Davanzati, Bernardo, *il Silente* (1529–1606), translator and editor of the works of Tacitus.

Del Bene, Giulio, *il Desioso*, a founder.

Del Nero, Agostino (*c.*1570–*c.*1591), son of Tommaso, amateur musician.

Del Nero, Nero, *l'Orrido*, brother of Tommaso, one of first admitted after founding.

Del Nero, Tommaso, *lo Sconcio* (1544–72), a founder, first host.

Doni, Giovanni Battista (1594–1647), Secretary of the Sacred College, author of works on ancient music.

Gabrielli, Lorenzo, *l'Agevole*.

Giacomini (de' Tebalducci Malespini), Lorenzo, *il Mesto* (1552–98), admitted 8 July 1583, classicist, literary critic.

Guicciardini, Francesco, *lo Smemorato*.

Malaspina, Torquato, *il Tardo*.

Medici, Don Giovanni de', *il Saldo*, son of Duke Cosimo I.

Mei, Girolamo, *il Pianigiano* (1519–94), classicist, literary critic, elected *in absentia* 2 September 1585.

Neroni, Baccio, *il Grave*.

Rinuccini, Alessandro, *l'Ardito* (1555–1621), poet, senator, three times regent.

Rinuccini, Ottavio, *il Sonnacchioso* (1562–1621), brother of Alessandro, admitted 4 September 1586, poet.

Rucellai, Carlo, *lo Sdegnoso*.

Rucellai, Cosimo, *il Travagliato*.

Rucellai, Piero, *l'Umido* (d. *c.*1625).

Strozzi, Filippo, *lo Svegliato*.

Strozzi, Giovanni Battista the Younger, *il Tenero* (1551–1634), poet, host to

Alterati after *c.*1572, four times regent.

Valori, Baccio (1535–1606), senator, connoisseur of arts.

Valori, Filippo (d. 1606), son of Baccio, admitted 29 July 1599, president of University of Pisa.

Vettori, Piero, *l'Assicurato* (1499–1585), senator, professor of moral philosophy and Greek and Latin rhetoric, inactive in Alterati.

16

The First Performance of Euridice

This essay was first published in the *Twenty-fifth Anniversary Festschrift (1937–62)*, commemorating the first twenty-five years of Queens College, edited by Albert Mell (New York: Queens College of the City University of New York, 1964), 1–23.

Even today, the music of Peri's *Euridice* is known more by reputation than actual sound. There still does not exist a critical edition of the score,[1] and there is not an acceptable recording of the entire work. Its reputation has suffered from its being dismissed by historians of music as consisting mostly of dry, rather deliberately archaic recitative, full of cadences, and falling short of the dramatic and musical success of Monteverdi's *Orfeo*.

Euridice's rehabilitation began in the 1960s. Nino Pirrotta, in a lecture at the Fondazione Giorgio Cini in Venice in 1963, published in 1971,[2] showed how both Rinuccini's libretto and Peri's music were a model for the *Orfeo* of Alessandro Striggio and Monteverdi. Barbara Russano Hanning dedicated a large part of her Yale dissertation of 1968 to Rinuccini's poems *Dafne* and *L'Euridice* and to Peri's music and surrounding questions of genre, theatrical and poetic conventions, and musical style.[3] As an introduction to a performance of *Euridice* that Howard M. Brown directed at the University of Chicago in 1967, he gave a lecture at the Renaissance Seminar of that university that was later published as 'How Opera Began: An Introduction to Japoco Peri's *Euridice* (1600)'.[4] This traces the emergence of the work from the theorizing of the Camerata, experiments with *Dafne*

---

[1] There is a performing edition, ed. Howard Mayer Brown (Madison, Wis.: A-R Editions, 1981), from which the original can be reconstructed, and two facs. edns. of the publication of 1601, *Le musiche di Iacopo Peri nobil fiorentino sopra L'Euridice del Sig. Ottavio Rinuccini* (Florence: Giorgio Marescotti, 1600): Rome: Reale Accademia d'Italia, 1934, with a preface by E. Magni Dufflocq; and Bologna: Forni, 1969, with a postface by Rossana Dalmonte.

[2] 'Monteverdi e i problemi dell'opera', in Maria Teresa Muraro (ed.), *Studi sul teatro veneto fra Rinascimento ed età barocca* (Florence: Leo S. Olschki, 1971), 321–43, repr. in N. Pirrotta, *Scelte poetiche di musicisti: Teatro, poesia e musica da Willaert a Malipiero* (Venice: Marsilio, 1987), 197–217; trans. in Pirrotta, *Music and Culture in Italy from the Middle Ages to the Baroque: A Collection of Essays* (Cambridge, Mass.: Harvard University Press, 1984), 235–53.

[3] 'The Influence of Humanist Thought and Italian Renaissance Poetry on the Formation of Opera', Ph.D. diss. (Yale University, 1969), published, with some revision, as *Of Poetry and Music's Power: Humanism and the Creation of Opera* (Ann Arbor, Mich.: UMI Research Press, 1980).

[4] In Eric Cochrane (ed.), *The Late Italian Renaissance, 1525–1630* (New York: Harper and Row; London: Macmillan, 1970), 401–43, repr. with revisions in Ellen Rosand (ed.), *The Garland Library of the History of Western Music* (New York: Garland, 1985), xi. 1–43.

432

and other pastorals, and other theatrical developments in Florence. Brown then appraises the score's originality and effectiveness, particularly in comparison with Caccini's setting of the same libretto. He concludes that Peri realized his aims remarkably well and that *Euridice* 'deserves repeated hearings and study, not merely for its historical significance as the first extant opera, but because it is capable of moving listeners even today'.[5] Tim Carter, for his doctoral dissertation at the University of Birmingham (1980), searched through a large number of documents for the facts of Peri's life and characterized the main features of the score in a chapter on Rinuccini's poem and Peri's setting.[6] Carter's distillation of these findings in 'Peri's "Euridice": A Contextual Study'[7] offered a fine synthesis of the historical background and an eloquent defence of the artistic merits of the work, based on close analysis of a variety of scenes and situations in the pastoral. My essay, 'Peri and the Theory of Recitative', which follows the present one in this collection, takes a more theoretical view of Peri's achievement.

Not much has been added since my article to our knowledge of the first performance of *Euridice*. Elvira Garbero Zorzi has identified the hall in the apartment of Don Antonio de' Medici in which the pastoral was produced as that now known as the 'Sala bianca'.[8] The identity of the scenic designer is still uncertain. C. Molinari has proposed that it was Ludovico Cigoli. Documents show that Cigoli was working on an unidentified comedy for the wedding.[9] A. M. Nagler assumed that Buontalenti did the design, though it was simple and did not require any machines.[10] According to Michelangelo Buonarotti the younger,[11] the first part was played in a beautiful wood, partly in relief and partly painted, lit up in such a way that it appeared to be full daylight. Then the scene changed to a desolate landscape of horrid masses of rocks, stumps, and livid grass, while in the background through a large opening in a rock could be seen the city of Dite burning, flames gushing from its towers, the air a copper colour.[12] After the scene in Hades, the first set returns.[13]

[5] Ibid. 443. I came to a similar conclusion in my *Baroque Music* (Englewood Cliffs, NJ: Prentice-Hall, 1968), 32 (3rd edn., 1991), 36: 'there is an intensity, nobility, and realism that could not have failed to move its first auditors and that can still affect us today'.

[6] Timothy Carter, 'Jacopo Peri (1561–1633): His Life and Works', Ph.D. diss. (University of Birmingham, 1980), published as *Jacopo Peri (1561–1633): His Life and Works* (New York and London: Garland, 1989). The chapter on *Euridice* is in vol. i. 157–204.

[7] *Music Review*, 42 (1982), 83–103.

[8] Mario Fabbri, Elvira Garbero Zorzi, and Anna Maria Petrioli Tofani (eds.), *Il luogo teatrale a Firenze . . . Firenze, Palazzo Medici Riccardi, Museo Mediceo, 31 maggio/31 ottobre, 1975* (Milan: Electa Editrice, 1975), 144. Caccini's *Euridice* was done in the same hall on 5 Dec. 1602, according to a note by Mario Fabbri, ibid. 144.

[9] C. Molinari, 'L'attività teatrale di Ludovico Cigoli', *La critica d'arte*, 8 (nos. 47, 48; 1961).

[10] *Theatre Festivals of the Medici, 1539–1637* (New Haven, Conn.: Yale University Press, 1964), 94–5.

[11] *Descrizione delle felicissime nozze della Cristianissima Maestà di Madama Maria Medici Regina di Francia e di Nauarra* (Florence: Giorgio Marescotti, 1600).

[12] A design for *Venere gelosa* (Venice, 1643) that fits this description of the scene in Hades may be seen among the *Apparati scenici* for the Teatro novissimo published in Venice, 1644, by Jacomo Torelli da Fano, reproduced in Simon Towneley Worsthorne, *Seventeenth Century Venetian Opera* (Oxford: Clarendon Press, 1954), Plate 20*b*, and in Ellen Rosand, *Opera in Seventeenth-Century Venice: The Creation of a Genre* (Berkeley: University of California Press, 1991), 167.

[13] See also Fabbri *et al.*, *Il luogo teatrale*, 144, item 10.2.

Since my research on these festivities around 1960, some new sources have emerged, including the diary of the journey of the Papal Legate, Cardinal Pietro Aldobrandino, nephew of the reigning Pope Clement VIII, from Rome to Florence to perform the wedding ceremony.[14] We learn in the account, attributed to Mgr. Agucchia,[15] that the Cardinal was accompanied by the singers of the Epistle and Gospel and other musicians of the Papal Chapel. His immediate party had twelve carriages, each drawn by six horses. Of the wedding ceremony on Thursday, the chronicler tells the 'ceremony and the sung mass was the same as that celebrated in Ferrara for the wedding of the Queen of Spain.[16] The music was excellent, and a big salvo of artillery was fired.'[17] Of the entertainment that night at 'a solemn wedding banquet that was done with great machinery and royally', Agucchia tells that outside the hall 'there was most excellent music, especially that coming out of the walls from the sides of the hall, but facing the head table were two bridges in the air, with clouds, on which fabulous deities sang some songs in praise of the wedding couple, and the festivity lasted until seven at night'.[18] This was the dialogue between Juno and Minerva by Guarini and Cavalieri, but what Agucchia thought were bridges were two carri, Juno's drawn by two peacocks, Minerva's by a unicorn. On Friday, 'in the evening, the principal comedy in music [*Euridice*] was done, which deserved much praise for its scenery and its intermedi, but the manner of singing easily became boring, and, besides, the movement of the machines was not always felicitous'.[19] The reference to intermedi is puzzling, since

[14] 'Diario Del viaggio del Card. Pietro Aldobrandino nell'andar Legato Apostolico á Firenze per il sponsalitio della Regina di Francia, e' doppo in Francia per la pace. Descritto dà Mons. Agucchia morto in Venetia Nuntio Apostolico.' New York, Pierpont Morgan Library, Feltrinelli Collection, No. 95. This is one of several manuscript copies of this 'Diario' in various libraries around the world. Other copies are listed in Sara Mamone, 'Feste e spettacoli a Firenze e in Francia per le nozze di Maria de' Medici con Enrico IV', *Quaderni di teatro*, Anno 2, no. 7 (Mar. 1980), *Il teatro dei Medici*, 208–28 at 208 n. 5.

[15] Actually Mgr. Agucchia, Secretary to the Cardinal, was too ill to undertake the trip and sent his brother, also an Agucchia, in his place. See Mamone, 'Feste', 208 n. 5.

[16] This was the wedding of Margaret of Austria, daughter of the Archduke of Styria, and Philip III, son of King Philip II of Spain, who had just died, which made it a royal wedding. It took place in Ferrara on 14 Nov. 1598, with Pope Clement VIII performing the ceremony and saying the mass in the duomo. The description of the event, *Relatione dell'entrata solenne fatta in Ferrara à di 13. di Nouembre 1598 per la sereniss. D. Margarita d'Austria Regina di Spagna* (Rome: Ottaviano Gabrielli, 1598); facs. in Bonner Mitchell, *1598, a Year of Pageantry in Late Renaissance Ferrara* (Binghamton, NY: Medieval & Renaissance Texts and Studies, 1990).

[17] 'Diario', fo. 44ᵛ: 'la Ceremonia e la messa cantata fù l'istessa celebrata à ferrara per lo Sponsalitio della Regina di Spagna. La musica fù ottima, e si fece una gran salua di artigliaria . . .'.

[18] Ibid., fos. 45ʳ–46ʳ: 'fuori ui erano musiche eccellentissime, especialmente uscirono fuori delle mura da' lati della sala mà dinanzi alla tauola principale due Ponti in aria con Nuuole, entro de quali erano delle Deita fauolose, che cantarono alcune canzoni in lode delli sposi, e la festa durò sino alle sett'hore di notte'. The windows that opened on the Salone dei Cinquecento, where the banquet was held, may have been used as loges for spectators not admitted to the hall itself, as was done at the theatre in the Uffizi for the 1589 intermedi, and it is through these that Agucchia must have witnessed the feast and heard the music. See Franco Berti, 'Studi su alcuni aspetti del diario inedito del Seriacopi e sui disegni buontalentiani per i costumi del 1589', *Quaderni di Teatro*, Anno 2, no. 7 (Mar. 1980), *Il Teatro dei Medici*, 157–68 at 163.

[19] 'Diario', fo. 46ʳ: 'La sera si fece la Comedia principale in Musica, che per l'apparato scenico, e gl'Intermedij, meritò molta lode, mà il modo di cantarla, uenne facilmente à noia, oltre che non sempre il mouimento delle maniche è riuscito felice.' The copyist incorrectly wrote 'maniche' for 'macchine',

the official description does not refer to them, but the remark about the machinery corroborates Cavalieri's complaint that the scenery was not altogether ready. Agucchia may have mistaken some of the choral and dance episodes in *Euridice* for intermedi.

Another manuscript source, which gives us no new information but reflects on the contemporary attitude towards the contribution of composers to these festivities, is the collection of drafts by Michelangelo Buonarotti the younger for his official description.[20] Whereas the published description does not give the names of the composers of *Euridice*, only that of the poet, Buonarotti's draft does give them credit, recording that Jacopo Peri and Giulio Caccini, 'excellent composers', shared in setting it to music. Here are the two versions.

Printed, fo. C2^v	Draft, fo. 79^r
La onde auendo il Signor Iacopo	Il perche auendo il Sr Jacopo
Corsi fatta mettere in musica	Corsi fatta mettere in musica
con grande studio la Euridice	con grande studio la euridice,
affettuosa, e gentilissima	affettuosa fauola del Sr Ottauio
fauola del Signor Ottauio	Rinuccini, parte da Iacopo Peri,
Rinuccini, e per li personaggi,	e parte da Giulio Caccini ottimi
ricchissimi, e belli,	compositori e per gli personaggi
uestimenti apprestati;	ricchissimi uestimenti, e belli
offertala a loro Altezze; fu	apprestati; offertala al
riceuuta, e preparatale nobile	palazzo; e fu riceuuta, e
scena nel Palazzo de Pitti . . .	preparatale nobile scena ne
	Pitti . . .

A set of notes indicating points for revision, probably handed down by a member of the Grand Duke's administration, includes the following as point no. 12: 'non occorre nominare tanti Musici'—'there is no need to name so many musicians'.[21] In a draft of a letter dated 19 November 1600 to one of the Duke's staff, Buonarroti concedes that 'in keeping with the wishes of His Highness I have added many things and omitted and changed others in my description'.[22]

THE first surviving example of a particular musical genre naturally looms large in the topography of history. When this genre is the ever-fascinating one of music drama, it is particularly difficult to see the first survivor, Peri's *Euridice*, as anything but a great landmark. It is time, however, to restore it to its proper scale, to ask not what it represents to us but what it was to its contemporaries.

Much of the data for such a reappraisal was published earlier in this

which is the reading in Paris, Bibliothèque nationale, fonds italien, MS 1323, fo. 33^v (quoted in Mamone, 'Feste', 218).

[20] Florence, Biblioteca Medicea Laurenziana, Archivio Buonarroti, MS 88.

[21] Ibid., fo. 220^r.

[22] Ibid., fo. 226^v: 'Conforme al uolere di S. Altezza ho aggiunte molte cose e leuate e mutate intorno alla mia descrizione.'

century by Angelo Solerti. Only recently have a few new facts been uncovered, and these are the immediate pretext for this review of the first performance. The purpose of this contribution, then, will be to set *Euridice* in its social, political, and artistic contexts.

The occasion for the performance of 6 October 1600 is well known: the marriage of Henry IV of Navarre, King of France, to Maria de' Medici, niece of Ferdinand I, Grand Duke of Tuscany. She was the daughter of the previous Grand Duke, Francis I, and his wife, Giovanna of Austria.

The performance of *Euridice* occupied one of six evenings in a series of festivities that called upon all the artistic resources of the Florentine court. The schedule of the most important events was as follows:

Monday, 2 October. Arrival of the Duke of Mantua.

Tuesday, 3 October. Arrival of the Ambassador of Venice.

Wednesday, 4 October. Solemn entry into the city of Cardinal Pietro Aldobrandini, the papal legate appointed to perform the marriage ceremony. The procession preceding him from the gates of the city included a group of monks and clergymen, the beadles and ministers of the city, the servants of the Cardinal and Duke, fifty horsemen in armour, six trumpeters, Florentine and Roman noblemen, twenty-one mules bearing the Cardinal's effects, numerous prelates of the Church, and young Roman noblemen. Finally, the Cardinal rode on horseback, covered by a canopy carried by eight Florentine noblemen. At the side was the Duke of Tuscany and behind them sixteen prelates from Rome and fifty more Florentine gentlemen bearing halberds.[23]

Thursday, 5 October. Henry IV, through his proxy, Grand Duke Ferdinand de' Medici, was married to Maria de' Medici in the Cathedral of Santa Maria del Fiore. The papal legate said mass. After cannon roared from all sides, the Duke's children, Lorenzo, born on 1 August 1599, and Maria, born on 22 June 1600, were baptized. In the evening a ball and grand banquet were held in the hall of banquets of the Palazzo Vecchio. The hall was richly decorated. A buffet in the shape of a fleur-de-lis encrusted with gems of all sorts alone cost 1,800 scudi.[24] The dancing began with courantes and branles at the wish of the Queen. During the dinner there were many magical transformations in the décor.[25]

---

[23] *Traicté du mariage de Henry IIII. Roy de France et de Navarre avec la Serenissime Princesse de Florence* (Paris: Jean Petit, 1601), 14.

[24] Anonymous letter printed in *Mémoires-Journaux de Pierre de l'Estoile*, ed. G. Brunet *et al.*, vii: *Journal de Henry IV, 1595–1601* (Paris: Librairie des Bibliophiles, 1879), 240.

[25] These are described at great length by Michelangelo Buonarotti, the younger, *Descrizione delle felicissime nozze della cristianissima maestà di madama Maria Medici, regina de Francia* (Florence: Giorgio Marescotti, 1600), sigs. B2ᵛ–C3ᵛ·

After the dessert, two goddesses descended in cloud-machinery designed by Bernardo Buontalenti. Juno in a chariot drawn by peacocks and Minerva in a chariot drawn by a unicorn vied with each other in praising the newly-weds in a dialogue by Giovanni Battista Guarini set to music by Emilio de' Cavalieri.[26]

Friday, 6 October. In the evening in a room of the apartment of Don Antonio de' Medici in the Pitti Palace, the princely guests and a small number of noblewomen saw performed Ottavio Rinuccini's *Euridice*, set to music by Jacopo Peri and Giulio Caccini. Ambassadors and the papal nunzio looked on from another room. The party afterwards danced for two hours.

Saturday, 7 October. In the afternoon a parade of horsemen and a race called the *palio*. In the evening a dress rehearsal of Giulio Caccini's *Il rapimento di Cefalo*, open to those who wished to see it.

Sunday, 8 October. In the afternoon a garden party at the Riccardi Palace, with chariot races, allegorical *trionfi*, songs, and dances.[27] Vincenzio Panciatichi's *tragicomedia pastorale*, *L'amicizia costante*, probably occupied the evening,[28] along with dancing.

Monday, 9 October. At the great theatre of the gallery of the Uffizi, *Il rapimento di Cefalo* by Gabriello Chiabrera, set to music by Giulio Caccini, with choruses by Stefano Venturi, Luca Bati, and Pietro Strozzi. Scenery and machinery by Bernardo Buontalenti and Alessandro Pieroni, intermezzi and staging by Don Giovanni de' Medici. The performance lasted from 1 to 5 a.m.

The Queen left Florence on the 13th, stopping at the Villa Ambrosiana for the night, proceeding to Pisa on the 14th and to Leghorn on the 15th. Accompanied by about sixty women, she embarked on the 17th at Leghorn. After stopping in La Spezia and being detained in Portofino for nine days during a storm, the fleet of seventeen galleys got under way again. Touching numerous Italian and French ports on the way, the Queen arrived in Marseilles on 3 November. She was not united with the King, however, until after three days of feasting in Avignon, and eight days of waiting in Lyons, where he arrived on 9 December. On the 17th they were married

[26] 'Il dialogo cantato nel convito reale da Giunone e Minerva'. The music is lost; the text is printed in Buonarroti, *Descrizione*, sigs. C3ᵛ–4ᵛ, and reprinted in Solerti, *Musica, ballo e drammatica alla corte medicea dal 1600 al 1637* (Florence: R. Bemporad e Figlio, 1905), 229–38.

[27] The poems were by Riccardi and published in *Rime cantate nel giardino del signor Riccardo Riccardi con l'occasione d'una festa quivi fatta per la reina* (Florence: D. Manzani, 1600).

[28] The anonymous letter quoted by l'Estoile states: 'Dimanche, il se doit faire une superbe Comoédie, et lundi, une Pastorelle, dont le dépense coutera plus de soixante mil ecus', in Brunet, *Journal*, 241. The 'Comoédie' was probably Panciatichi's tragicomedy, which Solerti could not assign to any of the evenings. Cf. Solerti, *Musica, ballo*, 25 n. 2.

once again by the papal legate Aldobrandini in the church of St Jean, and a banquet and ball followed.[29]

The climax of the Florentine festivities was *Il rapimento di Cefalo*. Upon this performance were lavished 60,000 scudi (roughly $300,000 [in 1962]), about 1,000 staff members, including 100 musicians and singers under the direction of Caccini, and elaborate scenery and machinery. It consisted of a prologue, five acts, and a final 'carro' and ballo. The official description of the wedding festivities by Michelangelo Buonarotti, the younger, which pauses only for about a page on *Euridice*, dwells for sixteen on *Cefalo*.[30] 'This production,' Buonarotti asserts, 'from the standpoint of the greatness of the apparatus, of the charm, and of the spectacle, is believed to have exceeded by far any other since the Romans.'[31]

The only singers identified by Buonarotti are the four women of Caccini's family and Melchior Palantrotti, who, he says, was borrowed from the Papal Chapel. Caccini identified two others in the *Nuove musiche*, where he printed the music for the final chorus. Three stanzas of this are for solo voices and they were intended for Palantrotti, Rasi, and Peri. The audience consisted, according to one of the court diarists, of 3,000 gentlemen and 800 gentlewomen. 'Marvellous machines', 'superb', 'a most beautiful comedy', 'one of the most ingenious comedies ever done here, and entirely in music, with the most beautiful intermezzi, as everyone reports': these were some of the comments elicited.[32] A French chronicler, who passed over *Euridice* silently, said of *Cefalo*: 'it filled the ears of all and the eyes of the spectators with such admiration that they were all astounded.'[33]

Next to this grand spectacle, *Euridice* was bound to suffer both in care of preparation and in public notice. *Euridice* achieved less celebrity also because fewer gained entrance to see it. It was staged in a room of the apartment of Don Antonio de' Medici in the Pitti Palace. How exclusive was the gathering is revealed by the Modenese ambassador, Count Giulio Thiene, in a letter of 7 October to his Duke.

yesterday [6 October] a pastoral represented in music was done, to which entered only a few besides the princes: some gentlewomen and foreign women. It was put

---

[29] These facts are from the *Traicté du mariage* and from *Le discours veritable de ce qui c'est passe au voyage de la Royne, depuis son departemen de Florence iusques a son arrivee, en la ville de Marseille, avec les magnificences faites à l'entree de sa Maiesté* (Paris: pour Benoist Chalonneau et Silvestre Moreau, 1600).

[30] Sigs. C4ᵛ–B+4ᵛ.

[31] Sig. B+4ᵛ. Chiabrera's text is printed in Solerti, *Albori*, iii. 29–58; music for lines 608–57 is in Giulio Caccini, *Le nuove musiche* (Florence: Marescotti, 1601/2), 19–24, ed. H. Wiley Hitchcock (Madison, Wis.: A-R Editions, 1970), 103–13.

[32] Settimani, quoted in Solerti, *Musica, ballo*, 26 n. 1.   [33] *Traicté du mariage*, 17.

on in a little hall in the upper part of the palace at Pitti. It turned out very well . . .[34]

The Venetian ambassador, Nicolò da Molin, reported on 7 October: 'Yesterday there was also a feast, and in the evening a comedy recited entirely by musicians on very sweet melodies (*suavissimi canti*).'[35] A French visitor, in a letter dated 7 October, describes the banquet of 5 October and notes the entertainments to come on 8 and 9 October, but omits mention of *Euridice* altogether.[36] Similarly, the author of the official French description sums up the activities between the banquet of 5 October and the spectacle of 9 October with the words: 'The three following days were employed in races and jousts, tilting at the ring, and other activities of kings and princes usual in such solemnities.'[37]

The staging of *Euridice* was apparently somewhat hastily prepared, for Cavalieri complained after the performance that among other shortcomings its scenic constructions (*prospettive*) were not finished. In the case of *Cefalo*, too, Cavalieri noted that because Buontalenti's counsels had not been followed the machinery was not finished.[38] The hurried preparations upon which Cavalieri lays part of the blame for the incomplete success of the entertainments must have been caused by the many misadventures that preceded the wedding. Since music historians have been silent about these, a review of the facts is necessary.

As far back as 1592, Henry IV, then still a Protestant and married to Marguerite de Valois, made a secret agreement with Tuscany through Cardinal Gondi, a native of Florence, who was Bishop of Paris. In return for Duke Ferdinand's financial help in the amount of about a million scudi, Henry, when conditions permitted, would dissolve his marriage to Marguerite, embrace Catholicism, and marry Maria de' Medici.[39] There were a number of formidable obstacles in the way of this plan. Pope Clement VIII was reluctant to encourage the conversion of Henry for fear of antagonizing the Spanish, who were sponsors of a pretender to the crown and controlled

---

[34] Solerti, *Musica, ballo*, 27.

[35] Ibid.

[36] L'Estoile, *Mémoires*, in Burnet, *Journal*, 241.

[37] *Traicté du mariage*, 17: 'Les trois iours suivants furent employez en chasses & en ioustes, courses de bagues & autres exercises de Rois & Princes en telles solemnitez accoustumees.'

[38] Letter to Belisario Vinta, Rome, 7 Oct. 1600 (misdated; probably of 7 Nov.), Florence, Archivio di Stato, Mediceo del Principato, Filza 899, fos. 416ᵣ–417ᵛ. This letter was published in full by Solerti in 'Laura Guidiccioni Lucchesini ed Emilio del Cavaliere', *Rivista musicale italiana*, 9 (1902), 817. He did not question the date, but see my reasons for doubting it in 'Musical Asides in the Diplomatic Correspondence of Emilio de' Cavalieri', above, Essay 14, n. 53.

[39] Iacopo V. R. Galluzzi, *Istoria del Granducato di Toscana sotto la Casa Medici* (Florence: G. Cambiagi, 1781), iii. 166.

a large party in the college of cardinals. Childless Marguerite recognized that Henry needed an heir, but was unwilling to agree to the annulment as long as she was convinced Henry would marry his mistress Gabrielle d'Estrées.

The diplomacy of Duke Ferdinand was mainly instrumental in easing the way in Rome for the conversion of the King and at the same time in keeping Henry to his resolution.[40] The reconciliation with the Church was solemnly declared in September 1595. The death of Gabrielle on 10 April 1599 removed the other obstacle. Meanwhile Henry had decided to put the plan of 1592 into operation and had sent the Marquis de Sillery, his ambassador in Rome, to the Grand Duke with a proposal of marriage for Maria. This was accepted, and negotiations soon began on a dowry agreement. The Duke authorized his representative Baccio Giovannini to offer 500,000 scudi, of which 400,000 would be a credit on the King's debts to Tuscany.[41] Henry's minister Villeroi insisted on a million. The King reasoned that if he could have got a million in 1592, now that he was powerful and reconciled with his internal enemies he was worth at least that and more. The Duke contended that he had already spent about two million on aiding the King, and to give him another million would look as if he had to pay heavily for this alliance. News of the haggling reached the Florentine nobility, and Jacopo Corsi (the sponsor of *Euridice*) appealed to the Duke in the name of the nobility, which was jubilant about the marriage, to allow them to raise the difference.[42] Duke Ferdinand held his ground, however, and eventually Sully, Henry's superintendent of finances, and Giovannini secretly compromised on 600,000 gold scudi, of which 350,000 was in credit on debts, the rest in cash. The agreement was signed in Paris on 7 March 1600, and on 25 April the marriage contract was proclaimed in Florence. The couple was to be married by proxy in Florence; then the bride was to be accompanied with great pomp to Marseilles in May, and the church wedding would take place there or in Lyons in June.

Even before receiving news of the signing and terms of the contract, Henry wrote to Sillery to seek a postponement of the wedding until the end of September. He also made clear his wish that the wedding be in

---

[40] Bojan Bujić has recently studied the symbolism of Rinuccini's libretto in terms of Duke Ferdinand's political and dynastic ambitions in ' "Figura poetica molto vaga": Structure and Meaning in Rinuccini's *Euridice*', *Early Music History*, 10 (1991), 29–64.

[41] Berthold Zeller, *Henry IV et Marie des Médicis d'après des documents nouveaux tirés des archives de Florence et de Paris* (Paris: Librairie académique, 1877), 15.

[42] Galluzzi, *Istoria*, iii. 169.

Marseilles and that the festivities not exceed eight or ten days.[43] The next day he received the articles of the agreement. He was angry at its publication in Florence and took exception to the clause that the marriage would be in Florence by proxy. He insisted on marrying the Princess de' Medici in person, in Marseilles, and not before September. Apart from the heat of the summer, the difficulty of preparing Marseilles for the festivities, and the time needed to organize the equipages, the King was concerned about an international situation. The Duke of Savoy was required to restore to France the Marquisate of Saluces (Saluzzo) by the treaty of Vervins signed with Spain in 1598 and had not yet done so. Henry expected he might have to drive him out.[44] The Duke of Savoy kept promising but delayed clearing the way for French rule of the territory because he expected any day to receive news of the King's death, having conspired with Philip III of Spain and several in Henry's court, including Marshal Biron, to have Henry assassinated. On 24 May, Henry wrote that on further deliberation he had decided to allow the marriage to be by proxy in Florence so that the Queen might travel more honourably to Marseilles, where the church wedding would be held.[45] Finally, on 24 July Giovannini informed the Grand Duke from Lyons that the bearer of the proxy would leave on 6 or 8 August and that the ceremony should proceed upon his arrival, whether Cardinal Aldobrandini, the papal legate designated to officiate, was there or not. Henry's Grand Equerry, the Duke of Bellegarde, did not actually leave with the proxy until 24 August, reaching Leghorn on 20 September and Florence on the 23rd. The marriage was now to take place in Avignon, because the King was busy at the front in Savoy. Still, the King wanted the Queen in Marseilles at the end of September.[46] On 30 August, however, Giovannini informed the Grand Duke that Marseilles would not be ready to receive the Queen before 10 October,[47] and that without any great solemnity.

It is evident from these negotiations that as late as August the principal marriage festivities were still being planned for Marseilles, and that consequently the Duke's projects until then for entertaining the guests must have been of limited scope and ill formed. Eventually the ceremonies and entertainments in Florence very much outweighed those in France. They

---

[43] Letter, Henry IV to Sillery, 11 May 1600, in *Lettres inédites du Roi Henri IV à Monsieur de Sillery du 1er avril au 27 juin 1600* (Paris: Auguste Aubry, 1866), 37–40.
[44] Letter, Henry IV to Sillery, 12 May 1600, ibid. 49–51.
[45] Letter, Henry IV to Sillery, 24 May 1600, ibid. 62–3.
[46] Letter, Giovannini to Grand Duke, Lyons, 21 Aug. 1600, summarized in Abel Desjardine, *Négociations diplomatiques de la France avec la Toscane*, v (Paris: Imprimerie royale, 1875), 436.
[47] Ibid. 437.

lasted ten days, from 4 to 13 October. We know that by August work had begun on the decorations for the cathedral, where the marriage ceremony by proxy was to take place, and some rehearsals were also under way. The Florentine representative of the court of the Este at Modena, Marchese Bartolomeo Malaspina, reported back to his home office on 29 August 1600:

The Queen[48] and the Grand Duke, together with the whole court, went to Pratolino. Meanwhile they are working unceasingly in the cathedral and in the hall of the Palazzo Vecchio with diligence, and every morning the comedy in music that is being done is rehearsed. For this purpose the Most Serene Grand Duke has had famous musicians come from Rome, among them Melchior.[49]

The rehearsals mentioned here are probably not of *Euridice*, which was performed not in the Palazzo Vecchio but in the Palazzo Pitti. Moreover, Melchior Palantrotti would not have been called away from Rome so early to sing a few lines—the part of Pluto has thirty lines in the libretto of *Euridice*, twenty-six bars in the score of Peri. Palantrotti was one of the principal soloists, as we have seen, in *Il rapimento di Cefalo*, which must be the work then being rehearsed at the palace. Another singer who had arrived by this time was Francesco Rasi. He wrote to his patron, the Duke of Mantua, on 14 August, shortly after his arrival:

My trip was a happy one, but even happier was my arrival. I was greeted by these Most Serene Princes most affectionately and provided with every accommodation. If I should believe their words, said with too much enthusiasm, I would report the honour and praise of this marvellous pastoral or fable or whatever I should call it.[50]

Could this remark refer to *Euridice*? We know from Peri's preface to the *Euridice* score that Rasi played Aminta in that performance. This part has 73 lines out of the 790 of the libretto, not one of the principal roles, but substantial compared to the Pluto of Palantrotti. On the other hand, Rasi had undoubtedly one of the principal roles in *Cefalo*, perhaps the title role, so his remark probably refers to this pastorale rather than *Euridice*. Only top billing would have justified borrowing the most famous tenor of his day from a neighbouring prince. There is no evidence, then, that *Euridice* was already in rehearsal, but it must have been before long. The production had barely a month and a half to go before its unveiling. The novelty of the work, and the fact that all the instrumental parts apart from the bass had to

[48] Although not yet married, Maria de' Medici was being accorded all the honours of a queen, including the title from the time of the public announcement of the marriage contract in April. Zeller, *Henry IV*, 28.
[49] Solerti, *Musica, ballo*, 23.
[50] Solerti, *Albori*, i. 67 n. 3.

be improvised, would have required much rehearsal. It is not to be wondered that the time was considered insufficient.

The official description by Buonarotti gives this account of the performance of *Euridice*:

Signor Jacopo Corsi had the very affecting and gentle story of Euridice of Signor Ottavio Rinuccini set to music with great care and had very rich and beautiful costumes prepared. He having offered it to Their Highnesses and they having accepted it, a noble setting was readied at the Pitti Palace. It was performed on the evening after the royal wedding. Here is the argument of this tale. While the loving bridal couple Orfeo and Euridice are enjoying a peaceful life, she dies from the bite of a snake hidden in the grass. Orfeo laments his loss and, upon the advice of Venus, who leads him to the mouth of hell, he calls to Euridice singing sorrowfully. Pluto, moved to pity by the sweetness of the singing and by the counsel of Proserpina, restores Euridice to him more beautiful than ever. They rejoice in their renewed love. In a noble hall, behind the curtains was revealed a magnificent apparatus. Inside a great arch were two niches, one at each end. In them Poetry and Painting were represented as statues—a nice touch on the part of the designer. Between these a forest was seen, very beautifully rendered through relief and painting. It was bathed with a light as bright as day by well-placed lamps. Later, when a hell was represented, these woods changed into horrible and frightening masses that seemed real. The twigs looked bare and the grasses livid. Further upstage, through the opening of a large rock the city of Dite could be seen burning, tongues of flame vibrating from the windows of its towers, the air all around blazing with a brassy colour. After this change of set, the first one returned, and there were no further scene changes. The whole was consummately performed, honouring everyone who had a part in it and giving varied pleasures to the mind and senses of the spectator.[51]

Buonarotti assigns the initiative for the production of *Euridice* to Corsi. This agrees with a statement by Marco da Gagliano, who tells that Rinuccini, having experienced the success of *Dafne* in Peri's musical setting, decided to write a more extended piece, which was *Euridice*. When Corsi heard the poem, he decided to have it staged at the wedding, and Jacopo Peri was asked to set it to music.[52] The scenic designs and sets were apparently supplied by the ducal house, as were the direction, most of the singers, and the instrumentalists.

Witnesses concur in giving credit to Emilio de' Cavalieri for the direction. The diarist Tinghi refers to *Euridice* as 'the comic pastorale in music of Sig. Emilio del Cavalieri'.[53] The author of the *Diario d'Etichetta* recorded

---

[51] *Descrizione*, sigs. C3ᵛ–4ʳ.

[52] Preface 'Ai Lettori' in *La Dafne di Marco da Gagliano* (Florence: Christofano Marescotti, 1608), reprinted in Solerti, *Le origini del melodramma* (Turin: Fratelli Bocca, 1903), 81.

[53] 'The 6th of the said month [October], on Friday, His Highness and all the princes rested a good part of the morning, and in the evening His Highness, having invited a good number of noblewomen,

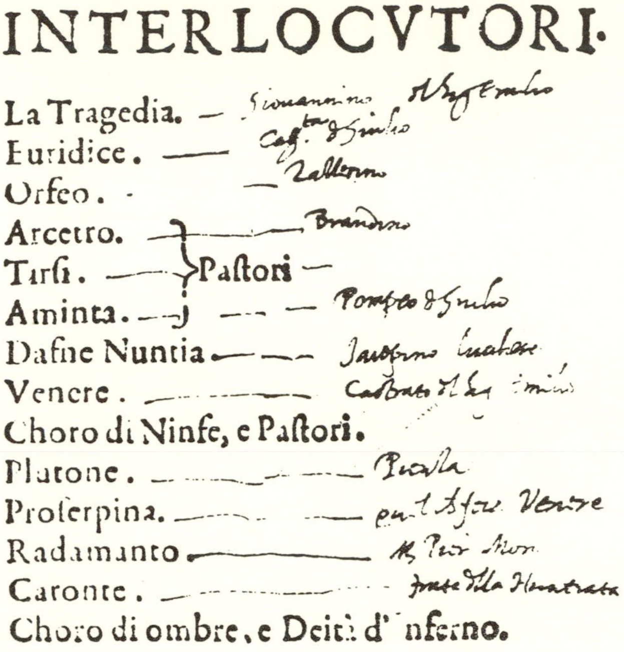
INTERLOCVTORI.

La Tragedia.

Euridice.

Orfeo.

Arcetro.

Tirsi. Pastori

Aminta.

Dafne Nuntia

Venere.

Choro di Ninfe, e Pastori.

Plutone.

Proserpina.

Radamanto

Caronte.

Choro di ombre, e Deità d'Inferno.

PL. 16.1. The cast in Peri's *Euridice* in a performance shortly after 6 October 1600, from Ottavio Rinuccini, *L'Euridice* (Florence, 1600). University of Illinois Library

that 'on the 6th there was done at the Pitti in the evening a pastoral that lasted two hours, set to music by Sig. Emilio de Cavalieri'.[54] Cavalieri himself refers to it as 'the music of the comedy I did'.[55] Another circumstance tying Cavalieri to the production is the presence in the cast, as will be seen, of singers who were his pupils and members of his household.

Peri, in his letter to the readers of his score of *Euridice*, identified a number of the singers taking part in the performance.[56] The cast, as he sets it out, consisted of Francesco Rasi as Aminta, Antonio Brandi as Arcetro, Melchior Palandrotti [*sic*] as Plutone, and Jacopo Giusti—'fanciuletto lucchese'—as Dafne. The parts of Euridice, portions of those

to give a little recreation to those princes, had performed a comic pastoral in music done by Sig. Emilio del Cavaliere in the rooms of Signor Don Antonio de' Medici at the Pitti, whither all the said princes and ambassadors repaired. It lasted two hours.' Solerti, *Musica, ballo*, 25.

[54] Ibid.

[55] Letter of '7 October'—see above, n. 36.

[56] Solerti, *Origini*, 48–9; trans. in Oliver Strunk, *Source Readings in Music History* (New York: Norton, 1950), 375–6.

TABLE 16.1. *Casts of the first and a later performance of* Euridice

Interlocutori	Peri, Preface	Illinois copy of libretto
La Tragedia		Giovannino del Sig. Emilio
Euridice	[Caccini dependant]	Cog.ta di Giulio [G. Caccini's sister-in-law]
Orfeo		Zazzerino [Peri]
Arcetro ⎫	Antonio Brandi	Brandino
Tirsi ⎬ Pastori		
Aminta ⎭	Francesco Rasi	Pompeo di Giulio
Dafne nunzia	Jacopo Giusti fanciuletto lucchese	Jacopino lucchese
Venere		Castrato del Sig. Emilio
Choro di Ninfe, e Pastori	[Caccini dependants]	
Plutone	Melchior Palandrotti	Pienza
Proserpina		quel che fece Venere [he who did Venus]
Radamanto		Ms. Piero Mon
Caronte		Frate della Nuntiata [Priest from the Church of the Annunciation]
Choro di ombre, e Deità d'Inferno		

of the Pastore del Coro, of the Ninfe del Coro, and certain choruses, were sung by members of Caccini's household. Peri did not identify the singers of the remaining parts, that is Orfeo, Tirsi, Venere, Proserpina, Radamanto, and Caronte.

A copy of the printed libretto marked by a contemporary supplies the identity of the singers at another performance (see Pl. 16.1). This copy, formerly belonging to the Wolffheim Library,[57] is now in the library of the University of Illinois.[58] If the two casts are set side by side (see Table 16.1), it becomes evident that the interpreters of Euridice, Arcetro, and Dafne coincide, while those of Aminta and Pluto, sung on 6 October by the imported singers Rasi and Palantrotti, were taken at the later performance by resident singers. That this was indeed a later performance is established by the fact that the marked libretto bears a dedication date of 4

---

[57] Cf. *Versteigerung der Musikbibliothek des Herrn Dr. Werner Wolffheim*, II. Teil (Berlin: Martin Breslauer–Leo Liepmannsohn, 1929), Texband, 212, No. 1084. A facsimile of the page is given in Tafelband, Tafel 17.

[58] *L'Euridice d'Ottavio Rinuccini rappresentata nello sponsalitio della Christianiss. Regina di Francia e di Navarra. In Fiorenza, 1600. Nella Stamperia di Cosimo Giunti.* Sig. A4r is headed 'Interlocutori'. The Library of the University of Illinois kindly supplied the photograph of this page reproduced here.

October. On the other hand, the performance documented in it cannot have been staged much later than the first, because of the number of common singers and because Cavalieri left Florence and his post definitively around the beginning of November 1600. The two singers referred to as 'Giovannino del Sign. Emilio' and 'castrato del Signor Emilio' would not have continued to bear these tags much after his departure.[59] It seems likely, then, that the members of the cast in the performance of 6 October not identified by Peri were the same as those of the later revival. Apart from Piero Mon and the priest of the Annunziata, they were all on the court's musical staff.

The only part not identified in the later performance is that of Tirsi. This may be because Tirsi and Aminta were sung on that occasion by one and the same person, namely Pompeo. In Caccini's setting Aminta's part is eliminated in the scenes in which Rinuccini gave lines to both Aminta and Tirsi. This permits one singer to do both, as must have happened in the second performance, after Rasi was gone. Whether Pompeo sang Tirsi in the first performance cannot be established, but it is unlikely because Peri did not name that part as one in which Caccini's music was used.

Peri had reason to boast modestly in his preface to the reader that, as compared with *Dafne*, *Euridice* was more successful, partly because it was sung 'by the most excellent musicians of our times'.[60] Francesco Rasi, tenor, was once a member of the Duke's musical staff, but he was lured away by the Duke of Mantua just before the presentation of *Dafne* at court. Melchior Palantrotti, bass, employed by Cardinal Montalto in Rome, was among the outstanding singers remembered by the chroniclers Vincenzo Giustiniani[61] and Pietro della Valle. Della Valle recalled that 'besides an excellent aptitude, he possessed techniques that after him have remained the rule of gracious singing for basses'.[62] Antonio Brandi was another Peri could be proud to have in his cast. On the occasion of Brandi's creation of the role of the Nunzio in Marco da Gagliano's *Dafne* (1608), the composer paid this tribute to him:

[59] It has been suggested that the cast noted in this copy of the libretto was that of the Caccini *Euridice*, performed on 5 Dec. 1602 (Nino Pirrotta, 'Caccini', *Enciclopedia dello spettacolo*, ii. 1451). The reference to Emilio de' Cavalieri, who died on 11 Mar. of that year, would then have been out of the question.

[60] Solerti, *Le origini*, 48.

[61] Vincenzo Giustiniani, 'Discorso sopra la musica de' suoi tempi', in Solerti, *Le origini*, 110; English translation in Carol MacClintock, 'Giustiniani's Discorso Sopra la Musica', *Musica disciplina*, 15 (1961), 215; also in Ercole Bottrigari, *Il Desiderio* and Vincenzo Giustiniani, *Discorso sopra la musica*, trans. Carol MacClintock (American Institute of Musicology, 1962).

[62] Pietro della Valle, 'Della musica dell'età nostra che non è punto inferiore anzi è migliore di quella dell'età passata', in Solerti, *Le origini*, 162.

He sang the part in such a way that more could not have been desired, I believe. His voice is an exquisite contralto; his diction and the grace of his singing are marvellous. He not only makes the words understood but with gestures and movements he seems to take possession of one's spirit.[63]

Concerning Jacopo Giusti, the boy-soprano from Lucca, nothing further is known.

The remaining singers, if we may assume that they were the same as those of the later performance, are, apart from Peri himself, obscure today. Giovannino, a castrato, was a pupil of Cavalieri and received at the time of the wedding six scudi a month as a member of the Duke's personnel. Cavalieri, shortly after his departure from Florence, wrote to the Duke's secretary to advise him to raise his salary by two scudi, because from Cavalieri he received only his room and furnishings (*masserizie*).[64] Cavalieri was disappointed to hear that he and another castrato, Fabio, were no longer studying diligently. Fabio Fabri may be the anonymous castrato who sang Venus and Proserpina, since the two, Giovannino and Fabio, were accustomed to sing duets together to the accompaniment of Peri.[65] Giulio Caccini's sister-in-law, whose name is not known, must be the fourth of the 'quattro donne di sua famiglia' who, according to Buonarotti, participated in the *Rapimento di Cefalo*.[66] Piero Mon and the Frate dell'Annunziata, who sang the two minor parts of Radamante and Caronte, are not otherwise known.

The two remaining singers taking part in the later performance, who

---

[63] Solerti, *Le origini*, 87.

[64] Letter to Marcello Accolti, Rome, 24 Nov. 1600: 'con Scudi sei il mese; non possono vivere, poichè da me non hanno altro ora che stanza; et massaricie; et Gioannino se troverà qualche comodo; serrà ancho lui necessitato; se il G. Duca le crescerà Scudi doi il mese per ciascheduno; potranno servire; altrimenti andaranno alla mala via . . .'. Florence, Archivio di Stato, Mediceo del Principato, Filza 3622, fo. 196ʳ.

[65] Later Giovanni Battista del Cornetto or 'del Franciosino', who played the lira, took over this duty from Peri. Cavalieri advised the Duke to try Giovanni Battista in this capacity in the letter of 24 Nov. 1600 cited above, fo. 195ᵛ. See also C. Lozzi, 'La musica e specialmente il melodramma alla Corte Medicea', *Rivista musicale italiana*, 9 (1902), 314, where we learn from a report to the Grand Duchess attached to a letter of 6 Aug. 1603 that Giovannino's name was Giovanni Boccherini. Both Giovannino and Fabio were still listed among the court personnel in a roll of 1606 in Archivio di Stato, Guardaroba, Filza 279, no. 16, cited by R. Gandolfi in 'La cappella musicale della corte di Toscana', *Rivista musicale italiana*, 16 (1909), 509. The two castrati were still favourite interpreters in 1607, when the poet Francesco Cini recommended them to the Duke of Mantua for two parts in his *Teti*, which was to be set to music by Monteverdi and Peri for the wedding of Prince Francesco Gonzaga: Giovannino for the part of the Ninfa Nuntia and Fabio for the title-role of Tetide. That libretto was set aside, however, in favour of Rinuccini's *Arianna*. Cf. Cini's letter of 26 Oct. 1607, quoted in Solerti, *Gli albori del melodramma*, i. 83–4. Several of the Florentine singers were requested for the Mantua wedding, including Brandi and Fabio, but the Grand Duke refused to allow them leave because he was using all his musicians in three different comedies being prepared at court—letter from Grand Duke Ferdinand to Duke Vincenzo Gonzaga, 4 Dec. 1608, quoted in Solerti, *Albori*, i. 104.

[66] *Descrizione*, sig. A+1ᵛ.

may have been understudies in the first, were well known to Florentines. Pompeo di Giulio, Caccini's son, was at this time quite young but apparently old enough to sing a tenor part. Aldobrando Trabocchi da Pienza, the Pluto of the later performance, was highly esteemed. On 18 December 1599 Cavalieri warned Lorenzo Usimbardi, a secretary of the Grand Duke: 'If he [Trabocchi] should come to Rome—there being a vacant place [in the Papal Chapel]—he would be immediately welcomed, since to my taste there is no voice like his today in the chapel.'[67] In a letter of around 1603 to the Grand Duchess, Trabocchi was recommended as having 'such a beautiful bass voice that perhaps no equal of it can be found in Italy'.[68] The letter recommended that he be raised by 120 scudi a year so that he would leave the town of Pienza, where he was canon, and establish himself in Florence.

A number of the instrumentalists who played from behind the scenes ('dentro alla scena') were also identified by Peri. These were Jacopo Corsi, gravicembalo; Don Grazia Montalvo, chitarrone; Giovanbattista (Jacomelli) dal Violino, lira grande; and Giovanni Lapi, large lute. Of these the most noted professional musician was Giovanni Battista del Violino, who 'was so called because he played this instrument most excellently' and was celebrated also for having introduced the double harp to Rome, Giustiniani informs us.[69]

Some of the best talents in Italy, then, were lavished upon the production. Still, there was divided opinion about its success. Among both musicians and lay listeners, some praised it highly, but others found it dull and ineffectual. The most authoritative of the appreciative critics was Marco da Gagliano, who wrote of *Euridice*:

I shall not grow tired of lauding it; indeed there is no one who does not bestow infinite praise upon it, no lover of music who does not have constantly before him the songs of Orfeo. Let me say truthfully that no one can completely understand the gentleness and the force of his [Peri's] airs if he has not heard him sing them himself. He gives to them such grace and so impresses on the listener the affection of the words, that he is compelled to weep and rejoice, as the composer wills. How much the representation of this *favola* pleased would be superfluous to relate, since there is the testimony of so many princes and lords, the cream of the nobility of Italy, one might say, who convened at those pompous wedding festivities.[70]

---

[67] Florence, Archivio di Stato, Mediceo del Principato, Filza 3622, fo. 173ʳ.
[68] Lozzi, 'La musica', 314–15.
[69] 'Discorso sopra la musica', Solerti, *Le origini*, 124; trans. MacClintock, 'Giustiniani's Discorso', 222; ead., *Desiderio*.
[70] Preface, 'Ai Lettori', *Dafne*, 1608, in Solerti, *Le origini*, 81.

We have seen that the Venetian ambassador found the melodies of *Euridice* 'very sweet'. The Parmesan ambassador Conti was also appreciative, saying that 'it was a most beautiful thing, though simple in its machinery'.[71]

If these accounts give a picture of unqualified success, equally authoritative and emphatic are the voices of those who were dissatisfied with *Euridice*. Emilio de' Cavalieri's reactions are doubly interesting because he was probably the musical director.[72] In the first letter that Cavalieri wrote from Rome after leaving Florence he expresses regret that his advice had not been followed with regard to the music of *Cefalo*, which he found inadequate to the vast proportions of the theatre. Concerning *Euridice*, though he does not name it, he gives the impressions communicated to him by some of the guests: 'The music . . . they say, did not give satisfaction, the scenic constructions [*prospettive*] not having been completed and also for other reasons. I replied to this that the shortness of time was to blame.'[73] Cavalieri elaborated upon these comments, perhaps at the request of Marcello Accolti, the Grand Duke's Secretary, in a postscript that has been detached from the letter to which it belonged and therefore of uncertain date, but probably of November 1600. He reports that those present at the performances to whom he had spoken had said 'the things of moderate size [for example, *Euridice*] did not succeed, and the big production [that is, *Cefalo*] particularly did not. [They say] that the music was tedious, that it seemed like the chanting of the passion.' Giovanni Bardi, Maestro di Camera of Pope Clement VIII, said that 'they should not have gone into tragic texts and objectionable subjects'. Cavalieri, comparing the effect of the Florentine pastorals on listeners with that of his own *Rappresentatione di Anima et di Corpo*, boasts that his own music 'moved them to tears and laughter and pleased them greatly, unlike this music of Florence, which did not move them at all, unless to boredom and irritation'.[74]

Allowances must be made in these judgements for bias stemming from the complex of rivalries that characterized Florentine court music at this time.[75] Cavalieri had clashed with Caccini on numerous occasions, and it

[71] E. Costa, 'Le nozze di Enrico IV Re di Francia con Maria de' Medici', *Rassegna emiliana*, 1 (1888), 114.

[72] Until recently it was believed that Cavalieri was absent from the performance of 6 Oct. because of a letter in his hand, dated Rome, 7 Oct., in the Archives in Florence (see above, n. 38). Elsewhere I have shown that this date must be mistaken and should be amended to 7 Nov. or thereabouts: see Essay 14, n. 53.

[73] Above, Essay 14, p. 403.

[74] See above, p. 404.

[75] These are discussed with great insight by Nino Pirotta in 'Temperaments and Tendencies in the Florentine Camerata', *Musical Quarterly*, 40 (1954), 169–89.

was Caccini who now took over the direction of music for the Grand Duke. This might explain Cavalieri's failure to appreciate *Cefalo*. On the other hand, no animosity is known to have existed between Cavalieri and Peri, although there was a difference of aesthetic philosophy. Cavalieri's principal witness was Giovanni Bardi, a friend and protector of Caccini. Bardi, the host of the Camerata and once a musical pioneer and experimenter himself, had apparently little sympathy for Peri's dry style or Rinuccini's tragicomedy.[76] Besides, he would have been inclined to see Corsi as a rival, since he had displaced Bardi as the principal patron of the new music at court. And Peri was Corsi's protégé, as Caccini had been Bardi's. Of those who had frequented Bardi's Camerata, only Caccini remained active in music, and his eminence was threatened by Peri's success with *Dafne* and *Euridice*. So for Bardi there were conditions predisposing his unfavourable reaction to *Euridice*. However much these personal biases may have affected the judgements of Cavalieri and Bardi, the most important factor was probably that they both had grown old and were sceptical of Peri's novel dissonances and untuneful vocal lines, and of Rinuccini's simple and unspectacular dramatic conception.

In the preface to his score, Peri glosses over what must have been the keenest rivalry of all—between himself and Caccini. He says there:

And although as far back as that time [the time of the performance] I had composed the score as it is now published, nevertheless Giulio Caccini (*detto Romano*), whose supreme merit is known to the world, wrote the airs of Euridice and some of those of the Shepherd and Nymphs of the Chorus, and of the choruses, 'Al canto, al ballo', 'Sospirate', and 'Poiche gli eterni imperi', and this because they were to be sung by persons dependent upon him. These airs may be found in his score, composed and printed however after my own was performed before Her Most Christian Majesty.[77]

Evidently Caccini, with characteristic possessiveness and insecurity, had refused to allow his singers to perform Peri's music, and this despite the fact that it would have been only a fair exchange for having Peri as one of the leading performers in his own *Cefalo*, which was moreover the most prominent production of the wedding. The result was that Peri, singing his own lines for Orfeo, had to suffer the affront of being answered by Caccini's sister-in-law singing the blander music composed for Euridice by Giulio Romano. The ratio of Peri to Caccini in the production of 6 October was

---

[76] I am using the term Camerata in the only way that is historically accurate—as referring to the group that met in Bardi's house in the 1570s and perhaps 1580s. The circle around Corsi should be regarded as a distinctly separate one. This view is amply defended in the article by Pirrotta, cited in n. 75, 169–76.

[77] Solerti, *Le origini*, 49.

about six to one, approximately 658 lines of Peri to 132 of Caccini. Euridice's part is a short one, only 26 lines. The choruses named by Peri total 74 lines and the portions of the Shepherd and Nymphs of the Chorus probably by Caccini are 17 lines each.

What effect did this forced marriage have on the performance? It deprived Euridice of the more expressive recitative that Peri wrote for her and was a violation, surely, of stylistic consistency. On the other hand, from the point of view of the listener it provided a welcome variety, for, compared stanza for stanza, the Caccini music that replaced Peri's was airier in its melody, more graceful in its use of embellished cadences and ornaments generally, and closer in spirit to the music the audience was already accustomed to hearing. It is doubtful if those who were present were aware of the pot-pourri or even of its composers' names. None of the ambassadors or guests who wrote home about the pastoral mentioned either of their names, though Peri's should have been known to them from the libretto's preface.

As is so often the case, the immediately recorded reactions to this historic performance came short of ascribing it any unique place in the music of its time. This is not surprising, since in its external features *Euridice* was not unlike a number of other musical pastorals composed entirely in music since 1595. The most important of these works were Cavalieri's *Il giuoco della cieca*, first performed in the Pitti Palace on 29 October 1595,[78] and Peri's *Dafne*, first produced in 1598 in Jacopo Corsi's house. Both were revived in January 1599. To a casual spectator *Euridice* must not have seemed exceptional, particularly because of the simple and modest staging. But the connoisseur would probably have remarked that in it Peri had matured his recitative style and in so doing had found a new idiom. Unfortunately, apart from the comments of Peri and Rinuccini themselves, we have no testimony to any immediate recognition of this. Only later in the writings of Marco da Gagliano (1608), Severo Bonini, and Pietro de' Bardi (1634) is there evidence of an understanding of Peri's unique contribution—dramatic recitative.[79] Perhaps the most significant commentary on Peri's *Euridice* was that of Claudio Monteverdi, who in his *Orfeo* seven years later adopted many essential features of Peri's recitative style.

---

[78] For a study of Cavalieri's early musical pastorals, see Warren Kirkendale, 'L'opera in musica prima del Peri: le pastorali perdute di Laura Guidiccioni ed Emilio de' Cavalieri', in *Firenze e la Toscana dei Medici nell'Europa del '500'*, ii: *Musica e spettacolo, scienze dell'uomo e della natura* (Florence: Leo S. Olschki, 1983), 365–95.

[79] The relevant passages by these three authors are cited in Solerti, *Le origini*, 81, 137, and 145. A brief account of Peri's contribution is to be found in Nino Pirrotta's article 'Peri' in *Enciclopedia dello spettacolo*, viii. 1–3. For an extended study, see Carter, *Jacopo Peri*, especially i. 157–204.

17

Peri and the Theory of Recitative

This essay was prepared as a chapter, 'Peri und die Theorie des Rezitativs', in the section 'Die Jahrzehnte um 1600 in Italien' of volume 7 of the series Geschichte der Musiktheorie, *Italienische Musiktheorie im 16. und 17. Jahrhundert: Antikenrezeption und Satzlehre*, by F. Alberto Gallo, Renate Groth, Claude V. Palisca, Frieder Rempp, edited by Frieder Zaminer under the sponsorship of the Staatliches Institut für Musikforschung, Preußischer Kulturbesitz, Berlin (Darmstadt: Wissenschaftliche Buchgesellschaft, 1989), 293–306. The original English version was published in *Studies in Music*, 15 (University of Western Australia, 1981), 51–61, and is reprinted here by kind permission of the Staatliches Institut. A related study is my article 'Rezitativ' for the *Handwörterbuch der musikalischen Terminologie* (11. Auslieferung, 1983–4), 1–16, which surveys the history of the term from the earliest usages until the nineteenth century.

I was pleased that Dr Zaminer was willing to consider the theory of recitative as falling within scope of the history of theory. No other general historical work on the subject has given recitative, particularly early recitative, much attention, since it does not fit into the usual categories of tonal systems, counterpoint, harmony, or form, which constitute the core of the discipline of music theory. Yet recitative is a genre of music that does have certain definable procedural standards. These have to do with the following: the method of adapting music to the syllables, accents, periodization, and rhythms of a poetic text; the metrical and rhythmic organization of the music in response to these aspects of the text as well as to its message; the relationship of the vocal line to the bass and its chordal realization, particularly with regard to consonance and dissonance and how these interact with the temporal characteristics; considerations of melodic construction, such as pitch content, range, steps and leaps, and tessitura; and, finally, how all these relate to the emotional, narrative, and cognitive content of a text. Although Peri does not consider these matters systematically, he touches on all of them. Christoph Bernhard, Johann David Heinichen, Johann Adolph Scheibe, and Friedrich W. Marpurg were later to incorporate recitative more systematically in an important way into their instructions on composition.[1] Peri deserves to be recognized not only as a composer and performer but as a pioneer in this line of theoretical thought.

---

[1] Bernhard, *Tractatus compositionis augmentatus* (MS, c.1660); Heinichen, *Der General-Bass in der Composition* (Dresden: Author, 1728); Scheibe, 'Abhandlung vom Recitativ', in *Critischer Musikus* (Leipzig: B. C. Breitkopf, 1745); Marpurg, 'Unterricht vom Recitativ', in *Kritische Briefe über die Tonkunst* (Berlin: F. Wilhelm Birnstiel, 12 June 1762).

MUSIC theory, it is said, follows practice, and that with some delay. We should not expect, then, to find in the years immediately surrounding 1600 an adequate theoretical exposition of the new idiom of recitative. Yet this is precisely what we do find, published simultaneously with the first full-length music drama. Indeed, in the preface to *Le musiche sopra l'Euridice* Jacopo Peri set down what I esteem the best theoretical description of early recitative ever written. Even granted that recitative was prematurely ripe for theoretical formulation because it was born largely of theoretical speculation, Peri's precocious realization of a theory of recitative was a significant achievement.

A careful study, point by point, of key passages from this preface will reveal the profound aptness of Peri's description of the new style.[2]

1. Ancient Tragedy Employed Continuous Music

Peri asserts that the ancients, in the opinion of many, sang entire tragedies on the stage:

Onde veduto, che si trattava di poesia Dramatica, a che però si doueua imitar col canto chi parla (e senza dubbio non si parlò mai cantando) stimai, che gli antichi Greci, e Romani (iquali secondo l'openione di molti cantauano su le Scene le Tragedie intere) vsassero vn'armonia, che auanzando quella del parlare ordinario, scendesse tanto dalla melodia del cantare, che pigliasse forma di cosa mezzana; . . .	Seeing that dramatic poetry was concerned, and that therefore one ought to imitate with song someone speaking (and without doubt people never spoke singing), I decided that the ancient Greeks and Romans (who according to the opinion of many sang entire tragedies on the stage) employed a melody that, elevated beyond ordinary speech, descended so much from the melody of song that it assumed an intermediate form . . .

Peri's source for the belief that the ancient tragedies were sung from beginning to end was the humanist and classical scholar Girolamo Mei,

[2] Jacopo Peri, *Le musiche sopra l'Euridice* (Florence: Giorgio Marescotti, 1600 [dedication dated 1601 modern style]); facs. edn., Bibliotheca musica Bononiensis, ed. Giuseppe Vecchi (Bologna: Forni, 1969), 'A Lettori'. All translations into English in this essay are mine. Concerning scholarly opinion on this question in the sixteenth century, see Barbara Russano Hanning, *Of Poetry and Music's Power: Humanism and the Creation of Opera* (Ann Arbor, Mich.: UMI Research Press, 1980), 15–19; and 'Apologia pro Ottavio Rinuccini', *Journal of the American Musicological Society*, 26 (1973), 247–52. See also C. V. Palisca, 'The "Camerata fiorentina": A Reappraisal', *Studi musicali*, 1 (1972), 220–1, repr. in *Opera I*, The Garland Library of the History of Western Music, xi. 45–79; and Egert Pholmann, 'Antikenverständnis, und Antikenmissverständnis in der Operntheorie der Florentiner Camerata', *Die Musikforschung*, 22 (1969), 5–13.

who had dealt with the music of the tragedy at some length in his treatise *De modis musicis antiquorum*, book iv. Mei sent a copy of it in 1573 to Piero Vettori, authorizing him to let a few members of his circle see it. The passage, not before published, that supports the contention that the entire tragedy was sung, is the following:[3]

Erat enim poematum genus, quod solis uersibus in sua imitatione quasi contentum esset; tametsi et illa quandoque cum sui poetae tum posteriores musicj quum ipsis modo aptassent ad lyram canendo recitare quodammodo instituerint quorum artifices a suo uersu epici praecipue dicebantur. Erant autem et quae contra omnibus istis propemodum gauderent, omniumque istorum ope, dum imitantur, munus suum quasi explerent. ut Tragoedia, comoedia uetus, satyri, Dithyrambus denique et eorum omnium imitamenta quos uno nomine, melicos ab ipso cantu posteriores uocitarunt.
Horum uero opera quae ista omnia in sua imitatione coniungerent, eo maxime discrimine distinguebantur, quod Dithyrambici semper et melicj, quum choros instituerent, omnibusque (ut dicitur) numeris absolutum melos conficerent, uersu, numero, et harmonia perpetuo uterentur.
Tragoedi uero et ueteres comoedi (nouorum enim non eadem fuit ratio) et satyri in ea sola suj operis parte, quae choro, qui multitudinem ipsam

There was a genre of poetry that was content, as it were, in its imitation with verses alone. Even this too sometimes either by the poet himself or later musicians was applied to a melody to recite singing to the lyre. Those who practised this art were in turn mainly called epic [poets]. There were others, however, who, on the contrary, well-nigh rejoiced in all these means, and fulfilled their duty, as it were, with the help of them all, as the tragedy, the old comedy, the satyr-play, and, finally, the dithyramb and imitations of all those whom later people referred to because of the singing, by one name: melic [poets]. Their works, then, which joined all of these resources in their imitation, were distinguished above all by the fact that the dithyrambic and melic poets, when they instructed choruses and made their melody complete in every respect (as the saying goes) always used verse, rhythm, and melody [*harmonia*] throughout. In the tragedy, however, and in the old comedy (the new comedy was not the same in nature) and the satyr-play [this perfect melos was used] only in that part of the work that was

---

[3] Girolamo Mei, *De modis musicis antiquorum*, Rome, Biblioteca Apostolica Vaticana, MS Vat. lat. 5323, bk. iv, pp. 17–18. This fourth book has recently been twice edited: in Donatella Restani, *L'Itinerario di Girolamo Mei: dalla 'Poetica' alla musica* (Florence: Leo S. Olschki, 1990), where this passage is at 122–3; and Girolamo Mei, *De modis*, ed. Tsugami Eisuke (Tokyo: Keiso Shobo, 1991), 112–13.

repraesentabat, tribuebatur,	assigned to the chorus that
idque quum chorus	represented the crowd and when
ipse non staret;	the chorus was not stationary.
in reliquis uero ipso tantum	In the other parts, only
uersu et harmonia: quemadmodum et	verse and melody were used, as we
in ijs euenisse suspicarj	may suspect happened in the case of
possumus, qui elegos at Tibiam	those who sang elegies to the aulos,
canerent, quum chorum non	since they had no chorus.
haberent.	

The substance if not the form of these beliefs was undoubtedly communicated by Mei to Galilei in one or more of his letters. Some notes, deriving from Mei, that Galilei used in preparing his *Dialogo della musica antica et della moderna* include the following statements:[4]

La tragedia la comedia la	The tragedy, the comedy, the
satira i Ditirambi ricevevano	satyr-play, the dithyrambs received—
oltre il verso canto numero e	besides verse—melody, rhythm, and
gesto. i ditirambi erano	action. Dithyrambs were recited by
recitati dal coro con verso	the chorus with perpetual verse,
numero et armonia perpetua.	rhythm, and melody.
La tragedia et la comedia et	The tragedy and the comedy and
la satira non sempre havevano	the satire did not always have the
il ritmo del saltare, ma la	rhythm of the dance, but melody
armonia sempre.	always.
Le tragedie eran cantate	Tragedies were sung to the
à la tibia ma non col coro.	aulos, but not the chorus.
La tibia si usava ne le	The aulos was used in tragedies
tragedie et ne le comedie.	and comedies.

The ancient model of a stage action in which all the words were sung, though not all in the rhythm of dance or regular rhythm, was fundamental to the development of a theory of recitative. The parts of the actors in ancient drama demanded a special style, one that united verse and melody but was free of the regular rhythm that characterized the songs assigned to the standing chorus. Similarly, the chants of the chorus that represented a crowd were also in free rhythm. On the other hand, whereas the actors in ancient times were accompanied by the aulos, the chorus was not. These

---

[4] C. V. Palisca, *Girolamo Mei: Letters to Vincenzo Galilei and Giovanni Bardi* (Rome: American Institute of Musicology; 2nd corr. edn., with addenda, Neuhausen-Stuttgart: Hänssler, 1977), 142–7. These notes, found in the only extant copy of Mei's letters to Galilei in Biblioteca Apostolica Vaticana, MS Regina lat. 2021, are, like the letters, in the hand of Giorgio Bartoli. Donatella Restani has identified them as a summary, though incomplete, of bk. iv of *De modis* and has edited them in *L'Itinerario di G. Mei*, 166–7. That Galilei had recourse to them is evident from his incorporation of the information into his *Dialogo della musica antica et della moderna* (Florence: Giorgio Marescotti, 1581); facs. edn. by Fabio Fano (Rome: Reale Accademia d'Italia, 1934), 63, 100, 145.

facts, researched and communicated by Mei and passed on to the circle of Florentine musicians around Galilei and Bardi, could not help but influence the solution that Peri eventually found for setting musically the speeches of dramatic characters.

2. Melody Intermediate between Song and Speech

E per cio tralasciata qualunque altra maniera di canto vdita fin quì, mi diedi tutto a ricercare l'imitazione, che si debbe a questi Poemi; e considerai, che quella sorte di voce, che dagli Antichi al cantare fu assegnata, la quale essi chiamauano Diastematica (quasi trattenuta, e sospesa) potesse in parte affretarsi, e prender temperato corso tra i mouimenti del canto sospesi, e lenti, e quegli della fauella spediti, e veloci, & accomodarsi al proposito mio (come l'accomodauano anch'essi, leggendo le Poesie, & i versi Eroici) auuicinandosi all'altra del ragionare, la quale continuata appellauano; Il che i nostri moderni (benchè forse ad altro fine) hanno ancor fatto nelle musiche loro.

For this reason, putting aside every other manner of singing heard up to now, I dedicated myself wholly to searching out the imitation that is owed to these poems. And I reflected that the sort of voice that was assigned by the ancients to song and which they called diastematic (as if to say sustained) could at times be hurried and assume a moderate course somewhere between the slow, sustained movements of song and the rapid movements of speech and thus suit my purpose just as the ancients adapted it too in reading their heroic poems and verses), approaching that other [voice] of speech, which they called continuous and which our moderns (though perhaps for other purposes) have also used in their music.

The notion of vocal style that is neither song nor speech had a venerable history before Peri elevated it to a principle of recitative. The concept is dependent on the classification of vocal utterances into *diastematic*, in which the voice moves from one discrete pitch to another by interval, and *continuous*, that is, gliding through various pitches without sustaining any precise pitches or paying attention to the intervals separating them. The diastematic is the voice of song; the continuous, the voice of speech. The distinction was first made by Aristoxenus,[5] but it was known to readers of Boethius,[6] who had cited the two Greek terms συνεχής, meaning con-

---

[5] Aristoxenus, *Harmonicorum*, i. 8–9.
[6] Boethius, *De institutione musica*, i. 12.

tinuous, and διαστηματική, meaning intervallic, without, however, giving his source. The source of this chapter has been identified as Nicomachus, who in turn, attributed the distinction to the Pythagoreans.[7] The terminology probably reached Peri through Galilei and Mei.[8]

Boethius spoke also of a third type of voice, which, he said, was recognized by Albinus: 'we read a heroic poem neither in a continuous flow as in prose nor in the sustained and more sluggish manner of voice as in song'.[9]

Peri may not have known this citation directly, since much of the contents of the five books on music by Boethius had been absorbed into common knowledge. But the idea of an intermediate kind of vocal utterance that was used by the ancients to read 'heroic poems and verses' offered a model for theatrical speech-song. Peri was led by this model to navigate a course between the diastematic voice of song and the continuous one of speech.

Before he could apply this model to an Italian poem, Peri had to formulate a theory of intonation-pattern in Italian speech.

Conobbi parimente nel nostro parlare alcune voci, intonarsi in guisa, che vi si puo fondare armonia, e nel corso della fauella passarsi per altre molte, che non s'intuonano, finchè si ritorni ad altra capace di mouimento di nuoua consonanza.	I recognized likewise that in our speech certain sounds are intoned in such a way that a harmony can be built upon them, and in the course of speaking we pass through many that are not so intoned, until we reach another that permits a movement to a new consonance.

An Italian speaker, Peri observed, sustained the pitch of certain vowels in a sentence, while he rushed through many other syllables without pausing upon any single vowel or pitch. Italian speech, Peri implied, did not exclusively use the 'continuous' voice. The proportion between sustained and gliding syllables varied with a speaker's state of mind and affection as did also the speed of utterance.

---

[7] Ubaldo Pizzani, 'Studi sulle fonti del *De institutione Musica* di Boezio', *Sacris erudiri, Jaarboek voor Godsdienstwetenschappen*, 16 (1965), 5–164, esp. 48–50, where the parallel passages of Nicomachus, *Manuale harmonicum* 2 and Boethius, *De inst. mus.* i. 12 are compared.

[8] Mei to Galilei, 8 May 1572, in Palisca, *G. Mei*, 116.

[9] Boethius, *De inst. mus.* i. 12, ed. G. Friedlein (Leipzig: G. Teubner, 1867), 199: 'His, et Albinus autumat, additur tertia differentia, quae medias voces possit includere, cum scilicet heroum poema legimus neque continuo cursu, ut prosam, neque suspenso segnioriorique modo vocis, ut canticum.' Pizzani, in 'Studi sulle fonti', 50, identifies Albinus' source as Aristides Quintilianus, *De musica*, i. 4.

3. Liberation of the Voice from the Bass

We come now to the operative part of Peri's description:

& hauuto riguardo a que' modi,
& a quegli accenti, che nel
dolerci, nel rallegrarci, & in
somiglianti cose ci seruono, feci
muouere il Basso al tempo di
quegli, hor piu, hor meno, secondo
gli affetti, e lo tenni fermo tra
le false, e tra le buone
proporzioni, finchè scorrendo per
varie note la voce di chi ragiona,
arriuasse a quello, che nel
parlare ordinario intonandosi,
apre la via a nuouo concento; E
questo non solo, perchè il corso
del ragionare non ferisse
l'orecchio (quasi intoppando negli
incontri delle ripercosse corde,
dalle consonanze piu spesse), o
non paresse in vn certo modo
ballare al moto del Basso e
principalmente nelle cose, ò
meste, ò graui, richiedendo per
natura l'altre piu liete, piu
spessi mouimenti: Ma ancora,
perchè l'vso delle false, ò
scemasse, o ricoprisse quel
vantaggio, che ci s'aggiugne
dalla necessità dell'intonare
ogni nota, di che per cio fare
poteuan forse hauer manco bisogno
l'antiche Musiche. E però, (sì come
io non ardirei affermare questo
essere il canto nelle Greche, e
nelle Romane fauole vsato), così
ho creduto esser quello, che solo
possa donarcisi dalla nostra
Musica, per accomodarsi alla
nostra fauella.

Keeping in mind those manners
and accents that serve us in our
grief and joy and
similar states, I made the bass
move in time with these,
faster or slower according to the
affections. I held it fixed through
both dissonances and consonances
until the voice of the speaker,
having run through various notes,
arrived at a syllable that, being
intoned in ordinary speech, opened
the way to a new harmony. I did
this not only so that the flow of
the speech would not offend the ear
(almost stumbling upon the repeated
notes of more frequent consonant
chords), but also so that the voice
would not seem to dance to the
movement of the bass,
particularly in sad or severe
subjects, granted that other more
joyful subjects would require more
frequent movements. Moreover, the
use of dissonances
lessened or masked the
advantage gained from the
necessity of intoning every note,
which perhaps for this
purpose was less needed in ancient
music. Thus (though I would not
venture to assert that this was the
singing style used by the Greeks
and Romans in their plays), I
believed it was the only style
that our music could yield that
would be suited to
our speech.

The dynamic qualities of speech as analysed by Peri suggested to him the relationship that the voice should maintain with the notes of the bass and the harmonies built upon them. The vowels that are intoned in speech should meet the bass in a consonance, while those syllables that are passed over quickly between these sustained vowels would not be reflected in movements of the bass, which would hold firm until the next sustained syllable is intoned. The frequency of meetings in consonance of the voice and bass, moreover, should vary with the affection of the text. In moments of joy, a speaker intones or sustains syllables frequently, and this should lead the composer to move his bass relatively quickly so that it meets the frequent sustained syllables of the voice. Speaking excitedly or while gripped with fear or sorrow, the voice intones fewer syllables; so a single bass note should be held under numerous syllables before a new bass note meets the voice in a consonance. The syllables passed over quickly may be either consonances or dissonances, Peri reasoned; the ear hardly notices whether they are the one or the other.

Peri recognized three advantages in this method over normal singing. First, by sustaining the bass note under the flowing 'continuous' vocal part, he skirted the constant dissonant clashes that would occur if the bass repeated the same pitch in time with the syllables of the singer. Over the sustained bass the free movement of the voice, even when it hit some dissonances, did not offend the ear. Secondly, the syllables of the voice did not seem to dance to the movement of the bass as it did in the older recitational style, in which the bass moved in time to the syllables of the voice (as in the example to be demonstrated presently). Thirdly, by mixing dissonances with consonances, the composer diverted the listener's attention from the constant craving for sweet concordance of voice with bass, freeing the listener's taste to savour the continuous flow of the new style, or so Peri seemed to be saying.

This description of the dynamics of the new style of recitative is nearly as remarkable as the achievement of the new intermediate mode of speech-song. It documents Peri's dependence on ancient models and on theories concerning ancient Greek practice. At the same time it gives evidence of his analysis of his immediate situation, the context of Italian language and poetry, and the expectations of the contemporary listener as well as musician.

A few examples will show the operation of Peri's principles.

In Dafne's speech in *Euridice* Peri displayed the power of his new recitative, offering a striking example of the dynamics of the new style (see Ex. 17.1). The vertical boxes enclose the notes of the vocal part and harmony that set the syllables normally intoned in speaking these lines. The pitches of the voice meet the bass and harmony in consonances. The passages boxed horizontally are those which the voice pronounces rapidly and in singing imitates the 'continuous' voice of speech, passing through both consonances and dissonances (marked by asterisks). The intoned syl-

Ex. 17.1. Peri, *Le musiche sopra l'Euridice* (Florence, 1601), p. 15

lables are not only consonant with the harmony but are notes of longer duration. Most often they fall on a penultimate and/or final syllable of a line, but they may also fall on a caesura of a line. However, there is not a cadence at the end of each line (as some have said that Peri was wont to make). Indeed there is not a cadence in this whole example. The dissonances are not of a kind normally admitted in polyphonic writing, nor do they observe the structures of counterpoint but are of a different nature, although they can be interpreted in contrapuntal terms, as Christoph Bernhard showed in his treatise of around 1660.[10] For example, the second C in bar 1 is struck on the 'levare' or up-beat of the measure, where a dissonance is not permitted, and is anticipated in the previous beat. The A in this bar is also a dissonance, anticipating the next consonance. The counterpoint rules recognized neither the dissonance on the 'levare' unless by syncopation (suspension), nor the anticipation. In bar 2 the rapid notes are all consonances, but in bar 3 the Gs again break away from the norm. The first G, approached by leap, is not countenanced at all in counterpoint (Bernhard called it *quaesitio notae*). The two Gs at the end of the bar depart even from the anticipation pattern, for the syllable *pra* of *prato* is accented and would normally fall on a consonance. The succession in bar 4, A−B♭−A, all dissonant, includes an unprepared seventh. The Bs in bar 5 escape altogether from the reigning harmony. It is evident that Peri has found an idiom that, defying the contrapuntal rules, answers perfectly to his requirement that it imitate speech by liberating the voice from a dancing bass.

Peri's rhythmic precepts are also illustrated here. When Dafne speaks of the beautiful Euridice gracefully moving across the meadow, the harmony changes infrequently and the voice moves calmly, mainly in eighth-notes or longer of the transcription (semiminims in the original). As soon as Dafne begins to speak of the cruel snake that bit Euridice, the pace quickens, the bass moves twice or more per bar and many syllables carry only a sixteenth-note. So, as Peri set forth in his preface, the bass moves faster or slower according to the affections.

The novelty of this technique is set into relief by the more conventional recitational style of the Prologue to *Euridice*. For this poem of seven strophes Peri adopted the technique of the standard air for singing poetry—the *aria da cantar versi*. The same melodic formula is used to sing all seven stanzas. Each line ends in a cadence. All the notes of the melody meet the bass in consonance except for the 'accenti' before the cadence in bars 5 and 7, and the portamento of bar 10, vocal improvisatory ornaments common in sixteenth-century solo singing (see Ex. 17.2). The other dissonances that occur are in the accompaniment, and they follow the rules of the suspension (i.e. bars 3, 9, and 13).

Giovanni Battista Doni was justified in distinguishing this type of recitational style from the recitative proper. In differentiating the styles of

---

[10] Christoph Bernhard, *Tractatus compositionis augmentatus*, chs. 14 ff., ed. in Joseph Müller-Blattau, *Die Kompositionslehre Heinrich Schützens in der Fassung seines Schülers Christoph Bernhard* (2nd edn.; Kassel: Bärenreiter, 1963), 61 ff. For an English translation, see Walter Hilse, 'The Treatises of Christoph Bernhard', *Music Forum*, 3 (1973), 1−106.

Ex. 17.2. Peri, *Le musiche sopra l'Euridice*, p. 2

La Tragedia:

monody (*stile Monodico*) used on the stage, he identified the Prologue of *Euridice* as belonging to the 'special recitative' style, a manner intermediate between the 'narrative', to which he assigned Dafne's speech, and the 'expressive', to which he assigned Monteverdi's lament of Ariana. He noted the many cadences used in this 'special recitative' type of singing, making it somewhat tedious in a drama but effective in recitations of heroic and other poems composed of numerous stanzas, such as *ottave rime*.[11] He characterized the 'narrative' style, on the other hand, as 'remaining a great deal on the same notes (the Greeks call this *moniotonè*) which were almost always those of the fundamental tone (mode), with a quick pace, similar to that of speech'.[12]

Peri's description of his own recitative style, evocative as it is, is not self-sufficient as a theory of recitative, and one must seek elsewhere to complement it. Caccini's letter of dedication to Giovanni Bardi of his *Euridice*, published several months before Peri's, reflects some of the same principles.[13] There, he explained, in the 'basso continuato' which he wrote under the parts that are recited, he

hauendo legato alcune volte le corde del basso, affine che nel trapassare delle molte dissonanze, ch'entro vi sono, non si ripercuota la corda, e l'vdito ne venga offeso; Nella qual maniera di canto, ho io vsata vna certa sprezzatura, che io ho stimato, che habbia del nobile, parendomi con essa di essermi appressato quel piu alla natural fauella . . .	tied some of the bass notes, so that in passing through the many dissonnances among the notes [of the voice part], the [bass] note is not restruck in such a way that the ear is offended. In this manner of song, I used a certain carelessness that I valued as having a noble quality, for it seemed to me that with it I approached natural speech that much more . . .

Caccini used the term *sprezzatura* again in a similar context in the preface to the reader of his *Le nuove musiche* (1601/2). Later in the same preface, after introducing numerous fragmentary musical examples, a strophe of a Romanesca, and a complete madrigal, he clarified further his concept of *sprezzatura*:[14]

avvenga che nobile maniera sia cosi appellata da me quella che va usata senza sottoporsi a misura ordinata,	for I called noble that manner of not submitting oneself to a regular measure, as when the value of

---

[11] Giovanni Battista Doni, *Annotazioni sopra il Compendio de' generi e modi della musica* (Rome: Andrea Fei, 1640), 61, note to the *Compendio del trattato de' generi e de' modi* (Rome: Andrea Fei, 1635), 101.

[12] Ibid. 60: 'trattenersi assai su le stesse corde (i Greci ciò dicono μονιοτονή) e quasi sempre fu quelle del Tuono fondamentale; e con tempi veloci, e simili a quelli della favella'. For an extended discussion of Doni's theories of recitative see Margaret Rosso Grossman, 'G. B. Doni and Theatrical Music', Ph.D. diss. (University of Illinois, 1977), 168–85.

[13] Giulio Caccini, *L'Euridice composta in musica in stile rappresentativo* (Florence: Giorgio Marescotti, 1600), dedication, signed 20 Dec. 1600, sig. A2ʳ.

[14] Giulio Caccini, *Le nuove musiche* (Florence: I Marescotti, 1602 [1 Feb. 1601, Florentine style]), 'Ai lettori', ed. Angelo Solerti, in *Le origini del melodramma* (Torino: Bocca, 1903), 57. See the edn. of *Le nuove musiche* by H. Wiley Hitchcock (Madison, Wis.: A–R Editions, 1970), 44–5.

Ex. 17.3. Caccini, *Le nuove musiche* (Florence, 1602), Preface

senza misura, quasi favellando in armonia con la sudetta sprezzatura

Au — re au - re di - vi - ne, Ch'er - ra - te pe - re - gri - ne in

que - sta par - t'e in quel - la.

11   ♯10   14

| facendo molte volte il valor delle note la metà meno secondo i concetti delle parole, onde ne nasce quel canto poi in sprezzatura, che si è detto. | notes is often cut in half in keeping with the meaning of the text, whence arises the kind of song *in sprezzatura*, as I called it, {that takes certain liberties}. |

The madrigal contains a passage of three measures over which Caccini wrote the instruction 'senza misura, quasi favellando in armonia con suddetta sprezzatura' (without measure, almost speaking in melody with the said licence) (see Ex. 17.3).

From the notation, the bass line appears to move in regular rhythm; only Caccini's verbal instruction would lead a singer to perform it otherwise. Peri's recitative, on the other hand, is inherently 'without measure', that is free of metronomic recurrence of beat and metre. For example, in Dafne's speech, the line 'Che celato giacea tra fiori, e l'erba' truly fails to submit to regular measure in that the accented syllable *l'er* of *l'erba* falls on the fourth beat of bar 7. The infrequency of chordal accompaniment, as determined by the bass, throughout permits disregard of regular rhythm, in effect a real *sprezzatura*.

When in the preface to *Nuove musiche e nuova maniera di scriverle* (1614) Caccini finally defined the term *sprezzatura*, he departed even more from the idea of speech-song.[15]

| La sprezzature è quella leggiadria la quale si dà al canto co'l trascorso di piu crome | *Sprezzatura* is that gracefulness conferred upon singing by passing through a number of eighth-notes |

[15] Florence: Zanobi Pignoni e Compagni, 1614, ed. in Solerti, *Le origini*, 75.

e semicrome sopra diverse	and sixteenths over various notes
corde, co'l quale,	[of the bass], through which, when
fatto a tempo, togliendosi al	done in time, removing from the
canto una certa terminata angustia	singing a certain bare poverty and
e secchezza, si rende piacevole,	dryness, it is rendered pleasing,
licenzioso e arioso . . .	unhindered, and airy . . .

Caccini's understanding of the term had shifted in 1614 to embrace the florid singing of his airs and madrigals, just as he had abandoned the free speech-like recitative of his *Euridice*, a borrowed style that never really suited him.

More relevant than Caccini's *sprezzatura* to the theory of recitative are some standards for the composition of monody set forth by Vincenzo Galilei, who, though deceased by the time of *Euridice*, had experimented with monody in the early 1580s. In an essay that he planned as a sequel to his counterpoint treatise and in which he intended to deal mainly with the origins and use of the enharmonic and chromatic genera, and in a supplement to this essay, Galilei laid down some principles that ought to govern the composition of vocal music, which in effect would all be monodic music.[16] The essay and supplement date from the last year of his life, 1590–1.

1. In natural speaking, and, therefore, in singing that expresses the ideas of a text, only a narrow range of the voice needs to be used. A wide range is artificial and more suited to instruments than voices. The most beautiful and popular melodies rarely span a range of more than six notes.

2. This narrow range should be in a register of the voice suited to the subject of the text: high for an excited or querulous speech; intermediate for a tranquil speech; and low for a lament or a speech characterized by somnolence.

3. Slow metres are apt for the last, moderate rapidity for the tranquil, and rapid for the excited.

4. Only those rules of counterpoint ought to be applied that serve to provide an accompaniment to the voice, not those that would produce independent parts to compete with it.

Peri, although he made no point of some of these precepts in his preface, seems to have followed them in his music. The passage of Dafne's speech from 'Ma la bella Euridice' up to 'Punsele il piè' (Ex. 17.1) only once exceeds the range of the fifth G–D, in bar 6, where F♯ breaks the lower

[16] *Discorso intorno all'uso dell'enharmonio*, Florence, Biblioteca Nazionale Centrale, MSS Galilei, 3, fos. 3ʳ–34ᵛ, and *Dubbi intorno a quanto io ho detto dell'enharmonio con la solutione di essi*, fos. 62ʳ–68ʳ, especially fo. 67ʳ⁻ᵛ. See my English translation of relevant passages above, Essay 12, pp. 351–2.

barrier. Later, in the last five bars of the same speech, where Dafne laments the loss of Euridice, the range occupies the sixth D—B, a third lower than the previous ambitus. Thus, in accord with Galilei's theory, the lamenting voice occupies a lower register of the voice than the excited passage that preceded it. We have already observed that the bass notes shift more frequently in the excited passage. Peri, as Galilei advised, avoided according any individuality to the bass of the recitative, so that it would serve simply as a foundation.

Although it may have seemed presumptuous to seek a theory of recitative in the literature that surrounded the first continuously musical pastoral, such a theory was indeed expressed in those early years of the style, and that with urgency. It lacked the didactic character of contrapuntal theory, its prescriptions and prohibitions. It invited support and understanding of the new style by patrons and public, not emulation by other composers. The prefaces and dedications were manifestos rather than treatises; fortunately, they contained more than empty rhetoric, for they captured in the heat of creation the essence of the new *recitar cantando*.

Even from the short-range perspective of eight years Marco da Gagliano could recognize the uniqueness of Peri's invention:[17]

Allora ritrovò il sig. Jacopo Peri quella artificiosa maniera di recitare cantando, che tutta Italia ammira. Io non m'affaticherò in lodarla, per ciò che non è persona che non le dia lodi infinite, e niuno amator di musica è che non abbia sempre d'avanti i canti d'Orfeo: dirò bene, che non può interamente comprendere la gentillezza e la forza delle sue arie chi non l'ha udite cantare da lui medesimo; però che egli dà loro una si fatta grazia e di maniera imprime in altrui l'affetto di quelle parole, che è forza e piangere e rallegrarsi secondo che egli vuole.	Then Sig. Jacopo Peri discovered that artful manner of *recitare cantando*, which all Italy admires. I shall not exhaust myself in praising it, for there is not a person who does not heap infinite praises on it. There is no lover of music who does not have always before him the songs of Orfeo. To speak truthfully, whoever has not heard him [Peri] sing them himself will never fully experience the gentleness and force of his airs. For he gives them such grace and impresses in others the affection of the words in such a manner that he forces everyone to weep and rejoice according to his will.

[17] Marco da Gagliano, *La Dafne* (Florence: Christofano Marescotti, 1608), 'Ai lettori', ed. in Solerti, *Le origini*, 81.

18

G. B. Doni, Musicological Activist, and his Lyra Barberina

This essay was first published in *Modern Musical Scholarship*, edited by Edward Olleson (Stocksfield, Boston, Henley, and London: Oriel Press, 1980), 180–205. This volume contained the papers presented in the fall of 1977 at the Oxford International Symposium at Christ Church, organized and chaired by Denis Arnold, then Heather Professor of Music. The theme of the symposium was 'Modern Musicology and the Historical Tradition of Musical Scholarship'.

The impetus for this paper was the discovery of the illustrations that Doni planned to publish with his treatise, *Lyra Barberina*, which were lost for more than three hundred years. As in many such discoveries, good fortune played a major part. I happened to be in Paris for the academic year 1972–3, on leave from Yale University as Senior Fellow of the National Endowment for the Humanities, and while there was fulfilling one of my assignments for the *New Grove Dictionary of Music and Musicians*: the article 'Giovanni Battista Doni'. I conscientiously inspected whatever Doni manuscripts the Bibliothèque nationale possessed, and when I saw there the copy of the *Lyra Barberina* that Doni had destined for a Parisian printer I realized that the illustrations were altogether different from those published with the treatise in the two-volume collection of Doni's works edited in the eighteenth century. The editors of that collection had searched in vain for the copious iconographical documentation that Doni had assembled and referred to, never suspecting that it was in Paris. The Paris manuscript persuaded me, which the 1763 edition did not, that Doni aimed to produce a carefully documented history of Greek stringed instruments.

My present essay was preparatory to the publication of a corrrected edition, with commentary, of Doni's *Lyra Barberina*. Arnaldo Forni of Bologna had announced plans to reprint the two-volume collection of Doni's writings, originally published in 1763 by Giovanni Battista Passeri under the titles *Lyra Barberina* for volume i, and *De' trattati di musica di Gio. Batista Doni, Tomo secondo* for volume ii. I proposed through Professor Giuseppe Vecchi of the University of Bologna to supplement that reprint with my corrections, the original iconography, and a commentary for the essay *Lyra Barberina*. However I was not able to satisfy the schedule set by Forni—the facsimile was issued in 1974—and Professor Vecchi kindly offered to publish my work on Doni's essay, with a facsimile of only that part of the 1763 edition, as a separate volume in his series Antiquae Musicae Italicae Studiosi. This

467

publication was accomplished in 1981 (the date on the title-page) under the title *G. B. Doni's* Lyra Barberina, *Commentary and Iconographical Study, Facsimile Edition with Critical Notes* in the series Miscellanee Saggi Convegni as Number 18. It was issued simultaneously as Fascicle 2 of the periodical edited by Vecchi, *Quadrivium*, 22 (1981). The book consists of a commentary (1–61), 32 unnumbered pages of plates, facsimile of the 1763 edition (65–144, with five folding plates from that edition), notes concerning illustrations missing or incorrectly placed in the Gori–Passeri edition (145–50), correction of and collation of the 1763 edition with the Paris manuscript (151–80), and material in the Paris manuscript not published in 1763 (181–94), including Doni's 'Onomasticon'—'Interpretatio vocum musicarum graecarum et latinarum obscuriorum'.

For reasons that are not altogether clear, but having to do with the death and the settlement of the estate of Arnaldo Forni, the printed copies of the book and periodical number remained in storage, and no copy of either the separate book or the volume of *Quadrivium* was made available either to me or the public before 1987. Even since then, either version has been difficult to procure, and few copies exist in public libraries besides those I donated from a small stock that I received in 1989.[1] Because this larger work will probably remain scarce, I decided to include my paper of 1977 in the present collection. Eventually I plan to prepare a proper edition with notes and commentary of Doni's important study.

In my article I make the statement that Doni's essay was 'the most ambitious history of the Greek lyre ever written'. This is no longer true. A truly definitive such history has recently been published by Martha Maas and Jane McIntosh Snyder (New Haven, Conn.: Yale University Press, 1989). However, it complements rather than altogether replaces Doni's history. The modern authors focused their study on instruments known through iconographical and literary sources from the earliest periods up to around 324 BC, the majority of the visual evidence being from pottery. Doni, on the other hand, did not have access to ancient pottery, almost all of it excavated since his time, and had to rely on coins, sculpture, and paintings, most of them dating from Roman times. He was rarely able to assign any dates, though he knew the approximate age of some of the Roman coins.

The exemplar that most fascinated Doni was the cithara represented in the Sarcophagus of the Muses (see below, Pl. 18.5*a*), which served Raphael as a model for the cithara held by Erato in the fresco of Parnassus in the Stanza della Segnatura in the Vatican. The sarcophagus is a late example of the Sidamara type, originating probably from Asia Minor and dated second to third quarter of the third century.[2] Two citharae of this type may be seen being played in sculptures in the Vatican Museum, Sala delle Muse (nos. 511 and 516).[3] None of the instruments discussed

[1] As of Dec. 1990 the distributor of the series Antiquae Musicae Italicae Studiosi is 'Il Fabbro Armonioso', Via Bersaglieri 5 E, I-40125 Bologna, Italy.

[2] See Charles Rufus Morey, *The Sarcophagus of Claudia Antonia Sabina and the Asiatic Sarcophagi* in Sardis, 5, pt. 1 (n.p.: American Society for the Excavation of Sardis, 1924), 49–50 and pls. 87–9.

[3] No. 516, a statue of Apollo playing this instrument, from the Villa of Crassus in Tivoli, is shown in Günter Fleischhauer, *Musikgeschichte in Bildern: Etrurien und Rom* (Leipzig: Deutscher Verlag für Musik, 1964), 115, pl. 63. Photographs and description of the cithara discussed by Doni are in Emanuel Winternitz, 'Musical Archaeology of the Renaissance in Raphael's *Parnassus*', in *Musical*

or pictured in Maas—Snyder is of this type. However, for most of the other instruments described and illustrated by Doni, comparable types may be found in Maas—Snyder.

The following essay serves to introduce Doni's remarkable pioneering effort in musical iconography.

IT is fitting in a symposium on the traditions and present state of musical scholarship to ask the question: why has musicology in the past so rarely been a field of pure research, unlike other fields of the humanities? Why has it tended, rather, to be directed—some might say corrupted—by practical goals? In Britain, in particular, the study of early music has often been the servant of the performer and composer. 'Modal' counterpoint was for a long time studied as a tool for the composer, organist, and choir director rather than as a means to knowing how music was composed in the past. Editions of early music, such as those of Edmund Fellowes, were published to serve as vehicles for choirs and to permit the music to be heard as living art, not as documents of an otherwise distantly dim culture.

This tendency has been characteristic of musicology from its very first practitioners. I shall cite two scholars whom I have come to know intimately over the years. The first is Girolamo Mei. As a member of a scholarly team around Piero Vettori in Florence in the 1540s he worked towards the establishment and reconstruction of the texts of several of the Greek tragedies. The object was not to perform them, though some were eventually translated or adapted and performed, but to reclaim them from the ravages and accretions of the centuries. Similarly, in assisting Vettori to understand the musical references in Aristotle's *Poetics* towards the preparation of Vettori's *Commentarii in primum librum Aristotelis de arte poetarum,*[4] Mei was engaged in a disinterested search for an understanding of the Greek past. This was also his object in preparing the four books on the history of the Greek tonal system, *De modis musicis antiquorum.*[5] But these were barely finished in 1573, when Mei, who had never studied music and could not play or sing, became a musical reformer, urging his musical

---

Instruments and their Symbolism in Western Art (New Haven, Conn.: Yale University Press, 1979), 185 ff. and pls. 82*a*, 86, 87, and 88; pl. 77*b*, from a Roman wall-painting, not otherwise identified, shows a seven-string cithara of this type.

[4] Florence: Successors of Bernardo Giunti, 1573.

[5] Rome, Vatican Library, MS Vat. lat. 5323. For other copies see C. V. Palisca, *Girolamo Mei: Letters on Ancient and Modern Music to Vincenzo Galilei and Giovanni Bardi* (Rome: American Institute of Musicology, 1960; 2nd edn., Neuhausen-Stuttgart: Hänssler, 1977). The fourth book is edited in Donatella Restani, *L'Itinerario di Girolamo Mei: dalla 'Poetica' alla musica* (Florence: Leo S. Olschki, 1990); and the entire treatise is edited in Girolamo Mei, *De modis*, ed. Tsugami Eisuke (Tokyo: Keiso Shobo, 1991).

associates through essays and letters to reshape the music of their time in the image of ancient Greek music.

My second and central case history is that of Giovanni Battista Doni, who was inspired by reading one of Mei's crusading letters to embark on a similar programme of research, the focus of which also soon converged on the so-called Greek 'modes'. Mei had pointed to the 'modes'—or more properly *tonoi*—as the key to the power that ancient music had to communicate human emotions. If one wanted to regain this power, Doni became convinced, the ancient system of *tonoi* needed to be revived. As a classical scholar, which he was by profession if not always occupation (like so many humanists he made his living as a secretary), Doni seemed content to pursue Greek letters and antiquities quite apart from any practical application. For example, he compiled 6,000 ancient inscriptions for publication (they were eventually published posthumously), for no other purpose than to make them available to antiquarians. He also collected drawings of lyres and citharae, but these he set out to collect not out of a pure desire for knowledge but because he was searching for a model for a modern instrument that could be a medium for restoring the Greek tonal system. In the course of this campaign he became so interested in the ancient instruments themselves that he decided to write a history of the ancient lyre and cithara.

Thus Doni's motivation for research into the Greek lyre was deeper than an antiquarian curiosity. To be sure, he was fascinated by antiquity in general and Greek music in particular. But curiosity alone would not have led him down the thorny path of investigating instruments of which only iconographic and literary evidence remained. Like humanists in the previous century, he wanted musicians to revive certain qualities of ancient Greek music that he felt the modern lacked. The aura that surrounded the ancient 'modes' had cast its spell over musicians from Boethius to Glareanus, but now there was a further reason to try to revive these 'modes'. It had been definitively established by Mei, Galilei, and Bardi that the system of the Greeks was altogether different from the church modes. Therefore the modes to which Glareanus gave the ancient Greek names could not be expected to work the marvellous effects that the ancient authors attributed to Greek music. If the real Greek system could be brought to life again, perhaps music could get a brave new start. Doni was the first to try to realize a revival of the Greek tonoi through practical strategies.

Doni recognized that modern musical instruments were incompatible with the ancient *tonoi*, because they could not accommodate the ancient system's unlimited possibilities of transposition and modulation. Moreover, within each *tonos* there were—besides the diatonic—the chromatic and enharmonic genera. Instruments that were capable of performing in multiple keys and in the three genera needed to be developed. Doni designed among other instruments diharmonic viols and violins, triharmonic harpsichords, a theorbo with three fingerboards, a panharmonic viol, and—the most famous—the amphichordal lyre or lyra Barberina, named after Maffeo Barberini, whom Doni briefly served before Maffeo in 1623 became Pope Urban VIII. The investigation of ancient string instruments was thus an essential part of the project of reviving the ancient tonal systems, for Doni expected to find in lyres and citharae models for new string instruments on which one might play all the ancient modes and genera.

Until now it has not been possible to retrace Doni's search for exemplars of the old Greek and Roman instruments, because the only existing edition of his essay 'Lyra Barberina', in which he reported his findings, lacked his iconographical documentation. Thus the route to the Barberini lyre and certain details of the instrument itself have been obscured. And what in retrospect is even more important, Doni's contribution to musical iconography and organology has been altogether lost from sight. If we are to evaluate his dual role of scholar and reformer, it is essential to consider the essay 'Lyra Barberina' in the state in which Doni left it for publication.

In 1763 Giovanni Battista Passeri published an edition prepared by Antonio Francesco Gori of the writings on music of Giovanni Battista Doni.[6] The opening essay, 'Lyra Barberina', was probably Doni's major scholarly work, left in manuscript when he died at the age of 53 in 1647. The title of the first volume is misleading, because the essay 'Lyra Barberina' occupies only the first seventy pages, while the remaining 354 contain other works of Doni, some previously published, such as *De praestantia musicae veteris*, but also many shorter essays not before printed. And what has been the bane of librarians and cataloguers is that the second volume has a totally different title: *De' trattati di musica di Gio. Batista Doni Patrizio fiorentino, Tomo secondo*.[7]

---

[6] *Io. Baptistae Doni Patrici Florentini Lyra Barberina* ΑΜΘΙΧΟΡΔΟΣ *accedunt eiusdem opera pleraque nondum edita, ex autographis collegit, et in lucem proferri curavit Antonius Franciscus Gorius Basilic. Bapt. Flor. olim Praep. distributa in tomos ii. Absoluta vero studio et opera Io. Baptistae Passeri Pisaurensis cum praefationibus eiusdem.* Florentiae Typis Caesareis Anno M. D. CC. LXIII.

[7] I have published in the series Antiquae Musicae Italicae Studiosi of the University of Bologna, edited by Giuseppe Vecchi, a more extensive study of Doni's essay than the present one, accompanied by a facsimile edn. of the 1763 edition, with corrections, all of Doni's illustrations, together with their sources, and the glossary of Greek and Latin terms that Doni intended to publish with the essay: *G. B. Doni's 'Lyra Barberina', Commentary and Iconographical Study, Facsimile Edition with Critical Notes* (Miscellanee Saggi Convegni, 18; Bologna: Antiquae Musicae Italicae Studiosi, Università degli Studi di Bologna, 1981). See the introduction to this essay.

Deceptive also is 'Lyra Barberina' as the title of the lead essay. It is not simply a description and presentation of Doni's new instrument: rather, it is a history of the Greek lyre, cithara, and similar instruments, to which Doni tacked on a too brief description of his novel hybrid lute-lyre. It is the most ambitious history of the Greek lyre ever written; yet it is practically unknown to historians of instruments or of Greek music, who have omitted it from all their bibliographies.[8]

The greatest deception of all in this publication is that the many representations of lyres, citharae, psalteries, and elegantly robed and unrobed men and women playing them were, with few exceptions, not at all the illustrations prepared and intended by Doni but drawings compiled and commissioned by the eighteenth-century editors, when, after exhaustive efforts—or so they claimed—to find the authentic illustrations, they gave them up as lost.[9] Even before Gori's edition was out Angelo Maria Bandini, Doni's biographer, complained that it was incomplete, lacking an *onomasticon*, or lexicon of Greek and Latin musical terms, and some poems that Bandini knew belonged to the book from a letter which Doni had written to Gaspar Scioppius.[10] Bandini, in his biography of 1755, speculated that the complete autograph must have remained with Doni's friend Gabriel Naudé in Paris or with Cardinal Francesco Barberini in Rome.[11]

Both of Bandini's guesses were good. The Barberini collection in the Vatican Library possesses what must have been the presentation copy to Pope Urban VIII (Maffeo Barberini). This elegantly copied manuscript, Barberinus latinus 1897, must represent the earliest version of the treatise, as it stood around 1632. It is illustrated with ink-drawings of lyres and citharae (Pl. 18.1) sketched by an artist from frescoes, bas-reliefs, coins, gems, and other art objects. Unfortunately, the writing shows through from the reverse side (see Pl. 18.4*b*).

Gori eventually located this manuscript, but only after the volume

---

[8] The first part of this statement is no longer true, with the appearance of *Stringed Instruments of Ancient Greece* by Martha Maas and Jane McIntosh Snyder (New Haven, Conn.: Yale University Press, 1989), but that work too fails to mention Doni.

[9] Passeri wrote from Bologna to Abbot Annibale Camillo Olivieri in Pesaro on 26 Sept. 1761 that Gori had printed two volumes in folio of Doni's works after working on the project for thirty years, but a number of lacunae had still to be filled. Now he was almost finished. 'But I cannot find anywhere the engravings of antiquities that Doni cites, and I see that Gori had the idea of putting others in their place. I have written to Florence about these apprehensions, but if they do not satisfy me, it would be proper that I derive the plates from the relics that he cites according to his intention.' Quoted in Francesco Vatielli, *La 'Lyra Barberina' di G. B. Doni* (Pesaro: Annesio Nobili, 1908), 23.

[10] Angelo Maria Bandini, *Commentariorum de vita et scriptis Joannis Baptistae Doni* (Florence: Typis Caesareis, 1755), p. lxix n. 6. Doni's letter to Scioppius is in Doni, *Commercium litterarium*, ed. Antonio F. Gori (Florence: Typis Caesareis, 1754), cols. 156–8.

[11] *Commentariorum*, p. lxix.

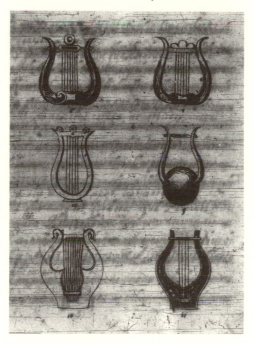

PL. 18.1. Illustrations for Doni, 'Lyra Barberina'. Rome, Vatican Library, MS Barb. lat. 1897, fo. 17ʳ

containing 'Lyra Barberina' was in print, though not yet published. As an addendum on the last pages of the first volume (414–24) he recorded the variants from his printed version as reported by Abbot Simone Ballerini, prefect of the Barberini Library, who collated the codex with the printed text. In listing the variants Gori noted that the Barberini manuscript had some pictures of lyres not unlike those in Johannes Bottari's *Roma sotterranea*,[12] to which Gori referred the reader.

The other possibility Bandini mentioned, that Doni's manuscript had remained with Naudé in France, was the better hunch, for a manuscript written partly in Doni's hand, with instructions for the printer, did remain in Paris and is now at the Bibliothèque nationale. Doni had sent it to Gabriel Naudé, who was to have found a French publisher for the essay, and it was still in France when Doni suddenly died of a fever in Florence on 1 December 1647. This manuscript (shelf-mark latin 10274) presents a

---

[12] Giovanni Gaetano Bottari, *Sculture e pitture sagre estratte dai cimiteri di Roma; pubblicate gia dagli autori della Roma sotterranea* (Rome: Stamperia Vaticana, 1737–54) ii. 55–61. Doni cites this on p. 415 of the Gori–Passeri edition.

version that, compared with the Barberini manuscript, is much enlarged and revised. It is approximately equivalent to the draft published by Gori—Passeri, which was copied from Doni's working duplicate of the Paris manuscript now in Pesaro.[13] The Paris manuscript contains, however, a few later revisions and additions. More importantly, it has the full complement of pictures that Doni intended for publication.

How Doni's definitive manuscript happened to remain unpublished in Paris in 1647, fifteen years after the dedication to Pope Urban VIII was signed ('Anno 1632' in the printed edition; 'Rome 9 August 1632' with autograph signature in the Paris manuscript) is a fascinating story in itself, of which I shall give here only the briefest outline. The sequence of events can be reconstructed from Doni's correspondence with Marin Mersenne, Gabriel Naudé, Nicolas-Claude Peiresc and the brothers Dupuy, among others. On 15 October 1633 Doni announced to Mersenne that he had just finished the essay. A month later he told Peiresc that he hoped 'to bring to light in this discipline [of music] many recondite and notably useful things: starting with the work on the lyra Barberina, which in a few weeks will begin to be printed'.[14] But then he became engrossed in other matters, and, he confessed to Mersenne in April 1634, the book had not begun to be printed.[15] In September 1635 he doubted that publishers in Rome would undertake it because of the many illustrations.[16] He decided in 1638 to try to get it printed in France.[17] Gabriel Naudé promised to find a publisher there through Jacques and Pierre Dupuy (the Signori Puteani, as he often referred to them).[18]

In July 1645 the Dupuys still hoped to find a printer, but Doni, getting

---

[13] The manuscript on which the Gori—Passeri edition was based, according to Vatielli (*La 'Lyra'*, 20), was an autograph later acquired by the Biblioteca Oliveriana in Pesaro, where he saw it. Actually this codex, Biblioteca Oliveriana, MS 68, is written by a scribe with corrections in Doni's hand. It once belonged to Antonio Francesco Gori, whose brother continued to claim it even after Passeri had donated it to the Olivieri collection. It must have been the prototype for the fair copy written by Gori that served the printer of the Gori—Passeri edition: Florence, Biblioteca Marucelliana, MS A294. This, which contains marks for paragraphing, italics, and decorated capitals, was followed by the printer in every detail, including some misspellings.

[14] Richard Schaal, 'Ein unbekannter Brief von G. B. Doni', *Acta musicologica*, 25 (1953), 88–91. The letter to Mersenne is in *Correspondance du P. Marin Mersenne*, ed. Paul Tannery and Cornelius De Waard, iii (Paris: Presses universitaires de France, 1946), 497 ff.

[15] Mersenne, *Correspondance*, iv (1955), 90.

[16] Ibid., v (Paris: Éditions du CNRS, 1959), 391–2.

[17] Ibid., vi (1960), 384.

[18] Naudé had already intervened to arrange for the publication of Doni's two French treatises, and while reporting that they were still with Doni's cousin, Bishop of Riez, to whom they were dedicated, he urged Doni to send the manuscript of the 'Lyra'. Naudé's letter to Doni, of 18 Apr. 1642, is in Mersenne, *Correspondance*, xi (1970), 123. Naudé had reported on 16 Feb. 1641 to Doni (ibid., x (1967), 509) that Robert Ballard was ready in January to take something else off the press and to put Doni's two treatises on, but he still lacked the manuscript.

impatient, asked to have the manuscript returned, because he was angling to get Cardinal Francesco Barberini to sponsor its publication in Italy.[19] He hoped that when the Cardinal saw the *De praestantia musicae veteris libri tres*, which came out in 1647, he would be eager to have also the 'Lyra' essay see the light under his patronage.[20] In one of his last letters Doni urged Dupuy to consign the essay to Naudé, who would have it returned to Doni in Florence.[21] Doni died in December of that year, and nothing more was done to see 'Lyra Barberina' to press until, a hundred years later, Antonio Francesco Gori embarked on the project of publishing Doni's complete works.

Although the motive for writing 'Lyra Barberina' must originally have been to describe the new instrument, only the last six chapters pertain to the lyra specifically. The first eight report the fruit of research undertaken to find ancient models for modern instruments. Doni set out in the first chapter to distinguish among the numerous terms used to designate ancient plucked string instruments, for example *kithara, chelys, testudo, phorminx, kitharis, psalterium, magadis,* and *sambuca*. While the first chapter dealt with literary evidence, the second presented iconographic evidence. In the third chapter Doni dealt specifically with the psaltery, magadis, and sambuca. He devoted chapter 4 to distinguishing the lyre from the cithara and to enumerating different types of each, while in the following chapter he detailed their parts. The plectrum receives special attention in the sixth chapter, and in the seventh Doni tried to solve the mystery of the pecten, which he believed was a comb-like device used to pluck more than one string at a time. Doni's final chapter on the history of the lyre and cithara concerned the manner of holding and playing the instruments.

Throughout these chapters the text contains references to illustrations. Most of these references are retained in the text of the printed edition, but the figures supplied by the editors rarely illuminate the text, and, what is worse, the references in the text are not correctly co-ordinated with the

---

[19] Doni was already trying to get the manuscript back in 1644, for Naudé wrote to him on 15 Dec. 1644 from Paris assuring him that he was trying to retrieve the book from the Dupuys, 'who esteem it very much' (Paris, Bibliothèque nationale, MS ital. 1671, fos. 24–5). On 29 July 1645 Naudé, now in Rome, wrote that before leaving Paris he urged the Dupuys to let him have the 'Lyra' manuscript, but they still were optimistic about getting it printed.

[20] In an undated letter, but obviously of 1647, Doni sent to an assistant of Cardinal Mazarin, to whom the book is dedicated, copies of *De praestantia musicae veteris libri tres*, intimating that Cardinal Francesco, who was now in exile in France, might support the publication of the 'Lyra' essay (Doni, *Commercium litterarium*, cols. 239–40).

[21] Florence, Biblioteca Marucelliana, MS A290, fo. 92ᵛ (Doni's draft of the letter). However, so far as getting anything printed in Florence, Doni was extremely disappointed with the work of the printer Amator Massa, who did the *De praestantia*. See *Commercium litterarium*, col. 231.

plate numbers. In a few cases, though, thanks to Doni's identification of his sources, Passeri was able to track down Doni's intended illustration, and he included two figures of which Doni spoke that are not found in any of the manuscripts, namely the representation of Orpheus playing the magadis from a Vatican manuscript of Virgil and a detail from the Sarcophagus of the Muses.[22]

In the Paris manuscript Doni gave the source, whether an engraving in a printed book or a collection of antiquities, from which each figure was drawn. A variety of monuments are represented; for example on the two sides of folio 90 (see Pll. 18.2 and 18.3) there are gems (nos. 1, 3, 28), coins (2, 4, 5, 6, 12, 13, 16–27, and 30–5), marble bas-reliefs (7, 8, 10, 11, and 36), and illuminations from a Bible (37 and 38). The greater part of the monuments are of Roman origin. From Greece there are a number of coins: no. 12, from Perinthus; 13, from Chalcidice; 16, from Mytilene; 18 and 19, from Delphi; 20, from Cranii; 23, from Chersonesus; 30, from Megara; 31, from Centuripae in Sicily; 34, from Lappa in Crete.

Justifiably, Doni applied a good measure of scepticism to the analysis of available representations of the lyre and cithara and its associated forms. He warned the reader to bear in mind that instruments portrayed on coins and astronomical charts served a symbolic function and often had little to do with instruments actually used by Greeks and Romans. As an example of the difficulties and contradictions that iconographic evidence posed, Doni scrutinized the lyre in the fresco known as the 'Aldobrandini Wedding' (Pl. 18.4*a*)[23]:

But it is important to present [for consideration] yet another form of cithara, from a very ancient picture, which, cut from the wall of a certain crypt, we find transferred to the Quirinal villa of the Aldobrandini. In it an ancient celebration of a wedding is graphically represented. The most noble Cassiano dal Pozzo engraved it in bronze,[24] and it was commented upon with erudite observations by

[22] 'Orpheus in pictura antiquissimi Codicis Virgiliani in Bibl. Vaticana' is Tab. III, no. II, a plate prepared by Passeri. Tabula V, nos. I, II, IV, V, and VII, prepared by Gori, are drawn from the figure of the Mattei Sarcophagus of the Muses in Ridolfino Venuti, *Vetera monumenta Matthaeiorum*, ii (Rome: Sumptibus V. Monaldini, 1778), Tab. xvi.

[23] This fresco was excavated in 1604 or 1605 near the Arch of Gallieno on the Esquiline Hill in Rome. It was purchased by Cardinal Pietro Aldobrandini for the villa given to him by Pope Clement VIII in 1601. In 1818 Pius VIII gained possession of the fresco, and in 1838 Gregory XVI had it placed in the public gallery of the Vatican Library, where it may be seen today. See Leonard von Matt, *The Art Treasures of the Vatican Library* (New York: Harry N. Abrams, 1974), 19–20, including a colour reproduction. The work dates from the beginning of the Christian era.

[24] A drawing showing the wedding in reverse, as if it were a sketch for an engraving, is in the collection of the British Library, which contains many drawings formerly owned by Cassiano dal Pozzo. It is illustrated in Cornelius C. Vermeule, III, 'The Dal Pozzo–Albani drawings of Classical Antiquities in the British Museum', *Transactions of the American Philosophical Society*, NS 50/5 (1960), 77, fig. 97. The drawing is in vol. 2, fo. 79[r], no. 414 of the collection.

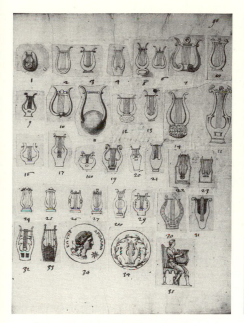

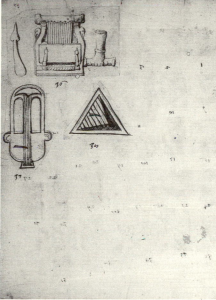

PL. 18.2. Illustrations for Doni,
'Lyra Barberina'. Paris,
Bibliothèque nationale, MS lat.
10274, fo. 90^r

PL. 18.3. Illustrations for Doni,
'Lyra Barberina'. Paris,
Bibliothèque nationale, MS lat.
10274, fo. 90^v

Pignorio.[25] There, among other [human] figures is seen one of a girl holding a cithara suspended by a strap [*balteus*] and striking the strings with the right and left hands. This is the figure: [Pl. 18.4*b*].

It is true that the painter portrayed few strings in the cithara of the Aldobrandinian player, and the rings around the yoke by means of which the strings are tied seem somewhat thick. On this account such a one is not to be considered truly a species of it exactly but rather something conjured up by some fertile Minerva. Where are the pegs [*claviculi*] or *kollaboi*, which, the grammarians teach, were provided in citharae and lyres and without which the strings cannot easily be tightened? Or are we to believe that they are lower, where the *echeum* appears? But, on the other hand, they can hardly be comfortably placed there, for they clearly tell us that they were above the yoke. Then, where are the twenty-four strings, which the author of the letter to Dardanus attributed to St Jerome assigns to the cithara? Nor ought we conclude that when this picture was made the cithara had not yet reached that number of strings. The times of Epigonius and Simicius, whose

[25] Lorenzo Pignoria, *Antiquissimae picturae quae Romae visitur typus . . . accuratè explicatus* (Padua: Donatus Pasquardus, 1630), contains a commentary and a folding engraving of the fresco. A copy is in Florence, Biblioteca Nazionale Centrale, Palat. Misc. 2.G.16.4.

477

Left PL. 18.4*a*. Fresco, 'Aldobrandini Wedding', detail. Rome, Vatican Museum
Right PL. 18.4*b*. Drawing of lyre-player from 'Aldobrandini Wedding'.
Rome, Vatican Library, MS Barb. lat. 1897, fo. 18ᵛ

[instruments] consisted of forty and thirty-five strings, according to Atheneus, were much more ancient. Besides, music did not significantly develop beyond this point, so far as we know, under the Roman Caesars.[26]

Bolstered by the study of perhaps hundreds of representations of lyres and citharae and informed by reading the Greek and Latin sources, Doni was able to apply a critical eye to the Aldobrandini lyre-player's instrument. He returned to it repeatedly in his study, resolving some of the questions just posed.

The instrument that most fascinated Doni and to which he returned most often is that in the Sarcophagus of the Muses, then in the Villa Mattei and now in the Museo delle Terme in Rome. Strangely, it is not represented among the figures in the manuscripts, but Doni must have intended to

---

[26] Translated by the author from Doni's Latin in 'Lyra Barberina', Gori–Passeri edn., i. 12–13, as corrected through the Paris manuscript, fo. 11ʳ. Folio 11ᵛ, which once contained a pasted drawing of the Aldobrandini lyre-player, is now blank.

478

Left PL. 18.5*a*. Drawing of the Mattei Sarcophagus from the collection of Cassiano dal Pozzo, detail. Windsor, The Royal Library, No. 8706. Crown copyright reserved

Right PL. 18.5*b*. Drawing of a marble sculpture formerly in the Sacchetti Palace, Rome. Paris, Bibliothèque nationale, MS lat. 10274, fo. 12ʳ

illustrate it, as he spoke of details that would have been meaningless without a picture. He deplored the mutilated state of the bas-relief, but he probably knew it in much better preservation than it is now. Plate 18.5*a* shows the detail in question as drawn by a contemporary of Doni for the collection of Cassiano dal Pozzo. As Emanuel Winternitz has shown,[27] this cithara was copied by Raphael in his *Parnassus* in the Stanza della Segnatura in the Vatican.

Doni speculated on the function of what appeared to be tables above and below, but he had no conclusive answer as to how they were used. He also wondered about the simultaneous use of the plectrum in the right hand and the fingers of the left hand on the strings such as may be seen in the figure from the Sacchetti palace (Pl. 18.5*b*). What does the right hand do with

[27] 'Musical Archaeology of the Renaissance', 185 ff. and pls. 82*a*, 86, 87, and 88.

479

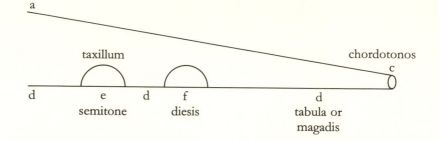

FIG. 18.1

the plectrum? In 1924 Curt Sachs proposed that the lyre and cithara were tuned pentatonically, for example $e-g-a-b-d'-e'$; the missing notes f and c', semitones above the lower boundary notes e and b of each tetrachord, would be produced through stopping with the finger.[28] In 1939 Otto Gombosi modified this theory, suggesting that the stopping was done between the bridge and the string fastener (*chordotonos*) by the plectrum, held by the right hand, and he pointed to several representations as evidence.[29]

Three hundred years earlier Doni had proposed a similar theory in a passage not in the early Barberini version, therefore dating from around 1640. The passage is in the Gori–Passeri edition but in a slightly earlier version than that of the Paris manuscript.[30] Little rounded blocks, Doni explained, are placed on the surface of the table (tabula) or magas to mark the place where the plectrum will depress the string to stop it, one for the semitone, point e, and one for the diesis, point f (see Fig. 18.1). In this way it was possible with a four-string lyre to obtain a descending scale such as $e'-c'-b-a-f-e$ or an enharmonic variant of this. Doni admitted that this interpretation of the iconographic evidence was conjectural, but it was the best explanation he could offer.

The sceptical modern scholar naturally asks: are Doni's monuments themselves authentic, and how well do the drawings represent them? The drawing of the lyre-player from the Aldobrandini wedding in the Barberini manuscript can be compared with the photograph of the existing fresco (Pl. 18.4). Doni's artist endowed the figure of the girl and her dress with a certain seventeenth-century elegance, but the lyre itself is quite faithfully rendered, with perhaps excessive reconstruction of the circular resonating

[28] 'Die griechische Instrumentalnotenschrift', *Zeitschrift für Musikwissenschaft*, 6 (1924), 289–301.
[29] *Tonarten und Stimmungen der antiken Musik* (Copenhagen: E. Munksgaard, 1939).
[30] Gori–Passeri edn., 42; Paris MS, fo. 50ᵛ.

Left PL. 18.6*a*. Drawing of detail from the tomb of Atilia Urbica. Paris,
Bibliothèque nationale, MS lat. 10274, fo. 14^v

Right PL. 18.6*b*. Engraving of detail from the tomb of Atilia Urbica. From
Ottavio Rossi, *Le memorie bresciane*, p. 38

chamber. The instrument held by the girl in the tomb of Atilia Urbica in
Brescia, which Doni called the 'lyra posterior' or 'later lyre', is not rendered
at all faithfully by Doni's artist, who transformed it into a lute (Pl. 18.6*a*).
A truer likeness must be that of the engraving published by Ottavio Rossi,
on which Doni's was based (Pl. 18.6*b*).

A number of other illustrations of coins and gems may be compared with
the printed sources from which they were copied. The coins numbered 22
and 23 in the Paris manuscript (Pl. 18.2), the first a Neapolitan coin, the
second from Chersonesus, may be compared with the representation in
Agostini's *Dialoghi intorno alle medaglie* (Rome: Guglielmo Faciotto, 1592).
Similarly, the lyre that Doni identified as 'from an ancient gem, in which is
carved the contest between Apollo and Marsyas, with the inscription

' "Neronis Caesar", after Simeonius' (Pl. 18.2, no. 28), may be compared with the representation of the medal in Gabriele Simeoni's *Discorso della religione antica de' romani* (Lyons: Guglielmo Rouillio, 1559), which in turn is translated from Guillaume de Choul's *Discours de la religion des anciens romains* (Lyons: Guillaume Rouille, 1556).[31] In all these Doni's artist scrupulously followed the traits of the originals. Some of the instruments were extracted from engravings of marbles represented in Jean Jacques Boissard's *Antiquitates Romanae*.[32] Here too Doni's artist followed his models punctiliously.

A number of Doni's figures were copied from the drawings made of classical antiquities by artists employed by Cassiano dal Pozzo, secretary and librarian to Cardinal Francesco Barberini, for his *Museum chartaceum*. Ten volumes of the collection are now in the Royal Library at Windsor Castle, and a smaller group of 500 drawings are in the British Museum.[33] Doni had at least six of these copied. Comparison of the illustrations that Doni ascribed to the Dal Pozzo collection reveal that they were copied accurately. For example, the cithara from what Doni described as a 'round base in which the figures of the ancient gods are represented in the gardens of the Farnesi Palace' (Pl. 18.7, lower left) may be compared with the drawing in the Dal Pozzo collection of a puteal now in the Naples Museo Nazionale (Pl. 18.8*a*). Similarly, the cithara from 'a marble of the Farnesi palace in which bacchanales are carved' (Pl. 18.7, upper right) may be verified through the Dal Pozzo drawing in Windsor (Pl. 18.8*b*).

Whether, apart from iconography, Doni's scholarship on the ancient instruments will stand the test of deeper research remains to be seen. The history of the lyre and cithara still awaits definitive work.[34] The publications of Theodore Reinach,[35] Hermann Abert,[36] and Tobias Norling,[37]

---

[31] I am indebted to Mark Lindley for locating the Choul and Simeoni volumes in the British Library.

[32] *Romanae urbis topographiae & antiquitatum . . . iiii* (Frankfurt: Theodor de Bry, 1597–1602). The lyre numbered 6 in the Barberini MS (Pl. 18.1, top left), equivalent to Paris MS no. 7, identified by Doni as 'from a marble that was in the Villa of the Carpi, after Boissard', is from Boissard, Pars iv, p. 82. Barberini no. 9 (Paris no. 11), 'from another marble with the inscription, IOVI SANCTO BRONTONTI . . . at the Paulini according to the same Boissard', is from Boissard, Pars iv, p. 137.

[33] The figures that were copied directly for Doni from the Cassiano dal Pozzo collection in Windsor are in the Paris MS, fo. 9ᵛ, no. 36, and fos. 12ᵛ–13ʳ. They correspond to the following volumes and numbers in the Windsor Royal Library, MSS A40 to A52, as catalogued in Cornelius C. Vermeule, III, 'The Dal Pozzo–Albani Drawings of Classical Antiquities in the Royal Library at Windsor Castle', *Transactions of the American Philosophical Society*, NS 56/2 (1966): vol. iv, fo. 17, Cat. no. 8417; vol. vi, fo. 32, Cat. no. 8584; vol. iv, fo. 15, Cat. no. 8415; vol. ii, fo. 49, Cat. no. 8304; vol. ii, fo. 47, Cat. no. 8302; vol. vii, fo. 45, Cat. no. 8673.

[34] But see above, n. 8.

[35] 'Lyra', *Dictionnaire des antiquités grecques et romaines* (Paris: Hachette, 1904), iii. 1437–51.

[36] 'Lyra', *Real Encyclopädie der classischen Altertumswissenschaft*, xiii/2 (1927), 2479–89.

[37] 'Lyra und Kithara in der Antike', *Svensk Tidskrift för Musikforskning*, 16 (1934), 77–98.

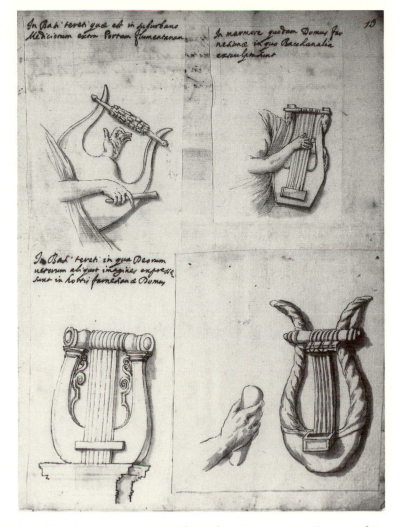

PL. 18.7. Four instruments copied from drawings in the collection of Cassiano dal Pozzo. Paris, Bibliothèque nationale, MS lat. 10274, fo. 13ʳ

the most recent of which are more than forty years old, do not contradict Doni's basic information, though they do introduce some chronological order into the history of the instruments. The pictorial anthologies of Max Wegner[38] have extended the iconographic repertory back to more remote periods of Greek history, thanks to the many vases excavated since the

---

[38] *Das Musikleben der Griechen* (Berlin: de Gruyter, 1949); *Griechenland* (Musikgeschichte in Bildern, 2/iv; Leipzig: Deutscher Verlag für Musik, 1963).

PL. 18.8*a*. Drawing of the Puteal Farnese in the Dal Pozzo collection.
Windsor, The Royal Library, No. 8302. Crown copyright reserved

PL. 18.8*b*. Drawing of a bacchanale in the Dal Pozzo collection.
Windsor, The Royal Library, No. 7673. Crown copyright reserved

seventeenth century going back to the archaic geometric period of the
seventh century and the black-figured and red-figured vases of the sixth and
fifth centuries BC.

Doni's 'Lyra Barberina' must be assessed as a conscientious product of
one of the earliest musicologists and iconographers, one who based his
conclusions on hard facts and documents. Once the illustrations are joined
to the text, the essay can be read with profit by anyone interested in

PL. 18.9. Sketch of the lyra Barberina, front view. Paris, Bibliothèque
nationale, MS lat. 10274, fo. 87ʳ

the state of musical scholarship in Doni's age or in the history of ancient
string instruments.

Turning now to Doni's activist side, it must be said that his amphichordal lyre (Pl. 18.9) is very much a compromise between an ancient
lyre and a large lute or chitarrone. Its ample, almost human torso, is
fundamentally modelled on the ancient lyre of the type represented in no. 4
of the Paris manuscript (Pl. 18.2), drawn from a coin from the reign of

Emperor Antoninus Pius (AD 138–61). Its archaic features may be identified by reference to the sketch in the Paris manuscript (Pl. 18.9; the labelling of parts and the inventory are faulty in the Gori–Passeri edition): the *ancones* or arms (D), the *iugum* or yoke (G), the *cornua* or hollow horns, here built into the body as resonating cavities, and the *chordotoni* (T, S, V), through which strings are attached to the table. Perhaps also the two-faced lyra Barberina was inspired by the three-faced *trigonon*, which could be pivoted to change *tonos*.

The construction of the instrument appears to have preceded the completion of the essay, for in a letter to Mersenne of 15 October 1633 Doni remarked: 'In general the instrument is successful; it has a very sweet tone, so that it surpasses the lute and the harp, while partaking of both.'[39] Six months later he wrote: 'my amphichord turns out to have a sweeter tone every day, such that it surpasses by far the lute.'[40]

The amphichordal lyre was one of several instruments Doni devised to play the ancient *tonoi*. Among others were the diharmonic viols and violins, triharmonic harpsichords, a theorbo with three fingerboards, and a panharmonic viol.[41] Doni persuaded several composers to experiment with his instruments and in the ancient modes, notably Girolamo Frescobaldi,[42] Domenico Mazzocchi, Pietro Eredia, Gino Capponi, Ottaviano Castelli, Luigi Rossi, and Pietro della Valle.

Doni was disappointed that a truly first-rate composer had not taken up his system. He tried to interest Monteverdi in his ideas in 1633,[43] describing to him his new instrument, and in 1634 even sent him a sketch of the lyra Barberina, which Monteverdi acknowledged in a letter of 2 February

---

[39] Mersenne, *Correspondance*, iii (2nd edn., 1969), 508–9.

[40] 8 Apr. 1634; ibid., iv (1955), 90.

[41] Sketches for a number of other instruments, some of them prototypes for the Barberini lyre, are in Florence, Biblioteca Nazionale Centrale, MS Palatino 959, fasc. 3. In a letter to Mersenne of 27 Mar. 1640 Doni apologized for not being able to invite Mersenne to hear the lyra Barberina or the diharmonic viols, not having anyone at the moment who played them. However, Doni promised that if Mersenne were to come to Rome he could hear the diharmonic and triharmonic harpsichords, the big panharmonic viol, and the diharmonic violin: *Correspondance*, ix (1965), 218–19.

[42] Doni reported to Mersenne in a letter of 22 July 1640 that Frescobaldi had obtained permission from Cardinal Barberini to have an organ built to play the various *tonoi* on the model of the triharmonic harpsichord. Still, Doni did not have much faith in him as an exponent of the new music: 'As for Frescobaldi, he is the least well bred of all, seeing that he is a very coarse man, although he plays the organ most perfectly and is an excellent composer of fantasias, dance pieces, and similar things, but as for setting the words, he is very ignorant and devoid of judgement. You might say that he has all his erudition on the tips of his fingers. And I do not doubt that he is esteemed more far from here than where he is!' Translated from Mersenne, *Correspondance*, ix (1965), 486–8.

[43] Monteverdi's reply of 22 Oct. 1633 is in G. F. Malipiero, *Claudio Monteverdi* (Milan: Fratelli Treves, 1929), 291–4, translated in *The Monteverdi Companion*, ed. Denis Arnold and Nigel Fortune (London: Faber and Faber, 1968), 83–5 and Denis Stevens, *The Letters of Claudio Monteverdi* (London: Faber and Faber, 1980), no. 123, p. 409.

1634.[44] Probably piqued at not having received acknowledgement from Monteverdi for a copy of the *Compendio del trattato de' generi e de' modi della musica* (Rome: A. Fei, 1635), Doni, in a letter to Mersenne, coupled praise for Monteverdi's lament of Ariadne with the remark that the composer was, 'after all, like almost all of them, of little understanding, which is precisely the opposite of the ancient [musicians], who were generally persons of distinction and the most beautiful spirits and the most polished of those times'.[45]

Of the experiments made by various composers with Doni's restored ancient tonalities, the most extensive were those of Pietro della Valle. A manuscript survives of his *{Dialogo} per la festa della Santissima Purificazione a cinque voci con varietà di cinque tuoni diversi, cioè Dorio, Frigio, Eolio, Lidio, et Hipolidio*.[46] Here Della Valle utilized two instruments that were built for him to accommodate the rapid changes of tonality, a cembalo triarmonico and a viola panarmonica. The cembalo triarmonico (Pl. 18.10) was built by Giovanni Pietro Polizzino for Della Valle. It consisted of three keyboards. The middle one played the Dorian tonality, and its black keys were suited to the Iastian; the top keyboard, which sounded a third higher than written, accommodated the Phrygian, with split keys permitting Aeolian and Lydian. The lowest keyboard supplied the Hypolydian and sounded a tone lower than written. Just tuning prevailed throughout.

The notation and tonal system used in Della Valle's *Dialogo* were devised by Doni to restore to use the ancient *harmoniae* and *tonoi*, in which he believed resided the expressive vigour of ancient Greek music. Doni derived his understanding of the ancient system mainly from Ptolemy, according to whom there were two types of mutation possible in melody-writing, one of mode or *harmonia*, the other of key or *tonos*. In the first—of octave species or mode—the melodic intervals and their order and relationships changed, in the second—modulation of key—only the pitch level changed.

In the *Compendio del Trattato de' generi e de' modi della musica*,[47] Doni gave a chart of modulations for two of the modes and *tonoi*, the Dorian and Phrygian (Exx. 18.1—4). The Dorian mode has the rising melodic form *mi*,

[44] Malipiero, *Monteverdi*, 296; *The Monteverdi Companion*, 87; Stevens, *The Letters*, no. 124, 414—16. Doni had sent similar sketches to others, for example to Mersenne with a letter of 15 Oct. 1633 (*Correspondance*, iii (2nd edn., 1969), 509) and to Michelangelo Buonarroti, the younger, with a letter of 23 Dec. 1633 in Florence, Biblioteca Medicea Laurenziana, Archivio Buonarroti, MS 46, fo. 822.

[45] Mersenne, *Correspondance*, vi (1960), 30.

[46] Rome, Biblioteca Nazionale, MSS musicali 123. See the facs. in Joyce L. Johnson and Howard E. Smither (eds.), *Oratorios by Pietro della Valle, Francesco Foggia, Bonifazio Graziani, Marco Marazzoli* (The Italian Oratorio, 1650–1800, 1; New York: Garland, 1986).

[47] Rome: A. Fei, 1635, 33—4.

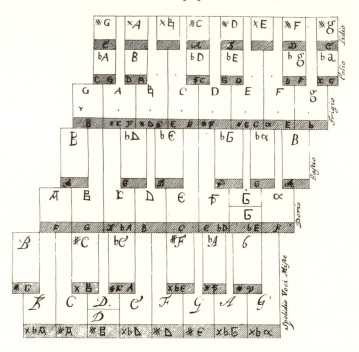

PL. 18.10. Cembalo triarmonico, from Doni, 'Trattato secondo sopra gl'instrumenti di tasti', in *Lyra Barberina*, ed. A. F. Gori and G. B. Passeri (Florence, 1763), p. 330

fa, sol, la, mi, fa, sol, la. In the second stave Doni showed how it may be transposed to the Phrygian *tonos*, a whole tone higher. The melody remains the same, while the pitch rises by a whole tone. (We would say that it has been transposed from its natural key to the higher key of two sharps.) If one wished to sing a Phrygian mode in the Dorian *tonos*, one would remain in the *e–e'* octave but use the necessary accidentals to produce the succession characteristic of the Phrygian mode: *re, mi, fa, sol, re, mi, fa, sol* (Ex. 18.1*b*). In going from Ex. 18.1*a* to 1*b* a mutation of mode occurs, the melody remaining on the pitch level of the Dorian *tonos*. Supposing instead that one wished to sing the Phrygian mode in the Phrygian *tonos*; then the same syllables, *re, mi, fa, sol, re, mi, fa, sol*, would be sung starting on *f♯*, because the Phrygian *tonos* is a whole tone higher than the Dorian. This is represented in Ex. 18.3*b*. The Phrygian melody is now at its normal Phrygian pitch level.

Doni devised a simplified notation that eliminated the multitude of sharps in the transpositions. Ex. 18.4 shows how the modulation from Dorian *tonos* and mode to Phrygian *tonos* and mode would be notated. The

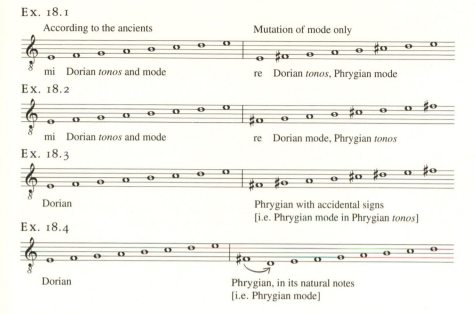

Ex. 18.1

According to the ancients — mi Dorian *tonos* and mode

Mutation of mode only — re Dorian *tonos*, Phrygian mode

Ex. 18.2

mi Dorian *tonos* and mode

re Dorian mode, Phrygian *tonos*

Ex. 18.3

Dorian

Phrygian with accidental signs
[i.e. Phrygian mode in Phrygian *tonos*]

Ex. 18.4

Dorian

Phrygian, in its natural notes
[i.e. Phrygian mode]

initial *f♯* would indicate the modulation to the Phrygian *tonos*; then the Phrygian mode would be given in its natural notes, as we would today indicate an instrument in E. This is demonstrated in Ex. 18.4*b*.

Pietro della Valle modified Doni's notation in that he provided a key to the transposition just before the shift of tonality, the change of pitch being signalled by a *custos*. Della Valle thus realized the variety of tonality that Doni felt was missing from the music of their time, while preserving the pure intonation of intervals. One passage in the *Dialogo* reaches F♯ minor from the original D major, then, shifting from Phrygian to Hypolydian, makes an enharmonic change to E♭ major (notated as D♯ major). Then through a C♯ major chord it leads back to the starting-point, D major.[48] The panharmonic instruments assure just intonation throughout the rather strained chordal juxtapositions.

The starting-point of Doni's research on ancient instruments was the conviction that a medium had to be found for performing the ancient tonalities. An observer and critic of the contemporary musical scene, he responded to what he perceived as a deficiency of the music of his time. He had welcomed the new dramatic style of monody; indeed he was one of the

[48] See Agostino Ziino, 'Pietro della Valle e la "musica erudita", nuovi documenti', *Analecta musicologica*, 4 (1967), 97–111 (including facsimile of the original notation and transcription of passage in question).

most intelligent and articulate critics of this new music. But by the 1630s the novelty of recitative had worn off, and composers were turning towards more lyric styles, which Doni also applauded. He deplored, however, the lack of tonal and harmonic and therefore expressive variety in this music, which tended to stay within a narrow range of keys. On the one hand, he wanted to see more modal variety and more liberal use of modulation; on the other, he realized that the tuning systems in use did not permit them. This led him to the search for instruments that in his time could expand the range of tonalities and modes and bring to life the ancient effects.

The mingling of practical goals and scholarly research exemplified in Doni's work has been a source of strength and vitality in the discipline of musicology. The stimulus that scholarship and practice have exerted on each other is not unique to music but has decisively affected the directions of musical scholarship since its earliest practitioners. Doni's work illustrates both the enthusiastic creativity and the methodological immaturity that this alliance bred.

19

The Recitative of Lully's Alceste:
French Declamation or Italian Melody?

This article was first published in *Actes de Baton Rouge*, edités par Selma A. Zebouni, as volume 25 (1986) of the annual *Biblio 17*, Papers on French Seventeenth-Century Literature (Paris, Seattle, Tübingen, 1986). These were the proceedings of a conference held in March 1985 at Louisiana State University in Baton Rouge by the North American Society for Seventeenth-Century French Literature. The topic of the meeting was the year 1674 in French literature and music. My paper was delivered at a session entitled '1674 et la musique', organized by Georgia Cowart of the University of South Carolina.

The invitation to participate at this meeting gave me a chance to reconsider the question of the relationship of Lully's recitative to that of Italian opera of his contemporaries and immediate predecessors. This topic came up in my teaching almost every year, and I had written about it briefly in my *Baroque Music* (Englewood Cliffs, NJ: Prentice-Hall, 1968; 3rd edn., 1991). This was an opportunity to confront it seriously. I expected the thesis expressed here to be controversial, but it seems to have caused hardly a ripple.

A NUMBER of our assumptions and theories about the origin and nature of Lully's recitative deserve fresh evaluation. One is that Lully developed a new kind of musical declamation based on that of French tragic actors and actresses. Another is that French versification required him to depart from the uniform barring of Italian recitative, which he had adopted in some of his *récits* for the comédies-ballets. A third received opinion is that French recitative as found in the early tragédies lyriques, and specifically *Alceste* (1674), belongs to a genre different from Italian recitative.

Before addressing these issues, I should review the categories of solo vocal music found in *Alceste* in order to isolate the genre that is central to this discussion. No adequate terminology in 1674 distinguished between the various levels of declamation and lyricism practised by Lully. A term that did appear in the scores, particularly of the ballets, *récit*, covered a variety of musical types and was defined by A. Furetière in his *Dictionnaire universel* (1690) as 'that which is sung by a solo voice, particularly by a soprano. A beautiful music ought to be interspersed with *récits* amd choruses.'[1] Unfortunately, this is too general to be useful. Some of the passages designated *récit* in Lully's early works are in a free declamatory style, while others are in an airy, rhythmic style. The term *air* is also sometimes marked in the scores over dancelike, somewhat tuneful, metrically regular, closed musical periods. Another category of solo vocal music usually bears no designation of genre—this is the recitative, the normal style for dialogues and monologues. But even this comes in more than one variety. Only in the mid-eighteenth century was an essential distinction made between two kinds of recitative. Pierre Estève in 1753 classified them into *simple* and *mesuré*, and this became the standard terminology.[2] It is with what he calls *récitatif simple* that I shall be concerned. Without employing the term *récitatif simple*, Rameau in 1722, before he had written his first opera, described what it ideally should be:[3]

il faut che le Chant imite la parole, de sorte qu'il semble que l'on parle, au lieu de chanter; ainsi les Cadences parfaites ne doivent y être employées qu'aux endroits où le sens se termine . . . en s'attachant encore à exprimer les syllabes longues du discours par des Nottes d'une valeur convenable, & celles qui sont breves par des Nottes de moindre valeur . . . pourvû que l'on fasse entendre les longues dans le premier moment de chaque temps, & surtout, dans le premier temps.	the melody should imitate speech, so that it seems like speaking rather than singing. Thus perfect cadences should not be used except where the thought concludes . . . striving besides to set long syllables of a speech with suitable note-values and short ones with notes of lesser value . . . provided that the longs are heard on the first part of a beat and above all on the first beat of each measure.

What Rameau meant by long and short syllables is unclear, since other witnesses of that time and before tell us that the language had no short and long syllables.[4] He probably meant that the syllables with the principal

[1] Antoine Furetière, art. 'Recit', *Dictionnaire universel* (The Hague and Rotterdam: A. & R. Leers, 1690; repr. Geneva: Slatkine, 1970), iii: 'ce qui est chanté par une voix seule, & sur tout par un dessus. Une belle musique doit être entremêlée de recits & de chœurs.'

[2] *L'esprit des beaux-arts* (Paris: C. J. Baptiste Bauche fils, 1753), ii. 25–30.

[3] Jean Philippe Rameau, *Traité de l'harmonie reduite à ses principes naturels* (Paris: Jean-Baptiste-Christophe Ballard, 1722; repr., ed. Erwin R. Jacobi in Rameau, *Complete Theoretical Writings* (n.p.: American Institute of Musicology), i (1967), ii, ch. 27, p. 162).

[4] For some illuminating discussions of this question see Louis E. Auld (ed.), *The Lyric Art of Pierre Perrin, Founder of French Opera*, ii (Henryville, Pa.: Institute of Mediaeval Music, 1986), ch. 6, commentary, section 4; and David Tunley, 'The Union of Words and Music in Seventeenth-Century French Song—The Long and Short of It', *Australian Journal of French Studies*, 21 (1984), 281–307.

accents should fall on the first beat of a bar. But it is clear that he spoke of *récitatif simple*.

Estève defined *récitatif mesuré* as 'a sort of blending of *récitatif simple* with song that tends more towards melody than towards declamation'.[5] This more songful manner, he said, was used to give vent to sentiments of joy, sadness, hate, or fury. Such moments of lyricism are analogous to the arioso or mezz'aria of the contemporary Italian opera, triple-time melodious passages in the midst of recitative speeches and dialogue in duple time. A good example of this juxtaposition is in *Alceste*, Act V, scene 2. In this scene Straton is in chains and asks Lychas, his rival for the love of Céphise, to liberate him: 'M'ostera-tu point la chaine qui m'accable . . .'. On this happy day, when Alcide is leading Alceste back from Hades, Lychas will relieve Straton of his chains. So far the dialogue has been in simple recitative, with the time signature shifting between ₵ and 3. Then in measured recitative in 3, Lychas sings: 'Qu'on ne porte point d'autres fers / Que ceux dont l'Amour nous enchaîne' (Let us not suffer any other chains than those of love). The juxtaposition of the two styles of declamation is evident in the excerpt in Ex. 19.1.[6]

This could be a scene out of a mid-seventeenth-century Italian opera. The *récitatif simple* gives way to a triple-time passage, partly written over a recurrent bass that is built on the descending fourth, which is filled in by diatonic steps. It is the latter style that comes to be called *récitatif mesuré*.

The next scene, in which Straton and Lychas agree to stop fighting and to ask Céphise to choose between them, offers an example of the next higher level of lyricism, the air. Céphise's reply, although not marked 'air' in some scores, is 'Je n'ai point de choix à faire'. Marriage destroys the charms of love, she declares, and counsels: 'Amants, n'épousez jamais' (Ex. 19.2).[7] This exhibits the air's typical features—flowing dance-like melody, tidily wrapped, moreover, in a closed form, AAB, in which the B section also has internal repetition.

It is essential to keep clearly separated these three levels of solo vocal music when speaking about Lully's recitative. Jean-Léonor Le Gallois, Sieur de Grimarest, who wrote a *Traité du récitatif*, a general treatise on declamation—both spoken and sung—published in 1707, failed to observe this distinction. He theorizes that the composer ought to follow natural speech as

---

[5] *L'esprit des beaux-arts*, ii. 29: 'une sorte d'union du Récitatif simple avec le chant, et qui tient de plus près à la modulation des sons qu'à la déclamation'.

[6] For the entire scene, see Lully, *Œuvres complètes*, Part II, vol. ii, ed. Henry Prunières (Paris: Éditions de la Revue musicale, 1932), 280–3.

[7] Ibid. 285–8. Céphise's piece is marked 'air' in the edition by Théodore Lajarte, Chefs-d'œuvre classiques de l'opéra français, 16 (Paris: T. Michaelis, 1881?; repr. New York: Broude Bros., 1971), Act V, scene 3, 257–8.

Ex. 19.1. Lully, *Alceste*, V. ii

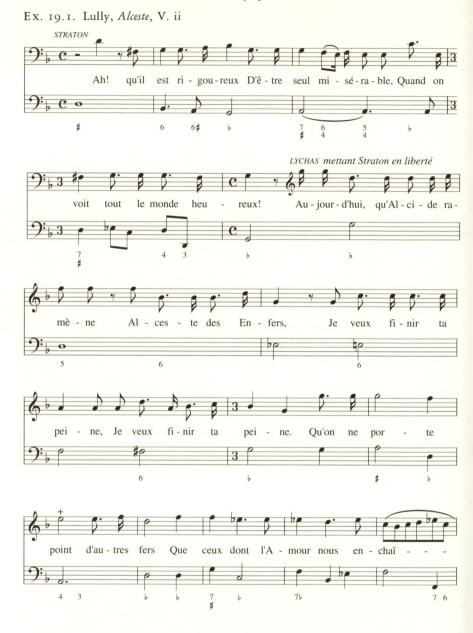

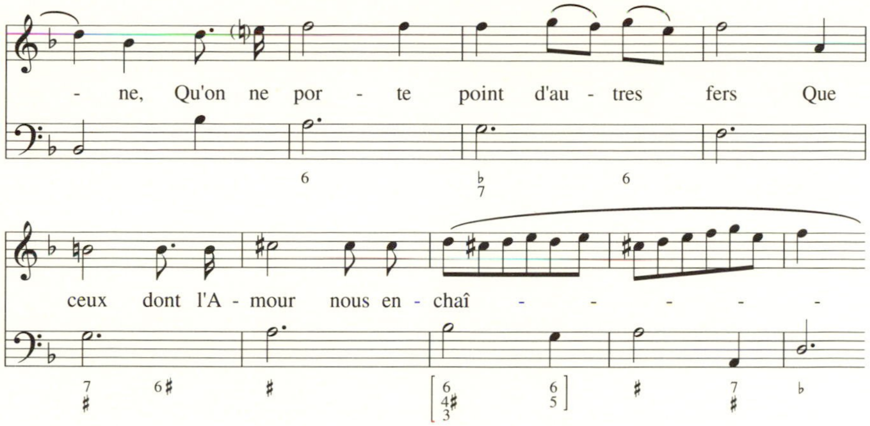

Ex. 19.2. Lully, *Alceste*, V. iii

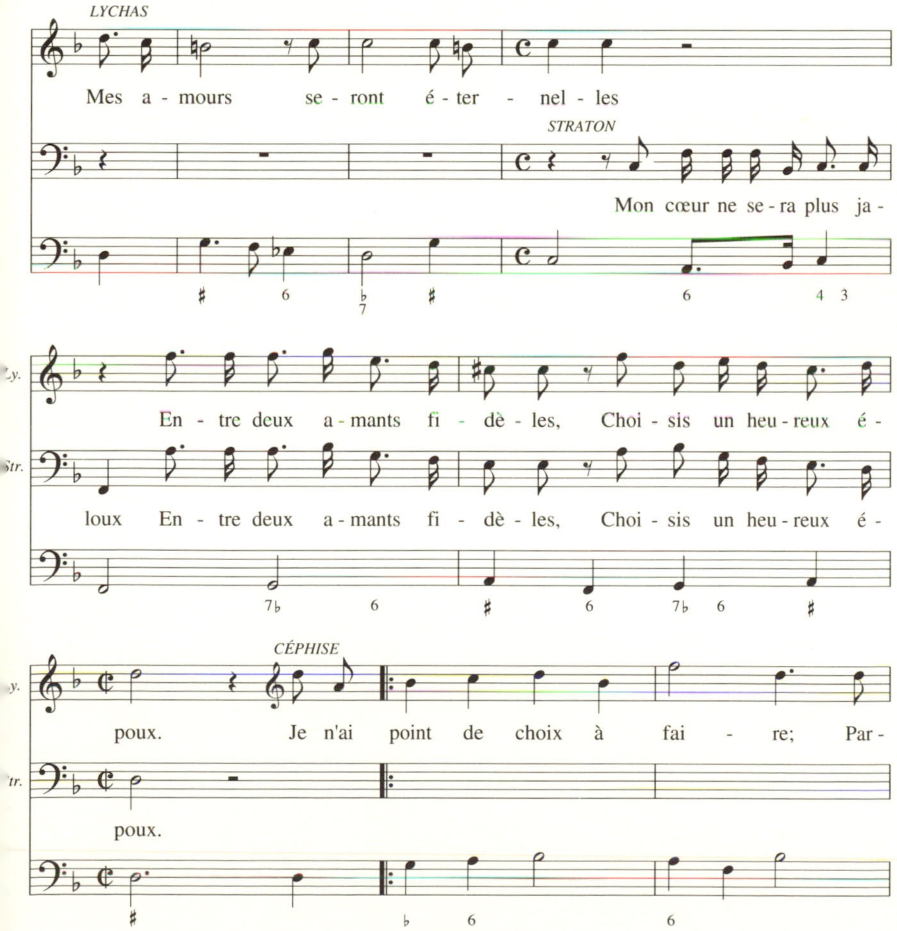

lons d'ai - mer et de plai - re   Et vi - vons tou - jours en

paix.   Je n'ai paix.   L'hy - men dé - truit la ten -

dres - se,   Il rend l'a - mour sans at - traits   Vou - lez -

vous ai - mer sans ces - se,   A - mants, n'é - pou - sez ja -

mais,   Vou - lez - vous ai - mer sans ces - se,   A -

mants,   a - mants, n'é - pou - sez ja - mais,

much as possible: 'In the length or brevity of the syllables, in the character of the expression, [the music] must maintain a proportion closest to the natural pace of speech . . . '.[8] Lully, he says, excelled at this, and he cites 'Bois épais' from *Amadis* (Act II, scene 4)[9] and 'Ah! j'attendrai long tems' from *Roland* (Act IV, scene 2).[10] As a model of good declamation he points also to the passage from *Armide*, sung by Armide herself: 'Le vainqueur de Renaud, si quelq'un le peut être, / Sera digne de moi'.[11] All these texts are set to measured recitative or air, in which, contrary to Grimarest's precepts, faithful speech-like declamation was not a major consideration, even though Lully did not flagrantly violate the normal stresses. Whatever value the treatise may have as evidence of spoken declamation, its authority on sung declamation is severely compromised by Grimarest's failure to distinguish between free and measured recitative. If he wanted to put Lully's recitative to the test, he should have cited passages of *récitatif simple*.

Much has been made of the remark of Jean Laurent Le Cerf de la Viéville, Seigneur de Freneuse, in which he recalled that Lully fashioned his recitative in imitation of the style of delivery of the actress Champmeslé.[12]

Il le vouloit le recitatif si uni, dit la Comtesse, qu'on prétend qu'il alloit le former à la Comedie sur les tons de la *Chanmêlé*. Il écoutoit déclamer la Chanmêlé, retenoit ses tons, puis leur donnoit grace, l'harmonie & le degré de force qu'ils devoient avoir dans la bouche d'un Chanteur, pour convenir à la Musique à laquelle il les aproprioit de cette maniere.

He wanted the recitative to be so uniform, said the Countess, that it is claimed that he aimed to model it on the inflections of Chanmêlé at the Comédie. He listened to Chanmêlé declaim, retained her tones, to which he added grace, harmony, and the level of force that they must have in the mouth of a singer to suit the music for which he appropriated this manner.

Champmeslé began attracting public attention in 1670, when she played Bérénice.[13]

---

[8] Jean-Léonor Le Gallois, Sieur de Grimarest, *Traité du récitatif dans la lecture, dans l'action publique, dans la déclamation, et dans le chant* (Paris: Jacques Le Fèvre et Pierre Ribou, 1707; repr. New York: AMS Press, n.d.), 124–5: 'Ainsi dans la longueur, ou dans la brieveté des silabes, dans le caractere de l'expression, il doit garder la proportion la plus approchante de leur mesure naturelle . . .'.

[9] Lully, *Œuvres compliètes, Les Opéras*, iii, ed. Henry Prunières (Paris: Éditions Lully, 1939), iii. 95–7.

[10] Lully, *Roland* (Paris, 1685), 220.

[11] Lully, *Armide*, ed. T. Lajarte, Chefs-d'œuvre classiques de l'opéra français, 17 (Paris: T. Michaelis, 1880?; repr. New York: Broude Bros., 1971), Act I, scene 2, p. 64.

[12] Le Cerf de la Viéville, *Comparaison de la musique italienne et de la musique françoise* (2nd edn., Brussels: Foppens, 1705; repr. Geneva: Minkoff, 1972), 204.

[13] Georges Lote, 'La Déclamation du vers français à la fin du XVIIe siècle', *Revue de phonétique*, 2 (1912), 319.

Le Cerf, who informs us of Lully's admiration for her, was born in the year celebrated in the present conference, 1674. He was only 13 years old when Lully died, so the reliability of his interlocutor's testimony is questionable. But assuming that it is true, what in Champmeslé's manner of performance could Lully have imitated? Rameau and Grimarest both emphasize the importance of being faithful in musical setting to the long and short syllables of the poetry. But are there long and short syllables in French? Would Champmeslé have recited the lines of Ex. 19.3 in the rhythm assigned them by Lully?

Ren - dez   à   vo - tre fils   cet - te ai - ma - ble prin - ces - se

Tout est sou - mis,   la guer - re ces - se,

Or did Lully find in her delivery tonal accents and inflections that he wanted to imitate? The author of *Entretiens galants*, which appeared in 1681, was struck by her quasi-musical delivery:[14]

Le récit des comédiens, dans le tragique, est *une manière de chant*, et vous m'avouerez bien que la Champmeslé ne vous plairoit pas tant, si elle avoit une voix moins agréable, mais elle sait la conduire avec beaucoup d'art, et elle y donne à propos des inflexions si naturelles, qu'il semble qu'elle ait vraiment dans le cœur une passion qui n'est que dans sa bouche.

The speech of the actors in a tragedy is a kind of song, and you will surely admit that Champmeslé would not please you as much if she had a less pleasing voice, but she knows how to use it with great art, and she gives it the required natural inflections, so that it seems as if she truly has in her heart the passion that is only on her lips.

Of course, we do not know how Champmeslé declaimed her lines. One scholar suggested we might infer this from the way Lully set French verses to music.[15] But if Lully's rhythm for the two lines I just cited is typical—and it is—we would be deceived, I believe.

What Lully evidently did follow were the caesuras and accents of the lines, and he probably did this more faithfully than any actor would.[16] Indeed he was quite rigid in respecting the line form in *Alceste*, though he loosened up in later operas.

[14] Ibid. 321–2.
[15] Ibid. 359.
[16] There is a good analysis of this aspect of Lully's text-setting by Lois Rosow, 'French Baroque Recitative as an Expression of Tragic Declamation', *Early Music*, 11 (1983), 468–79.

Ex. 19.3. Lully, *Alceste*, II. vi

Line	Number of quarter-notes
alex.	6
alex.	6
alex.	6
octon.	4
octon.	4
six	3
octon.	$2\frac{3}{4}$

The Recitative of Lully's Alceste

501

It is frequently said that Lully used a variety of metres or time signatures in his recitatives because the changing syllabic count of Quinault's lines, shifting particularly from alexandrine to octonary lines, compelled him to vary the length of the measure so as to reach each terminal accent on a first beat. But a close look at the settings in *Alceste* shows that the number of syllables in a poetic line does not determine the duration of the musical line. If we calculate the number of quarter-note values (including rests) used to set the two most common lines, the alexandrine and the octonary in, for example, the dialogue among Alcide, Phérès, and Alceste in Act II, scene 6, we find that the alexandrine occupies anywhere from four and a half to eight beats, and the octonary may occupy as few as two and three-quarters and as many as five (see Ex. 19.3). This range of musical line-lengths demonstrates that the alternation of different verse-types did not force Lully into mixed metres, because there is a great variety within a given syllabic count. Moreover, the flexibility and diversity of musical line-length shows that Lully could have written music organized in regular bars, if he had chosen to do so.

What accounts, then, for his varying the length of the measures? Sometimes the rate of declamation is faster, based on the sixteenth-note per syllable, as in 'allez la rendre à son heureux époux'; at other times it is based on the eighth-note per syllable, as in the first line, 'Rendez à votre fils'. This depends, at least much of the time, as in these examples, on the meaning and mood of a line. Lully also pauses longer on a caesura (the *coupe*), or line-end (the *rime*) in certain places, chiefly for dramatic effect. This pacing he may well have learnt from hearing the recitation of tragedians, but it is also true to natural speech.[17] It is this irregularity of measure that most distinguishes French from Italian recitative. But is it a fundamental stylistic difference or a superficial notational difference? The great distance that a number of celebrated commentators observed between the French and Italian recitative was owed largely, I believe, to an anachronism between the objects compared. Le Cerf, Raguenet,[18] Rousseau,[19] and Graun[20] compared the Lullian recitative with the Italian recitative of their own times, that is, the eighteenth century. Le Cerf had in mind

---

[17] See, for example, *Alceste*, Act II, scene 6, in *Œuvres complètes, Les Opéras*, ii, ed. Henry Prunières (Paris: Éditions Lully, 1932), 159–62; Chefs d'œuvre edn., 146–50.

[18] François Raguenet, *Paralèle des Italiens et des François, en ce qui regarde la musique et les opéra* (Paris: Jean Moreau, 1702).

[19] Jean-Jacques Rousseau, *Lettre sur la musique françoise* (n.p., 1753). Rousseau was aware of the fact that earlier the recitative was sung more rapidly, less songfully, with fewer ports-de-voix and ornamented cadences (61–2).

[20] Carl Heinrich Graun, correspondence with Georg Philipp Telemann in *Georg Philipp Telemann Briefwechsel*, ed. Hans Grosse and Hans Rudolf Jung (Leipzig, 1972), 264–306.

Alessandro Scarlatti or Bononcini, both of whom he names. Rousseau and Graun compared Rameau (who followed Lully's formula) with such composers as Pergolesi and Hasse, whereas Graun referred to his own practice as a standard. Further, all these critics had heard Lully's recitative as performed in the eighteenth century, by which time the pace of delivery had slowed down and many ornaments were introduced.[21] Lully's recitative, particularly performed in the eighteenth-century manner, when compared with Italian recitative of this period, does, indeed, seem unique.

But it is with mid-seventeenth-century Italian recitative that Lully should be compared. Such a comparison leads us to suspect that it was there, and not on the French stage, that Lully found his model. But, as we shall see, he transformed that model in certain ways.

Compare the scene in Ex. 19.3 with a scene from Cesti's *Orontea*, one of the most frequently performed operas of the Italian repertoire. It was first produced in Venice in 1649, three years after Lully left Italy. Lully must have been exposed to similar works while in Florence.[22] He may have heard Luigi Rossi's *Orfeo* in Paris in 1647 and is known to have taken part in 1654 in a performance of Cavalli's *Le nozze di Peleo e di Teti*. Lully wrote dance music for his *Serse* in 1660.[23] He may have been involved also in Cavalli's *Ercole amante* in 1662.

Unlike Lully, Cesti does not vary the length of the measure—it always contains four quarters—and he lets the final accent of the line fall almost as often on the third beat as on the first, for example on *genitríce*, *peregrinándo*, *quella córte*, and *sventúra*. He too varies the length of the measure within any line-type. So the *endecasillabi* in this sample are allocated between six and eleven quarter-note values, and the *settenari* between four and six quarter-note values. Again, the pacing is dictated by the content of the text and the composer's dramatic strategy. If we rebar Cesti's recitative to conform

---

[21] D'Alembert felt that performers in his time were dragging out the recitative. 'On assure que du temps de Lully le récitatif se chantait beaucoup plus vite . . . Depuis le temps de Lully, notre récitatif, sans rien gagner d'ailleurs, a même perdu le debit que cet artiste lui avait donné, et qu'il faudrait tâcher de lui rendre.' *De la liberté de la musique* (1754), p. xxii, in *Œuvres*, i (Paris: A. Bellin, 1821), 531–2; also in Denise Launay (ed.), *La querelle des bouffons* (Geneva: Minkoff Reprint, 1973), 425–6. Le Cerf tells that Lully reacted angrily to the introduction of ornaments in his recitative and reproached one singer with the admonition: 'Il n'y a pas comme cela dans vôtre papier, & ventrebleu, point de broderie; mon Récitatif n'est fait que pour parler, je veux qu'il soit tout uni.' *Comparaison*, Deuxième Partie, 204. The score of *Alceste* published in 1708 and followed by Lajarte in the Chefs-d'œuvre edn. contained added ornaments that are a testimony to this embellished, more flowing style. The version given in Ex. 19.4 was based on manuscripts closer to Lully's own autograph, which is lost. The edition in the *Œuvres complètes*, ii. 160–2, is the source for this example.

[22] See Robert L. and Norma W. Weaver, *A Chronology of Music in the Florentine Theater, 1590–1750* (Detroit: Information Coordinators, 1978).

[23] See James Anthony, *French Baroque Music from Beaujoyeulx to Rameau* (New York: Norton, 1974), 47–9.

to Lully's practice of placing the terminal accent and other main accents (as before the caesura) on the first beat of a bar, we get a result not unlike Lully's (these hypothetical bars are represented on Ex. 19.4 above the staff).[24] A figure after the vertical line indicates a hypothetical change of grouping of quarter-notes. The similarity is even more striking if we set to Cesti's recitative a French translation of the Italian text, as is done in Ex. 19.4.

One anomaly emerges in this process. Whereas Cesti's recitative mixes measures of four and two quarters, in this sample there are no bars of three quarters, and it is the interpolation of the triple measures that gives Lully's recitative its unmetrical sound. However, allowing for the faster pace of Italian recitative, we should look at the organization of the half-note pulses, and here we do find groups of three mixed with groups of two. But because the bar is divided according to quarter-notes, no irregular barring is necessary.

Some questions remain. What compelled Lully to make the accent fall on the first beat of a bar? And why for this purpose did he introduce bars of three units within the traditionally duple metre of recitative? These are matters for conjecture rather than documentary evidence. I propose that he discovered that French singers, because they were accustomed to performing airs de danse, had the habit of overstressing the first beat of a measure, and if he did not arrange to place the accented syllables there, whatever syllable did fall on the first beat would wrongfully have received an accent. As Tunley has aptly put it, all French music in this period 'aspired to the condition of dance'.[25] Lully's was thus a practical accommodation to singers in a country then lacking a recitative tradition.

As to the intermixing of duple and triple bars, two reasons may be conjectured. One is that Lully wanted to prevent a metrically marked and songful rendition of his recitative. By interrupting the steady duple with occasional triples in places suited to the text, the composer defeated any attempt by the singer to 'dance' the phrases. Another reason for the triple bars is related to some French traditions. The air de cour, perhaps because of the influence of the *vers mesurés à l'antique*, mixed duple and triple configurations in its setting of quantitative poetry. This music was not at first published with measure-bars, but when they were introduced, the barring had to be irregular, and the changes of time signature signalled the

---

[24] The example is based on the edition by William Holmes (Wellesley: The Wellesley Edition, 1973), 67–8.
[25] David Tunley, *Couperin* (London: British Broadcasting Corporation, 1982), 13.

Ex. 19.4. Cesti, *Orontea*, I. ix

	Line	Number of quarter-notes
ALIDORO		
Al - i - do - ro è il mio no - me, [A - li - do - re je m'a - pel - le,	settenario	5
Fu mio pa - dre un cor - sa - ro, Et mon pè - re un cor - sai - re,	settenario	4
E la vec - chia A - ri - stea ‖ mia gen - i - tri - ce. Et la vieil - le A - ri - stée é - tait ma mè - re	endecasillabo	6
Con lei pe - re - gri - nan - do Dans un pè - le - ri - na - ge	settenario	4
In Fe - ni - cia n'an - da - i, ‖ e in quel - la cor - te jus - qu'à la Phé - ni - cie nous som - mes al - lés, où	endecasillabo	9
Mi fe' re - gio pit - tor, ‖ be - ni - gna sor - te. m'ont - ils pein - tre nom - mé de ce roy - au - me.]	endecasillabo	8
I - vi la Prin - ci - pes - sa Ar - ne - a	settenario	6
Del Re Si - don - i - o ‖ l'u - ni - ca e - re - de,	endecasillabo	8

505

irregularities. Lully, who married the daughter of a celebrated composer of airs, Michel Lambert, was well acquainted with this convention.[26]

My conclusion is not surprising: Lully's recitative is a combination of Italian and French elements. The declamation aspires to natural speech and perhaps to stage speech, though it is rhythmicized, melodized, and stylized in ways foreign to speaking in any language. In Italian recitative the method had evolved of translating stresses into prolonged durations, and Lully embraced this technique. Neither Italian nor French speech of the

---

[26] See the airs sérieux by Michel Lambert in the appendix to Théodore Gérold, *L'art du chant en France au XVII* siècle (Strasburg: Faculté des Lettres, 1921), 243–6, drawn from airs printed by Ballard in Paris in 1659 and 1689.

period is believed to have been quantitative, for in it quantity evidently varied unpredictably in both normal and stage delivery.[27] But it was through quantity as well as down-beat that stress was normally expressed in music. The pitch content and contour of Italian recitative was also transferred to the French. By the mid-seventeenth century, Italian recitative had lost the free dissonance of earlier days and the pitches of the voice were limited to the notes of the accompanying chord and to passing and neighbouring notes on weak beats. Lully adopted this convention too. Thus Lully's *récitatif simple* in *Alceste*, like a spoken dialect that died out in its native land but survives in an isolated colony on foreign soil, is a musical dialect of an earlier Italian idiom.

[27] In the discussion of this paper in Baton Rouge, Louis Auld quoted Perrin's comment that the quantity of syllables in French are 'presque toutes douteuses'. This phrase is from Perrin's 'Avant-propos' to his *Recueil des paroles de musique*, paragraph *h* in Auld's edition. Margaret Seares has used Bénigne de Bacilly's rules (in *L'art de bien chanter*, Paris, 1679) to assign length to particular syllables and showed that Lully was sensitive to the quantitative requirements of certain combinations in 'Aspects of Performance Practice in the Recitative of Jean-Baptiste Lully', *Studies in Music*, 8 (1974), 8–16.

INDEX